Macon County, North Carolina

Marriages

1829-1939

By:

James E. Wooley

Please direct all correspondence and orders to:

www.southernhistoricalpress.com
or
SOUTHERN HISTORICAL PRESS, Inc.
PO BOX 1267
375 West Broad Street
Greenville, SC   29601
southernhistoricalpress@gmail.com

ISBN #0-89308-342-9

Printed in the United States of America

INTRODUCTION

Macon County was formed in 1828 from Haywood. The Court House was located in Franklin. No loss of marriage records known.

These marriage records were taken from a microfilm of the register. The register is a book of the original bonds and licenses as they were returned and verified that the marriage had taken place.

On a bond the name of the groom and his bondsman, the bride, and witnesses. The bond date is when it was issued. The marriage may have taken place the same day, a week or more later. In 1868 the bond was discontinued, although marriage licenses and certificates had been issued for many years. Only after 1851 was the J.P. or minister required to return the license to the Clerk of the County Court office. In the 1868 law the marriage license was to be kept in the Register of Deeds Office. In this same law the age, race, residence and place of marriage was to be recorded, with the other information.

In the Macon County Register the residence is shown only if out of the County or State. In a few places is found "Original not Found" means that the officiating person did not return the bond or license, record the marriage date, and sign his name. The date in such cases is the date issued in the Clerk's office.. Some are shown as "Retd. not executed" means that the bond or license was returned, but the marriage did not take place.

The mark / is used to separate the bride's age from the date of marriage.

There are a few marriages recorded in the register, that were performed in the State of Georgia, they were performed by an Ordinary (Ord) now the Probate Judge..

```
Abernathy,James to Louiza R.Clure          9-25-1855  John Hall,Clk.
Anernathy,M.V.22 to Sarah J.Moses 21       12-23-1883 M.L.Rickman,J.P.
Abernathy,John F.21 to Willie Gregory 22   2-15-1892  J.M.Keener,M.G.
Abernathy,Jacob L.26 to Nannie E.Totherow 19/2-27-1896 M.Ghomley,M.G.
Abernathy,J.D.20 to Bertha E.Mashburn 18   12-25-1907 J.M.Keener,M.G.
Adams,Nipper to Polly Carrell              12-29-1842 J.K.Gray,Clk.
Adams,Martin to Elizabeth Shanks           2-15-1844  J.K.Gray,Clk.
Adams,Beverly to Alvire Frady              11-20-1847 B.Adams.
Adams,Bannister to Jane Brown              5- 3-1850  T.P.Siler,D.Clk.
Adams,Johnson to Jane Deweese              1-30-1867  R.C.Slagle,Clk.
Adams,William J.to Mary J.Stewman          1- 7-1869  R.C.Slagle,Reg.
Adams,Marion 21 to Sarah Moore 14          2- 9-1875  J.S.Woodard,M.G.
Adams,Mead 21 to Adaline Ridley 19         9-28-1879  E.H.Franks,J.P.
Adams,Joshua A.23 to Jennie McKinney 19    3- 1-1888  D.L.Miller,M.G.
   He from Jackson Co.N.C.
Adams,Jasper 26 to Nancy Hasket 22         5-19-1892  J.W.Parker,J.P.
Adams,John P.26 to Lola Fox 19             1-24-1895  J.B.Elmore,J.P.
Adams,Allen 22 to Lydia Fox 25             6-10-1906  J.D.Sitton,M.G.
Adams,J.Parker 26 to Polly Price 22        3-10-1907  Jas.M.Corbin,J.P.
Adams,O.L.22 to Ruth Webb 18               9-20-1916  J.P.Moore,J.P.
Adams,P.N.55 to Mae B.Burrell 25           4- 8-1919  W.T.Thompson,M.G.
Adams,Charles 20 to Elizabeth Simonds 33   9- 7-1923  J.B.Stallcup,M.G.
Adams,Leroy 21 to Hester Higdon 18         5-17-1924  J.R.Pendergrass,MG
Adams,Parker 22 to Elsie Jones 18          10-17-1936 Sam.J.Murray,J.P.
Adams,Tom 21 to Addie Sisk 18              8-18-1936  Geo.Carpenter,J.P
   Both from Clarksville,Ga.
Addington,Jacob to Mary Dobson             9-26-1840  John Hall,Clk.
Addington,Wm.A. to Adeline Kelly           10-16-1845 J.K.Gray,Clk.
Addington,S.D. to V.A.Connelly             2- 3-1847  J.K.Gray,Clk.
Addington,J.B. to C.A.Wykle                10-27-1857 C.D.Smith,M.G.
Addington,W.M. to V.R.Trotter              3- 1-1864  L.F.Siler,Clk.
Addington,J.B. to Mary L.McPherson         1-17-1866  R.C.Slagle,Clk.
Addington,Dick to Emily Conley  Colored    8- 4-1866  James McGee,J.P.
Addington,Franklin Jr.to Francis Angel Col. 10-26-1871 M.Rickman,M.G.
Addington,William A.25 to Roxanna L.Siler 19/10-7-1874 J.W.Boman,M.G.
Addington,Colonel 22 to Carolin Gray 20 Col.9- 4-1879 J.H.Addington,M.G.
Addington,M.E.23 to Ella C.Munday 22       10-7-1879  Geo.A.Maiden,M.G.
Addington,Ben 26 to Callie Obe 18 Colored  1-21-1894  Jas.T.Kannedy,M.G.
Addington,Colonel 56 to Julia Johnson 26 Col.1-4-1912 B.H.Davis,M.G.
Addington,W.C.52 to Fanny Haynes 49        8-11-1918  E.Jno.McKay,M.G.
Addington,Richard 28 to Eva Love 23Colored 2- 7-1925  Geo.Carpenter,J.P.
Addington,J.H.54 to R.M.Hurst 36           7-14-1880  G.A.Oglesby,M.G.
Alexander,Freeman 23 to Nancy A.Barnes 20  10-2-1892  B.W.Wells,J.P.
Alexander,Jacob C.21 to T.Maud Keener      8-18-1926  Geo.C.Steed,M.G.
   He from Danville,Va... She from Raburn Co.Ga.
Alexander,Bascus 23 to Nobia Mason 23      4- 6-1913  T.J.Vinson,M.G.
Allen,D.H. to Emeline Welch                12-31-1845 J.K.Gray,Clk.
Allen,Daniel to Sarah Kelly                9-16-1858  R.C.Slagle,Clk.
```

```
Allen,Burr to Catherine Berry                          1-20-1859   Joshua Allen,M.G.
Allen,W.J. to Mary R.Kelly                             2-17-1864   R.C.Slagle,Clk.
Allen,T.W. to Elizabeth P.Deal                         11-2-1868   E.W.Moore,M.G.
Allen, Henry E.23 to Margaret Ann Potts 17             3- 6-1873   Thos.Mashburn,J.P.
Allen,D.W.21 to Martha M.Ramsey 20                     9- 1-1875   Thos.Mashburn,J.P.
Allen,C.E.25 to Sarah Cunningham 22                    1-19-1876   J.S.Woodard,M.G.
Allen,W.S.27 to M.A.Burnett 22                         3-20-1879   J.S.Gibson,J.P.
Allen,John H.21 to Ellie N.Potts 23                    1-23-1890   A.B.Dalton,J.P.
Allen,John H.26 to Nannie Leatherman 22                3- 7-1895   W.J.Jenkins,J.P.
Allen,Judson 34 to Emma Curtis 26                      1-13-1897   D.F.Carver,J.P.
Allen,Charles H.20 to Ivy Bradley 19                   10-18-1899  J.S.Woodard,M.G.
Allen,W.S.57 to Mrs.I.L.Potts 33                       8-15-1909   T.C.King,M.G.
Allen,A.P.25 to B.L.Robinson 28  Colored               9- 2-1911   J.M.Bristol,M.G.
Allen,J.H.51 to Mrs.Lillie Calhoun 28                  12-14-1912  M.H.Tuttle,M.G.
Allen,J.E.36 to Ella Childers 25                       9-15-1918   Theadore McCoy,JP
Allen,D.A.34 to Ruth Rickman 21                        6- 1-1919   J.L.Bryson,J.P.
Allen,Logan A.66 to Fannie Shepherd 38                 7-21-1926   J.R.Pendergrass,MG
Allen,W.Burr 56 to Emma J.Stillwell 48                 8-14-1933   W.R.Jenkins,M.G.
   He from College Park,Ga... She from Atlanta,Ga.
Allen,William to Martha Carson                         1-24-1839   A.Hester.
Allgood,George P.35 to Eugenia E.Manning 23/4- 3-1926  B.C.Reaves,M.G.
   Both from Marietta,Ga.
Allison,John to Rebecca Bryson                         12-24-1835  John Tatham,Clk.
Allison,Ephraigrin to Elizabeth Zachary                1- 9-1838   J.K.Gray,Clk.
Allison,W.P. to Sarah Ann Waldroop                     7-27-1866   J.R.Ammons,M.G.
Allison,Jno.W.23 to Amanda Collett 20                  12-15-1878  Rev.M.Ghomley,M.G.
Allison,Benjamin 22 to Martha Abernathy 18             1-30-1887   M.Ghormley,M.G.
Allison,O.M.34 to Emma Reid 32                         2-12-1896   A.W.Davis,M.G.
Allison,John 21 to Lillie Evans 18                     4- 2-1919   John Allison,J.P.
Allison,Fred 23 to Mary Ferguson 24                    8-11-1827   A.P.Ratledge,M.G.
   Both from Waynesville,N.C.
Allman,George to Martha Crawford                       1-18-1854   J.R.Roane,J.P.
Allman,William C.to Callie A.Addington                 11-1-1870   T.E.Glenn,M.G.
Allman,L.T.23 to Sarah Downs --                        11-11-1880  C.Campbell,M.G.
Allman,W.N.46 to Mary Johnston 27                      7- 6-1881   W.C.Carden,M.G.
Allman,L.H.40 to Myra Siler 21                         1-26-1886   C.D.Smith,M.G.
Allman,Nathan A.21 to Maggie Campbell 19               6----1893   D.H.Cowan,M.G.
Allman,Lee 31 to Mamie Angel 29                        3- 7-1906   L.P.Bogle,M.G.
Allman,Robert L.27 to Essie Lewis 25                   5- 1-1910   J.R.Pendergrass,MG
Alley,Thomas D.28 to Fannie Thompson 28                4-26-1892   Samuel Rhodes,M.G
Alley,Z.B.30 to Cora Davis 27                          1-26-1893   D.H.Carman,M.G.
Alley,Morris 28 to Ida Moses 22                        12-16-1922  A.W.Jacobs,M.G.
Alloway,J.T.51 to Sallie Shields 25                    3-13-1901   J.R.Pendergrass,MG
Alloway,G.C.20 to Ollie Jacobs 18                      1-26-1905   John H.Moore,M.G.
   He from Athens,Tenn.
Alston,Henry L.26 to May Ray 18  Colored               7-16-1900   G.W.Herbert,M.G.
Ammons,Vass to Rebia Collins                           3-19-1838   Alford Hall,Clk.
Ammons,David to Mary Carson                            11-12-1840  John Hall,Clk.
```

Ammons,John to N.C.Rogers	1- 6-1845	David Ammons.
Ammons,Thos.H. to R.A.Knight	6-21-1845	J.K.Gray,Clk.
Ammons,John to Martha Buchanan	11-17-1847	John Elmore,J.P.
Ammons,John A.to Rhoda R.Carson	1-16-1850	J.K.Gray,Clk.
Ammons,Samuel to Jane Pilkerton	9-18-1863	T.P.Siler,Clk.
Ammons,Joshua to Sally Buchanan	1-16-1870	Jas.K.Bryson,Reg.
Ammons,James W.24 to Margaret J.Blaine 18	8- 4-1872	W.H.Higdon,J.P.
Ammons,J.F.20 to M.E.Saunders 16	12-28-1875	J.S.Woodard,M.G.
Ammons,Wm.W.S.21 to Mary P.McDowell 21	2-16-1879	W.W.Henry,J.P.
Ammons,W.S.30 to Sarah Buchanan 35	3-25-1884	J.L.Strain,J.P.
Ammons,W.E.23 to P.A.Shepherd 21	11-1-1885	J.R.Ammons,M.G.
Ammons,William T.21 to Mary Keener 17	9-11-1887	J.G.Ammons,M.G.
Ammons,William M.19 to Nancy C.Clark 23	8- 2-1889	G.W.Loudermilk,MG
Ammons,Wm.David 22 to Ida Mashburn 18	2- 5-1893	N.J.Rush,J.P.
Ammons,Irvin 24 to Kansas Henry 26	8- 2-1896	J.M.Keener,M.G.
Ammons,W.T.19 to Sarah Ammons 18	2- 4-1897	J.W.Parker,J.P.
Ammons,William E.38 to Sarah M.Leatherman 24/8-24-1899		D.C.McCoy,J.P.
Ammons,Colombus 25 to Laura Henry 18	8-15-1900	J.M.Keener,M.G.
Ammons,T.W.29 to H.L.Mashburn 19	4- 9-1901	T.R.Arnold,J.P.
Ammons,Lon 26 to M.C.Henry 25	1-29-1901	G.W.Stiwinter,J.P
Ammons,William 21 to Isabel Parker 23	2-23-1902	W.L.Higdon,J.P.
Ammons,James 21 to Ada Elders19	6- 8-1902	J.W.Ammons,J.P.
Ammons,Elias29 to Margie Sellers 20	9- 4-1906	W.L.Bradley,M.G.
Ammons,John G.24 to Jane Mashburn 20	5-27-1907	J.M.Keener,M.G.
Ammons,Albert 19 to Nora Cross 18	4-30-1908	J.W.Duvall,J.P.
Ammons,T.W.35 to Ritter Coggins 20	9- 8-1909	S.L.Loudermilk,MG
Ammons,John T.21 to Nellie M.Williams 18	2-22-1911	J.A.Gibbs,M.G.
Ammons,James B.21 to Laura C.Gregory 18	1- 8-1911	James M.Corbin,JP
Ammons,Alex 33 to M.A.Leatherman 24	9-28-1913	W.T.Jennings,J.P.
Ammons,Richard 21 to Ruth Henry 15	4-23-1916	J.P.Moore,J.P.
Ammons,Albert 24 to Grady Mae Cabe 16	6-11-1933	A.J.Smith,M.G.
Ammons,Wiley R.23 to Helen Justice 20	9-10-1938	J.I.Vinson,M.G.
Anderson,J.B.to Eliza Battle	1- 7-1852	J.K.Gray,Clk.
Anderson,Joseph B.to Eliza Battle	1- 7-1852	J.K.Gray,Clk.
Anderson,W.T.to Martha A.Thomas	5-19-1864	R.C.Slagle,Reg.
Anderson,James to Lucinda Jacobs	7-14-1864	R.C.Slagle,Reg.
Anderson,J.R.to A.J.Justice	8- 8-1865	R.C.Slagle,Reg.
Anderson,James N.to Molly Horten	3-10-1869	R.C.Slagle,Reg.

Anderson,James B.19 to Hariett R.Pendergrass 19/10-16-1873-Albert Siler.
Anderson,William M.18 to Elizabeth Baldwin 17/10-30-1873-Albert Siler,JP.
Anderson,Mansfield 21 to Eliza Leatherwood 21/1-15-1873-Albert Siler,J.P.
   He from Clayton,Ga.
Anderson,Joseph H.21 to Eliza G.Pendergrass 23/1-14-1875-Albert Siler,JP

Anderson,Robert A.18 to L.T.Pendergrass 16	12-22-1875	Albert Siler,J.P.
Anderson,James B.46 to Mary M.Parker 29	5- 9-1875	Albert Siler,J.P.
Anderson,Hiram 23 to Priscilla Cody 31	4-12-1880	Hosa Moses,J.P.
Anderson,J.V.22 to Mary C.Gray 22	2-24-1884	J.J.McConnell,J.P.

```
Anderson,John 18 to Josie Gipson 17              4-11-1894   John C.Russell,JP
Anderson,Joseph Wm.20 to Ida L.Bates 24          12-6-1894   Thos.M.Slagle,J.P
Anderson,James R.20 to Betty Greenwood 20        6-17-1896   J.C.Weaver,J.P.
Anderson,H.L.35 to Lela Sellers 21               10-21-1896  J.A.Deal,M.G.
Anderson,Alex R.35 to Lydia M.Johnson 21         8- 8-1898   J.T.Wade,M.G.
Anderson,R.C.23 to L.M.DeHart 22                 12-21-1899  J.J.McCoy,J.P.
Anderson,G.W.21 to Lew Anderson 20               11-1-1899   W.A.Setser,J.P.
Anderson,H.M.20 to Emma Carpenter 18             8-26-1900   W.A.Setser,J.P.
Anderson,Mike 24 to Nevada Mason 18              10-12-1902  P.H.Justice,J.P.
Anderson,G.W.21 to Martha Ladford 20             2- 8-1903   W.P.Allison,J.P.
Anderson,H.B.22 to Nannie L.Lewis 22             11-5-1904   W.P.Allison,J.P.
Anderson,W.P.60 to Ernestine Keener 32           4- 8-1907   J.W.Ammons,J.P.
Anderson,Sam 35 to Julia Slagle 23               12-20-1909  F.M.Morgan,M.G.
Anderson,C.T.24 to Bessie Thomas 17              7-16-1911   J.T.Watts,J.P.
Anderson,R.A.54 to Grace E.Cloer 47              4-13-1913   C.A.Battles,J.P.
Anderson,John V.46 to Mattie Scroggs 35          12-21-1913  J.C.Farmer,M.G.
Anderson,E.F.20 to Annie Womack 18               8- 6-1916   J.R.Pendergrass,M.
Anderson,Maden 38 to Sallie Collier 33           11-3-1918   G.A.Clore,M.G.
Anderson,Lyle 24 to Flora Bates 18               1-17-1918   D.C.McCoy,M.G.
Anderson,John 20 to Elsie Roper 21               3-30-1919   Jacob Anderson,JP
Anderson,Vester 18 to Hallie Dills 18            7-11-1920   G.M.Johnson,J.P.
Anderson,George 26 to Maud Sweatman 19           4-11-1920   G.M.Johnson,J.P.
Anderson,J.N.25 to Ellen Frazier 20              12-22-1921  J.R.Pendergras,MG
Anderson,Fred H.21 to Jessie L.Blaine 16         9-12-1923   C.S.Slagle,J.P.
Anderson,Zeb 20 to Bessie Emory 21               3-22-1925   Geo.Carpenter,J.P
Anderson,Fred H.25 to Parilee Dills 25           10-30-1931  Sam J.Murray,J.P.
Anderson,Willie 22 to Flonnie B.Davis 14         10-25-1934  Geo.Carpenter,J.P
  He from Swain,Co.N.C.
Angel,William to Mary Ann Patton                 2- 2-1835   J.R.Allman.
Angel,James to Margaret Hughs                    10-12-1838  Johathan M.Bryson
Angel,James to Elenor Nichols                    2-26-1842   J.K.Gray,Clk.
Angel,Marvel to Narcissa Bryson                  11-7-1846   J.K. Gray,Clk.
Angel,James to Martha L.Brooks                   9-15-1847   J.K.Gray.
Angel,William to Sarah Nichols                   3-29-1848   N.H.Palmer,Wit.
Angel,G.W.to Mary E.Hayes                        4-11-1849   J.K.Gray,Clk.
Angel,Alfred to Julianna Thomas                  12-17-1850  J.K.Gray,Clk.
Angel,James P.to Eretta L.Reid                   9-21-1854   John Hall,Clk.
Angel,Adam to Lettie Angel          Colored      8-30-1866   Seth H.Hyatt,J.P.
Angel,Stephen to Jane Martin        Colored      12-27-1866  R.C.Slagle,C.C.C.
Angel,G.W. to A.E.Panland                        3- 6-1866   R.C.Slagle,C.C.C.
Angel,George W.to Rachel E.Gribble               9- 5-1868   R.C.Slagle,Reg.
Angel,Andrew P.to M.E.A.Dobson                   3-12-1870   J.K.Bryson,Clk.
Angel,T.A. to Ada Miller                         8- 9-1870   R.C.Slagle,D.Reg.
Angel,Benj.F.22 to Ida M.Siler 21                11-25-1874  Jno.W.Bowman,M.G.
Angel,Alfred 26 to Mattie Nevels 27 Colored      5-12-1877   Jno.McDowell,M.G.
Angel,Mel N.27 to Eliza J.Angel 25               12-26-1877  E.H.Franks,J.P.
Angel,M.L.20 to L.L.Benfield 20                  5- 3-1878   E.H.Franks,J.P.
```

Marriage	Date	Official
Angel,Squire 50 to Adalin England 36 Col.	10-28-1880	E.H.Franks,J.P.
Angel,Chas.L.20 to Lou S.Addington 19	3- 2-1882	C.D.Smith,M.G.
Angel,Thomas W.25 to Martha Berry 24	2-24-1887	Jas.H.Brendle,M.G
Angel,Jesse E.21 to Minnie Davis 17	12-8-1892	J.R.Pendergras,MG
Angel,Joseph D.22 to Alice Wall 24	11-8-1893	W.G.Mallonee,M.G.
Angel,Charles G.24 to Addie Rogers 22	1-15-1895	G.A.Bartlett,M.G.
Angel,W.F.19 to Addie Sanders 19	7-21-1897	John H.Fulton,J.P
Angel,B.M.52 to Cora Higdon 20	1- 5-1902	J.W.Briggs,M.G.
Angel,Samuel 25 to Lizzie Guffee 20	3- 8-1903	W.L.Higdon,J.P.
Angel,Walter M.20 to Fannie B.Mashburn 19	8- 9-1903	W.L.Higdon,J.P.
Angel,W.L.28 to Molly Neely 23	2- 7-1904	T.Baxter White,JP
Angel,E.M.25 to M.E.Ashe 22	7- 4-1905	F.L.Towsend,M.G.
Angel,John 31 to Lizzie Reese 17	1-28-1907	J.R.Pendergras,MG
Angel,Andrew 38 to Lula McDonnell 24 Col.	10-4-1908	J.H.Morrison,M.G.
Angel,A.P.Jr.27 to Florence C.Oliver 23	9-30-1908	R.E.Atkinson,M.G.
Angel,Brab.30 to Nina Myers 30	1-26-1908	W.R.Bulgin,J.P.
Angel,Archie Allen 20 to Olva El Dora/Ramey 24	2-26-1911	Robert Stamey,J.P
Angel,Thos.29 to Florence Blaine 29	10-4-1911	W.H.Roane,J.P.
Angel,Geo.T.26 to Sallie Stevens 24	1-10-1913	M.H.Tuttle,M.G.
Angel,E.M.29 to Julia Tallent 26	3-31-1916	Geo.Carpenter,J.P
Angel,Terrill 43 to Ella Addington 22 Col.	1-28-1917	S.Fincher,M.G.
Angel,J.B.41 to Nannie Reece 18	1-22-1917	Geo.Carpenter,J.P
Angel,Dave 24 to Belle Sorrels 19	10-27-1917	Geo.Carpenter,J.P
Angel,C.L.27 to Lou Cloer 19	4-15-1917	W.H.Roane,J.P.
Angel,Auburn 22 to Anner Franks 19	2- 8-1920	J.R.Pendergras,MG
Angel,Charlie 37 to Lillie McConnell 30	9-14-1926	R.A.Truitt,M.G.
Angel,T.W.Jr.24 to Alice Carmichael 21 She from Greensboro,N.C.	8-25-1927	A.P.Ratledge,M.G.
Ansly,Logan to Jane Ansly	12-14-1839	James Ansly,Wit.
Arnold,William to Polly Redman	3-27-1837	John Tatham,Clk.
Arnold,John to Althea Ledford	8-22-1869	J.K.Bryson,Reg.
Arnold,James 26 to Sarah Patterson 19	9-12-1885	Original not found
Arnold,Oscar 20 to Julia Crisp 18	12-22-1898	W.L.Higdon,J.P.
Arnold,John 19 to Lennie Love 18 Colored	8-21-1900	E.B.Angel,J.P.
Arnold,Frank 18 to Minnie Phillips 19	3- 2-1908	Robert Stamey,J.P
Arnold,Ishmal 22 to Jennie Guffee 27	8-27-1914	M.A.Love,M.G.
Arnold,Fred M.26 to Fannie M.Reece 22	11-11-1928	Robt.F.Mock,M.G.
Arnold,John 19 to Carrie Coward 22	10-6-1933	J.B.Taylor,M.G.
Arrowood,James to Lavina Hunter	12-12-1840	H.G.Woodfin,D.Clk
Arrowood,David to Susannah Truitt	8-25-1855	John Hall,Clk.
Arrowood,Humphrey P.69 to Mary Crisp 35	2-11-1889	M.B.Dockery,J.P.
Arrowood,Boyd 28 to O'Dell Bryant 21 He from Marble,N.C.	11-5-1938	Geo.W.Stepp,J.P.
Arthur,T.S.36 to Nettie J.C.Siler 24	5- 6-1883	J.A.Deal,M.G.
Arthur,James S.25 to Pearl B.Rector 22	9-16-1917	J.Q.Wallace,M.G.
ʌvey,Otto 22 to Harriet Lakey 19	2- 6-1883	Joseph Morgan,J.P
A vey,J.H.20 to Ella Queen 18	2- 7-1904	W.L.Bradley,M.G.

Arvey,W.C.24 to Ruby Bryson 18	4-18-1915	J.A.Lakey,J.P.
Ashe,Elcana to Mary Mayson	8-18-1843	J.K.Gray,Clk.
Ashe,Amos to Malinda Frizzle	7-24-1843	J.K.Gray,Clk.
Ashe,D.H. to Martha M.Elmore	8-13-1866	R.C.Slagle,C.C.C.
Ashe,I.J.26 to Fannie M.Bell 21	9-26-1877	M.P.Swain,M.G.
Ashe,Jesse A.21 to Margaret E.Moore 16	2- 6-1881	C.S.Buchanan,M.G.
Ashe,Robert T.23 to Mary Poindexter 23 He from Swain Co.N.C.	3-26-1885	B.G.Wild,M.G.
Ashe,B.M.32 to Harriet Peek 28	12-12-1897	J.W.Parker,J.P.
Ashe,Felix 21 to Mary Morrison 20	1-29-1899	T.E.Weaver,M.G.
Ashe,Charley 33 to Annie Tyler 19	12-10-1899	J.M.Carpenter,J.P
Ashe,Lon W.20 to Miner Wilkes 20	11-3-1906	J.B.Ramsey,J.P.
Ashe,Amos 45 to Ida Hall 19	5-22-1907	W.R.Bulgin,J.P.
Ashe,T.B.33 to Arie Potts 28	5-30-1915	Geo.Carpenter,J.P
Atkinson,Jep.24 to Lena Speed 28	1-31-1921	J.C.Mell,J.P.
Ayers,Lee 21 to Laura Mason 19	8-25-1898	F.M.Morgan,M.G.
Ayers,Crawford 22 to Grace Wilson 23 Both of Swain Co.N.C.	3-17-1930	Geo.Carpenter,J.P
Bailey,J.W. to Nancy Woodard	5-24-1864	John Ammons,J.P.
Bailey,J.T.27 to Tiny Kinsland 22	5- 8-1898	J.B.Elmore,J.P.
Bailey,J.K.21 to Texie Caler 21	10-6-1900	E.N.Dalrymple,J.P
Bailey,H.F.35 to Lila McPherson 25	7- 3-1914	J.Q.Wallace,M.G.
Bailey,Dewey 35 to Willie Tippett 17	11-13-1920	Geo.Carpenter,J.P
Bailey,Goldman 21 to Bell Burleson 18	12-24-1921	Geo.Carpenter,J.P
Bailey,H.Grady 26 to Zula Ray 24	7-12-1922	A.J.Smith,M.G.
Bailey,Wade H.23 to Mary McGinnis 21 He from Beckly,W.Va.	6- 9-1933	J.L.Teague,M.G.
Baines,W.S. to Mary Fuller	1-27-1867	R.C.Slagle,C.C.C.
Baird,Zebulon to Emma D.Smith 20	10-18-1876	L.K.Haynes,M.G.
Baird,Adolphus E.28 to Clara Conley 18	7- 5-1908	J.R.Pendergras,MG
Baker,David to Mary Baker	9- 3-1838	John Hall,Clk.
Baker,John B.22 to Callie Burnett 19	2-26-1896	Original not found
Baker,Robert 26 to Corrie Shepherd 18 Col.	9- 6-1915	Chas.L.Stewart,MG
Barker,Jason to Catherine Cabe	11-8-1838	John Hall,Clk.
Barker,Warren to Hannah Cabe	3-19-1838	John Hall,Clk.
Barker,Alfred to Martha A.Bailey	12-16-1871	William Sloan,Reg
Barker,Henry S.22 to Polly Robbins 19	12-25-1885	S.A.Dixon,J.P.
Barker,J.C.21 to Lillie Gibson 15	9-17-1921	J.L.Bryson,J.P.
Barker,Henry 23 to Bessie Davis 18	1-17-1928	Geo.Carpenter,J.P
Baldwin,Joseph to Mirah Johnson	7-22-1829	W.B.Hyatt,Wit.
Baldwin,Alexander to Martha Pendergrass	12-31-1851	J.K.Gray,Clk.
Baldwin,John 19 to Allie Ray 18	9-12-1880	P.C.Wild,J.P.
Baldwin,William 24 to Hattie Jacobs 16	12-26-1883	B.G.Wilds,M.G.
Baldwin,James 21 to Effie Bateman 18	9- 8-1893	J.T.Barnes,M.G.
Baldwin,Harley 21 to Allie Humphreys	10-7-1906	W.H.Solesbee,J.P.
Baldwin,Lee 19 to Ila Smith 16	6- 1-1913	Frank T.Gettis,JP
Baldwin,Bass 22 to Lotie Ray 19	2-15-1914	D.A.Younce,M.G.
Baldwin,Lyle 21 to Annar Pendergrass 18	1- 8-1927	J.H.Grant.

```
Baldwin,W.E.20 to Geneva Parrish 18          4- 8-1917  J.L.Younce,M.G.
Ball George C.17 to Martha Woods 18          7-13-1889  J.M.Keener,J.P.
Ballard,Marshall Jr.29 to Eleanor E.Terhune 25/9-3-1941-A.F.Rohrbacher,MG
Ballew,Charley to Margaret Gibby             10-26-1834 John Tatham,Clk.
Ballew,David to Melinda Leopard              10-10-1835 John Tatham,Clk.
Ballew,L.J. to Elizabeth Justice             9- 7-1839  H.G.Woodfin,Clk.
Ballew,David to Jane Higdon                  9-29-1843  J.K.Gray,CLK.
Ballew,Archileus to Mary Justice             3- 3-1853  J.K.Gray,Clk.
Ballew,William 23 to S.J.Blaine 16           10-31-1882 E.T.Long,J.P.
Ballew,Bud 44 to Margaret Talley 32          6-15-1901  T.N.Ford,M.G.
Ballew,Jesse J.23 to Nancy J.Mize 19         10-22-1911 E.P.Brown,J.P.
Ballew,Carl W.25 to Fannie E.Wilson 23       10-22-1914 E.P.Brown,J.P.
Ballew,S.C.24 to Ella Mason 22               3-26-1915  J.E.Vinson,J.P.
Balton,Alonzo D.29 to Lois M.Davis 28        12-29-1920 S.H.Hillard,M.G.
Banks,J.M. to Mary Jane Bryson               4- 7-1870  J.K.Bryson,Reg.
Barclay,Richard S.30 to Virginia L.Gates 24/10-12-1936 Sam J.Murray,J.P.
   He from Miami,Fla.. She from Atlanta,Ga.
Barnard,William D.22 to Ellen Winsted 19     12-17-1885 W.A.Thomas,M.G.
Barnard,H.Lackstone 22 to Jennie S.Ray 21    8-29-1889  J.P.Campbell,J.P.
Barnard,J.Lee 23 to Addie Ray 20             8-18-1892  W.J.Jenkins,J.P.
Barnard,J.E.28 to Etta Wood 20               8- 2-1907  A.S.Solesbee,M.G.
Barnard,W.M.22 to Nobie Sweatman 18          11-15-1915 W.G.Warren,M.G.
Barnes,Elihu to Mary Rowland                 2-18-1833  John Hall,Clk.
Barnes,John to Milley Martin                 2- 8-1844  J.K.Gray,Clk.
Barnes,Zebada to Becky Roland                10-13-1851 J.K.Gray,Clk.
Barnes,Floyd F.to Elmire McCall              3-15-1854  John Hall,Clk.
Barnes,Milton to Martha May                  2-28-1869  R.C.Slagle,Reg.
Barnes,John T.to Susan C.Evans               3-16-1871  Mark May,M.G.
Barnes,Jas.A.24 to Sarah L.Coleman 20        3-18-1880  John D.Howard,J.P
Barnes,Joseph 22 to May Lunsford 21          2-19-1882  Z.Barnes,J.P.
Barnes,Andrew J.18 to Taxas Killpatrick 16   3- 1-1885  James M.Barnes,JP
Barnes,J.M.23 to Cilla Wilson 24             12-1-1898  G.W.Matney,M.G.
Barnes,William L.22 to Mary G.Nichelson 18   12-28-1900 G.W.Matney,M.G.
Barnes,Manson 22 to Mary E.Hedden 18         10-21-1902 G.W.Stiwinter,J.P.
Barnes,C.H.24 to Elizabeth Tilson 18         6-22-1912  Z.P.Peek,J.P.
Barnes,Thomas 20 to May Woodall 15           6-25-1912  J.M.Keener,M.G.
Barnes,John H.21 to Sallie A.Woodall 17      1-24-1918  D.M.Rogers,J.P.
Barnes,Robert 42 to Laura Conner 44          9-19-1933  John W.Edwards,JP
Barnes,Harvey 23 to Charlotte Tilson 19      4- 2-1938  W.G.Wood,M.G.
Barnett,Joseph L.38 to Melvina L.Vanhook 45/3-17-1892  G.R.McPherson,J.P
Barnett,Hubert 22 to Mamie Dockery 21        1- 7-1936  Geo.W.Stepp,J.P.
Barr,Augustus C.30 to Laura O.Kelsey 18      10-14-1885 Jas.E.Fogarite,MG
Barrett,John 25 to Emma Dean 24              12-29-1887 A.A.Justice,M.G.
Barrett,George W.34 to Louise R.Bascom 32    9- 3-1918  Joseph T.Ware,M.G
Barrett,Thomas 54 to Bessie Davis 40         8-20-1927  J.R.Pendergras,MG
Barrington,J.C.53 to Lola Penland 36         8-22-1922  Chas.S.Plyler,M.G
Bascom,Henry M.30 to F.C.Davis 20            2-24-1887  J.E.Forgartie,M.G
```

```
Bateman,Archibald to Mahota Lambert            11-12-1846  J.K.Gray,Clk.
Bateman,Jacob to Celia E.Evans                  4- 2-1871  Mark May,M.G.
Bateman,Leander 21 to Lasaphine Davis 18       12-26-1872  Mark May,M.G.
  He from Nantahala,N.C.
Bateman,J.W.28 to Elizabeth M.Jones 20          5- 5-1873  Wm.Deweese,J.P.
Bateman,Thomas D.21 to Sylvester C.Batey 17/4-19-1874  Z.Barnes,J.P.
Bateman,Arch T.21 to Laura Cole 19              3-25-1895  R.P.Garrison,J.P.
Bateman,Alex 23 to Malia Waters  19             3-23-1899  W.J.Evans,M.G.
Bateman,John 20 to Docie Younce 20             11-26-1899  W.J.Evans,M.G.
Bateman,Ben 22 to Tiney Cope 20                 6-30-1901  W.L.Solesbee,J.P.
Bateman,Ruben P.25 to Dora Yonce 20            11-26-1901  W.A.Solesbee,J.P.
Bateman,Rube 27 to Elizabeth Owenby 25          8-19-1906  W.A.Solesbee,J.P.
Bateman,Charles 25 to Cleo Fouts 20             1- 8-1910  J.L.Fouts,J.P.
Bateman,George 21 to Maud Baldwin 19            8-29-1920  D.A.Younce,M.G.
Bateman,Chas.L.30 to Belva Roper 23            10-1-1923   L.P.Roper,J.P.
Bateman,Howard 21 to Maude Wilhide 22           8-10-1929  T.S.Roten,M.G.
Bates,William J.to Elizabeth Clure              3- 1-1858  R.C.Slagle,Reg.
Bates,J.G. to Martha A.McClure                  1-26-1867  R.C.Slagle,Clk.
Bates,Robert W.to Elmira Gray                   3-14-1870  J.K.Bryson,Reg.
Bates,Jas.A.33 to M.M.Henson 34                 1-30-1879  F.Poindexter,J.P.
Bates,Robert H.25 to Sarah E.Gray 23            3- 4-1886  J.M.Carpenter,J.P
Bates,William J.22 to Sarah L.DeHart 19         2- 7-1889  J.S.Woodard,M.G.
Bates,Henry C.29 to Ava Cloer 16                8-26-1900  J.M.Carpenter,J.P
Bates,J.R.28 to Mary Phillips 22                5-10-1903  Robert Stamey,J.P.
Bates,Hannibal 26 to Octie Holbrooks 25         1-17-1904  J.A.Brendle,M.G.
Bates,H.A.20 to Maggie Garland 21               2-28-1904  J.C.Shope,J.P.
Bates,Napolean S.26 to Thence Stockton 21       1- 4-1906  Robert Stamey,J.P
Bates,S.M.25 to Maude Long 18                  11-11-1906  J.R.Pendergras,MG
Bates,W.B.22 to Allie Sanders 22                1- 9-1910  Robert Stamey,J.P
Bates,Harley A.26 to Ada Bell 24                2-27-1910  Robert Stamey,J.P
Bates,Robt.H.21 to Viola Watts 18               9- 7-1934  John W.Edwards,JP
Bates,H.H. 45 to Margie Dalrymple 29            2-20-1936  Robert Stamey,J.P
Battles,James M.to Susanah Gibbs                9-30-1832  Mark Coleman,Wit.
Battles,John W.to Mary Hughes                   1-30-1833  John Hall,Clk.
Battles,Asoph to Nancy Hicks                    1- 9-1836  J.M.Bryson,.
Battles,John W.to Miriam H.Anderson             9- 6-1858  Wm.Witcher,M.G.
Battles,B.F. to Sarah Poindexter                7-19-1863  T.B.Siler,Clk.
Battles,M.T.to S.A.Shular                       3-31-1865  R.C.Slagle,Clk.
Battles,G.W.to Mary J.Wyant                     9-19-1866  J.H.Bryson,J.P.
Battles,C.Swain 19 to T.D.McDowell 17          10-21-1894  T.M.Slagle,J.P.
Battles,Ed 21 to Mary Southards 17              3-10-1901  W.P.Allison,J.P.
Battles,William 27 to Callie Guffey 26         12-30-1905  W.P.Allison,J.P.
Baty,John W.68 to R.E.Guy 35                    3-25-1876  Jno.McDowell,M.G.
Baty,John S.19 to E.M.Vinson 21                 8-14-1881  D.L.Miller,M.G.
Baty,J.W.17 to Eva Crunkleton 19                2-26-1899  T.J.Vinson,J.P.
Baty,Henry 21 to Silla Craine 19               12-24-1911  P.C.Galloway,J.P.
Baty,Augustus 27 to Genelia Crain 17            7-21-1912  J.E.Vinson,J.P.
```

Baxter,Andrew 63 to Mary Hyatt 53 Colored   6-10-1897 J.C.Hemphill,M.G.
Baxter,A,Owen 28 to Mary L.Scott 23   10-30-1926 B.C.Reavis,M.G.
  He from Atlanta,Ga... She from Stone Mountain,Ga.
Beach,C.W.27 to Noma A.Taylor 19   6-16-1920 L.B.Hayes,M.G.
Beal,James 60 to Lidia Butler 32   5-28-1892 J.L.Corbin,J.P.
Beal,James H.18 Callie V.Moss 21   4-13-1913 R.H.Munger,J.P.
Beal,Robert 21 to Ruth Holt 18   7- 3-1913· D.L.Miller,M.G.
Beam,Jess R. to May Kerby   8-30-1838 John Hall,Clk.
Bearden,W.W.28 to Mary Hill 24   11-29-1899 J.M.McGuire,M.G.
Beasley,Reubin to Jenny Hubbard   4-13-1832 John Hall,Clk.
Beasley,William to Rhoda Quilliams   9-27-1851 J.K.Gray,Clk.
Beasley,S.J.19 to Pheriba O.Franks 16 10-18-1891 A.B.Dalton,J.P.
Beasley,Jeremiah 22 to Mattie Leatherman 21/12-23-1888 P.R.Rickman,M.G.
Beasley,Geo.W.19 to Bessie B.Dotson 19 9-29-1911 ·C.R.Cabe,J.P.
Beasley,R.Van 21 to Cyntha Ammons 22 12-1-1912 J.W.Rickman,J.P.
Beaty,John E.22 to Mary Harrison 21   4-23-1886 F.M.Morgan,M.G.
Beaver,Perry 23 to Malinda Yonce 23   10-11-1891 P.C.Wild,M.G.
Beaver,George 23 to Bethie Allman 23   2-17-1907 C.H.Caviness,M.G.
Beaver,Gordon 27 to Ellen D.Johnson 22 2- 7-1920 T.G.Wilson,M.G.
Beck,W.M. to Rachael Elders   5-25-1849 J.K.Gray,Clk.
Beck,Samuel 68 to Hester E.Dalrymple 40 12-3-1874 Sam Gibson,M.G.
  He from Jackson,Co.N.C.
Beck,James 23 to Iowa A.Dills 17   8-28-1890 Wm.C.Kimzey,J.P.
Beck,John 21 to Florence Ritchie 18 Col. 10-1-1890 James Bristol,MG.
Beck,J.H.23 to Rebecca Stonecypher 21 Col. 3- 7-1901 J.W.Burston,M.G.
Beck,John 53 to Mary McCombs 40   Col. 12-8-1921 J.R.Pendergras,MG
Beck,Lawrence 25 to Annie Anderson 22 10-2-1925 Geo.Carpenter,J.P
Beeco,Bettex 19 to Leona Henson 18   9- 7-1913 J.R.Pendergras,MG
Beeco,C.C.21 to Bessie Brendle 18   1-27-1919 Robert Stamey,J.P
Beerdine,George to Susey Carter Colored 11-10-1868 R.C.Slagle,C.C.C.
Belk,Hiawatha to Shirley Grasty   12-7-1933 Will Smith,Ord.
Belk,Charles R.Jr.37 to Carole Collins 27 12-12-1941 J.L.Stokes,M.G.
   Both from Atlanta,Ga.
Bell,Sam H.24 to Amanda Sellers 26 Colored 2- 4-1886 J.J.McConnell,J.P
Bell,Charles W.22 to Callie V.Henson 22 2-25-1894 G.R.McPhearson,JP
Bell,Joseph R.26 to Savanah Shope 20   1-21-1906 Robert Stamey,J.P
Bell,James W.32 to Lizzie Simons 17   6- 3-1906 W.J.Morgan,J.P.
Benfield,John to Leannah Vanhook   8-31-1852 Wm.Angel,J.P.
Benfield,A.A. to Martha A.Morgan   3-29-1862 R.C.Slagle,Clk.
Benfield,J.L.19 to B.C.Roper 18   4-12-1873 John Ingram,J.P.
Benfield,Joseph 37 to Malinda Worley 23 10-14-1890 John B.Gray,J.P.
Bennett,Joseph L.38 to Melvina L.Vanhook 45/3-17-1892 G.R.McPherson,J.P
Bennett,M.S.20 to Callie Vinson 23   9- 7-1913 H.O.Miller,M.G.
Bennett,J.G.28 to Edna A.Rice 21   5-29-1921 S.H.Hilliard,M.G.
Bennett,Loyed 21 to Heerble Holland 18 9- 8-1934 Geo.Carpenter,J.P
Berry,John to Rachel Kirkland   12-23-1833 John Tatham,Clk.
Berry,William H. to Mary A.Moore   11-26-1855 J.D.Franks,J.P.

Berry,J.P.22 to L.E.Penland 19	11-21-1880 C.D.Smith,M.G.
Berry,Logan 75 to Frankie Blaine 65	2-10-1889 John Elmore,J.P.
Berry,Alexander J.23 to Minnie Sellers 20	11-15-1893 G.A.Bertlett,M.G.
Berry,Logan A.26 to Minnie Henry 16	4- 9-1896 G.A.Bartlett,M.G.
Berry,Fred 50 to Laura Mashburn 28	2-21-1900 T.R.Arnold,J.P.
Berry,W.A.24 to T.J.Higdon 24	12-24-1902 W.L.Higdon,J.P.
Berry,Jack 46 to Gertie Coggins 16	12-8-1918 J.M.Raby,J.P.
Berry,J.R.23 to Minnie Mincey 18	3-15-1920 J.R.Pendergrass,MG
Beshears,James to Elizabeth Roper	8-10-1837 Jesse Chastain.
Beshears,R.G.24 to Ruby Dowdle 27	9-13-1917 D.S.Richardson,M.G
Betts,Jep.L.29 to Lenna Lewis 30	4-26-1920 J.Q.Wallace,M.G.
Bentley,M.R.20 to Marietta Currier 18	9-20-1909 J.R.Pendergrass,MG
Bidwell,Frank E.32 to Mary L.Enloe 25	9-12-1893 D.H.Carnam,M.G.
Billingsley,James 26 to Lillie Brown 19	3- 1-1935 Geo.Carpenter,J.P
Bingham,Rufus to Nancy Cocern	7-28-1858 R.C.Slagle,Clk.
Bingham,J.F. to Jane Dickey	2-19-1859 R.C.Slagle,Clk.
Bingham,R.H.to Altha Griggs	11-20-1861 R.C.Slagle,Clk.
Bingham,G.N.to Sarah Lausen	3-31-1866 R.C.Slagle,C.C.C.
Bingham,C.L.21 to M.A.Hodgin 20	1-22-1880 J.H.Addington,J.P
Bingham,William A.21 to A.E.Fulcher 18	4-10-1882 E.L.Long,J.P.
Bingham,G.W.21 to Louisa Hodgins 18	2- 4-1884 W.C.Kimsey,J.P.
Bingham,J.Rickman 19 to Mary Elliott 18	11-3-1886 L.H.Enloe,J.P.
Bingham,Cicero L.30 to Rosetta N.Hodgins 26/8-10-1887 W.C.Kimsey,J.P.
Bingham,Charles 21 to Nannie Guy 19	11-10-1889 D.M.Matheson,M.G.
Bingham,R.L.25 to S.E.Bingham 19	5-15-1898 W.C.Sanders,J.P.
Bingham,Thomas 26 to Ella Blaine 28	2- 1-1899 M.A.West,M.G.
Bingham,Thos.A.33 to Fanny Dills 22	5-18-1899 H.H.Dills,J.P.
Bingham,J.N.26 to A.N.Dills 18	9-11-1899 W.A.Setser,J.P.
Bingham,W.A.31 to Lizzie Long 19	8- 8-1902 Jas.N.McConnell,JP
Bingham,Bart.L.20 to Nerva Gregory 20	10-22-1903 W.P.Allison,J.P.
Bingham,C.Oscar L.21 to Mamie T.Ledford 22	12-30-1906 A.M.Ledford,M.G.
Bingham,John R.26 to Lula Blaine 31	9- 8-1907 J.R.Pendergrass,MG
Bingham,Geo.N.22 to Belle Patton 22	1- 7-1910 W.H.Roane,J.P.
Bingham,Geo.N.Jr.22 to Jennie Sanders 29	1- 3-1910 Retd.Not executed
Bingham,Raleigh 19 to Sarah E.Ledford 22	5-22-1911 J.T.Watts,J.P.
Bingham,Monroe 19 to Anner Ledford 18	3-30-1914 Retd.Not executed
Bingham,Monroe 21 to Laura Ledford 16	12-21-1916 Robert Stamey,J.P
Bingham,Lawrence 21 to Bethel Bradley 21	4- 5-1918 W.C.Ledbetter,J.P.
Bingham,W.M.25 to Dora Wilson 19	6-20-1920 J.Q.Wallace,M.G.
Bingham,William L.20 to Willie M.Thomas 18	9-27-1925 J.J.Mann,J.P.
Bingham,Bill 21 to Arie Anderson 23 He from Gastonia,N.C.	11-28-1927 J.R.Pendergras,MG
Birchfield,David to Avaline Shuler	4-18-1846 J.K.Gray,Clk.
Birchfield,George 19 to Mattie Holland 19	7-23-1918 W.W.Marr,M.G.
Birchfield,Seth 19 to Hattie Skidmore 19 He from Bryson City,Swain Co.N.C.	12-21-1938 Lester L.Arnold,JP
Bird,Bonner to Elizabeth Redman	8-24-1834 Elijah Underwood,JP

Name	Date	Officiant
Bird,Benjamin to C.M.Connelly	8-16-1843	J.K.Gray,Clk.
Bird,Felix W.to Elza Watts	9- 3-1846	J.K.Gray,Clk.
Bird,John W.to Jane M.Moore	2-23-1848	J.K.Gray,Clk.
Bird,Joshua C.to Sophronia Wild	10-24-1849	T.C.Siler,Reg.
Bird,Johnathan to Martha A.Pevis	6- 3-1852	I.A.Reagan,M.G.
Bird,J.S. to N.C.Dean	4-27-1861	R.C.Slagle,Reg.
Bird,Robert to Mary Jane Battle	12-30-1866	J.F.Mashburn,J.P.
Bird,Clark to Melinda West	1- 2-1868	R.C.Slagle,C.C.C.
Bird,Benjamin A.to Mary A.Morrison	1- 6-1872	William Sloan,Reg
Bird,C.T.20 to L.O.Nichols 22	11-18-1875	W.H.Roane,J.P.
Bird,Jno.C.20 to Lucy Morrison 20	1- 8-1882	G.W.Dean,J.P.
Bird,John 21 to Ella Shields 16	10-30-1891	R.H.Anderson,M.G.
Bird,Geo.E.24 to Allie Anderson 26	1- 7-1903	W.A.Solesbee,J.P.
Bird,William L.23 to Jane Dean 18	6-11-1908	J.R.Pendergrass,MG
Bishop,Andrew 22 to Ella Mashburn 20	3-18-1897	W.A.Peek,J.P.
Bishop,Jake 24 to Vina Cantrell 17	12-26-1900	W.H.Morrison,J.P.
Black,Robert to Elizabeth Shields	3- 2-1833	J.K.Gray,Clk.
Blackburn,Levi A.to Nancy A.Franks	5- 9-1861	R.C.Slagle,Reg.
Blackburn,J.C.to A.M.Moore	5- 7-1870	Jas.K.Bryson,Reg.
Blackburn,J.P.to C.A.Parker	10-10-1902	W.A.Peek,J.P.
Blackburn,E.A.22 to Fannie Young 21	3- 3-1902	Original not found
Blackburn,O.C.38 to Mrs.Jane Lee Sherard 26/	9- 2-1908	T.C.King,M.G.
Blackwell,David to Margaret Wilson	3-31-1859	J.H.McCloud,J.P.
Blackwell,Frank 33 to Oma McIntyre 23	7- 8-1919	Geo.Carpenter,J.P
Blaine,Wilson N.to Francis Allen	11-1-1851	John McDowell,J.P
Blaine,William to Hester Daves	5- 8-1856	J.L.Robinson,Reg.
Blain,James to Matilda Carpenter	1-12-1859	R.C.Slagle,Clk.
Blain,B.F. to Sarah Forester	12-16-1869	J.H.Addington,J.P
Blain,John 21 to Jane Justice 20	7-15-1886	L.H.Garland,J.P.
Blaine,Charles L.24 to Hattie Sanders 24	3-23-1895	R.B.Shelton,M.G.
Blaine,J.W.24 to Ola Bingham 17	5-30-1901	C.W.Dowdle,J.P.
Blaine,Charles T.27 to Minnie G.Ashe 19	7- 2-1903	J.C.Postell,M.G.
Blain,Lawrence 22 to Ann Setser 22	11-28-1908	J.C.Shope,J.P.
Blaine,T.J.35 to Myra Potts	4-21-1909	A.W.Jacobs,M.G.
Blaine,D.W.40 to Maud Green 22	7-19-1911	J.R.Pendergrass,MG
Blaine,Phillip 40 to Bessie Corpening 31	4-17-1922	Geo.W.Moffitt,J.P
Blain,Arthur 23 to Lizzie Hodgins 19	12-27-1924	Geo.Carpenter,J.P
Blaine,Paul 22 to Annie Mae Lewis 18	9-16-1926	C.S.Slagle,J.P.
Blalock,Lester 36 to Emma Ghrmley 27	2-24-1918	J.W.Gregory,J.P.
Blankenship,Foeest 24 to Pauline McCoy 24	6- 9-1937	T.S.Denny,M.G.
He from Bryson City,Swain Co.N.C.		
Bleckley,Charles 18 to Laura Rogers 21 Col.	3- 4-1897	F.W.Wallace,M.G.
Bleckley,Thomas 30 to Linnie Allen 24	7-25-1897	E.Allison,M.G.
Bleufort,W.M. to Elizabeth Rogers	11-23-1848	Siler McDowell,JP
Bly,Robert 22 to Nan Bronson 17 Colored	12-17-1907	J.H.Morrison,M.G.
Bly,Q.L.24 to Octa Bronson 18 Colored	5-15-1897	A.B.Morrow,Deacon
Bolick,Gabriel to Polly Ammons	3- 1-1843	J.K.Gray,Clk.

```
Bolick,Jno.22 to Louisa George 18           8- 2-1876  J.S.Woodward,M.G.
Bolick,J.C.26 to S.F.Carpenter 22           12-4-1884  R.A.Owen,M.G.
Bolick,J.A.21 to Amanda Rogers 18           11-11-1900 A.G.Wood,J.P.
Bolick,Perry 21 to Florence Gibson 20       6-25-1905  J.H.Rogers,J.P.
Bolick,Sidney R.19 to Sarah J.Ashe 18       1- 3-1906  J.H.Roper,J.P.
Bolick,Carl 20 to Eva Rogers 18             8-28-1926  J.D.McCoy,J.P.
Bolick,John D.25 to Alma Moss 18            3-17-1935  W.G.Wood,J.P.
Bolinger,William 23 to Cordia Seabolt 19    4-20-1918  J.A.Brawner,M.G.
Boone,L.A.35 to Anna May 20                 1- 1-1903  F.M.Morgan,M.G.
Boring,James to Catherine Setser            11-26-1857 R.C.Slagle,D.Clk.
Boston,Jesse to Jane Woods                  8-31-1856  I.N.Keener,J.P.
Boston,Mack19 to Elizabeth Garret 21        7- 2-1883  A.S.Bryson,J.P.
Boston,Green 21 to Etter Carpenter 20       9-15-1901  W.P.Allison,J.P.
Boston,William 21 to Ezra McCracken 18      5-26-1912  Robt.Stamey,J.P.
Boston,Eugene 25 to Belle Leatherwood 26    12-31-1917 W.H.Roane,J.P.
Boston,Lee 48 to Jane Leatherwood 23        4-21-1918  W.W.Marr,M.G.
Boulton,Spencer to Nancy Brown              12-17-1840 John Hall,Clk.
Bolton,Claude 29 to Margaret Slagle 26      6-23-1941  J.A.Flanagan,M.G.
Bowers,Charles D.33 to Ivy Symonds 28       10-15-1889 W.R.Barnett,M.G.
Bowers,Robert 20 to Zora Wilson 18          3-23-1935  Carl Slagle,J.P.
Bowers,Charlie 26 to Lelia Wilson 20        3-28-1935  Geo.Carpenter,J.P
Bowman,John to Mary A.Stiwinter             3- 4-1857  I.N.Keener,J.P.
Bowman,Geo.S.28 to Sarah A.Wood 19          8-26-1888  J.M.Keener,J.P.
Bowman,James 22 to Flora Peek 22            5-11-1913  H.O.Miller,M.G.
Bowman,J.E.25 to Dora Gregory 23            3-21-1917  D.M.Rogers,J.P.
Boyd,James I.to Sarah G.Williams            2-16-1850  T.P.Siler,D.Clk.
Boyd,George Thos.to Jane Dalton             3-16-1871  William Sloan,Reg
Boyd,W.H.20 to H.L.Brendle 19               12-5-1880  E.H.Franks,J.P.
Boyd,J.A.21 to Cora Collins 18              2-10-1917  Geo.Carpenter,J.P
Boyd,H.T.22 to Lealer Johnson 20            5- 1-1920  J.B.Henry,J.P.
Boyd,Julius 21 to Beulah M.Ferguson 21      12-7-1929  Walter M.Lee,M.G.
   Both from Waynesville,Haywood Co.N.C.
Boyd,Thomas W.27 to Willie M.Newman 28      9-23-1933  W.A.Jenkins,M.G.
   He from Hendersonville,N.C... She from Water Town,Fla.
Boynton,Chas.L.30 to Mary E.Anderson 19     7-15-1894  Henery Emerson,MG
Brabson,A.C.39 to C.A.Rush 18               3-24-1881  M.R.Kirkpatrick,MG
Brabson,John M.28 to Mary McDowell 21       1- 1-1914  J.L.Teague,M.G.
Bracker,Abadiah to Agnes Cockerham          7-18-1829  W.B.Hyatt,Clk.
Bradford,George W. to Nancy Hopkins         7-28-1847  J.K.Gray,Clk.
Bradley,George to Elizabeth Bradley         1-18-1843  J.K.Gray,Clk.
Bradley,S.P.to Martha M.Long                4-14-1846  J.K.Gray,Clk.
Bradley,James to Altha Long                 1-31-1857  A.J.Carpenter,J.P
Bradley,J.H.to F.A.Hooper                   12-28-1865 R.C.Slagle,Reg.
Bradley,Joseph N.to Margaret Allen          1- 7-1869  S.H.Hyatt,J.P.
Bradley,Ely Morris to Margaret A.Burnett    1-10-1872  William Sloan,Reg
Bradley,Henry J.22 to Rachel M.Burnett 21   8-21-1873  M.Rickman,M.G.
Bradley,L.M.28 to L.J.Morrison 24           5- 8-1879  J.S.Woodard,M.G.
```

Bradley,J.A.24 to N.C.Bradley 23	2-21-1884	L.Howard,J.P.
Bradley,W.L.24 to Nicy A.Shuler 20	3-12-1884	John S.Gibson,J.P
Bradley,S.J.19 to M.E.Dickeson 18	3-29-1885	L.Howard,J.P.
Bradley,Alexander 18 to Selah Moore 16	8-16-1885	M.Ghormley,M.G.
Bradley,Andrew B.25 to Elizabeth Cabe 18	10-7-1886	L.Howard,J.P.
Bradley,Riley B.28 to Mary J.Howard 24	1-28-1887	L.Howard,J.P.
Bradley,Samuel P.70 to Marinda A.Dryman 40	4-14-1887	S.A.Dixon,J.P
Bradley,John H.46 to Sarah Jones 48	5-19-1889	S.A.Dixon,J.P.
Bradley,John P.21 to Mary Hopper 21	4- 4-1895	W.A.Norton,J.P.
Bradley,Martin 21 to Mrs.Ollie Reed 21	11-20-1898	M.Ghormley,M.G.
Bradley,G.R.24 to Ora Dillard 20	12-17-1902	J.C.Postell,M.G.
Bradley,C.N.25 to G.B.Parrish 17	2-20-1903	J.C.Postell,M.G.
Bradley,Ray 22 to Mittie Tallent 16	8-24-1904	W.L.Bradley,M.G.
Bradley,Everett 23 to Bula Byrd 19	10-1-1905	W.J.Morgan,J.P.
Bradley,Frad 21 to Lula Norton 23	1-14-1909	W.A.Norton,J.P.
Bradley,Judd 24 to Lillie Byrd 19	4- 4-1909	P.H.Justice,J.P.
Bradley,Avery 24 to Elna Hall 16	9- 4-1909	J.L.Younce,M.G.
Bradley,Mack 21 to Nora Rogers 15	12-17-1910	T.J.Vinson,M.G.
Bradley,W.W.23 to Tim Shepherd 26	5-17-1911	J.R.Pendergrass,MG
Bradley,Hillard 25 to Myrtle Welch 18	1- 3-1915	J.A.Lakey,J.P.
Bradley,I.E.35 to Alma Ghormley 23	2-26-1917	Z.Baird,J.P.
Bradley,E.R.42 to Bessie Rogers 21	1-20-1918	A.M.Ledford,M.G.
Bradley,Charles T.25 to Ruby Lee Gibson 17	8- 6-1926	G.A.Cloer,M.G.
Bradshaw,John to Sarah Freeman	1-20-1841	John Hall,Clk.
Bradshaw,Robert to Margaret Nichols	8- 7-1843	J.K.Gray,Clk.
Bradshaw,John to R.L.DeLozier	10-11-1859	R.C.Slagle,Clk.
Bradshaw,James to Martha Culbertson	11-8-1860	T.P.Siler,D.Clk.
Bradshaw,Horace F.23 to Elizabeth Howard 20/4- 3-1892		J.J.McConnell,J.P
Braselton,J.B.35 to Harriett Estes 25 Col.	11-27-1879	H.G.Woodfin,J.P.
Brownell,Abram 58 to Irena A.Morgan 50	11-28-1894	M.Ghormley,M.G.
Breedlove,Jessie to Mary A.DeHart	10-13-1855	William DeHart,JP
Breedlove,John to Sarah DeHart	8- 3-1860	T.P.Siler,Clk.
Breedlove,B.W.20 to B.L.Deuval 19	7-27-1879	T.J.Dawson,M.G.
Breedlove,J.Patton 22 to Dora Byrd 18	4-28-1892	J.S.Woodard,M.G.
Breedlove,Elbert 21 to S.J.Bates 36	10-5-1902	P.H.Justice,J.P.
Breedlove,Wiley 21 to Margaret Craig 21	2-11-1904	Joseph L.Fouts,JP
Breedlove,Robert 23 to Mae Deweese 17	3-28-1907	F.M.Morgan,M.G.
Breedlove,Harley 27 to Maggie Bradley 23	9-18-1917	D.C.McCoy,J.P.
Breedlove,T.E.21 to Ethel McCoy 17	8-17-1917	Theo.McCoy,J.P.
Breedlove,R.E.37 to Leila Bradley 33	7-21-1923	J.R.Pendergrass,MG
Brendle,Henry to Palsy M.Pilkerton	6-25-1848	J.K.Gray,Clk.
Brendle,Alfred M. to Martha I.Miller	11-1-1855	John Hall,Clk.
Brendle,Joseph to Amanda L.Sanders to	11-2-1855	B.W.Craig,J.P.
Brendle,Joseph to Sarah McDowell	8- 8-1859	H.G.Woodfin,J.P.
Brendle,John D.to Mary L.Galion	7-27-1863	T.P.Siler,Reg.
Brendle,J.D. to Rachel Grant	7-15-1864	R.C.Slagle,Clk.
Brendle,John to M.M.Chasteen	10-6-1866	R.C.Slagle,C.C.C.

```
Brendle,William to Jane Cline                        7-13-1869  J.K.Bryson,Reg.
Brendle,Harman D.22 to C.Virginia Gibbs 17   9- 4-1884  E.H.Bogle,M.G.
Brendle,Mathew M.21 to Mary Reid 18              5-27-1885 Original Not found
Brendle,Edmond H.22 to Harriett M.Saunders 19/10-23-1887-Jno.Elmore,J.P.
Brendle,John T. to Orrie G.Gibbs 21              1-16-1890  W.J.Mashburn,J.P.
Brendle,George 20 to Lilly Downs 20              1-23-1893  W.J.Jenkins,J.P.
Brendle,Alex J.H. 35 to Lizzie E.C.Mincy 22/8-16-1894  J.W.Parker,J.P.
Brendle,John 25 to Nannie Ray 16                 1-22-1896  J.S.Woodard,M.G.
Brendle,R.D.30 to Annie Ledford 22               10-29-1896J.R.Pendergrass,MG
Brendle,William T.25 to Sarah Childers 27   11-5-1899  R.D.Sellers,J.P.
Brendle,W.T.33 to Adna Childers 44               8-16-1908 J.R.Pendergrass,MG
Brendle,D.F.23 to Myrtle Painter 22              7-26-1910 J.R.Pendergrass,MG
Brendle,Joe 18 to Bertha Brendle 15              10-30-1910 Geo.Carpenter,J.P
Brendle,M.T.19 to Lula Sanders 21                6-30-1918  J.B.Henry,J.P.
Brendle,H.T.36 to Pearl Sanders 25               7- 6-1919  J.B.Henry,J.P.
Brendle,W.T.42 to Evalee Scroggs 25              10-29-1919 Retd.not Executed
Brendle,C.J.24 to Martha Pressley 20             1- 1-1920  G.L.Jones,M.G.
Brendle,W.T.44 to Eva M.Shepherd 23              5-15-1920  Geo.Carpenter,J.P
Brendle,F.M.24 to Nobia B.Sanders 18             8-30-1924 J.R.Pendergrass,MG
Brendle,Jule R.to Louisa Shepherd 21             11-6-1926  Geo.Carpenter,J.P
Brendle,John A.24 to Fannie Moore 19             3-10-1928 J.R.Pendergrass,JP
Brendle,L.G.28 to Alice R.Rickman 26             3-24-1928  Geo.Carpenter,J.P
Brendle,David W.22 to Josephine Martin 20   9- 4-1940  R.F.Mayberry,M.G.
   He from Morganton,Burke Co.N.C.
Bridgers,Rupert C. 22 to Dorthy Hunnicutt 16  11-24-1934 Will Smith,Ord.
   He from Rowland,Robeson Co.N.C.
Briggs,Wm.Robert 33 to Margaret E.Wild 19   11-1-1896  J.P.Campbell,J.P.
Briggs,J.W.49 to Coedelia Bryson 38              2- 9-1910  T.C.King,M.G.
Bristol,J.M.52 to Hattie Gudger 48 Colored  1- 7-1903  Jas.T.Kenedy,M.G.
Bristol,James M.58 to Elva Prater 46 Col.   10-12-1910 W.H.Roane,J.P.
Britton,Lawson to Eliza Laney                    1- 3-1840  John Hall,Clk.
Britton,Thomas U.to Sarah H.Steel                4- 6-1842  J.K.Gray,Clk.
Brooks,Robert P.to Mary A.Ford                   7-15-1870  .J.K.Bryson,Reg.
Brooks,John T.25 to Margaret D.McCall 17    1-12-1896  G.W.Matney,M.G.
Brooks,Jonathan R.29 to Elizabeth Chastain 22/1-1-1903 T.Baxter White,JP
Brooks,James 21 to Dolly Jones 19                6-29-1904  J.E.Woosley,M.G.
Brooks,Candler 22 to Rosa Brendle 18             8-27-1907  C.H.Caviness,M.G.
Brooks,Eddie 20 to Kansas Pickens 20             12-11-1910 J.L.Bryson,J.P.
Brooks,Robert C.29 to Iris M.Porter 21           9-14-1912  J.A.Deal,M.G.
Brooks,Roy 22 to Bell Tallent 19                 5-20-1916  Geo.Carpenter,J.P
Brooks,Robert 19 to Maggie Sanders 18            3- 2-1919  J.M.Raby,J.P.
Brooks,C.T.21 to Almetta Picklesimer 21          9-20-1924  J.W.Baty,M.G.
Broom,Hobert 21 to Exie Mathis 18                12-22-1924 Geo.Carpenter,J.P
Bronson,Albert 22 to Margaret Upton 18 Col. 3-10-1881  M.J.Mashburn,J.P.
Bronson,Frank 28 to Bessie Williams 22 Col. 12-26-1913 J.R.Pendergras,MG
Brown,R.A. to Elizabeth Corn                     10-6-1831  D.H.Jarrett,J.P.
Brown,James to Elvira Parker                     7-12-1842  N.M.Patton.
```

Brown,Robert S. to Elizabeth Moss	9- 4-1844	N.H.Palmer,Wit.
Brown,D.F. to Dulcena Patton	3-31-1866	R.C.Slagle,C.C.C.
Brown,Aron W.to Marharett H.Moore	12-1-1866	R.C.Slagle,C.C.C.
Brown,William S.19 to Lucy Fuller 23	9- 7-1873	James McGee,J.P.
Brown,John 37 to Martha Buchanan 23	8- 5-1876	W.W.Henry,J.P.
Brown,G.W.30 to N.M.Vanhook 23	5-15-1879	M.L.Kelly,J.P.
Brown,Edward 18 to Maggie Fretwell 19 Col.	5-14-1886	Jas.Bristol,M.G.
Brown,Ransom U.28 to Jennie Cochran 21	11-1-1888	A.B.Thomas,M.G.
Brown,James M.22 to Cassie Hill 20	10-13-1892	D.H.Cowan,M.G.
Brown,Robert 20 to Mary Rogers 17	12-12-1893	James C.Weaver,JP
Brown,Caleb·A.23 to Nannie M.Long 23	2-24-1895	L.H.Garland,J.P.
Brown,Alfred 20 to Mary J.Ballew 18	1-23-1897	G.R.McPherson,J.P
Brown,Bedford 29 to Mary Sanders 18	2- 1-1899	T.F.Glenn,M.G.
Brown,William20 to Effie Watts 14	3-18-1900	M.A.West,M.G.
Brown,J.M.25 to Julia Dowdle 16	11-18-1900	C.W.Dowdle,J.P.
Brown,J.W.25 to Bell Angel 22	10-6-1901	John H.Moore,M.G.
Brown,Cling 20 to Sarah Houston 17	10-29-1901	J.H.Fulton,J.P.
Brown,Charles 20 to Mamie Fulcher 20	11-17-1901	C.W.Dowdle,J.P.
Brown,William 23 to Flora Garland 30	2-22-1902	T.N.Ford,M.G.
Brown,Otto 18 to Hattie Cloer 16	1-20-1903	J.G.Bates,J.P.
Brown,F.E.29 to A.E.Justice 22	8-12-1906	J.E.Cabe,J.P.
Brown,William 28 toEthel Cadon 22	9-13-1908	J.T.Vinson,M.G.
Brown,Frank H.26 to Hattie S.Norton 29	2-23-1909	J.A.Peeler,M.G.
Brown,David 21 to Lucy Williams (Shank)?	9-27-1909	T.C.King,M.G.
Brown,Thomas 24 to Laura McClure 18	12-2-1909	C.R.Cabe,J.P.
Brown,Lee Jr.19 to Sarah I.Chasteen 18	11-28-1912	R.H.Munger,J.P.
Brown,E.H.24 to Flora Ballew 24	7- 2-1916	E.B.Bell,M.G.
Brown,Bryant 24 to Lula Young 18	1-20-1919	W.W.Marr,M.G.
Brown,T.E.38 to Maud Barnard 31	6-24-1919	L.B.Hayes,M.G.
Brown,G.E. 32 to Julia Cunningham 26	5-23-1920	J.R.Pendergrass,MG
Brown,W.S.22 to Helen Allison 28	6-13-1920	J.Q.Wallace,M.G.
Brown,Harry 25 to Marinda Smart 25	8- 6-1924	W.M.Smith,M.G.
Brown,George T.40 to Annie B.Henson 31 He from Athens,Ga.	11-10-1926	J.A.Flanagan,M.G.
Brown,Edgar 27 to Ruby Ashe 22 He from Barto,Ga... She from Whittier,Swain Co.N.C.	9-24-1927	A.P.Retledge,M.G.
Brown,T.Wiley 27 to Annie B.Angel 28	10-17-1931	H.C.Freeman,M.G.
Brown,Benj.B.31 to Gladys Parham 22 He from Griffin,Ga... She from Greenville,Ga.	4- 7-1934	E.R.Eller,M.G.
Brown James H.26 to Eugene Ramey 26 Hé from Atlanta,Ga... She from Clayton,Ga.	4-29-1934	Geo.Carpenter,J.F
Brown,Clarence S.23 to Mildred Cozad 22	8-4-1934	J.A.Flanagan,M.G.
Brown,William to Malinda Moss	9-19-1835	-------
Brown,Cornelius to Minervie Anderson	1-16-1836	U.Keener,D.Clk.
Brown,George W.26 to Bernice Broom 22 He from Darrington,Wash....She from Monroe,N.C.	11-26-1937	A.A.Angel,M.G.
Brown,William J. to Dora Brown	2-21-1838	J.K.Gray,Clk.
Brown,David A. to Rachel Hyde	7-13-1838	John Hall,Clk.

```
Brown,David Carroll 23 to Mahalie King 23      6-28-1939  J.G.Benfield,M.G.
  He from Anderson,S.C.
Browning,Charlie 18 to Kansie Caler 17         1-21-1886  Jas.A.Morrison,JP
Browning,William 21 to Frona Carver 18         3-27-1904  C.L.Rickman,J.P.
Browning,Newton 19 to Cora Jones 28            11-24-1912 W.H.Guffey,M.G.
Browning,V.A.24 to Nannie West 26              7-21-1915  W.G.Warren,M.G.
Browning,George 21 to Jane Scott 34            8- 4-1918  Geo.Carpenter,J.P
Browning,Humphery 20 to Gladys Shuler 20       10-17-1920 D,C.McCoy,M.G.
Brocker,Abadiah to Agnes Cockerham             7-18-1829  W.B.Hyatt.
Bruce,Climan C.45 to Texie Lunsford 23         1-13-1899  E.N.Evans,J.P.
Bryant,Willie 21 to Caroline Forrester 18      11-18-1897 E.N.Dalrymple,J.P
Bryant,Henry 21 to Elizabeth T.Ray 16          2- 4-1892  P.C.Wild,J.P.
Bryant,Henry 21 to Sarah Haney 19              10-14-1900 M.Ghormley,M.G.
Bryant,Walter 22 to Nannie Wilkes 18           5-20-1910  J.L.Fouts,J.P.
Bryant,Grady 20 to Minnie Ashe 18              12-22-1912 W.E.Welch,J.P.
Bryant,Marion 62 to Martha McConley 45         5-31-1917  D.F.Howard,J.P.
Bryant,Mark 25 to Lucinda Poindexter 19        7- 2-1922  A.S.Solesby,M.G.
Bryant,Horace 28 to Nora Taylor 26             8-25-1933  David F.Howard,MG
Bryant,J.H.22 to D.C.Haney 22                  2-11-1904  D.F.Howard,M.G.
  Both from Nantahala,N.C.
Bryson,James M.to Margaret Young               11-20-1832 William McKee,D.C
Bryson,John to Olivia Jones                    9-23-1833  John Hall,Clk.
Bryson,William to Mary Loudermilk              7-18-1835  ------.
Bryson,Samuel N.to Nancy Arnold                4-14-1838  John Hall,Clk
Bryson,Uel G.to Precilla Kerby                 10-13-1838 ------.
Bryson,Samuel to Sarah Moore                   2-27-1839  H.G.Woodfin,D.Clk
Bryson,Andrew to Jane Peek                     9-11-1840  Milton McCoy,J.P.
Bryson,Joseph to Mary C.Phillips               10-17-1840 John Hall,Clk.
Bryson,James to Elizabeth E.Shepherd           11-13-1843 J.K.Gray,Clk.
Bryson,Hugh B. to Elizabeth Angel              9-28-1847  J.K.Gray,Clk.
Bryson,George W. to Mary E.Connelly            10-30-1848 E.Dowdle,Reg.
Bryson,James H. to Caroline Siler              12-13-1848 S.G.Garrett,D.Clk
Bryson,Lefayett to Jane Mathis                 12-11-1850 J.K.Gray,Clk.
Bryson,William to Cyntha Moore                 7-27-1854  John Hall,Clk.
Bryson,Samuel to Mary Morrison                 2-11-1861  R.C.Slagle,Reg.
Bryson,A.F.to Angeline Williams                1- 4-1869  W.H.Higdon,J.P.
Bryson,James K.to Maggie Higdon                10-1-1871  H.H.Elmore,J.P.
Bryson,John N.25 to Sarah Ann Haskett 16       2-13-1874  I.S.Woodward,M.G.
  He from Jackson Co.N.C.
Bryson,John T.23 to Martha Jane Deal 22        3-29-1874  J.W.Bowman,M.G.
Bryson,Albert S.23 to Leona L.Lyle 20         .1-20-1875  L.H.Haynes,M.G.
Bryson,A.M.22 to Amanda Crisp 20               1-19-1879  Hosea Moses,J.P.
Bryson,T.C.27 to Mary S.Morrison 16            1-29-1879  A.Ammons,M.G.
Bryson,Virgil 42 to Eve Siler 38   Colored     11-6-1884  S.H.Harrington,M.G
Bryson,Columbus 19 to Mary Ingram 18           7-10-1887  M.J.Skenner,J.P.
Bryson,George T.26 to Rebecca T.Matlock 20     11-13-1887 A.B.Thomas,M.G.
Bryson,Abraham 21 to Callie Thomas 17 Col.     11-28-1888 M.J.Mashburn,J.P.
Bryson,James L.25 to Fannie Mallonee 21        12-20-1888 C.B.Lefew,M.G.
```

Bryson,Simeon D.33 to Eliza Shepherd 33Col.   3- 3-1889   E.J.Harris,M.G.
Bryson,Robert L.19 to Laura Wild 17   3- 8-1889   J.E.Morgan,M.G.
Bryson,Chas.S.25 to Beulah Watkins 17   3- 7-1895   Geo.T.Bryson,J.P.
Bryson,T.M.21 to Toledo Wilson 20   2-18-1897   A.W.Young,M.G.
Bryson,W.H.22 to Ida Adams 20   1-23-1898   J.M.Williams,J.P.
Bryson,D.V.22 to Mary A.Hall 22   8-13-1899   J.A.Young,J.P.
Bryson,Zeb V.23 to Rosa Allen 20   1- 4-1900   W.R.Rickman,M.G.
Bryson,William M.25 to Mary E.Bell 23   8-18-1901   R.S.Howe,M.G.
Bryson,Monroe 23 to Ivalee Holland 18   5- 3-1903   J.H.Fulton,J.P.
Bryson,G.L.C.26 to Lela Carter 19 Colored   6-28-1903   C.L.Stewart,M.G.
Bryson,Robert T.19 to Nora West 17   11-29-1903 J.H.Moore,M.G.
Bryson,John23 to Naoma Raby 27   11-9-1904   I.T.Peek,M.G.
Bryson,Bulon 21 to Tula Penland 19   12-24-1905 W.R.Bulgin,J.P.
Bryson,Felix 21 to Paralee Brooks 22 Col.   4- 4-1906   A.Z.Robinson,M.G.
Bryson,Geo.E.26 to Fannie B.Thomas 20   2-10-1907   C.H.Caviness,M.G.
Bryson,L.Lee 21 to Mary J.Wilks 20   3- 5-1907   Jos.L.Fouts,J.P.
Bryson,Bert. 32 to Joanna Clark: 28   2-21-1909   J.W.Ammons,J.P.
Bryson,Frank 22 to Selma Bryson 18   7- 9-1911   P.C.Calloway,J.P.
Bryson,C.A.44 to Nannie Matlock 34   2-29-1912   J.F.Starnes,M.G.
Bryson,Charles B.24 to Maggie Gregory 22   3- 9-1902   J.R.Pendergrass,MG
Bryson,Frank 26 to Carrie Moore 22   7-21-1912   J.A.Bryson,M.G.
Bryson,Elbert 25 to Eliza Bolick 30   12-15-1889 J.W.Keener,M.G.
Bryson,Edward 21 to Elvia Anderson 19   9- 4-1912   Retd.Not executed
Bryson,J.A.28 to Doris Dean 23   9-10-1912   R.P.McCracken,M.G.
Bryson,Dee 21 to Lillie Vinson 19   11-22-1913 H.O.Miller,M.G.
Bryson,A.F.25 to Hattie Raby 21   9- 5-1915   J.A.Lakey,J.P.
Bryson,J.P.25 to Arphia Raby 21   11-21-1917 E.O.Rickman,J.P.
Bryson,T.N.24 to Leona Evans 18   2- 8-1918   Geo.Carpenter,J.P
Bryson,Roy 20 to Annie Raby 16   10-12-1918 J.A.Morrison,J.P.
Bryson,Roy 22 to Cassie McCall 27   6-16-1920   D.L.Miller,M.G.
Bryson,Carr 32 to Frances Rickman 20   8-12-1926   G.A.Cloer,M.G.
Bryson,D.H.24 to Ivalee Childers 22   10-4-1927   J.A.Flanagan,M.G.
   He from Sylva,N.C.
Bryson,Theodore 23 to Ella Young 19   5- 7-1933   J.M.Keener,M.G.
Bryson,Ray 23 to Amelia Wright 18   7- 5-1933   Will Smith,Ord.
Bryson,Joe 26 to Viola Tallent 17   12-23-1933 V.C.Ramey,M.G.
Bryson,Sam Jr.22 to Bertha Higdon 18   1-18-1934   W.Frank Gillespie
Bryson,Edward B.23 to Zena McLean 18   8-10-1935   S.J.Murray,J.P.
Bryson,Marion 25 to Evelyn Sandheimer 18   12-6-1941   C.W.Modder,M.G.
Buchanan,James to Martha Cowin   4- 3-1841   H.G.Woodfin,D.Clk
Buchanan,Charles S. to Minerva Green   10-14-1848 Jonathan Neill.
Buchanan,James to Sarah Cabe   7- 4-1849   E.Dowdle.
Buchanan,Joseph to Martha A.Raby   2-17-1849   Jno.Buchanan,Wit.
Buchanan,William H.to Elvira Brooks   2-25-1852   H.G.Woodfin,Clk.
Buchanan,John A.to Name not given   3-10-1857   John Hall,Clk.
Buchanan,L.D. to Martha A.Peek   1- 7-1867   R.C.Slagle,Reg.
Buchanan,D.W.21 to Louella Blain 18   7-27-1876   W.H.Higdon,J.P.

```
Buchanan,B.M.22 to Catherine Tilson 19        12-16-1880  J.M.Keener,J.P.
Buchanan,M.R.22 to F.B.Keener,17              10-21-1880  Hosea Moses,J.P.
Buchanan,James M.48 to Jemima E.Elmore 38     8-13-1886  S.H.Harrington,M.G
Buchanan,James L.19 to Callie F.Long 20       10-13-1887  T.J.Vinson,J.P.
Buchanan,James A.26 to Mary Wiggins 18        12-20-1888  A.B.Dalton,J.P.
Buchanan,E.W.23 to Philadelphia Williams 18/9- 4-1898  W.A.Peek,J.P.
Buchanan,M.R.40 to Lydia J.Clark 22           4-10-1898  G.W.Stiwinter,J.P
Buchanan,Jack 22 to Ella Williams 18          5-19-1898  W.A.Peek,J.P.
Buchanan,J.W.22 to D.A.Hasket 25              10-8-1899  E.C.Stewman,J.P.
Buchanan,R.J.23 to D.M.Franks 18              12-21-1902  W.H.Hasket,J.P.
Buchanan,George 23 to Dovie Wood 19           1- 3-1906  J.W.Ammons,J.P.
Buchanan,Ben E.47 to Isabelle Thompson 27     8-23-1907  C.L.Rickman,M.G.
Buchanan,Oscar 18 to Edna Picklesimer 15      10-26-1911  J.M.Conley,J.P.
Buchanan,Elias 21 to Albie Cabe 16            12-31-1914  J.B.Hensley,M.G.
Buchanan,James 48 to Nora Conley 64           4- 8-1914  C.R.Cabe,J.P.
Buchanan,Verlin 22 to Willie Rickman 18       11-2-1914  P.R.Rickman,M.G.
Buchanan,Dan 29 to Minnie Gregory 19          7- 5-1916  J.P.Moore,J.P.
Buchanan,Dewey 17 to Iris Morgan 17           5-21-1916 Geo.Carpenter,J.P.
Buchanan,W.J.23 to Sallie Gregory 17          9- 5-1916  J.M.Williams,J.P.
Buchanan,J.L.60 to Mrs.Georgia Wilson 61      3- 3-1928 Geo.Carpenter,J.P.
   She from Cornelia,Ga.
Buchanan,Ellis 41 to Ruby Mason 22            5-25-1935  W.R.Rowland,J.P.
Buckner,Albin to Elizabeth Guyer              8- 5-1842  J.K.Gray,D.Clk.
Buckner,Shadrick to Martha Johnston           11-3-1842  J.K.Gray,D.Clk.
Buckner,Elijah to Margaret Dills              5-18-1854  John Hall,Clk.
Buckner,William to Mary A.Tippett             8-11-1857  T.P.Siler,D.Clk.
Buckner,Dock H.22 to Louella Bird 20          9-19-1896  Jno.H.Bradley,M.G
Bulgin,William G.42 to Virginia R.Moore 27    9- 3-1874  A.W.Miller,M.G.
Bulgin,Geo.M.35 to Blanche Brabson 27         6-21-1911  W.P.Chedester,M.G
Bulgin,Lawrence B.40 to Mildred McGuire 29    2-22-1923  J.Q.Wallace,M.G.
Bulgin,John 24 to Margaret A.Slagle 20        11-26-1937 J.A.Flanagan,M.G.
Bullock,Eugene C.32 to Virginia A.McGuire 25/6-18-1938 J.A.Flanagan,M.G.
   He from Hamlet,N.C.
Bumgarner,George to Eliza A.Tatham            2-27-1847  J.K.Gray,D.Clk
Bumgarner,J.N.23 to May Norton 22             11-25-1875 Chas.B.Fugate,M.G
   He from Jackson Co.N.C.
Bumgarner,Geo.E.24 to Margaret Clark 25       9- 2-1900  J.M.Keener,M.G.
Burch,Dyer to Name not given                  4-15-1836  --------
Burch,Barnett to M.M.Johnston                 9-22-1860  R.C.Slagle,Reg.
Burch,James A.to Mary Patton                  4-14-1863  R.C.Slagle,Reg.
Burch,M.C. to A.A.Moffatt                     11-4-1865  --------
Burch,J.P.20 to Margaret J.Ledford 21         4-11-1878  Z.Barnes,J.P.
Burch,M.L.21 to Iowa Davis 17                 8- 7-1879  Mark May,M.G.
Burch,Lee 22 to Mary Parker 20                4-18-1907  D.F.Howard,M.G.
Burch,Robert H.32 to Minnie M.Vinson 21       8-25-1913  A.W.Donaldson,J.P
Burgess,Samuel to Sharlotte Justice           10-19-1867 R.C.Slagle,Reg.
Burgess,Julius 25 to Georgia L.McDonnel 16 Col./2-12-1886 Z.Barnes,J.P.
Burgess,Thomas 20 to Lucinda Beck 16 Col.     8- 6-1887 Original not found
```

```
Burgess,Julius 50 to Roxie Burston 50 Col.   8-30-1911   M.J.Mashburn,M.G.
Burgess,Frank 27 to Vick Love 28         Col.  12-29-1912 M.J.Mashburn,J.P.
Burgess,Thomas 23 to Ella Scruggs 22  Col.  2-12-1917 J.R.Pendergrass,MG
Burgess,Charles 22 to Carrie Penland 18 Col.2- 1-1919   E.G.Siler,M.G.
Burgess,John 23 to Ola M.Shepherd 19   Col.  3-20-1920   W.F.Love,M.G.
Burgess,Billie 24 to Maggie Hall 32     Col.  8-10-1933 Geo.Carpenter,J.P
Burgin,Otis O.28 to Ruth Nolen 22           4-28-1927  A.P.Ratledge,M.G.
   Both from Waynesville,N.C.
Burleson,S.L.32 to Bida Penland 23          12-18-1907 J.R.Pendergras,MG
Burnett,Geo.W.to Sarah McHan                12-27-1942? J.K.Gray,Clk.
Burnett,James to Sarah Potts                12-26-1853 John Hall,Clk.
Burnett,Henry to Matilda DeHart             10-28-1856 ---------
Burnett,E.J.A. to Martha Matlock             9-13-1859  J.H.McLoud,J.P.
Burnett,Francis to Eliza Duvall              2-15-1859  R.C.Slagle,Reg.
Burnett,Henry C.to Louisa Bird              11-12-1869 B.G.Wild,M.G.
Burnett,James W.20 to Mary E.Ray 20          1- 9-1881  G.W.Dean,J.P.
Burnett,M.S.50 to Adeline Burrell 22         1-22-1882  J.N.Arnold,J.P.
Burnett,J.E.19 to Elizabeth Lakey 17        12-25-1884 Jno.S.Gibson,J.P.
Burnett,Henry 20 to Laura Shuler 21          1- 9-1890  A.A.Justice,M.G.
Burnett,Fred 22 to Mary Queen 18            12-25-1906 W.L.Bradley,M.G.
Burnett,Vernel 18 to Gertrude Wilson 17      2-14-1909  P.H.Justice,J.P.
Burnett,Frank 23 to Pansy Hughes 19          4-25-1915  J.A.Brendle,M.G.
Burnett,Dewey 22 to Esther DeHart 18         8- 6-1921  W.L.Bradley,M.G.
Burnett,M.S.20 to Callie Vinson 23           9- 7-1913  H.O.Miller,M.G.
Burnett,E.V.26 to Ima B.Rose 18              5-25-1921  Geo.Carpenter,J.P
Burnett,Wade 26 to Eva Arvey 28              3-25-1921 J.R.Pendergrass,MG
Burnett,J.D.26 to Mary McConnell 20         12-22-1922 Chas.S.Plyler,M.G
Burnett,John 25 to Emma Dean 24             12-29-1887 A.A.Justice,M.G.
Burns,W.F.45 to Martha Boston 20             4-16-1908 J.R.Pendergrass,MG
Burrell,W.L.17 to Mary M.Ridley 16          10-17-1880 J.T.Berry,J.P.
Burrell,B.26 to Lillie Ridley 25             2- 5-1905  C.L.Rickman,J.P.
Burrell,J.G.20 to Cordelia Holland 19        3-14-1909  T.J.Vinson,M.G.
Burrell,Lee 50 to Mrs.Ada E.Bates 48         5- 7-1935  J.L.Teague,M.G.
Burrell,Clark Lewis 20 to Anna Jean Moore 20/10-13-1940 Ivon L.Roberts.
Burris,Fernando 21 to Della Meadows 21       3- 9-1890  D.F.Howard,J.P.
Burston,Fletcher 22 to Roxie Carter 20 Col. 3-10-1881  M.J.Mashburn,M.G.
Burston,James 20 to Arie Moore 18       Col.  12-28-1899 A.B.Morrow,M.G.
Butler,W.O.44 to Lydia Keener 23             9-26-1884  J.M.Keener,J.P.
Burt,Edward 23 to Stella G.Marett 21        10-1-1937  J.A.Flanagan,M.G.
   He from Sarsota,Fla.
Burton,S.V.21 to Ida Hodgins 22              7- 9-1893  G.R.McPherson,J.P.
Burston,Jerry M.21 to Addie Jones 22        10-22-1896 J.M.Farmer,J.P.
Burton,Virgil 35 to Cora E.Ledford 25        9-29-1910  C.W.Slagle,J.P.
Burton,Joe M.23 to Isabell S.Richardson 23  8-24-1938 J.A.Flanagan,M.G.
   Both from Atlanta,Ga.
Byrd,D.C.25 to Mary Bradley 25               5-31-1903  T.S.DeHart,M.G.
Byrd,B.A.60 to Emeline Mason 40             10-4-1906  W.J.Morgan,J.P.
Byrd,Austin 20 to Lola Arvey 22              5- 9-1907  P.H.Justice,J.P.
```

Byrd,D.C.34 to Mrs.Josie Essansa 32	2- 5-1913	W.L.Bradley,M.G.
Byrd,Don W.22 to Gordia Younce 24	2-13-1936	D.F.Howard,M.G.
Cabe,Thomas to Nancy C.McClure	10-25-1836	U.Keener,D.Clk.
Cabe,Samuel to Martha McConnell	4- 4-1837	J.K.Gray,Clk.
Cabe,Z. to Elizabeth Penland	10-3-1842	J.K.Gray,Clk.
Cabe,Thomas B.to Purthine Willson	2-22-1843	John Hall,D.Clk.
Cabe,James to Dicy A.Hayes	12-9-1843	J.K.Gray,Clk.
Cabe,W.R.to Joannah Sutton	6-14-1845	J.K.Gray,Clk.
Cabe,John V.to Artelia Jones	1- 9-1850	T.P.Siler,D.Clk.
Cabe,Zacheriah to Matilda Fulcher	10-15-1850	James Russell,Wit
Cabe,James M.to Sarah A.Dowdle	11-4-1852	R.C.SLagle,D.Reg.
Cabe,Loranzo D.to Elenor Fulcher	1-16-1855	John Hall,Clk.
Cabe,William W.to R.A.Russell	10-4-1855	A.G.Vanhook,Wit.
Cabe,H.P.to Martha Collins	9-16-1858	R.C.Slagle,Reg.
Cabe,Leander to Amanda Fulcher	9-13-1860	R.C.Slagle,Reg.
Cabe,Z.P.to Mary A.Mann	7-31-1861	R.C.Slagle,D.Reg.
Cabe,William to Rebecca Hall	10-2-1868	R.C.Slagle,C.C.C.
Cabe,George W.to Sarah R.Glidewell	4-17-1869	R.C.Slagle,D.Reg.
Cabe,Lucius to Rachel Hopper	5-20-1869	J.K.Bryson,Reg.
Cabe,Leander to Mary M.Bradley	8-26-1869	J.K.Bryson,Reg.
Cabe,John L.to Amanda L.Sanders	1-19-1871	J.E.T.Long,J.P.
Cabe,Lorenzo F.to Margaret A.Russell	7-10-1871	William Sloan,Reg
Cabe,James L.to Sarah E.Cabe	9- 4-1871	William Sloan,Reg
Cabe,William T.21 to Mary E.Guffey 21	2-19-1874	T.F.Glenn,M.G.
Cabe,George 19 to Julia Bradley 19	12-17-1874	P.Howard,J.P.
Cabe,T.M.28 to Caroline McKiney 20	11-30-1876	M.L.Kelley,J.P.
Cabe,S.R.20 to E.A.Vanhook 16	1-24-1879	M.L.Kelley,J.P.
Cabe,Jno.L.D.26 to A.E.Kimzey 23	4- 8-1879	M.L.Kelley,J.P.
Cabe,J.M.49 to I.M.Russell 37	8- 7-1879	E.H.Franks,J.P.
Cabe,D.L.23 to Teletha C.Henson 21	1- 1-1884	M.L.Kelley,J.P.
Cabe,L.E.18 to Indiana McDowell 25	8- 9-1888	John Elmore,J.P.
Cabe,Robt.Lee 23 to Ellen Guffey30	9-27-1888	W.S.Ballard,M.G.
Cabe,Chas.A.24 to Fannie Sanders 18	2-12-1891	Jonathan Phillips
Cabe,Samuel A.21 to Arie Dryman 23	8- 2-1891	J.J.McConnell,J.P
Cabe,Harvy G.20 to Addie V.Sanders 18	2-18-1894	John Elmore,J.P.
Cabe,William A.51 to Margaret E.Rhodes 43	8-22-1894	Samuel Howard,J.P
Cabe,David P.28 to Emma I.Penland 29	10-31-1894	J.W.Bowman,M.G.
Cabe,S.R.37 to Millie Lee 18	7-12-1896	J.M.Carpenter,J.P
Cabe,Robert 21 to Lula Campbell 18	9-29-1897	W.H.Mann,J.P.
Cabe,J.E.21 to Nora Campbell 18	7-15-1900	Sam Howard,J.P.
Cabe,H.G.23 to Martha O.Cabe 23	1-27-1901	D.P.Cabe,J.P.
Cabe,John 22 to Nannie Justice 18	9-19-1901	P.H.Justice,J.P.
Cabe,E.C.21 to Becky Shook 24	3-13-1902	I.T.Peek,M.G.
Cabe,J.M.30 to Bell Norton 25	1-28-1904	J.C.Postell,M.G.
Cabe,J.H.Jr.22 to Estell McClure 18	1-26-1905	J.E.Cabe,J.P.
Cabe,Charlie C.31 to Mary E.Dowdle 26	2- 1-1905	J.H.Moore,M.G.
Cabe,Mell 23 to Mamie Penland 18	3- 8-1905	J.E.Cabe,J.P.

Cabe,J.T.27 to Daisy L.McPherson 25	3-22-1905	L.P.Bogle,M.G.
Cabe,Stephen L.32 to Roxie L.Talley 23	12-17-1905	S.S.Long,J.P.
Cabe,Harley,W.34 to Bertie Penland 17	3-29-1906	L.P.Bogle,M.G.
Cabe,Chalmers 23 to Ella Justice 22	9-18-1907	J.R.Pendergrass,MG
Cabe,P.F.22 to Ivale Cabe 22	10-9-1907	J.E.Cabe,J.P.
Cabe,J.H.28 to Arie Cabe 20	2-19-1908	J.E.Cabe,J.P.
Cabe,Thomas L.26 to Dorothy McCall 22	2-23-1908	J.E.Cabe,J.P.
Cabe,Burgess 24 to Blanche Downs 21	3-11-1908	F.L.Townsend,M.G.
Cabe,Henry G.33 to Martha M.Rhodes 37	10-10-1909	C.R.Cabe,J.P.
Cabe,George L.23 to Norah H.Frazier 19	12-5-1909	J.R.Pendergrass,MG
Cabe,W.H.30 to Bland Penland 22	8- 8-1910	J.R.Pendergrass,MG
Cabe,Harley M.20 to Effie Brendle 19	3- 5-1912	J.F.Starnes,M.G.
Cabe,Hillard 22 to Viola Grist 17	11-24-1912	J.R.Pendergras,MG
Cabe,Lindon 21 to Hattie Rickman 19	6-20-1914	Geo.Carpenter,J.P
Cabe,Lenzie 27 to Mary Ledford 22	12-24-1914	Robert Cabe,J.P.
Cabe,C.W.23 to Eva M.Moses 19	8-12-1917	L.H.Higdon,J.P.
Cabe,Frank 25 to Mimie McCoy 18	6-11-1918	Geo.Carpenter,J.P
Cabe,Annie 27 to Minnie Grant 20	5-17-1919	J.L.Bryson,J.P.
Cabe,A.P.20 to Sallie Sanders 19	5-27-1919	Geo.Carpenter,J.P
Cabe,L.R.21 to Ellen Collins 20	10-25-1919	J.R.Pendergras,MG
Cabe,Frank L.25 to Zora Seay 25	12-23-1919	J.R.Pendergras,MG
Cabe,J.E.40 to Minnie Norris 31	1-11-1920	James J.Mann,J.P.
Cabe,Fred D.21 to Jessie Sutton 17	1-16-1921	J.L.Kinsland,M.G.
Cabe,Thomas R.22 to Emma Callahan 21	11-7-1926	J.T.Lawrence,M.G.
Cabe,Chas.S.19 to Minnie L.McCall 22	3-26-1928	T.S.Roten,M.G.
Cabe,Elbert N.40 to Margaret R.Moore 32	4-28-1928	Robt.F.Mock,M.G.
Cabe,Paschal to H.Esther Thomas He from Dillard,Ga.	5-26-1933	Will Smith,Ord.
Cabe,Alex to Ruby Blaine	8-19-1934	Will Smith,Ord.
Cabe,Herschel 29 to Eula G.Burrell 19	10-3-1936	J.L.Teague,M.G.
Cabe,Cary 28 to Veo Burrell 25	12-8-1940	J.C.Swaim,M.G.
Cable,G.W.30 to Artie E.Moore 25	12-10-1902	D.F.Howard,M.G.
Caden,Jno.C.45 to Martha A.Justus 35	2-21-1878	L.Howard,J.P.
Cagle,Arthur C.20 to Ella M.Mason 20	2- 1-1906	W.L.Bradley,M.G.
Caldwell,M.C.29 to Elvira E.Garrison 16	9-13-1894	M.Ghormley,M.G.
Caldwell,Paul 29 to Dora E.Gibson 21 Col. He from Pennsylvania.	1- 2-1938	E.Johnson McKay.
Calhoun,W.J.30 to Burdell Deweese 20	7- 5-1922	Geo.Carpenter,J.P
Callet,H.H.54 to Jane Conley 32	8-24-1881	S.D.Smith,M.G.
Callyar,Albert 21 to Rittie Angel 21	8- 1-1902	C.W.Dowdle,J.P.
Caylor,Jeptha to Rachel Miller	2- 4-1846	J.K.Gray,Clk.
Caylor,Thomas I.to Martha I.Rogers	10-6-1863	R.C.Slagle,Reg.
Caylor,Thomas J.to Rebecca Daves	7- 1-1869	J.K.Bryson,Reg.
Caylor,W.W.20 to M.C.Howard 18	7- 6-1887	Z.Barnes,J.P.
Caylor,Vance W.26 to Catherine M.McCoy 18	4-21-1889	T.S.DeHart,M.G.
Caylor;Alfred 27 to Alie Deweese 20	10-12-1902	F.M.Morgan,M.G.
Caylor,A.W.26 to Mary J.Hampton 21	4-19-1903	S.J.May,J.P.

```
Caloway,Albert to Louhanna Angel                    4-10-1873 Original not found
Calloway,A.J.20 to L.L.Benfield 20                  5- 3-1878 Original not found
Calloway,A.J.25 to Nancy Benfield 25                8-28-1879 E.H.Franks,J.P.
Calloway,L.C.21 to Sarah Cansler 18                 11-13-1879 B.G.Wild,M.G.
Calloway,Prince 19 to Lotty Chambers 16             5- 6-1880  E.H.Franks,J.P.
Calloway,J.E.28 to Julia E.Parrish 20               3- 6-1895  G.A.Bartlett,M.G.
Calloway,A.J.Jr.22 to Martha Evitt 21               7-10-1898  T.J.Vinson,J.P.
Calloway,E.T.19 to Nellie O.Keener 18               5-13-1900  J.T.Peek,M.G.
Calloway,Green 23 to Delia Martin 18                1- 5-1901  J.B.Elmore,J.P.
Calloway,James 20 to Cary Jacobs 20                 2- 4-1901 J.R.Pendergrass,MG
Calloway,Robert A.19 to Rosetta Gibson 16           3- 2-1902  J.H.Fulton,J.P.
Calloway,Thomas 21 to Susie Houston 18              11-12-1905 Henry Stewart Jr.
Calloway,William 24 to Lillie Shields 25            3-26-1907  W.L.Bradley,M.G.
Calloway,Sam L.20 to Jenely Speed 18                12-20-1908 P.C.Calloway,J.P.
Calloway,Frank 21 to Ina Hawkins 22                 7-15-1910  M.J.Mashburn,J.P.
Calloway,Frank 22 to Louise Conley 25               11-26-1912 G.M.Bulgin,J.P.
Calloway,J.P.20 to Pearl Craine 23                  8- 6-1918  P.C.Calloway,J.P.
Calloway,C.L.Jr.22 to Lillie Bell Chastain 21/7-29-1922 W.T.Potts,M.G.
Calloway,Harley 17 to Lillian Hedden 15             7-11-1926  W.T.Potts,M.G.
Calloway,James J.25 to Ruth McMahan 18              12-22-1935 G.A.Calor,M.G.
Calloway,Sam D.18 to Emma L.Potts 18                6-28-1936  R.D.Bedinger,M.G.
Calloway,Hunter 22 to Barbara Darnell 18            9-13-1937  C.C.Herbert Jr.MG
Campbell,Joseph S.to Mary E.Bird                    11-14-1867 L.F.Siler,M.G.
Campbell,Charles C.26 to Urena C.Bird 24            8-10-1873  W.H.Bates,M.G.
Campbell,Thos.E.20 to Laura K.Bird 20               12-9-1875  L.K.Haynes,M.G.
Campbell,John P.22 to Ella Bird 18                  6-13-1877  Daniel Atkins,M.G
Campbell,J.W.18 to Catharine Hasket 24              4- 3-1881  C.S.Buchanan,M.G.
Campbell,Leslie 23 to Lou Deweese 21                11- 3-1890 T.M.Morgan,M.G.
Campbell,Edwin 28 to Emma Fouts 25                  1- 1-1902  J.A.Brendle,M.G.
Campbell,E.K.33 to Hannah R.Baird 22                1-26-1904  J.E.Woosley,M.G.
Campbell,Lonie 26 to Mattie Gibson 23               4-11-1907  Joseph L.Fouts,JP
Campbell,Walter 30 to Ella Poindexter 20            1- 8-1908  W.I.Hughes,M.G.
Campbell,Robert 21 to Bertha Collins 20             1-8-1908   W.I.Hughes,M.G.
Campbell,Richard 23 to Bell Winstead 18             12-5-1909  C.R.Cabe,J.J.
Campbell,J.P.62 to Mrs.Lala M.McCoy 48              10-8-1916  R.H.Dougherty,MG.
Campbell,Charles L.28 to Lavada Angel 21            2-19-1934  Geo.Carpenter,J.P
Campbell,G.Glen 26 to Pearl Buchanan 19             10-20-1935 R.L.Poindexter,MG
Cannon,E.D.30 to Margaret Cochran 23                10-10-1900 H.M.Thompson,M.G.
Cansler,Phillip to Elizabeth Jacobs                 9- 8-1854  John Hall,Clk.
Cansler,John to Louisa Grant                        6-26-1856  T.P.Siler,D.Clk.
Cansler,W.B.21 to Jennie Calloway 20                9-27-1885  M.J.Mashburn,J.P.
Cansler,R.L.27 to Maud Myers 18                     8-18-1915  W.G.Warren,M.G.
Cansler,W.B.50 to Hattie Hall 34                    11-11-1917 J.L.Younce,M.G.
Cantey,O.L.31 to Sarah E.Justice 18                 5-17-1891  W.J.Grist,J.P.
Cantrel,John 50 to Jane Raby 57                     2-19-1900  W.L.Bradley,M.G.
Capps,George 31 to Minnie Marr 20                   3- 7-1900  N.P.Rankin,J.P.
Capps,Z.G.18 to Stella Smith 21                     6- 1-1919  W.G.Barker,J.P.
```

```
Cardin,Wm.B.to Mary A.Childers              8-18-1857 T.P.Siler,D.Clk.
Carden,James T.to Mary Higdon               8-15-1860 T.P.Siler,D.Clk.
Carden,J.B.21 to N.A.Gibson 18              12-25-1881 M.J.Mashburn,J.P.
Carden,Floyd 21 to Bertha Elmore 19         5- 8-1910 R.R.Rickman,J.P.
Cargle,John to Mary Grant                   10-15-1861 R.C.Slagle,Reg.
Carpenter,Sanford to Patience McConnell     12-21-1835 John Tatham,Clk.
Carpenter,David to Sarah M.Ballew           5-29-1839 H.G.Woodfin,D.Clk.
Carpenter,Balavan to Martha Bateman         9-16-1845 David Carpenter.
Carpenter,Humphrey P.to Elizabeth Allen     12-20-1851 John McDowell,J.P
Carpenter,Henry to Mary L.Allen             2- 9-1854 A.B.Donaldson,J.P
Carpenter,Jackson to Martha Curtis          8- 9-1854 John Hall,Clk.
Carpenter,Benjamin B.to Jane Johnston       7-29-1858 R.C.Slagle,Clk.
Carpenter,W.D. to Amanda Cabe               11-15-1866 R.C.Slagle,C.C.C.
Carpenter,David N.to Margaret E.Grant       12-6-1866 R.C.Slagle,C.C.C.
Carpenter,David H.to Synthia D.Ledford      2-11-1869 R.C.Slagle,Reg.
Carpenter,Jackson T.to Sarah R.Bradley      3-29-1870 R.C.Slagle,D.Reg.
Carpenter,Damascus 19to Sarah Jane Quarles 19/1-24-1875 M.P.Long,M.G.
Carpenter,D.R.21 to Eddy Henry 17           1-13-1876 J.T.Woodard,M.G.
Carpenter,E.M.21 to Mary Penland 21 Col.    7- 5-1878 Thos.Warren,M.G.
Carpenter,W.H.21 to Mary Nichols 18         8-28-1878 W.H.Roane,J.P.
Carpenter,T.A.25 to C.J.McKinney 28         11-7-1878 M.L.Kelley,J.P.
Carpenter,J.E.25 to W.H.Long 18             12-14-1882 L.Howard,J.P.
Carpenter,G.B.24 to Alby Shope 16           2- 3-1884 L.Howard,J.P.
Carpenter,J.E.28 to Alice L.Bates 16        1-22-1886 S.A.Dixon,J.P.
Carpenter,David H.40 to Avey Landon 33      2- 4-1886 J.M.Carpenter,J.P
Carpenter,James M.31 to Sarah A.Sellers 19  3-22-1887 S.H.Harrington,MG
Carpenter,Edward E.20 to Lilly May Luther 19/3-1-1888 J.J.McConnell,J.P
Carpenter,Geo.B.30 to Sarah Norton 32       2-10-1889 W.C.Kimzey,J.P.
Carpenter,William 21 to Talitha I.Scroggs 23/8-23-1894 G.P.Mann,J.P.
Carpenter,George 23 to Frances E.Tally 20   12-22-1895 A.W.Young,M.G.
Carpenter,W.J.24 to C.M.Glidewell 17        9-12-1897 J.M.Carpenter,J.P
Carpenter,Henry 67 to Sarah McConnell 68    11-23-1897 W.A.Norton,J.P.
Carpenter,W.F.22 to Mary Knight 18          4- 2-1899 W.C.Sanders,J.P.
Carpenter,W.I.46 to Laura B.Clark 40        8- 5-1899 J.T.Wade,M.G.
Carpenter,B.H.36 to Levada Thomas 22        3-31-1901 J.R.Pendergrass,MG
Carpenter,James 23 to Ida Kell 20           2-29-1901 A.W.Young,M.G.
Carpenter,Geo.R.21 to Octie Ledford 17      10-25-1901 W.P.Allison,J.P.
Carpenter,Judson 21 to Jane Wadkins 20      3-22-1903 L.M.Mann,J.P.
Carpenter,John W.21 to Callie Jones 20      10-26-1905 W.P.Allison,J.P.
Carpenter,Charlie 19 to Ida Lewis 21        12-17-1905 W.P.Allison,J.P.
Carpenter,W.Vance 45 to Alby Stiles 39      3-25-1906 J.A.Brendle,M.G.
Carpenter,A.L.20 to Dona Byrd 18            6-22-1906 W.P.Allison,J.P.
Carpenter,Henry W.20 to Lorina Mason 19     12-9-1906 J.E.Cabe,J.P.
Carpenter,Harley 23 to Jennie Norton 20     2- 2-1908 J.C.Shope,J.P.
Carpenter,Fred 21 to Willie Conley 16       7-24-1908 W.A.Norton,J.P.
Carpenter,U.N.27 to Ada Garland 19          8- 2-1908 A.M.Ledford,M.G.
Carpenter,Robert L.19 to Dona Ann Sanders 19/2-25-1909 J.T.Watts,J.P.
```

```
Carpenter,Thomas 22 to Nannie Scruggs 21Col.6- 6-1909 J.R.Pendergrass,MG
Carpenter,John 19 to Ada Norton18          7- 7-1910  C.R.Cabe,J.P.
Carpenter,Arthur 23 to Ida Norton 21       10-2-1910  J.T.Watts,J.P.
Carpenter,Raleigh 20 to Alice Norton 23    8-15-1912  J.T.Watts,J.P.
Carpenter,David N.67 to Martha Ledford 37  8-15-1912  J.T.Watts,J.P.
Carpenter,W.T.44 to Bassie Ledford 29      1-15-1914  J.M.Griggs,M.G.
Carpenter,Charlie 25 to Mamie Conley 22    3- 8-1914  A.W.Donaldson,J.P
Carpenter,J.T.67 to Ernestine Keener 43    4-15-1916  Geo.Carpenter,J.P
Carpenter,E.J.18 to Eula Dean 19           4-29-1917 J.R.Pendergrass,MG
Carpenter,Walter B.19 to Hattie Anderson 19/8-19-1917  G.W.Moffitt,J.P.
Carpenter,William 21 to Lillie Southards 18/10-17-1918 J.E.Womack,M.G.
Carpenter,Oscar S.28 to Annis O.Brown 16   12-21-1924 Geo.Carpenter,J.P
Carpenter,Arthur L.40 to Emma C.Southards 23/11-7-1926 Geo.Carpenter,J.P
Carpenter,Paul B.33 to Dora Lee Garner 27  2-11-1933  E.R.Eller,M.G.
Carpenter,Drew 30 to Bertha Bell 21        12-26-1933 W.A.Norton,J.P.
Carpenter,Geo.64 to Lalar Wiggins 29       2-20-1937 W.B.Underwood,M.G.
Carpenter,R.L.22 to Durleen Scroggs 19     7-25-1937  Frank A.Smith,Ord
Carpenter,Sanford 27 to Recie Strobridge 29 Col.9-1-1937 Lester L.Arnold
Carrell,Thomas 58 to Ella Ashe 43          4-15-1918  J.L.Kinsland,M.G.
Carrington,Alfred to Emely Jane Stewart    11-7-1871  L.F.Glenn,M.G.
Carrol,Miles to Rue Setser                 12-6-1834  ----------
Carroll,Daniel to May Selsear              8-15-1838  John Hall,Clk.
Carrol,Absolom to Nancy Ledford            8-10-1839  John Hall,Clk.
Carroll,Absolom to Rebecca Ledford         4-28-1855  John Hall,Clk.
Carson,John H. to Nancy Bird               7-9-1844   J.K.Gray,Clk.
Carson,A.M. to Martha Poindexter           3- 3-1857  John Hall,Clk.
Carson,Jesse to Sarah E.Angel              8-12-1857  C.D.Smith,M.G.
Carson,Richard D.26 to Georgina McGee20    2-29-1937  W.B.Underwood,M.G
Carter,Thomas to Matilda Pendergrass       12-29-1840 ----------
Carter,James to Caroline Hurst             9-10-1845  J.K.Gray,Clk.
Carter,Wm.Edward 22 to Margaret A.Gibson 21/12-13-1874 J.W.Brown,M.G.
Carter,James W.25 to Callie E.Bradley 21   6- 4-1889  John Howard,J.P.
Carter,Thomas Wm.30 to Maggie B.Greenwood 16/10-13-1890 Jas.C.Weaver,J.P
Carter,Cicero 27 to Fannie Gray 35  Col.   3- 1-1891  D.H.Comame,M.G.
Carter,Dan 39 to Avaline Parrish 24  Col.  5-23-1905  L.A.Farm,M.G.
Carter,Arthur 25 to Prazy Thomas 21  Col.  6-23-1924  Geo.Carpenter,J.P
Carver,Henry to Polly Hill                 10-19-1856 John Hall,Clk.
Carver,John to Adaline Teague              10-28-1868 R.C.Slagle,Reg.
Carver,G.C.18 to F.J.Carpenter 16          11-28-1878 M.L.Kelley,J.P.
   He from Rabun Co.Ga.
Carver,W.H.50 to Mary M.Burnett 57         11-23-1885 J.A.Morrison,J.P.
   He from Swain Co.N.C.
Carver,J.Z.22 to Mary Ledbetter 18         1-22-1903  G.P.White,J.P.
Carver,Oscar 29 to Beulah Cabe 17          3-14-1921  Geo.Carpenter,J.P
Carver,Wayne 24 to Sallie Castle 18        11-28-1922 Geo.Carpenter,J.P
Carver,William R.22 to Manilla Gertrude Reese 18/12-24-1939 J.G.Benfield
   He from Clemson,S.C.
Cathey,Thomas to Mary A.Ingram             6-20-1831  N.B.Hyatt,D.Clk.
```

Caution,James 19 to Desda Huggins 20	2- 5-1882	P.C.Wild,J.P.
Chambers,Phillip to Ruth Sawyers	12-11-1849	Joseph Welch,J.P.
Chambers,Thos.B.to Nancy J.Taylor	4-28-1862	R.C.Slagle,C.C.C.
Chambers,John W.28 to Josie M.Allison 23	2-24-1891	S.J.May,J.P.
Chambers,S.R.23 to Laura Haney 20	3-31-1894	Z.Barnes,J.P.
Chambers,Isaac E.23 to Julia A.Allison 21	12-24-1890	S.J.May,J.P.
Chambers,Moses E.22 to Annie Haney 18	4- 1-1894	Z.Barnes,J.P.
Chambers,Isaac E.60 to Rhoda I.Allison 41	1-29-1900	M.Ghormley,M.G.
Chambers,Thomas R.21 to Mary Henry 18	5-10-1891	John Allison,J.P.
Chastain,James 22 to Etta Carpenter 21	4-21-1891	L.H.Garland,J.P.
Chastain,Aylor 21 to Amanda Littleton 19	3- 3-1895	D.L.Miller,M.G.
Chastain,John D.25 to Nancy A.Reed 19	10-10-1901	J.D.Vinson,M.G.
Chastain,J.W.25 to Rosaline Ledbetter 24	6- 7-1903	G.P.White,J.P.
Chastain,Zeke 23 to Martha Picklesimer 16	12-19-1907	Ed..Picklesimer,JP
Chastain,D.E.22 to Ada Bryson 20	3-21-1911	E.P.Picklesimer,JP
Chastain,M.L.24 to Nina Rogers 20	7- 8-1916	E.B.Bell,M.G.
Chastain,C.A.21 to Hattie Miller 17	7-23-1916	J.E.Vinson,J.P.
Chastain,Thomas 24 to Texas McDowell 22	6- 2-1917	Robert Stamey,J.P
Chastain,E.D.21 to Nettie M.B.Keener 19	2-20-1924	W.T.Potts,M.G.
Chavis,Jeff 42 to Charity Shepherd 28 Col.	12-5-1872	D.W.Wells,M.G.
Chavis,Jim 23 to Ellen Shepherd 21 Col.	7-29-1888	James Bristol,M.G
Chavis,Arthur 20 to Ellen Shepherd 20 Col.	8-12-1914	L.W.Thomas,M.G.
Chavis,Thomas 23 to Mae Bell Cline 21 Col.	3-21-1915	C.L.Stewart,M.G.
Chavis,Charley 22 to Dettie Hawshaw 20 Col.	9-13-1924	John A.Dunn,M.G.
Chavis,Bob 26 to Hassie McDonnell 22 Col.	10-24-1925	J.R.Pendergras,MG
Childers,Humphrey to Sarah Wilson	2-16-1849	W.H.Roane,D.Clk.
Childers,Slijah to Lucinda Quilliams	11-7-1849	T.P.Siler,Clk.
Childers,Allen to M.R.Cloer	8-24-1860	R.C.Slagle,Clk.
Childers,Thos.C.25 to Emma McCoy 18	9- 4-1892	J.W.Rickman,J.P.
Childers,Humphrey 21 to Alice Morrison 18	1-22-1896	Jos.Morrison,J.P.
Childers,Reuben 40 to M.J.Quilliams 19	5-15-1897	J.B.Cardon,J.P.
Childers,Marion 21 to Jane Bragg 19	9-16-1900	J.J.McCoy,J.P.
Childers,Wm.R.23 to Bell Hughes 14	9- 4-1904	J.T.Raby,J.P.
Childers,Herman Lee 31 to Josephine Snyder 23/4-14-1929-Robt.F.Mock,M.G.		
Childers,Burr A.to Sallie B.Blaine	4-23-1933	Will Smith,Ord.
Chapman,Jay F.21 to Eula May Potts 19 He from Atlanta,Ga.	1-31-1937	W.T.Beedle,M.G.
Chote,Iredele D.to Martha S.Green	4-27-1843	J.K.Gray,Clk.
Christy,Thos.H.24 to Carrie T.Corpening 21	4-18-1930	W.E.Abernathy,M.G
Clampett,James C.to Mary Jones	1-20-1855	Jos.Poindexter.
Clampett,George to Mira Mashburn	9-13-1860	R.C.Slagle,Reg.
Clampett,John to Ida Roxanna West	6- 1-1871	William Sloan,Reg
Clampett,Rufus 21 to Hattie Cochran 20	11-15-1903	Joseph L.Fouts,JP
Clampett,N.G.25 to Pearl Cochran 23	11-17-1912	C.T.Ray,J.P.
Clanton,Alfred B.to Eliza Anderson Col.	10-17-1869	R.C.Slagle,D.Clk.
Clanton,Pearl 20 to Lillie Gibson 18 Col.	11-19-1905	A.B.Morrow,M.G.
Clapp,C.G.35 to Cora Lee Mock 28	4- 5-1930	Robt.F.Mock,M.G.

```
Clark,James A. to Margaret Gribble          2-24-1849  Thad.P.Siler,Clk.
Clark,Hiram  to Martha Evans                9-24-1851  J.K.Gray,Clk.
Clark,Joseph to Elis E.Stiwinter            11-22-1860 T.W.Owen,J.P.
Clark,James P. to Mira M.Mashburn           2-13-1869  R.C.Slagle,Reg.
Clark,John  to Mary M.Bentley               9- 3-1869  J.W.Wilson,J.P.
Clark,James 20 to Aucybell Hodge 24         9-18-1887  J.E.Sanderson,M.G
Clark,Ervin 23 to Alice Grant 20            8-11-1898  ·N.P.Rankin,J.P.
Clark,W.F.21 to Carie Queen 16              10-30-1898 M.L.Rickman,J.P.
Clark,J.Logan 22 to Hattie Taylor 18        10-14-1905 J.W.Ammons,J.P.
Clark,Robin 21 to Sudie Bowman 19           2-13-1910  J.M.Keener,M.G.
Clark,Jim 24 to Rettie Hoilman 21           2-15-1921  W.L.Bradley,M.G.
Clark,Thomas 24 to Mae Smith 22             11-12-1924 Z.Baird,J.P.
Clark,Ted 24 to Julia Lakey 15              6-24-1933  Geo.Carpenter,J.P
Clark,Woodrow 21 to Laura Bradley 20        1-26-1935  W.G.Barker,J.P.
Clark,John D.25 to Nolita Bradley 22        12-27-1935 W.L.Bradley,M.G.
Clark,Clyde 31 to Katherine Ray 19          12-25-1938 J.A.Flanagan,M.G.
Clark,Oscar 37 to Mrs.Eliza Barker 37       1-27-1939  J.F.Browning,J.P.
Clark,T.A.22 to Allie Fair Houston 17       5-21-1939  W.L.Bradley,M.G.
Clayton,S.M.27 to Minnie Brendle 20         5-12-1920  J.R.Pendergrass,MG
Clement,A.B.24 to Mirian Killian 19         7-29-1883  T.Carter,M.G.
Cleveland,William 22 to Bessie Reese 22     11-12-1905 N.H.Starbuck,M.G.
Cleveland,James F.25 to Helen Lee McKinney 23/5-28-1911-W.L.Griggs,M.G.
Cleveland,J.D.37 to Irene Guye 19     Col.  8-31-1919  James Bristol,M.G
Cleveland,Reppard 30 to Timox Guy 20 Col.   9- 1-1919  E.J.McKay,M.G.
Cline,Absolem to Rody Kirkland              3-19-1831  Wm.McConnell.
Cline,John to Elizabeth Hyde                10-21-1837 J.K.Gray,Clk.
Cline,Jesse to Adeline Ausburn              3-28-1838  John Hall,Clk.
Cline,John to Elizabeth Sorrels             12-2-1845  J.K.Gray,Clk.
Cline,Michael to Catharine Hyde             2-13-1849  Thad.P.Siler,Clk.
Cline,John 22 to Otelia Parter 20     Col.  7-28-1912  C.L.Stewart,M.G.
Cloer,N.P. to Elizabeth McGathey            4-20-1849  J.K.Gray,Clk.
Cloer,N.J. to Matilda Carpenter             11-4-1852  J.F.Slagle,J.P.
Cloer,John to Grace Ammons                  12-16-1852 A.B.Donaldson,J.P
Cloer,Joshua to Louiza Bates                2-29-1856  M.Rickman,M.G.
Cloer,W.M. to Susannah Ledford              11-17-1856 G.W.Q.Moore.
Cloer,William R.to Margaret Moore           3-12-1859  R.C.Slagle,Reg.
Cloer,John F. to Palina Somex               9-20-1859  R.C.Slagle,Reg.
Cloer,William M.35 to Charity Cloer(widow)40/11-26-1872-J.H.Addington,JP
Cloer,D.W.21 to Josaphine Childers 15       12-23-1875 J.D.Wright,M.G.
Cloer,Jacob M.22 to Anna L.Anderson 16      12-22-1881 Wm.C.Kimsey,J.P.
Cloer,J.N.20 to H.E.Anderson 18             1-19-1882  W.C.Kimsey,J.P.
Cloer,W.R.26 to Fannie Roane 24             11-7-1883  F.M.Jordan,M.G.
Cloer,A.Jehu 24 to Caledonia Payne 18       10-21-1888 J.G.Ammons,M.G.
Cloer,A.J.26 to Callie Estes 16             3- 6-1890  P.R.Rickman,M.G.
Cloer,W.R.22 to A.M.Elders 20               10-30-1890 J.B.Elmore,J.P.
Cloer,James N.36 to Margaret E.Henson 40    9- 6-1896  J.M.Carpenter,J.P
Cloer,George 21 to Flora Dills 18           8-25-1904  W.P.Allison,J.P.
```

Cloer,Ed.23 to Temsie Price 21	10-13-1907 J.W.Ammons,J.P.
Cloer,Thad 21 to Pearl Fair 18	3-12-1908 J.L.Kinsland,M.G.
Cloer,J.C.23 to Ella McCracken 21	12-10-1911 Robert Stamey,J.P
Cloer,Andrew 22 to Roxie Passmore 20	9-16-1934 Geo.Carpenter,J.P
Clouse,M.C.22 to C.M.Mincy 19	9-20-1881 Hosea Moses,J.P.
Clouse,M.C. 39 to Addie Ammons 20	7-22-1898 J.W.Parker,J.P.
Clouse,Parker 24 to Delia Harris 23	10-26-1911 J.P.Moore,J.P.
Clouse,Z.M.25 to Nellie Reese 25	6- 3-1917 J.R.Pendergrass,MG
Coates,I.W.20 to Jane Tallent 21	8-11-1883 R.H.Cunningham,J.P
Cobb,R.J. 26 to Louise Zoeliner 21	6- 2-1910 T.J.Vinson,M.G.
Cockerham,John to Delphia Hall	9-16-1832 John Hall,Clk.
Cockerham,A.N. to Amanda Stalcup	5-11-1844 J.K.Gray,Clk.
Cockerham,Madison to Mira Cockerham	12-21-1844 J.K.Gray,Clk.
Cockerham,David Rebecca Upton	2- 9-1847 J.K.Gray,Clk.
Cockerham,J.W.to Mandy Daves	1-24-1861 L.F.Siler.
Cockerham,Aaron 19 to Martha Love 19 Col.	8- 1-1872 D.W.Wells,M.G.
Cockerham,Geo.W.21 to Alice I.Burnett 22	1-17-1886 J.A.Morrison,J.P.
Cochran,Moses to No name given	12-23-1846 J.K.Gray,Clk.
Cochran,Wm.H.to Harriett Deweese	12-23-1858 J.H.McLoud,J.P.
Cochran,John to Mary A.Craige	4-26-1861 R.C.Slagle,Reg.
Cochran,John A.to Blenders Cochran	12-21-1861 R.C.Slagle,Reg.
Cochran,Jerry F.to Silva A.Johnston Col.	3-17-1870 J.K.Bryson,Reg.
Cochran,Wash 41 to Addie Cabe 27	2-11-1877 J.S.Woodard,M.G.
Cochran,Wash 44 to Lou Potts 30	3-21-1880 J.S.Woodard,M.G.
Cochran,E.T.38 to Janny Walker 36 Col.	11-18-1888 Ransom Powell,M.G
Cochran,Thomas 25 to Sarah Hall 22	12-15-1892 P.C.Wilds,J.P.
Cochran,Moses 26 to Florence Ramsey 21	5- 2-1897 W.J.Evans,M.G.
Cochran,James 22 to Minnie Wilson 19	11-27-1898 S.J.May,J.P.
Cochran,William 21 to Emma Ledford 22	4- 1-1902 Mark Deweese,J.P.
Cochran,Aaron 20 to Julia Burgess 22 Col.	5-17-1905 G.H.Jackson,M.G.
Cochran,R.E.26 to Sallie Cabe 21	6-17-1906 A.S.Solesbee,M.G.
Cochran,J.M.45 to Docia Miller 32	4-21-1907 I.T.Peek,M.G.
Cochran,A.J.32 to Rosa Henry 20	3-30-1908 J.H.Mincey,J.P.
Cochran,W.R.22 to Jerusha Morgan 24	4-11-1915 J.H.Grant,J.P.
Cochran,McKinley 21 to Minnie Herron 19	9-26-1919 Original not found
Cochran,Ararat 20 to Agnes E.Burston 17 Col.	4- 4-1925 Geo.Carpenter,J.P
Cochran,Ted 22 to Daphine Grant 18	10-7-1933 L.A.Boone,J.P.
Cochran,J.L.18 to Viola Burston 20 Col.	8- 3-1936 E.Johnson McKay.
Coffee,John to Manerva Coffee	4-14-1838 J.K.Gray,Clk.
Coffee,Jessie to Elizabeth Thompson	2- 2-1835 Lenard Swanager.
Cogdill,J.B.33 to Martha J.Williams 23	11-8-1905 J.W.Ammons,J.P.
Coggins,Sam E.23 to Lucy Coggins 16	4- 3-1920 J.M.Raby,J.P.
Coggins,Western 23 to Callie Mathew 18	9- 4-1921 J.M.Raby,J.P.
Coggins,Eldon M.21 to Virginia Franks 18	4- 6-1935 J.M.Keener,M.G.
Coker,Newton 65 to Rachel Baty 47 Col.	5-24-1893 R.P.Powell,M.G.
Coker,W.B.22 to Emma Bingham 19	5- 9-1898 Retd.not executed
Cole,James L.to Sallie Knight	12-20-1834 John Tatham,Clk.

Cole,William to V.J.Stillwell	11-6-1851	Thos.Mashburn,J.P
Cole,William 21 to Samantha Phillips 19	11-26-1898	R.Q.Garrison,J.P.
Cole,John 22 to Ella Willie 19	12-12-1903	Joseph L.Fouts,JP
Cole,Garland 22 to Laura Seagle 22	4-18-1930	C.F.Farriss,M.G.
Collatt,J.P.29 to Mrs.Anna Drake Roper 21	11-21-1920	David F.Howard,MG
Collett,James 23 to Beulah Phillips 18	6- 4-1911	D.F.Howard,M.G.
Collier,William A.23 to Mary E.Jones 26	1-14-1873	J.H.Addington,J.P
Collier,John 30 to Elizabeth Mason 22	5-28-1907	C.A.Setser,J.P.
Collier,Henry L.28 to Dessie Anderson 26	1-27-1910	F.N.Johnson,J.P.
Collier,William Jr.26 to Lula Anderson 22	6-15-1913	C.S.Battles,J.P.
Collier,Oscar 21 to Josa Greenwood 21	9- 1-1915	C.S.Battles,J.P.
Collier,H.H.19 to Dovie Anderson 17	9- 1-1915	Robert Stamey,J.P
Collier,C.L.41 to Mrs,Carrie M.Wright 32	6-25-1919	J.C.Owen,M.G.
Collier,Arthur 20 to Annie Anderson 34	4-24-1937	Geo.Carpenter,J.P
Collins,Adolphas to Jane Watson	4-12-1840	H.G.Woodfin,D.Clk
Collins,Minor W. to Nicy Evans	7- 1-1840	H.G.Woodfin,D.Clk
Collins,Michal W. to Martha Marr	2-24-1855	John Hall,Clk.
Collins,William to Eliza Jacobs	12-22-1857	R.C.Slagle,Reg.
Collins,W.to Angeline Welch	10-25-1866	J.F.Mashburn,J.P.
Collins,Andrew T. to Sarah A.Franks	1-30-1869	R.C.Slagle,Reg.
Collins,Andrew to Sarah A.Franks	1-30-1869	R.C.Slagle,Reg.
Collins,E.C.to Virginia Gribble	8-19-1869	J.K.Bryson,Reg.
Collins,Jacob A.26 to M.J.Oliver 26	3-25-1875	J.H.Addington,J.P
Collins,George B.22 to Susanna F Stockton 28/	5-4-1875	J.H.Addington,J.P
Collins,Hugh E.21 to Lavina Moore 21	4- 2-1876	John Elmore,J.P.
Collins,Thos.A.23 to Amanda Downs 32	9-27-1877	Thos.Mashburn,J.P
Collins,W.Z.23 to S.C.Corbin 18	10-21-1877	J.Woodard,M.G.
Collins,J.B.22 to M.V.Cunningham 20	5-30-1880	C.Campbell,M.G.
Collins,George R.21 to Sarah R.Bailey 15	4- 6-1884	John T.Berry,J.P.
Collins,J.R.17 to Anna V.Fisher 17	1- 3-1885	J.R.Ammons.
Collins,B.E.24 to Quincy L.Shepherd 17	4-16-1885	P.P.McLean,M.G.
Collins,George R.23 to Roxie Hedden 16	11-15-1896	J.B.Elmore,J.P.
Collins,John 18 to Flora Nations 18	12-7-1897	D.C.McCoy,J.P.
Collins,James 26 to Vianna Teague 22	2-20-1898	George Bryson,J.P
Collins,Charley 18 to Mary McGaha 22	2-22-1900	George Bryson,J.P
Collins,J.B.44 to Inda Sellers 38	10-28-1903	J.H.Moore,M.G.
Collins,W.L.32 to Addie Fouts 41	7-16-1908	J.L.Younce,M.G.
Collins,J.B.50 to Arie Morrison 40	2-27-1910	W.L.Bradley,M.G.
Collins,B.E.50 to Rachel White 20	1- 7-1912	M.J.Mashburn,J.P.
Collins,Jacob 55 to Elizabeth Williamson 51/	10-28-1913	Robert Stamey,J.P
Colman,Wesley 19 to Minday Butler 18 Col.	3- 9-1876	Thos.Mashburn,J.P
Coleman,Jesse 17 to Louisa Gray 17 Col.	12-6-1878	E.H.Franks,J.P.
Coleman,James 21 to Sapharonia Lunsford 18	9-23-1883	J.M.Forrester,J.P
Coleman,J.D.51 to Catherine Passmore 35	4-14-1885	Jas.M.Barnes,J.P.
Coleman,Benj.F.17 to Margaret Land 15	5- 5-1887	W.J.Evans,J.P.
Coleman,Joseph C.20 to Margaret Frady 30	7-15-1888	Z.Barnes,J.P.
Coleman,Simond 24 to Lillie Shepherd 20 Col.	3-30-1909	R.R.Rickman,J.P.

Colvard,James to Mahala Sherrill	7-19-1832	John Hall,Clk.
Compton,T.B.22 to Lavada Penland 19	8-23-1908	P.R.Young,M.G.
Connelly,Jason to Polly Ann Bryson	12-3-1846	J.K.Gray,Clk.
Connelly,William to Caroline Blaine	1-20-1847	J.K.Gray,Clk.
Conley,S.C. to M.E.Angel	1-17-1856	P.Howard,J.P.
Conley,C.P. to Elizabeth R.Patton	1-12-1860	R.C.Slagle,Reg.
Conley,William A.to Sarah A.Wyant	9-19-1866	J.H.Bryson,J.P.
Conley,S.C.24 to Addie F.Howard 23	2- 7-1877	C.D.Smith,M.G.
Conley,W.E.21 to Ella S.Addington 20	9-25-1878	C.D.Smith,M.G.
Conley,Joseph A.21 to Laura E.Porter 16	1-12-1882	W.C.Corden,M.G.
Conley,J.D.21 to Nancy Wright 20	11-15-1882	J.J.Arnold,J.P.
Conley,Lee to Mary West 18 Col.	11-30-1882	J.E.Kilgore,M.G.
Conley,J.W.21 to Allice Shepherd 17 Col.	4- 1-1883	W.M.Lee,M.G.
Conley,Albert 21 to Henretta Carpenter 20	4-26-1883	M.P.Long,M.G.
Conley,George 24 to Callie Poindexter 18 Col.	12-20-1883-	T.P.Moulden,M.G.
Conley,Burgess G.22 Agness J.White 21	2-18-1886	S.H.Harrington,MG
Conley,Isaac 39 to Sallie Harrison 20	4-13-1887	J.O.Shelley,M.G.
Conley,William A.24 to Mary A.Justice 17	4-17-1887	J.O.Shelley,M.G.
Conley,Sidney W.36 to Mary E.Allman 30	11-24-1887	W.S.Ballard,M.G.
Conley,Robt.Lee 26 to Annie L.Mann 15	5-14-1891	W.J.Grist,J.P.
Conley,N.C.23 to Minnie Young 18	11-5-1891	W.J.Grist,J.P.
Conley,George 37 to Louisa Parrish 32 Col.	1-26-1893	J.C.Hemphill,M.G.
Conley,James P.29 to Eunice S.Wallace 25	5- 3-1893	W.G.Mallonee,M.G.
Conley,James L.49 to Lydia Harris 27	12-10-1893	W.C.Mason,M.G.
Conley,Edwin B.24 to Ada Bradley 19	10- 7-1894	W.A.Norton,J.P.
Conley,Eddy B.22 to Mary E.Guy 20	9-29-1895	D.F.Carver,M.G.
Conley,James M.20 to Abbie P.Cabe 20	6- 4-1899	S.C.Conley,J.P.
Conley,W.L.25 to Daisy Hester 18	1-31-1903	J.A.Brendle,M.G.
Conley,George 21 to Ellie Myers 20	2-15-1906	N.H.Starbuck,M.G.
Conley,W.Henry 24 to Mary Justice 25	11-3-1907	J.E.Cabe,J.P.
Conley,Ingram 25 to Sadie Justice 17	10-24-1912	Jas.Hensley,M.G.
Conley,Jess 25 to Mary B.Addington 23	12-24-1914	R.H.Dougherty,M.G
Conley,Lester S.30 to Velma McGaha 23	4- 5-1915	T.J.Vinson,M.G.
Conley,F.C.19 to Hattie Roane 18	12-3-1916	R.H.Dougherty,M.G
Conley,Jessie 21 to Maud Love 18 Col.	8-24-1918	James Ritchie,M.G
Conley,Gordie 33 to Mattie Deal 22 Col.	8-27-1918	Jim Bristol,M.G.
Conley,Karr 20 to Hallie Hall 19	9-21-1919	Geo.Carpenter,J.P
Conley,G.C.29 to Isabelle Dryman 21	2- 8-1920	Jessie Ballew,J.P
Conley,Charles E.22 to Lois V.Garner 18	3-23-1928	J.A.Flanagan,M.G.
Conner,William H.to Rachael A.Hill	1-18-1843	---------
Conner,John H. to Martha M.Hodgins	7-31-1847	J.K.Gray,Clk.
Conner,Edward A.28 to Flora Guffey 20	1-30-1892	G.P.Mann,J.P.
Conner,W.A.25 to Pearl Nix 26 Both from Atlanta,Ga.	9- 6-1926	J.M.Raby,J.P.
Conseen,Buck 34 to Anna Oocumma 39 Indians Both from Cherokee,N.C.	12-27-1937	Lester L.Arnold.
Constance,John J. to Elizabeth S.Delozier	12-11-1859	R.C.Slagle,Reg.
Cook,John to Elizabeth Hurst	4-13-1848	J.K.Gray,Clk.

```
Cook,Barnard R. to Caroline M.Reed             12-9-1858   R.C.Slagle,Reg.
Cook,John 23 to Martha Smith 21                 1-12-1896   Joseph Morgan,J.P
Cook,J.A.41 to Nannie Mae Kinnebrew 25          12-22-1919  L.B.Hayes,M.G.
Cook,Everett28 to Pauline DeHart 17             9- 8-1928   Geo.Carpenter,J.P
Cook,H.M.40 to Blanche Fouts 21                 3-21-1931   J.R.Pendergrass,MG
  He from Winston,N.C.
Cook,John 23 to Minnie McClain 15               2- 9-1935   Sam.J.Murray,J.P.
Cook,Lon 31 to Rachel Ammons 20                 3-18-1939   W.R.DeHart,M.G.
Cookston,S.M.22 to Beulah Forrester 20          7-11-1916   J.A.Lakey,J.P.
Cooper,Cornelus to Cynthea Conley               1- 5-1830   John Hall,Clk.
Cooper,William C.74 to Margaret M.Saunders 50/11-30-1882-Geo.D.French,MG
Cooper,A.F.28 to Modena Franks 23               2-11-1906   J.H.Rogers,J.P.
Cooper,Jno.R.39 to Mamie E.West 33              1- 1-1917   R.H.Dougherty,M.G
Cooper,J.W.26 to Margaret McGuire 24            6- 5-1937   J.A.Flanagan,M.G.
  He from Cleveland,Tenn.
Cope,Andrew to Rebecca Ray                      11-6-1865   R.C.Slagle,Reg.
Cope,Elbert C.23 to Sallie Bateman 16           6-26-1890   S.J.May,J.P.
Cope,James 22 to Paralee Haney 18               11-21-1903  W.A.Solesbee,J.P.
Cope,Tomie 21 to Pearl Evans 18                 8-30-1913   D.A.Yonce,M.G.
Cope,Will 22 to Lillie Martin 18                9-29-1916   Retd.not executed
Cope,William 23 to Texie Wishon 18              7- 8-1917   J.H.Grant,M.G.
Cope,Elza 19 to Revena Clampet 19               10-10-1920  A.S.Solesbee,M.G.
Cope,Grady 24 to Cleo Douthit 21                12-24-1930  A.S.Solesbee,M.G.
Corbin,William to Mary Ann Ford                 11-26-1844  ----------
Corbin,Pinkney 22 to Sarah Henry 21             4-19-1874   J.S.Woodard,M.G.
Corbin,N.J.28 to Polly S.Bolick 21              10-26-1881Original not found
Corbin,H.L.42 to Georgea A.McDowell 40          3-31-1885   R.A.Owen,G.M.
  He from Jefferson County,Col.
Corbin,J.Landon 21 to Ella M.Donaldson 24       12-21-1902  T.J.Vinson,M.G.
Corbin,J.M.38 to Sallie Moore 24                12-24-1902  W.H.Hasket,J.P.
Corbin,J.J.21 to Eva E.Higdon 21                12-23-1902  M.A.Love,M.G.
Corbin,H.D.26 to Maggie Seay 18                 12-30-1915  Geo.Carpenter,J.P
Corbin,J.M.27 to Elsie Stewart 27               1- 3-1916   J.R.Pendergrass,MG
Corbin,M.P.31 to Lillian Norton 21              9-30-1918   J.R.Pendergrass,MG
Corbin,Chas.Dewey 25 to Minnie B.Williams 20/1-16-1925-J.R.Pendergras,MG
Corbin,James L.35 to Sarah Adams 27             8-13-1938   A.L.Dills,J.P.
Corn,Samuel 21 to Lena Norton 21                3-30-1899   Samuel Howard,J.P
Corn,L.A.21 to Flora Norton 20                  5-10-1903   J.C.Shope,J.P.
Corn,Clyde H.25 to Louise Walker 23             6-25-1938   Lester L.Arnold.
  He from Arden,N.C... She from Asheville,N.C.
Cornelius,Sandy 33 to Hallie Moore 23 Col.      12-28-1899  T.J.Floyd,M.G.
Cornett,Samuel to Ann Adams                     3-16-1847   J.K.Gray,Clk.
Cornish,Noah 36 to Bertha Guynn 17    Col.      11-29-1908  Chas.Stewart,M.G.
Corpening,A.L. to Amanda B.Siler                6-19-1854   John Hall.
Corpening,J.T.42 to Mary Oliver 24              1- 1-1904   J.C.Postell,M.G.
Corpening,Will 24 to Mirtle Lewis 16            12-26-1910  F.N.Johnson,J.P.
Corpening,Roscoe 32 to Ivey Stamey 17           7- 6-1920   G.M.Johnston,J.P.
Coward,Nathan to Jane Rogers                    2-17-1844   A.M.Russell,J.P.
```

```
Coward,J.Shaw 22 to Saphrona A.Stewart 23 Col./9-8-1878 Thos.Warren,M.G.
Coward,W.H.21 to C.L.Stamey 16              11-6--1904  J.C.Shope,J.P.
Coward,Claud 21 to Hettie Farmer 18         12-26-1919 Robert Stamey,J.P
Cowen,William to Ellener Buchanan           11-16-1829 John D.Corn,J.P.
Cowen,Berdit to Martha Vaughn               2- 1-1853  J.F.Slagle,J.P.
Cox,O.C.42 to Mrs.Lula Ammons 38            10-9-1919  J.M.Raby,J.P.
Cozad,Henry O.29 to Hallie E.Conley 21      7-12-1905  L.P.Bogle,M.G.
Craig,James to Amanda Wilson                8-23-1849  T.P.Siler,D.Clk.
Crane,Ed.26 to Olive Burrell 19             12-10-1910 J.D.Vinson,J.P.
Crane,W.A.25 to Bettie Burrell 17           3-12-1912  J.D.Vinson,M.G.
Crane,Frank J.18 to Lora C.Holland 16       5-11-1918  W.T.Potts,M.G.
Craver,W.Sandford 23 to Ollie V.Sanders18   10-4-1894  G.R.McPhearson,JP
Crawford,Enos to Abrigail Gill'espie        9- 6-1835  Robt.Clayton,Clk.
Crawford,James to Name not given.           3- 7-1837  William Henry.
Crawford,George to Margaret Robinson        11-25-1855 John Hall,Clk.
Crawford,George to Margaret Robinson        11-25-1856 John Hall,Clk.
Crawford,Jas.G. to Virginia Butler          8-10-1858  R.C.Slagle,Reg.
Crawford,James to Elizabeth Butler          12-13-1859 R.C.Slagle,Reg.
Crawford,Robt.M.21 to Margaret Roper 22     10-10-1879 P.C.Wild,J.P.
Crawford,E.G.37 to Ellen V.Conley 16        3-29-1882  Geo.D.French,M.G.
Crawford,L.F.47 to Mysa Quisenbury 25       11-11-1896 J.R.Pendergras,MG
Crawford,W.R.30 to Hallie Porter 20         8-24-1898  Chas.F.Sherrill.
Crawford,S.N.35 to Jane Webb 19             1-28-1900  A.C.Queen,M.G.
Crawford,Lee 34 to Carrie Sloan 37          1- 1-1902  Ira Erwin,M.G.
Crawford,Harlie 24 to Minnie Tallent 24     10-18-1908 J.L.Yonce,M.G.
Crawford,C.W.26 to Lillie Higdon 26         10-10-1909 J.R.Pendergras,MG
Crawford,Wm.M.19 to Belle Yonce 22          1-16-1910  Jos.L.Fouts,J.P.
Crawford,R.L.22 to Bertha Cope 22           3-26-1916  Frank T.Gettis,JP
Crawford,John L.22 to Annie Childers 16     3-10-1918  W.W.Marr,M.G.
Crawford,Cecil M.22 to Flora M.Robinson 18  6-18-1924  J.Q.Wallace,M.G.
Crawford,Willie 21 to Mrs.Arie Webb 35 Col. 8-20-1924  Jno.A.Dunn.M.G.
Crawford,Gilmer L.23 to May Hunnicutt 20    12-31-1925 B.C.Reavis,M.G.
Crawford,Eugene E.24 to Mary E.Snyder 21    6-24-1931  G.C.Ervin,M.G.
Crawford,J.L.23 to Sara Kelpin 20           10-28-1939 C.F.Rogers,M.G.
   Both from Atlanta,Ga.
Crawford,Elmer Wilson 30 to Lucy Sue Gray 24/12-31-1939 J.A.Flanagan,M.G
Crawford,Emerson G.23 to Margarie Honeycutt 26/6-9-1941 Walter L.Lanier.
Crenshaw,Leroy F.44 to Bessie S.Durham 44   11-12-1935 Geo.Carpenter,J.P
   Both from Charleston,S.C.
Crisp,George to Leana Roper                 8-22-1836  U.Keener,D.C.S.C.
Crispe,Merrill to Maletha Ramsey            6-22-1837  J.K.Gray,Clk.
Crisp,Simpson to Emily Ramsey               8-14-1838  ----------
Crisp,Hiram to Mira Dills                   9-14-1844  J.K.Gray,Clk.
Crisp,Madison to Elizabeth Dills            11-27-1852 J.F.Slagle,J.P.
Crisp,John to Margaret Cabble               1- 7-1855  Joseph Welch,J.P.
Crisp,Joel to Manda Stillwell               9- 2-1865  A.B.Welch,J.P.
Crisp,W.T. to Margaret Rose                 4-27-1866  R.C.Slagle,C.C.C.
Crisp,A.P.25 to Phoeba Rogers 19            12-21-1882 Jno.L.Corbin,J.P.
```

```
Crisp,H.M.68 to Mary C.McCoy 41              1-29-1888   M.B.Dockery,J.P.
Crisp,M.Pinkney 22 to Delina L.Strain 20     1- 6-1888   M.B.Dockery,J.P.
Crisp,George 19 to Zettie Woods 19           9-30-1888   J.M.Keener,J.P.
Crisp,Joab 43 to Julia Henry 32              2- 3-1889   John B.Gray,J.P.
Crisp,Charley 26 to Annie Arnold 24          11-1-1898   J.R.Crisp,M.G.
Crisp,Millard 25 to Hesper Justice 20        5-21-1905   T.J.Vinson,M.G.
Crisp,Miller 27 to Mally Baty 19             4- 7-1907   T.Baxter White,JP
Crisp,G.F.32 to Emma Corbin 26               1-31-1911   J.L.Kinsland,M.G.
Crisp,Lon 22 to Lura Cagle 21                2-16-1913   C.R.Cabe,J.P.
Crisp,Ed 21 to Elizabeth Teems 21            3-18-1914   T.J.Vinson,M.G.
Crisp,C.E.25 to Bertha Houston 18            12-26-1916  J.M.Keener,M.G.
Crisp,Iva 22 to May Teem 18                  8-12-1917   L.H.Higdon,J.P.
Crisp,Ralph 22 to Delena Peek 20             4-16-1927   J.M.Keener,M.G.
Crisp,Iva 34 to Della V.Bryson 21            12-21-1929-J.R.Pendergras,MG
Crisp,H.Grady 23 to Elva Elliott 20          5-18-1935   Walter Taylor,J.P
Crook,Robt.L.39 to Annie I.Gray 33           3-15-1927   R.P.Smith.
   He from Biltmore,N.C.
Cross,Elijah to Elizabeth Lowe               7-18-1833   John Hall,Clk.
Cross,Jas.A.to Elizabeth Robins              2- 2-1858   R.C.Slagle,C.C.C.
Cross,W.F.20 to Mary A.Baty 16               9-12-1878   Wm.Deweese,M.G.
Cross,Frank 19 to Allie Dalrymple 18         12-22-1904  L.J.Mashburn,J.P.
Cross,J.H.38 to Etta Douthit 22              8- 1-1915   J.H.Grant,M.G.
Crowell,George H.38 to Elizabeth L.Gaston 24/6-24-1903 Edwin L.Blain,M.G
Crummer,Harry J.24 to Winifred H.McCord 23   7-28-1938   R.B.DuPree,M.G.
   He from Orlando,Fla... She from Macon Ga.
Crunkleton,John to Sarah A.Keener            12-18-1856  ---------
Crunkleton,Thos.28 to Octa Rogers 25         10-15-1899  M.A.West,M.G.
Crunkleton,Seth H.31 to Docia Rogers 26      12-23-1906  H.Stewart,Jr.,J.P
Crunkleton,James L.26 to Katie Talley 18     8- 4-1935   J.W.Baty,M.G.
Cruse,Edward 21 to Ida Dills 21              12-19-1902  W.P.Allison,J.P.
Cruze,C.E.20 to Eleanore Carpenter 18        3- 7-1918   E.O.Rickman,J.P.
Cruze,L.D.19 to Clara Woods 19               1- 9-1919   Retd.not executed
Cuthberson,David to Nancy Stilwell           11-28-1853  Jas.M.Thomason,JP
Culbertson,Wm.21 to Louise Tallent 20        10-13-1935  C.R.McCarty,M.G.
Curtis,David to Polly Alexander              6- 6-1832   John Hall,Clk.
Curtis,Asbury to Elizabeth Addington         8-11-1832   Cents Ledford,Wit
Curtis,G.W.to Elizabeth Carson               1-11-1866   R.C.Slagle,Reg.
Curtis,W.L.to Nancy Sanders                  1- 5-1871   W.T.Anderson,J.P.
Curtis,Jonathan B.to Jane Allen              2-22-1872   Wm.Sloan,Reg.
Curtis,M.H.28 to Julia Garland 23            2- 3-1881   E.L.Long,J.P.
Curtis,John H.20 to Angie Ladford 21         8-17-1881   E.L.Long,J.P.
Curtis,H.Terrell 22 to Arzela Woodall 19     8- 3-1890   W.C.Kimsey,J.P.
Curtis,John 56 to Arennida Curtis 40         9-11-1895   J.M.Gillespie,J.P
Curtis,Julius H.24 to Mary Messer 18         8-16-1896   W.A.Norton,J.P.
Curtis,W.F.23 to Mary Gaston 24              9-17-1901   Ira.Erwin,M.G.
Curtis,Frank 26 to Aileen Baird 21           2-15-1906   V.H.Starbuck,M.G.
Curtis,R.B.23 to Minnie Sanders 22           8-11-1909   A.W.Jacobs,M.G.
```

```
Curtis,Gaston 21 to Gradybelle Turner 23      3-13-1924  Geo.Carpenter,J.P
Curtis,Charlie S.19 Minnie L.McCall 22         3-26-1928  T.S.Rotea,M.G.
Curtis,Edward 21 to Myrtle Jones 21            11-13-1937 Lester L.Arnold.
  He from Dillard,Ga.
Cunningham,Robert to Viney Reece               6-20-1835  ----------
Cunningham,Thadius to Martha M.Tothrow         4-21-1848  J.K.Gray.
Cunningham,William to Amanda Cansler           6-29-1852  T.P.Siler,D.Clk.
Cunningham,Aaron to Rody Sanders               12-2-1852  J.F.Slagle,J.P.
Cunningham,Dewit C.to Henretta Gray            4- 2-1853  J.K.Gray,Clk.
Cunningham,Enoch to Martha Cansler             8-16-1854  John Hall,Clk.
Cunningham,John B.to Sarah Moore               4-17-1855  John Hall,Clk.
Cunningham,Jas.M.to Nancy Shepherd             9-18-1856  I.A.Odum.
Cunningham,Jas. to Sarah Mallonee              10-23-1859 R.C.Slagle,Reg.
Cunningham,Havel to Mary Ann Lindsey           5-23-1864  R.C.Slagle,Reg.
Cunningham,R.H.to Sarah Campbell               12-19-1865 R.C.Slagle,Reg.
Cunningham,T.M.to R.M.Duvall                   3-30-1866  R.C.Slagle,C.C.C.
Cunningham,J.E.to Nancy McHard                 10-21-1866 R.C.Slagle,C.C.C.
Cunningham,A.P.53 to Loucinda Sanders 42       3- 6-1877  John Elmore,J.P.
Cunningham,W.A.22 to E.L.Cansler 21            8-17-1877  Thos.Mashburn,J.P
Cunningham,William 50 to Joanna Drake 41       3-18-1880  B.G.Wild,M.G.
Cunningham,Charles C.22 to Maggie Stalcup 22/4-24-1889 J.A.Deal,M.G.
Cunningham,George 29 to Emma Jacobs 24         2-26-1893  G.R.McPherson,J.P
Cunningham,John 21 to Minnie Jacobs 18         3-26-1893  R.E.Lentz,M.G.
Cunningham,Sam 27 to Elen Jacobs 23            2-24-1897  W.A.Norton,J.P.
Cunningham,Jean 23 to Eva Collins 21           12-6-1903  John H.Moore,M.G.
Cunningham,Frank C.24 to Emma Mashburn 21      8-30-1905  W.L.Bradley,M.G.
Cunningham,A.E.22 to Birdie Gregory 18         9-19-1907  J.R.Pendergrass,MG
Cunningham,C.B.40 to Ella Tippett 19           1-28-1910  N.P.Rankin,J.P.
Cunningham,Wade H.21 to Lela Stiles 19         9-21-1911  S.W.King,M.G.
Cunningham,Aaron 22 to Ethel Fulcher 23        11-24-1915 J.L.Teague,M.G.
Cunningham,Rufus 22 to Jessie Franks 19        5- 2-1917 Original not found
Cunningham,C.M.Jr.20 to Edith Jacobs 19        7-31-1918 Original not.found
Cunningham,C.M.Jr.21 to Edith Jacobs 19        5- 3-1919 J.R.Pendergrass,MG
Cunningham,Neuton L.21 to Lucy Jones 23        11-15-1919 J.E.Womack,M.G.
Cunningham,Grady 22 to Nina Curtis 20          11-8-1919  M.L.Angel,J.P.
Cunningham,Roy F.23 to Eva E.Baird 20          2-16-1927  E.J.Pipe?,M.G.
Cunningham,W.R.32 to Sophie E.Peacock 24       2-24-1928  T.S.Roten,M.G.
  She from Eastman,Ga.
Cunningham,Paul B.24 to Hattie Lee Cabe 21     4-30-1930  H.C.Freeman,M.G.
Cunningham,Carl P.28 to Amanda B.Carringer 23/8-6-1930 Geo.Carpenter,J.P
Cunningham,Robt.R. to Myrtle Shields 19        8- 6-1933  Will Smith,Ord.
Cunningham,John L.24 to Mary Teague 20         1-23-1937  J.A.Flanagan,M.G.
Cunningham,Howard M.23 to Virginia Zachary 19/12-20-1941-Dallas Young,JP
  He from Pontica,Mich... She from Holgate, Ohio.
Dalrymple,T.W.to Amanda Kimzey                 1-25-1868  R.C.SLagle,C.C.C.
Dalrymple,E.Jr. 21 to H.Cailor 24              8-19-1877  Mark May,M.G.
Dalrymple,John C.21 to Mary O.Lewis 19         12-10-1898 S.B.Yoden,M.G.
Dalrymple,T.J.28 to L.R.Cockram 22             4-28-1901  J.L.Kinsland,M.G.
```

33

```
Dalrymple,James 23 to Annie Cross 19            1-12-1902  W.A.Solesbee,J.P.
Dalrymple,Geo.H.35 to Mary E.Dean 25           11-26-1902  W.A.Bradley,M.G.
Dalrymple,Thos.J.30 to Emily Bailey 22          1-30-1904  C.L.Rickman,J.P.
Dalrymple,Samuel E.36 to Obra Gillespie 17      4-15-1906  J.L.Kinsland,M.G.
Dalrymple,Thos.J.34 to Mary Brendle 24         12-27-1906  J.H.Mincy,J.P.
Dalrymple,Wm.N.23 to Blanche Martin 19          7-19-1925  A.J.Smith,M.G.
Dalrymple,Kermit 22 to Julia Kilpatrick 18     11-5-1933   T.D.Denny,M.G.
Dalton,James to Catherine Shepherd              4- 4-1848  J.K.Gray.
Dalton,C.W. to Mary Raby                        1-13-1849  J.K.Gray.
Dalton,John M.to Margaret Boyd                  3-25-1871  William Sloan,Reg
Dalton,Alfred 40 to Verlincha Raby 25           2-16-1873  P.R.Rickman,M.G.
Dalton,J.C.21 to M.C.Mashburn 21                1-25-1882  M.J.Mashburn,J.P.
Dalton,J.Lane 26 to Laura Shuler 18             8-17-1884  E.C.Stewman,J.P.
Dalton,C.W.59 to Nancy J.Kingree 30             5- 5-1888  J.T.Berry,J.P.
Dalton,Geo.B.23 to Adela Shepherd 19            9-20-1891  W.J.Jenkins,J.P.
Dalton,J.R.24 to Tallahasee Dillingham 18      10-26-1894  J.Kilpatrick,J.P.
Dalton,John H.24 to Emily A.Gibson 17           2- 8-1896  J.B.Cardon,J.P.
Dalton,T.E.22 to Hattie Fox 18                  1- 7-1897  J.B.Cardon,J.P.
Dalton,W.H.23 to Lillie Shepherd 23             5-25-1902  John E.Rickman,JP
Dalton,B.C.24 to Callie Tippett 26             12-31-1903  P.R.Rickman,M.G.
Dalton,George 27 to Artie McGaha 21             9-11-1904  P.R.Rickman,M.G.
Dalton,Edd 20 to Nellie London 16              12-3-1905   J.N.McConnell,J.P
Dalton,Fred 19 to Ivlee Hurst 19                4-21-1907  P.R.Rickman,M.G.
Dalton,C.T. 27 to Callie Ammons 18             11-25-1914  N.L.Jolly,J.P.
Dalton,Carl 24 to Nina Raby 18                 11-4- 1922  Geo.Carpenter,J.P
Dalton,Manuel B.49 to Mrs.Minnie Painter 48/11- 1-1933  G.A.Cloer,M.G.
   He from Salisbury,N.C.
Dalton,Robt.L.26 to Martha Buchanan 20          4- 4-1936  W.R.Rowland,J.P.
Daniels,James 31 to Louisa Hurst 27             3- 3-1879  P.P.McLean,M.G.
Daniels,Chas.C.28 to Mary S.Robinson 22        12-22-1892  D.H.Cowan,M.G.
Daves,Wm. to Elizabeth Middleton                8-13-1852  J.K.Gray.
Daves,Marcus to Emeline Shope                  12-3-1858   R.C.Slagle.
Daves,Robert to Adaline Yonce                   3- 2-1871  Mark May,M.G.
Daves,James M.25 to Adaline Cabe 23             2-17-1874  John McDonald,MG
Daves,Kope 24 to Addie Ramey 22                 4-16-1899  C.W.Dowdle,J.P.
Daves,Alfred 35 to Roxanna Tallent 28           2-12-1885  D.A.Younce,J.P.
Daves,George M.22 to Betty Huggins 17          12-16-1894  P.C.Wild,J.P.
Daves,Joseph 25 to Lizzie Holbrook 26          12-14-1906  J.F.Tippett,M.G.
Daves,J.H.37 to Annie Phillips 23               2-10-1915  W.G.Warren,M.G.
Daves,Frank 33 to Mattie Angel 33               7-19-1916  A.M.Ledford,M.G.
Daves,G.M.47 to Mrs.Ivalee Scroggs 26          11-8-1919   A.S.Solesbee,M.G.
Daves,C.C. 30 to Celia Bateman 18              11-6-1920   D.A.Younce,M.G.
Daves,Early 23 to Florence Waters 18            8-26-1934  D.L.Miller,M.G.
Daves,J.M.87 to Laura Holland 72                9- 8-1934  Geo.Carpenter,J.P
Davidson,Lee 26 to Minnie Stanfield 18         11-29-1912  J.R.Pendergras,MG
Davis,Thomas to Jane Kelly                      2- 2-1838  Risdon Cooper.
Davis,David to Reveny Hogin                     3-16-1837  U.Keener,Wit.
```

Davis,Peter to Sarah Davis	6- 2-1838	James Parson,Wit.
Davis,Ephriam to Manerva Peek	12-23-1840	H.G.Woodfin,Wit.
Davis,John to Polly Deweese	12-29-1840	H.G.Woodfin,Wit.
Davis,Mathew to Sophria Gibbs	1-24-1841	John Hall,Clk.
Davis,Thomas to Nany Grant	11-12-1844	J.K.Gray,Wit.
Davis,John to Louisa Deweese	9-26-1845	J.K.Gray,Wit.
Davis,Isaac H.to Elizabeth E.Rogers	3-29-1847	J.K.Gray,Wit.
Davis,W.M. to Naoma Ray	4- 3-1850	---------
Davis,James L. to Althia Daves	12-27-1854	---------
Davis,T.W.P. to Minerva A.Tethero	8-15-1865	---------
Davis,Henry to Cotherin Sheets	9-14-1866	R.C.Slagle,C.C.C.
Davis,T.J. to I.M.Thomason	8- 5-1870	J.K.Bryson,Reg.
Davis,D.A. 21 to Sarah A.Buckner 21 He from Cleveland,Tenn.	3-27-1873	B.G.Wild,M.G.
Davis,F.P.25 to N.D.M.Poindexter 23	1-15-1879	C.D.Smith,M.G.
Davis,Alf W.22 to Martha Cowan 19 He from Oconee Co.,S.C.	11-11-1879	W.H.Higdon,J.P.
Davis,L.G.26 to Mary Young 23	2-10-1884	John Elmore,J.P.
Davis,Robt.L.24 to E.Etta Morrison 24	5-11-1892	G.A.Bartlett,M.G.
Davis,Jason26 to Susy Ray 15	3- 4-1894	J.T.Barnes,M.G.
Davis,Kope 24 to Addie Ramey 22	9- 2-1899	Original not found
Davis,William S.51 to Rebecca L.Pierson 37	5-20-1915	W.T.Thompson,M.G.
Davis,Billie 29 to Olive G.Norton 25	9- 9-1915	D.P.Proffitt,M.G.
Davis,Jim 24 to Velma Shepherd 21	5-10-1919	J.L.Bryson,J.P.
Davis,N.Don 27 to Eva Mae Hyatt 22 He from Sylva,N.C.	1-21-1925	J.Q.Wallace,M.G.
Davis,R.Franklin 27 to Margie A.Gray 18	3- 4-1928	J.A.Flanagan,M.G.
Davis,D.L. 21 to Opal Ashe 18 Both from Whittier,N.C.	4-10-1929	Geo.Carpenter,J.P
Davis,Furman 25 to Clara Mae Fisher 16	7-25-1929	J.R.Pendergrass,MG
Davis,J.R.21 to Bertha McLean 21	11-4-1929	Robert Mock.M.G.
Davis,Otis 24 to Ruth Medford 21 Both from Waynesville,N.C.	1- 7-1930	R.F.Mock,M.G.
Davis,Willis H.53 to Mary J.DeHart 37	10-15-1931	J.A.Lakey,J.P.
Davis,Sandy 31 to Maud Lunsford 22	12-1-1931	J.R.Pendergrass,MG
Davis,Virgil 24 to Josie Dowell 15	2-12-1935	W.G.Barker,J.P.
Davis,George 27 to Kate Ross 23 Both from Cherokee,N.C.	12-22-1936	J.J.Edward,M.G.
Davis,Ross,30 to Ellie McKinnish 20 Both from Almond,N.C.	12-26-1936	C.C.Welch,M.G.
Davis,Robert N.24 to Francis E.Tallent 18	11-5-1938	S.R.Crockett,M.G.
Davis,Charles H.25 to Thelma Holt 20 He from Dillard,Ga.	12-23-1938	C.T.Rogers,M.G.
Davis,John B.29 to Vinnie Alice Holbrooks 20/12-14-1941-G.W.Davis,M.G.		
Dawkins,Willie P.22 to Bertha E.McClure 17	11-10-1907	J.R.Pendergras,MG
Deadwyler,J.G.46 to Dora P.Smith 40	12-21-1922	W.T.Potts,M.G.
Deal,William to Martha Jennings	3-13-1838	John Hall,Clk.
Deal,T.N.to Lucinda C.Arnold	2- 9-1860	Joshua Ammons,MG
Deal,James 18 to C.J.Shepherd 20	12-25-1873	D.W.Wells,M.G.

Deal,M.C.26 to Martha Elmore 18	10-6-1881	J.S.Woodard,M.G.
Deal,W.P.30 to Lydia C.Berry 23	12-6-1883	J.S.Woodard,M.G.
Deal,Chas.30 to Maria Bradley 19 Col.	12-20-1917	E.J.McKay,M.G.
Deal,James 64 to Myrtle West 22 Col.	10-31-1918	W.L.Bradley,M.G.
Dean,Alexander B.to Mary Wilds	5-26-1855	M.Rickman,J.P.
Dean,George W.to Aletha A.Parrish	2- 8-1858	R.C.Slagle,Clk.
Dean,G.B. to Margaret Bryson	1-29-1859	R.C.Slagle,Clk.
Dean,Sydney to Sarah J.Henry	3-11-1861	L.M.Bena,Wit.
Dean,J.H.to Mary Dills	5-27-1865	Jesse S.Moore,Wit
Dean,William L.to Florence I.Hill	11-1-1887	W.S.Ballard,M.G.
Dean,Henderson D.26 to Alice Morgan 18	12-25-1887	W.L.Bird,J.P.
Dean,Geo.B.22 to Myra J.Cody 16	2-23-1890	A.A.Justice,J.P.
Dean,John H.26 to Candis McCoy 18	11-8-1900	Joseph L.Fouts,JP
Dean,Silas J.27 to Florence Dillard 20	3- 8-1908	D.C.McCoy,J.P.
Dean,Walter 24 to Timmie Clouse 20	4-23-1916	J.P.Moore,J.P.
Dean,Herman 23 to Alma Berry 18	12-31-1916	J.B.Henry,J.P.
Dean,Ralston 19 to Mahota Arvey 19	4- 6-1925	J.R.Pendergrass,MG
Dean,Furman B.27 to Myrtle Shelton 19	9-20-1930	D.C.McCoy,M.G.
Deaver,William to Jane Downs	11-15-1851	J.K.Gray,Wit.
DeHart,Martin to Eliza Elders	3-31-1840	John Hall,Clk.
DeHart,John P.to Margaret L.Miller	8-30-1849	T.P.Siler,D.Clk.
DeHart,J.P. to Mary Thompson	1-13-1855	---------
DeHart,Jas.W.to Sarah Thomason	11-28-1857	R.C.Slagle,C.C.C.
DeHart,A.J.to Lorenda Parrish	4- 2-1861	R.C.Slagle,C.C.C.
DeHart,W.J.to Eliza A.Gipsen	12-9-1865	R.C.Slagle,Clk.
DeHart,Dallas to Sarah S.Neel	9-16-1869	J.K.Bryson,Reg.
DeHart,Thomas S.to Cordelia E.Painter	8-30-1870	J.K.Bryson,Reg.
DeHart,A.M.20 to H.M.Rickman 21	12-9-1881	J.S.Woodard,M.G.
DeHart,Jacob R.19 to Tilithe C.Rickman 19	9-29-1887	Jno.S.Smiley,M.G.
DeHart,John T.22 to Nannie M.Myers 18 He from Swain Co.N.C.	12-17-1887	E.A.Sample,M.G.
DeHart,Allen 42 to Clemontine Potts 30	5-30-1896	H.D.Dean,J.P.
DeHart,J.A.B.35 to Martha Mason 22	9-11-1897	W.C.Hamrick,M.G.
DeHart,Geo.R.30 to Callie McCoy 22	11-5-1899	D.C.McCoy,J.P.
DeHart,James 32 to Emma May 22	2-15-1906	F.M.Morgan,M.G.
DeHart,John 26 to Isabel Anderson 25	2-28-1908	W.L.Bradley,M.G.
DeHart,J.Robert 34 to Mamie Parrish 22	1-21-1909	W.L.Bradley,M.G.
DeHart,D.M.25 to Fannie Elmore 23	8-31-1910	R.P.Rickman,J.P.
DeHart,Earnie 21 to Leona Hasting 18	12-27-1917	Robert Stamey,J.P
DeHart,J.H.45 to Iona Hurst 27	11-9-1918	W.W.Marr,M.G.
DeHart,Bryan 28 to Edna Cabe 18	1- 8-1927	Geo.Carpenter,J.P
DeHart,James R.57 to Nola Gibson 48 He from Bryson City,N.C.	5-12-1935	C.C.Herbert,M.G.
DeHart,Wint 23 to Pearl Guffey 18	11-11-1936	D.C.McCoy,M.G.
DeHart,Earl 27 to Florence Byrd 18 Both from Bryson City,N.C.	3-18-1938	Lester L.Arnold.
Deitz,Toban F.to Sarah Buchanan	11-26-1844	J.K.Gray,Wit.
Deitz,Nantahiel to Margaret J.Buckhanan	8-23-1848	J.K.Gray,Wit.

Deitz,Lorenzo 20 to Alice Wilson 18	10-8-1891	W.J.Jenkins,J.P.
Deitz,Richmond 25 to Myra Webb 20	5-16-1921	Geo.Carpenter,J.P
Delozier,Edward to Elizabeth Poindexter	5-24-1834	B.G.Wild,M.G.
Delozier,J.R.to Emiline Stillwell	7-12-1869	Jas.K.Bryson,Reg.
Dempsey,James to Caroline Scoggins	8-23-1839	H.G.Woodfin,D.Clk
Dendy,Floyd E.24 to Mae Henry 17	1-28-1917	W.T.Potts,M.G.
Denny,Edward 32 to Margie Cope 21	8- 3-1935	Phillip Passmore.
Denny,Will 24 to Ella Dills 19	1-18-1937	G.A.Lee,M.G.
Denton,Isaac to Jane Roland	6- 7-1847	J.K.Gray,Wit.
Derreberry,Cross 23 to Beulah Byrd 15	9-11-1921	Geo.W.Stepp,J.P.
Deweese,Wm.W.to Rachel Solesbee	12-2-1848	J.K.Gray,Wit.
Deweese,Garrett to Elizabeth Wilson	8-18-1857	T.P.Siler,D.Clk.
Deweese,John to Nicey Wilson	1-28-1860	T.P.Siler,D.Clk.
Deweese,Jesse to H.T.Clampett	1-29-1862	R.C.Slagle,Clk.
Deweese,Julean to Angalin Drenon	6- 6-1865	J.M.Weldes,Wit.
Deweese,Wm.D.24 to Winnie Jones 15	10-11-1896	F.M.Morgan,M.G.
Deweese,Joseph 23 to Lucinda Wilkes 19	3- 3-1898	J.P.Campbell,J.P.
Deweese,William H.36 to Rosa Tippett 25	3-21-1899	J.F.Wilks,J.P.
Deweese,Jesse 23 to Sarah Cochram 25	8- 6-1899	W.C.Hanrick,M.G.
Deweese,John A.26 to Callie Tippett 18	4-15-1900	Mark Deweese,J.P.
Deweese,G.W.24 to Manda Grant 19	1-12-1902	W.A.Solesbee,J.P.
Deweese,Theodore 25 to Nannie Wilson 18	7-19-1906	A.S.Solesbee,M.G.
Deweese,John 28 to Florence Roper 22	1-12-1908	H.P.Ray,J.P.
Deweese,Malcomb 23 to Mattie Willie 18	10-26-1923	J.R.Pendergras,MG
Deweese,Floyd 23 to Elsie Solesbee 18	3- 5-1928	T.G.Wilson,J.P.
Dewey,Isaac H.27 to O.A.Owenby 18	4- 8-1888	F.M.Morgan,M.G.
Dickerson,Mart 24 to Clara Sawyers 24	2-24-1914	J.L.Kinsland,M.G.
Dickey,Jas.21 to Liza Siler 19 Col.	5-29-1880	E.H.Franks,J.P.
Dickey,James 25 to Lou McCoy 19 Col.	12-6-1900	A.B.Morrow,M.G.
Dickey,Harley 22 to Martha McDonald 21 Col.	4- 4-1909	W.F.Love,M.G.
Dillard,George W.29 to M.M.Howard 25	1-20-1881	G.A.Ogelsby,M.G.
Dillard,Jno.M.22 to Margaret R.Foster 23	10-15-1882	J.S.Dixon,M.G.
Dillard,Arthur 25 to Carrie Edwards 23	12-24-1911	A.P.Foster,M.G.
Dillard,Charlie 19 to Eva Williams 25	12-26-1920	J.M.Williams,J.P.
Dills,Henry to Susa Furr	12-18-1838	J.K.Gray.
Dills,William to Mary McGaha	3-24-1842	J.K.Gray.
Dills,John Jr. to Lucenda Cabe	12-6-1847	J.K.Gray.
Dills,John to Margaret Gibson	5- 9-1851	J.K.Gray.
Dills,Phillips to Jane Henderson	1-31-1856	John Dills.
Dills,Bartlett to Nancy A.Patton	8-30-1859	J.H.McLoud.
Dills,Erwin to Abrgail Brooks	1-21-1860	R.C.Slagle.
Dills,Levi to Martha Love	11-26-1860	L.F.Siler,J.P.
Dills,John S.to Mary A.Frazier	1-27-1863	R.C.Slagle,Clk.
Dills,Jeremiah to Rachel Payne	2- 7-1863	R.C.SLagle,Clk.
Dills,H.H.to M.E.Carpenter	3-18-1865	P.C.Slagle.
Dills,Henry H.to Henrietta Nichols	1- 4-1871	Jos.Conley,J.P.
Dills,J.R.18 to Elizabeth Lunceford 18	7-20-1873	Albert Siler,J.P.

```
Dills,H.T.20 to Mary Gipson 19                        9- 2-1876   I.N.Keener,J.P.
Dills,David B.21 to R.E.Grant 17                      9-16-1877   Mark May,M.G.
Dills,W.T.28 to Emily Houston 30                      10-17-1877  J.D.Vinson,M.G.
Dills,Rufus V.20 to Martha R.Nichols 20               1-17-1878   Albert Siler,J.P.
Dills,Samuel M.17 to Ellen J.Drake 19                 11-17-1878  M.Gormley,M.G.
Dills,Geo.L.25 to Rutha Peek 18                       3-23-1882   J.L.Corbin,J.P.
Dills,J.M. 40 to Rachael D.Simons 22                  1-21-1883   Joseph Morgan,J.P
Dills,J.H.21 to Kanzada Mason 22                      2- 3-1883   J.M.Forester,J.P.
Dills,E.B.21 to Malinda Dalrymple 18                  8-19-1883   J.M.Forester,J.P.
Dills,Henry N.20 to Malinda Hascusson 15              12-7-1884   M.S.Dills,J.P.
Dills,Levi 55 to Mary A.Lee 33                        8- 4-1885   M.S.Dills,J.P.
Dills,Geo.L. 29 to Juda Peek 18                       6-24-1886   M.B.Dockney,J.P.
Dills,Thomas 21 to Louisa Bennett 18                  2-24-1887   Original not found
Dills,A.J. 35 to Cora A.Dryman 21                     9-18-1887   J.J.McConnell,J.P
Dills,James A.21 to Margaret Pendergrass 22/4- 8-1888 Z.Barnes,J.P.
Dills,Henry G.20 to Maggie A.Stalcup 22               7- 7-1888   Retd.not executed
Dills,Asa M.21 to Emma Guffey 16                      11-17-1889  W.C.Kimzey,J.P.
Dills,James A.20 to Iowa A.Anderson 20                9-19-1890   S.J.May,J.P.
Dills,Chas.L.20 to Bettie A.Holbrooks 22              9-24-1891   W.C.Mason,M.G.
Dills,Chas.P.22 to Tine Tallent 17                    12-4-1892   N.J.Rush,J.P.
Dills,Thos.S.20 to Laura Norton 18                    8-22-1894   Wm.Kimzey,J.P.
Dills,S.E.55 to Margaret Dills 40                     8-16-1896   J.C.Burrell,M.G.
Dills,J.L.21 to S.C.Smith 19                          3- 3-1897   M.B.Setser,J.P.
Dills,Lom 21 to Mary Patton 18                        12-23-1897  Thos.M.Slagle,J.P
Dills,J.C.23 to Sophronia Holland 14                  3-10-1898   J.T.Peek,M.G.
Dills,Thomas S.23 to Alice Davis 18                   7-31-1898   Thos.M.Slagle,J.P
Dills,W.M.21 to Coralee M.Holland 15                  8-24-1899   T.J.Vinson,J.P.
Dills,A.J.22 to Mary B.Jones 18                       10-1-1899   J.B.Elmore,J.P.
Dills,Berry 21 to Bell Gregory 22                     9-20-1900   J.M.Keener,M.G.
Dills,Charlie 20 to Lelah Curtis 23                   1-26-1901   J.L.Kinsland,M.G.
Dills,Harley 20 to Tiney West 18                      5- 9-1901   W.A.Setser,J.P.
Dills,Archie E.23 to Ida Ledford 19                   11-16-1902  J.L.Kinsland,M.G.
Dills,G.P.36 to Telitha Webb 18                       1- 4-1903   H.Stewart,J.P.
Dills,W.Zeb 21 to Mrs.Addie Beck 27                   2-12-1903   J.W.Greenwood,J.P
Dills,J.H.22 to Rosey Mason 16                        9-20-1903   L.I.Mashburn,M.G.
Dills,Harlie M.22 to Darcus Buchanan 20               3-13-1904   J.M.Keener,M.G.
Dills,Oscar W.18 to Sarah E.Holland 15                11-24-1905  T.J.Vinson,M.G.
Dills,Wesley 22 to Sallie Morgan 22                   12-22-1905  W.C.Mason,M.G.
Dills,W.A.20 to Sarah Mason 16                        2-21-1906   J.W.Greenwood,J.P.
Dills,W.Sherman 21 to Rosie Mashburn 17               5- 6-1906   L.J.Mashburn,M.G.
Dills,Hez 18 to Hassie Cloer 17                       6-23-1907   C.A.Setser,J.P.
Dills,Matason 23 to Nora Tallent 21                   8-27-1908   T.J.Vinson,M.G.
Dills,Homer 22 to Iley Anderson 18                    11-24-1909  C.W.Slagle,J.P.
Dills,Richard 25 to Lettie McCoy 14                   6-29-1911   J.M.Keener,M.G.
Dills,Allen 21 to Ida Shope 18                        9-16-1911   T.B.Enloe,J.P.
Dills,George 21 to Angie Bradley 20                   12-31-1911  C.R.Cabe,J.P.
Dills,Judson 23 to Jane Pendergrass 19                3-20-1912   Robert Stamey,J.P
```

Dills,Harley 21 to Ida Cagle 18	3-17-1913	A.W.Donaldson,J.P
Dills,John 21 to Bula Cabe	12-21-1913	C.R.Cabe,J.P.
Dills,Lester 22 to Exie Henderson 19	7- 4-1917	J.R.Pendergrass,MG
Dills,Lonnie 21 to Hester Anderson 17	7-30-1920	G.M.Johnson,J.P.
Dills,M.E.19 to Maud Passmore 19 Both from Nantahala,N.C.	11-1-1925	W.C.Mason,M.G.
Dills,A.L.55 to Elmer Higdon 47	9- 2-1926	J.M.Raby,J.P.
Dills,Lonnie E.28 to Charlotte B.McCall 19	6- 6-1927	J.L.Kinsland,M.G.
Dills,Grady L.25 to Florence Robbins 21 He from Nantahala,N.C... She from Wesser,N.C.	5-30-1932	W.C.Mason,M.G.
Dills,W.M. to Mae B.Crisp	10-2-1933	Will Smith,Ord.
Dills,Fred 23 to Bertie Holland 20	10-28-1933	Will Smith,Ord.
Ditmore,Dave 51 to Elvie Deweese 54	1- 5-1936	J.R.Wikle,J.P.
Dobson,W.W. to Mrs.Clearinda Byers	3- 3-1835	---------
Dobson,Joseph W.to L.W.Dobson	12-16-1839	John Hall,Clk.
Dobson,Mac 24 to Mary Blackburn 28	11-9-1873	E.H.Franks,J.P.
Dobson,B.W.22 to M.E.Sellers 24	3-28-1877	C.D.Smith,M.G.
Dobson,W.B.58 to Laura A.Wood 43	4-20-1910	W.I.Hughes,M.G.
Dobson,O.L.35 to Nora Mashburn 29	1- 9-1924	J.L.Teague,M.G.
Dodson,Wm. to Mary Henderson	12-10-1831	John Hall,D.Clk.
Donaldson,Wm. to Rachel McConnell	6-18-1844	J.K.Gray,Clk.
Donaldson,Wm.C.to Sarah Mann	5-10-1869	J.K.Bryson,Reg.
Donaldson,J.C. to E.T.Gray	8-12-1869	J.K.Bryson,Reg.
Donaldson,Ivey S.23 to Susan A.Dowdle 22	9-24-1873	John McDowell,M.G
Donaldson,C.A.25 to Mollie M.Dowdle 19	8-10-1874	John McDowell,M.G
Donaldson,H.P.23 to M.F.Cabe 16	11-9-1876	E.H.Franks,J.P.
Donaldson,M.N. 30 to Elizabeth A.McDowell 24/	9-5-1878	J.D.Wright,M.G.
Donaldson,J.B.21 to Mary E.Conley 26	10-12-1881	L.H.Garland,J.P.
Donaldson,Geo.21 to Mary A.Norris 23	1- 8-1882	L.H.Garland,J.P.
Donaldson,A.W.23 to M.M.Rhodes 25	5- 6-1883	L.Howard,J.P.
Donaldson,Henry P.35 to Lizzie Kimzey 24	10-31-1888	Jona.Phillips,J.P
Donaldson,R.N.28 to Elba V.Donaldson 20	4- 9-1911	Robert Stamey,J.P
Donaldson,Joseph F.27 to Fannie B.Guffee 26/	6- 4-1911	J.T.Watts,J.P.
Donaldson,Wymer 32 to Hattie Setser 29	10-1-1911	Robert Stamey,J.P
Donaldson,Oscar 20 to Jennie Smith 26	3-25-1917	Robert Stamey,J.P
Donaldson,Carl 23 to Lela Tallent 20	7- 4-1918	J.R.Pendergrass,MG
Donaldson,W.J. 32 to Estell Dryman 18	1-24-1919	J.J.Mann,J.P.
Donaldson,Clint 34 to Jessie Jennings 20	2-22-1926	J.J.Mann,J.P.
Donaldson,Harvey 36 to Dochia McFalls	11-4-1929	J.A.Young,J.P.
Dooley,Summer 24 to Francis Sanders 20 He from Jackson Co.N.C.	7-11-1925	J.R.Pendergrass,MG
Dotson,Edd 20 to Nellie London 16	12-3-1905	Jas.N.McConnell.
Dotson,Henry 23 to Minnie Leatherwood 21	7-17-1910	F.N.Johnston,J.P.
Douthit,C.H.22 to Addie Owenby 22	1- 8-1899	E.N.Delrymple,J.P
Douthit,A.I.26 to A.L.Welch 19	12-19-1909	H.J.Hogen,M.G.
Douthit,Alfred 28 to Hassie Owenby 22	10-22-1914	A.S.Solesbee,M.G.
Dowdle,Felix to A.C.Addington	9-24-1846	E.Dowdle.
Dowdle,F.A. to Sary S.Cabe	9-30-1852	J.F.Slagle,

Dowdle,Thomas to Elizabeth Bird	11-5-1853	John Hall,Clk.
Dowdle,J.W. to Mary W.Vanhook	11-26-1861	R.C.Slagle,Wit.
Dowdle,E.P. to Jane Huggins	3-15-1870	J.K.Bryson,Reg.
Dowdle,Benjamin F. to Sarah M.Guffey	11-29-1871	William Sloan,Reg
Dowdle,Felix A.to Ellen Moore	12-3-1871	William Sloan,Reg
Dowdle,J.M.26 to Mary M.Huggins 22	8- 3-1876	J.W.Bowman,M.G.
Dowdle,C.W.24 to Ida Patton 22	3-26-1884	R.A.Owens,M.G.
Dowdle,Thos.C.23 to Emma Tallent 20	8-29-1897	J.H.Bradley,M.G.
Dowdle,J.E.22 to Arizona McConnell 22	1- 4-1899	T.R.Arnold,J.P.
Dowdle,Chas.W.26 to Ollie McPhearson 20	9-20-1899	E.A.Sample,M.G.
Dowdle,Geo.C.23 to Sallie Campbell 19	11-16-1899	C.M.Campbell,M.G.
Dowdle,J.Harve 32 to Laura McClure 26	10-3-1906	John H.Moore,M.G.
Dowdle,Robert T.23 to Naomi Fulcher 21	11-21-1906	J.H.Moore,M.G.
Dowdle,Thad O.23 to Jane Daves 18	5-10-1908	J.R.Pendergrass,MG
Dowdle,Tilman 29 to Hester Elliott 23	6-30-1909	W.I.Hughes,M.G.
Dowdle,George 21 to Erma Ray 19	6-11-1911	J.R.Pendergrass,MG
Dowdle,Marcus L.22 to Mary E.Barnard 23	10-7-1914	E.E.Williamson,MG
Dowdle,E.A.22 to Bertha Cowart 22	2-15-1924	J.L.Teague,M.G.
Dowdle,Lee 27 to Sallie Henry 20	8-31-1935	Lester Sorrels,MG
Dowell,James to Vicy Redman	4-14-1848	J.K.Gray,Clk.
Dowell,Martin to Margaret M.Adams	6-19-1860	A.Ammons,M.G.
Dowell,W.R.21 to Louisa C.McCoy 25	9- 4-1881	G.W.Dean,Esq.
Dowell,Richard M.35 to Sarah Smith 25	1-18-1885	A.A.Justice,M.G.
Dowell,Wm.C.26 to Nancy Anderson 17	7-21-1910	Joseph L.Fouts,JP
Downs,Alexander to Catherine Guyer	11-25-1841	E.Collins,Wit.
Downs,William to Mary C.Garrett	8-12-1863	R.C.Slagle,C.C.C.
Downs,M.C.to Rachel Vaughn	12-7-1864	H.Parrish,J.P.
Downs,Wm.to Laura C.Davis	9- 8-1870	W.Sloan,Reg.
Downs,Zachariah to Amanda Drennon	11-12-1870	Wm.Sloan,Reg.
Downs,Ezekiel 20 to M.L.Buckner 19	9- 5-1878	Joseph Morgan,J.P
Downs,Z.A.31 to Eunice Ray 38	7-20-1879	P.C.Wild,J.P.
Downs,Thos.A.30 to A.R.Roper 18	2- 4-1880	C.Campbell,M.G.
Downs,William 22 to Nannie L.Bell 16	1-25-1883	Geo.D.French,M.G.
Downs,Alexander 64 to Mary C.Glymps 49	4-15-1886	F.M.Morgan,M.G.
Downs,Wilford 32 to Minnie Ray 23	7-21-1892	A.W.Jacobs,M.G.
Downs,N.B.L.19 to Florence Sheffield 23	8-15-1901	Robt.Howie,M.G.
Downs,Ira 21 to Hattie Lowe 19	7-13-1902	Jas.L.Fouts,J.P.
Downs,Charles 21 to Rosa Houston 21	3-15-1914	J.A.Morrison,J.P.
Downs,Sammie 21 to Laura Holbrooks 18	12-15-1919	Geo.Carpenter,J.P
Downs,W.W. 22 to Trixie Dryman 17	12-24-1919	L.B.Hayes,M.G.
Downs,Robert 23 to Margie Hughes 23	2-25-1926	J.J.Mann,J.P.
Drake,Pauley to Sarah I.Clark	10-30-1851	J.K.Gray,Clk.
Drake,John to Elizabeth Rowland	5-20-1856	John Hall,Clk.
Drake,L.D. to R.S.Moore	9-10-1867	R.C.Slagle,Clk.
Drake,W.T.24 to Adelia Baldwin 16	12-24-1882	E.B.Padgett,J.P.
Drake,Arthur A.20 to Delia Dills 16	8-25-1907	W.T.Griggs,M.G.
Drake,Carl 22 to Maud Bateman 18	12-27-1914	E.G.Ledford,M.G.

Drake,Norman 21 to Hester Hodgins 18	7- 1-1915	G.A.Cloer,M.G.
Drenin,Thomas 48 to Addie Ray 45	10-18-1906	J.L.Yonce,M.G.
Drenning,Hensly to Isabella Shope	9- 4-1846	J.K.Gray,Clk.
Drenning,Ervin 23 to Lillie I.Reeves 17	3- 4-1896	C.S.Ray,J.P.
Drenon,Wm. to Altha Davis	3-17-1860	D.H.Allen,Wit.
Drinnon,Wm. to Maron Welch	10-16-1847	A.Hall.
Drinon,D.E.38 to Mary Teague 24	1-16-1911	J.R.Pendergrass,MG
Dryman,John to Rachel McConnell	10-10-1835	James Robinson,Wt
Dryman,William to Polly Penland	5-30-1843	Jno.Connely,Wit.
Dryman,V.M. to Mary M.Allen	1-21-1858	C.D.Smith,M.G.
Dryman,James A.to Harriet Allen	3-16-1864	R.C.Slagle,Clk.
Dryman,W.M. to Susan Sanders	11-9-1865	John A.Green,Wit.
Dryman,George N.to Eliza Phillips	9- 1-1869	J.K.Bryson,Reg.
Dryman,William J.35 to Elizabeth L.McClure 33	4-7-1874	W.T.Anderson,J.P.
Dryman,Wm.P.22 to Myra L.Dills 21	2-16-1898	D.P.Cabe,J.P.
Dryman,Charles 21 to M.J.Cabe 26	8-24-1898	D.P.Cabe,J.P.
Dryman,J.B.21 to Lydia Gregory 26	10-16-1898	J.W.Parker,J.P.
Dryman,W.J.57 to Mary R.Carpenter 45	1- 4-1899	A.W.Young,M.G.
Dryman,Roy 19 to Minnie Justice 20	8-20-1905	T.J.Vinson,M.G.
Dryman,Ray 22 to Mamie McConnell 16	7- 7-1910	S.S.Long,J.P.
Dryman,Earl 19 to Mae Garland 17	2-26-1911	H.O.Miller,M.G.
Dryman,Ray 29 to Dovie McCall 32	1-12-1915	H.O.Miller,M.G.
Dryman,F.O.29 to Matilda Gray 27	6-11-1918	A.W.Jacobs,M.G.
Duckworth,Robert to Lucinda Hall	3- 7-1833	Thomas Cathey,Wit
Duncan,Daniel to Nancy Gillespie	11-20-1832	Elisha Duncan,Wit
Duncan,Wm.M. to Sarah A.Gillespie	9-18-1845	J.K.Gray,Clk.
Duncan,Murray A.23 to Virginia Stephens 26 Both from Newman,Ga.	1-30-1932	J.A.Flanagan,M.G.
Dunn,Allen 21 to Frona Young 19	7-17-1904	W.H.Hasket,J.P.
Duvall,B.L.to R.E.Bryson	3-30-1856	M.Rickman,M.G.
Duvall,J.R. to R.M.Bird	7-24-1861	John Spears,M.G.
Duvall,James A.21 to Jane H.Deweese 21	12-19-1872	Mark May,M.G.
Duvall,William L.24 to Sarah E.Morrison 19	12-14-1873	G.W.Parrish,J.P.
Duvall,B.L.50 to Elizabeth Lakey 30	1-26-1881	G.W.Dean,J.P.
Duvall,John 20 to Docia Cochran 20	2-21-1881	Joseph Morgan,J.P
Duvall,J.B.24 to M.M.Bradley 19	1-13-1882	G.W.Dean,J.P.
Duvall,S.W.22 to Jennie Morgan 19	3- 2-1883	A.A.Justice,M.G.
Duvall,Cleaburn A.22 to Lillie Morgan 21	2-17-1887	A.A.Justice,M.G.
Duvall,Joshua 22 to Lillie Davis 18	11-20-1887	Z.Barnes,J.P.
Duvall,Joseph K.24 to S.E.Buckner 21	9-18-1892	A.L.Wild,J.P.
Duvall,Lewis 17 to Belle Byrd 18	7-31-1898	J.B.Justice,J.P.
Duvall,Bascom 19 to Texie Morgan 19	11-26-1905	S.J.May,J.P.
Duvall,William 21 to Minnie Guy 18	12-3-1905	M.L.Rickman,J.P.
Duvall,Earnest 22 to Vixie Owenby 22	6-18-1911	J.A.Lakey,J.P.
Duvall,Robert R.19 to Hallie B.Parrish 17	9-24-1911	Joseph L.Fouts,JP
Duvall,Moses 23 to Paralee Edwards 22	11-26-1911	Ben S.West,M.G.
Duvall,Edward B.28 to Lillie Liner 18	4-22-1914	T.J.Vinson,M.G.

Duvall,Claude 21 to Lucy Myers 18	4- 6-1919	D.C.McCoy,M.G.
Duvall,Lee 22 to Tallie Solesbee 15	4-28-1919	J.L.Yonce,M.G.
Duvall,J.M.31 to Oma Tallent 19	7- 7-1920	Not Executed
Duvall,J.M. 32 to Ollie Postell 24	12-18-1920	W.C.Mason,M.G.
Duvall,W.H.26 to Novia Brendle 20	1-14-1924	Frank L.Henry,J.P
Duvall,Steve 28 to Bell Cody 20	4-18-1927	Retd.not executed
Early, John to Sarah Reyner	6- 9-1838	D.Hicks,Wit.
Early, William M.22 to Mary J.Holland 18	2-16-1893	J.M.Keener,M.G.
Early, John 23 to Mamie Estes 18	5-19-1922	J.R.Pendergrass,MG
Easton,Irvin L.22 to Hattie C.Sloan 23 He from Rockfish,Va.	10-1-1925	W.M.Smith,M.G.
Edmundson,Robert to Catherine Saunders	9- 4-1855	W.Edmundson,Wit.
Edwards,George to Marget Allen	11-21-1832	---------
Edwards,John R.to Sarah Truitt	5-10-1853	J.F.Slagle,Wit.
Edwards,Lem to Susannah Morrow	3-31-1855	Westly Truitt,Wit
Edwards,James M.to Elizabeth Mann	2-11-1860	R.C.Slagle,Reg.
Edwards,J.R. to Sarah Guyer	2-13-1865	R.C.Slagle,Reg.
Edwards,Phillip 20 to Luthenia Guyer 16	8-18-1885	B.G.Wild,M.G.
Edwards,Mack D.31 to May P.Bolick 15	9- 4-1898	M.P.Alexander,M.G
Edwards,A.J.22 to Daisy Baldwin 18	3-20-1904	Joseph L.Fouts,JP
Edwards,Andrew E.24 to Hattie Bryson 24	4- 2-1905	W.L.Bradley,M.G.
Edwards,James G.21 to Hettie Harris 23	5- 6-1906	Joseph Fry,M.G.
Edwards,W.I.30 to Haseltine Bailey 28	12-31-1908	J.R.Pendergras,MG
Edwards,W.Robert 23 to Bulah Welch 17	11-13-1910	J.L.Yonce,M.G.
Edwards,Grover D.26 to Helen Heacock 19	11-5-1911	W.T.Potts,M.G.
Edwards,A.C.23 to Callie Stewart 22	3-19-1913	J.P.Moore,J.P.
Edwards,Loyd 21 to Bertha Duvall 20	8-11-1916	Fred Cochran,M.G.
Edwards,J.W.28 to Thelma Jones 18	4-15-1919	James C.Mell,J.P.
Edwards,W.M.66 to Mrs.Jane Teague 42	8- 5-1922	A.J.Smith,M.G.
Edwards,Ralph 21 to Georgia Rogers 19	3- 9-1929	J.R.Pendergrass,MG
Edwards,W.W.49 to Mimie Z.Edwards 46 He from Douglas,Wyo.	9-15-1931	Chas.R.McCarty,MG
Edwards,Wilbur J.27 to Maude Autley 24	8-20-1933	Robert White Jr.
Edwards,F.Darrell 22 to Emma L.Carter 19	5-12-1934	J.F.Burrell,M.G.
Elders,R.L.22 to Polly A.Wikle 17	2-20-1890	P.R.Rickman,M.G.
Elders,C.L.20 to N.M.Stewman 18	11-5-1902	J.W.Ammons,J.P.
Elders,Bob 39 to Lillie Pickens 22	2-24-1917	Geo.Carpenter,J.P
Elders,Thurman 21 to Alta Davis 21	4- 2-1930	J.R.Pendergrass,MG
Elias,Thomas J. to Sally Phillips	10-5-1834	Jno.Tatham,Clk.
Elias,K.26 to Tim Siler 20	1-11-1876	L.K.Haynes,M.G.
Ellard,Lamar M.22 to Myra Ida Stribbling 18/	11-19-1931	J.A.Flannagan,M.G
Ellenburg,Luther 43 to Martha Sanders 20	10-22-1938	Geo.Carpenter,J.P
Ellenby,John C.to Celia Butler	11-20-1839	B.Wilson.
Eller,J.A.21 to Nancy Curtis 17	9-24-1900	J.L.Kinsland,M.G.
Eller,Martin 24 to Maggie Yonce 17	12-25-1921	D.A.Yonce,M.G.
Elliott,Eugene A.18 to Elizabeth Caloway 22/	4-13-1873	E.H.Franks,J.P.
Elliott,Geo.W.23 to Nancy McConnell 22	1-17-1877	E.H.Franks,J.P.

```
Elliott,Robt.Jr.22 to Rebecca J.Brendle 16    9-7-1884    M.S.Rickman,J.P.
Elliott,Robt.66 to Mary C.Williamson 44       4-20-1892   G.R.McPhearson,J.P
Elliott,Charley 21 to Hattie Wooten 22        10-3-1897   J.B.Elmore,J.P.
Elliott,William 22 to Mary I.Benfield 19      4- 5-1897   N.J.Rush,J.P.
Elliott,Henry 22 to Cardelia Vinson 14        3-20-1900   T.J.Vinson,J.P.
Elliott,James 23 to Florence Angel 23         8-26-1900   J.B.Elmore,J.P.
Elliott,Walter D.21 to Susan E.Benfield 18    8-31-1902   J.B.Elmore,J.P.
Elliott,James 26 to Jane Morgan 25            8-10-1904   J.W.Kesterson,M.G.
Elliott,Jesse 21 to Mary Corbin 25            10-15-1905  M.A.Love,M.G.
Elliott,Walter 26 to Ida Bell Corbin 24       2-10-1907   C.L.Rickman,J.P.
Elliott,Joseph 22 to Ida Kinsland 27          5- 5-1907   C.L.Rickman,J.P.
Elliott,W.A.26 to Eva Corbin 30               2-16-1913   J.L.Kinsland,M.G.
Elliott,Oscar 22 to Hattie Guffee 23          1-18-1917   W.H.Carpenter,J.P.
Elliott,Chas.W.23 to Reva McCracken 18        3- 2-1919   J.M.Raby,J.P.
Elliott,Perceval 28 to Marie Virginia Thomas 24/6-24-1919- Not Executed
Elliott,Geo.W.23 to Tim Cunningham 24         8-26-1929   Geo.Carpenter,J.P.
Elmore,William to Lucinda M.Hurst             5-13-1841   H.G.Woodfin,D.Clk.
Elmore,Hugh H.to Elizabeth Vaughan            2-22-1854   Joshua Ammons,M.G.
Elmore,John 63 to Sarah Mashburn 40           4- 7-1889   J.B.Elmore,J.P.
Elmore,J.B.,Jr.27 to Dora B.Jemkins 22        12-28-1905  M.L.Rickman,J.P.
Elmore,James M.26 to Callie Lakey 26          2- 6-1908   W.L.Bradley,M.G.
Elmore,John G.21 to Fannie L.Shepherd 20      3-12-1911   J.W.Rickman,J.P.
Elmore,Omar 18 to Ethel Rickman 19            8- 2-1915   J.A.Lakey,J.P.
Emory,James P.24 to Elizabeth Blain 24        9- 7-1004   S.F.Harrington,M.G
Emory,John 21 to Connie Childers 29           4- 7-1907   L.P.Bogle,M.G.
Emory,James 22 to Ellie Anderson 23           6-22-1910   W.H.Roane,J.P.
Emory,John 60 to Callie Teague 44             10-17-1918- J.L.Yonce,M.G.
Emory,Furman 20 to Oma M.Payne 15             8-28-1930   J.R.Pendergrass,MG
Emory,Robert 22 to Gladys Dills 19            4- 4-1934   Geo.Carpenter,J.P.
England,Lon 23 to Sarah Angel 22      Col.    11-7-1893   Geo.T.Bryson,J.P.
England,H.P. 23 to Julia Wilson 19            8-19-1900   T.N.Ford,M.G.
England,Clifton 22 to Ella Mae Love 24 Col.   10-10-1926  J.B.Meekins,M.G.
England,Gus 20 to Helen Ledford 18     Col.   10-28-1927  Geo.Carpenter,J.P
England,John P.29 to Essie Love 20     Col.   2-16-1936   E.S.Wiley,M.G.
English,Augustus 21 to Cora Taylor 19         12-2-1918   J.R.Pendergras,MG
Enloe,William W.to Mary E.Angel               8-14-1843   J.K.Gray,Clk.
Enloe,L.H. to Mary E.Roane                    4- 9-1857   John Hall,Clk.
Enloe,T.B.27 to Clara Allman 23               4- 9-1885   R.A.Owen,M.G.
Enloe,J.T.32 to Nannie C.Carpenter 22         3-11-1894   L.H.Garland,J.P.
Enloe,W.A.65 to Delia Slagle 40               7-20-1898   T.E.Hagg,M.G.
Enloe,James T.46 to Callie Glidewell 21       8- 1-1908   A.M.Ledford,M.G.
Enloe,G.O.46 to Dollie E.Stanfield 28         11-27-1912  J.L.Teague,M.G.
Erwin,Mercer 23 to Lillie L.Caler 25          10-1-1897   W.H.Morrison,J.P.
Estes,D.E. to Amanda Pannel                   4-21-1866   A.A.Justice,M.G.
Estes,William A.19 to Isabella Mason 17       12-3-1894   J.B.Carden,J.P.
Estes,Asbury 19 to Theadocia Rickman 21       2- 3-1899   J.H.Dalton,J.P.
Estes,C.L.23 to Julia Justice 18              12-29-1907  J.D.Vinson,M.G.
```

Estes,Alonzo 24 to Maggie Reese 17	6-22-1913	J.R.Pendergrass,MG
Estes,Jess L.to Maude Angel	5- 5-1933	Will Smith,Ord.
Estes,G.Willy 23 to Edna Shook 21	8-16-1934	Geo.Carpenter,J.P
Estes,James D.20 to Velma Wooten 18	1-15-1936	Frank W.Holland.
Estridge,William 22 to Mary Pannell 18	8- 6-1872	J.D.Vinson,M.G.
Estridge,Jesse E.18 to Mary H.Wilson 16	11-13-1878	P.R.Rickman,M.G.
Evans,Thomas M.to Martha Garland	11-12-1835	---------
Evans,Reuben P.to Rebecca Waters	2-20-1849	T.P.Siler,D.Clk.
Evans,Jackson to Amanda Rowland	11-24-1853	John Hall,Clk.
Evans,Abratham L.to Martha J.Russell	7-19-1869	J.K.Bryson,Reg.
Evans,J.M.21 to M.C.Fuller 18	3-12-1878	G.W.Dean,J.P.
Evans,Albert 28 to Emma Ledford 18	8-29-1886	M.Ghomley,M.G.
Evans,John 23 to Hattie Slagle 25	3-21-1888	E.A.Sample,M.G.
Evans,W.R.28 to Louisa Roper 18	3-10-1889	J.E.Morgan,M.G.
Evans,J.S.23 to Ellen Haney 18	5-31-1890	Z.Barnes,J.P.
Evans,Andrew J.23 to Millie Peek 21	12-25-1890	J.M.Keener,M.G.
Evans,Charles 18 to Rose Yonce 18	9-25-1892	M.Ghormley,M.G.
Evans,William J.35 to Alice S.Garrison 18	12-4-1892	S.J.May,J.P.
Evans,Erastus N.24 to Jane Hicks 22	9-10-1896	Z.Barnes,J.P.
Evans,Jesse 21 to Ollie Hampton 14	11-7-1907	D.A.Yonce,M.G.
Evans,Carl 21 to Mattie Shook 17	5- 2-1916	T.C.Vinson,J.P.
Evans,Cline 22 to Lora Rowland 21	2-24-1917	J.W.Gregory,J.P.
Evans,J.A.23 to Bulah Mason 21	4-13-1919	W.L.Bradley,M.G.
Evans,Norman H.24 to Nettie Deweese 22	9-27-1920	J.L.Fouts,J.P.
Evans,Claud 21 to Ethel Moore 18 She from Rabun Gap,Ga.	6- 1-1928	Geo.Carpenter,J.P
Evans,E.N.48 to Ida McConnell 34	6- 6-1928	A.S.Solesby,M.G.
Evans,Albert 21 to Luella Rowland 18	5-21-1933	R.M.Lambert,J.P.
Evans,Shirdan 27 to Dollie Pendergrass 26	10-14-1933	Geo.Carpenter,J.P
Evitt,D.M. to Meekey Vaughn	12-22-1859	I.N.Keener,J.P.
Evitt,J.C.24 to Mary M.White 19 She from Jackson Co.,N.C.	2-27-1876	J.D.Vinson,M.G.
Evitt,Jackson C.34 to Sarah J.Rogers 27	12-3-1886	J.M.Keener,J.P.
Evitt,Columbus 20 to Rosetta E.Houston18	4- 8-1894	John L.Corbin,J.P
Evitt,James 30 to Mennie J.Caloway 21	6-21-1898	Henry Stewart,J.P
Evitt,Dock,26 to Addie Steward 35	9-12-1932	Geo.Carpenter,J.P
Extine,John M. to Mary Beam	3-30-1833	John Hall,Clk.
Fagg,T.H.30 to Rachel Slagle 23	7- 6-1940	J.A.Flanagan,M.G.
Fair,Pinkney 19 to Mary Anderson 21	6-25-1900	W.A.Setser,J.P.
Fair,James A.20 to Maggie N.McDonnell 19	Col./12-25-1904-	J.T.Kennedy,M.G
Farley,William to Fanny Conley	12-26-1833	Silas McDowell,Wi
Farmer,John 21 to Mary Saunders 18	12-15-1888	W.C.Kimsey,J.P.
Farmer,George 23 to Francis McDowell 18	5-11-1919	Robert Stamey,J.P
Farmer,J.F.21 to Zoah DeHart 19	1- 2-1921	J.E.Womack,M.G.
Farmer,J.M.57 to Mrs.Lula Taylor 36	6-24-1924	Geo.Carpenter,J.P
Farmer,E.H.24 to Margaret Ann Wolf 22	3-11-1925	John S.Green,M.G.
Ferguson,R. to Martha Oliver	4-22-1858	L.F.Siler,J.P.
Ferguson,Lewis 21 to Lillie Bingham 21	10-6-1887	W.C.Kimzey,J.P

Ferguson,E.G.27 to Mary A.Gray 29	3-20-1907	J.C.Hardin,M.G.
Ferguson,John C.25 to Myrtle E.Gray 22	8- 7-1907	H.C.Bradley,M.G.
Ferguson,Charles 21 to Reta Cunningham 20	6- 2-1940	R.F.Mayberry,M.G.
Fessender,Prier D.23 to Eva Stephens 26	9- 1-1924	E.J.Pipes,M.G.
Field,J.E.29 to Louise H.Connata 28	9-26-1911	Wm.P.Chedester,M.G
Feezell,Asbury 26 to Tabitha Young 18	6- 4-1905	J.M.Keener,M.G.
Fine,Peter L. to Ann E.Harshaw	2- 2-1838	D.Weeks,D.Clk.
Finney,A.D.24 to Mary Willis 30	11-16-1895	Thos.W.Mansfield.
Fish,A.C.39 to Martha J.Wilson 28	10-8-1918	J.M.Raby,J.P.
Fish,Charlie 23 to Bertha Dietz 18 He from Jackson Co.,N.C.	1-18-1928	J.M.Raby,J.P.
Flanagan,J.L.21 to Annie M.Calloway 18	12-24-1919	G.L.Jones,M.G.
Flood,James 21 to Onie Phillips 25 He from Eton,Ga... She from Crandall,Ga.	9- 3-1937	Jasper N.Dills,MG
Flowers,Patty 22 to Dart Beasley 25	11-29-1899	George Bryson,J.P
Flowers,A.R.22 to Addie Herron 21	5- 6-1900	Wm.R.McCall,J.P.
Flowers,Jessie 17 to Fannie Hurst 23	4- 1-1919	E.O.Rickman,J.P.
Flowers,William P.60 to Elsie Shepherd 24	3- 7-1935	Sam J.Murray,J.P.
Flynt,John W.22 to Helen Stanley 19	8-18-1934	C.C.Herbert,M.G.
Foister,Jonathan to Lucinday Millsaps	5-20-1831	Wm.McConnell,Wit.
Ford,T.N.21 to R.S.McKinney 18	3- 8-1881	Jno.L.Corbin,J.P.
Ford,Thos. to Barbara Tilley	12-18-1844	J.K.Gray,Clk.
Ford,Horatio to Polly Brown	5- 9-1850	J.K.Gray,Clk.
Ford,Jonathan to Margaret A.Rogers	10-8-1853	John Hall,Clk.
Ford,Jonathan to Nancy P.Rogers	7-30-1865	R.C.Slagle,Clk.
Ford,Landon C.to Elizabeth A.Marrow	9-10-1870	C.D.Smith,M.G.
Ford,Jackson to Josephine V.McDonald Col.	6- 6-1872	Wm.Sloan,Clk.
Ford,John B.26 to Martha A.Rogers 18	4-12-1885	J.M.Arnold,J.P.
Ford,James 25 to Mrs.Lassie Guffie 28	12-22-1912	J.B.Hensley,M.G.
Fore,Joseph U. to Sarah Nouland	10-22-1842	J.K.Gray,Clk.
Fore,Thomas 26 to Lacie Vaughn 20	11-5-1899	C.T.Peek,M.G.
Fore,Morris 20 to Lillie Woods 15	2-19-1905	J.M.Keener,M.G.
Fore,Horrace 23 to Fannie Houston 19	12-24-1908	J.M.Keener,M.G.
Forester,J.P. to Elizabeth Mason	7-23-1861	R.C.Slagle,Clk.
Forester,Andrew J. to Sarah C.Mason	12-14-1870	Wm.Sloan,Reg.
Forester,John A.20 to Elizabeth Wilson 18	1- 5-1879	Wm.Deweese,M.G.
Forester,M.C.21 to Rosa A.McClure 15	12-24-1889	John Howard,J.P.
Forrester,Eli to Irene McConnell	5-26-1855	L.F.Siler,Wit.
Forrester,James to Martha Mason	6-11-1855	John Hall,Clk.
Forrester,Wm.A.23 to Rachel R.Wilson 17	1-15-1880	J.M.Forrester,J.P
Forrester,M.M.18 to Modene Passmore 18	11-9-1884	Mark May,M.G.
Forrester,Wm.C.18 to Harriette L.Forrester 19/	8-18-1889-	W.C.Mason,M.G.
Forrester,James M.22 Susie Guffee 18	10-27-1897	E.N.Dalrymple,J.P
Forrester,D.C.21 to Lydia Flowers 18	12-17-1899	E.N.Dalrymple,J.P
Forrester,H.S.20 to Lona McConnell 18	3-12-1900	E.P.Brown,J.P.
Forrester,Clingman 20 to Lillie Mason 18	6-10-1900	W.C.Mason,M.G.
Foster,Ray 19 to Fannie Norton 22	1- 3-1915	C.R.Cabe,J.P.
Foster,F.S.29 to Zonie Crunkleton 19	3-11-1918	D.V.Howell,M.G.

Foster,A.B.21 to Edith Mozely 21	5-15-1920	W.A.Norton,J.P.
Foster,Adam 23 to Hattie Nicholson 18	5-11-1925	A.J.Smith,M.G.
Fortenberry,James H.to Elizabeth Curtis	2- 2-1843	J.K.Gray,Clk.
Fortins,William to M.Ann Russell	1-26-1861	J.N.Keener,Wit.
Fouse,Earnest to Laura Chavers 22 Col.	12-15-1915	C.L.Stewart,M.G.
Fouts,William P.to Jane A.Wild	3-16-1839	H.G.Woodfin,Wit.
Fouts,Jacob to Sarah Yonce	9-22-1853	H.H.Ray,Wit.
Fouts,John to Rebecca Ray	4-14-1855	John Hall,Wit.
Fouts,Tall to Lassa Addington Col.	10-25-1866	L.F.Siler,M.G.
Fouts,Toliver to Eliza Love	2- 8-1870	J.K.Bryson,Reg.
Fouts,Toliver 57 to Lucy Angel 27 Col.	8-10-1874	B.F.Hemphill,M.G.
Fouts,Noah 22 to Uceba West 19	10-25-1879	J.S.Woodard,M.G.
Fouts,Jas.E.20 to Sarah F.Baldwin 18	12-4-1879	Mark May,M.G.
Fouts,Brag 22 to Elizabeth Roland 24	3-24-1881	P.C.Wild,J.P.
Fouts,A.E.32 to Addie Penland 25	11-5-1891	W.G.Mallonee,M.G.
Fouts,William 65 to Molly Anderson 45	2- 7-1893	S.J.May,J.P.
Fouts,C.H.22 to Rosie Downs 21	12-26-1897	Jacob L.Yonce,M.G
Fouts,Sicero 25 to Mittie Jacobs 21	3- 4-1904	J.A.Brendle,M.G.
Fouts,Green T.24 to Minnie Rowland 22	4-26-1907	Joseph L.Fouts,JP
Fouts,D.C.39 to Effie Kimsey 18	1- 2-1910	T.C.King,M.G.
Fouts,W.T.34 to Bell Barnard 22	8-23-1913	W.T.Potts,M.G.
Fouts,W.T.30 to Dora Rickman 21	3- 4-1917	T.J.Vinson,M.G.
Fouts,J.H.53 to Leah Fouts 32	2-16-1921	J.Q.Wallace,M.G.
Fowler,E.W.57 to Vianna Cloer 49	7-22-1897	J.R.Pendergras,MG
Fowler,E.W.64 to Mataline Angel 20	6- 1-1905	J.H.Moore,M.G.
Fox,George to Nancy Mathis	5-18-1833	John Hall,Clk.
Fox,Robert to Ann Adams	3- 9-1850	Bannister Adams.
Fox,James W. to Mary Ann Ammons,	12-12-1866	I.N.Keener,J.P.
Fox,Elisha 21 to Mary C.Corbin 25	10-4-1874	F.Poindexter,J.P.
Fox,James 21 to Rebecca C.Teems 17	12-18-1888	Jno.B.Gray,J.P.
Fox,Thos.L.21 to Margaret Haskett 19	2-24-1895	J.P.Moore,J.P.
Fox,Luther 20 to Nora Burrell 18	12-25-1899	J.B.Elmore,J.P.
Fox,Robert L.18 to Jane Scott 18	10-29-1901	J.B.Elmore,J.P.
Fox,Elisha 25 to Millie Blackburn 18	9- 7-1902	J.D.Sitton,M.G.
Fox,Henry 22 to Lavada Houston 19	7-22-1906	Jas.M.Corbin,J.P.
Fox,Thos.L.35 to Elizabeth Stiles 29	8-22-1909	Geo.W.Seay,M.G.
Fox,J.W.36 to Ermia Sykes 27	4- 2-1919	L.B.Hays,M.G.
Fox,G.N.21 to Hattie Wood 17	4-19-1920	J.M.Keener,M.G.
Fox,Zollie 23 to Sallie Ashe 21	8-17-1920	J.M.Raby,J.P.
Fox,Wm.R.22 to Alice L.Gregory 21	11-23-1923	J.R.Pendergras,MG
Frady,Levi to Rebeckah Corn	9- 9-1838	John & Adam Corn.
Frady,Soloman to Margaret C.Frizle	3-22-1845	J.K.Gray,Clk.
Frady,Edmond to Hulda A.McCall	1-12-1846	J.K.Gray,Clk.
Frady,William to Sally Case	1-23-1849	W.G.Woodfin,D.Clk
Frady,A.J.to Sarah Barnes	5-15-1853	E.Collins,J.P.
Frady,G.W. to May E.Night	9-18-1856	J.G.Crawford,Wit.
Frady,Erwin to Sarah Ammons	3-21-1859	T.W.Owen,J.P.

Frady,Jackson to Caroline Scroggs	3-10-1860	R.C.Slagle,Clk.
Frady,G.L.20 to Laura A.Ammons 17	3- 1-1883	Hosea Moses,J.P.
Frady,Coleman 21 to Catherine Downs 20	2-18-1885	M.E.Welch,J.P.
Frady,Wm.A.28 to Nancy Glase 23	9-30-1888	John Reid,J.P.
Frady,Coleman M.27 to Mrs.Amanda E.Wilson 34	/8-23-1893-	J.S.Woodard,M.G.
Frady,W.S.26 to Jane Frizelle 18	12-6-1896	E.D.Franks,J.P.
Frady,G.W.22 to Timmie Tallent 22	3-27-1897	E.B.Angel,J.P.
Frady,Annis 21 to Lizzie Green 18 Both from Jackson Co.,N.C.	7-12-1897	John Elmore,J.P.
Frady,Thomas 22 to Rhoda J.Frady 18	6- 2-1899	H.H.Dills,J.P.
Frady,J.A.21 to Emma J.Low 21	6- 2-1901	James L.Bryson,JP
Frady,B.F.23 to Minnie Tallent 21	9- 1-1901	Jacob Yonce,M.G.
Frady,G.J.21 to Mandy Tallent 33	10-10-1903	Robt.Stamey,J.P.
Frady,Kelse 18 to Evie McCoy 16	8-13-1917	O.C.Corbin,J.P.
Frady,G.W.43 to Maggie Teems 30	3-17-1918	A.W.Jacobs,M.G.
Francis,J.M.22 to Bessie Inman 20	8- 1-1909	J.T.Watts,J.P.
Franklin,John 18 to Mary J.Justice 18	12-30-1886	J.E.Morgan,M.G.
Franklin,W.F.23 to Fannie Dills 18	8- 5-1894	D.L.Miller,M.G.
Franklin,Joseph 20 to Anna Dills 21	8- 9-1894	D.L.Miller,M.G.
Franks,William to Pheoba Hunter	9-27-1832	John Hall,Clk.
Franks,James D. to Name not given	1-23-1839	John Davis,Wit.
Franks,Isam to Sarah Jennings	2-16-1846	J.K.Gray,Wit.
Franks,John R.to Nancy A.Ammons	10-17-1871	H.H.Elmore,J.P.
Franks,Wm.J.to Mary F.Hampton	6-30-1872	William Sloan,Reg
Franks,Josiah 22 to Martha Moses 22	8-18-1873	Revoked
Franks,John 20 to Nancy C.Franks 19	6-27-1875	E.H.Franks,J.P.
Franks,J.I.24 to Lucy Morgan 23	9-15-1876	E.H.Franks,J.P.
Franks,Harrison 22 to Harriett Brindle 21	10-7-1877	J.A.Franks,J.P.
Franks,David 21 to Sophronia Kinsland 19	10-25-1877	S.H.Harrington,MG
Franks,William F.25 to Loucinda Forrester 18	/8-8-1878	Wm.Deweese,M.G.
Franks,G.F.18 to L.A.Southards 18	11-18-1880	J.D.Vinson,M.G.
Franks,Everett D.21 to Florence Rogers 19	1- 4-1881	W.C.Carden,M.G.
Franks,J.T.20 to Mary E.Haskett 17	12-3-1882	C.S.Buchanan,M.G.
Franks,Henry 19 to Sarah Cloer 21	11-12-1882	M.J.Mashburn,J.P.
Franks,John H.25 to Tisha Bishop 28	7- 5-1922?	J.R.Pendergrass,MG
Franks,William 20 to Polly Shepherd 22	5- 1-1892	J.C.Ammons,M.G.
Franks,John R.54 to Jene Sanders 48	5-18-1895	J.B.Elmore,J.P.
Franks,S.C.20 to Ella Kinsland 18	1-10-1895	G.A.Bartlett,M.G.
Franks,John R.18 to Mattie Beasley 19	5- 7-1896	P.R.Rickman,M.G.
Franks,John A.22 to Maggie Tramel 22	6-21-1902	L.I.Mashburn.
Franks,S.H.21 to Emma Sorrels 22	8- 6-1902	J.L.Kinsland,M.G.
Franks;E.D.42 to Lillie Justice 24	12-20-1902	J.A.Brendle,M.G.
Franks,W.R.23 to Kittie Conley 20	12-14-1905	M.A.Love,M.G.
Franks,M.J.23 to Meekie Bryson 19	7-26-1911	J.D.Vinson,M.G.
Franks,J.I.65 to Minnie Myers 43	3-28-1919	J.M.Corbin,J.P.
Franks,John T.25 to Mary Shitles 19	9-19-1919	J.R.Pendergrass,MG
Franks,Jake 33 to Nancy B.Barnes 16	12-21-1919	D.M.Rogers,M.G.

Franks,Tillman 21 to Jessie Tranthan 19	8-26-1920	J.M.Raby,J.P.
Franzini,C.J.18 to Anora Misner 22	11-14-1918	J.R.Pendergras,MG
Frazier,Van 27 to Florence Anderson 21	5-11-1921	J.R.Pendergrass,MG
Frazier,Milton 22 to Dorothy Fish 18	10-23-1936	A.A.Angel,M.G.
Freeman,John to Ibby Watson	3-11-1838	Allen Freeman.
Freeman,Samuel to Martha Ammons	4-12-1860	M.J.Morgan,J.P.
Freeman,John L.to Malinda DeHart	5- 2-1861	T.P.Siler,Clk.
Freeman,Thos.N.to Lusinda Jones	12-25-1863	R.C.Slagle,Clk.
Freeman,John to Nancy Lockaby	3-29-1869	R.C.Slagle,Reg.
Freeman,Robert H.to Mary J.Smiley	12-22-1870	William Sloan,Reg
Freeman,Samuel 21 to Jennie Bird 21	10-21-1900	Jos. Morgan,J.P.
Freeman,T.W.38 to Rebecca Phillips 20	11-29-1905	A.S.Solesbee,M.G.
Freeman,Lee 22 to Evy Mashburn 18	11-20-1919	J.H.Grant,M.G.
Freeman,Glen 21to Edith M.Rhodes 16 He from Hendersonville,N.C.	12-26-1927	Robert Mack,M.G.
Freezell,Asberry 26 to Tolietha Young 18	6- 4-1905	J.M.Keener,M.G.
Fretwell,Jeff to Amanda Cochram Col.	2-12-1870	R.C.Slagle,Clk.
Fretwell,H.B.30 to Mary Love 19 Col.	9-16-1903	J.T.Kenedy,M.G.
Frizel,John A. to Nancy Monteath	5-22-1848	J.K.Gray,Clk.
Frizzle,Mack 29 to Ellen Shepherd 30	5- 1-1921	R.Neal,M.G.
Frost,C.L.(MD) 57 to Meta Norton 24	6-12-1888	J.H.Weaver,M.G.
Fulbright,John 24 to Iva Wilds 18	10-27-1901	N.P.Rankin,J.P.
Fulbright,Robt.L.53 to Martha Deal 39 He from Waynesville,N.C.	12-18-1929	R.P.McCracken,M.G
Fulbright,Johnie F.24 to Adlee McGaha 23 He from Eastonlee,Ga.	9-22-1934	Geo.Carpenter,J.P
Fulcher,J.C.to Rachel Tatham	12-14-1846	J.K.Gray,Clk.
Fulcher,J.B. to Jane McConnell	1- 3-1865	J.B.Sanders,Wit.
Fulcher,Wm. to Margaret E.Morgan	11-4-1866	R.C.Slagle,C.C.C.
Fulcher,J.A.23 to S.A.Cabe 24	7- 6-1876	M.L.Kelley,J.P.
Fulcher,Eddie 25 to Ada McClure 24	10-15-1902	C.W.Dowdle,J.P.
Fulcher,James B.70 to Mrs.Syndia Teague 30	8-22-1913	Robert Stamey,J.P
Fuller,J.B.to Arintha Cunningham	9-25-1867	R.C.Slagle,Clk.
Fuller,John to Nancy Morrow	1-21-1871	T.F.Green,M.G.
Fuller,Sam 22 to Margaret Angel 20 Col.	2- 4-1881	Thos.Taylor,M.G.
Fuller,Sam 29 to Eliza Jackson 28 Col.	3-13-1892	R.E.Lentz,M.G.
Fulton,John H.33 to Jane Higdon 30	1- 3-1900	W.R.Rickman,M.G.
Fulton,Mack 24 to Marion Munger 18	5-24-1925	J.W.Baty,M.G.
Furr,W.E.28 to Burdell Williams 22	6-29-1921	L.B.Hayes,M.G.
Gabby,Daniel Jr. to Roina Rowland	3- 3-1840	John Hall,Clk.
Galloway,Alonzo 21 to J.Ann Shepherd 22	12-9-1894	P.R.Rickman,M.G.
Galbrath,James M.to E.C.Coleman	3-26-1849	J.K.Gray,Clk.
Gallian,James to Name not given	11-7-1856	Jacob Waldroop.
Garey,Edward M.29 to Letha Trammell 16	3-16-1901	S.J.May,J.P.
Garland,Humphry to Elvira Williams	3- 4-1843	John Hall,Clk.
Garland,William P.25 to C.S.Allen 24	11-28-1876	E.T.Long,J.P.
Garland,William M.22 to A.S.Bradley 18	4-24-1877	M.L.Kelley,J.P.
Garland,John 21 to M.L.Bradley 19	1-18-1880	M.P.Long,J.P.

Garland,H.P.21 to I.E.Young 15	3- 2-1882	M.P.Long,M.G.
Garland,H.W.21 to Mattie E.Justice 19	5-16-1889	L.H.Garland,J.P.
Garland,J.M.18 to Lelia C.Justice 17	11-7-1889	L.H.Garland,J.P.
Garland,Geo.W.25 to Flora Long 20	11-7-1889	L.H.Garland,J.P.
Garland,Noah L.28 to Virginia Angel 21	10-1-1891	W.G.Mallonee,M.G.
Garland,Geo.M.18 to Annie S.Beasley 17	12-25-1892	J.R.Pendergras,MG
Garland,David L.22 to Minnie A.Franks 14	11-19-1893	G.A.Bartlett,M.G.
Garland,H.L.22 to Hannah Wilson 14	2-11-1894	L.H.Garland,J.P.
Garland,R.J.24 to Mary·Carpenter 24	11-22-1894	G.A.Bartlett,M.G.
Garland,Andy 25 to Bell Rush 20	9- 8-1897	R.B.Shelton,M.G.
Garland,Doc 20 to Mary Guffee 20	3-10-1900	T.N.Ford,M.G.
Garland,Barnet 25 to Bell Daves 23	12-17-1903	W.E.Mozley,J.P.
Garland,Robert L.26 to Bessie Daves 21	8-27-1908	Robt.E.Atkinson.
Garland,Lee 20 to Bertha Carpenter 21	2- 7-1909	A.M.Ledford,M.G.
Garland,Chas.L.24 to Ida Glidwell 18	4-23-1911	C.R.Cabe,J.P.
Garland,G.L.22 to Nina Talley 17	10-27-1912	R.P.McCracken,M.G
Garner,A.Jackson 28 to Elie I.Wright 21	6-21-1891	John Reid,J.P.
Garner,James Grady 37 to Blanch A.Cabe 33	7-16-1935	B.W.Lefler,M.G.
Garrett,Andrew to Sarah West	1-14-1842	J.K.Gray,Clk.
Garrett,Julius to Mary West	3-14-1843	Silas McDowel,Wit
Garrett,William R.to Martha A.Freeman	10-30-1850	B.M.Bell.
Garrett,Walter V.23 to Nellie Gillespie 18	4-29-1888	J.A.Deal,M.G.
Garrett,James F.49 to Emmer Gentry 29	12-29-1904	D.F.Howard,M.G.
Garris,Arnold 22 to Marion Day 16	12-12-1936	Frank Bloxham,M.G
Garrison,John to Sarah Roland	4- 8-1871	William Sloan,Reg
Garrison,Samuel 23 to Harriet J.Davis 19	3- 5-1874	Mary May,M.G.
Garrison,O.L.28 to Mary J.Dockery 19	3-11-1883	Jno.A.Mathason,MG
Garrison,Caleb A.25 to Sarah E.Sweatman 16	9-11-1887	I.D.Wright,M.G.
Garrison,R.B.26 to Addie Kilpatrick 20	10-24-1897	Z.Barnes,J.P.
Garrison,Hurshel 21 to Nola Drake 20	10-8-1905	A.S.Solesbee,M.G.
Gather,Jacob to Dora Cunningham	7- 1-1832	John Hall,Clk.
Gaston,Parley C. to Margaret A.Moore	9-26-1871	C.D.Smith,M.G.·
Gash,Alla to Margaret Siler	2- 9-1830	J.R.Siler,J.P.
Gaziway,John 21 to E.J.Mason 18	9-12-1880	J.M.Forester,J.P.
Gennett,N.W.34 to Mrs.Nina Porter Mizner 31	10-16-1912	M.H.Tuttle,M.G.
Gentry, A.E.25 to Carrie Wilson 18	4-18-1914	Frank T.Gettis,JP
Gettis,F.T.28 to Sallie Cochran 27	9-26-1897	F.M.Morgan,M.G.
Gettis,Frank T.47 to Hermie Liner 31	12-2-1913	J.R.Pendergrass,MG
Ghormley,M.D.18 to Georgia S.Howard 17	11-23-1892	J.H.Morgan,J.P.
Ghormley,W.D.21 to Loula Solesbee 17	4- 6-1902	A.H.Gregory,J.P.
Ghormley,M.D.30 to Lexie Evans 17	9-29-1907	A.B.Barnes,J.P.
Gibbs,John W. to Rachel L.Queen	9-23-1840	John Hall,Clk.
Gibbs,John N. to Sarah Ann Enloe	7-15-1846	J.K.Gray,Clk.
Gibbs,Charles W. to Harriett Addington	12-3-1856	C.D.Smith,M.G.
Gibbs,William to Cynthia A.Battles	8-31-1850	T.P.Siler,D.Clk.
Gibbs;Bryant to Elizabeth Ballew	9- 1-1848	J.K.Gray,Clk.
Gibbs,Andrew to Mary Cross	2-22-1845	J.K.Gray Clk.

```
Gibby,Bryant to Elizabeth Balew                    9- 1-1848  J.K.Gray,Clk.
Gibby,Elisha to Mary Jenkins                       1- 5-1859  R.C.Slagle,Reg.
Gibby,J.S. to Lousea Panther                       10-7-1865  J.M.Thomas,Wit.
Gibby,William 20 to Susan Gregory 25               1- 9-1879  M.Ghormley,M.G.
Gibby,James C.19 to Florence Bird 18               1- 7-1886  Jno.S.Gibson,J.P.
Gibby,Logan C.23 to Lucinda Brookshire 20          2-21-1886  J.A.Brawner,M.G.
Gibson,Harrison to Jane Mayfield                   8-14-1834  B.Bell,Wit.
Gibson,Hiram to Margaret Jones                     3-30-1835  Beecher Guy,Wit.
Gibson,Isaac to Sally Price                        11-5-1840  Solomon Newton,Wi
Gibson,Hugh to Mary A.Gray                         2-14-1848  J.K.Gray,Clk.
Gibson,S.W.to Sealy Loomis                         3- 6-1852  A.B.Welch,Wit.
Gibson,Walter to Mary Kirby                        3-15-1854  I.N.Keener,Wit.
Gibson,John to Catherine A.Chambers                3-17-1854  John Hall,Clk.
Gibson,Jason to Emily Kerby                        3-26-1856  John Hall,Clk.
Gibson,Jas.G.to Emeline Gibson                     5- 2-1860  R.C.Slagle,Reg.
Gibson,Leander to Rebecca Guy                      4-17-1865  I.N.Keener,Wit.
Gibson,W.A.to Nancy Justice                        10-29-1865 R.C.Slagle,Clk.
Gibson,S.B.to Sarah J.Earls                        11-17-1865 E.T.Gibson,Wit.
Gibson,J.S. to Polina Shepherd                     7-17-1866  M.Rickman,M.G.
Gibson,Sam to Charity White                        12-18-1866 T.J.Kimsey,J.P.
Gibson,Elias P.to Valintia Cochram                 3-12-1870  R.C.Slagle,D.Reg.
Gibson,Leander 28 to Rhody Gibson 28               2-19-1875  S.W.Hill,J.P.
Gibson,John P.21 to Elizabeth A.Guy 24             10-28-1875 J.D.Vinson,M.G.
Gibson,J.C.22 to M.A.Allen 20                      2-29-1878  M.P.Wain,M.G.
Gibson,H.M.19 to M.E.Passmore 19                   8-10-1879  J.T.Berry,Esq.
Gibson,G.H.24 to Emma L.Owen 23                    11-16-1881 C.Campbell,M.G.
Gibson,John L.25 to Sarah Raby 21                  12-7-1882  E.H.Bogle,M.G.
Gibson,Joseph 22 to Louisa Siler 20    Col.        12-14-1882 J.E.Kilgore,M.G.
Gipson,P.A.26 to M.E.Wilson 24                     12-6-1883  John Ammons,J.P.
Gibson,John P.32 to Josephine  Guy 17              9-27-1885  J.D.Vinson,M.G.
Gibson,Sandy A.29 to Elizabeth Shepherd 20 Col.9-23-1888-Robt.Smith,M.G.
Gipson,Joe Dendy 24 to Catherine E.Gipson 20/7-18-1890-Jno.L.Corbin,J.P.
Gipson,James 23 to Florence Waldroop 17            5- 3-1891  W.G.Mallonee,M.G.
Gibson,Benjamin 20 to Dolly Jennings 18            8-28-1896  J.C.Russell,J.P.
Gibson,Robt.J.21 to Arie Coward 18  Col.           2-17-1898  C.W.Walten,M.G.
Gibson,Alexander 21 to Hattie Sorrels 18           4-17-1898  John H.Fulton,J.P
Gibson,H.L.48 to Sallie Sorrels 23                 10-9-1899  T.R.Arnold,J.P.
Gibson,Elijah 29 to Palina Bradley 28              1-21-1900  D.P.Cabe,J.P.
Gibson,Thomas E.20 to Lyda Adams 19                3- 6-1901  J.A.Deal,M.G.
Gibson,Asbury 22 to Belle Hurst 20                 12-20-1903 C.C.Rickman,M.G.
Gibson,W.Henry 21 to Addie Sorrels 17              3-25-1904  W.L.Hidgon,J.P.
Gibson,D.Walter 23 to Allice Higdon 18             12-29-1904 J.R.Pendergras,MG
Gipson,Joseph 25 to Mamie Jones 17                 1-20-1905  W.R.Bulgin,J.P.
Gibson,Jake 25 to Allean McDonnell 20 Col.         12-29-1907 J.T.Kenedy,M.G.
Gibson,Joseph 42 to L.V.Peek 33                    3- 8-1908  I.T.Peek,M.G.
Gibson,Jay C.23 to Cora Jacobs 24                  11-24-1908 J.P.Campbell,J.P.
Gibson,Newton G.27 to Nannie Mallonee 21 Col.10-10-1910-J.S.McKinney,M.G
```

```
Gibson,Ira D.31 to Leila Dryman 18              5-21-1911   J.R.Pendergras,MG
Gibson,Benjamin 22 to Catherine Tilman 19       8-17-1911   Z.J.Peek,J.P.
Gibson,J.Thomas 24 to Sarvilla Henry 17         12-24-1916  P.C.Calloway,J.P.
Gibson,Willie 19 to Maggie Shepherd 22          8-11-1918   J.A.Morrison,J.P.
Gibson,N.F.30 to Myrtle Clark 18                12-16-1920  J.L.Bryson,J.P.
Gibson,Roy C.28 to Bessie Rickman 18            12-26-1923  G.A.Cloer,M.G.
Gibson,Frank W.22 to Leobelle Bradley 22        2-23-1929   D.C.McCoy,M.G.
Gibson,Neil 21 to Mamie Talley 20               3- 8-1933   W.Frank Gillespie
Gibson,Luther 22 to Mrs.Minnie Gibson 36        7- 1-1933   A.A.Angel,M.G.
Gibson,Joseph R.21 to Martha L.Henderson 25/3-11-1934  Guy A.Gulleth.
Gibson,Ellis 31 to Lillie B.Jones 28 Col.       4- 4-1934   G.W.Rose,M.G.
  He from Clarksville,Ga.
Gibson,Weaver 47 to Francis Parrish 41          9-30-1934   A.S.Solesbee,M.G.
Gillespie,Marion to Margaret Potts              11-3-1859   R.C.Slagle,Clk.
Gillespie,Henry 21 to Nannie Wild 18            6-20-1897   C.S.Ray,J.P.
Gillespie,L.T.55 to Sarah M.Tallent 33          3- 5-1898   Jas.C.Weaver,J.P.
Gilliam,Daniel to Elviry Laird                  10-3-1829   William F.McKee.
Gilliland,Robert E.39 to Clara V.Mashburn 36/11-25-1926-Geo.Carpenter,JP
  He from Asheville,N.C.
Glaze,G.M. to M.L.Barnes                        9-14-1866   Z.Barnes,J.P.
Glidwell,J.H.30 to M.E.Henson 20                11-17-1876  E.T.Long,J.P.
Glidwell,T.A.18 to L.C.Williamson 21            11-9-1901   T.N.Ford,M.G.
Glimpes,Leonard to Mary Deweese                 10-13-1860  R.C.Slagle.
Godwin,E.M. 22 to Catheryn Cunningham 25        6-13-1920   R.P.McCracken,MG
Godwin,Sidney 32 to Helen A.Moses 26            1-14-1930   Dee Woolum,M.G.
  He from Wilson,N.C.
Goodson,Joseph 23 to Orrie Rogers 23            1-16-1890 Original not found
Goss,Louie J.31 to Margie Elizabeth Rochester 19/6-15-1940-J.A.Flanagan.
  He from Asheville,N.C.
Gottwals,John Z.65 to Martha Norton 42          3- 6-1896 G.W.Matney,M.G.
Graham,Swan to Marg. C.Trammel                  4- 7-1841 H.G.Woodfin,D.Clk.
Graham,James H.26 to Nellie Laney 28 '          1-18-1936 Geo.Carpenter,J.P
Grahl,William M.to Emily Curtis                 11-13-1858 R.C.Slagle,C.C,C.
Grant,A.B. to Sarah Smith                       10-11-1841 J.K.Gray,Clk.
Grant,James to Nancy Mayfield                   12-6-1845  J.K.Gray,Clk.
Grant,Wilkey to Mary A.Tothrow                  3-21-1848  Joel Sawyer.
Grant,Joseph A.to Celo E.Price                  12-11-1855 John Hall,Clk.
Grant,Joseph to Sarah Forister                  1-16-1856  John Hall,Clk.
Grant,Henry to Elizabeth Morrison               8- 6-1857  John Hall,Clk.
Grant,William C.to Eliza C.Totherow             12-8-1857  T.P.Siler,D.Clk.
Grant,William H.to Elizabeth J.Gipson           5- 6-1858  R.C.Slagle,Clk.
Grant,G.C.to M.M.Queen                          8-11-1861  R.C.Slagle,Clk.
Grant,Jessie to Sarah Queen                     6-28-1870  J.K.Bryson,Reg.
Grant,John P.to Betsy Ann Low                   9-24-1871  J.S.Buchanan,M.G.
Grant,John to Margaret Clure                    11-20-1871 William Sloan,Reg
Grant,William M.21 to Mary L.Low 21             1- 6-1873  A.L.Wild,J.P.
Grant,J.R.31 to Nancy M.Martin 19               12-10-1876 P.P.McLean,M.G.
Grant,W.M.17 to H.E.Dalrymple 18                9- 1-1878  J.M.Forester,J.P.
```

Grant,G.W.28 to Harriett L.McGaha 30   10-1-1878   Thos.Mashburn,J.P
Grant,V.D.20 to R.J.Rickman 22   7- 7-1881   J.S.Woodard,M.G.
Grant,Chas.T.21 to Anna Shepherd 18   9-18-1881   M.J.Mashburn,J.P.
Grant,V.M.22 to S.E.Potts 21   10-7-1881   J.S.Woodard,M.G.
Grant,Thomas 22 to Elizabeth Grant 24   3-24-1885   Jas.M.Barnes,J.P.
Grant,John S.21 to Carie A.Hurst 21   12-27-1885 John Elmore,J.P.
Grant,John 23 to Emily V.Smith 19   4-22-1888   A.A.Justice,M.G.
Grant,J.Henry 17 to Tiny A.Martin 18   8-16-1889   W.C.Mason,M.G.
Grant,A.Sherman 22 to Susan M.Love 18   12-22-1889 J.Reid,J.P.
Grant,J.J.21 to Lizzie Guffee 16   8-10-1890   J.D.Wright,M.G.
Grant,J.W. 21 to Lilly McGaha 22   10-23-1892 J.W.Rickman,J.P.
Grant,William 21 to Laura Key 26   8-21-1895   Joseph Morgan,J.P.
Grant,W.C.20 to Amanda McMahan 19   12-21-1895 W.C.Mason,M.G.
Grant,Wilkie N.22 to Mary Mason 20   5-10-1896   F.M.Morgan,M.G.
Grant,James S.21 to Rachel A.Grant 17   12-16-1897 E.N.Dalrymple,J.P.
Grant,Richard 22 to Balm Grant 20   5-27-1903   S.J.May,J.P.
Grant,Frank 21 to Jennie Tallent 18   9- 1-1907   John C.Hurst,J.P.
Grant,D.A.21 to M.E.Grant 18   9-13-1908   L.I.Mashburn,M.G.
Grant,Mart 17 to Tally Owenbey 19   2-25-1917   P.H.Passmore,M.G.
Grant,Arthur 21 to Maude Grant 21   8-17-1925   Geo.Carpenter,J.P
    He from Gastonia,N.C.
Grant,Olsen A.23 to Helen Dalrymple 20   7- 3-1935   Geo.Carpenter,J.P
    He from Bessemer City,N.C.
Grant,James M.23 to Mollie Pendergrass 21   4- 5-1936   Geo.W.Stepp,J.P.
Grant,Noel 23 to Carolina Owenby 20   10-17-1937 Geo.W.Steppe,J.P.
    He from Mantahala,N.C.
Grant,J.H.67 to Elisha Passmore 53   4-20-1939   T.D.Denny,M.G.
Grant,Fred 34 to Ida Bryant 25   3-28-1942   C.F.Rogers,M.G.
Grasty,M.C.23 to Bertha Myers 22   7-14-1909   Geo.Carpenter,J.P
Grasty,Taylor 25 to Dora Hopkins 20   9-23-1917   Geo.Carpenter,J.P
Gray,James K.to Faney W.Grant   7-31-1833   John Hall,Clk.
Gray,William to Sofiah McClure   5- 7-1834   John Tatham,Clk.
Gray,James G.to Mary Thomas   2-28-1836   John Tatham,Clk.
Gray,J.K.to Matilda S.Robinson   11-4-1845   B.K.Dickey,Wit.
Gray,Enos to Elmira Allen   5- 5-1859   H.K.Kimsey,J.P.
Gray,John J.to H.H.Roane   8-26-1861   J.C.Anderson,Wit.
Gray,Isaac to Fannie Gray   Col.   10-5-1866   R.C.Slagle,C.C.C.
Gray,Jno.P.21 to Margaret M.Long 19   9-26-1872   W.T.Anderson,J.P.
Gray,George W.22 to Eugenia Slagle 20   11-23-1875 J.A.J.Morrison,MG
Gray,Thos.R.35 to Ellen L.Crawford 22   4- 5-1882   W.C.Carden,M.G.
Gray,William H.21 to Orah McConnell 18   10-6-1892   G.R.McPherson,J.P
Gray,Dallas 23 to Sallie Patton 19   Col. 7-18-1895 Original not found
Gray,William 30 to Adalaide Burgess 20 Col. 9- 5-1899 Chas.L.Stewart,MG
Gray,H.R.23 to Ella Thomas 23   1-28-1903   E.A.Sample,M.G.
Gray,W.H.35 to Mary McConnell 36   11-8-1903   Robert Stamey,JP
Gray,Thomas R.58 to Mary Slagle 53   4-19-1905   John H.Moore,M.G
Gray,Joe 28 to Emma Moore 23   11-18-1905 A.B.Padgett,M.G.
Gray,Javan J.24 to Mary May Stiles 21   11-6-1907   P.R.Young,M.G.

```
Gray,Joseph Burk 21 to May Hattie Blaine 19/3-12-1913  F.M.Morgan,M.G.
Gray,Clifford 29 to May McCall 18            10-6-1920  J.Q.Wallace,M.G.
Gray,J.S.22 to Bessie Cabe 22               12-29-1920 J.Q.Wallace,M.G.
Gray,J.E.45 to Carrie Moore 21              12-27-1931 J.L.Teague,M.G.
  He from Lyman,Washington.
Green,William to Ione Parson                 1-29-1838  John Hall,Clk.
Green,Jourdan to Matilda Curtiss             8-29-1840  John Hall,Clk.
Green,E. to Ann Justice                      5-19-1847  Jos.McClure,Wit.
Green,Pleasant to Isabel Cabe                7-29-1852  J.F.Slagle,J.P.
Green,Silas J. to Mary A.Grilliany          10-18-1852 J.R.Siler,D.Clk.
Green,John A.to W.N.Slagle                    4-27-1865 R.C.Slagle,Clk.
Green,Silas 25 to P.E.Cloer 24               2-15-1880  P.R.Rickman,M.G.
Green,Robert 21 to N.E.Rickman 23            1-10-1882  C.L.Buchanan,M.G.
Green,J.A.23 to D.A.McCall 18                6-11-1882  J.N.Arnold,J.P.
Green,R.C.22 to Maggie Holland 17            2-10-1885  J.R.Ammons,M.G.
Green,A.Judson 30 to Ruth A.Watkins 17       1-24-1889  L.H.Garland,J.P.
Green,W.T.25 to Hattie Hurst 18             12-15-1889  P.R.Rickman,M.G.
Green,Joseph 28 to Lethe Cody 20            11-3-1893   P.C.Wild,J.P.
Green,Chris C.22 to Mennie Estis 16          3- 1-1900  D.C.McCoy,J.P.
Green,W.Thomas 25 to Mary M.Estes 21         4-30-1903  John Shepherd,J.P
Green,Elmer D.22 to Ida Sanders 19           9-13-1908 J.R.Pendergrass,MG
Green,E.H.38 to Texie A.Norris 20           11-4-1908 Original not found
Green,Hillard 18 to Hattie Beasley 16        1-17-1911  J.W.Rickman,J.P.
Green,R.C.50 to Mrs.Jennie Shular 46         9-22-1912 J.R.Pendergrass,MG
Green,R.C.57 to Octa Deal 55                11-12-1919 J.R.Pendergras,MG
Green,Cecil S.19 to Nora L.Gillespie 22     10-18-1921  Geo.Carpenter,JP
Green,Homer C.25 to Ester Reece 20          12-31-1921  Robert E.Ward,MG
Green,Thad M.19 to Ruth Wallace 18           1- 2-1922 J.R.Pendergrass,MG
Green,C.M.23 to Lucy Wiggins 18              8-14-1924  Leroy Woods,M.G.
Green,Arthur L.18 to Annie Lou Pressley 21  12-31-1929 J.R.Pendergras,MG
Green,Luther 24 to Geneva Pine 27           12-28-1937  J.A.Flanagan,M.G
  He from Keystone,W.Va.... She from Athens,W.Va..
Greenwood,Madison to Isabel Morrow           2-10-1852  J.K.Gray,Clk.
Greenwood,W.H.A. to M.I.Carter               8-15-1866  R.C.Slagle,C.C.C.
Greenwood,John D.W. to Elizabeth Carter     10-25-1870  Wm.Sloan,Reg.
Greenwood,Jas.W.20 to Mary Ann Lewis 19      7-24-1873  Albert Siler,J.P.
Greenwood,William H.20 to Octa Kelly 19     11-9-1895   R.B.Shelton,M.G.
Greenwood,G.H.20 to Della Huscusson 17       5-31-1900  W.A.Setser,J.P.
Greenwood,Thomas 25 to Hattie Wilson 25 Col.12-30-1903 C.L.Stuart,M.G.
Greenwood,William 23 to Maggie Cloer 17      1-27-1907  C.A.Setser,J.P.
Greenwood,F.M.23 to Josie Anderson 17        3- 9-1910  C.W.Slagle,J.P.
Greenwood,Thomas 31 to Nannie Bly 20   Col. 10-23-1910 C.L.Stewart,M.G.
Greenwood,Clarance G.21 to Zannie Collier 17/7-27-1935 S.R.Crockett,M.G.
Gregory,Archabald to Elizabeth Younce        4- 3-1846  J.K.Gray,Clk.
Gregory,Henry to Polly Blackburn            12-18-1851  J.K.Gray,Clk.
Gregory,John C.to Polly Dills                9-28-1860  R.C.Slagle,Reg.
Gregory,Andrew to Aner Teague                8-28-1863  Z.Barnes,J.P.
```

Gregory,William to C.S.Ammons	2-29-1866	I.N,Keener,J.P.
Gregory,George W.19 to Sarah Neal 18	8-16-1874	Z.Barnes,J.P.
Gregory,William R.18 to Tempy Ledford 16	1-21-1877	Z.Barnes,J.P.
Gregory,J.C.28 to M.A.Mincy 18	3-10-1881	Hosea Moses,J.P.
Gregory,William 24 to Sarah Ledford 21	4-19-1883	Z.Barnes,J.P.
Gregory,W.Alex 23 to Fannie Stanfield 21	8-29-1888	J.M.Keener,J.P.
Gregory,Wm.T.35 to Mary E.Parker 29	3- 9-1890	J.W.Parker,J.P.
Gregory,Charley 22 to Emma Jones 19	8- 8-1890	Z.Barnes,J.P.
Gregory,Adolphus 28 to Jane Young 27	4-15-1894	J.W.Parker,J.P.
Gregory,Charley M.25 to Louvinie Vaughn 17	8-25-1895	T.J.Vinson,J.P.
Gregory,A.H.52 to Aveline Rowland 40	4-14-1897	Jacob Yonce,M.G.
Gregory,John 21 to Delia Riddle 19	10-26-1897	R.B.Sheltain,M.G.
Gregory,J.H.22 to Callie Sorrels 18	5- 1-1898	U.A.Peek,J.P.
Gregory,John 20 to Julia Wood 18	9- 2-1900	D.F.Howard,M.G.
Gregory,Asbury 24 to Laura Tilson 18	12-23-1900	J.H.Fulton,J.P.
Gregory,W.J.22 to Peggie Fox 20	4- 6-1902	M.A.Love,M.G.
Gregory,John 23 to Nora Lunsford 22	10-16-1902	J.T.Taylor,M.G.
Gregory,J.H. 30 Addie Willis 22	9-25-1904	W.A.Solesbee,J.P.
Gregory,Joseph W.23 to Lela Garrison 21	11-20-1904	D.F.Howard,M.G.
Gregory,R.A. 21 to Flora Neal 18	9-29-1905	A.S.Solesbee,M.G.
Gregory,J.M.21 to Connie Plemons 21	11-1-1906	A.S.Solesbee,M.G.
Gregory,George 27 to Amanda Stiwinter 25	4-22-1908	Z.P.Peek,J.P.
Gregory,B.H.24 to Mary Taylor 19	12-28-1915	L.J.Young,M.G.
Gregory,Maden 34 to Vina Stilwinter 17	9-24-1918	J.M.Keener,M.G.
Gregory,J.A.23 to Amanda Houston 19	7-23-1922	J.M.Keener,M.G.
Gregory,Geo.L.to Vallie Holland	6- 3-1924	M.H.James,J.P.
Gregory,Chas.M.22 to Gladis A.Berrong 23 Both from Hiawasi,Ga.	11-12-1932	J.M.Raby,J.P.
Gribble,Robert W. to Sarah Buckhanan	10-8-1833	James Gray,Wit.
Gribble,John to Rachael Willison	2- 8-1847	J.K.Gray,Clk.
Gribble,Thomas to Clarissa Rogers	8-15-1849	T.C.Siler,D.Clk.
Gribble,William M. to Elizabeth Pendergrass	1-20-1858	T.P.Siler,D.Clk.
Gribble,James L.to Mary C.Dills	1-12-1861	R.C.Slagle,C.C.C.
Gribble,Lucius M.to Sarah A.Carpenter	11-4-1869	J.K.Bryson,Reg.
Gribble,J.Wilburn 24 to Mary E.Higdon 21	10-26-1873	Jas.McGee,J.P.
Gribble,Jno.J.25 to Lidia Moore 19	12-22-1877	W.W.Henry,J.P.
Gribble,William A.22 to Elizabeth T.Mathews	26/8-21-1879-	C.D.Smith,M.G.
Gribble,William A.34 to Sallie Holland 20	2- 5-1891	J.R.Pendergrass,MG
Gribble,John 24 to Annie Davis 14	1-10-1897	N.P.Rankin,J.P.
Gribble,Ted 22 to Willie Mae Bullock 23	9-18-1927	J.A.Flanagan,M.G.
Griffin,J.H.23 to Annie Pickens 16	11-20-1897	M.L.Rickman,J.P.
Griffin,Alfred 22 to Lassie Brown 22	7-27-1913	J.B.Hensley,M.G.
Griffin,Lawson 19 to Ader Mae Winstead 17	3-14-1915	C.W.Ramey,J.P.
Griffin,Lawrence 21 to Lula Dietz 18 Both from Sylva,N.C.	5-23-1929	Geo.Carpenter,J.P
Griggs,Woody to Airy McKinzy	10-31-1846	J.K.Gray,Clk.
Greggs,William to Mary Ledford	9-13-1847	S.M.Dowdle,Wit.

Griggs,J.M.20 to T.L.McDowell 24	11-2-1882	E.T.Long,J.P.
Griggs,R.A.24 to Ollie Sanders 24	11-27-1900	C.W.Dowdle,J.P.
Griggs,E.L.20 to May Sanders 19	8-18-1901	C.W.Dowdle,J.P.
Gringstaff,C.S.29 to Berdie West 24	9-28-1920	J.R.Pendergrass,MG
Grisham,A.F.23 to H.A.McDonnell 19 Col.	11-27-1875	D.W.Wills,M.G.
Grisham,Jule 21 to Laura McDonnell 17 Col.	12-25-1881	F.Poindexter,J.P.
Grist,William J.23 to Mary E.Garland 22	4-16-1876	M.L.Kelley,J.P.
Grist,A.J.23 to M.C.Garland 22	10-25-1877	M.L.Kelley,J.P.
Gross,George W.to Catherine S.Huggins	2-26-1839	H.G.Woodfin,D.Clk
Groves,William to Addie A.Gray	11-8-1866	R.C.Slagle,C.C.C.
Gudger,Benjamin M.to Hariet L.West Col.	12-10-1871	William Sloan,Reg
Gudger,William 54 to Roda Gibson 23	4-11-1903	J.P.Bryson,J.P.
Gudger,Bishop 22 to Florence Ammons 18 He from Sylva,N.C.	7- 1-1934	Jake Henry,J.P.
Guess,James C.16 to Addie Gribble 19	10-5-1882	T.S.Siler,J.P.
Guest,Geo.A.17 to Rebecca M.Love 14	4- 8-1883	I.D.Wright,M.G.
Guest,George 17 to Martha Kinsland 19	4-14-1901	J.B.Elmore,J.P.
Guest,James 20 to Fannie Kinsland 18	8-31-1910	A.S.Ammons,J.P.
Guest,Charlie 25 to Vinnie Thompson 22	5- 2-1919	J.M.Raby,J.P.
Guest,R.Holland 23 to Lela E.Sullivan 23 He from Anderson,S.C.	8- 3-1929	John E.White,M.G.
Guffee,William to Martha Lowry	9-11-1839	H.G.Woodfin,D.Clk
Guffee,Jesse R.to Elizabeth Magaha	10-21-1846	J.K.Gray,Clk.
Guffee,Thomas to Margaret Lowery	11-3-1851	Jacob Siler,J.P.
Guffee,J.L.23 to Matilda A.Dowdle 18	9- 4-1872	T.F.Glenn,M.G.
Guffee,William C.21 to Harriett C.Jones 22/	11-13-1873	Albert Siler,J.P.
Guffee,James 21 to Eliza Jones 18	12-21-1877	.Albert Siler,J.P.
Guffee,Henry 24 to S.E.Merritt 22	8-16-1883	M.Lee Rickman,J.P
Guffee,J.L.50 to Mary Pressley 33	10-9-1898	R.L.Cabe,J.P.
Guffee,E.N.25 to N.L.Buirl 16	12-16-1899	Retd.not executed
Guffee,David 20 to Bettie Anderson21	8-30-1900	W.A.Setser,J.P.
Guffee,E.N.25 to Lillie Buchanan 18	11-25-1900	J.B.Elmore,J.P.
Guffee,Samuel 20 to Bell Buchanan 19	11-24-1901	J.B.Elmore,J.P.
Guffee,Joseph E.22 to Lassie Donaldson 20	3- 2-1904	T.N.Ford,M.G.
Guffee,Henry 28 to Bular Potts 22	4- 9-1908	N.P.Rankin,J.P.
Guffee,John H.21 to Jessie M.Rickman 18	12-11-1910	P.R.Rickman,M.G.
Guffee,Ben 24 to Laura Sorrels 22	1-12-1914	J.R.Pendergrass,MG
Guffee,David 36 to Allie Williamson 26	7- 5-1916	A.M.Ledford,M.G.
Guffey,O.B.24 to Ruth M.McCullum 17	11-9-1919	L.B.Haynes,M.G.
Guffey,Henry L.45 to Mary E.Cabe 36 He from Young Harris,Ga.	8- 1-1935	J.B.Tabor,M.G.
Guffey,Rolen S.23 to Francis Key 18	8- 2-1937	Lester L.Arnold.
Guillians,William B.to Martha M.Lindsay	9-13-1850	T.P.Siler,D.Clk.
Guinn,James W.to Catherine Dobson	2- 2-1830	W.M.McConnell,Wit
Guinn,Jerry 17 to Sallie Gipson 15 Col.	7-23-1890	N.P.Rankin,J.P.
Guinn,Ben 19 to Mary McClure 17 Col.	11-29-1894	J.R.Pendergras,MG
Guinn,Hiley 21 to Lou Cox 21 Col.	11-24-1901	S.B.Cornelius,MG
Gunter,T.B. to Sophia Huggins	10-8-1859	R.C.Slagle,Clk.

Guy,Clark to Caroline Gibson	7-13-1836	John Tatham,CSC.
Guy,James to Susan Kerby	5-14-1839	H.G.Woodfin,D.Clk.
Guy,Daniel to Mary Foster	8-23-1854	John Hall,Clk.
Guy,Albert to Angeline Waldroop	1-19-1855	John F.Mashburn.
Guy,W.W. to Nancie Kerby	8-27-1855	John Hall,Clk.
Guy,Henry to Martha Ann Guy	3-26-1861	R.C.Slagle,Reg.
Guy,Joseph to Martha McCurry	7-19-1865	R.C.Slagle,Reg.
Guy,Joshua R.to Amanda Phillips	6-29-1867	R.C.Slagle,Clk.
Guy,George 24 to Margaret Sweatman 19	1- 3-1875	F.Poindexter,J.P.
Guy,Johnston 21 to Georgia A.Gibson 16	8- 5-1883	J.D.Vinson,M.G.
Guy,D.N.26 to Annie Kilpatrick 19 Col.	3-12-1885	John B.Gray,J.P.
Guy,William P.19 to Laura A.Peek 20	2-19-1887	D.L.Miller,M.G.
Guy,Ed 22 to Anna Madcap 20 Col.	2-24-1895	John C.Russell,JP
Guy,William 36 to Lucinda Burgess 30 Col.	10-8-1903	J.M.Bristol,M.G.
Guy,William 49 to Fannie Mallonee 25 Col.	12-30-1906	G.H.Jackson,M.G.
Guy,George 24 to Lena Clark 24 Col.	5- 2-1915	E.O.Cowan,M.G.
Guy,Furman 22 to Minnie Morrison 18	8- 1-1915	J.A.Lakey,J.P.
Guy,Albert 21 to Mary Gregory 18	7-18-1915	W.G.Woods,J.P.
Guyer,David to Louisa Buckner	--13-1841	J.K.Gray,Clk.
Guyer,G.H.to Soprana Roper	1-30-1861	R.C.Slagle,Reg.
Guyer,Phillip to May Ann Tallent	2-14-1873	License revoked
Guyer,James 22 to Maggie Tallent 19	12-3-1899	Jos.L.Fouts,J.P.
Halderman,Dan 26 to Sudie Burton 19	4-18-1917	Geo.Carpenter,JP
Hall,M.M. to Jane C.Hyde	12-2-1839	H.G.Woodfin,D.Clk
Hall,James A.to Jane Clemons	10-12-1840	John Hall,Clk.
Hall,Alfred to Margaret McCoy	12-8-1842	J.L.Brindle,Wit.
Hall,Jamison to Elizabeth Hyde	2-13-1843	J.K.Gray,Clk.
Hall,David L.to Rachel Wilson	7-16-1844	J.K.Gray,Clk.
Hall,M.M. to Sarah C.Turner	12-11-1860	R.C.Slagle,Clk.
Hall,David R.to Francis Love	12-1-1861	R.C.Slagle,Clk.
Hall,R.H. to Lucy Morrison	9- 6-1862	R.C.Slagle,Clk.
Hall,John W.to Francis Love	2- 7-1866	R.C.Slagle,C.C.C.
Hall,Robert S.21 to Mary N.Myers 21	2- 8-1874	F.Poindexter,J.P.
Hall,A.M.22 to Nina M.Beasley 20 He from Jackson Co.,N.C.	11-9-1879	P.R.Rickman,M.G.
Hall,H.A.21 to B.Drinnon 17	9-30-1882	Jos.Morgan,J.P.
Hall,Albey 39 to Nannie Ford 19 Col.	1-16-1883	E.H.Bogle,M.G.
Hall,Elbert 20 to Josie McCoy 18	12-23-1888	M.J.Mashburn,J.P.
Hall,Dewitt C.20 to Lizzie J.Welch 20	1-28-1892	J.A.Morrison,J.P.
Hall,Aleck 26 to Laura Moore 18 Col.	10-16-1892	N.J.Rush,J.P.
Hall,Cary McD. 20 to Lucy J.Bradley 21	9- 8-1895	H.D.Dean,J.P.
Hall,Tudor T.51 to Mrs.Meta N.Frost 32	3- 5-1896	J.A.Deal,M.G.
Hall,Rufus H.54 to Margaret R.Slagle 28	6-13-1896	Original not found
Hall,John W.51 to Ella D.Sweatman 24	6-16-1897	Jas.C.Weaver,J.P.
Hall,Lena 24 to Mary Jacobs 25	12-4-1898	J.R.Pendergrass,MG
Hall,D.A.26 to Pearl Bradley 23	3- 2-1905	W.L.Bradley,M.G.
Hall,Clingman to Lydia B.Ammons 22	11-21-1908	J.W.Ammons,J.P.

Hall,R.Sam 57 to Fannie Meadows 31	1-16-1910	M.J.Mashburn,J.P.
Hall,Furman 18 to Mamie Shuler 18	4- 2-1911	W.L.Bradley,M.G.
Hall,Wm.G.25 to Pauline Penland 22	12-2-1911 Original not found	
Hall,Rufus 18 to Viola York 18	8-28-1914	C.S.Battles,J.P.
Hall,F.H.21 to Jennie Smith 20	11-10-1917	J.L.Fouts,J.P.
Hall,Oliver V.21 to Mrs.Bertha Byrd Winstead 22/7-24-1918-Geo.Carpenter.		
Hall,Lester 23 to Maggie Conley 18 Col.	9-28-1919	E.G.Siler,M.G.
Hall,A.W.27 to Birdell Gibson 19 Col.	10-17-1920	E.G.Siler,M.G.
Hall,Tudor N.23 to Margaret S.Gilbert 16	9-19-1928	S.L.McCarty,M.G.
Hall,John M.31 to Sue Ruckner 24 She from Hartwell,Ga.	5- 5-1931	Chas.R.McCarty,MG
Hall,Will 54 to Nan Riddle 50	7- 1-1933	Geo.Carpenter,J.P
Hall,Ligah 21 to Bertie Leatherman 20	2-20-1937	N.E.Holden,M.G.
Hall,James 23 to Jaunita Gibson 23	2-20-1937	N.E.Holden,M.G.
Halleck,Joseph 57 to A.E.Stephenson 23	11-15-1881	M.C.Smith,M.G.
Halloway,Champ 22 to Bonnie Pendergrass 17 He from Topton,N.C.	4-17-1937	D.F.Howard,M.G.
Hamby,John C.22 to Margaret L.Garland 21 He from Rabun Co.Ga.	2- 3-1878	L.Howard,J.P.
Hamilton,F.A.35 to Mamie Deal 23 Col.	10-17-1900	A.B.Morrow,M.G.
Hamilton,Robert 23 to Martha Taylor 18	5-31-1909	D.F.Howard,M.G.
Hamilton,Gilbert A.24 to Mary E.Bulgin 33	8-22-1923	J.Q.Wallace,M.G.
Hampton,B.F.21 to Phebe A.Dalrymple 20	1- 5-1880	J.M.Forester,J.P.
Hampton,Thomas G.19 to Viana Bates 19	11-17-1895	H.D.Dean,J.P.
Hampton,E.R.56 to Florence M.Curtis 35	2-25-1903	Edwin L.Bain,M.G.
Hampton,Robert 21 to Pinkie Dalrymple 24	2-13-1910	J.W.Duvall,J.P.
Hampton,John 20 to Emmer Roane 21	2-24-1915	J.L.Teague,M.G.
Haney,Mathew to Jane Tanner	8-27-1836	John Tatham,Clk.
Haney,Mathew to Dicy Marr	5-24-1838	J.S.Gray,Clk.
Haney,Charles to Elizabeth Keener	1-14-1854	T.W.Setzer,Wit.
Haney,I.B.24 to Anna R.Reid 18	6- 6-1886	B.W.Wells,J.P.
Haney,J.M.20 to Callie Ledford 18	7-10-1887	Z.Barnes,J.P.
Haney,Ambrose 18 to Lou Dalrymple 20	10-11-1891	M.Ghormley,M.G.
Haney,J.N.34 to Sarah T.Bryant 21	11-3-1902	J.H.Gregory,J.P.
Haney,Frank 21 to Jane Cope 18	12-13-1906	A.S.Solesbee,M.G.
Haney,Riley 17 to Sarah J.Wilson 20	2-21-1907	W.C.Mason,M.G.
Haney,John 41 to Laura Tramel 21	6-25-1907	S.A.Rains,M.G.
Haney,W.C.20 to Alice Wilson 21	8-13-1911	W.C.Mason,M.G.
Haney,Mark 24 to Maud Wilson 22	11-21-1913	J.L.Fouts,J.P.
Haney,Charley W.22 to Mrs.Ferry Moore 25	7-24-1922	Geo.Carpenter,J.P
Haney,J.H.24 to Doshia Lunsford 18	6-20-1933	T.D.Denny,M.G.
Haynie,Clarence 30 to Hattie P.Huggins 23	9- 7-1921	W.L.Bradley,M.G.
Hanner,James to Lucea Lovell	8-22-1840	John Hall,Clk.
Harbison,Thos.G.34 to Jessie M.Cobb 28	8- 6-1896	G.W.Mateny,M.G.
Harbison,Thomas C.24 to Suzanne E.Rice 26	1- 8-1933	Chas.R.McCarty,MG
Hardie,William E.23 to Jane E.Wilson 22	9- 5-1886	J.W.Wilson,J.P.
Hardman,John B.26 to Nannie M.Trotter 26	10-18-1899	A.H.Sims,M.G.
Harkins,Jeefia 20 to Bessie Stamey 18	1-27-1901	C.W.Dowdle,J.P.

```
Harness,Richard 23 to Blanch Teem 22              2-27-1934   Geo.Carpenter,J.P
Harper,William B.21 to Hattie Deal 17    Col. 12-27-1893 J.Williams,M.G.
Harper,W.B.30 to Martha Parrish 18       Col. 11-2-1902  A.B.Morrow,M.G.
Harrell,Clifford 19 to Christine Hogan 19    7-29-1937   Lester L.Arnold,JP
   Both from Waynesville,N.C.
Harrington,S.H.26 to Anna E.Ingram 24        10-14-1879  C.D.Smith,M.G.
Harris,John H.37 to Lydia O.Mason 20          3-10-1886  J.M.Forester,J.P.
Harris,Charley 28 to Vergie Wykle 19    Col. 10-2-1915   J.H.Crosby,M.G.
Harris,Will 34 to Carrie Brown 33        Col. 10-30-1926 Geo.Carpenter,J.P
   Both from Clarksville,Ga.
Harris,Jas.G.21 to Lena M.Lovingood 18        9-26-1928  A.T.Medford,M.G.
Harrison,Ryly to Elizabeth Ledbetter          4-30-1842  J.K.Gray,Clk.
Harrison,Jeramiah to Mary S.Gelispie          8-13-1858  R.C.Slagle,Clk.
Harrison,E.L.27 to Mary E.Dowdle 25           8- 2-1880  B.G.Wild,M.G.
Harrison,John O.24 to Allie O.Nolen 24       10-30-1883  E.H.Bogle,M.G.
Harrison,J.M.27 to Allie McGee 19             1- 8-1902  J.H.Moore,M.G.
Harrison,Horace 26 to M.Rebecca Smith 20      5- 7-1911  M.H.Tuttle,M.G.
Harrison,Benjamin 37 to Margaret Zoellner 21/11-15-1926-Geo.C.Steed,M.G.
Harrison,Earl M.23 to Clara B.Shope 20        6- 3-1927  Geo.M.Steed,M.G.
Harshaw,Cale 29 to Hattie Shepherd 24   Col. 1- 5-1903  C.L.Stewart,M.G.
Harshaw,Jesse 22 to Ice Greenwood 20    Col. 3-18-1914  C.L.Stewart,M.G.
Harwood,Patton 23 to Carrie L.Killian 20      9-23-1886  L.H.Garland,J.P.
Hasket,John T.21 to Amanda J.Keener 21       12-13-1874  J.S.Woodard,M.G.
Hasket,J.C.20 to M.J.Moore 18                 9-27-1881  Hosea Moses,J.P.
Hasket,Andrew C.19 to Mary A.Blackburn 16     4-25-1891  J.W.Parker,J.P.
Hasket,Levi 21 to Alice Parker 21             8- 8-1909  James M.Corbin,JP
Haskett,Parker 21 to Stella Williams 21       5-15-1913  J.P.Moore,J.P.
Hastin,Franklin to Elizabeth Nichols          9-14-1854  John Hall,Clk.
Hasting,Albert to Hannah M.Ledford            9-24-1863  R.C.Slagle,C.C.C.
Hasting,F.Columbus 21 to Mary Battles 18     12-18-1889  W.B.Setser,J.P.
Hasting,Jason A.25 to Mary A.Sanders 19       9-17-1896  G.R.McPherson,J.P
Hasting,Wimer 21 to Mattie Ledford 16         2-28-1901  Robert Stamey,J.P
Hasting,Joe 25 to Allie Bird 18               8-22-1920  J.W.Moffit,J.P.
Hausier,Luther 30 to Bettie Roane 28          1-24-1900  T.F.Gleen,M.G.
Hauser,Love H.55 to Hattie M.Wood 50          7- 8-1929  H.C.Freeman,M.G.
Hauser,Thermon F.40 to Helen K.Blankenship 24/8-8-1936 C.C.Herbert,M.G.
Hawkes,B.H.34 to Jane Pendergrass 22          4-28-1916  Frank T.Gettis,JP.
Hawkins,Manson to Lucinda Queen               4- 4-1859  R.C.Slagle,Clk.
Hawkins,Ralph 22 to Florence Wild 20          5- 8-1905  Baylus Code,M.G.
Hawshaw,Gale 50 to Mrs.Octie Bly 30     Col. 8- 1-1920  J.Q.Wallace,M.G.
Hay,Neil C.23 to Levada R.Howard 24           6-25-1913  D.F.Howard,M.G.
Hay,Thomas R.21 to Ardith M.Hodges 16         6-23-1935  David F.Howard,MG
   He from Andrews,N.C.... She from Dunwoody,Ga.
Hay,Neil C.Jr.22 to Sue W.Almond 18           7- 2-1938  David F.Howard,MG
   Both from Andrews,N.C.
Hayes,Charles to Sarah Donnaldson            11-14-1844  John McDowell,Wit.
Hayes,Andrew 53 to Martha McCurry 35    Col. 6-14-1884  John Reid,J.P.
   He from Rabun Co.,Ga.
Hays,Jacob 75 to Hulda Powell 57        Col. 12-27-1834 Jona.Phillips,J.P.
```

Hayes,Geo.23 to Fannie Clanton 15   Col. 12-25-1891 M.J.Mashburn,J.P.

Hayes,George 29 to Jennie McDonald 25   Col. 12-12-1897 E.B.Angel,J.P.

Hays,G.W.28 to Mabel E.Cleveland 21   11-23-1901 G.W.Matney,M.G.

Hays,William R.28 to Lula Brownson 22   Col. 10-16-1905 N.P.Rankin,J.P.

Hays,Henry 21 to Ida Stewart 20   Col. 3- 7-1906 C.L.Stewart,M.G.

Hays,Thomas 25 to Alice Tallent 29   1- 3-1909 W.L.Bradley,M.G.

Hayes,Henry 38 to Mrs.Mary Wikle 46   Col. 5- 6-1923 J.J.Mann,J.P.

Hayes,Jas.N.21 to Lethea Greenwood 19   Col. 8-27-1927 E.S.Wyly,M.G.

Hayes,Wm.A.24 to M.Francis Paul 20   10-25-1928 W.T.Potts,M.G.

Hayes,Leonidas B.41 to Margaret Rogers 36   2- 5-1929 Chas.C.Weaver,M.G
   He from Winston Salem,N.C.

Hays,Iverson 28 to Edna Carpenter 21   Col. 10-18-1938 E.J.McKay,M.G.

Heaton,Oscar 30 to Emma Tallent 18   4- 4-1900 T.R.Arnold,J.P.

Heaton,Oscar 33 to Lizzie Tallent 35   10-26-1902 Jos.L.Fouts,J.P.

Hedden,J.V.to Almina Barnes   1-24-1864 W.Picklesimer,J.P.

Hedden,William N.to Charity Frada   8- 2-1865 R.C.Slagle,Clk.

Hedden,D.B.to Selma A.Picklesimer   7-14-1866 R.C.Slagle,Clk.

Hedden,Wm.V.25 to Martha Reid 22   10- 7-1873 J.S.Woodward,M.G.

Hedden,Stanhope 20 to L.Hasseltine Brindle 15/10-8-1875-J.S.Woodward,M.G.

Hedden,Blake 24 to Jane Bowman 22   6- 9-1880 J.M.Keener,J.P.

Hedden,William 36 to M.L.Thompson 24   8-13-1885 John Elmore,J.P.

Hedden,H.T.21 to Sophronia Peek 24   9- 4-1898 J.W.Parker,J.P.

Hedden,W.Ransom 24 to Mary M.Hicks 25   8- 8-1905 Thos.B.White,J.P.

Hedden,J.M.24 to Rouie Wood 18   1- 6-1907 G.W.Stiwinter,J.P.

Hedden,Geo.D.23 to Callie Buchanan 20   1- 7-1907 G.W.Stiwinter,J.P.

Hedden,Benjamin 22 to Fannie Wood 16   7-14-1911 J.M.Keener,M.G.

Hedden,Will W.22 to Rosetta Leopard 15   3-31-1912 J.M.Keener,M.G.

Hedden,W.Jasper 20 to Nellie Wood 18   10-12-1913 Frank Peek,J.P.

Hedden,P.M.21 to Eva Russell 18   10-25-1914 J.M.Keener,M.G.

Hedden,Wm.P.25 to Ruby Phillips 20   10-12-1921 J.Q.Wallace,M.G.

Hedden,John Q.26 to Thelma Howell 19   11-22-1925 J.Q.Wallace,M.G.

Hedden,Frank P.29 to Nellie M.Davis 16   11-17-1933 W.G.Barker,J.P.

Hedgecock,Minten to Teletha Elders   11-13-1844 J.K.Gray,Clk.

Helms,Wadsworth 26 to Dorothy Evelyn Burress 24/3-9-1939-Lester Arnold,JP
  He from Monroe,N.C.... She from Waynesville,N.C.

Hemphill,Joseph to Peggy Thomas   12-27-1847 J.K.Gray,Clk.

Hemphill,B.Frank 28 to Sophronia Thompson 24,Col.1-13-1874-D.W.Wells,M.G
   He from Henderson Co.N.C.

Hemphill,Albert 33 to Lula Norton 24   3-14-1905 Original not found

Henderson,Wm.to Margaret Moss   3-22-1845 J.K.Gray,Clk.

Henderson,George W.to Milley Peek   10-9-1858 R.C.Slagle,Clk.

Henderson,J.C.30 to Catherine Russell 22   4-23-1882 Jno.L.Corbin,J.P.

Henderson,Miles A.41 to Margaret A.Slagle 25/9-22-1886 E.A.Sample,M.G.

Henderson,C.Fredreck 22 to Allie Hoppar 19   10-20-1895 G.R.McPherson,J.P

Henderson,Chas.W.21 to Annie Keener 21   2- 8-1903 J.H.Fulton,J.P.

Henderson,C.Ted 38 to Annie M.Watts 20   12-9-1911 Robert Stamey,J.P

Henderson,W.A.28 to Minnie Dills 18   7-19-1914 T.C.Vinson,M.G.

Henderson,Fitz J.24 to Charlotte Ledbetter 19/3-13-1921-J.L.Teague,M.G.

```
Henderson,Tillery T.43 to Margarite Fulton 31/4- 9-1932-H.C.Freeman,M.G.
Henderson,Don L.23 to Beulah Z.Houston 20    11-23-1935 J.O.Nix,M.G.
Henry,John to R.L.Cogebourn                   8-31-1848  J.K.Gray,Clk.
Henry,W.W.to Cathrine Moore                   9-23-1857  R.C.Slagle,C.C.C.
Henry,J.T.to M.A.Moore                        1-25-1865  R.C.Slagle,Clk.
Henry,John to Elmira Franks                   3-18-1865  R.C.Slagle,Clk.
Henry,Calvin C.22 to Mary E.Thompson 19       2- 2-1873  Joshua Ammons,M.G
Henry,John 20 to Eliza Miller 20              1-15-1877  J.D.Vinson,M.G.
Henry,William H.22 to Coradine Grey 16        9-13-1877  I.N.Keener,J.P.
Henry,Joseph 23 to Mary L.Gipson 16           2-16-1890  D.W.Matheson,M.G.
Henry,R.A.24 to Elizabeth J.Bryson 18         6-22-1890  Jacob W.Parker,JP
Henry,Jacob W.H.22 to Caroline Moses 18       11-2-1890  J.W.Parker,J.P.
Henry,Joseph 21 to Sarah Cabe 27              3-10-1892  S.H.Harrington,MG
Henry,John P.23 to Jennie Sherrill 26         3-12-1893 J.R.Pendergrass,MG
Henry,James J.22 to Martha Talley 21          6-16-1895  Marion Wright,J.P
Henry,Isaac 23 to Nancy A.Wooten 20           2- 8-1896  J.B.Elmore,J.P.
Henry,Millard H.19 to Dora T.J.Webb 21        8- 2-1896  B.W.Wells,J.P.
Henry,Robert F.22 to Ruth Berry 22            10-15-1896 G.A.Bartlett,M.G.
Henry,B.H.40 to Jane Downs 40                 10-14-1897 C.S.Ray,J.P.
Henry,Thomas 21 to Margaret Southard 26       8- 7-1898  W.W.Moss,J.P.
Henry,Frank P.21 to Ida E.McCall 19           8-25-1898  Marion Wright,J.P
Henry,Geo.A.25 to Rebecca L.Pierson 21        1- 1-1899  J.T.Wade,M.G.
Henry,Love 20 to Hulda Tally 19               8- 6-1900  G.W.Matney,M.G.
Henry,Ryfus A.35 to Elizabeth J.Bryson 29     2-15-1902  J.W.Ammons,J.P.
Henry,W.H.45 to Mrs.Mary Dills 36             1- 4-1903  D.L.Miller,M.G.
Henry,Isaac 33 to Mrs.Millie Cabe 26          10-18-1905 M.A.Love,M.G.
Henry,Thomas 26 to Cora I.Vinson 16           12- 6-1906 J.D.Vinson,M.G.
Henry,Frank L.21 to Carrie Kinsland 18        9-30-1909  T.C.King,M.G.
Henry,Frank F.21 to Ester B.Collins 19        12-20-1912 J.P.Moore,J.P.
Henry,John B.29 to Vera Hudson 22             3- 2-1913  R.P.McCracken,M.G
Henry,Fate 20 to Daisy Henry 17               4- 3-1914  P.C.Calloway,J.P.
Henry,Charlie 22 to Eveline McCall 18         7-18-1915  P.C.Calloway,J.P.
Henry,Z.V.37 to Ethel Franks 21               2-12-1916. E.V.Ammons,J.P.
Henry,Claud 20 to Lucy McCall 16              3-21-1916  P.C.Calloway,J.P.
Henry,Robert D.19 to Laura Williams 16        5-24-1916  L.J.Young,M.G.
Henry,L.C.29 to Eliza J.Peek 24               7-23-1916  J.P.Moore,J.P.
Henry,N.J.24 to Carrie Stewman 19             11-3-1917  W.I.Jennings,J.P.
Henry,Love 39 to Addie Justice 45             2- 5-1918  W.C.Ledbetter,J.P
Henry,Noah 23 to Sarah Young 22               9- 7-1919  James C.Mell,J.P.
Henry,C.M.25 to Brettie Webb 22               1-28-1920  McKinley Webb,J.P
Henry,Charlie 21 to Bessie Harris 19          12-27-1920 W.T.Jennings,J.P.
Henry,Canton 25 to Lillian Elliott 22         6-17-1933  William Henry,J.P
Henry,W.T.25 to.Lelia E.Houston 23            11-5-1933  G.A.Hovis,M.G.
Henry,Grady J.21 to Eula Houston 21           8-10-1935  William Henry,J.P
Henry,Thomas L.23 to Pearl Dills 22           11-23-1935 William Henry,J.P
Henry,Walter L.20 to Mildred Stewart 18       7-16-1937  P.N.Moses,J.P.
Henry,Joseph M.21 to Martha L.Southards 16    1-16-1938  Arthur Mosteller.
```

```
Hensley,Hillard 26 to Nettie Anderson 19     11-11-1926 J.R.Pendergrass,MG
Herbert,Robt.C.21 to Josephine Porter 22 Col.11-6-1894 D.F.Carver,M.G.
Herbert,Fred L.21 to Ida Garrison 17          12-28-1895 M.Ghormley,M.G.
Herbert,Carl 25 to Sophrina Thompson 24 Col.10-27-1897 E.B.Angel,J.P.
Herrin,Levi to Cloe A.Picklesimer            8-14-1844  J.K.Gray,Clk.
Herren,Judson to Jane Moore                  11-29-1865 R.C.Slagle,Clk.
Hester,Carr to Polly Painter                 7- 6-1833  J.K.Gray,Clk.
Hester,A. to Jane Hall                       2- 3-1842  J.K.Gray,Clk.
Hester,Davis to Phoeba West                  12-19-1854 Thos.Mashburn,J.P.
Hester,John H.26 to Ann Conley 25            12-10-1873 J.W.Bowman,M.G.
Hewitt,Melvin 21 to Elsie Robinson 18        11-27-1937 J.E.Abernathy,M.G.
   He from Carthage,Tenn.... She from Sylva,N.C.
Henson,Edmon to Lucinda Ledford              9-18-1838  J.K.Gray,Clk.
Henson,Eli to Elizabeth Ledford              7-24-1839  H.G.Woodfin,Wit.
Henson,Ephriam to Anna Carpenter             5-13-1841  H.G.Woodfin,D.Clk.
Henson,Isaac to Elizabeth Lowery             4-30-1842  J.K.Gray,Clk.
Henson,Lazarus to Rebecca Hodges             2-20-1843  J.K.Gray,Clk.
Hanson,Eli to Leaner E.Ledford               4-29-1854  Joshua Ammons,M.G.
Henson,D.L. to Nancy C.R.Sanders             1-29-1870  R.C.Slagle,D.Clk.
Henson,John A. to Huldy Anderson             10-20-1870 T.J.Martin,M.G.
Henson,A.J.26 to Mary L.Rush 20              12-25-1878 G.H.Maden,M.G.
Henson,Benj.F.24 to Mat Allen 19             9-14-1879  E.T.Long,J.P.
Henson,Joseph 45 to Elenda Cross 40          10-26-1879 E.T.Long,J.P.
Henson,John A.33 to E.R.Long 23              1-18-1880  M.L.Kelly,J.P.
Henson,John W.24 to L.C.Wilson 21            5-14-1885  J.N.Arnold,J.P.
Henson,William 22 to Lilly Stockton 18       9- 9-1890  D.M.Matheson,M.G.
Henson,Ely 21 to Ada Glidwell 17             8-19-1894  G.R.McPhearson,JP
Henson,M.C.18 to Hastletine Freeman 19       10-4-1900  J.R.Edwards,M.G.
Henson,Lafayett 54 to Ella Carpenter 28      9- 7-1905  Robert Stamey,J.P.
Henson,Robert 21 to Rosa Keener 28           6- 4-1906  W.A.Norton,J.P.
Henson,G.R.22 to C.C.Liner 28                10-31-1906 R.M.Taylor,M.G.
Henson,Lonie 19 to Mattie Henderson 22       1-10-1913 Original not found
Henson,Madison 22 to Ivy Bryson 21           11-23-1913 R.H.Munger,J.P.
Henson,Lonie 21to Ora Norris 19              9-24-1914  Robert Stamey,J.P
Henson,Grady 21 to Eula Leadford 22          1-16-1916  J.M.Bennett,M.G.
Henson,Claud 20 to Ornessie Norris 18        7-29-1917  A.M.Ledford,M.G.
Henson,Prince C.21 to Meril Grist 19         8- 5-1917  J.B.Stalcup,M.G.
Henson,James 23 to Mary Howard 27            4- 4-1920  W.A.Norton,J.P.
Henson,J.L.21 to Ollie Wood 23               5-30-1920  Noah L.Jolly,J.P.
Henson,Carl 19 to Gussie Ledford 17          12-25-1924 V.B.Harrison,M.G.
Hibberts,Cornelius to Cyntha L.Parks      .  1- 6-1833  John Hall,Clk.
Hickerson,J.T.26 to Margaret H.Gay 22        1- 1-1912  J.E.Gay,M.G.
Hicks,Theodore to Eliza F.Grant              5- 2-1850  J.K.Bell,D.Clk.
Hicks,A.L.to Cynthia J.Tatham                9-13-1857  John Hall,Clk.
Hicks,John to E.C.Yonce                      8- 6-1861  Joseph Roland,J.P
Hicks,J.L.22 to R.E.Chambers 23              6- 9-1881  E.B.Padget,J.P.
Hicks,J.H.26 to Maggie Hayles 16             12-5-1897  M.Ghormley,M.G.
```

```
Hicks,J.B.24 to Carrie Wood 18            8-16-1900   D.F.Howard,M.G.
Hicks,Oscar 25 to Lillie Baldwin 18       5- 5-1908   D.A.Yonce,M.G.
Hicks,Arthur 30 to Martha Waters 23       3-11-1914   Frank T.Gettis,JI
Hicks,James 25 to Molly B.Crisp 26        12-17-1916  W.P.Wilson,J.P.
Hicks,Harrison 23 to Hester Jones 19      5- 4-1919   F.M.Morgan,M.G.
  Both from Nantahala,N.C.
Hicks,Edgar 22 to Catherine Waters 22     8-26-1936   P.H.Passmore,M.G.
  She from McAdenville,N.C.
Higdon,John to No name given              9-17-1834   John Higdon,Wit.
Higdon,William H.to Jincy Buchanan        12-2-1837   Joel Simmonds,Wit
Higdon,Leander to Rebecca Stewman         10-10-1853  I.N.Keener,J.P.
Higdon,William to Sarah Brindle           4-10-1861   John S.Gibson,J.I
Higdon,J.H.to Margaret Berry              9-24-1865   J.L.Buchanan,M.G.
Higdon,William to Jane Moore              11-9-1869   J.K.Bryson,Reg.
Higdon,Joseph to Sarah J.Cowart           9- 9-1870   Wm.Sloan,Reg.
Higdon,Thos.B.20 to Molly J.West 20       8- 7-1875   J.W.Bowman,M.G.
Higdon,J.A.25 to Lou A.Coggins 24         1- 6-1876   L.K.Haynes,M.G.
Higdon,Samuel A.30 to Harriett M.Berry 23 10-15-1879  J.S.Woodard,M.G.
Higdon,W.L.23 to Emma McDowell 23         4- 9-1890   J.M.Hillard,M.G.
Higdon,James L.23 to Lavada Strain 18     11-31-1893  J.M.Keener,M.G.
Higdon,John S.21 to Nola Cabe 21          3-28-1895   J.R.Pendergrass,MC
Higdon,Wm.H.79 to Charlotte Matthews 25   2-12-1896   J.T.Wade,M.G.
Higdon,T.B.49 to Lula Shepherd 19         3-26-1905   J.R.Pendergrass,MC
Higdon,Mack 30 to Mattie Franks 22        11-4-1908   T.C.King,M.G.
Higdon,Major 20 to Mary B.Cunningham 16   2-27-1910   T.C.King,M.G.
Higdon,W.R.29 to Georgia Corbin 23        7-29-1913   J.B.Stalcup,M.G.
Higdon,L.A.33 to Lula Corbin 21           11-9-1913   J.R.Pendergrass,MC
Higdon,Mack M.28 to Liza C.Loudermilk 22  8-20-1914   J.P.Moore,J.P.
Higdon,J.W.22 to Maude E.Berry 20         9- 9-1915   J.P.Moore,J.P.
Higdon,Johnson 22 to Birdie Upton 18      10-13-1915  J.A.Lakey,J.P.
Higdon,Roscoe 28 to Elizabeth Murray 18   5-29-1916   T.J.Vinson,M.G.
Higdon,Horace 27 to Ollie Stepp 19        7- 2-1916   J.H.Vinson,J.P.
Higdon,A.W.24 to Myrtle Bryson 18         5-13-1917   J.R.Pendergrass,MC
Higdon,C.F.25 to Sallie Bell Crawford 22  3-28-1920   L.H.Higdon,J.P.
Higdon,L.C.23 to Francis C.Moody 23       7-23-1921   L.B.Hayes,M.G.
Higdon,Jeter 28 to Vernon Dean 33         12-23-1923  J.M.Woodard,M.G.
Higdon,F.J.28 to Birdie Younce 25         12-25-1927  Will Smith,Ord.
Higdon,Alfred R.38 to Annie M.Crawford 28 4- 3-1930   J.A.Flanagan,M.G.
Higdon,Paul 24 to Callie Jones 18         7- 2-1933   O.E.Moses,J.P.
Higdon,Carl  to Hilda Ashe                10-1-1933   O.J.Withrow,M.G.
Higdon,T.B.Jr.23 to Otelia Haskett 18     10-25-1937  Arthur Mosteller.
Higgins,W.H.28 to Minnie Siler 20         8- 8-1888   J.A.Deal,M.G.
Higgins,Harry 23 to Agness Zachary 22     12-27-1912  Original not found.
Higgs,Norris V.36 to Bertha L.Patterson 38 Col.8-16-1936-J.C.Smith,M.G.
  He from Miami,Fla... She from Atlanta,Ga.
Hill,Jonathan to L.N.Garrett              1-27-1852   T.P.Siler,Clk.
Hill,J.H.to Ruth A.Pilkinton              9-20-1861   R.C.Slagle,Clk.
Hill,Christopher C.24 to Annie Roland 24  8-27-1874   Original not found
```

Hill,F.H.27 to S.O.Frost 20	1- 1-1882	Geo.French,M.G.
Hilton,Kenney R.30 to Willie M.Ledford 28 He from Clemson,S.C.	7- 9-1936	W.L.Griggs,M.G.
Hix,William N.28 to Oma Bateman 14	2-14-1894	Jno.T.Barnes,M.G.
Hobart,William 57 to Kate I.Robinson 40	6-27-1917	R.H.Dougherty,M.G.
Hockel,Thos.B.22 to Dicy C.Patton 16 Col.	1-20-1880	H.G.Woodfin,J.P.
Hodgins,Andrew to Rosanna L.Donnaldson	3- 7-1838	J.K.Gray,Clk.
Hodgins,W.L. to Sarah A.Ledford	8-26-1858	R.C.Slagle,C.C.C.
Hodgins,M.D.to Julia A.Moffitt	5-26-1867	R.C.Slagle,Clk.
Hodgins,J.C.23 to Margaret A.Ledford 24	4-30-1878	J.H.Addington,J.P
Hodgins,Wm.L.56 to Margaret Jones 43	11-23-1890	Wm.C.Kimzey,J.P.
Hodgins,J.S.19 to Martha J.Bird 18	12-16-1894	Geo.R.McPherson,JP.
Hodgins,Wm.M.19 to Mary E.Bird 18	3-21-1896	J.M.Carpenter,J.P
Hodgins,Chas.D.19 to Leona Bird 15	10-25-1896	J.M.Carpenter,J.P
Hodgins,Geo.T.17 to Carry Hopkins 19	2-21-1901	Robert Stamey,J.P
Hodgins,W.M.24 to Nettie Parker 20	6-13-1905	Robert Stamey,J.P
Hodgins,Edward 19 to Flora McClure 17	9-13-1911	Robert Stamey,J.P
Hodgins,C.R.21 to Alice Drake 18	11-14-1915	D.F.Howard,J.P.
Hodgin,Wm.18 to Nannie Ledford 18	5-18-1919	Robert Stamey,J.P
Hodgin,Edd 24 to Arlee Tallent 18	1-24-1928	Geo.Carpenter,J.P
Hogan,John to Elizabeth Holt	2-21-1834	John Tatham,Clk.
Hogshead,George 22 to Julia L.Slagle 25	11-23-1875	A.J.Morrison,M.G.
Hogue,John to Caroline Rich	6-16-1837	U.Keener,Clk.
Hoilman,Joseph 22 to Tinnie Byrd 22	1- 8-1899	Ira Erwin,M.G.
Hoilman,Dwight 29 to Edna Clark 24	9-26-1936	J.H.Fleming,J.P.
Holbrooks,William to Catharine Setser	12-6-1836	Ul.Keener,Clk.
Holbrooks,A. to Sarah Bryson	8-31-1865	R.C.Slagle,Clk.
Holbrooks,Larkin S.to Sary A.Moore	12-22-1866	R.C.Slagle,C.C.C.
Holbrooks,W.P.20 to Sarah Roper 18	7-11-1880	P.C.Wild,J.P.
Holbrooks,Henry 21 to Mary E.Hughes 22	12-6-1881	John S.Gibson,J.P
Holbrooks,Ezra 30 to W.D.Jacobson 23	6-17-1883	Jas.E.Fogartie,MG
Holbrooks,Ira L.20 to Nannie Fulcher 17	11-6-1887	J.E.Morgan,M.G.
Holbrooks,Jonah 20 to Della Robbins 20	12-27-1891	W.C.Mason,M.G.
Holbrooks,Moses 20 to Amanda Mason 17	8-27-1893	W.C.Mason,M.G.
Holbrooks,James H.20 to Julia Mason 16	3-17-1895	W.C.Mason,M.G.
Holbrooks,Jerry M.20 to Arie Mason 19	8- 3-1895	W.R.Rickman,M.G.
Holbrooks,Wm.T.24 to Eva A.Higdon 21	12-14-1895	Original not found
Holbrooks,A.H.67 to Artie Waldroop 35	8- 8-1897	Joseph Morgan,J.P
Holbrooks,William 24 to Cathaline Shepherd 24/	1-16-1901-	John Shepherd,JP
Holbrooks,J.R.25 to Pearl Gibson 19	12-20-1903	John H.Moore,M.G.
Holbrooks,Wm.F.37 to Eva A.Higdon 34	1-29-1908	F.M.Morgan,M.G.
Holbrooks,John Jr.22 to Bell Rowland 19	2-19-1910	Joseph L.Fouts,JP
Holbrooks,F.H.27 to Nina Dalton 17	8-17-1917	W.W.Marr,M.G.
Holbrooks,W.M.22 to Texie Morgan 22	7- 5-1920	L.B.Hayes,M.G.
Holbrooks,J.S.19 to Berdie Icenhower 18	1-16-1921	J.L.Fouts,J.P.
Holden,Madison J.24 to H.Josephine Anderson 22/	3-27-1887-	M.B.Setser,J.P.
Holden,Robt.H.23 to Fannie E.Anderson 15	9- 8-1892	W.C.Kimzey,J.P.

```
Holden,J.R.18 to Emeline Wilson 24           7- 2-1900  W.C.Mason,M.G.
Holden,H.F.17 to Rachel Mason21              10-20-1901 L.I.Mashburn,M.G.
Holden,M.J.47 to M.C.Jones 28                11-2-1901  W.P.Allison,J.P.
Holden,Isaac T.18 to Clara McMahan 15        7-16-1905  W.C.Mason,M.G.
Holden,Arthur H.22 to Ella B.Fisher 18 Col.  9- 6-1906  J.T.Kennedy,M.G.
Holden,Wm.F.35 to Ellen Burnett 23           3- 9-1913  E.P.Brown,J.P.
Holden,Coburn 22 to Beulah McCoy 24          2-10-1935  A.S.Solesbee,M.G.
Holland,Benjamin to Phebe Burrell            12-12-1844 J.K.Gray,Clk.
Holland,Anthony to Elizabeth Corbin          8- 6-1846  J.K.Gray,Clk.
Holland,W.M. to Nancy C.Burnes               11-13-1850 J.K.Gray,Clk.
Holland,James to Mary Rogers                 1- 1-1854  James Rogers,Wit.
Holland,David G.to Sarah Gregory             9-25-1860  R.C.Slagle,Clk.
Holland,Bright to Martha Wilson              1-22-1868  R.C.Slagle,C.C.C.
Holland,Marvin 26 to Laura A.Wood 14         1-23-1876  I.N.Keener,J.P.
Holland,James H.22 to Addie Dills 17         9- 6-1884  J.M.Keener,J.P.
Holland,W.S.20 to Mary C.Crisp 21            3-31-1889  J.M.Keener,J.P.
Holland,Anthony 64 to Martha Elmore 60       12-15-1889 J.B.Elmore,J.P.
Holland,William J.29 to Martha E.Rogers 24   2-19-1892  Henry Stewart,J.P
Holland,Perry G.20 to Hulda J.Houston 20     1- 1-1893  J.W.Keener,M.G.
Holland,Lee H.40 to Harriett Justice 35      1- 5-1893  J.M.Keener,M.G.
Holland,Soloman 20 to Emma Prater 17         4-10-1895  Napolen R.Rush,JP
Holland,W.M.23 to T.L.McCoy 18               12-1-1897  I.T.Peek,M.G.
Holland,Radford 21 to Bessie McCoy 16        3- 3-1898  Retd.not executed
Holland,R.L.22 to Jennie Crisp 17            12-17-1898 Retd.not executed
Holland,Radford 22 to Bessie McCoy 18        7-16-1899  I.T.Peek,M.G.
Holland,T.Luther 23 to Octa Tilson 15        10-15-1905 T.J.Vinson,M.G.
Holland,Frank 21 to Carrie Watkins 21        4-28-1907  T.J.Vinson,M.G.
Holland,Tillman 21 to Mattie Tilson 14       7-14-1907  T.J.Vinson,M.G.
Holland,J.M.25 to Hettie Dills 14            8-11-1907  I.T.Peek,M.G.
Holland,Girlie 20 Temperance Moore 20        12-22-1907 T.J.Vinson,M.G.
Holland,Benjamin 21 to Lula Russell 18       10-2-1914  T.C.Vinson,J.P.
Holland,Harlie 21 to Zelmer Estes 18         11-27-1915 O.W.Wells,J.P.
Holland,John 29 to Minnie Tippett 20         8-19-1917  J.B.Henry,J.P.
Holland,James 24 to Nettie Dills 15          5-19-1918  O.C.Corbin,J.P.
Holland,L.L.22 to Emma Teem 18               2- 1-1919  N.L.Jolley,J.P.
Holland,R.L.20 to Pearl Shook 19             9-17-1920  Geo.Carpenter,J.P
Holland,Cecil 22 to Leona Higdon 16          12-25-1927 W.T.Tilson,J.P.
Holland,M.Troy 25 to Margie Fox 20           11-21-1935 Geo.Carpenter,J.P
Holt,Andrew to Elizabeth Baloo               12-29-1852 Samuel Justice.
Holt,John M.21 to Margaret McCall 20         6- 4-1903  J.D.Vinson,M.G.
Holt,George 21 to Margaret Green 19          12-31-1905 J.E.Cabe,J.P.
Holt,Marvin 21 to Fannie Cabe 29             10-16-1910 P.C.Calloway,J.P.
Huneycutt,Leonard 21 to Addie Williams 21    4-15-1906  James M.Corbin,J.P
Hood,William to Elizabeth Moore              3-21-1833  John Hall,Clk.
Hood,Iseral P.to Ann Mashburn                10-24-1835 John Tatham,Clk.
Hood,James N.27 to Anna C.Siler 22           3-12-1879  D.Athins,M.G.
Howell,John D.to Ann Setser                  4-27-1838  Henry I.Garrison.
```

Howell,A.R.41 to Sarah Adams 41   12-25-1878 John T.Berry,J.P.
Howell,Henry 45 to Elizabeth McDonnall 35 Col.12-25-1881-F.Poindexter,JP
Howell,E.W.21 to Elizabeth Dowdle 26   5-10-1902 C.W.Dowdle,J.P.
Howell,John 25 to Eva Gudger 23   Col. 9-22-1907 A.B.Morrow,M.G.
Howell,Denver 22 to Sallie McCracken 24   9- 2-1923 R.E.Ward,M.G.
Howell,Harry 23 to Zelma Jaynes 21   12-13-1829 Walter M.Lee,M.G.
  Both from Waynesville,N.C.
Howell,Luke 71 to Mamie Angel 49   5- 8-1930 J.R.Pendergrass,MG
Howard,Lafayete to Mary L.Wikle   12-8-1848 J.K.Gray,Clk.
Howard,Noah I.to Mary Jenkins   11-3-1855 John Hall,Clk.
Howard,P.21 to L.A.Norton 38   8-22-1878 Geo.A.Maiden,M.G.
Howard,Geo.E.23 to M.J.Garrison 21   12-12-1878 M.Ghomley,M.G.
Howard,D.F.22 to Sarah Barnes 18   3- 3-1881 E.B.Padgett,J.P.
Howard,George 24 to Nancy A.Hemphill 18 2- 4-1883 L.Howard,J.P.
Howard,William 22 to Sarah C.Cabe 17   3-12-1885 L.H.Garland,J.P.
Howard,Alexander 22 to Hulda Womack 19 7-20-1885 Original not found
Howard,Nicholas F.24 to Miranda R.Bradshaw 18/8-7-1890 W.G.Mallonee,M.G.
Howard,W.Sylvanus 20 to M.E.Kilpatrick 19 1- 1-1891 M.Ghormley,M.G.
Howard,Virgil 33 to Anna Curtis 15   1-24-1895 W.A.Norton,J.P.
Howard,Robert 22 to Cordelia Norton 20   7- 1-1895 Retd.not executed
Howard,Samuel 25 to Alma S.Cabe 20   11-1-1895 W.A.Norton,J.P.
Howard,Wm.A.20 to Bellzora Neal 17   10-24-1897 H.H.Hyde,M.G.
Howard,Robert L.27 to Cordelia Norton 25 8-26-1900 Jack Forester,J.P.
Howard,W.W.21 to Annie Neal 15   3-31-1904 A.H.Gregory,J.P.
Howard,Larence 21 to Ada Painter 20   3- 4-1907 W.R.Bulgin,J.P.
Howard,Marvin 21 to Emma Dills 21   12-25-1910 C.R.Cabe,J.P.
Howard,Alex 30 to Blanche Vinson 29   12-28-1937 A.A.Angel,M.G.
Howard,Carl 38 to Lola Ramsey 28   5-26-1940 C.F.Rogers,M.G.
Hooper,Andrew to Sarah Woodring   10-14-1837 J.K.Gray,Clk.
Hooper,L.C. to Sarah Watson   11- 4-1837 H.C.Wilson,Wit.
Hooper,Wm. to Margarette Carroll   3-17-1847 J.K.Gray,Clk.
Hooper,James M.to Margaret M.Rogers   12-3-1850 T.P.Siler,Wit.
Hooper,Thos.J.to Sophia Ann Willson   10-16-1855 Joshua Ammons,M.G
Hooper,B.H.21 to Viney Williams 18   9- 5-1897 J.W.Parker,J.P.
Hooper,M.M.31 to Fannie Henderson 20   1-30-1901 John H.Moore,M.G.
Hooper,Edward 23 to Lassie McDowell 21 1-13-1909 A.P.Foster,M.G.
Hooper,Joseph 24 to Alice Martin 18   12-14-1913 D.F.Howard,M.G.
Hope,Radford 26 to Helen A.Bathuck 20   8-26-1879 H.M.Thompson,M.G.
Hopkins,Samuel T.to Jane Lewis   4-22-1857 J.P.Angel,Wit.
Hopkins,John to Mary Guffee   3-15-1859 R.C.Slagle,Clk.
Hopkins,Sam L.to Jane Liner   4-22-1859 J.P.Angel,Wit.
Hopkins,James to Louisa Burch   2- 9-1860 Jacob Siler,J.P.
Hopkins,William E.22 to Elizabeth Anderson 18/10-18-1880-Albert Siler,JP
Hopkins,William 38 to Lillie D.Woods 26 4-11-1897 H.H.Dills,J.P.
Hopkins,W.R.38 to Callie McClure 24   9-25-1898 W.A.Norton,J.P.
Hopkins,Ellis 19 to Blanche Watts 18   12-23-1915 G.A.Cloer,J.P.
Hopkins,S.O.31 to Mattie Sorrells 19   10-28-1917 A.M.Ledford,M.G.

```
Hopkins,Ellis 24 to Mary Davis 19              9-10-1919  Geo.Cloer,M.G.
Hopkins,Raleigh 23 to Alma Carpenter 20        1- 4-1920  Jesse Ballew,J.P.
Hopkins,F.Ray 23 to Mae Cloe 23                3-11-1933  J.R.Pendergrass,MG
Hopper,Andrew to Sarah Woodring                10-14-1837 J.K.Gray,Clk.
Hopper,William 23 to Elizabeth J.Long 22       1- 9-1876  E.J.Long,J.P.
Hopper,Jasper 50 to Harriett A.Dryman 40       1- 7-1883  E.T.Long,J.P.
Hopper,Geo.29 to Evelyn E.Cleveland 27         11-26-1933 W.A.Reid,M.G.
Hopper,Joseph 24 to Alice Martin 18            12-14-1913 D.F.Howard,M.G.
Horn,Wm.to C.M.S.Mashburn                      8- 9-1860  R.C.Slagle,Clk.
Horn,Edward F.27 to Nancy M.Fulton 21          1-21-1892  John B.Gray,J.P.
Horn,Alfred W.24 to Ida L.Barnard 19           2- 1-1893  J.P.Campbell,J.P.
Horn,Leonard 31 to Leota McCracken 23          2- 9-1930  H.C.Freeman,M.G.
Horsley,James W.22 to Lasca Evans 20           7- 9-1938  J.A.Flanagan,M.G.
Horton,David 24 to Martha McDonnell 23         11-16-1882 Geo.D.French,M.G.
Houk,G.L. 29 to Lynn Johnston 33               6- 8-1924  R.H.Dougherty,M.G
Houston,Alexander to Dicy R.Gregory            12-26-1871 J.D.Vinson,M.G.
Houston,Geo.I.22 to May Frady 16               9-30-1876  W.W.Henry,J.P.
Houston,Calvin 24 to E.Caroline Gregory 17 /2-17-1878  J.M.Keener,J.P.
Houston,J.W.22 to Ann Holbrooks 19             3-30-1884  John Elmore,J.P.
Houston,Richard H.51 to Nebraska Vaughn 31     8-28-1887  M.B.Dockery,J.P.
Houston,George W.21 to Mary M.Miller 18        5- 7-1890  Retd.not executed
Houston,Emulus G.20 to Lula McCoy 22           3-18-1894  J.L.Corbin,J.P.
Houston,R.Hensley 58 to M.J.Vinson 27          7-10-1894  J.L.Corbin,J.P.
Houston,Chas.P.22 to Ella Vaughn 19            1-28-1895  Original not found
Houston,J.Thomas 27 to Sallie Ammons 27        3- 7-1895  G.A.Bartlett,M.G.
Houston,Monroe 23 to Vina Ingram 20            3-11-1896  J.M.Keener,M.G.
Houston,Floyd 34 to Alva Allen 29              3-31-1898  J.R.Pendergrass,MG
Houston,Isaac 23 to Mollie Brown 17            3-24-1901  S.C.Conley,J.P.
Houston,Mel 23 to L.B.Ballew 19                1-26-1902  G.W.Stiwinter,J.P
Houston,Robert H.19 to Mattie Calloway 18      3-22-1905  Henry Stewart,Jr.
Houston,E.G.36 to Emma McCoy 26                8-14-1910  J.M.Keener,M.G.
Houston,Calvin C.56 to Lydia McCoy 36          10-12-1913 Frank Peek,J.P.
Houston,Floyd 23 to Belle Franks 18            12-21-1913 A.B.Miller,J.P.
Houston,W.A.28 to Lela Bolick 17               7- 4-1919  Geo.Carpenter,J.P
Houston,G.G.30 to Dovie Southards 18           9-21-1919  O.C.Corbin,J.P.
Houston,Grady 21 to Inez Parrish 20            5-27-1921  Geo.Carpenter,J.P
Houston,Charlie I.23 to Margaret G.Keener 19/12-24-1935-H.L.Valentine,JP
Houston,Don 21 to Mary Rogers 18               3-11-1937  Geo.Carpenter,J.P
Hughston,John W. to L.M.Miller                 12-5-1860  R.C.Slagle,Clk.
Hubbard,J.G.25 to S.S.Anderson 16              3- 3-1914  W.E.Welch,J.P.
Hubbard,Lewis MacBride 80 to Ethel Howell Kirkley 65/3-25-1941 A.Morgan,M.
     Both from Asheville,N.C.
Huckaby,John to Mary A.McCall                  9- 8-1856  W.Picklesimer,Wit.
Hudson,Arthur S.23 to Blanche Addington 19     1-25-1910  Chas.L.Stewart,MG
Hudson,Mike 23 to Ethie Hancock 20             4- 1-1933  Sam J.Murray,J.P.
     Both from Atlanta,Ga.
Hudspeth,Leonard R.18 to Mellie Anderson 16/1-25-1936  R.F.Anderson,J.P.
```

Huggins,John H.to Susan R.Carson	9-23-1845	J.K.Gray,Clk.
Huggins,John to Frances C.Lackey	9- 2-1849	J.R.Siler,J.P.
Huggins,James 29 to Margaret C.Davis 17	8-14-1887	D.A.Yonce,J.P.
Huggins,J.W.67 to Elizabeth Cabe 39	10-26-1892	W.G.Mallonee,M.G.
Huggins,E.A.36 to Eliza Wishon 19	6-30-1898	F.M.Morgan,M.G.
Huggins,W.A.35 to Ethel Welch 30	7-14-1917	J.L.Fouts,J.P.
Hughes,George to Mary Poindexter	5-30-1832	----------
Hughes,Jackson to Elizabeth Thomas	4-15-1835	Dillard Love,Wit.
Hughes,James W.to Rebecca Ensley	10-21-1836	R.Morgan,Wit.
Hughes,Gilbert to Louisa J.Mason	8-17-1852	T.P.Siler,D.Clk.
Hughes,William P.22 to L.M.Lindsay 21	5-13-1877	Thos.Mashburn,J.P
Hughes,G.D.46 to E.A.Morgan 34	9- 2-1877	A.A.Justice,M.G.
Hughes,B.M.23 to Sarah Cloer 20	10-28-1882	J.P.Painter,Elder
Hughes,Andrew H.24 to Alice F.Ramey 22	2- 1-1888	M.J.Mashburn,J.P.
Hughes,Heab 21 to Bessie Stepp 18	3-22-1903	D.F.Howard,M.G.
Hughes,W.V.21 to Addie Totherow 21	6-11-1905	D.F.Howard,M.G.
Hughes,Ed.T.19 to Ida Welch 18	3-27-1906	Retd.not executed
Hughes,Ed. 21 to Mary Ann Pickens 19	11-17-1907	W.L.Bradley,M.G.
Hughes,Rev.W.I.39 to Mary Ann Dowdle 22	9- 6-1910	J.E.Gay,M.G.
Hughes,Frank 24 to Maud Blaine 17	12-20-1912	J.R.Pendergras,MG
Hughes,Walter M.27 to Myrtle M.Dean 18	3- 1-1918	W.L.Bradley,M.G.
Hughes,J.B.31 to Lillie Martin 18	5- 3-1918	J.R.Pendergrass,MG
Hughes,John E.24 to Cuba Houston 19	2- 3-1922	J.L.Fouts,J.P.
Hughes,Mack 22 to Lizzie Shields 18	10-24-1927	Geo.Carpenter,J.P
Hughes,Ralph 21 to Mae West 18	10-27-1933	Geo.W.Stepp,J.P.
Hughes,H.L.Grady 23 to Lonie Belle Ellison 19/9-2-1934		D.F.Howard,M.G.
Hughes,Robert 22 to Julie Lee 18	3-20-1937	Geo.W.Stepp,J.P.
Hughston,John W.to L.M.Miller	12-5-1860	R.C.Slagle,Clk.
Huneycutt,Josiah 21 to Minnie Rogers 21	1-15-1900	E.J.Dalrymple,J.P
Hunt,T.R.30 to Effie Neely 20	12-30-1919	W.T.Potts,M.G.
Hunt,J.B. to Isabella Brazeal	12-20-1835	John Tatham,Clk.
Hunter,Jason H.to E.S.Sherrill	7-17-1843	J.K.Gray,Clk.
Hunter,Mitchel 27 to Maggie Holden 25 Col.	12-20-1900	G.W.Washington.
Hunter,Nicholas A.38 to Pearl Dowdle 19	1- 1-1907	L.P.Bogal,M.G.
Humphreys,William 22 to Mary J.Gregory 21	8-30-1888	J.M.Keener,J.P.
Humphrey,Chas.G.18 to Zadie Anderson 19	11-17-1895	S.J.May,J.P.
Humphrey,J.H.18 to Lizzie Rogers 17	12-5-1897	W.T.Long,J.P.
Humphrey,George 21 to Louella Anderson 18	11-27-1904	W.A.Solesbee,J.P.
Humphrey,John D.37 to Bertha Binkley 20	11-15-1911	J.E.Gray,M.G.
Humphrey,Glenn 22 to Maggie Bryson 18	9-14-1921	D.F.Howard,M.G.
Hurst,William to Judeth Ann Morrow	12-11-1851	J.K.Gray,Clk.
Hurst,Madison to Rebecca Ammons	12-18-1854	I.N.Keener,J.P.
Hurst,G.N.to Angeline Dalton	11-25-1866	R.C.Slagle,C.C.C.
Hurst,William T.20 to Nancy Beasley 16	12-26-1875	Samuel Gibson,M.G
Hurst,B.J.19 to Eliza Ann Grant 18	1-20-1881	M.J.Mashburn,M.G.
Hurst,James E.27 to Elizabeth I.Ramsey 26	9- 6-1883	S.H.Harrington,MG
Hurst,John A.24 to Mary A.Dalton 26	8- 9-1891	P.R.Rickman,M.G.

```
Hurst,Geo.B.25 to Lula Shepherd 17              11-18-1895  P.R.Rickman,M.G.
Hurst,G.J.22 to Hattie Wilson 21                1-22-1900   J.B.Elmore,J.P.
Hurst,Emlis 25 to Dolly Shepherd 27             3- 8-1903   P.R.Rickman,M.G.
Hurst,J.M.23 to Elsie Cardon 19                 12-23-1906  P.R.Rickman,M.G.
Hurst,Jesse C.28 to Bell Beasley 19             4- 1-1908   M.L.Rickman,J.P.
Hurst,B.Judson 28 to Lillian M.Jenkins 19       9-10-1908   M.L.Rickman,J.P.
Hurst,Albert T.25 to Nellie Raby 18             8-14-1910   C.T.King,M.G.
Hurst,Horace J.24 to Ella M.Miller 25           12-24-1911  J.R.Pendergras,MG
Hurst,Geo.Bascomb 39 to Arie Tippett 22         1- 7-1912   M.J.Mashburn,J.P.
Hurst,John C.29 to Mary Jenkins 26              4- 3-1912   M.H.Tuttle,M.G.
Hurst,Horace C.27 to Mary Lou Gray 25           3- 4-1914   A.W.Jacobs,M.G.
Hurst,J.D.22 to Ella Allen 22                   2-29-1920   J.L.Bryson,J.P.
Hurst,Chas.T.23 to Maude Evans 18               8- 8-1928   J.R.Pendergrass,MG
Husscusson,Wm.Taylor 20 to Ola Love 18          7-27-1893   W.C.Kimsey,J.P.
Husscusson,John 22 to Mary M.Greenwood 17       3- 2-1899   W.A.Setser,J.P.
Husscusson,B.H.23 to M.J.Anderson 21            7-31-1902   Jas.N.McConnell,J.P
Husscusson,Harley 19 to Vana Anderson 20        2-22-1907   C.A.Setser,J.P.
Huskey,Cecil G.21 to Martha R.Stribbling 21/3-20-1937  W.B.Underwood,M.G
    He from Spartinburg,S.C... She from Asheville,N.C.
Huston,Hensley  to Martha Gregory               11-1-1859   R.C.Slagle,D.Clk.
Huston,James R.to Mary C.Gregory                12-8-1870   William Sloan,Reg
Huston,James C.18 to Sallie E.Gregory 18        9-13-1888   J.M.Keener,J.P.
Huston,Elbert I.22 to Cincinnati Buchanan 19/10-27-1889-J.P.Yarborough.
Hutson,Thos. 21 to Lou McDonnell 18             3-13-1880   H.G.Woodfin,J.P.
Hutson,J.H.29 to Cora Dills 24                  8-17-1917   W.W.Marr,M.G.
Hyatt,John to Margaret Johnston                 12-17-1842  James Witherow.
Hyatt,Shadrick to Jane Garrett                  10-28-1848  J.K.Gray,D.Clk.
Hyatt,S.H.to E.A.Wikle                          1- 8-1860   C.D.Smith,M.G.
Hyatt,Filetes 19 to Zettee Gray 16     Col.     8-24-1882   F.Poindexter,M.G.
Hyatt,Robert B.25 to Ada C.Shope 22             8- 5-1896   J.R.Pendergras,MG
Hyatt,Early M.22 to Birdie L.Johnson 20         8-24-1923   J.L.Kinsland,M.G.
Hyatt,Early M.25 to Bonnie Brooks 19            2-15-1927   J.M.Raby,J.P.
Hyatt,Edgar 20 to Mattie Coggins 18             8-12-1933   Geo.Carpenter,J.P
Hyde,William to Elizabeth Kirkland              12-22-1847  J.K.Gray,Clk.
Hyde,John B.to Jane Nickles                     1- 6-1848   J.K.Gray,Clk.
Hyde,David to Margaret Crisp                    4-16-1858   A.B.Welch,J.P.
Hyde,Perley 21 to Nettie Cruse 22               12-22-1928  Geo.Carpenter,J.P
    He from Bryson City,N.C.
Hylton,N.J.31 to Mrs.Minnie Rowland 31          10-22-1913  D.F.Howard,M.G.
Icenhower,Loyd 21 to Lucella Holbrooks 19       12-23-1914  J.H.Lakey,J.P.
Icenhower,J.C.57 to Artie Shepherd 47           10-13-1927  W.L.Bradley,M.G.
Inman,L.L.28 to Flora Green 20                  3-24-1907   J.R.Pendergrass,MG
Ingram,John to Martha Moore                     8-26-1847   E.Dowdle.
Ingram,John to L.M. Downes                      11-11-1854  L.F.Siler.
Ivan,John to Elizabeth Garland                  1-21-1836   Paul Smith.
Ivester,Julius P.26 to Martha Forrester 18      5-14-1889   W.C.Mason,M.G.
Ivester,Sidney J.18 to Callie Trammell 19       6-28-1900   E.N.Dalrymple,J.P
```

Name	Date	Officiant
Jackson,Andrew 33 to Eliza Clanton 19 Col.	10-3-1885	B.G.Wild,M.G.
Jackson,James S.19 to Hazel E.Brock 19 Both from Atlanta,Ga.	9- 4-1933	Geo.Carpenter,J.P.
Jackson,Oscar H.22 to Mildred E.Day 20	12-30-1936	Frank Bloxham,M.G.
Jacobs,John to Ceily Clampett	3-25-1856	John Hall,Clk.
Jacobs,W.B. to Jane Tallent	10-2-1856	John Hall,Clk.
Jacobs,B.P. to Margaret Stalkup	9-29-1865	E.A.Deweese,M.G.
Jacobs,David to Roxanna Russell	6-10-1869	R.C.Slagle,D.Clk.
Jacobs,Solomon 19 to Mary Russell 21	9- 9-1874	Thos.Mashburn,J.P.
Jacobs,J.T. 20 to Rachel Cunningham 19	12-13-1878	Thos.Mashburn,J.P.
Jacobs,A.W.27 to M.Louisa Gray 20	2-19-1880	G.A.Oglesby,M.G.
Jacobs,R.P.22 to Mary Cunningham 20	7-17-1881	M.J.Mashburn,J.P.
Jacobs,B.P.43 to Mary Fouts 25	8-10-1882	M.J.Mashburn,J.P.
Jacobs,Chas.T.25 to G.A.Reece 25	10-24-1885	Original not found
Jacobs,Jas.P.21 to Beuna Dalton 19	12-10-1885	Jno.S.Gibson,J.P.
Jacobs,Solomon 31 to Maggie Roper 25	2-17-1887	Jno.P.Campbell,JP
Jacobs,John M.50 to Martha M.Allen 32	9- 1-1887	M.J.Mashburn,J.P.
Jacobs,J.Logan 21 to Martha Deweese 23	5-24-1891	Jno.P.Campbell.
Jacobs,William A.27 to Judith A.Hurst 19	5-12-1895	G.A.Bartlett,M.G.
Jacobs,Chas.E.17 to Fannie C.Anderson 18	11-14-1896	R.P.Garrison,J.P.
Jacobs,C.S.20 to Lucy Morrison 22	9-21-1902	Ira Erwin,M.G.
Jacobs,David A.54 to Nannie Myers 21	3-29-1905	J.R.Ramsey,J.P.
Jacobs,Bird 21 to Mattie Palmer 19	3-16-1908	J.R.Pendergrass,MG
Jacobs,B.P.27 to Bell Tallent 27	6- 6-1916	Geo.Carpenter,J.P
Jacobs,Frank 21 to Mattie Snyder 20	9-28-1916	J.R.Pendergrass,MG
Jacobs,G.L.25 to Bessie Baldwin 18	1- 1-1917	J.L.Fouts,J.P.
Jacobs,A.T.38 to Lydia Buchanan 26	2- 4-1920	Geo.Carpenter,J.P
Jacobs,Sol 67 to Nannie Sanders 54	1-17-1923	Robert E.Ward,M.G
Jacobs,B.P.36 to Dora Ramsey 26 She from Almond,N.C.	3- 4-1927	Geo.Carpenter,J.P
James,Samuel to Mary Whitaker	2- 2-1833	Mikel Wikel,Wit.
James,Benjamin to Adaline Trusty	10-8-1864	R.C.Slagle,Reg.
James,Charles to Harriett Mashburn	1-16-1871	William Sloan,Reg
James,Andrew J.21 to Bettie Harrison 18	4-20-1886	Retd.not executed
James,John 21 to Callie Taylor 19	9-19-1899	John H.Dalton,J.P
James,Dank 20 to Mae Blakely 19	1- 1-1915	J.R.Pendergrass,MG
James,Lawton P.27 to Irene Picklesimer 24	10-11-1929	J.O.Nix,M.G.
Jameson,T.P.to Mary C.Conley	4-29-1852	H.G.Woodfin,D.Clk.
Jamison,Grover 26 to Mary E.Brown 31	6- 4-1911	J.R.Pendergrass,MG
Jamison,Carl 26 to Ida Mae Cabe 27	5-13-1923	J.Q.Wallace,M.G.
Jarrett,Daniel to Hannah Addington	10-29-1832	George McClure.
Jarrott,Devereaux to Elizabeth McClasky	7-13-1843	J.N.Siler.
Jarrett,John to Name not given	12-24-1853	John Hall,Clk.
Jarrett,Robt.F.28 to Sallie C.Wild 24	12-25-1892	G.A.Bartlett,M.G.
Jenkins,Jonas to Rachel Hyde	10-19-1840	John Hall,Clk.
Jenkins,Thomas to Elizabeth Cline	12-9-1845	Moris Mayfield.
Jenkins,Peter to Judian Brendle	3-20-1849	J.K.Gray,Clk.

69

Jenkins,Charley to May Nichles	5-18-1850	J.K.Gray,Clk.
Jenkins,John to Lucenda Watkins	5-18-1853	D.C.Newton,J.P.
Jenkins,John to Elizabeth Bain	3-16-1856	E.Collins,J.P.
Jenkins,F.M. to Rutha Hide	5- 5-1866	R.C.Slagle,C.C.C.
Jenkins,S.W.to Eliza Rose	5- 6-1866	R.C.Slagle,C.C.C.
Jenkins,Wm.J.23 to Beunavesta Allen 16	11-9-1876	P.P.McLeon,M.G.
Jenkins,Melvill 22 to Callie Bingham 21	7-29-1894	Geo.R.McPherson.
Jenkins,John 21 to Creasy Webb 18	9-13-1898	Original not found
Jenkins,Butler 19 to Jennie Webb 18	2- 4-1900	M.A.Russell,J.P.
Jenkins,J.Allen 19 to Sarah Webb 18	11-20-1903	Henry Stewart,Jr.
Jenkins,Lawson 20 to Clara McCall	9-10-1911	P.C.Calloway,J.P.
Jenkins,Thomas 21 to Betsey Webb 19	2- 3-1911	P.C.Calloway,J.P.
Jenkins,W.B.33 to Jennie Matlock 29	2-16-1911	J.F.Starnes,M.G.
Jenkins,George 24 to Rose Mozinsky 21	9- 1-1929	Geo.Carpenter,J.P
Jenkins,Silas 18 to Zelma Hedden 18	3-15-1934	W.G.Wood,J.P.
Jentry,John to Polly Jentry	4- 9-1864	R.C.Slagle,Reg.
Jennings,James J.to Polly L.Caylor	1-24-1842	J.K.Gray,Clk.
Jennings,John to Elizabeth A.Kilpatrick	1-18-1847	Harvy Stalcup,Wit
Jennins,James to Lucinda P.Evit	9-25-1849	J.K.Gray,Clk.
Jennings,James to Sarah Henderson	6-14-1861	J.Keener.
Jennings,J.J.22 to Louiza Mashburn 21	10-29-1874	J.D.Vinson,M.G.
Jennings,J.J.19 to Myra Mashburn 19	12-25-1882	J.B.Gray,J.P.
Jennings,Charles C.24 to Mary E.Horn 16	2-20-1887	Jno.B.Gray,J.P.
Jennings,John 20 to Love Angel 22	9- 2-1896	N.J.Rush,J.P.
Jennings,E.C.26 to Ethel Ammons 16	11-19-1923	J.M.Keener,M.G.
Jennings,Elmer 21 to Imogene Stiwinter 18	5-13-1937	Ennis R.Tilson,JP
Jennings,V.V.21 to Ollie M.Allen 24	7-18-1916	J.L.Bryson,J.P.
Jerome,Robert L.34 to Jean Porter 24 He from Burlington,N.C.	11-4-1935	C.P.Jerome,M.G.
Johnson,John to Loas Grigg	9-24-1836	Felix Axley.
Johnson,Jacob L.to Margaret Huggins	7-11-1840	H.G.Woodfin,D.Clk
Johnson,William 22 to Mary E.Angel 26	11-13-1887	John Elmore,J.P.
Johnson,Alfred A.31 to Mary Clark 25	8- 3-1890	J.W.Parker,J.P.
Johnson,John 25 to Hattie Rowland 18	10-25-1894	T.M.Slagle,J.P.
Johnson,T.B.32 to Mary V.Conley 22	3- 4-1897	T.E.Wagg,M.G.
Johnson,Geo.M.22 to Maggie J.Dalrymple 18	11-18-1897	M.B.Setser,J.P.
Johnson,Homer D.22 to Bessie R.McConnell 22/	1-15-1907	F.L.Townsend,M.G.
Johnson,Wm.S.28 to Maye McConnell 25	11-11-1908	F.L.Townsend,M.G.
Johnson,L.H.18 to Mary Nix 18	10-23-1911	N.P.Alexander,M.G
Johnson,Luther 22 to Missouri Talley 21	10-29-1911	P.C.Calloway,J.P.
Johnson,E.L.21 to Eugenia M.Landrum 20	9-22-1913	D.P.Waters,M.G.
Johnson,Elmer 25 to Bessie Smart 21	3-15-1914	J.L.Teague,M.G.
Johnson,W.I.23 to Latha McCall 22	11-7-1915	W.P.Wilson,J.P.
Johnson,James Riley 19 to Ivey Webb 21	6-25-1916	W.T.Thompson,M.G.
Johnson,John 30 to Lillie Mason 30	9- 1-1917	W.R.Lunsford,M.G.
Johnson,Thomas H.27 to Rhoda Jacobs 25	10-25-1918	J.R.Pendergras,MG
Johnson,P.N.30 to Hattie Huggins 18	11- 6-1918	J.L.Fouts,J.P.

```
Johnson,S.M.23 to Mary Will Ritchie 20 Col. 12-24-1919 Geo.Carpenter,J.P
Johnson,L.J.24 to Bertha Morgan 19           9-12-1923 Geo.Carpenter,J.P
Johnson,Homer D.33 to Grace E.Moore 25      11-20-1927 J.L.Teague,M.G.
Johnson,Clyde 23 to Margie Roper 18          3-25-1929 Geo.Carpenter,J.P
  He from Hiawasea,Ga.
Johnson,G.Frank 23 to May Carpenter 23       9- 2-1929 Walter M.Lee,M.G.
Johnson,Claude 21 to Dollie Pendergrass 23  10-26-1929 Geo.Carpenter,J.P
Johnson,Willard 19 to Nina Duvall 16         4-24-1937 Geo.Stepp,J.P.
Johnson,James C.26 to Nellie Henry 20       10-22-1938 J.O.Nix,M.G.
Johnston,Henry H.to Sarah McDowle            8- 3-1832 John Hall,Clk.
Johnston,Benjamin to Name not given          2- 7-1833 John Hall,Cl.
Johnston,Jackson to Eugenia Siler            3-23-1859 R.C.Slagle,Reg.
Johnston,Chas.D.37 to Letty Conley 31  Col. 5-12-1878 F.Poindexter,J.P.
Johnston,H.C.C.21 to H.M.J.Moore 16    Col. 4- 3-1880 E.H.Franks,J.P.
Johnston,Harvey 22 to Anna Stonesipher 22 Col.2-4-1881 ------------
Johnston,Reid 22 to Minda Stonecipher 22 Col.10-26-1882 J.E.Kilgore,M.G.
Johnston,Reid 24 to Amanda Shaver 18   Col. 12-24-1884 Jas.M.Bristol,M.G
Johnston,James H.28 to Sela H.L.Fuller 16 Col.11-3-1886 J.M.Bristol,M.G.
Johnston,Allen 23 to Mary Baxter 19    Col. 12-13-1888 M.J.Mashburn,J.P.
Johnston,Thos.J.28 to Mary Ethelwyn Deal    12-9-1903 J.A.Deal,M.G.
Johnston,John L.20 to Minnie Yonce 18        4-21-1906 W.A.Solesbee,J.P.
Johnston,Roe 23 to Clara Justice 21          6-16-1907 J.D.Vinson,M.G.
Johnston,Grover 18 to Oliva Lowery 18        10-6-1907 L.I.Mashburn,M.G.
Johnston,James L.28 to Elizabeth W.Deal 23  11-25-1908 J.A.Deal,M.G.
Johnston,Thos.Jr.21 to C.Ann Cunningham 23  12-23-1928 Robt.F.Mock,M.G.
Jollay,John G.21 to R.C.Holbrooks 18        12-5-1885 J.M.Keener,J.P.
Jolly,Marshall A.23 to Cornelia Cabe 32     12-2-1894 Jno.L.Corbin,J.P.
Jolly,Noah 28 to Miss Addie Bryson 20       11-24-1901 John W.Briggs,M.G
Jollay,Lyman 26 to Selma Young 26            6- 7-1933 V.C.Ramey,M.G.
Jones,William to Mary Jones                  9- 6-1838 John Hall,Clk.
Jones,Henderson to Mahala Ashe               3- 9-1841 John Hall,Clk.
Jones,H. to Mary Buchanan                    2-24-1842 J.K.Gray,Clk.
Jones,E.J.to Elizabeth Norton               10-26-1842 J.K.Gray,Clk.
Jones,John G.to Mira Ashe                    3-10-1846 J.K.Gray,Clk.
Jones,Richard to Nancy Higden                3-17-1847 J.K.Gray,Clk.
Jones,Joseph D.to Mary McGee                 3-16-1848 J.K.Gray,Clk.
Jones,Leanard to Mary M.Green                8-25-1851 J.K.Gray,Clk.
Jones,Stephen D.to Dicy Cabe                12-28-1854 L.F.Siler,J.P.
Jones,Joshua to Emeline Waldroop             8-21-1855 Jno.F.Mashburn,JP
Jones,Elias to Elizabeth Hicks               8-21-1858 R.C.Slagle,Clk.
Jones,Stephen to Sarah T.Cabe                2-11-1861 R.C.Slagle,Clk.
Jones,H.C.to Margaret Demosey               12-28-1861 W.A.Trotter,D.Clk
Jones,T.J.to D.C.Wilson                     12-15-1862 Martin DeHart,J.P
Jones,J.M.to H.L.Saunders                   11-23-1865 R.C.Slagle,C.C.C.
Jones,Rufus to Ruth Ann Linsey               4-25-1870 J.K.Bryson,Reg.
Jones,Wilson Taylor to Rachel R.Ledford     12-15-1870 Wm.Sloan,Reg.
Jones,John S.23 to Susanah Ray 23            2-14-1875 Z.Barnes,J.P.
```

Jones,William to Rachel Carel	10-18-1836	Samuel Carrol,Wit
Jones,John W.19 to Delia Stamey 19	6-10-1875	Albert Siler,J.P.
Jones,Samuel 31 to Sarah J.Burgess 23	7-17-1875	Albert Siler,J.P.
Jones,Marcus 21 to Martha J.Mason 20	7-25-1875	Thomas Mashburn.
Jones,Nichols W.22 to Martha M.Guffee 18	2-11-1875	Albert Siler,J.P.
Jones,Thomas C.21 to Sarah M.Stamey 21	10-21-1875	Jno.H.Addington.
Jones,William R.18 to L.A.Baty 17	12-9-1875	Wm.Deweese,M.G.
Jones,Geo.A.26 to Lilly E.Lyle 22	12-29-1875	L.K.Haynes,M.G.
Jones,M.W.21 to Mary A.Oliver 24	3- 9-1876	J.H.Addington,J.P
Jones,L.E.24 to M.A.Peek 27	2- 3-1880	J.M.Keener,J.P.
Jones,Thomas 22 to Sallie Gregory 21	10-8-1884	John D.Howard,J.P
Jones,James 22 to Hetta Baldwin 18	11-25-1880	E.B.Padget,J.P.
Jones,S.J.20 to E.Elizabeth Ammons 29	11-30-1884	Hosea Moses,J.P.
Jones,H.F.22 to C.D.Brown 18	12-18-1884	M.L.Kelly,J.P.
Jones,William 21 to Ellen Gibson 18	10-25-1885	Jno.B.Gray,J.P.
Jones,Alfred L.to Ella Wikle 21 Col.	2- 2-1888	John Reid,J.P.
Jones,W.H.21 to Martha D.Saunders 18	2-18-1888	J.P.Yarborough,M.G
Jones,Wm.L.29 to Martha Moore 22	11-13-1888	Hosea Moses,J.P.
Jones,A.Jackson 24 to Lou Rany Bell May 17	1-28-1889	H.B.Cook,M.G.
Jones,Martin F.50 to Lydia J.Henry 22	10-31-1889	J.E.Moore,M.G.
Jones,John F.20 to Kittie Baldwin 18	12-14-1890	John Allison,J.P.
Jones,James A.21 to Mary L.Martin 19	2- 8-1891	M.Ghormley,M.G.
Jones,Fenton 22 to Mary C.Burnett 19	10-5-1891	J.S.Woodard,M.G.
Jones,Riley 46 to Mary J.Raby 25	8-22-1894	Original not found
Jones,George A.45 to Hattie B.Sloan 32	1-31-1895	D.F.Carver,M.G.
Jones,Joseph D.65 to Mrs.Elizabeth Huggins 43/	5-26-1896-	J.M.Keener,M.G.
Jones,Larkin 22 to L.A.Franklin 25	1-23-1898	Henry Stewart,J.P
Jones,John W.23 to Etta May 19	12-18-1898	S.J.May,J.P.
Jones,Benjamine 32 to Nancy E.Bowman 31	1-12-1899	W.W.Moss,J.P.
Jones,Thomas 21 to Lelia Ledford 20	3-18-1900	M.A.West,M.G.
Jones,Chas.A.22 to Rebecca Brown 38	2-24-1902	C.W.Dowdle,J.P.
Jones,W.M.21 to M.O.Saunders 21	10-23-1902	C.W.Dowdle,J.P.
Jones,Charley N.20 to Ella Keener 16	11-27-1902	G.W.Stiwinter,J.P
Jones,G.A.20 to Cara Morgan 19	3-22-1903	W.A.Solesbee,J.P.
Jones,James S.23 to Lena Bingham 19	9-24-1903	J.R.Pendergrass,MG
Jones,W.L.25 to Annie Duvall 19	12-18-1904	F.M.Morgan,M.G.
Jones,Virgil L.30 to Isabell Elias 26	6-20-1905	F.L.Townsend,M.G.
Jones,Zeb 18 to Lonie Anderson 18	1-13-1907	F.N.Johnson,J.P.
Jones,Joe 24 to Carie Donaldson 21	10-22-1908	J.C.Shope,J.P.
Jones,W.A.21 to Jane Houston 22	12-15-1908	J.M.Keener,M.G.
Jones,Lewis 21 to Hattie Davis 22	6-11-1910	N.P.Rankin,J.P.
Jones,Robert 22 to Hattie Mashburn 18	9-22-1912	Geo.Carpenter,J.P
Jones,Thos.S.24 to Damaris Blain 18	1-27-1913	W.H.Roane,J.P.
Jones,Charley 21 to Bardie Tippett 15	3-31-1913	M.J.Mashburn,M.G.
Jones,Joe Brown 26 to Florence Leatherwood 21/	10-12-1913-	Pendergrass,M.G
Jones,James M.22 to Maggie Welch 18	6-21-1914	J.A.Lakey,J.P.
Jones,Oscar 23 to Zola Wishon 20	7- 5-1914	L.A.Boone,J.P.

Jones,B.C.24 to Grace Clark 18	3-29-1915	Original not found
Jones,L. A.22 to Rosa McCall 18	11-25-1916	J.R.Pendergras,MG
Jones,Gilmer A.26 to Maud E.Jacobs 27	8- 4-1917	R.H.Dougherty,M.G
Jones,L.C.26 to Minnie Gibson 19	9- 8-1918	E.O.Rickman,J.P.
Jones,James 28 to Belle Conley 24	5-19-1919	E.J.McKay,M.G.
Jones,George L.26 to Maggie Bingham 19	11-13-1919	Retd.not executed
Jones,Zeb 29 to Mary Evans 18	5-22-1920	Geo.Cloer,M.G.
Jones,Geo.L.29 to Virginia Lenoir 27	9-22-1922	J.Q.Wallace,M.G.
Jones,Henry R.26 to Maude Corpening 27	8-25-1923	Z.Baird,J.P.
Jones,George 28 to Floy Belle 18	10-22-1925	Geo.Carpenter,J.P
He from Hayesville,N.C.... She from Clay Co.N.C.		
Jones,Frank H.28 to Alma E.Stalcup 30	6-30-1926	J.R.Pendergrass,MG
Jones,Arthur 23 to Lona Gibson 19	2-11-1934	Sam J.Murray,J.P.
Jones,O.Howard 23 to Carolyn Farmer 19	8-29-1936	Geo.Carpenter,J.P
He from Weaverville,N.C... She from Asheville,N.C.		
Jones,Jim 50 to Mrs.Leona Walker 36	9-20-1936	N.E.Holden,M.G.
Jones,Vincen 21 to Pauline Owenby 18	6-20-1937	P.H.Passmore,M.G.
Justice,Andrew to Avaline Carpenter	2-11-1840	F.Long.
Justice,Isaac to Rachel Plemons	3-15-1841	T.V.Oliver.
Justis,Amos A.to L.M.Shope	9-22-1847	J.K.Gray,Clk.
Justice,S.P.C.to Matilda Carson	8- 7-1856	John Hall,Clk.
Justice,A.A. to Mary J.Simons	10-24-1862	R.C.Slagle,C.C.C.
Justice,S.P.C. to Jane Carpenter	9-30-1865	R.C.Slagle,C.C.C.
Justice,Henry N.20 to Hattie Anderson 19	10-25-1872	Jas.H.Addington,MG
Justice,J.D.21 to C.J.A.Duvall 21	11-7-1878	G.W.Dean,J.P.
Justice,J.W.22 to M.A.Sullins 14	6-25-1882	J.S.Woodard,M.G.
Justice,Andrew J.63 to Harriet Rhodes 35	9-14-1884	M.P.Long,M.G.
Justice,John B.23 to Lucy J.Meadows 23	11-19-1893	Joseph Morgan,J.P
Justice,Wm.A.25 to Chole Articia Talley 20	12-6-1896	A.W.Young,M.G.
Justice,Henry P.25 to Mary Owneby 24	6- 4-1899	Mark Deweese,J.P.
Justice,A.M.22 to A.B.Woody 18	1-12-1902	Mark Deweese,J.P.
Justice,J.M.27 to Nettie Carver 18	5-10-1903	G.P.White,J.P.
Justice,W.V.22 to Ettie Cabe 19	10-18-1903	A.W.Young,M.G.
Justice,Manson L.24 to Mattie Howell 21	10-22-1905	T.J.Vinson,M.G.
Justice,Alex 20 to Olive Mason 17	9-16-1906	S.S.Long,J.P.
Justice,A.M.23 to Nancy E.Conley 23	1- 2-1883	M.P.Long,M.G.
Justice,Emory 21 to Harriet Cabe 19	1-20-1907	Joseph L.Fouts,
Justice,John W.60 to Calra Ledford 37	10-18-1908	J.R.Pendergras,MG
Justice,Allen 22 to Naomia Lona 19	3- 7-1909	C.R.Cabe,J.P.
Justice,Badger 23 to Maud Conley 18	2- 4-1912	J.M.Conley,J.P.
Justice,Horace 24 to Beulah Houston 16	4-14-1912	J.R.Pendergrass,MG
Justice,Lester 31 to Paradie Conley 28	4-15-1914	J.B.Hensley,M.G.
Justice,T.B.26 to Laura Norton 25	5-24-1914	J.L.Fouts,J.P.
Justice,James 21 to Toledo Cabe 18	3-12-1921	J.E.Womack,M.G.
Justice,T.C.32 to Lillie Penland 23	8-28-1925	W.M.Smith,M.G.
He from Clayton,Ga.		
Justice,Rufus 21 to Eva Roper 23	12-29-1930	Fred Anderson,J.P
She from Asheville,N.C.		

```
Kee,T.A.21 to Mary A.Hall 20                          8- 9-1885  C.S.Ray,J.P.
Keener,Isaac N.to Mary Jennings                       1-19-1837  U.Keener,D.Clk.
Keener,Ulrech to Carolina S.Ledford                   1-24-1846  J.K.Gray,Clk.
Keener,James M.to R.V.Holebrooks                      11-3-1871  William Sloan,Reg
Keener,Brownlow 21 to Martha Hollen 19                10-20-1872 J.L.Strain,J.P.
Keener,Hiram A.23 to Mary M.Keener 22                 9-17-1874  J.L.Strain,J.P.
Keener,James C.21 to Sarah M.Picklesimer 17/9-23-1875 S.W.Hill,J.P.
Keener,Alex I.19 to Mary E.Young 17                   8- 7-1879  Hosea Moses,J.P.
Keener,Jno.S.45 to Iowa Queen 42                      9- 6-1886  D.McCracken,M.G.
  He from Jackson Co.N.C.
Keener,William W.22 to C.Earnestine Brown 17/1-13-1889 Hosea Moses,J.P.
Keener,Ben I.20 to Melvina Crunkleton 19             8-30-1896  A.G.Wood,J.P.
Keener,E.N.22 to Hulda Holbrook 22                   12-22-1897 J.M.Keener,M.G.
Keener,W.A.24 to Fannie J.Jones 18                   12-23-1897 G.W.Stiwinter,J.P
Keener,T.M.23 to M.V.Calloway 19                     1-12-1902  J.H.Fulton,J.P.
Keener,Isaac 18 to Martha N.Calloway 17              3-11-1902  J.H.Fulton,J.P.
Keener,W.C.42 to Addie Stewman 27                    7-27-1902  J.E.Rickman,J.P.
Keener,Geo.26 to Callie Russell 15                   1-19-1908  J.E.Vinson,J.P.
Keener,Isaac 28 to Eva C.Higdon 25                   12-29-1909 J.R.Pendergras,MG
Keener,J.U. 20 to Fannie E.Williams 17               12-21-1913 W.T.Jennings,J.P.
Keener,Alex 36 to Pearl Houston 18                   2-22-1914  I.T.Peek,M.G.
Keener,T.M.36 to Edna Corbett 23                     11-15-1916 Geo.Carpenter,J.P
Keener,R.A.19 to Lillie Stanfield 18                 12-16-1917 A.W.Jacobs,M.G.
Keener,Charlie 18 to Grace Conley 16                 1- 6-1918  W.A.Norton,J.P.
Keener,Henry 21 to Millie McClure 18                 1-26-1920  J.M.Keener,J.P.
Keener,Wm.A.24 to Nana Fox 21                        8-25-1923  J.R.Pendergrass,MG
Keener,Randolph 21 to Pearl Miller 20                10-12-1928 Will Smith,Ord.
Keener,William P.44 to Icie Ethel Dickerson 35/4-5-1933 Carl Slagle,J.P.
  Both from Rabun Gap,Ga.
Keener,Truman 29 to Ruby Johnson 18                  8- 8-1937  Lester Arnold,J.P
Keenon,Robert T.24 to Nannie May West 16             12-29-1924 A.J.Smith,M.G.
  He from Buncombe Co.N.C.
Keever,W.C.42 to Addie Stewman 27                    7-27-1902  Jno.E.Rickman,J.P
Kelsey,S.T.,Jr.24 to Mrs.Ivey S.Bowers 32           6- 6-1893  J.A.Deal,M.G.
Kell,J.R.19 to Martha A.Tally 18                     11-20-1887 J.W.Wilson,J.P.
  He from Rabun Co.Ga.
Kell,Leonard 26 to Lathey Talley 17                  12-24-1888 J.M.Wilson,J.P.
Kell,M.L.22 to Elizabeth Miller 24                   9-15-1912  H.O.Miller,M.G.
Kell,James F.22 to Clare Miller 20                   12-1-1912  H.O.Miller,M.G.
Kell,Mathew 26 to Ida Dryman 18                      3-25-1917  W.C.Ledbetter,J.P
Kelley,Marcus L.to Ann Eliza Hyatt                   12-8-1870  Wm.Sloan,Clk.
Kemp,Homer Robert Jr.27 to Eula Lee King 20 Col.1-28-1939-Johnson McKay.
  She from Sylva,N.C.
Kerby,Wm.R.to Francis Picklesimer                    10-19-1841 J.K.Gray,Clk.
Kerby,W.W. to Sarah Martin                           9-22-1855  J.V.Trammill.
Kirby,Jess B.to Nancy M.Passmore                     8-15-1871  Wm.Sloan,Reg.
Kerby,Alvey F.31 to Elmyra L.Owenby 31               5- 2-1886  F.M.Morgan,M.G.
Kerby,A.F.52 to Mrs.Sarah Cochran 31                 9-19-1903  Joseph L.Fouts,JP
```

Key,James 37 to Martha Roper 24   2- 9-1879   P.C.Wild,J.P.
Key,John F.42 to Jane Hall 30   8-29-1879   P.C.Wild,J.P.
Key,Samuel 18 to Catherine Franklin 24   10-5-1886   A.A.Justice,M.G.
Key,John 20 to Josephine Dalton 30   9- 4-1887   M.J.Mashburn,J.P.
Key,John 24 to Mollie Daves 17   9-24-1891   J.E.Morgan,M.G.
Key,James A.52 to Margaret J.Jones 22   5-12-1892   W.J.Jenkins,J.P.
Key,Jas.Albert 21 to Kansas Painter 18   9- 3-1893   W.J.Jenkins,J.P.
Key,James Henry 22 to Maggie Daves 19   8- 1-1894 Original not found
Key,T.L.23 to Annie Painter 18   3-30-1899   E.B.Angel,J.P.
Key,William 24 to Flora Collins 22   1-13-1901   P.H.Justice,J.P.
Key,Frank 21 to Dove Bryson 25   10-27-1907 J.E.Cabe,J.P.
Killian,W.B.21 to Leona Passmore 16   12-5-1911   T.B.Enloe,J.P.
Kilpatrick,B.E. to Sarah A.Morrow   1- 5-1835   John Tatham,Clk.
Kilpatrick,J.Morgan 19 to Iowa T.Wood 19   8-19-1886   Z.Barnes,J.P.
Kilpatrick,Elisha A.21 to Basha A.Stephens 18/12-7-1893-Z.Barnes,J.P.
Kilpatrick,Athen 21 to Minnie Freeman 19   10-2-1899   S.J.W.McCoy,J.P.
Kilpatrick,A.A.24 to Lillie Roesbell Wilson 20/8-17-1902-W.C.Mason,M.G.
Kilpatrick,W.Francis 21 to Eloise Hooper 18/4-20-1935   E.R.Eller,M.G.
   Both from Clyde,N.C.
Kimsey,David to Ann McClure   5-19-1831   Romelus Brown.
Kimsey,Thos.J.to Laurina Sellers   1-26-1848   J.K.Gray,Clk.
Kimsey,Elisha L.to Margaret A.Philips   8-31-1851   W.M.Angel,J.P.
Kimzey,W.C.to Harriet R.Ledford   11-29-1865 R.C.Slagle,Reg.
Kimsey,William B.23 to S.L.Dowdle 27   1-15-1881   Jno.Addington,J.P
Kimzey,Marshall P.23 to A.G.Shields 18   7-20-1882   E.B.Padgett,J.P.
Kimzey,Charles R.38 to M.Catherine Sellers 36/12-31-1890-W.G.Mallonee,MG
Kimsey,Charles O.28 to Nancy A.Waldroop 22 9-25-1895   G.R.McPherson,J.P
Kimsey,Harold D.24 to Helen Hall 19   10-30-1935 Eugene R.Eller,MG
   He from Kingsport,Tenn.
King,J.W.to Nancy A.Coleman   5- 5-1841   H.G.Woodfin,D.Clk
King,Peter to S.C.Cook   2-19-1852   J.F.Slagle,J.P.
King,Jackson 22 to Lydia Moore 18   9-25-1887   Hosea Moses,J.P.
   He from Rabun Co.Ga.
King,Martin 25 to Rosa Carpenter 19   12-24-1899 T.R.Arnold,J.P.
King,W.H.24 to Lizzie Stiles 22   6- 5-1902   J.W.Briggs,M.G.
King,W.H.25 to Carrie Dills 17   5-13-1906   J.L.Kinsland,M.G.
King,Allen L.21 to Alice M.Parrish 23   7- 6-1930   J.A.Flanagan,M.G.
   He from Washington,D.C.
Kinnebrew,Edwin R.33 to Nannie P.Sloan 19   3-18-1886 C.D.Smith,M.G.
Kinsland,John to Sarah A.Corbin   12-21-1852 W.R.Slagle,J.P.
Kinsland,John to Sarah Ann Holland   9-24-1871   H.H.Elmore,J.P.
Kinsland,M.G.29 to Betty Angel 19   12-3-1884   S.H.Harrington,MG
Kinsland,Charley 21 to Lillie Morgan 18   12-16-1888 J.B.Elmore,J.P.
Kinsland,John L.30 to Margaret Higdon 24   1- 9-1895   G.A.Bartlett,M.G.
Kinsland,E.C.42 to Mary D.Guest 18   8-24-1904   M.A.Love,M.G.
Kinsland,A.G.25 to Mary Lee Robinson 18   7-22-1916   Geo.Carpenter,J.P
Kinsland,Paul 23 to Ruby Mason 19   12-26-1927 Geo.Carpenter,J.P
Kinsland,Roy 40 to Glady Lorine Pannell 30 9- 9-1941   C.F.Rogers,M.G.

Kirkland,James to Fanny Watkins	4-17-1850	T.P.Siler,D.Clk.
Kirkland,Pat 18 to Lillie Truitt 15	8- 9-1914	J.A.Lakey,J.P..
Kiser,J.B.22 to Nina Gillispie 16	9-12-1915	R.P.McCracken,M.G
Kiser,T.W.26 to Lola Stillwell 21	5- 6-1922	J.R.Pendergrass,MG
Kitchens,Jason to Rebecca Hooper	5- 9-1845	J.K.Gray,Clk.
Knight,J.H.32 to Yoncey Duncan 16	3-29-1883	M.I.Skiner,J.P.
Knight,James 70 to Mary Dills 20	4-10-1883	J.J.Arnold,J.P.
Knight,Narvel 27 to Ada Bird 19	3-28-1886	J.W.Bird,M.G.
Knox,Cornelius 23 to Vina Prater 19 Col.	11-15-1877	E.H.Franks,J.P.
Krom,Stanford 24 to Mildred Bryson 19	7-20-1941	J.L.Stokes,M.G.
He from Ellenville,N.Y.		
Lackey,Lloyd 22 to Florence Solesbee 19	10-14-1933	S.J.Murray,J.P.
He from Lenoir,N.C.		
Locount,V.M.22 to Cora Ashe 15	7-25-1897	W.L.Higdon,J.P.
Ladd,Ed.L.37 to Lizzie Curtis 25	4-11-1907	F.L.Townsend,M.G.
Lakey,Samuel to Nancy Poindexter	1-22-1855	John Hall,Clk.
Lakey,Hiram to Sarah Grant	11-5-1859	J.C.McLoud,J.P.
Lakey,C.J. to Nancy Collins	7-24-1865	R.C.Slagle,Reg.
Lakey,W.J.to Nancy Ann Cross	9-15-1866	Martin DeHart,J.P
Lakey,J.B. to Nancy A.Ammons	8- 4-1870	R.M.Roberts,J.P.
Lakey,James P.25 to Elizabeth Russell 25	10-28-1875	B.G.Wild,M.G.
Lakey,John B.23 to Mary M.Briggs 17	10-4-1896	H.D.Dean,J.P.
Lackey,W.A.26 to Lelah Parrish 22 Col.	10-22-1898	Jas.Bristol,M.G.
Lakey,W.B.23 to Ader West 19	9-10-1899	W.H.Morrison,J.P.
Lakey,C.R.22 to Eva Bishop 18	12-31-1901	W.H.Morrison,M.G.
Lakey,J.A.31 to Minnie Tallent 16	7-20-1904	W.L.Bradley,M.G.
Lakey,W.J.61 to Maggie Green 35	3-21-1917	D.C.McCoy,M.G.
Lakey,Vivon 20 to Berdie Ledford 18	12-7-1920	Retd.not executed
Lakey,J.E.37 to Abie Shepherd 19	3- 2-1921	J.L.Bryson,J.P.
Lakey,Vivian 21 to Berdie Ledford 18	10-26-1921	R.P.McCracken,M.G
Lamb,David 53 to Allice L.Linsey 21	3-26-1883	John Elmore,J.P.
Lamb,John J.43 to Maud A.Lightfoot 28	9- 3-1913	M.H.Tuttle,M.G.
Lamb,Borgis to Charlotte Justice	10-19-1867	R.C.Slagle,Clk.
Lambert,Samuel C.to Sarah Tetherow	2-13-1869	R.C.Slagle,Reg.
Lambert,Robt.P.45 to Catherine Rowland 30	7- 3-1873	Jesse Stepp,J.P.
Lambert,Samuel C.40 to Martha A.Whitlock 42/2-28-1877		Z.Barnes,J.P.
Lambert,Columbus 22 to Elizabeth Barnes 23 /7-13-1884		M.Ghormley,M.G.
Lambert,Samuel C.25 to Emeline Passmore 18 /11-30-1890		M.Ghormley,M.G.
Lambert,R.A.24 to Alice E.Passmore 18	5-14-1898	T.J.Taylor,M.G.
Lambert,W.T.19 to Roxie Coleman 18	7-30-1901	A.H.Gregory,J.P.
Lambert,J.S.20 to Dora.Cheeks 24	5-12-1908	J.T.Taylor,M.G.
Lambert,T.O.26 to Ollie May 18	1- 7-1917	F.M.Morgan,M.G.
Lance,Peter 70 to Jane Rickman 58	9-26-1901	W.L.Bradley,M.G.
Land,Isaac to Matilda Lewis	4-22-1834	John Tatham,Clk.
Land,B.J.26 to L.J.Barnes 27	6-27-1882	E.B.Padgett,J.P.
Land,Henry 20 to Nannie Brown 20	12-26-1887	John Reid,J.P.
Land,William H.30 to Eloise McConnell 27	5- 2-1943	Frank Godfred,J.P

```
Landrum,Wm.P.21 to Arie F.Watkins 21          1-14-1892   John B.Gray,J.P.
Landrum,Weaver W.26 to Ruth Deal 26           6-10-1922   A.J.Smith,M.G.
Lanning,Tom 20 to Nellie Shapherd 20          5- 6-1917   T.J.Vinson,M.G.
Lawrence,Clifford 24 to Annie W.Love 22 Col.9-12-1925     E.S.Wyly,M.G.
    He from Seneca,S.C.
Lawson,David to Caroline Wilson               1-16-1865   H.H.Ray,J.P.
Lawson,Elmer 28 to Hermey Stiles 21           7-28-1909   T.C.King,M.G.
Lawing,James A.27 to Samantha A.Frady 17      2- 9-1873   W.H.Higdon,J.P.
    He from Rabun Co.Ga.
Lea,James M.20 to Catherine C.Lambert 24      3-27-1873   Jesse Stepp,J.P.
    He from Nantahala,N.C.
Lea,William J.20 to Elizabeth Allison 24      2- 7-1877   Z.Barnes,J.P.
Lea,J.W.20 to Harrett E.Grahl 20              3-21-1882   Joseph Morgan,J.P
Lea,Elihu 23 to Margaret Gibby 21             2-14-1886   Z.Barnes,J.P.
Lea,Richard M.21 to Cornelia Allison 19       10-9-1887   Ephram Norris,M.G
Leach,Frank to S.C.Cunningham                 9- 1-1864   R.C.Slagle,Reg.
Leas,Leonard M.60 to Laura Wright 25          12-16-1907  T.J.Vinson,M.G.
Leatherman,L.J.23 to Nannie Shepherd 16       9-13-1896   J.B.Cardon,J.P.
Leatherman,W.A.21 to Valzora Hurst 20         11-7-1907   John C.Hurst,J.P.
Leatherman,S.C.23 to Nancy Mason 24           3-11-1916   T.J.Vinson,M.G.
Leatherman,Dock I.29 to Mae Buchanan 20       6-10-1917   E.O.Rickman,J.P.
Leatherwood,J.H.21 to Margaret S.Lewis 20     12-1-1875   Albert Siler,J.P.
Leatherwood,R.71 to Polly Pendergrass 66      1-25-1882   Joseph Morgan,J.P
Leatherwood,Andy 21 to Amanda Siler 21 Col.11-15-1883 Original not found
Leatherwood,John 29 to Bonnie Reece 26        1-16-1918   J.C.Umburger,M.G.
Ledbetter,Daniel to Pressan Tabor             11-15-1850  T.M.Angel,Wit.
Ledbetter,Daniel to Elizabeth Forrester       1-28-1853   J.K.Gray,Clk.
Ledbetter,Wm.I.21 to Ann Oliver 20            10-25-1877  I.D.Wright,M.G.
Ledbetter,John T.21 to Mary Oliver 18         12-26-1877  I.D.Wright,M.G.
Ledbetter,Harley 22 to Essie Carpenter 16     9- 3-1903   J.D.Vinson,J.P.
Ledbetter,W.C.36 to Sallie Garland 28         3- 4-1913   J.B.Stalcup,M.G.
Ledbetter,Homer 25 to Beulah Mae Sanders 18/11-8-1933     J.G.Fleming,J.P.
Ledford,Watson to Nancy Saunders              9-22-1834   John Tatham,Clk.
Ledford,John to Sarah B.Bell                  12-22-1835  John Tatham,Clk.
Ledford,Lester to Rebeccah Jollay             10-14-1836  U.Keener,D.Clk.
Ledford,Noah C.to Elizabeth Peek              3- 1-1842   Jno.H.Ledford.
Ledford,William to Martha Guffey              10-13-1843  J.K.Gray,Clk.
Ledford,John to Amy Nickles                   3-28-1844   J.K.Gray,Clk.
Ledford,Stephen to Vina Gibson                10-9-1849   J.K.Gray,Clk.
Ledford,Jessie to Polly Pressley              8-12-1851   J.K.Gray,Clk.
Ledford,George to Mary Williamson             12-25-1853  John Hall,Clk.
Ledford,Amos to S.P.Saunders                  9-12-1860   R.C.Slagle,Reg.
Ledford,Jesse to Louisa Ledford               10-24-1861  R.C.Slagle,Reg.
Ledford,Madison M.to Mary D.Nicholas          12-5-1867   R.C.Slagle,C.C.C.
Ledford,James W.to Martha A.Carpenter         10-14-1869  J.K.Bryson,Reg.
Ledford,Jason to Letty Carpenter              9-10-1871   Wm.Sloan,Reg.
Ledford,Benj.T.19 to Emily Jones 19           1- 8-1873   J.H.Addington,J.P
Ledford,John 19 to Sarah S.Collyer 18         12-25-1873  C.D.Smith,M.G.
```

```
Ledford,John R.22 to Cornelia Ledford 21        9-15-1874  J.H.Addington,J.P
Ledford,Thomas 22 to Margaret V.Baldwin 18      12-16-1874 Albert Siler,J.P.
Ledford,A.I.35 to Mary A.Ingram 21              3-22-1876  L.K.Haynes,M.G.
Ledford,Jesse W.20 to Emma F.Saunders 18        3-14-1878  J.H.Addington,J.P
Ledford,J.E.23 to Sarah Brock 20                1-11-1880  J.C.Addington,J.P
  He from Habersham Co.Ga.
Ledford,John W.23 to L.J.Guffee 19              2-19-1880  Albert Siler,J.P.
Ledford,Julius 24 to Marthana Ledford          2-26-1880 Original not found
Ledford,William 21 to Rosetta Nichols 18        10-6-1881  Albert Siler,J.P.
Ledford,George W.22 to C.D.Jones 21             2- 2-1882  I.D.Wright,M.G.
Ledford,William L.22 to Anna A.Allen 24         1-21-1883  L.Howard,J.P.
Ledford,Rufus 22 to Ella Griggs 17              3-27-1885  M.S.Dills,J.P.
Ledford,Jason K.26 to Adda E.Garland 25         12-31-1885 L.Howard,J.P.
  He from Rabun Co.Ga.
Ledford,Charlie L.17 to Cora A.Jones 17         3- 4-1886  M.S.Dills,J.P.
Ledford,Lucius M.19 to Callie Blaine 19         1-29-1890  C.L.Ledford,M.G.
Ledford,Montraville 25 to Cora Messer 19        10-11-1891 C.L.Ledford,M.G.
Ledford,William Z.21 to Allie Z.Oliver 24       1-17-1895  G.R.McPherson,J.P
Ledford,W.Z.22 to Hattie Patton 15              12-17-1896 J.R.Pendergras,MG
Ledford,Miller D.21 to Lula Stanfield 21        8- 4-1897  G.R.McPherson,J.P
Ledford,Abe 28 to Callie Sanders 20             10-28-1897 J.M.Carpenter,J.P
Ledford,George 21 to Lola Gillespie 16          10-3-1900  J.L.Kinsland,M.G.
Ledford,W.R.35 to Hattie Conley 20              10-28-1900 M.G.Ledford,M.G.
Ledford,Colman 22 to Cally Stonesipher 21 Col.12-27-1900-T.R.Arnold,J.P.
Ledford,J.M.21 to Florence A.Blaine 18          12-17-1902 D.M.Matheson,M.G.
Ledford,James 25 to Hattie Hall 18              2- 8-1903  Mark Deweese,J.P.
Ledford,Ed.23 to Ida Moffitt 22                 7- 6-1904  J.C.Postell,M.G.
Ledford,A.Ben 21 to Flora Ann Watts 14          3-15-1905  Robert Stamey,J.P
Ledford,Robert M.38 to Lowellen Johnson 23 5-15-1907 J.R.Pendergrass,MG
Ledford,Lester 18 to Anna Reed 16               12-29-1907 J.L.Kinsland,M.G.
Ledford,Raleigh 22 to Mary Norton 24            8-23-1908  W.A.Norton,J.P.
Ledford,Oscar 21 to Lexie Farmer 18             10-21-1908 W.L.Griggs,M.G.
Ledford,Frank 22 to Millie Sellers 19  Col. 9-26-1909  G.M.Bulgin,J.P.
Ledford,Andy 25 to Bertha Dills 18              12-21-1910 Robert Stamey,J.P
Ledford,F.W.18 to Cordie Bingham 17             1-15-1911  J.T.Watts,J.P.
Ledford,Fred 21 to Dora Poindexter 16           1- 7-1912  Chas.T.Ray,J.P.
Ledford,John W.56 to Lizzie Long 31             4- 5-1914 J.R.Pendergrass,MG
Ledford,Spurgeon 24 to Maybelle Burton 19       8-16-1916  R.P.McCracken,M.G.
Ledford,Ransom 28 to Elsie Cabe 18              12-20-1916 A.M.Ledford,M.G.
Ledford,H.B.28 to Nellie May Watts 18           2- 7-1917  W.H.Carpenter,J.P
Ledford,M.R.31 to Franchie Sanders 16           6-21-1917  Geo.Carpenter,J.P
Ledford,Laurence 20 to Gertrude Brendle 20      10-14-1917 J.R.Pendergras,MG
Ledford,D.A.25 to Ida Ashe 28                   1-27-1918  J.L.Fouts,J.P.
Ledford,J.A.42 to Ada Raby 18                   2-14-1919  L.P.Roper,J.P
Ledford,J.A.Sr.66 to Addie Dills 45             8-22-1919  Geo.Carpenter,J.P
Ledford,Sam 26 to Ida Guy 20           Col. 12-22-1919  E.J.McKay,M.G.
Ledford,Robert 23  to Ella Stewart 23 Col.  12-23-1919 E.J.McKay,M.G.
```

```
Ledford,Clint 22 to Henrietta Love 21    Col. 12-24-1919 E.J.McKay,M.G.
Ledford,Mack 26 to Sallie Guy 23         Col. 11-6-1920  E.J.McKay,M.G.
Ledford,John 22 to Willie Guy 19         Col. 1-20-1921  W.C.Vanhook,M.G.
Ledford,L.Nelson 22 to Edna Ledford 21        6-15-1933  A.T.Medford,M.G.
Ledford,Thomas L.20 to Gertrude R.Clampitt 18/7-21-1935-Geo.Carpenter,JP
Ledford,Geo.R.58 to Lula Ellen Long 48        11-25-1937 E.N.Evans,J.P.
   She from Walhala,S.C.
Lee,James to Elizabeth Johnston               11-10-1842 James Stenson,Wit
Lee,Stanford to Mary J.Barnes                 12-8-1852  G.W.Yonce,Wit.
Lee,Joseph M.to Martha A.Smith                12-26-1864 M.S.Bona,Wit.
Lee,James W.to Fanny Fulcher                  1- 3-1869  R.C.Slagle,Reg.
Lee,Thomas 27 to Lanna Fulcher 18             9-12-1874  Albert Siler,J.P.
Lee,George W.18 to Ellen Dalrymple 18         12-16-1888 Z.Barnes,J.P.
Lee,Jesse B.20 to Sophrany Dalrymple 17       3- 5-1892  S.H.Waters,M.G.
Lee,Charlie 18 to Pearl Howard 17             12-20-1905 D.F.Howard,M.G.
Lee,James 27 to Isabell Greenwood 18          9-10-1933  Thomas Wyley,M.G.
Lee,Thad 19 to Lillie Mae Willis 19           6-22-1940  Jas.S.Higgins,M.G
   He from Lawndale,N.C.... She from Vale,N.C.
Lenoir,B.B.to Mary V.Siler                    5-14-1872  William Sloan,Reg
Leopard,Alfred 19 to Dortha Ammons 17         7-18-1918  W.T.Jennings,J.P.
Lequire,William to Jane Thomasson             1-30-1855  T.P.Siler,Reg.
Leslie,O.J.28 to Ethel Sutton 25              9-16-1926  Geo.Carpenter,J.P
   He from Wetupha,Ala.
Lewis,Thomas 21 to Mary A.Lunsford 22         1- 2-1876  J.M.Forester,J.P.
Lewis,John 20 to Ellen Setser 19              9- 9-1878  Albert Siler,J.P.
Lewis,David W.23 to Sallie L.Conley 24        12-9-1880  C.D.Smith,M.G.
Lewis,John H.24 to Martha C.Shuler 15         1-17-1892  W.J.Jenkins,J.P.
Lewis,W.D.20 to Minnie Shuler 15              5-19-1893  P.R.Rickman,M.G.
Lewis,Andrew N.28 to Maymee Rice 25           1-28-1908  R.M.Taylor,M.G.
Lewis,Fred 24 to Bessie Corpening 19          10-30-1910 F.N.Johnston,J.P.
Lewis,W.O. 27 to Vastie Kiser 18              11-22-1915 C.S.Slagle,J.P.
Lewis,E.M.24 to Lonie Moffitt 23              6-19-1917 J.R.Pendergrass,MG
Lewis,Grover 28 to Jennie Waldroop 32         8-27-1917 J.R.Pendergrass,MG
Lewis,Frank 22 to Ida Moffitt 19              2-24-1918  W.H.Roane,J.P.
Lewis,James L.22 to Beulah Nichols 25         1-29-1921  J.E.Womack,M.G.
Lindburg,Charles 32 to Dora Cochran 20        7-11-1920  J.H.Cochran,M.G.
Liner,Matt 34 to Levada Bell Bradley 28       1- 1-1911  C.R.Cabe,J.P.
Liner,D.T.27 to Nina E.P.Patton 20            3- 9-1912  J.L.Teague,M.G.
Liner,Lawrence B.25 to Tressie Russell 25     10-16-1927 J.A.Flanagan,M.G.
   She from Maysville,Tenn.
Littlejohn,J.B.23 to Georgia Bly 22    Col. 12-5-1925   J.R.Watson,M.G.
   He from Gaffney,S.C.
Lindsy,Larkin to Rachel Stiles                8-24-1839  John Hall,Clk.
Lendsey,George to Ollyan Miller               11-9-1839  John Hall,Clk.
Linzey,Timothy to Mary A.Boyd                 10-13-1853 Thos.Mashburn,J.P
Lindsay,R.A.to Sarah Beasley                  4- 5-1862  R.C.Slagle,Reg.
Lindsey,W.C.to M.A.Elmore                     8- 1-1863  R.C.Slagle,Reg.
Lindsay,W.E.35 to Nancy E.Hurst 27            8-14-1879  John S.Gibson,J.P
```

```
Lindsey,Alan 28 to Mary Alstaetter 27          9-19-1936  Frank Bloxham,M.C
   He from Savannah,Ga.
Lipman,Edward 21 to Bulah Wikle 18      Col.  1- 4-1910  Retd.not executed
Loeffel,Henry J.30 to Caroline E.Forrester 23/2-23-1893-G.P.Mann,J.P.
Logan,Dewey to Mary Addington                  9-13-1829  W.B.Hyatt,D.Clk.
London,T.M.to M.A.Owen                        12-6-1859  R.C.Slagle,Reg.
London,Robert 62 to Sarah E.Mullins 56        5- 2-1876  I.D.Wright,M.G.
London,Jno.A.27 to D.F.Huggins 21             9-10-1882  F.Poindexter,J.P
London,William R.25 to Jennie Cabe 26         8-10-1886  J.Reid,J.P.
London,William R.42 to Mrs.Eva Franks 32      11-13-1904 Jas.McConnell,J.P
Long,Martin L. to Dorcas A.Dryman             12-23-1835 Samuel Smith.
Long,Labon to Caroline Carpenter              3-19-1838  John Hall,Clk.
Long,John to Nancy Jackson                    6- 6-1844  J.K.Gray,Clk.
Long,Simeon to Sarah L.Allen                  2-26-1848  J.K.Gray,Clk.
Long,J.W. to E.J.Dryman                       10-18-1865 R.C.Slagle,Reg.
Long,Wm.T.to Sarah E.Justice                  10-23-1866 R.C.Slagle,C.C.C.
Long,L.72 to Elizabeth Phillips 71            12-5-1882  L.Howard,J.P.
Long,George W.21 to Martha A.Gray 20          1-16-1873  J.H.Addington,J.P
Long,Martin L.65 to Louiza Jane Dryman 47     10-9-1873  W.T.Anderson,J.P.
Long,Marrion N.20 to Rosetta J.Carpenter 16/1-30-1875 Original not found
Long,Frank 21 to Loucinda Beck 30      Col.   4- 4-1878  J.S.Gibson,J.P.
Long,Harrison P.22 to Mary L.Rhodes 21        11-15-1880 M.L.Kelly,J.P.
Long,Napoleon 17 to R.H.Norris 23             6- 5-1881  E.L.Long,J.P.
Long,L.L.22 to M.H.Dailey 24                  2-12-1882  L.Howard,J.P.
Long,N.B.22 to Flora L.Killian 21             3-22-1883  R.A.Owen,M.G.
Long,Simeon S.23 to Nancy C.Mize 22           12-4-1889  John Howard,J.P.
Long,Robert Lee 21 to Georgia A.White 24      10-23-1890 G.P.Mann,J.P.
Long,Simeon M.22 to S.Clementine Young 15     7-16-1891  L.H.Garland,J.P.
Long,Nathan 20 to Cansada A.Dryman 18         6-11-1893  W.A.Norton,J.P.
Long,William P.26 to Ellen Watkins 17         1-24-1894  N.J.Rush,J.P.
Long,J.H. 25 to Mattie Setser 28              7-30-1902 J.R.Pendergrass,MG
Long,H.M. 24 to Belle Blaine 21               3-23-1904  Jas.C.Postell,M.G
Long,Javan 30 to Minnie Jacobs 18             10-7-1905  V.H.Starbuck,M.G.
Long,E.I.32 to Emma McCoy 25                  12-12-1906 W.L.Bradley,M.G.
Long,Raleigh W.23 to Nellie Campbell 19       12-25-1908 W.I.Hughes,M.G.
Long,W.Bascom 24 to Cora Talley 21            1- 3-1909  J.D.Vinson,M.G.
Long,S.S.43 to Lula Ellen Watts 20            5-15-1910  J.M.Fowler,M.G.
Long,Ervin W.26 to Zoah Dowdle 19             5- 9-1917  D.S.Richardson,MG
Lord,C.S.28 to Ellen Dalton 22                1- 1-1896  Z.Barnes,J.P.
Lord,Elsie S.22 to Matilda Morgan 17          1- 1-1896  Z.Barnes,J.P.
Lord,Carl F.24 to Virginia M.Roper 16         11-27-1923 L.P.Roper,J.P.
Loudermilk,John to Sarah Davis                7-27-1829  W.B.Hyatt,D.Clk.
Loudermilk,W.W.to Ann Wilson                  -- 3-1841  J.K.Gray,Clk.
Lowdermilk,G.W.to Sarah Clark                 8-23-1844  J.K.Gray,Clk.
Lowdermilk,Joseph I.20 to Nancy C.Jones 21    5- 4-1873  J.T.Strain,J.P.
Loudermilk,William 23 to Sarah C.Rogers 23    2-12-1883  John Elmore,J.P.
Love,Andrew to Mary S.Hopkins                 1-29-1846  J.K.Gray,Clk.
```

```
Love,Berryman to Francis Satterfield          8-30-1855   J.P.McConnell,Wit
Love,Andrew to Mandy Siler             Col. 8- 4-1866   B.R.Cook,J.P.
Love,John C.to Louisa Sloan            Col. 8-30-1866   B.R.Cook,J.P.
Love,William L.to Margaret A.Allman         10-9-1866   R.C.Slagle,C.C.C.
Love,John A.to Nancy C.Dills                8-22-1867   R.C.Slagle,Clk.
Love,James to Nancy Love               Col. 11-24-1869  J.K.Bryson,Reg.
Love,Ben to Jane West                  Col. 2- 5-1870   A.L.Wild,J.P.
Love,Thomas G.to Augustus McCall            5-11-1871   H.H.Elmore,J.P.
Love,Andrew B.21 to Alice Neagle 20    Col. 9-28-1872   D.W.Wells,M.G.
Love,Andrew J.50 to Margaret R.Pendergrass 28/5-8-1873  Albert Siler,J.P.
Love,Samuel P.23 to Sarah C.Smith 17        7-15-1875   Albert Siler,J.P.
Love,M.Dillard 19 to H.E.Gray 17            12-31-1880  J.H.Addington,J.P
Love,J.W.27 to Hattie Ray 22                12-15-1881  P.C.Wild,J.P.
Love,John E.25 to Albie Moore 23            9-21-1882   W.C.Corden,M.G.
Love,Isam 21 to Teletha Hyatt 18       Col. 11-11-1885  J.M.Bristol,M.G.
Love,James M.47 to Elizabeth C.Dills 40     1-26-1889   M.Ghormley,M.G.
Love,Nicodemiss 20 to Margaret Ritchie 20 Col.5-6-1894 James Bristol,M.G
Love,Charley S.23 to Julia Sellers 18  Col.5- 6-1894   James Bristol,M.G.
Love,G.Washington 21 to Hattie Conley 18 Col.2-20-1895 Geo.Bryson,J.P.
Love,Burton 29 to Mary Carter 24       Col.3-24-1897   F.W.Wallace,M.G.
Love,J.Frank 23 to Nannie B.Jacobs 21       2-14-1904   J.H.Moore,M.G.
Love,James T.25 to Ella McDonnell 26   Col. 12-17-1905  N.P.Rankin,J.P.
Love,D.Wimer 31 to Nina B.Higdon 25         1-19-1910   J.R.Pendergrass,MG
Love,Otto A.35 to Mary E.Siler 29           1- 2-1916   R.H.Dougherty,M.G
Love,Geter 19 to Ollie Harper 21       Col. 8- 5-1917   E.G.Siler,M.G.
Love,Harry 20 to Estell Thomas 19      Col. 12-6-1926   Geo.Carpenter,J.P
Love,Theodor T.25 to Pauline Snyder 28      11-25-1930  Clifton Ervin,M.G
  He from Clarksville,Ga.
Love,Graham 22 to Sophia Conley 19     Col. 9-27-1933   W.L.Bradley,M.G.
Love,Jesse   to Mary A.Butler               1-10-1853   James McKinney,JP
Lovingood,Harmon to Winny Weeks             11-26-1830  W.B.Hyatt,D.Clk.
Lowe,Adam to Cynthia Mason                  11-2-1837   John Hall,Clk.
Low,Jesse to Mary Mason                     10-30-1838  J.K.Gray,Clk.
Low,Nathen to Elizabeth Mason               1- 3-1839   J.K.Gray,Clk.
Low,Jesse to Mary A.Butler                  1-10-1853   J.K.Gray,Clk.
Low,Jess N.22 to Charlotte Lindsay 23       10-29-1882  M.J.Mashburn,J.P.
Low,D.H.27 to Delia Taylor 18               10-1-1903   D.F.Howard,M.G.
Low,John L.21 to Lillie C.Martin 16         8-21-1904   J.T.Taylor,M.G.
Low,J.N.53 to Laura Bryson 40               8-28-1913   J.R.Pendergrass,MG
Low,W.F.25 to Eva Houston 22                9- 7-1917   D.C.McCoy,M.G.
Lowe,Ed 28 to Edna Childers 16              12-20-1920  Geo.Carpenter,J.P
Lowe,James N.25 to Bernice Rice 19          6-12-1937   W.F.Beadle,M.G.
  He from Lilesville,N.C.
Lowery,T.A.to Mary Ann Patton               4-15-1856   J.T.Patton,D.Clk.
Lowery,J.B.21 to Annie Smith 21             4-16-1899   W.C.Hanrick,M.G.
Lowery,R.R.21 to Florie May 18              5-11-1902   L.I.Mashburn,M.G.
Lowery,Charles A.48 to Lelia J.Allison 39   8-26-1908   A.J.McKelway,M.G.
```

```
Lowman,Carl M.28 to Sallie B.Younce 20        5- 8-1936  C.C.Herbert,M.G.
Loyd,John to Narcissis Spivy                  9-29-1832  John Hall,Clk.
Lunsford,Micayah to Anna Barnes              12-25-1843  J.K.Gray,Clk.
Lunsford,William to Elizabeth Ray            11-30-1845  J.K.Gray,Clk.
Lunsford,John to M.M.Pendergrass              2- 4-1856  Thos.Lunsford.
Lunsford,M.M.to Susan Pendergrass             9- 7-1865  R.C.Slagle,Reg.
Lunsford,Michael to Nancy Guffee              1- 2-1867  R.C.Slagle,Clk.
Lunsford,William R.to Mary Ann Wilson         2-18-1872  William Sloan,Reg
Lunsford,John W.21 to Nancy Jones 21          3- 8-1874  Z.Barnes,J.P.
Lunsford,Thos.21 to Martha A.Howard 37        2-29-1880  J.M.Forester,J.P.
Lunsford,Thomas 22 to Mary Gibby 16           8- 1-1886  Z.Barnes,J.P.
Lunsford,Willie 22 to Artie Neal 16           7-24-1898  W.J.Evans,M.G.
Lunsford,D.M.45 to Maud Willis 26            11-16-1931  A.S.Solesbee,M.G.
Lyle,John to Laura Siler                      9-25-1850  J.R.Siler,J.P.
Lyle,J.M. to Nannie A.Moore                   1-22-1867  R.C.Slagle,C.C.C.
Lyle,Daniel 23 to Carrie A.Parrish 20         1-10-1893  D.H.Cowan,M.G.
McAfee,A.McDuffie 21 to Mary Logan 21    Col.5-14-1891  J.C.Hemphill,M.G.
Mack,Horace 21 to Anner McMahan 16            3-17-1901  W.C.Mason,M.G.
Mahaffey,D.F.to Jane Tetherow                 6- 3-1869  Merrit Rickman,MG
Major,Chas.S.34 to Lucia E.Sullivan 24       10-13-1928  W.N.Seay,M.G.
Malonee,Adam to M.V.Cansler                  11-30-1861  R.C.Slagle,Reg.
Mallonee,Jackson to Susy A.Parrish       Col. 2-15-1868  R.C.Slagle,C.C.C.
Mallonee,Comodore B.23 to Laura J.Reid 18     9- 4-1873  W.H.Bates,M.G.
Mallonee,Elbert S.28 to Mary J.McDonald 21   12-30-1874  Jno.W.Bowman,M.G.
Mallonee,Abraham 48 to L.A.Leatherwood 28     1-27-1878  B.G.Wild,M.G.
Mallonee,W.G.43 to Lou A.Ledford 36           7- 2-1890  W.B.Barnett,M.G.
Mallonee,John 21 to Minnie Allen 18           1- 4-1891  W.J.Jenkins,J.P.
Mallonee,Charles R.29 to Belle Cansler 20     6-23-1907  J.P.Campbell,J.P.
Mallonee,E.Harley 25 to Mary Cansler 18       7-16-1911  J.R.Pendergrass,MG
Mallonee,John 33 to Rebecca Wright 23    Col.12-4-1913  L.E.Carr,M.G.
Mallonee,Jack 60 to Callie West 40       Col.9-30-1916  J.L.Bryson,J.P.
Maney,Mack 19 to Margaret West 19        Col.12-4-1874  D.W.Wells,M.G.
Manley,John 20 to Nannie Carpenter 17        10-16-1910  J.T.Watts,J.P.
Manley,Ben 21 to Bonnie Holt 29              12- 6-1913  R.H.Monger,J.P.
Manley,John 58 to Nancy Barnes 24            10-13-1896  G.W.Matney,M.G.
Mann,G.P.25 to C.E.Bradley 18                 2-24-1876  E.L.Long,J.P.
Mann,W.H.21 to Julia M.McClure 19             3-21-1877  J.H.Addington,J.P
Mann,J.C.50 to Georgia A.Sherrill 24         11-9-1895  W.H.Mann,J.P.
Mann,J.H.21 to Mamie Sanders 20              11-9-1898  R.B.Shelton,M.G.
Mann,James J.21 to Hattie Smart 18            3-27-1910  C.R.Cabe,J.P.
Mann,H.C.23 to Lela Bleckley 19              12-3-1918  Roy Dryman,J.P.
Mantooth,John to Margaret Penland             8-22-1843  Chas.M.Penland.
Marcuss,Ruphus to Carolina Hoag              12-11-1854  Jonah Welch,Wit.
Marr,Lemuel to Caroline Duvall               12-6-1836  Eli Collins.
Marr,Joseph to Mary Taber                     9-22-1855  John Hall,Clk.
Marr,Benj.F.to Mary T.Carden                  8-23-1862  R.C.Slagle,C.C.C.
Marr,Thomas to Elizabeth Welch                9- 4-1866  A.A.Justice,M.G.
```

```
Marr,William 58 to Alcy A.Stepp 58          1- 6-1878  Z.Barnes,J.P.
Marr,W.W.21 to Nettie Smith 18              7-31-1898  J.B.Justice,J.P.
Marr,Lambert 24 to Vinnie M.M.Dean 28       7-25-1938  W.L.Bradley,M.G.
   She from Cherokee,N.C.
Marshall,George D.26 to Nellie M.Womack 21  10-14-1933 J.F.Burell,M.G.
   He from Graham,N.C.
Martin,Riley to Elizabeth Downs             1-27-1841  John Hall,Clk.
Martin,Joseph to Nancy Hicks                2-25-1850  T.P.Siler,D.Clk.
Martin,Jefferson to Elizabeth Caylor        1- 7-1862  R.C.Slagle,Reg.
Martin,Walker to Mary I.Moose               9-11-1865  J.A.Tramell,J.P.
Martin,John to Mary Edmonson                6- 4-1868  R.C.Slagle,C.C.C.
Martin,W.D.to Margaret B.Magaha             6-25-1869  J.K.Bryson,Reg.
Martin,Nathaniel 20 to Rachel Morgan 21     12-12-1878 M.Ghormley,M.G.
Martin,B.F.21 to Easter Simpson 19    Col.  1-11-1883  E.H.Bogle.
Martin,Henry 27 to Alley Morgan 18          9- 3-1887 Original not found
Martin,John M.30 to Jane A.McGaha 22        4-20-1890  A.A.Justice,M.G.
Martin,Charley R.19 to Mary Mason 18        10-22-1890 F.M.Morgan,M.G.
Martin,Richmond 21 to Amanda Shields 20     4-10-1892  J.H.Morgan,J.P.
Martin,John J.18 to Mary Beasley 20         10-16-1895 C.S.Buchanan,M.G.
Martin,Ben C.51 to Mandy Johnston 42  Col.  7-16-1907  C.L.Stewart,M.G.
Martin,H.Z.22 to Sarah Ammons 18            8-22-1911  J.L.Bryson,J.P.
Martin,T.P.21 to Hessie Barker 19           7-13-1916  J.A.Lakey,J.P.
Martin,Dan 23 to Leona Hayes 22       Col.  11-28-1916 C.L.Stewart,M.G.
Martin,J.F.26 to Ola Raby 21                3- 6-1918  D.C.McCoy,J.P.
Martin,Harley 18 to Ida Tramel 21           2-13-1920  M.C.Mason,M.G.
Martin,Dan 26 to Rosa Bly 20          Col.  7- 7-1920  E.J.McKay,M.G.
Martin,John 42 to Lou Passmore 35           8-27-19?? Lester Arnold,J.P
   Both from Nantahala,N.C.
Martin,Ellis James 25 to Eleanor Irish 22   3-12-1939  Ivon L.Roberts,MG
   She from Concord,N.C.
Mashburn,William to Rachel Guffey           4-20-1839  H.G.Woodfin,D.Clk
Mashburn,Drury W.to Temperance Reid         1-11-1843  John Hall,Clk.
Mashburn,Louis to Rachael Reid              12-23-1847 S.McDowell,Wrt.
Mashburn,T.W.to Hariet Moore                11-27-1851 J.K.Gray,Clk.
Mashburn,Mathew A.to Nancy C.Moore          8-15-1855  John Hall,Clk.
Mashburn,James M.to Nancy S.Nicholds        6-19-1858  R.C.Slagle,C.C.C.
Mashburn,William P.to Jane M.Corbin         3- 9-1859  R.C.Slagle,C.C.C.
Mashburn,David to Isabell Miller            8-15-1866  R.C.Slagle,C.C.C.
Mashburn,T.W.to S.J.Clark                   8- 5-1870  J.K.Bryson,Reg.
Mashburn,L.S.to Mary A.Love                 9-25-1870  William Sloan,Reg
Mashburn,Alfred to Octava Ramsey            4-18-1872  William Sloan,Reg
Mashburn,H.Leander 22 to Cynthia Bentley 21/10-3-1875  F.Poindexter,J.P.
Mashburn,Jesse 22 to Lassie Guffee 21       8-13-1879  H.G.Woodfin,J.P.
Mashburn,Gilbert 22 to Mary Stiles 18       12-29-1881 W.C.Carden,M.G.
Mashburn,D.W.26 to Georgia E.Huggins 27     3-23-1885  C.C.Smith,J.P.
Mashburn,M.J.47 to Menervia Mashburn 37     6- 8-1885 Original not found
Mashburn,Manson 20 to Rebecca Shields 20    8-30-1888  F.M.Morgan,J.P.
Mashburn,J.Harvey 26 to Mary Lakey 26       10-3-1889  M.J.Mashburn,J.P.
```

```
Mashburn,Thomas 20 to Caroline Wilson 16      6-15-1890  W.C.Mason,M.G.
Mashburn,Elbert 20 to Myra Angel 21
                                               9-15-1892  N.P.Rankin,J.P.
Mashburn,George W.20 to Nellie Wilson 15       8-27-1893  W.C.Mason,M.G.
Mashburn,W.W.26 to Roxie Angel 22              3-11-1894  N.J.Rush,J.P.
Mashburn,John R.20 to Melvina Mason 16         3-31-1895  W.C.Mason,M.G.
Mashburn,Allen 19 to Latishu Painter 19        11-22-1897 John H.Fulton,J.P
Mashburn,Harley 20 to Ethel Heaton 21          10-13-1898 T.R.Arnold,J.P.
Mashburn,J.D.41 to Buna Stiles 24              1-27-1901  W.L.Higdon,J.P.
Mashburn,George 28 to Cora Holden 19           3- 9-1902  W.C.Mason,M.G.
Mashburn,Thomas 31 to Samantha Mason 41        8-26-1902  W.C.Mason,M.G.
Mashburn,M.E.20 to Mandy J.Dills 24            8-16-1903  W.C.Mason,M.G.
Mashburn,Isaac 19 to Mary Kilpatrick 15        6-24-1906  H.J.Hogue,M.G.
Mashburn,Amos 24 to Cora Holland 19            3-13-1910  J.M.Keener,M.G.
Mashburn,Burt 31 to Florence Bryson 21         12-18-1911 T.J.Vinson,M.G.
Mashburn,W.C.23 to Jennie Angel 23             3- 8-1903  W.L.Higdon,J.P.
Mashburn,L.H.22 to Florence Kilpatrick 15      3-11-1913  J.H.Grant,M.G.
Mashburn,W.G.27 to Minnie Reece 19             4-13-1913  T.J.Vinson,M.G.
Mashburn,Eddie 22 to Alice Reece 21            6-17-1913  J.R.Pendergrass,MG
Mashburn,R.R.25 to Anna Bryson 21              7-12-1914  J.P.Moore,J.P.
Mashburn,J.H.,Jr.23 to Mary Bell Ashe 25       4- 2-1915  R.H.Dougherty,M.G
Mashburn,A.J.32 to Florence Jacobs 22          9-15-1915  J.R.Pendergrass,MG
Mashburn,Gilbert 58 to Tina Ramey 34           6-31-1918  L.J.Young,M.G.
Mashburn,F.E.37 to Fay Moses 29                4- 2-1921  W.A.Keener,J.P.
Mashburn,Larce 20 to Alma Holden 19            8-30-1932  J.H.Grant,J.P.
   He from Nantahala,N.C.... She from Wesser Creek,N.C.
Mashburn,Odas 21 to Carrie Brendle 18          7- 4-1936  Sam J.Murray,J.P.
Mason,John to Mary Robinson                    12-7-1832  John Hall,Clk.
Mason,Peter to Mary Drinnon                    6-16-1840  John Hall,Clk.
Mason,Peter to Jane Hughes                     10-1-1845  J.K.Gray,Clk.
Mason,Joseph B.to Nelly Willson                4-18-1846  J.K.Gray,Clk.
Mayson,Isaac to Martha Buchanan                2-14-1842  J.K.Gray,Clk.
Mason,Jacob to Elizabeth Cabe                  1- 7-1852  W.H.Roane,J.P.
Mason,William,Jr.to Susan Malinda Benfield     11-6-1865  E.A.Deweese,M.G.
Mason,Jacob to Nancy Beasley                   12-18-1866 R.C.Slagle,C.C.C.
Mason,Gilbert P.to Sarah C.Waldroop            4-30-1871  William Sloan,Reg
Mason,William M.to Margaret Lindsey            6-28-1871  William Sloan,Reg
Mason,William C.to Sarah J.Wilson              2-25-1872  William Sloan,Reg
Mason,Isaac 17 to Letty C.Beasley 17           2- 9-1873  P.R.Rickman,M.G.
   He from Swain Co.N.C.
Mason,John T.21 to Samantha L.Wilson 18        8-25-1873  J.M.Forrester,J.P.
Mason,James N.26 to Carolina Forester 25       5-30-1875  J.M.Forrester,J.P
Mason,A.M.20 to Emaline Lindsay 20             11-27-1879 Thos.Mashburn,J.P
Mason,Thos.C.21 to Julia A.Parker 20           9-11-1883  M.J.Mashburn,J.P.
Mason,J.A.19 to Finettea Wilson 19             12-7-1884  J.M.Forrester,J.P
Mason,Jacob M.39 to M.C.Shepherd 27            12-2-1886  Jno.S.Gibson,J.P.
Mason,James 20 to Addie Crawford 25            11-17-1887 M.J.Mashburn,J.P.
Mason,James H.19 to T.A.Mashburn 21            9- 2-1888  P.P.McLean,M.G.
```

Mason,Jesse J.H.22 to Temple Parker 19	10-7-1888	P.R.Rickman,M.G.
Mason,Marion 20 to Minnie Pendergrass 18	10-21-1888	W.J.Evans,J.P.
Mason,Andrew A.20 to Elizabeth Goode 20	3-23-1891	Jno.P.Campbell,JP
Mason,Martin 21 to Ida Jones 18	2-27-1897	P.R.Rickman,M.G.
Mason,Charlie 24 to Jane Scroggs 25	5-19-1901	M.L.Kelly,J.P.
Mason,J.N.53 to Cordelia Marr 23	6-30-1901	S.J.May,J.P.
Mason,W.R.22 to Maggie Gibson 21	1-29-1905	John C.Hurst,J.P.
Mason,John 28 to Pallie Holden 23	1-10-1909	W.C.Mason,M.G.
Mason,Harley 21 to Roseta Anderson 23	4-11-1909	F.M.Morgan,M.G.
Mason,Henry 23 to Margaret Morgan 18	8-30-1910	W.C.Mason,M.G.
Mason,J.N.26 to Margaret Vinson 18	11-5-1910	J.D.Vinson,M.G.
Mason,R.A.22 to Lillie Waters 27	1-26-1912	D.A.Yonce,M.G.
Mason,Thomas 21 to Lillie Owenby 20	12-15-1912	S.J.Mashburn,M.G.
Mason,Edward 19 to Martha Smith 18	2-19-1913	P.H.Justice,J.P.
Mason,Dan 21 to Pearl Sanders 19	8- 6-1915	Original not found
Mason,Wavery 19 to Estell Rogers 17 Col.	8-18-1915	J.R.Pendergrass,MG
Mason,Dan 21 to Ida Hasting 21	2-10-1916	Robert Stamey,J.P
Mason,Buel 22 to Nena Dalton 19	7- 4-1919	J.R.Pendergrass,MG
Mason,Arthur 20 to Fay Plemmons 18	8- 8-1919	J.R.Pendergrass,MG
Mason,Oscar 21 to Delphia McMahan 18	12-24-1919	W.C.Mason,M.G.
Mason,Felix 21 to Ida Wilson 18	12-10-1920	W.C.Mason,M.G.
Mason,Sheridan 21 to Elvie Anderson 19	10-10-1922	D.C.McCoy,M.G.
Mason,Ralph 24 to Kate Daves 18	8-28-1928	Geo.Carpenter,J.P
Mason,Marion W.47 to Eva Drendle 37	4-11-1936	Geo.Carpenter,J.P
Mason,John 38 to Lillie B.Roper 18	12-3-1936	Geo.W.Stepp,J.P.
Mathews,James 23 to Lindia Holden 19 He from Graham Co.N.C.	12-20-1883	Wm.Deweese,M.G.
Mathews,David 22 to Rebecca Webb 18	10-6-1886	Original not found
Mathews,John 22 to Telitha Jane Webb 21	2-27-1904	Henry Stewart,Jr.
Mathis,W.M. to Elizabeth West	8-11-1848	J.K.Gray,Clk.
Mathis,Levi to Lucinda Robbins	9- 9-1857	J.L.Robinson,D.Cl
Mathis,Christine to Elizabeth Ray	6-14-1869	David Sheets,M.G.
Mathis,Wm.W.20 to Mary M.Kirklan 22	7- 6-1879	J.S.Gibson,J.P.
Mathis,Henry C.19 to Margaret Connard 20	9- 4-1880	John S.Gibson,J.P
Mathis,James 22 to Cordelia Flowers 18	12-22-1892	W.J.Jenkins,J.P.
Mathis,J.D.35 to Fanny Dills 22	4-21-1898	E.B.Angel,J.P.
Mathis,G.W.69 to Adaline Watts 67	11-1-1902	W.P.Allison,J.P.
Mathis,Tom 25 to Mrs.Mary B.Dalrymple 29	7-22-1911	J.R.Pendergrass,MG
Mathis,Andy 26 to Ellen Smith 24	3- 3-1913	J.L.Bryson,J.P.
Mathis,Grover 23 to Urella McCall 20	10-7-1916	J.J.Carver,J.P.
Matheson,E.F.to Abigail Roland	4-25-1856	J.L.Robinson,J.P
Matheson,Wm.F.19 to Julia A.Dalrymple 22	9- 2-1889	T.W.Brown,M.G.
Matlock,J.H.to Alvira J.West	5-28-1864	W.M.Downes,D.Clk.
Matlock,Thomas to Jane Allman Col.	2-12-1867	B.G.Wild,J.P.
Matlock,Andrew to Mary I.Browning	8-20-1869	R.C.Slagle,D.Reg.
Matlock,Thomas 19 to Laura Bailey 16	10-27-1889	J.B.Elmore,J.P.
Matlock,John B.22 to Lillie Mason 18	9-27-1894	Geo.T.Bryson,J.P.

```
Mauldin,H.L.52 to Sallie Shope 40                7- 6-1910  J.T.Watts,J.P.
May,Palmer to Mary Cochran                       2- 4-1869  R.C.Slagle,Reg.
May,Sam 20 to Sarah Wishon 19                    11-19-1919 F.T.Gettis,J.P.
May,Mark 60 to Cecilla Gillespie (widow)44       11-22-1874 Albert Siler,J.P.
May,S.J.25 to Nancy R.Burch 16                   1- 7-1877  Z.Barnes,J.P.
May,S.J.28 to Jane Jones 20                      8- 1-1880  Wm.Deweese,M.G.
May,Marcus M.24 to Lavada Smith 18               7- 8-1894  F.M.Morgan,M.G.
May,W.B.23 to Rachel Mann 20                     3-26-1899  W.C.Hanrick,M.G.
May,M.J.23 to Rosa B.Mason 17                    4- 7-1901  S.J.May,J.P.
May,Tim A.22 to Nora Hurst 19                    5- 7-1910  Joseph L.Fouts,JP
May,William O.37 to Eliza V.Green 27             1- 9-1927  Geo.C.Steed,M.G.
   He from Atlanta,Ga.
May,John 25 to Lola Cochran 18                   8- 6-1933  P.H.Passmore,M.G.
May,James B.21 to Gladys Cochran 21              5- 1-1934  T.D.Denny,M.G.
Mayfield,Moses W.to Marthey Bradley              12-2-1833  Pleasant Bradley.
Medlin,Franklin to M.C.Welch                     3-21-1850  J.K.Gray,Clk.
Medlin,William to Rebecca Lindsey                5-12-1860  R.C.Slagle,Reg.
Meadows,Daniel to Nancy C.Elmore                 9- 1-1865  L.F.Siler,J.P.
Meadows,Willis 24 to Martha Duvall 21            7-31-1892  W.J.Jenkins,J.P.
Meadows,Emlius 23 to Ethel Morgan 14             11-25-1900 J.B.Justice,J.P.
Meadows,Crude 21 to Kattie Cansler 18            3- 2-1910  J.L.Bryson,J.P.
Meadows,Seth 25 to Hattie Potts 24               3-31-1910  R.R.Rickman,J.P.
Medford,James B.61 to Sue Gray 33                9- 7-1927  J.A.Flanagan,M.G.
   He from Haywood Co.N.C.
Medford,C.H.28 to Anna V.Myers 19                9-30-1928  J.A.Flanagan,M.G.
   He from Andrews,N.C.
Medford,Elmer 22 to Beatrice Byrd 21             2-14-1932  W.L.Buchanan,M.G.
   Both from Bryson City,N.C.
Meroney,W.R.to Zelphan Belk                      11-19-1836 John Tatham,C.S.C
Merritt,William 26 to Susannah Thomasson 19/12-19-1885 W.A.Thomas,M.G.
Merritt,Melvill S.26 to Rachel A.Sanders 20/10-1-1891  J.B.Elmore,J.P.
Messer,Henry to Catherine Sutton                 11-9-1851  J.K.Gray,Clk.
Messer,W.J.28 to Elizabeth Ramsey 22             12-23-1875 I.D.Wright,M.G.
   He from Jackson Co.N.C.
Messer,Thadus 22 to Sarah H.McKinney 18          2-22-1876  Jno.McDowell,M.G.
Messer,W.T. to Anice Allen                       9- 4-1880  John T.Gibson,J.P
   He from Haywood Co.N.C.
Messer,John L.26 to Kittie E.Luther 25           6-28-1896  T.Baxter White,JP
Messer,John L.26 to Kittie Luther 25             12-24-1896 G.R.McPherson,J.P
Messer,Jason 52 to Nannie Rhodes 33              9- 6-1900  R.S.Howell,M.G.
Messer,Charles 24 to Lona Henson 16              9-14-1908 J.R.Pendergrass,MG
Messer,Granvill 22 to Della Parrish 22           10-13-1935 Geo.Carpenter
   She from Alarka,N.C.
Miles,John A.,Jr.30 to Mary Ives Stuart 25       8-22-1907  F.L.Townsend,M.G.
Mills,James to Jane Morrow                       10-10-1865 J.M.Thomas, Wit.
Miller,Noah to Elizabeth Taber                   3-15-1842  J.K.Gray,Clk.
Miller,John K.to Arlena Tabor                    12-22-1846 J.K.Gray,Clk.
Miller,Henry to Elizabeth Forriester             12-4-1849  T.P.Siler,D.Clk.
Miller,Henry to Elizabeth Moore                  7- 1-1858  R.C.Slagle,C.C.
```

```
Miller,Joel B.to Elizabeth Hughston          2-28-1859   R.C.Slagle,Reg.
Miller,David to Louisa Vaughn                3-14-1866   I.N.Keener,J.P.
Miller,Joseph I.22 to Mary I.Henderson 24    8-10-1873   J.D.Vinson,M.G.
Miller,Charles 20 to Tolitha McCoy 18        8-19-1881   J.A.Deal,M.G.
Miller,John 32 to Sallie Cypher 30     Col. 12-10-1882 J.E.Kilgore,M.G.
Miller,David F.29 to Rebecca Angel 22        11-22-1885 John Elmore,J.P.
Miller,D.I.20 to Margaret Watkins 19         2- 7-1886   D.L.Miller,M.G.
Miller,Geo.L.20 to Elvira Rogers 18          11-17-1892 J.M.Keener,M.G.
Miller,Geo.B.21 to Julia Ann N.Watkins 16    8- 5-1894   L.H.Garland,J.P.
Miller,Aaron B.24 to Laura S.Rogers 17       2- 3-1895   D.L.Miller,M.G.
Miller,Jeremiah 20 to Arizona Corbin 19      12-27-1896 I.T.Peek,M.G.
Miller,D.L.,Jr.21 to Sarah Carpenter 18      5-13-1900   I.T.Peek,M.G.
Miller,Jeremiah 28 to Fannie Bryson 17       12-11-1904 J.I.Miller,M.G.
Miller,Archie 22 to Parazadie Peek 18        7- 9-1905   J.D.Vinson,M.G.
Miller,H.O.26 to Thedocia Peek 25            2-13-1907   T.J.Vinson,M.G.
Miller,Bynum 19 to Riffie Benfield 16        1-25-1908   C.L.Rickman,J.P.
Miller,Henry 23 to Bessie Ballew 20          10-15-1911 J.D.Vinson,M.G.
Miller,Lemuel 19 to Fannie Talley 21         5-24-1914   R.H.Munger,J.P.
Miller,Evit 18 to Addie Henry 16             1-17-1915   T.M.Keener,J.P.
Miller,Edgar 21 to Lidda Adams 22            9-10-1917 Original not found
Miller,W.E.25 to Eva Woodard 21              1-14-1922 J.R.Pendergrass,MG
Miller,John A.36 to Bessie Wiggins 18        5- 8-1926   B.C.Reavis,M.G.
   Both from Bryson City,N.C.
Miller,Aaron H.21 to Lillie A.Tilson 16      2- 5-1935   Edgar Miller,J.P.
Millsaps,Logan to Lettie A.Cailor            11-25-1855 John T.Millsap.
Mincy,Henry R.to Mary Peek                   1-26-1859   R.C.Slagle,Reg.
Mincey,James A.to Susan C.Peek               2-26-1862   R.C.Slagle,C.C.C.
Mincy,Charles G.27 to Nannie J. Higdon 18    1-27-1895   J.P.Moore,J.P.
Mincy,David M.26 to Lillie Ammons 21         9-27-1895   J.W.Parker,J.P.
Mincy,O.V.23 to Ethel Rebecca Pressley 18    4- 4-1920   J.M.Raby,J.P.
Mincy,Lester L.32 to Kate Jones 25           10-1-1933   O.E.Moses,J.P.
Mingus,Shannon 22 to Lavada England 23  Col.11-5-1892   W.J.Jenkins,J.P.
Mingus,Ed 21 to Conie Malonee  18       Col.8-15-1901   J.L.Bryson,J.P.
Mingus,Frank 25 to Austa Burgess 19     Col.6- 3-1912   M.J.Mashburn,J.P.
Mingus,Bert 27 to Cora Wikle 23         Col.7-20-1913   Samuel Logan,M.G.
Mingus,Frank 35 to May Moore 19         Col.12-6-1926   Geo.Carpenter,J.P
Minters,William M.to Mary A.Owen             5-13-1858   T.P.Siler,D.Clk.
Mitchell,J.W. to Mary E.Ray                  7-27-1857   J.P.McConnell.
Mitchell,George 21 to Nancy Southards 19     10-26-1890 W.C.Kimzey,J.P.
Mitchell,E.W.,Jr. 23 to Lillie Johnson 20 Col./10-25-1909-E.S.Wyly,M.G.
Mize,Nathan 22 to Laura Norris 17            2-21-1904   S.S.Long,J.P.
Mize,Ray 22 to Minnie Palmer 19              9-27-1915   J.M.Bennett,M.G.
Mock,Will 21 to Ada Shepherd 18         Col.12-22-1897 Geo.Bryson,J.P.
Moffitt,Josiah to Sarah L.Huggins            1- 3-1840   John Hall,Clk.
Moffitt,Geo.W.to Amanda A.Johnston           7-25-1858   R.C.Slagle,Reg.
Moffitt,John to Ida Kimsey                   9-12-1862   R.C.Slagle,Reg.
Moffatt,William S.24 to Roxanna Elliott 22  2-12-1880   J.H.Addington,J.P
```

```
Moffatt,William S.24 to Roxanna Elliott 22      2-12-1880   J.H.Addington,J.P
Moffate,L.K.21 to M.A.McGee 20                  12-29-1881  J.H.Addington,J.P
Moffitt,G.W.20 to Margaret McGee 20             1- 8-1885   W.C.Kimzey,J.P.
Moffitt,L.K.30 to A.Slice Enloe 20              7-10-1890   W.G.Mallonee,M.G.
Moffitt,John M.24 to Bertha Blaine 20           11-11-1908  J.R.Pendergras,MG
Moffitt,Laurence 18 to Bertha Ledford 20        2-18-1909   J.R.Pendergras,MG
Moffitt,Lester 21 to Aline Donaldson 22         8-31-1910   J.T.Watts,J.P.
Moffitt,Dillard 22 to Gula May Sanders 18       12-24-1911  Robert Stamey,J.P
Moffitt,Charles 27 to Inez Dillard 26           11-12-1913  J.L.Teague,M.G.
Moffitt,Geo.Lester 25 to Ida Anderson 21        4- 1-1914   J.M.Griggs,M.G.
Moffitt,O.C.28 to Carrie Sellers 24             12-23-1914  J.M.Bennett,M.G.
Moffitt,B.M. 22 to Blanche C.Blaine 19          12-24-1916  D.S.Richardson,MG
Moffett,Howard R.24 to Zelma Jenkins 27         11-12-1938  J.L.Teague,M.G.
Moffitt,Earnest 20 to Eunice Stockton 18        3-16-1939   Lester L.Arnold.
Monroe,Washington 51 to Lou McDonnell 37 Col.11-7-1887 W.S.Ballard,M.G.
Monteith,D.W. 43 to C.M.Keener 55               7-21-1898   A.G.Wood,J.P.
Monteith,J.C. 26 to Lula London 19              11-6-1902   M.A.Love,M.G.
Monteith,W.O.24 to Sarah May Wilson 19          12-31-1911  A.P.Foster,M.G.
Montgomery,Oscar 20 to Bulah Wykle 20 Col.      10-10-1910  Chas.L.Stewart,MG
Moody,William H.26 to Mary R.Russell 17         4-26-1891   John L.Corbin,J.P.
Moody,C.T.29 to Lillie Calloway 26              8-14-1933   Chas.R.McCarty,MG
Mooney,Lucius P.28 to Lucinda Mashburn 21       12-2-1894   John Elmore,J.P.
Moore,Isaac to Rachel Bryson                    1-29-1839   M.Dowell,J.P.
Moore,G.W.J.to Lena Woodard                     10-15-1840  J.K.Gray,Clk.
Moore,Josiah to Elizabeth Bryson                9- 2-1841   John Hall,Clk.
Moore,Parker to Hulda Kilpatrick                3- 7-1844   J.K.Gray,Clk.
Moore,John to Mary Ann Berry                    11-19-1853  John Hall,Clk.
Moore,John J.to Sarah A.Bell                    8-22-1854   James T.Smith,M.G
Moore,T.H.to Ellen Bird                         7- 1-1858   R.C.Slagle,Clk.
Moore,B.W.to Roxana E.Siler                     11-15-1859  T.P.Siler,D.Clk.
Moore,J.D. to Louisa Blackburn                  12-17-1859  R.C.Slagle,Reg.
Moore,John W. to Mary A.Hyatt                   10-17-1861  R.C.Slagle,Reg.
Moore,A.J. to Mary C.Holbrooks                  4- 7-1862   R.C.Slagle,Reg.
Moore,William to Elizabeth Crunkleton           7-12-1862   R.C.Slagle,C.C.C.
Moore,John to Margaret Guyer                    11-4-1864   R.C.Slagle,C.C.C.
Moore,J.S. to Susan C.Wickle                    9-18-1865   R.C.Slagle,Reg.
Moore,William to Hanna Patton        Col.       9- 3-1866   T.S.Addington,J.P
Moore,William to Hanna M.Siler       Col.       11-27-1867  R.C.Slagle,Clk.
Moore,Marion to Mary Shepherd        Col.       6- 6-1869   J.K.Bryson,Reg.
Moore,Patt to Maria Greenwood                   12-25-1869  D.C.Harden,J.P.
Moore,John P.44 to Nancy V.Young 35             11-6-1873   J.S.Woodard,M.G.
Moore,Martin 19 to Harriett McDonnell 19 Col.12-4-1875 D.W.Wells,M.G.
Moore,T.L.20 to E.R.Benfield 16                 5-17-1876   E.H.Franks,J.P.
Moore,J.L.Jr.40 to Lillie A.McDonnell 23        12-20-1883  C.D.Smith,M.G.
Moore,W.M.26 to Mary Love  20            Col. 12-27-1883 F.P.Moulden,M.G.
Moore,H.W.26 to Martha Bryson 22                3-30-1884   John B.Gray,J.P.
Moore,A.T.23 to Theadocia Mason 16              4-20-1884   J.M.Forrester,J.P.
```

Moore,Simon 19 to Ada Anderson 14   Col. 12-12-1884 B.G.Wild,M.G.
Moore,James A.19 to Sudie E.Boyd 22   8- 1-1886 P.P.McLean,M.G.
Moore,Geo.W.18 to Pearlie M.Welch 16   8-22-1886 H.D.Dean,J.P.
Moore,David D.20 to Rutha A.Caler 18   12-12-1886 F.M.Morgan,M.G.
Moore,U.Emerson 19 to Julia H.Owen 18   9-11-1887 S.A.Dixon,J.P.
  He from Transylevana Co.N.C.
Moore,Simon 24 to Lassie McDonnell 18   Col. 10-24-1889 James Bristol,M.G
Moore,J.W.39 to Arie A.McDowell 24   11-7-1889 J.O.Shelby,M.G.
Moore,John J.Jr.,Dr.57 to Mrs.Louisa J.Wallace 27/6-11-1890-C.D.Smith,MG
Moore,William J.25 to Sallie E.Morgan 18   8- 2-1891 M.Ghormley,M.G.
Moore,William 45 to Emma Clanton 19   Col. 1-13-1894 Ransom Powell,M.G.
Moore,Larken A.22 to Darkey J.Mincy 21   12-23-1894 J.R.Pendergras,MG
Moore,Charley 21 to Mary Harper 20   Col. 12-28-1897 C.W.Walton,M.G.
Moore,Joab 18 to Mary Winfrey 19   8-19-1898 M.Ghormley,M.G.
Moore,J.H.49 to M.E.Mann 24   1- 1-1902 Ira Erwin,M.G.
Moore,J.P.33 to Allie P.Allen 27   12-25-1902 J.W.Briggs,M.G.
Moore,Andrew J.,Jr.30 to Jane McDowell 21   9-11-1904 J.W.Ammons,J.P.
Moore,James C.23 to Sallie Hooper 22   10-22-1905 J.W.Ammons,J.P.
Moore,J.Marion 30 to Ida Bryson 20   10-14-1906 W.R.Bulgin,J.P.
Moore,Rufus Alex 21 to Lillie Henry 16   11-25-1906 J.M.Keener,M.G.
Moore,William 48 to Elizabeth Obey 35   Col. 2-27-1906 J.T.Kennedy,M.G.
Moore,Harvey 20 to Eldie Allison 18   1-30-1907 Retd.not executed
Moore,Charles M.47 to Mary Carson 42   10-17-1907 F.L.Townsend,M.G.
Moore,Andrew 21 to Arie Jones 20   8-27-1908 J.W.Duvall,J.P.
Moore,S.W.25 to Ethel Crisp 16   9- 6-1908 W.L.Bulgin,J.P.
Moore,J.P.40 to Sarah S.Stewart 37   7- 4-1909 S.L.Loudermilk,MG
Moore,Alex 39 to Ida Corbin 25   12-24-1911 R.P.McCracken,M.G
Moore,Charley 19 to Eva Martin 18   3- 8-1913 Original not found
Moore,W.T.29 to Sallie E.Cunningham 20   12-30-1914 R.H.Dougherty,M.G
Moore,J.B.33 to Mary Robertson 21   4-27-1916 W.T.Potts,M.G.
Moore,C.G.24 to Jean Barnard 22   5-17-1916 R.H.Dougherty,M.G
Moore,C.E.39 to Mamie Rogers 18   4- 8-1917 L.J.Young,M.G.
Moore,T.L.62 to Mary Samantha Stewart 52   4-11-1918 N.L.Jolly,J.P.
Moore,Burt 39 to Balzora Leatherman 30   4- 2-1919 J.L.Bryson,J.P.
Moore,W.L.37 to Hattie Sanders 32   1-10-1923 R.E.Ward,M.G.
Moore,Clifford 27 to Bell Conley 30   Col.   12-22-1926 Geo.Carpenter,J.P
Moore,Fred S.29 to Leona Waldroop 25   4-16-1927 A.P.Ratledge,M.G.
Moore,Carl 28 to Carrie Gibson 19   Col.   6-24-1933 Sam J.Murray,J.P.
Moore,Wendell Wm.21 to Allie Jennings 18   5-19-1935 Earnest James,M.G
Moore,Howard A.25 to Cora Lee Higdon 20   12-8-1935 Geo Carpenter,J.P
Morgan,William B.to Mary Queen   2- 3-1833 John Hall,Clk.
Morgan,James to Elizabeth Kilpatrick   4- 7-1833 John Hall,Clk.
Morgan,Robert to Lydia Kilpatrick   12-11-1833 John Tatham,Clk.
Morgan,William to Anna James   6-21-1836 John Tatham,Clk.
Morgan,Barthew to Patsy Griffin   11- 6-1837 John Hall,Clk.
Morgan,M.P.to Catherine DeHart   1- 4-1853 T.P.Siler,D.Clk.
Morgan,B.L.to Susan C.Battles   4-22-1859 E.Collins,J.P.

```
Morgan,Joseph to Rebecca Deweese           1-18-1862   R.C.Slagle,Reg.
Morgan,George to Adaline Roper             2- 4-1860   R.C.Slagle,Reg.
Morgan,William C.to Mary L.Sheets          12-15-1860  R.C.Slagle,Reg.
Morgan,William to L.J.Watters              10-24-1861  R.C.Slagle,Reg.
Morgan,J.B.to A.I.Matheson                 2-27-1862   R.C.Slagle,Reg.
Morgan,James W.to Carolina M.Ridley        2-27-1869   R.C.Slagle,Reg.
Morgan,Jason H.to Mary E.Jones             2-18-1872   Joseph Morgan,J.P
Morgan,James L.19 to Amanda Adams 20       7-28-1881   E.H.Franks,J.P.
Morgan,Alf 26 to Fannie E.Siler 24         8- 4-1881   D.L.Miller,M.G.
Morgan,W.R.23 to Ellen Tallent 16          12-30-1884  Canara S.Ray,J.P.
Morgan,Joseph 49 to Lillie T.Owenby 26     10-2-1887   F.M.Morgan,M.G.
Morgan,Joseph W.26 to Callie Childers 20   4-24-1890   M.J.Mashburn,J.P.
Morgan,George 20 to Emma Cope 20           3-24-1892   A.B.Dalton,J.F.
Morgan,William R.21 to Mary R.Barnes 16    9-16-1894   M.Ghormley,M.G.
Morgan,Jonathan M.24 to Ella Bradley 18    1-30-1896   H.D.Dean,J.P.
Morgan,James R.21 to Emily Dean 18         5-15-1898   J.J.McCoy,J.P.
Morgan,Jesse 21 to Ever Hedden 16          6-26-1898   J.B.Elmore,J.P.
Morgan,W.J.22 to Beulah Dean 20            2-22-1898   J.B.Justice,J.P.
Morgan,G.A.21 to Agness Pendergrass 18     2- 5-1899   W.C.Mason,M.G.
Morgan,Charley 24 to Dora Wilson 19        8-20-1899   W.C.Mason,M.G.
Morgan,James J.26 to Laura Reid 21         11-12-1899  J.B.Elmore,J.P.
Morgan,Arthur 21 to Lener Winfrey 16       3-15-1903   D.F.Howard,M.G.
Morgan,Willard 20 to Fannie Winfry 19      4-16-1904   E.Norris,M.G.
Morgan,Martin Van 20 to Julia Pendergrass 19/3-3-1909 D.A.Yonce,M.G.
Morgan,E.J.19 to Claudie Barrier 19        4-23-1916   D.F.Howard,M.G.
Morgan,C.A.26 to Bertha Holland 19         11-22-1917  Geo.Carpenter,J.P
Morgan,A.C.20 to Minnie Sanders 20         11-25-1917  Geo.Carpenter,J.P
Morgan,F.D.18 to Mattie Sanders 18         2-17-1918   Geo.Carpenter,J.P
Morgan,Leeman 21 to Lydia Brooks 18        10-1-1918 J.R.Pendergrass,MG
Morgan,J.W.,Jr.27 to Mary Nichols 22       11-14-1920  Geo.Carpenter,J.P
Morgan,Frank W.19 to Ada Sanders 21        11-16-1921  J.R.Pendergras,MG
Morgan,John H.31 to Clara Shook 21         12-18-1921  R.C.Morgan,M.G.
Morgan,Arthur 21 to Zettie Mason 18        12-25-1921  P.H.Passmore,M.G.
Morgan,Jeff 24 to Esther Smith 22          12-12-1925  Geo.Carpenter,J.P
Morgan,Horace J.31 to Nellie M.Wilkes 22   11-16-1926  J.R.Pendergras,MG
Morgan,Arthur M.31 to Dorothy Roper 19     8- 9-1931   W.C.Mason,M.G.
   Both from Nantahala,N.C.
Morgan,Zeb 24 to Gladys Roland 19          9- 4-1938   T.D.Denny,M.G.
   Both from Nantahala,N.C.
Morris,John M.75 to Martha S.Collins 27    8- 9-1887   W.J.Jenkins,J.P.
Morris,Ben 30 to Laura Angel 19       Col. 12-22-1887 James Bristol,M.G
Morrison,James to Arminda Shepherd         11-7-1844   James Morrison,Wi
Morrison,Alfred to Sarah Burnett           11-28-1849  T.P.Siler,D.Clk.
Morrison,John to Cynthia Barnett           10-9-1851   E.Collins,J.P.
Morrison,Javan to Lelah Ann Pase           8-11-1853   J.K.Gray,Clk.
Morrison,William to Elizabeth Saunders     12-29-1855  Peter Davis.
Morrison,Joseph to Margaret M.Bryson       8-17-1856   J.T.Buchanan,M.G.
Morrison,William to Elizabeth Saunders     12-29-1858  John Hall,Clk.
```

Morrison,William to Clarinda Cansler	12-27-1866	R.C.Slagle,C.C.C.
Morrison,W.H.23 to M.J.Bradley 18	1-20-1876	I.D.Wright,M.G.
Morrison,W.S.20 to Margaret A.Patton 19	11-16-1876	I.D.Wright,M.G.
Morrison,James A.24 to L.E.Dean 18	7-31-1884	W.H.Conner,M.G.
Morrison,John 23 to Elizabeth Hasting 20 He from Jackson Co.N.C.	4- 5-1885	M.S.Dills,J.P.
Morrison,Joseph 52 to M.Jenney Watkins42	6-15-1889	J.W.Rickman,J.P.
Morrison,James M.26 to Margaret Meadows 19	10-23-1892	Joseph Morgan,J.P
Morrison,Juan 22 to Melie Dills 18	3-17-1909	J.R.Pendergrass,MG
Morrison,F.D.26 to Arie West 28	5-21-1924	A.J.Smith,M.G.
Morrison,Harley R.52 to Minnie Potts 27	7-28-1934	A.S.Solesbee,M.G.
Morrison,J.Don 28 to Virginia Kennedy 18 Both from High Point,N.C.	6-12-1937	D.C.McCoy,M.G.
Moose,Joe 50 to Callie Shields 25	12-6-1907	J.L.Fouts,J.P.
Moreland,John to Jane Robinson	6- 5-1835	J.M.Bryson,J.P.
Morrow,Patterson to Mary Morrow	2-15-1831	John Hall,Clk.
Morrow,James to Frances Hester	8-18-1833	John Hall,Clk.
Morrow,William to Nancy Belk	2-10-1834	John Tatham,Clk.
Morrow,E.G. to Selene Mauney	--26-1841	J.K.Gray,Clk.
Morrow,Jim to Mary Love Col.	7-28-1870	R.C.Slagle,D.Reg.
Morrow,James H.19 to Lila T.Mock 15 Col.	8-19-1893	J.D.Wadell,M.G.
Morrow,John P.50 to Cordelia Mathis 35 Col.	10-6-1935	Geo.Carpenter,J.P
Moses,Arthur to Manerva Peek	12-19-1850	J.K.Gray,Clk.
Moses,Anson B.18 to Emaline Jones 18	5-11-1873	J.T.Strain,J.P.
Moses,A.B.24 to Mary J.Gregory 18	4-29-1879	W.W.Henry,J.P.
Moses,David J.21 to Edith L.Brown 21	4- 1-1890	Hosea Moses,J.P.
Moses,William A.60 to Anna M.Justice 30	4-28-1891	Hosea Moses,J.P.
Moses,Byard 21 to Lydea Young 20	11-13-1892	J.T.Berry,J.P.
Moses,W.H.17 to Fannie Keener 17	12-30-1897	G.W.Stiwinter,J.P
Moses,A.B.45 to Ann Southards 24	1- 1-1901	J.M.Keener,M.G.
Moses,R.C.21 to Jane Buchanan 18	12-30-1901	J.M.Keener,M.G.
Moses,Clarence 19 to Latha Peek 26	1-12-1913	J.M.Keener,M.G.
Moses,Oliney 18 to Jessie Conley 18	12-9-1914	Original not found
Moses,Oleney 18 to Dessie Ammons 18	1-10-1915	J.P.Moore,J.P.
Moses,Zachary 22 to Minnie Moses 21	12-27-1915	J.P.Moore,J.P.
Moses,Athen 27 to Nora Holland 26	8- 8-1920	J.M.Keener,M.G.
Moses,Thurman 23 to Rebecca McCall 22	5-30-1923	J.M.Keener,J.P.
Moses,P.N.28 to Martha Taylor 21	5- 7-1927	Geo.Carpenter,J.P
Moses,Oliver H.20 to Tisha McFalls 21 She from Glenville,N.C.	3-29-1936	William Henry,J.P
Moss,Thomas to Melinda Sutton	3-27-1831	John Hall,Clk.
Moss,Howell to Lucinda Redmond	9-26-1834	John Tatham,Clk.
Moss,William to Nicy Deannon	12-17-1835	Henry Moss.
Moss,William to Martha Holbrooks	11-4-1869	James Bryson,Reg.
Moss,John 24 to Mattie Fox 24	6- 9-1895	J.P.Moore,J.P.
Moss,Frank 23 to Rosetta Holland 22	8-22-1909	Z.J.Peek,J.P.
Moss,Charles 26 to Jane Ammons 29	8-26-1915	W.G.Wood,J.P.
Moss,T.M.36 to Alice Wood 22	12-16-1922	A.B.Potts,J.P.

Moss,Fred J.29 to Fannie Smith 18	8-25-1923	Z.Baird,J.P.
Moss,Milton to Ruth Peak	3-10-1836	Ulrich Keener,Cl?
Mosteller,Jesse 22 to Lillie Passmore 18	11-30-1911	T.B.Enloe J.P.
Mattox,A.M.24 to La Delle Black 24	8- 2-1921	Geo.Carpenter,J.?
Mozeley,W.E.22 to A.H.Penland 25	4- 3-1897	R.B.Shelton,M.G.
Mozeley,Thomas 20 to Ada Greenwood 18 Col.	1- 5-1898	C.W.Walton,M.G.
Mozeley,James 20 to Grady West 20	9- 1-1918	J.C.Umburger,M.G
Munday,A.P.to A.A.Jarrett	9-17-1855	W.M.Adington.
Munday,Boice 21 to Mary Bell Ashe 23	2-13-1913	Original not retd
Munday,T.S.59 to Pauline M.Foust 35	6-20-1928	Robert F.Mock,M.?
Munger,Fred W.22 to Rebecca L.D.Cabe 23	11-24-1898	J.M.Carpenter,J.?
Munger,R.H.30 to Mrs.Nancy Manley 33	1-15-1905	Thomas B.White,J?
Munger,James S.26 to Nora L.Jones 16	8-31-1908	T.Baxter White,J?
Murray,James W.to Metilda Watters	3-20-1834	L.M.Dowdle.
Murray,John W.19 to Mattie J.Rickman 23	5-10-1884	P.R.Rickman,M.G.
Murray,Joseph 19 to Annie Franks 18	12-17-1891	P.R.Rickman,M.G.
Murray,Frank I.26 to Nobia Gibson 21	1-12-1919	T.J.Vinson,M.G.
Murray,S.J.30 to Mamie Higdon 29	6-27-1920	Joseph A.Bryson.
Murray,Frank I.26 to Nobia Gibson 21	1-12-1919	T.J.Vinson,M.G.
Murphy,F.C. to Lucinda Jane Moore	6- 8-1870	J.K.Bryson,Reg.
Murrow,Anderson 22 to Fannie McAfee 16 Col.	3- 2-1884	E.H.Bogle,M.G.
Mull,William E.to Margaret Plemmons	5-31-1841	John Hall,Clk.
Mull,Benjamin to Martha Hadgcock	9-16-1845	J.K.Gray,Clk.
Mull,Johnston to Polly Bradley	3- 1-1849	M.L.Sherrill.
Mullins,Asa to Nancy Jentry	8-19-1864	R.C.Slagle,Reg.
Myers,John C.to Susan Vanhook	1-19-1865	J.F.Mashburn.
Myers,L.P. to E.C.Collins	2-12-1867	R.C.Slagle,Clk.
Myers,Pinkney P.23 to Tina Mashburn 21	11-14-1875	Thos.Mashburn,J.?
Myers,D.A.21 to Lena Angel 23	11-26-1883	M.J.Mashburn,J.P
Myers,Jacob T.37 to Callie N.Jacobs 28	5-29-1889	M.J.Mashburn,J.P
Myers,James E.24 to Nannie B.Jacobs 18	8- 3-1896	E.Myers,M.G.
Myers,George B.29 to Carrie E.Palmer 20	10-30-1912	J.R.Pendergras,M?
McAfee,A.McDuffie 21 to Mary Logan 21	5-14-1891	J.C.Hemphill,M.G.
McCaley,Raymond D.21 to Mary L.Evans 21	10-24-1931	Clifton Ervin,M.?
McCall,John to Mary Smith	1-18-1852	J.K.Gray,Clk.
McCall,William M.to Rebecca Frady	3-25-1858	R.C.Slagle,Clk.
McCall,S.J.to Jane Morgan	10-9-1862	B.H.Jones.
McCall,Thomas J.to Isobeler H.Chastain	9- 1-1869	J.W.Wilson,J.P.
McCall,S.C.22 to L.E.Vinson 22	10-25-1877	J.W.Wilson,J.P.
McCall,Thomas R.23 to Elizabeth Webb 17	6- 3-1888	M.J.Skinner,J.P.
McCall,Rufus 23 to Albie Picklesimer 22	8-17-1890	M.J.Skinner,J.P.
McCall,George W.29 to Nancy J.Shepherd 27	4-21-1891	J.W.Rickman,J.P.
McCall,James A.25 to Laura S.Talley 22	12-29-1895	T.Baxter White,J?
McCall,Julius W.28 to Alice Neely 23	11-21-1896	J.M.Keener,M.G.
McCall,T.T.47 to M.A.Vinson 19	3-13-1898	T.J.Vinson,J.P.
McCall,J.A.34 to Margaret Teague 44	3-12-1900	I.T.Peek,M.G.
McCall,D.A.21 to Rosie McClure 18	10-10-1901	J.D.Vinson,M.G.

McCall,Tyra 31 to Lizzie Scroggs 21	11-16-1902 J.M.Keener,M.G.
McCall,Vest 21 to Mindy Webb 20	4- 2- 1905 Henry Stewart,J.P.
McCall,Julius 31 to Callie Brown 17	3- 8-1906 S.S.Long,J.P.
McCall,Luther 21 to Mary McCoy 25	6-11-1907 J.M.Keener,M.G.
McCall,John 20 to Zena Owens 21	7- 5-1908 T.Baxter White,JP
McCall,Thomas C.21 to Bruenettie Owens 15	11-29-1908 P.C.Calloway,J.P.
McCall,E.S.25 to Lela Owens 23	3-18-1909 P.C.Calloway,J.P.
McCall,Harley M.21 to Annie Martin 21	9-22-1915 J.Z.Carver,J.P.
McCall,Andy 25 to Cyntha Moses 16	1- 9-1920 J.M.Keener,M.G.
McCall,Jasper 21 to Leona Teague 18	3- 6-1920 O.C.Corbin,J.P.
McCall,Luther 36 to Roxie Wood 29	12- 3-1921 J.M.Keener,M.G.
McCall,Harry E.29 to Essie E.Pettus 22	8- 3-1936 James C.Mell,J.P.
McCullom,Phil 23 to Mildred A.Kinnebrew 18	2-19-1933 L.B.Haynes,M.G.
McCallister,Charley to Name not given	12-2-1833 John Tatham,Clk.
McCarty,Chas.R.29 to Nancy J.Crockett 24	12-27-1934 S.R.Crockett,M.G.
McClure,Reubin to Mary Reid	3-12-1833 Mathew Russell.
McClure,E.H.to Tabitha Savage	11-21-1834 John Tatham,Clk.
McClure,Andrew to Margaret Rogers	12-12-1836 U.Keener,Clk.
McClure,George to Mercilla Howard	11-13-1837 J.K.Gray,Clk.
McClure,John to Maria Ann McDowell	4- 4-1840 John Hall,Clk.
McClure,W.M.to Elizabeth Jones	3-13-1848 J.K.Gray,Clk.
McClure,William to Elizabeth C.McDowell	2-18-1850 T.P.Siler,D.Clk.
McClure,Jasper to Mary Vaughn	6-??-1865 I.N.Keener,J.P.
McClure,Jessey to Isabeler Ingram	10-22-1865 A.B.Welch.
McClure,John W.to Sarah Vaughn	12-3-1871 J.D.Vinson,M.G.
McClure,Masrus L.17 to Rosetta Forester 21	10-12-1872 W.H.Roane,J.P.
McClure,James 17 to Juliet M.Watts 17	2- 4-1874 W.H.Roane,J.p.
McClure,L.J.24 to M.A.Norton 21	1- 4-1877 E.T.Long,J.P.
McClure,W.D.24 to E.J.Norton 24	1- 3-1878 E.T.Long,J.P.
McClure,John 68 to Mary A.McConnell 58	10-23-1883 John Elmore,J.P.
McClure,A.L.22 to Martha A.Forester 21	4- 5-1885 J.J.McConnell,J.P
McClure,Wm.H.22 to Raxie Ledford 20	2- 4-1886 S.A.Dixon,J.P.
McClure,Bynam M.22 to Anzonettee Hodgins 15	/7-18-1889 C.L.Ledford,M.G.
McClure,Ervin 20 to Rosetta Sanders 22	8- 7-1892 S.A.Dixon,J.P.
McClure,John T.21 to Bessie Blaine 19	9-13-1894 G.R.McPherson,J.P
McClure,Lamb 22 to Ella Cabe 22	4- 6-1905 J.E.Cabe,J.P.
McClure,Chas.H.35 to Ethel Gray 20	10-31-1906 R.M.Taylor,M.G.
McClure,W.M.25 to Ida McConnell 18	7-21-1907 J.E.Cabe,J.P.
McClure,Zeb 28 to Julia Ledford 28	12-25-1907 A.M.Ledford,M.G.
McClure,Oscar 21 to Maude Stockton 20	1-22-1908 Robert Stamey,J.P
McClure,Carey 21 to May Hodgins 18	5-15-1910 Robert Stamey,J.P
McClure,J.E.30 to Dora Bell Angel 24	8-31-1910 Original not found
McClure,Parker,26 to Frances Keener 19	12-22-1912 D.L.Miller,M.G.
McClure,Lee 23 to Brunettie McCoy 17	2- 9-1913 N.L.Jollay,J.P.
McClure,Otto 31 to Bessie Angel 19	5-10-1914 W.J.Warren,M.G.
McClure,Willard 21 to Frances Foster 19	4- 7-1934 J.R.Pendergrass,MG
McClure,Norman 21 to Mattie Russell 18	12-23-1936 Geo.Carpenter,J.P

```
McCombs,W.M.35 to Mary McDaniel 20          Col.3-30-1893   C.S.Ray,J.P.
McCombs,William 21 to Eliza Porter 22       Col.9-13-1896   John H.Bradley,MG
McCombs,J.Thomas 23 to Cora Moore 18        Col.9-21-1907 J.R.Pendergrass,MG
McCombs,William 26 to Bulah Montgomery25 Col.7-8-1916    C.L.Stewart,M.G.
McConnell,William to Sarah Crawford           3-22-1830   John W.Carnes,J.P
McConnell,William to Nancy Phillips          12-8-1838    John Hall,Clk.
McConnell,E.M.to Carolina Moffitt             3- 7-1898   J.K.Gray,Clk.
McConnell,D.A.to Susan V.Jones                1- 2-1850   J.K.Gray,Clk.
McConnell,W.M.to Rachel Crisp                12-10-1850 J.K.Gray,Clk.
McConnell,J.M.to Eliza Conley                 3- 6-1856   T.P.Jamerson,J.P.
McConnell,C.B.to Elizabeth Moffitt            1-20-1857   G.W.Moore.
McConnell,John P.to E.A.Sellers               8- 4-1857   J.G.Crawford,Sher
McConnell,J.J.to Julia Ann Gray              12-16-1864 R.C.Slagle,Clk.
McConnell,David to Hariett Wyant              9-17-1868   E.W.Moore,M.G.
McConnell,Samuel H.to Edy Carpenter           3-16-1871   J.H.Elmore,J.P.
McConnell,Wm.A.24 to Roxana J.McLoud 24      11-23-1872   H.H.Elmore,J.P.
McConnell,John D.21 to Rosetta Russell 21     9- 9-1874   ---------
McConnell,J.C.19 to S.E.Mann 19              12-17-1876 M.L.Kelly,J.P.
McConnell,J.C.25 to A.A.Guffee 22            12-20-1876 M.P.Swain,M.G.
McConnell,Jas.N.21 to B.E.Roane 18            5-10-1882   W.C.Carden,M.G.
McConnell,G.R.21 to Mary Phillips 21          9-30-1883   R.A.Owen,M.G.
McConnell,W.A.36 to Eliza J.Hall 30           3-27-1884   C.D.Smith,M.G.
McConnell,Elisha W.24 to Lillia A.Elliott 19/11-12-1884-W.C.Kimsey,J.P.
McConnell,Jno.C.24 to Temperence O.McCall 19/2-7-1886   J.W.Wilson,J.P.
McConnell,James M.22 to Sarah C.Thomas 23    10-13-1887 E.A.Sample,M.G.
McConnell,Benjamin T.18 to Sarah Sanders 24/11-10-1887 C.T.Roane,J.P.
McConnell,Albert N.21 to Maggie McDowell 25/11-11-1888 W.C.Kimsey,J.P.
McConnell,Wiley B.21 to Eulala Gray 21        8-25-1889   J.J.McConnell,J.P
McConnell,John C.28 to Elizabeth J.Long 43   12-15-1889 John Howard,J.P.
McConnell,Judson 24 to Cora H.McConnell 22    1- 6-1891   Geo.A.Sparrow,M.G
McConnell,Chas.W.28 to Sarah B.Stamey 18      8- 7-1892   G.R.McPherson,J.P
McConnell,John D.42 to Martary Russell 23    12-2-1894    N.J.Rush,J.P.
McConnell,C.A.25 to Lulah Garland 21          4-17-1898   J.M.Carpenter,J.P
McConnell,W.R.22 to Elmira J.Rogers 17       10-25-1900 T.N.Ford,M.G.
McConnell,E.C.28 to Ida E.Sellers 24          3-12-1902 J.R.Pendergrass,MG
McConnell,George R.40 to Sallie Whitmire 35/7-15-1906 J.R.Pendergrass,MG
McConnell,Robert 20 to Mary Mize 18           7-18-1907   J.E.Cabe,J.P.
McConnell,Harley M.28 to Nellie McConnell21/10-26-1911 M.H.Tuttle,M.G.
McConnell,John A.21 to Etta May Moffitt 20   12-13-1911 J.L.Teague,M.G.
McConnell,John C.51 to Ida M.Penland 21       5-19-1914   C.R.Cabe,J.P.
McConnell,Harve 23 to Nany Dowdle 21          2- 3-1915   W.G.Warren,M.G.
McConnell,Loran 23 to Bessie Ledford 23       2-21-1915   J.L.Kinsland,M.G.
McConnell,W.D.21 to Edna Ledford 17          10-25-1915 J.A.Brendle,M.G.
McConnell,Dewey 19 to Rosa Hastings 23       12-24-1917 Robert Stamey,J.P
McConnell,Edward 37 to Blanche Watts 23       8-25-1918   G.W.Moffitt,J.P.
McConnell,G.R.24 to Ethel Zachary 17          8- 3-1919   W.T.Potts,M.G.
McConnell,J.M.59 to Mrs.Carrie Hodgins 43     7-17-1924   V.B.Harrison,M.G.
```

McConnell,Arthur 32 to Minnie Sorrels	1-21-1920	J.A.Bryson,M.G.
McConnell,George,Jr.35 to Sallie Dowdle 33	11-27-1941	Philip L.Green,MG
McCord,H.I.to Americas Hood	9-23-1856	W.N.Allman.
McCoy,Daniel to Elizabeth West	3-24-1835	Miles Killian.
McCoy,Milton to Jula Peek	11-10-1836	Ulrich Keener,D.C
McCoy,Martin to Mary Peek	2-14-1840	John Hall,Clk.
McCoy,James to Jane Kinsland	4- 8-1852	J.K.Gray,Clk.
McCoy,James C.to Sarah Ann Rogers	4-14-1858	R.C.Slagle,Clk.
McCoy,John W.to Hariett M.Rogers	3- 7-1861	R.C.Slagle,Clk.
McCoy,H.P.P.to Emily A.Welch	4- 6-1864	James Bryson,J.P.
McCoy,Wilson 21 to Arvy Poindexter 19 Col.	11-22-1877	John Gibson,J.P.
McCoy,Wm.N.20 to Juda Peek 19	1-30-1879	D.L.Miller,M.G.
McCoy,Hugh H.28 to Mary Cloer 25	3- 1-1888	John Elmore,J.P.
McCoy,Wm.S.23 to Jennie Dean 23	7-28-1889	W.J.Jenkins,J.P.
McCoy,D.Commodore 24 to Kansas Dean 17	4- 5-1891	J.A.Morrison,J.P.
McCoy,C.E.21 to Lalie M.Fouts 21	12-22-1892	J.D.Woodard,M.G.
McCoy,John W.26 to Drucilla Holland 17	2-16-1893	J.M.Keener,M.G.
McCoy,Edgar W.20 to Lydia Keener 16	2-22-1893	John L.Corbin,J.P
McCoy,Mell 21 to Lydia Houston 19	10-28-1896	G.W.Matney,M.G.
McCoy,Ulucus 21 to Margaret Calloway 18	3-25-1898	T.J.Vinson,J.P.
McCoy,William 45 to Mary Mallonee 23 Col.	11-15-1900	A.B.Marrow,M.G.
McCoy,Isaac 19 to Lula D.Miller 19	9-27-1903	J.I.Miller,M.G.
McCoy,D.A.27 to Fannie Bell Hall 22	4- 7-1905	J.R.Pendergrass,MG
McCoy,J.Welch 32 to Laura Hughes 15	1-23-1907	Jos.L.Fouts,J.P.
McCoy,D.W.31 to Dove Long 21	1-26-1908	F.M.Morgan,M.G.
McCoy,Montgomery 18 to Allafair Holland 19	2-16-1908	T.J.Vinson,M.G.
McCoy,David M.21 to Mary Bell Gregory 18	7- 3-1910	J.M.Keener,M.G.
McCoy,David 19 to Edith Henry 18	1- 7-1914	J.M.Keener,M.G.
McCoy,E.W.21 to Hattie Bradley 19	9- 4-1914	J.A.Lakey,J.P.
McCoy,Verlin 21 to Temasure Parrish 20	9-17-1916	J.A.Morrison,J.P.
McCoy,H.L.24 to Hallie Holland 18	4-21-1927	Geo.Carpenter,J.P
McCoy,Paul 24 to Nina M.Tippett 22	11-16-1929	Walter M.Lee,M.G.
McCoy,Dearl 30 to Ruth Welch 15	7-15-1937	C.C.Welch,M.G.
McCoy,Carl 22 to Emma DeHart 22	4- 3-1938	Sam Murray,J.P.
McCoy,S.E.28 to Mattie Houston 19	4-24-1920	D.L.Miller,M.G.
McCracken,J.M.L.67 to Mary M.Carpenter 42	6-27-1908	A.W.Jacobs,M.G.
McCracken,W.R.25 to F.L.Huggins 23	6- 7-1922	A.J.Smith.
McCracken,C.T.24 to Mattie Scott 22	1- 9-1924	R.A.Truitt,M.G.
McCracken,R.T.32 to Bernice Pendergrass 22	7- 4-1937	J.L.Teague,M.G.
McDade,R.E. 57 to Lena Wilson 49	8-22-1939	Lester Arnold,J.P
McDaniel,James to Jamima Deaton	4- 9-1840	J.H.McLoud.
McDaniel,Andrew to May Hall	5-18-1846	J.K.Gray,Clk.
McDaniel,T.H.to Jane Hester	6-16-1852	M.R.Slagle.
McDonnell,Ben to Nancy Anderson	8- 4-1870	J.K.Bryson,Reg.
McDonald,John to Mary Trotter	9-14-1871	A.W.Wells,M.G.
McDonald,Adam 21 to Lydia Thompson 19 Col.	8-14-1873	D.W.Wells,M.G.
McDonnell,Thomas 23 to Georgia Stewart 21 Col.	5-8-1908	J.R.Pendergras,MG

```
McDonald,Joe 56 to Carry Prater 21       Col.   11-21-1921  J.R.Pendergras,MG
McDonnel,Samuel to Margaret McDonnell Col.       9- 7-1866   T.S.Addington,J.P
McDonnell,Abner to Louisa Prater          Col.   7-16-1870   R.C.Slagle,D.Reg.
McDonnell,R.D.22 to Elizabeth Siler14 Col.       12-26-1883  F.P.Moulden,M.G.
McDonnell,Wilburn 19 to Ada Moore 18   Col.      5- 5-1887   M.Ghormley,M.G.
McDonnell,Wm.T.21 to Ticia Holden 23             1- 1-1889   M.B.Setser,J.P.
McDonnell,Thomas H.36 to Rosetta Dills 22        3-25-1894   W.C.Kimsey,J.P.
McDonnell,Samuel 26 to Dovie Morris 18 Col.      9- 2-1906   C.L.Stewart,M.G.
McDonnell,Lester 21 to Bessie Scruggs 21Col.3-   3-1913   J.M.Bristol,M.G.
McDonald,Richard 32 to Vivian V.Richardson 37/12-25-1940-J.L.Stokes,M.G
   Both from Gastonia,N.C.
McDowell,A.L. to P.C.Russell                     7-22-1861   R.C.Slagle,Reg.
McDowell,Joseph to Margaret A.Guy                6- 6-1867   R.C.Slagle,Reg.
McDowell,John L.34 to Amanda Norton 31           2-11-1875   M.L.Kelly,J.P.
McDowell,A.D.21 to H.A.Hastings 18               3- 1-1877   W.H.Roane,J.P.
McDowell,Jas.M.22 to M.J.L.Stewart 17   Col. 11-15-1877 C.D.Smith,M.G.
McDowell,Jas.E.35 to M.G.Stanfield 34            2-24-1881   G.A.Oglesby,M.G.
McDowell,John 18 to Susan Buchanan 16            4- 7-1881   Hosea Moses.
McDowell,James F.33 to Arie Ella Howard 30       5-16-1889   J.O.Shelly,M.G.
McDowell,Charley 18 to Lula Curtis 19            6- 4-1894   L.H.Garland,J.P.
McDowell,Millard 18 to Rosa Ledford 20           8-29-1901   W.P.Allison,J.P.
McDowell,Ab.D.48 to Ada Henson 38                2-27-1905   W.P.Allison,J.P.
McDowell,H.H.29 to Cora Norton 30                12-2-1907   J.E.Cabe,J.P.
McDowell,James H.27 to Bertha Higdon 21          12-28-1909  J.R.Pendergras,MG
McDowell,J.E.20 to Bessie Owen 18                9- 5-1915   D.F.Howard,M.G.
McDowell,W.F.25 to Cora Crisp 20                 12-22-1915  N.L.Jollay,J.P.
McDowell,T.M.32 to Bessie Cabe 26                10-7-1917   D.S.Richardson,MG
McFall,Edward to Nancy Price                     5- 4-1852   T.P.Siler,D.Clk.
McGaha,John to Caroline Patton                   11-25-1847  J.K.Gray,Clk.
McGaha,Samuel to Sarah Battles                   7-25-1853   Thos.Mashburn,J.P
McGaha,William C.to Rebecca Mashburn             12-29-1853  J.R.Roane.
McGaha,P.K. to Matilda Patton                    9-15-1859   R.C.Slagle,D.Clk.
McGaha,George to Jane Tippett                    4-19-1860   L.F.Siler.
McGahay,Alfred to Mary E.West                    9- 6-1867   Wm.B.Dean,J.P.
McGahey,James to Hariett G.West                  9-19-1867   Merit Rickman,M.G
McGaha,R.M.to Sarah Cochran                      9-28-1867   R.C.Slagle,C.C.C.
McGaha,Samuel to Annas Battles                   12-8-1868   R.C.Slagle,Reg.
McGaha,Wm.T.31 to Elizabeth Runnion 30           1-31-1878   P.P.McLean,M.G.
McGaha,William A.20 to Jennie Morrison 20        1-14-1886   J.A.Morrison,J.P.
McGaha,James T.19 to Jane Shuler 18              4- 1-1896   J.A.Morrison,J.P.
McGaha,William A.19 to Amanda Shuler 18          9- 6-1888   J.A.Morrison,J.P.
McGaha,W.T.53 to Margaret Morrison 44            3- 3-1901   M.L.Kelly,J.P.
McGaha,J.R.24 to Mary Smith 20                   2-19-1903   P.H.Justice,J.P.
McGaha,R.M.27 to Alice Byrd 18                   3- 5-1905   W.J.Morgan,J.P.
McGaha,Alfred 32 to Carey Welch 24               11-29-1906  W.L.Bradley,M.G.
McGaha,Charles 20 to Mary Clark 22               1-30-1908   Retd.not executed
McGaha,Charley 17 to Mary Clark 22               2-28-1908   W.L.Bradley,M.G.
```

```
McGaha,Harvey 21 to Nina Young 18           5- 9-1909  Geo,Carpenter,J.P
McGaha,Fred 26 to Vinnie Matlock 19         11-14-1915 T.J.Vinson,M.G.
McGaha,Joseph 22 to Ida Miller 25           9-18-1916  J.R.Pendergrass,MG
McGaha,Jud 26 to Cleo Truitt 15             2- 2-1936  D.C.McCoy,M.G.
McGaha,Boyd 22 to Joe ann Shepherd 20       4-19-1937  Lester Arnold,J.P
McGaughty,James to Nancy Bryson             3-10-1833  U.Keener,D.Clk.
McGee,James W.to Jane G.Gibbs               7-26-1847  J.K.Gray,D.Clk.
McGee,John to Martha Carpenter              2- 4-1860  R.C.Slagle,Clk.
McGee,Charles 21 to Jennie Potts 20         7-23-1875  Isaac C.Potts,M.G
McGee,E.S.29 to Mary Florence Roane 17      10-11-1905 L.P.Bogal,M.G.
McGee,G.W.26 to Anna Setser 28              4-22-1916  D.S.Richardson,MG
McGill,M.W.27 to Mildred Burch 23           6-17-1925  J.Q.Wallace,M.G.
    He from Davidson,N.C.... She from Chattanooga,Tenn.
McGuffey,Alexander to Cornelia Patton       9- 3-1868  R.C.Slagle,C.C.C.
McGuire,Thomas J.36 to Lela E.Watkins 22    11-27-1895 J.B.Gray,J.P.
McGuire,William B.26 to Maggie Moore 22     10-27-1891 W.R.Barnett,M.G.
McGuire,Wm.B.44 to Margaret Bulgin 32       9-15-1909  M.R.Kirlpatric,MG
McGuire,Fred 20 to Lucy Gregory 18          2- 1-1920  Noah Jollay,J.P.
McGuyer,Joseph 30 to Nannie C.Hall 29       3-18-1880  C.B.Fugate,M.G.
McHaffey,D.F.to Carolina McCoy              12-23-1852 N.G.Allman,J.P.
McHan,Burchet to Sally Truitt               2-17-1849  J.K.Gray,Clk.
McHan,James H.23 to Hariett Owen 19         3- 4-1873  B.G.Wild,M.G.
    He from Swain Co.N.C.
McHan,William A.20 to Jane A.Dean 16        12-2-1875  A.Ammons,M.G.
McHan,Noah 21 to Prissilla Byrd 17          9-10-1879  G.W.Dean,J.P.
McHan,W.J.24 to Tina Cabe 20                8-24-1911  J.S.Woodard,M.G.
McHan,Ellis 23 to Parcie Brendle 18         10-24-1923 J.R.Pendergras,MG
McHargen,W.P.to Nancy E.Boyd                11-27-1853 Thos.Mashburn,J.P
McIntyre,J.S.28 to Emaline Jones 25         2- 1-1877  J.S.Woodard,M.G.
McKee,W.F. to Elizabeth Bryson              9-28-1837  John Hall,Clk.
McKee,Eli to May Sherrill                   11-23-1843 Wm.Allman,D.Clk.
McKee,William to Mary M.Siler               2-15-1870  J.K.Bryson,Reg.
McKinzey,William to Ruth Gibbs              12-14-1844 J.K.Gray,D.Clk.
McKimsey,William W.19 to Emma Pierson 19    11-3-1909  T.J.Vinson,M.G.
McKinney,J.P.20 to Margaret J.Gribble 21    12-25-1875 John McDowell,M.G
McKinney,N.H.28 to T.A.Hill 28              2-27-1877  Geo.A.Jacobs,M.G.
McKinney,Zeb.V.35 to Lethie Ann Evitt 23    6-28-1896  T.Baxter White,JP
McKinney,Thomas G.20 to Florence Lena Zachary23/3-16-1913-R.H.Munger,J.P
McKinney,Mack H.50 to Gertrude Love 34 Col. 11-7-1937  E.G.Siler,M.G.
    He from Andrews,N.C.
McLane,Daniel S.to Nancy Calloway           7-18-1867  R.C.Slagle,Reg.
McLean,Pinkney P.23 to Emma V.West 16       10-6-1874  L.F.Green,M.G.
McLean,Melvin 24 to Maggie Humphrey 16      9- 6-1894  S.J.May,J.P.
McLean,A.L.25 to Ollie Ramsey 19            1- 5-1907  L.P.Bogle,M.G.
McLaughlin,John G.36 to Elsie Moore 24      3-29-1924  J.R.Pendergrass,MG
McLoud,Mason to Jane White                  12-26-1835 Lane Smith.
McLoud,E.to Jane Brawley                    8-26-1846  J.K.Gray,D.Clk.
McLoud,James H.to Catherine E.Wilson        1-22-1861  C.D.Smith,M.G.
```

McLoud,William M.to Mary Woods   10-9-1870   D.Mallonee,J.P.
McLoud,T.W.35 to Nancy Young 45   1-15-1878   H.G.Woodfin,J.P.
McLoud,Tilman W.47 to Martha Holt 28   3-22-1889   J.M.Keener,J.P.
McLoud,Jesse M.21 to Lelia Sanders 16   4- 9-1911   Geo.Carpenter,J.P
McMan,Leander to Mary L.Mason   2- 8-1872   William Sloan,Reg
McMahan,John 19 to Nancy J.Mason 18   9-10-1876   J.M.Forester,J.P.
McMahan,Robert 21 to Cora Lowery 14   2-22-1894   W.C.Mason,M.G.
McMahan,John 21 to Callie Dills 18   2-15-1903   L.I.Mashburn,M.G.
McMahan,J.C.22 to Alice Holden 16   9-17-1905   W.C.Mason,M.G.
McMahan,Lucius 21 to Hattie Pannell 22   7-22-1911   Geo.Carpenter,J.P
McMahan,Curtis 25 to Ellen Campbell 35   9-12-1912   J.L.Younce,M.G.
McMahan,J.L. 26 to Martha Welch 26   2-25-1917   J.H.Grant,M.G.
McMahan,Albert 19 to Ethel Morgan 18   10-31-1925   J.R.Pendergras,MG
McMahan,Fred 31 to Ollie Oliver 19   8-21-1934   Geo.Carpenter,J.P
    Both from Bryson City,N.C.
McMullen,Jason to Elizabeth Ann Atter   11-19-1838   J.K.Gray,Clk.
McNabb,Lloyd T.21 to Nottie Lois Henderson 22/12-24-1939-Frank Reed,M.G.
McNab,William H.33 to Dora Hicks Phillips 22/12-17-1912-M.H.Tuttle,M.G.
McPherson,John E.to Sarah M.Sellers   8- 9-1843   N.H.Palmer.
McPherson,Robert H.27 to S.A.Angel 23   11-23-1876   C.D.Smith,M.G.
McPherson,G.R.26 to Varina Dowdle 22   3-19-1885   R.A.Owen,M.G.
McPherson,Robert B.19 to Belle Clement 17   9- 1-1914   E.E.Williamson.MG
McPherson,Eugene R.38 to Bess Irene Cunningham32/8-27-1941-H.G.Wardlaw,M
    He from Chester,Pa.
Nall,A.R.51 to Lillian S.Pearson 40   11-24-1931   L.E.Cranson.
Nations,Samuel A.to Louvada Wilson   1-11-1871   Samuel Gibson,M.G
Neal,James 21 to Polly Roland 19   9-19-1874   Z.Barnes,J.P.
Neal,John H.18 to Emalin Woods 22   4- 8-1875   Z.Barnes,J.P.
Neal,Samuel 20 to Catherine Dill 20   3-21-1880   Mark May,M.G.
Neal,Geo.W.19 to Sallie Kilpatrick 15   4-25-1897   Z.Barnes,J.P.
Neal,James A.18 to Cora Dills 18   9- 3-1899   W.A.Setser,J.P.
Neal,W.D.20 to Mamie Jones 19   2-15-1903   J.W.Ammons,J.P.
Neal,John W.26 to Annie Lunsford 20   5-31-1903   D.F.Howard,M.G.
Neal,Thomas 18 to Rhobia Daily 18   4-17-1904   D.F.Howard,M.G.
Neal,Homer 19 to May Howard 18   11-6-1909   D.F.Howard,M.G.
Neely,H.B.21 to Mary Brooks 19   12-22-1898   G.W.Matney,M.G.
Neely,G.Y.24 to Maggie Brooks 22   12-24-1899   G.W.Matney,M.G.
Neely,Stinson 27 to Mollie Talley 20   9-23-1911   Ed.Picklesimer,JP
Neely,Harry 22 to Carrie Dendy 19   5- 1-1937   J.O.Nix,M.G.
Neel,Andrew J. to Janie Reid   11-25-1847   S.M.Dowell,D.Clk.
Nelson,W.L.28 to Laura Smith 22   5- 2-1920   L.P.Roper,J.P.
Nelson,Hughey 27 to Launa McConnell 19   8-25-1936   Geo.Carpenter,J.P
    He from Delaware City,Del.
Newell,I.C.33 to Nannie Wilson 28   6- 1-1918   J.W.Duvall,J.P.
Newman,John 37 to Lillie Lowe 37   1- 4-1920   J.R.Morrison,J.P.
Newson,Emmett E.29 to Martha Perry Buist 26/12-14-1911 W.T.Thompson,M.G.
Newton,John to Sarah McFarland   3-10-1831   W.W.Lawtop.
Nichols,James to Mira M.McGaha   9- 9-1833   John Hall,Clk.

Nichols,W.R. to Sarah Jones	10-18-1860	R.C.Slagle,Reg.
Nichols,J.F. to Altha McDowell	11-28-1865	John A.Green.
Nichols,John H.30 to Eva A.Southards 21	11-21-1889	John Reid,J.P.
Nichols,George L.30 to Henrietta A.Jones 36/	12-5-1889	C.L.Ledford,M.G.
Nichols,Charles D.22to Rachel A.Saunders 18/	2- 3-1892	G.R.McPherson,J.P
Nichols,Robert L.25 to Ella A.Angel 28	1-20-1896	G.R.McPherson,J.P
Nichols,D.I.54 to Sallie Sanders 45	10-2-1898	E.D.Franks,J.P.
Nichols,Robert L.33 to Effie Mann 24	6- 1-1904	J.C.Postell,M.G.
Nichols,G.R.20 to Mary Carpenter 18	12-10-1916	G.A.Cloer,M.G.
Nichols,J.T.18 to Martha E.Hodgins 17	4-27-1919	G.A.Cloer,M.G.
Nichols,Floyd 20 to Beulah Dills 18	11-7-1919	G.M.Johnston,J.P.
Nicks,Oscar 27 to Margaret Neely 19	9- 1-1917	P.C.Calloway,J.P.
Nickles,P.B. to Amy E.Palmer	7-21-1844	J.K.Gray,Clk.
Nickles,Wesly M. to Susanah Nickles	1-29-1848	J.K.Gray,Clk.
Nickles,William to Nancy Shuler	3-19-1850	J.K.Gray,Clk.
Nickles,Daniel to Martha Ann Jones	1-25-1859	R.C.Slagle,Reg.
Nolen,H.W. to M.C.Siler	9-27-1856	John Hall,Clk.
Nolen,F.H.37 to Flora Corpening 29	6- 9-1898	T.E.Wagg,M.G.
Nolen,Horace T.28 to Ruth E.McKinney 25	10-7-1939	J.A.Flanagan,M.G.
Norman,John 29 to Lonner Chavis 16 Col.	12-26-1912	C.L.Stewart,M.G.
Norris,J.W.to A.J.Curtis	12-9-1852	J.F.Slagle,J.P.
Norris,L.D.to Mersella Bingham	2- 8-1858	T.P.Siler,D.Clk.
Norris,Isaac to Nancy C.Long	1- 6-1859	R.C.Slagle,Reg.
Norris,N.C.to Mary S.S.Brown	9-13-1868	R.C.Slagle,Reg.
Norris,H.H.25 to Mary J.Carpenter 18	1-23-1879	W.H.Roan,J.P.
Norris,Lafayett 18 to Mary Long 18	12-5-1880	M.L.Kelly,J.P.
Norris,L.S.26 to Mary C.Bradley 23	1-15-1888	S.A.Dickson,J.P.
Norris,I.C.J. 46 to Mary A.Cabe 45	4-18-1901	J.H.Moore,M.G.
Norris,J.R.24 to Grace Henson 20	8-19-1917	W.C.Ledbetter,J.P
Norton,Calib to Jane Garland	11-3-1839	William Garland.
Norton,William to Susan Zachary	1- 8-1842	H.Cowart.
Norton,William P.to Rosetta S.Howard	3- 2-1858	T.P.Siler,D.Clk.
Norton,F. to S.L.Hill	11-9-1865	R.C.Slagle,Reg.
Norton,Virgil Z.to Rosetta G.Bradley	10-25-1871	L.Howard,J.P.
Norton,J.P.23 to H.E.Bradley 23	5-19-1878	L.Howard,J.P.
Norton,Albert 21 to L.A.Bradley 18	8-21-1881	L.Howard,J.P.
Norton,P.Lafayett 21 to M.Carolin Dickerson 19/	4-15-1888-	S.A.Dickson,J.P
Norton,C.A.29 to Emma Jollay 23	4-20-1899	M.A.West,M.G.
Norton,Robert L.22 to Nancy M.Howard 24	3- 8-1900	Sam Howard,J.P.
Norton,T.N.27 to Ada Thomas 18	2- 9-1902	D.P.Cabe,J.P.
Norton,Burrus 48 to Mrs.Alice Zachary 43	12-22-1904	J.E.Woosley,M.G.
Norton,Charley 24 to Lula Cabe 27	1-10-1906	L.P.Bogle,M.G.
Norton,James 25 to Anna McDowell 26	1-24-1907	J.R.Pendergrass,MG
Norton,Leonard 18 to Jane Crane 21	10-28-1910	Retd.not executed
Norton,Leonard 18 to Jane Crane 21	2- 3-1911	P.C.Calloway,J.P.
Norton,Nathan 24 to Mrs.Lassie Guffee 27	9-28-1911	Original not found
Norton,Nathan 25 to Edith Rogers 18	6-23-1912	A.P.Foster,M.G.

Norton,Fred 26 to Hattie Howard 15	10-6-1912	C.R.Cabe,J.P.
Norton,Ed.L.23 to Minnie Bell Bradley 19	11-15-1914	C.R.Cabe,J.P.
Norton,Mann 32 to Ethel Henry 18	4-20-1919	T.J.Vinson,M.G.
Norton,Earnest B.23 to Callie Mae Watson 20	5-27-1916	J.A.Bond,M.G.
Norton,Frank H.22 to Annie Mae Keener 21	12-21-1916	Geo.Carpenter,J.P
Norton,Homer 35 to Margie Vinson 18	1- 5-1921	G.J.Vinson,M.G.
Norton,J.P.20 to Mary Brendle 23	1-16-1921	Robert E.Ward,M.G
Norton,Zeb L.33 to Maud Hudson 39	6- 1-1922	J.Q.Wallace,M.G.
Nowland,James H.to Sarah Owens	12-29-1853	John Hall,Clk.
Nunn,W.L.42 to Sarah Mullin 33	7-24-1911	M.H.Tuttle,M.G.
Nunn,James G.29 to Fannie K.Womack 24	12-7-1933	E.R.Eller,M.G.
O'Dell,Ed 22 to Sallie Thompson 20	5- 7-1905	S.J.Ammons,J.P.
Officer,Marsh 39 to Nannie Conley 19	12-15-1910	G.W.Bulgin,J.P.
Ogden,Jonathan to Mary Sanders	7-26-1843	Jason Stalcup.
Oldham,John to Altha Cunningham	8- 5-1856	---------
Oldridge,J.E. to Mary Clampet	5-21-1859	R.C.Slagle,Reg.
Oliver,Joseph to Patsy Rodes	1-21-1856	U.Keener,D.Clk.
Oliver,Thomas W.to Mary Plemons	3-15-1841	Isaac Justice,J.P
Oliver,William P.to Catherine Nichols	7-19-1862	R.C.Slagle,Reg.
Oliver,J.C.to H.M.Nichols	1-16-1866	R.C.Slagle,C.C.C.
Oliver,Henry Ellis to Margaret A.Nichols	5-31-1871	William Sloan,Reg
Oliver,Geo.W.27 to Amilea J.Moore 20	2-19-1876	Albert Siler,J.P.
Oliver,Milus N.27 to Rachel A.Cabe 28	10-8-1876	M.L.Kelley,J.P.
Oliver,James M.23 to J.L.Huggins 23	12-2-1886	W.C.Kimzey,J.P.
Oliver,N.C.24 to Lillie Phillips 20	9- 7-1899	Samuel Holland,JP
Oliver,Burt 21 to Bertha Fouts 19	1-27-1906	M.A.Love,M.G.
Oliver,Jesse 21 to Florence Canada 17	10-25-1909	J.R.Pendergras,MG
Oliver,Zack 30 to Bertha Dowdle 29	4- 2-1911	W.I.Hughes,M.G.
Oliver,Hugh 23 to Grace Addington 19	10-20-1911	J.R.Pendergras,MG
Oliver,Fred S.21 to Rufus Stallcup 20	12-25-1911	F.N.Johnson,J.P.
Orr,Fidill 26 to Mary J.Daves 22	8-25-1885	D.A.Yonce,J.P.
Orr,James R.22 to Annie Lee Curtis 19	7- 3-1937	Frank Loyd,M.G.
Ormond,Alfred N.26 to Nancy Eliz.Hines 23 He from Pocatello,Idaho.	4-23-1941	A.Rufus Morgan,MG
Osborn,John G. to Mary A.Gash	7-21-1858	R.C.Slagle,Reg.
Osborn,Ezekiel 26 to Pink Hester 23	11-29-1899	E.A.Sample,M.G.
Overcash,Hayes E.30 to Villa P.Powers 26	11-25-1937	J.E.Abernethy,M.G
Overstreet,William C.to Minerva Ruell	2-17-1855	John Hall,Clk.
Owenby,Leander to Lucindy C.May	12-22-1871	William Sloan,Reg
Owenby,Thomas 21 to Ellen Grant 15	11-18-1880	J.M.Forester,J.P.
Owenby,Loranzo 19 to Martha R.May 17	12-27-1885	F.M.Morgan,M.G.
Owenby,Alfred F.21 to Alice Martin 18	2-21-1892	W.C.Mason,M.G.
Owenby,R.L.30 to Martha M.Grant 28	4- 5-1895	F.M.Morgan,M.G.
Owenby,Lorenzo 28 to Emma Welch 17	12-9-1897	F.M.Morgan,M.G.
Owenby,Samuel 23 to Meranda Passmore 18	5-14-1899	W.C.Mason,M.G.
Owenby,Alex 22 to Ruth May 19	10-15-1899	F.M.Morgan,M.G.
Owenby,John E.21 to Mary E.Welch 17	11-16-1899	W.C.Mason,M.G.

Owenby,David 22 to Nola Cochran 18	12-9-1906	J.W.Duvall,J.P.
Owenby,T.M.24 to Effie Yonce 21	4-10-1910	J.H.Grant,M.G.
Owenby,Lester 21 to Nolie Shields 21	5- 4-1913	D.A.Yonce,M.G.
Owenby,J.R.33 to Thelma Cochran 17	12-14-1919	H.O.Miller,M.G.
Owenby,Eckel 25 to Julia Martin 21 Both from Nantahala,N.C.	3-28-1934	T.D.Denny,M.G.
Owenby,Edgar R.26 to Sallie Ledford 18	8-11-1934	D.L.Miller,M.G.
Owenby,Beuford 21 to Vera Cochran 20	9-21-1934	T.D.Denny,M.G.
Owenby,Voyd 22 to Ruby Dills 21	11-6-1934	T.D.Denny,M.G.
Owenby,Agrie 24 to Gertrude Mashburn 18 Both from Nantahala,N.C.	11-17-1936	J.Fred Bryson,J.P
Owenby,Addie 22 to Mayberl Rowland 19 He from Asheville,N.C.	12-22-1936	Geo.W.Stepp,J.P.
Owenby,Elmer 25 to Gladys Owenby 20	9-26-1937	Geo.Stepp,J.P.
Owenby,Roy 27 to Gladys Dills 22	10-13-1938	Phil.Passmore,M.G
Owens,Thomas W.to Jane Neil	9-12-1851	W.M.Angel,J.P.
Owens,John W.to Nancy Russell	5- 4-1859	R.C.Slagle,Reg.
Owens,Jesse C.22 to Mary S.McConnell 21	11-23-1876	M.L.Kelly,J.P.
Owens,William J.43 to Ellen Penland 27	9-11-1884	L.M.Garland,J.P.
Owens,William S.21 to Sarah E.Rhodes 17	11-26-1885	L.Howard,J.P.
Owen,John A.40 to Rachel Rhodes 26	4- 8-1890	W.G.Mallonee,M.G.
Owen,Henry M.19 to Hester R.Howard 16	3-19-1894	J.T.Plott,M.G.
Owens,Jesse G.25 to Kansada Parker 28	12-13-1894	John B.Gray,J.P.
Owens,Evan 20 to Dora Brown 17	11-17-1907	Thos.B.White,J.P.
Pace,C.A.22 to Mary E.Bryson 19	11-13-1881	Z.Barnes,J.P.
Padgett,Elijah B.to Elmira Stepp	11-20-1867	L.J.Martin,M.G.
Paine,Dink 31 to Jamima McCinnis 19	3- 7-1880	W.H.Higdon,J.P.
Painter,S.G.18 to E.V.Dalton 15	10-3-1877	P.P.McLeow,M.G.
Painter,William L.20 to N.E.Dalton 24	7-27-1882	M.J.Mashburn,J.P.
Painter,John 27 to Lola Bailey 21	9-29-1900	D.R.Sellers,J.P.
Painter,Eastman 27 to Cora Lee Elmore 17	1- 1-1904	W.L.Bradley,M.G.
Painter,John 34 to Callie Sanders 32	3-23-1907	J.H.Mincy,J.P.
Painter,Robert 21 to Ruth Brendle 18	12-1-1912	Geo.Carpenter,J.P
Painter,James C.26 to Jennie Jones 17	6-25-1921	E.N.Evans,J.P.
Palmer,J.F.23 to M.J.Merritt 21	10-14-1880	Albert Siler,J.P.
Palmer,W.T.22 to Sarah Hicks 19	12-30-1900	D.F.Howard,M.G.
Palmer,J.F.42 to Allie Harrison 25	1- 9-1901	T.Bright,M.G.
Palmer,Jake F.52 to Jennie Ray 47	3- 3-1909	W.I.Hughes,M.G.
Palmer,James A.27 to Lexie Love 24	8-24-1910	J.R.Pendergras,MG
Palmer,Joe 28 to Elcie Jones 24	2-29-1915	W.G.Warren,M.G.
Palmer,Frank 32 to Bettie Jacobs 20	5- 4-1916	J.R.Pendergras,MG
Pannell,Elias 17 to Martha J.Dockery 17 He from Loudon,Tenn.	8-13-1874	F.Poindexter,J.P
Pannell,James 19 to Eliza Southards 22	9- 6-1875	W.Henry,J.P.
Pannell,W.T.20 to D.T.Waldroop 20	12-10-1880	J.M.Keener,J.P.
Pannell,A.E.19 to Rhema Calloway 26	3- 1-1883	John Elmore,J.P.
Pannell,William 22 to Hattie Clayton 14 Col.	9-12-1884	John S.Gibson,J.P
Pannell,Arthur 24 to Callie Hall 23	1-19-1910	G.M.Bulgin,J.P.

```
Pannell,Harrison 19 to Mary Bell McGaha 19   6-18-1910   Geo Carpenter,J.P
Panter,S.C. to Nancy T.Hyde                   11-6-1865   R.C.Slagle,Reg.
Panter,John 23 to Vallie Dalton 15            2-18-1894   W.R.Rickman,M.G.
Panther,Jacob to Angeline Shepherd            6- 8-1839   John Hall,Clk.
Panther,Aurzema to Sarah M.Boyd               5- 9-1845   J.K.Gray,Clk.
Panther,Robert E.33 to Laura A.Tippett 22     1-14-1894   T.S.DeHart,M.G.
Pardon,Pascal L.20 to Barbary M.Carpenter 16/12-29-1887-L.H.Garland,J.P.
Paris,Jackson to Margaret Brooks              9- 8-1851   J.K.Gray,Clk.
Parker,John to Mary Hide                      8- 2-1836   W.F.McKee,D.Clk.
Parker,Franklin to Charlotte Sanders          8-21-1847   William Conner,JP
Parker,William to May Watts                   3-14-1855   John Hall,Clk.
Parker,W.M. to Mary S.Robbins                 5-18-1859   R.C.Slagle,Reg.
Parker,Jacob Wm.19 to L.A.Moses 19            8-11-1872   Wm.H.Higdon,J.P.
Parker,C.W.23 to M.A.Moses 19                 12-13-1877  J.M.Keener,J.P.
Parker,William M.23 to Louisa Hopkins 20      10-21-1880  Joseph Morgan,J.P.
Parker,Alexander L.31 to Florence Sanders 20/9-12-1896  H.H.Dills,J.P.
Parker,Samuel 23 to Cordelia Mason 18         12-19-1897  W.M.Downs,J.P.
Parker,C.L.21 to Birdell Hedden 18            3- 4-1900   J.A.Young,J.P.
Parker,Samuel 19 to Ellen Patton 20           10-21-1900  J.L.Kinsland,M.G.
Parker,Booth 18 to Parthena Houston 21        11-26-1901  J.M.Keener,M.G.
Parker,John 21 to Emma Shope 20               11-23-1904  W.P.Allison,J.P.
Parker,Dock 26 to Hattie Riddle 19            11-16-1907  W.P.Allison,J.P.
Parker,Homer 21 to Nettie Rhodes 18           7- 2-1911   C.R.Cabe,J.P.
Parker,Ledger 22 to Minnie Nichols 21         11-1-1914   J.L.Teague,M.G.
Parker,D.B.21 to Eva Russell 17               4- 8-1917   W.T.Jennings,J.P.
Parks,Jefferson to Mira Dickey                8-26-1832   Hiram Hartness.
Parish,William M.to R.E.Bryson                8-31-1854   John Hall,Clk.
Parrish,E.W.to Amanda West                    1-22-1860   M.J.Morgan,J.P.
Parrish,N.H.to Sarah J.Vanhook                11-5-1860   R.C.Slagle,Reg.
Parrish,G.W.to Josephine Ramsey               10-27-1865  J.H.Green.
Parrish,Henry 28 to Minnie DeHart 18      Col.10-12-1881  M.J.Mashburn,J.P.
Parrish,Green 60 to Loucinda Beck 40      Col.10-29-1882  P.P.McLean,M.G.
Parrish,J.W.24 to Louisa Beck 21          Col.2- 4-1883   John S.Gibson,J.P
Parrish,John 21 to Mary Lakey 19              1- 5-1890   W.J.Jenkins,J.P.
Parrish,James A.23 to Catherine G.Roone 23    2-16-1892   I.D.Wright,M.G.
Parrish,Nathaniel H.50 to Laura Hall 16       5-15-1892   J.R.Pendergras,MG
Parrish,James R.19 to Callie Downs 18         9-27-1898   J.J.McCoy,J.P.
Parrish,E.H.24 to Ethel Wadkins 20            1-26-1902   W.E.Conner,M.G.
Parrish,Geo.W.60 to Mrs.Lillie E.Berry 41     3-10-1903   J.G.Bates,J.P.
Parrish,George 22 to Visa Moore 18        Col.7-21-1905   J.B.Ramsey,J.P.
Parrish,Major 60 to Fannie Thomas 40      Col.10-29-1911  E.G.Siler,M.G.
Parrish,R.P.23 to Lucy Fouts 18               10-8-1916   J.L.Fouts,J.P.
Parrish,Carl 21 to Julia Arvey 19             9- 1-1918   Geo.Carpenter,J.P
Parrish,William M.37 to M.B.Higdon 19         11-19-1918  W.W.Marr,M.G.
Parrish,J.R.24 to Beulah C.Jollay 24          4- 7-1927   Geo.C.Steed,M.G.
Parrish,Fred 19 to Wilma Parker 26            7-29-1936   Geo.Carpenter,J.P.
  Both from Alarka,Swain County,N.C.
```

Parton,G.W. to Nancy Belk	3-16-1846	Thos.Welch.
Parton,G.W.to Desia C.Sheets	8- 4-1866	R.C.Slagle,Reg.
Parton,Marion F.to Sarah Morgan	1-19-1871	William Sloan,Reg
Parton,James 21 to Birdie Williams 20	10-6-1928	J.R.Pendergras,MG
Passmore,William F.to Elizabeth Ledford	4-12-1832	Samuel Jones.
Passmore,David to Margaret A.Bell	1-30-1837	U.Keener,D.Clk.
Passmore,John to Nancy Hegan	6-15-1839	Henry Franks,Wit.
Passmore,Thomas J.to Martha Louisa Cleveland	7-20-1840	H.G.Woodfin,D.Clk.
Passmore,Harden to Emeline Sanders	2-22-1851	J.K.Gray,Clk.
Passmore,W.C.to Alis Cerby	7-29-1867	R.C.Slagle,Reg.
Passmore,T.L. to Nancy Adams	8- 7-1867	John Ammons,J.P.
Passmore,Elisha to T.Jane Palmer	8-24-1871	William Sloan,Reg
Passmore,Wm.Thomas 20 to Fannie J.Lea 19	9- 7-1873	Mark May,M.G.
Passmore,N.H.22 to S.H.Franks 19	3-18-1880	E.H.Franks,J.P.
Passmore,Wm.C.43 to Martha M.Owenbee 46	5-25-1886	F.M.Morgan,M.G.
Passmore,C.P.30 to L.Anna McDonnell 17	9- 5-1886	W.C.Kimsey,J.P.
Passmore,Travis L.46 to Maria Wallis 23	2- 6-1888	J.W.Parker,J.P.
Passmore,Hugh D.22 to Eleanor M.Owenby 21	1-28-1891	W.C.Mason,M.G.
Passmore,Thos.M.23 to Betty Waldroop 20	5-24-1896	N.J.Rush,J.P.
Passmore,S.H.21 to Lillie Nelson 20	12-23-1897	Z.Barnes,J.P.
Passmore,T.B.28 to Roxie Owenby 19	4-21-1898	W.C.Mason,M.G.
Passmore,P.H.23 to Ellender Owenby 18	6-16-1898	W.C.Mason,M.G.
Passmore,James L.21 to Nancy J.Lea 22	6-14-1901	A.H.Gregory,J.P.
Passmore,S.T.18 to Dora E.Owenby 18	1- 5-1902	W.C.Mason,M.G.
Passmore,T.M.27 to Lyda Bingham --	8-24-1902	J.A.Deal,M.G.
Passmore,Robert 21 to Jessie Clark 20	10-24-1916	J.W.Gregory,J.P.
Passmore,Ray 19 to Martha Wilson 21	1- 2-1917	W.C.Mason,M.G.
Passmore,J.T.27 to Lorena Haskett 18	2-24-1917	J.P.Moore,J.P.
Passmore,N.H.65 to Mrs.Margaret Valentine 47/	3-22-1923	Geo.Carpenter,J.P
Passmore,Homer 21 to Azalee Mason 15 Both from Nantahala,N.C.	9-26-1925	W.C.Mason,M.G.
Passmore,Dave 23 to Eta Dills 19	10-15-1925	W.C.Mason,M.G.
Passmore,Troy C.23 to Eula E.Morgan 18	7-23-1935	Geo.Carpenter,J.P
Passmore,Fred 18 to Marie Frazier 15 He from Brevard,N.C.	5-23-1938	Sam J.Murray,J.P.
Pate,Monroe 21 to Palace Yonce 17	1-31-1913	D.A.Yonce,M.G.
Patrick,Jessie C.Jr.25 to Florence Pendergrass24/	10-1-1921-	J.R.Pendergrass.
Patterson,Sam to Jane Moore	3- 8-1830	John D.Carne.
Patterson,John 21 to Hester A.Watts 15	1-14-1875	W.H.Roan,J.P.
Patterson,W.S.23 to Julia Hicks 19	9-18-1898	Z.Barnes,J.P.
Patterson,John 22 to Sarah E.Teems 17	1-17-1886	John B.Gray,J.P.
Patterson,J.D.A.22 to Amanda J.Jenkins 20	1-27-1886	M.C.Warlick,M.G.
Patterson,John A.35 to Amanda Cabe 30	4- 9-1888	S.H.Harrington,MG
Patterson,J.C.23 to Lelia Grant 21	7-23-1905	John C.Hurst,J.P.
Patterson,John H.21 to Bessie Guffee 18	12-14-1908	R.R.Rickman,J.P.
Patterson,W.E.30 to Clemie Beck 38	3-13-1910	J.L.Kinsland,M.G.
Patterson,Hawlass 19 to Ida Crain 21	11-17-1912	E.P.Brown,J.P.

Patterson,William 22 to Lizzie Haskett 18	6- 6-1921	L.J.Young,M.G.
Patterson,Polk 35 to Nannie E.Elliott 23	8-11-1926	J.R.Pendergras,MG
Patterson,M.C.24 to Sue Fisher 21	9-12-1931	G.Cliff.Ervin,M.G
Patton,Alfred S.to Margaret Trotter	11-21-1870	William Sloan,Reg
Patton,John 26 to Jane Wright 21	4- 4-1878	C.D.Smith,M.G.
Patton,George R.34 to Annie Phillips 22	11-5-1884	J.A.Deal,M.G.
Patton,William J.18 to Jenny Thomas 16 Col.	11-7-1889	Jas. Bristol,M.G.
Patton,J.Thad 42 to Elbie Penland 24	9-24-1890	W.G.Mallonee,M.G.
Patton,W.Ramsey 20 to Nannie Rogers 19	12-3-1891	J.C.Weaver,J.P.
Patton,L.A.22 to Ella Guy 21	11-25-1896	G.A.Bartlett,M.G.
Patton,Bartlett 21 to Martha Hooper 20	12-4-1895	H.H.Dills,J.P.
Patton,J.Thad 48 to Addie McDowell 26	2-30-1897	R.B.Shelton,M.G.
Patton,Ervin 41 to Maggie Crawford 27	12-8-1897	Frank Siler,M.G.
Patton,William 45 to Margaret Frady 29	12-8-1898	E.B.Angel,J.P.
Patton,R.21 to Nannie Dills 21	8-21-1901	W.A.Setser,J.P.
Patton,Ervin 46 to Melvie Roane 29	4-30-1902	John H.Moore,M.G.
Patton,William Jr.20 to R.Jane Frady 21	3-19-1904	M.A.Love,M.G.
Patton,John B.59 to Henrietta Boston 45	11-14-1907	J.R.Pendergras,MG
Patton,Robert A.25 to Mamie D.Slagle 24	11-17-1912	J.E.Gray,M.G.
Patton,T.W.21 to Blanche Farmer 22	1-18-1914	J.M.Griggs,M.G.
Patton,Arthur 20 to Mae Rogers 16	4- 2-1916	J.Z.Carver,J.P.
Patton,C.B.23 to Gertrude Cunningham 16	10-24-1920	J.R.Pendergras,MG
Patton,George B.29 to Kate Panland 24	4-30-1928	Robert F.Mock,M.G
Patton,William to Leaner Grigge	9- 5-1835	James Griggs,J.P.
Patton,John to Oma Waldroop	7-31-1838	John Hall,Clk.
Paul Hiram T.27 to Clara Babcock 29	2-11-1900	J.T.Wade,M.G.
Paul,Guy 22 to Ethel Mae Potts 17	10-31-1907	T.J.Vinson,M.G.
Paul,Hiram 37 to Carrie Edna McKinney 28	10-17-1909	P.C.Calloway,J.P.
Payne,Samuel 20 to Sarah A.Payne 22	8-17-1883	T.S.Siler,J.P.
Payne,Cley 20 to Belle Arvey 19	2- 6-1927	J.M.Woodard,M.G.
Payne,Clay 28 to Ella Ledford 24	2-13-1935	J.B.Tabor,Jr,M.G.
Pearce,Ed.23 to Laura Williams 21 Col.	12-24-1923	J.M.Bristol,M.G.
Pearson,Moses to Martha Teague	1-11-1855	J.L.Robinson,J.P.
Pearson,Jefferson 21 to Roxanna Burrell 19	7-23-1882	L.H.Garland,J.P.
Pearson,W.D.19 to Florence Welch 20	11-11-1900	D.C.McCoy,J.P.
Pebeley,J.A. to Catherine Angel	1- 4-1834	Joshua Whitaker,JP
Peek,Isaac to Elizabeth Carrol	12-22-1847	J.K.Gray,D.Clk.
Peek,William C.to Elizabeth Henderson	7-29-1848	Beuford Henderson
Peek,D.L. to Jane Moss	10-26-1850	J.R.Siler,D.Clk.
Peek,Jas.M.Jr.to Clarissa Wright	8-24-1856	Joshua Ammons,M.G
Peek,James M.to Eliza J.Keener	10-17-1868	R.C.Slagle,Reg.
Peek,J.K.25 to Mary A.McClure 21	3- 4-1875	J.D.Vinson,M.G.
Peek,Wm.M.24 to Sarah H.Ammons 19	4-11-1876	W.W.Henry,J.P.
Peek,Isaac T.23 to Josephine Peek 22	12-8-1878	David L.Miller,MG
Peek,Z.J.22 to Margaret A.Peek 18	3- 6-1884	J.M.Keener,M.G.
Peek,Henry 30 to Mary A.Rogers 24	11-14-1895	D.L.Miller,M.G.
Peek,I.H.35 to Ann Houston 26	10-7-1900	J.M.Keener,M.G.

```
Peek,W.A.27 to Eliza J.Cantrell 25              1-10-1909   W.I.Hughes,M.G.
Peek,Frank 24 to Minnie Shook 15                8-17-1912   W.A.Keener,J.P.
Peek,Truman 20 to Charlotte Holland 20          10-6-1912   W.A.Keener,J.P.
Peek,Carl 25 to Clista Shook 20                 8-19-1925   W.G.Wood,J.P.
Peek,John M.29 to Ella Keener 17                2-27-1926   J.D.McCoy,J.P.
Peek,William P.31 to Mary M.Fulton 24           5- 8-1927   G.A.Cloer,M.G.
Peek,G.R.24 to Honor Cabe 25                    4-29-1928   Geo.Carpenter,J.P
Peek,Martin J.25 to Ollie Ammons 18             3-22-1936   J.M.Keener,M.G.
Peek,Paul 28 to Burdell Jennings 18             7-31-1938   Arthur Mosteller.
Peek,James 21 to Idolene Roberts 19             9-28-1940   E.Getty Nunn,J.P.
   He from Monks Corner,S.C.... She from Lowell,N.C.
Pell,Hampton A.32 to Addie Bradburn 20          9-28-1909   P.C.Calloway,J.P.
Pendergrass,Miles to May Lowery (blurred)   11-18-1832? John Hall,C.C.C.
Pendergrass,John to Jane Lowery                 12-5-1835   John Tatham,Clk.
Pendergrass,Jesse to Martha Hill                8- 3-1844   J.K.Gray,Clk.
Pendergrass,Humphery to Fanny Hastings          4-29-1854   L.F.Siler.
Pendergrass,John to Nancy Dills                 1- 7-1860   R.C.Slagle,Reg.
Pendergrass,J.D.20 to L.E.Dills 19              1-24-1881   Albert Siler,J.P.
Pendergrass,Henry M.19 to Nancy E.Ledbetter 18/8-19-1888-J.E.Morgan,M.G.
Pendergrass,Jacob D.29 to Malinda E.Mason 18/4- 3-1890 W.C.Mason.
Pendergrass,Jesse R.32 to Mrs.F.I.Dean 28    3-31-1891   S.H.Harrington,MG
Pendergrass,John S.20 to Mary A.Holbrooks 18/3-12-1893 S.J.May,J.P.
Pendergrass,Miles 22 to Harriet H.Morgan 18/5-14-1899  W.C.Mason,M.G.
Pendergrass,C.L.24 to Elsie Richardson 20    12-24-1916 D.D.Richardson,MG
Pendergrass,George 36 to Sarah Cope 28          11-23-1919 D.A.Yonce,M.G.
Pendergrass,Floyd 22 to Etta Willis 21          12-4-1926  A.S.Solesbee,M.G.
Pendergrass,Alex. 21 to Iler Roper 19           1-27-1920  L.P.Roper,J.P.
Pendergrass,William 26 to Leona Pendergrass 17/8-3-1920 T.G.Wilson,M.G.
Pendergrass,Wiley 26 to Vinnie Roper 18         12-2-1920  A.S.Solesbee,M.G.
Pendergrass,Fred C.19 to Lucy Neal 19           9-29-1934  D.F.Howard,M.G.
Pendergrass,Troy 22 to Lassie Hall 19           8- 1-1936  Geo.Carpenter,J.P
Penland,Chamberlain to Nancy Conley             12-25-1851 John McDowell,J.P
Penland,Robert N.20 to A.P.Patton 21            2-15-1876  Albert Siler,J.P.
Penland,H.P. to S.E.Conley                      2-21-1854  John Hall,Clk.
Penland,James to Elizabeth S.Runnon             3-15-1855  John Hall,Clk.
Penland,Leander H.to Martha I.Angel             12-15-1869 C.D.Smith,M.G.
Penland,Geo.N.25 to H.P.Phillips 18             1- 9-1873  C.D.Smith,M.G.
Penland,David W.32 to Sarah Moseley 16          12-22-1886 L.H.Garland,J.P.
Penland,William 22 to Lena A.McDonnell 18 Col.8-17-1890-Jnos.Phillips,JP
Penland,Henry A.35 to Callie Bradley 22         12-16-1891 W.J.Grist,J.P.
Penland,Eddy C.21 to Lucy Downs 21              6-29-1892  C.D.Smith,M.G.
Penland,Melville.E.32 to Lizzie G.Downs 19      7-13-1892  C.D.Smith,M.G.
Penland,Ham 22 to Mary Cochran 21         Col. 7-29-1894  J.C.Hemphill,M.G.
Penland,Enoch 28 to Parchina Moore 18  Col. 9-30-1894  M.Ghormley,M.G.
Penland,Homer 23 to Annice Donaldson 19         10-31-1896 John C.Russell,JP
Penland,J.W.20 to I.C.Philipps 21               7-30-1908  T.C.King,M.G.
Penland,Homer R.35 to Mattie E.Crawford 23  9- 6-1908  W.L.Griggs,M.G.
```

```
Penland,Witham 21 to Sadie E.Stiles 16          11-25-1917 A.M.Ledford,M.G.
Penland,Fred 21 to Mary Will Love 21       Col.12-14-1919 Geo.Carpenter,J.P
Penland,Lawrence 19 to Gorda Stiles 18          11-14-1920 Noah L.Jollay,J.P
Penland,William 37 to Beulah M.Cabe 30           3- 8-1927 J.H.Strickland,JP
Penland,Louis 28 to Grady Burgess 23       Col.3-10-1928 J.E.Chambers,M.G.
Pennington,Nathaniel 27 to Inda Kinsland 19 12-29-1907 C.L.Rickman,J.P.
Perkins,Basil C.34 to Elna Donilson 23          12-11-1924 E.J.Pipes.
  Both from Boise,Idaho.
Perry,Charles 31 to Kate M.Slagle 21            9-14-1891  C.D.Smith,M.G.
Perry,Charles H.25 to Laura Kate Baird 19       5-12-1928  Robert F.Mock,M.G
Phillips,Wiley to Laurine Morgan                11-19-1838 J.K.Gray,Clk.
Phillips,E.H. to Claressa Russell               12-1-1838  J.K.Gray,Clk.
Phillips,Archable to Belinda Ammons             1- 2-1840  John Hall,Clk.
Phillips,Gilpin to Hariett Hayes                12-22-1842 A.Hester,J.P.
Phillips,Samuel H.to Amanda A.Vanhook           1-28-1852  Wm.Angel,J.P.
Phillips,Joseph to Lydia Cross                  7-25-1861  L.F.Siler,J.P.
Phillips,John L.21 to Sarah E.McConnell 20      3-15-1876  E.H.Franks,J.P.
Phillips,Jonathan 29 to Adda Hicks 21           11-11-1885 R.A.Owen,M.G.
Phillips,R.J.29 to Mary E.Wright 32             12-5-1886  J.H.Weaver,M.G.
Phillips,James 23 to Mary Colvard 28            1-14-1889  George Bryson,J.P
Phillips,Clayton J.30 to Jenny Sanders 19       10-31-1896 R.B.Shelton,M.G.
Phillips,James 19 to Dora Knight 17             10-4-1900  E.P.Brown,J.P.
Phillips,Samuel 25 to Ida Guest 20              10-9-1904  J.R.Pendergras,MG
Phillips,D.M.50 to Mrs.Lula J.Ghormley 30       10-20-1912 W.W.Howard,J.P.
Phillips,Frank 21 to Augusta Garner 21          4-14-1915  J.R.Pendergras,MG
Phillips,C.C.33 to Niza Arnold 21               8-21-1917  Robert Stamey,J.P
Phillips,Roy 36 to Octa Henry 20                12-25-1925 W.T.Potts,M.G.
Phillips,L.B.29 to Nina B.Setser 28             4- 3-1926  E.J.Pipes,M.G.
Phillips,Wendell 23 to Hariett E.Straine 19/9-11-1926 R.A.Truitt,M.G.
Phillips,Thos.W.28 to Mrs.Avis Trimmer 30       2-23-1927  J.R.Pendergras,MG
Phillips,Nat.M.27 to Emma J.Sanders 19          9- 3-1933  J.N.Dulin,M.G.
Pickens,Ceborn 22 to Catherine Martin 25        7-24-1880  H.G.Woodfin,J.P.
Pickens,Marvin 21 to Edith Hurst 20             6-10-1934  Lee Mason,J.P.
Pickens,Wade 23 to Evelyn Sanders 19            8- 6-1933  Geo.Carpenter,J.P
Picklesimer,Watson to Jane Cathey               7-16-1839  H.G.Woodfin,D.Clk.
Picklesimer,Wilson to Jane McCall               12-6-1842  John Hall,C.C.C.
Picklesimer,Benson to M.C.Thompson              1-18-1864  R.C.Slagle,Reg.
Picklesimer,D.A.19 to Elizabeth Watkins 19      1-20-1884  J.N.Arnold,J.P.
Picklesimer,Andrew J.21 to Salina C.Wilson 18/8-5-1886 J.W.Wilson,J.P.
Picklesimer,Edward 27 to Cora Rogers 31         1-21-1900  G.W.Matney,M.G.
Picklesimer,John 37 to Gerdie Rogers 24         10-24-1909 P.C.Calloway,J.P.
Picklesimer,Bascomb 27 to Francis Jones 21      10-20-1912 C.R.Cabe,J.P.
Picklesimer,J.H.31 to May Bell Keener,          3-24-1918  W.C.Ledbetter,J.P
Picklesimer,H.A.27 toNora Sawyer 25             11-22-1918 J.R.Pendergras,MG
Pierce,John to Rebecca Ledbetter                3-23-1841  John Hall,C.S.C.
Pierson,Evan to Rebecca Norton                  3-20-1849  Elias Norton,J.P.
Pierson,Mack 23 to Annie A.Whipp 25             4-14-1909  T.J.Vinson,M.G.
```

Pierson,A.F.21 to Susan Rogers 17   10-17-1909 T.J.Vinson,M.G.
Pierson,J.Q.31 to Lillie F.Moore 26   7-17-1910 J.R.Pendergrass,MG
Pilketon,James T. to Mary Collins   1- 6-1864 R.C.Slagle,Reg.
Pilkington,John A.to Elizabeth Kirkland   10-12-1870 William Sloan,Reg
Pitman,William to Jane Robinson   9-19-1829 Robert Huggins,JP
Pittman,Reubon 20 to Ida Duvall 16   8- 7-1899 Jacob Younce,M.G.
Plemmons,Archibald to Judah Hipps   7- 7-1830 John D.Carne,J.P.
Plemmons,James to Linsey Murray   7- 3-1836 D.Weeks,J.P.
Plemmons,M.A.22 to Myrtle Hurst 21   9-21-1919 T.J.Vinson,M.G.
Plemmons,Thos.A.to Lucinda Cunningham   1-19-1843 J.K.Gray,D.Clk.
Poindexter,Francis to Margaret J.Bryson   2-20-1855 John Hall,Clk.
Poindexter,Jasper to Martha J.Dewze   9-22-1856 John Hall,Clk.
Poindexter,John 21 to Margaret Jacobs 18   11-14-1880 B.G.Wild,M.G.
Poindexter,J.L.22 to C.J.Moore 19   2-15-1892 W.C.Carden,M.G.
Poindexter,Albert L.32 to Lavada E.Wilkes 21/6-17-1894 J.P.Campbell,J.P.
Poindexter,William A.26 to Kittie Tallent 21/3-27-1909 W.I.Hughes,M.G.
Poindexter,Robert 21 to Launa Barnard 20   11-1-1910 W.I.Hughes,M.G.
Poindexter,A.L.52 to Mrs.Lula Phillips 30   1-30-1915 A.S.Solesbee,M.G.
Poindexter,George 23 to Lalie Angel 20   9-27-1916 J.R.Pendergras,MG
Poindexter,James 19 to Lula Ledford 20`   12-17-1915 J.L.Yonce,M.G.
Poindexter,Lee 21 to Bessie Holland 21   12-18-1920 J.R.Pendergras,MG
Poindexter,R.L.,Jr.24 to Eddis Tallent 22   10-18-1936 R.E.Mayberry,M.G.
Pope,David 41 to Mrs.Sallie Conley 42   11-19-1908 J.R.Pendergras,MG
Pool,William L.23 to Nannie C.Potts 22   1-14-1890 W.R.Barnett,M.G.
Porter,Stephen to E.S.Moore   5-23-1865 R.C.Slagle,Reg.
Porter,R.L.27 to F.M.Cunningham 20   1- 1-1878 M.P.Swain,M.G.
Porter,Stephen 37 to T.F.Adams 25   8-29-1878 M.P.Swain,M.G.
Porter,Robert L.22 to Emily Ramsey 18   10-13-1874 Thos.Mashburn,J.P
Porter,Jesse W.25 to Flora Roane 22   4-17-1895 J.J.Gray,M.G.
Porter,J.A.28 to Mary V.Addington 25   3-30-1897 T.E.Nagg,M.G.
Porter,Thomas W.28 to Leona C.Bryson 23   10-19-1904 Thos.Winecoff,M.G
Porter,J.D.22 to Ruth Zachary 22   11-15-1910 J.R.Pendergras,MG
Porter,R.L.20 to John William Daugherty 21?/5- 1-1917 R.H.Daugherty,M.G
Porter,Lester 28 to Pauline Bell 24   Col. 10-27-1917 R.H.Daugherty,M.G
Porter,J.S.22 to Margaret Cunningham 22   1- 7-1924 W.M.Smith,M.G.
Porter,Thomas W.Jr.30 to Mabel Parker 26   12-30-1937 J.E.Abernathey,MG
Postell,John to Nancy Passmore   2-26-1844 J.K.Gray,Clk.
Potts,William F.to Amanda Morrison   6- 9-1848 W.F.Robinson,J.P.
Potts,D.W. to Carolina Addington   2-21-1855 J.B.Little,M.G.
Potts,J.S. to S.A.Addington   8-15-1855 J.G.Crawford,D.Ck
Potts,M.L. to Mary C.Addington   8-16-1859 Jacob Siler,J.P.
Potts,T.S. to Sarah Tippett   12-29-1859 T.P.Siler,D.Clk.
Potts,Wm.F. to Mary C.Dean   8-22-1867 R.C.Slagle,Clk.
Potts,Miles to Sarah McGaha   12-8-1868 R.C.Slagle,Clk.
Potts,William W.24 to E.B.Matlock 17   4-27-1882 P.P.McLean,M.G.
Potts,J.H.22 to Susie S.Morrison 21   3- 1-1883 M.J.Mashburn,J.P.
Potts,W.T.25 to Martha J.Ammons 20   1-11-1883 S.H.Harrington,JP

```
Potts,John F.21 to Alice M.Shepherd 17        2-21-1884  M.J.Mashburn,J.P.
Potts,Robert 23 to Stacy P.Stewart 18         3-29-1886  M.B.Dockery,J.P.
Potts,Judson 23 to Isabella Raby 24           12-3-1893  W.R.Rickman,M.G.
Potts,Albert J.22 to Cora B.Matlock 19        8-30-1894  Geo.T.Bryson,J.P.
Potts,J.T.38 to Dollie Elmore 20              12-23-1900 John E.Rickman,JP
Potts,Walter 21 to Sarah C.Hurst 18           12-20-1908 John C.Hurst,J.P.
Potts,J.Edward 22 to Ella Pierson 21          2-28-1909  T.J.Vinson,M.G.
Potts,William Royal 18 to Meta Frost Pierson 17/11-22-1910-P.C.Calloway.
Potts,Frank Huffman 22 to Eula Bell McKinney 23/5-28-1911-W.L.Griggs,M.G
Potts,Edward C.24 to Eva Earl McCoy 26        10-22-1912 W.T.Thompson,M.G.
Potts,C.W.27 to Margaret Higdon 24            7-18-1915  L.J.Young,M.G.
Potts,Charles C.22 to Helen G.Zachary 19      10-12-1916 W.T.Potts,M.G.
Potts,Samuel E.21 to Alice O.Reese 18         6-12-1917  P.C.Calloway,J.P.
Potts,A.B.25 to Fannie McClure 19             5- 5-1917  O.C.Corbin,J.P.
Potts,J.T.20 to Virginia Bryant 18            4- 6-1919  D.C.McCoy,M.G.
Potts,Floyd 33 to Maude Bradley 23            10-19-1921 R.P.McCracken,M.G
Potts,J.L.25 to Esther Calloway 18            1- 8-1922  Geo.Carpenter,J.P
Potts,Paul 30 to Allie Ray 25                 1-13-1925  Geo.Carpenter,J.P
Potts,Paul 20 to Mabel Cabe 18                4-24-1937  J.J.Edward,M.G.
Potter,D.A. 19 to Bessie Fish 18              6-29-1918  J.R.Davis,M.G.
Poteet,Barnard to Rachel Russell              7-26-1831  James Poteet.
Powell,Doc 30 to Pallie Burnett 22            4-25-1897  J.Ammons,M.G.
Powers,Lon 24 to Omah Young 22                7- 7-1901  S.J.May,J.P.
Powers,W.N.42 to Mrs.Minnie A.Garland 35      9- 8-1914  J.R.Pendergras,MG
Powers,R.M.29 to Effa Love 33                 1-15-1916  R.H.Daugherty,M.G
Prater,Elijah 20 to Elva Beck 19        Col. 2-27-1878  E.H.Franks,J.P.
Prater,Jule 55 to Jane Logan 30         Col. 12-28-1881 J.E.Kilgore,M.G.
Prater,Walter 21 to Jennie Burgess, 22  Col. 11-21-1910 J.R.Pendergras,MG
Prater,George W. to Martha C.Love             9-19-1829  W.B.Hyatt,J.P.
Presnell,David to Nancy Lee                   11-29-1851 J.K.Gray,D.Clk.
Pressley,Dunon 20 to Maria Jones 24           10-28-1879 Hosea Moses,J.P.
Pressley,D.H.23 to Amanda Roper 19            8- 3-1884  Canaro S.Ray,J.P.
Pressley,Mack M.19 to Nancy C.Dills 17        8-10-1890  F.M.Morgan,M.G.
Pressley,Andrew M.19 to Queen Vashti Parker 18/8-17-1893-J.P.Moore,J.P.
Pressley,Fidille 24 to Laura Gregory 20       9-16-1894  A.W.Davis,M.G.
Pressley,S.E.21 to Henrietta Sanders 20       3-21-1921  J.R.Pendergras,MG
Pressley,Geo.E.30 to Lola Bailey 18           12-23-1933 Geo.Carpenter,J.P
Pressley,Walter 22 to Dollie Shepherd 15      5-12-1934  Geo.Carpenter,J.P
Previtt,Smith to Vina Peek                    11-23-1844 James Peek,J.P.
Price,Phillips 28 to Sarah J.Ammons 19        12-1-1881  J.M.Keener,M.G.
Price,Zeb.V.24 to T.V.Owenby 22               3-14-1886  F.M.Morgan,M.G.
Price,Robert 30 to Martha Bateman 15          4-27-1890  F.M.Morgan,M.G.
Price,James R.32 to Bertha W.Gaston 26        9-26-1900  C.M.Campbell,M.G.
Price,W.S.66 to Annie Watkins 45              12-28-1916 A.W.Jacobs,M.G.
Price,Raymon J.24 to Lora L.Cabe 19           6- 3-1926  J.R.Pendergras,MG
Price,Glenn 24 to Francis Palmer 22           8-30-1930  Geo.Carpenter,J.P
Prichard,James to Francis Ridley              3- 7-1839  H.G.Woodfin,D.Clk
```

```
Pruitt,George W.to Mary Breedlove          5-25-1852  Jas.M.Murray,J.P.
Pruitt,Thomas to Martha Tatham             10-26-1859 Felix Kilpatrick.
Pullam,Bariston to Nancy Ingram            2-22-1833  John Hall,C.C.C.
Plonk,T.M. 30 to Louise McGuire 24         9- 1-1920  J.Q.Wallace,M.G.
Plott,Smith H.24 to Norah Smith 16         11-22-1896 Jas.C.Weaver,J.P.
Query,James to Lorata Briton               2-22-1835  Joel Simons,J.P.
  She from Haywood Co.N.C.
Quesinberry,James W.49 to Octie Ingram 36  1-12-1887  S.H.Harrington,MG
Queen,Maxwell to Sela Rose                 12-20-1832 Wm.Morgan,J.P.
Queen,J.W. to Martha Hickey                10-3-1840  H.G.Woodfin,D.Clk
Queen,John to Mary Holcomb                 11-8-1852  Caleb Holcomb.
Queen,William to Susan West                1-18-1853  W.H.Higdon,J.P.
Queen,Timothy to Clarissa Young            11-11-1857 John Elmore,J.P.
Queen,T.B.J.to D.P.Matlock                 9-22-1865  R.C.Slagle,Reg.
Queen,D.P. to H.I.Jarrett                  4-23-1870  Jas.K.Bryson,Reg.
Queen,S.M.21 to Etter Tippett 18           11-18-1880 J.S.Gibson,J.P.
Queen,William 25 to Mary F.Rickman 22      1- 4-1883  John S.Gibson,J.P
Queen,Osco 20 to Martha Johns 23           7-14-1895  M.Ghormley,M.G.
Queen,James A.50 to Mrs.Maggie McGaha 49   9-21-1907  J.R.Pendergras,MG
Queen,Wesley C.24 to Bessie Tallent 16     11-10-1907 J.P.Campbell,J.P.
Queen,Thomas H.21 to Mamie Icenhower 17    12-8-1908  W.L.Bradley,M.G.
Queen,William 57 to Sarah Painter 23       5-12-1912  J.L.Bryson,J.P.
Queen,Edgar 19 to Maude Roper 18           1-24-1927  G.A.Cloer,M.G.
Queen,Lloyd 21 to Essie Jamison18          6-22-1927  G.A.Steed,M.G.
  He from Dillsboro,N.C.... She from Sylva,N.C.
Queen,Fred W.23 to Ruth Houston 18         5-16-1936  W.L.Bradley,M.G.
Queen,Lon 21 to Lois DeHart 18             11-6-1936  T.D.Denny,M.G.
  She from Bryson Cith,N.C.
Raby,Frederick to Hannah Jones             1-17-1839  John Hall,C.C.C.
Raby,Alfred to Sarah Ann Raby              1-13-1853  D.C.Newton,J.P.
Raby,Elijah to Carolina Boyd               9-27-1857  R.C.Slagle,C.C.C.
Raby,Henry to Mary Wilson                  10-18-1857 Joseph Buchanan.
Raby,Tilghman  to Polly Ann Lowe           8- 4-1860  R.C.Slagle,C.C.C.
Raby,M.A. to N.T.Shepherd                  8-14-1863  R.C.Slagle,C.C.C.
Raby,Jas.to Margaret Blackwell             10-18-1865 H.H.Raby,J.P.
Raby,Josiah 22 to Candes Webb 18           9-19-1878  P.R.Rickman,M.G.
Raby,Elijah 53 to Jane Burnett 40          12-9-1883  E.C.Stewman,J.P.
Raby,C.A.17 to Clearcy L.Bird 17           3- 4-1886  J.A.Morrison,J.P.
Raby,Jas.T.23 to Melvina Wiggins 16        1-16-1890  A.B.Dalton,J.P.
Raby,J.R.55 to Rowena Shields 27           2-14-1897  W.M.Downs,J.P.
Raby,John F.27 to Pearl V.Bryson 18        3-19-1899  A.H.Sims,M.G.
Raby,James M.21 to Annie Corbin 22         9- 9-1904  S.J.Ammons,J.P.
Raby,H.H. 72 to Nannie Reaves 47           9-22-1904  J.R.Morrison,J.P.
Raby,Albert L.24 to Leina Fowler 18        7- 9-1905  W.L.Bradley,M.G.
Raby,Charlie D.21 to Ellie Reeves 19       5- 6-1906  Joseph L.Fouts,JP
Raby,Oscar A.22 to Hester Sanders 19       3- 8-1908  J.E.Vinson,J.P.
Raby,John F.38 to Elzie Allen 30           2- 3-1910  R.R.Rickman,J.P.
Raby,J.R.68 to Dora Payne 38               12-18-1910 J.R.Pendergras,MG
```

```
Raby,James M.29 to Inda Corbin 25            3-16-191?  Geo.Carpenter,J.P
Raby,J.J. 24 to Ada B.Welch 20              12-15-1917 J.L.Fouts,J.P.
Raby,George C.42 to Ethie Shepherd 26        8-27-1919 W.L.Bradley,M.G.
Raby,Luther 26 to Genevive Bryson 22         3- 7-1925 Geo.Carpenter,J.P
Raby,William Algia 28 to Grace Shuler 24     3-12-1939 R.C.Rickman,J.P.
Ragland,Thomas R.25 to Cathryn E.Rice 18    12-1-1929  Albert New,M.G.
    He from Miami,Fla.
Rainwater,Brown V.27 to Elizabeth Brown 28  9-25-1940  Frank Bluxham,M.G
    He from Pensaola,Fla.... She from Dallas,Tx.
Ramsey,James M.to H.E.Hicks                 12-3-1851  W.M.Angel,J.P.
Ramsey,James Kerr 49 to Georgia Lee Morton 46/9-22-1940-S.R.Crockett,M.G
    Both from Madisonville,Ky.
Ramsey,John  to Martha Bryson               11-1-1842  J.F.Padgett,
Ramsey,Samuel to Nancy Parrish              10-10-1869 M.Rickman,M.G.
Ramsey,Henry 50 to Lucinda Beasley 39        3-18-1875 P.R.Rickman,M.G.
Ramsey,W.A.33 to R.A.West 28                12-21-1882 C.D.Smith,M.G.
Ramsey,John B.23 to Texas V.Caler 19        12-23-1885 M.J.Mashburn,J.P.
Ramsey,John H.22 to Laura C.Morgan 14       12-21-1893 A.A.Justice,M.G.
Ramsey,George T.25 to Pearlie F.McCoy 19     4-10-1899 J.B.Justice,J.P.
Ramsey,James R.24 to Pearl Byrd 17           1- 8-1905 W.L.Bradley,M.G.
Ramsey,Charles O.22 to Virgie D.Bryson 16    3- 6-1909 J.R.Pendergras,MG
Ramsey,Albert L.23 to Margarett Higdon 22    5-12-1918 A.W.Jacobs,M.G.
Ramsey,Robert 32 to Ardenia Hurst 21         6-15-1910 J.R.Pendergras,MG
Ramsey,W.L.34 to Clare Faye Hyatt 23         5-20-1923 J.Q.Wallace,M.G.
Ramsey,Floyd 22 to Lillie Smith 18           7- 4-1928 A.S.Solesbee,M.G.
Ramsey,G.T.58 to Trixie Justice 20           3- 8-1932 Geo.Carpenter,J.P
Ramph,E.M.50 to Stella Smith 31              2-24-1927 W.T.Potts,M.G.
    He from Atlanta,Ga.
Rankin,Wm.W. to Rebecca S.Drake              9- 6-1870 Wm.Sloan,Reg.
Rankin,W.W. 48 to Sarah R.Haxed 29           2- 7-1886 W.A.Thomas,M.G.
Rankin,Grant 21 to Lillian Smith 21          5-28-1927 Geo.Carpenter,J.P
Rakes,G.F. 19 to Elsie Sanders 19           10-12-1933 Will Smith,Ord.
    He from Draper,N.C.
Ray,Thomas to Sarah Phillips                 9-15-1835 Robert Clayton,Cl
Ray,Levy to L.Ann Deweese                    7-18-1850 T.P.Siler,D.Clk.
Ray,Henry H.to Mary E.Moore                  5- 8-1855 John Hall,Clk.
Ray,Wilbun to Eunice Deweese                 3-19-1864 R.C.Slagle,Reg.
Ray,Henry to Mary C.Gribble                  7-27-1866 R.C.Slagle,C.C.C.
Ray,William to Louisa Morgan                 9-30-1866 R.C.Slagle,C.C.C.
Ray,L.J.27 to Adie Fouts 19                 12-26-1877 C.Campbell,M.G.
Ray,J.R.20 to C.R.Fouts 17                   2-13-1878 Z.Barnes,J.P.
Ray,Mat 21 to Nancy Hacket 18      Col.      5-22-1879 H.G.Woodfin,J.P.
Ray,J.Frank 34 to Josephine Fouts 23        12-26-1889 J.S.Woodard,M.G.
Ray,Jesse Robt.23 to Hattie Harrison 18      9-16-1891 J.M.Roan,J.P.
Ray,Rufus 22 to Carrie A.Roper 21           12-22-1892 P.C.Wild,J.P.
Ray,Emulus 27 to Ida Roper 23               12-13-1894 P.J.Campbell,J.P.
Ray,Charles T.31 to Katie H.Wild 20          3-10-1895 J.P.Campbell,J.P.
Ray,James 21 to Susan Bateman 16             1-29-1896 W.J.Evans,M.G.
```

Ray,Newton H.24 to Mary Wild 20	2- 5-1899	James L.Fouts,J.P
Ray,H.P.28 to Minnie Yonce 21	4-11-1901	Jos.L.Fouts,J.P.
Ray,Jeff 35 to Lassie Bateman 40	1-24-1902	W.A.Solesbee,J.P.
Ray,Jake 28 to Mrs.Docia Bateman 24	10-17-1903	W.A.Solesbee,J.P.
Ray,J.Robert 49 to Jennie Wild 39	5-26-1907	J.L.Yonce,M.G.
Ray,R.A.24 to Susie Waters 18	1- 2-1910	D.A.Yonce,M.G.
Ray,Lewis B.20 to Daisy Grisham 26 Col.	10-1-1911	Chas.L.Stewart,MG
Ray,John W.26 to Burdelle Jenkins 18	1- 4-1914	T.J.Vinson,M.G.
Ray,N.H.38 to Elizabeth Edwards 31	10-25-1914	W.E.Welch,J.P.
Ray,Andrew 19 to Grace Love 17 Col.	2-17-1916	J.W.Henderson,J.P
Ray,A.R.22 to Mae West 22	4- 7-1915	Geo.Carpenter,J.P
Ray,J.Frank,Jr.24 to Hellen R.Penland 21	7-29-1917	R.H.Dougherty,M.G.
Ray,Robert 19 to Bulah Dowdle 22	8-16-1917	A.W.Jacobs,M.G.
Ray,John 20 to Georgia Wishon 15	10-7-1917	D.A.Yonce,M.G.
Ray,W.E.52 to Blanche Carter 27	12-28-1919	M.L.Angel,J.P.
Ray,Jess R.30 to Alice M.Cunningham 24	4-23-1932	E.R.Eller,M.G.
Raymond,Henry 31 to Bunnie Carter 29	5-30-1913	D.F.Howard,M.G.
·Ramey,James to Margaret Moffat	2-23-1871	J.H.Addington,J.P
·Ramey,James J.42 to Nancy R.Watkins 26	8- 5-1894	L.H.Garland,J.P.
Ramey,Martin 16 to Pallie L.Watkins 18	4- 7-1895	L.H.Garland,J.P.
Ramey,J.R.42 to to Ella Dotson 18	1-21-1899	Jas.C.Weaver,J.P
Ramey,Nevil 19 to Texie McDonald 16	7-16-1907	W.P.Allison,J.P.
Ramey,Jeff 22 to Ida Norris 18	2- 5-1908	J.R.Pendergras,MG
Ramey,Frank 21 to Nellie Mashburn 18	1- 2-1910	J.M.Keener,M.G.
Ramey,Luther 20 to Effie Angel 19	6- 2-1912	Geo.Carpenter,J.P
Ramey,Cordia 25 to Emma Jones 25	1-26-1913	C.R.Cabe,J.P.
Ramey,Ed 26 to Floy Dills 16	8-28-1915	J.R.Pendergras,MG
Ramey,V.C.20 to Willie Grist 16	1- 6-1917	J.B.Stalcup,M.G.
·Ramey,Fred 24 to Allie Dills 21	8-30-1919	G.A.Cloer,M.G.
Rector,E.L.58 to Lena Phillips 43 He from Andrews,N.C.	12-27-1928	Robt.F.Mock,M.G.
Redmond,J.L. to Eliza H.Evett	9-22-1860	R.C.Slagle,Reg.
Redmond,Geo.Frank 22 to Flomire M.Patterson 21	10-9-1929	Robt.F.Mock,M.G
He from Whittier,N.C..... She from Bryson City,N.C.		
Redden,J.M.31 to Martha Ellon Watts 23	11-8-1910	J.T.Watts,J.P.
Reece,R.W.22 to O.Womack 20	2-11-1880	C.D.Smith,M.G.
Reece,Charles 23 to Nora Lewis 17	10-1-1884	R.A.Owen,M.G.
Reece,S.J.21 to Olive Moss 18	1-18-1915	T.M.Keener,J.P.
Reece,Frank 24 to Margie Waldroop 18	12-25-1919	L.B.Hayes, M.G.
Reece,Wade A.30 to Birdell Waldroop 23	4-30-1928	Robert F.Mock,M.G
Reese,William M.27 to Mattie Luther 26	12-26-1883	R.A.Owen,M.G.
Reese,William D.22 to Roxie Potts 22	12-31-1889	C.D.Smith,M.G.
Reese,R.M.32 to Ivy Stepp 18	3-10-1898	Z.Barnes,J.P.
Reese,R.W.45 to Arie Tallent 26	1- 1-1902	J.C.Postell,M.G.
Reese,Robert 22 to Myrtle C.Henderson 20 She from Jackson Co.,N.C.	11-23-1924	J.G.W.Holloway,MG
·Reed,Wilborn to Sarah Brendle	2-25-1845	J.K.Gray,Clk.
Reed,John to Salina Moore	2-11-1852	J.K.Gray,Clk.

Reed,N.W.,Jr.19 to Rosa C.Revis 22   12-11-1881 J.N.Arnold,J.P.
Reed,Lee 23 to Addie Miller 24   1-13-1895 D.L.Miller,M.G.
Reed,Sim 21 to Mary Justice 18   11-21-1907 Original not found
Reed,Andrew 21 to Effie Keener 19   10-27-1913 I.T.Peek,J.P.
Reid,Wilburn to Name not given   1- 8-1855 John Hall,Clk.
Reid,Wilburn to Martha Rogers   1- 8-1856 John Hall,Clk.
Reid,Andrew J.25 to Rebecca A.Sanders 19   7-13-1890 J.B.Elmore,J.P.
Reid,J.Robert 30 to M.Dore Nichols 18   12-21-1890 M.J.Mashburn,M.G.
Reid,Robert 35 to Mrs.Iva Scroggs 32   8-10-1909 P.C.Calloway,J.P.
Reid,Charles 20 to Alice Dills 18   12-27-1915 C.A.Ramey,J.P.
Reid,George J.27 to Edith Anderson 23   12-24-1923 A.J.Smith,M.G.
Reeder,James H.45 to Althea Z.Graham 45   9-11-1895 W.T.Thompson,M.G.
Reeves,J.B.21 to Rebeca Roland 18   10-7-1880 J.S.Woodard,M.G.
Reeves,Thomas 22 to Ida Love 21   3-16-1905 H.P.Ray,J.P.
Reeves,Charley 21 to Addie Davis 26   8-11-1906 J.R.Pendergras,MG
Reeves,J.C.19 to Lora Patterson 16   1-14-1912 Chas.T.Ray,J.P.
Reeves,Charlie 29 to Arlesa Willis 19   11-9-1913 W.E.Welch,J.P.
Reeves,C.M.35 to Texie Roper 25   3-28-1920 L.P.Roper,J.P.
Renson,R.F.25 to Mary D.Foss 23   11-5-1915 W.P.Wilson,J.P.
Reneau,Charles A.21 to Irene M.Edwards 18   10-28-1914 A.C.Gibbs,M.G.
Rembert,Walter 21 to Florence Donaldson 18 3-13-1895 G.R.McPherson,J.P
Revell,James H.to Sarah Miller   5-31-1853 J.K.Gray,Clk.
Reynolds,James to Nancy Cabe   12-30-1850 T.P.Siler,D.Clk.
Reynolds,J.W.25 to Lucy Robinson 20   8- 9-1878 Hosea Moses,J.P.
Reynolds,David C.46 to Harriett L.Rickman 35/7-1-1886 David McCracken.
Reynolds,Jess O.17 to Mammie B.Gibson 19   3-10-1912 J.W.Rickman,J.P.
Reynolds,Harley 24 to Ora Curtis 22   4- 7-1920 W.A.Norton,J.P.
Reynolds,Frank T.23 to Anne Siler 26   5-20-1929 J.A.Flanagan,M.G.
Reynolds,Walter W.41 to Laura Samthers 31   9-26-1933 Geo.Carpenter,J.P
  Both from Canton,N.C.
Rhea,T.Bragg 35 to Alice Davis 18   3- 8-1887 F.M.Morgan.
Rhea,Jeff H.35 to Una Quisenberry 22   4-29-1896 A.B.Thomas,M.G.
Rhinehart,Joe W.,Jr.29 to Kate A.Moore 29   5- 7-1936 W.M.Burns,M.G.
  He from Sylva,N.C.
Rhodes,Thomas W.to Margaret H.Carpenter   1- 8-1864 R.C.Slagle,D.Clk.
Rhodes,T.W. to M.A.T.Carpenter   6-20-1865 A.W.Bell.
Rhodes,Z.T.to Mary Justice   8- 5-1870 Jas.K.Bryson,Clk.
Rhodes,Curtis N.23 to Margaret E.Penland 22/12-13-1873 W.T.Anderson,J.P.
Rhodes,Samuel 18 to Louisa M.Queen 25   8-29-1875 E.T.Long,J.P.
Rhodes,Z.T.33 to Margaret M.Conley 23   8- 6-1879 G.A.Maden,M.G.
Rhodes,James M.35 to Annie Justice 17   12-16-1896 S.C.Conley,J.P.
Rhodes,G.H.22 to Maggie Cabe 23   11-21-1897 D.P.Cabe,J.P.
Rhodes,W.N.21 to Penelope Henson 18   4-16-1898 J.M.Carpenter,J.P
Rhodes,J.M.30 to Adelia Young 23   3-21-1900 E.A.Sample,M.G.
Rhodes,Charley 25 to Mary Waldroop 19   1-30-1910 F.N.Johnston,J.P.
Rhodes,Wm.Lafayett 55 to Julia E.Carpenter 35/12-14-1911-J.M.Conley,J.P.
Rhodes,Frank 22 to Ethel Burres 18   11-15-1923 T.L.Taylor,M.G.

```
Rhodes,Thomas W. 84 to Mary J.Norris 70        1-15-1930  Geo.Carpenter,J.P
Rice,Irvin 25 to Lillie Womack 18              8- 2-1896  T.B.Johnson,M.G.
Rice,Lake C.23 to Elsie N.Rideout 21           10-5-1901  G.W.Matney,M.G.
Rice,Edwin 30 to Kate Landrum 27               10-22-1903 G.W.Stiwinter,J.P
Rice,Luther 22 to Christina Anderson 21        9-24-1905  J.E.Woosley,M.G.
Rice,Lewis Carl 25 to C.Alberta Carter 19      8- 7-1922  S.L.McCarty,M.G.
Rice,Tim 21 to Bertha Welch 21                 11-8-1929  Geo.Carpenter,J.P
Rich,J.H.26 to Lucy Collins 17                 5- 7-1916  Geo.Carpenter,J.P
Richardson,Tiny to Emma D.Gray        Col.     10-19-1885 J.E.Forgartie,M.G
Rickman,Phillip R.to Harietta A.Shepherd       11-27-1855 Jackson Johnson.
Rickman,John J.to Martha L.Caylor              2-26-1859  R.C.Slagle,Reg.
Rickman,Jessie W.to Mary L.Coggins             2- 4-1869  R.C.Slagle,Reg.
Rickman,Martin W.20 to Sarah I.Rickman 21      2-16-1873  A.L.Wild,J.P.
Rickman,C.L.26 to Margaret A.Deal 18           2-15-1880  J.S.Woodard,M.G.
Rickman,John D.22 to Sarah T.Shepherd 20       2-19-1881  J.G.Ammons,M.G.
Rickman,Jas.L.22 to Nora M.Welch 21            4-11-1883  J.S.Woodard,M.G.
Rickman,Merrit L.28 to Sarah A.Rickman 21      4-22-1883  John S.Gibson,J.P
Rickman,Jno.E.20 to Sallie C.Sanders 20        2-11-1887  J.S.Woodard,M.G.
Rickman,J.Wiley 27 to Alice M.Bryson 28        2-23-1890  J.M.Hillard,M.G.
Rickman,M.Lee 30 to Margaret Morrison 27       5-11-1892  G.A.Bartlett,M.G.
Rickman,Roland R.21 to Azbzena Leatherman 16/2-22-1894 W.R.Rickman,M.G.
Rickman,J.D.33 to Mrs.Amey Murray 27           11-23-1899 W.L.Bradley,M.G.
Rickman,J.E.34 to Mary J.Potts 32              3- 3-1901  W.L.Bradley,M.G.
Rickman,W.J.21 to Cora Tallent 18              4-20-1902  Jos.L.Fouts,J.P.
Rickman,Thomas N.20 to Nettie G.Ammons 24      12-11-1906 W.L.Bradley,M.G.
Rickman,J.B.25 to Effie Norton 25              11-5-1910  A.W.Jacobs,M.G.
Rickman,John P.26 to Angie Higdon 24           11-9-1910  J.R.Pendergras,MG
Rickman,R.C.28 to Berdie Elmore 24             6-28-1916  W.L.Bradley,M.G.
Rickman,E.B.22 to Jessie Sheffield 18          8- 5-1916  W.L.Bradley,M.G.
Rickman,Jno.P.32 to Nellie Waldroop 28         12-17-1916 D.S.Richardson,MG
Rickman,E.O.25 to Sissie Mason 23              2-18-1917  J.L.Bryson,J.P.
Rickman,W.P.28 to Inez Bryson 18               10-19-1918 J.R.Pendergras,MG
Rickman,Thomas M.25 to Fannie Holbrooks 19     6-20-1926  J.R.Pendergras,MG
Rickman,H.Sloan 22 to Pearl R.McCoy 21         8-12-1929  Geo.Carpenter,J.P
Rickman,Arthur E.26 to Lois Bradley 20         9- 5-1937  R.F.Mayberry,M.G.
Riddle,Theodore 21 to Kansas Mathis 19         7-18-1914  J.L.Bryson,J.P.
Ridley,James to Mary J.Sorrels                 11-10-1857 John Elmore,J.P.
Ridley,C.A.24 to Lida B.Wilson 22              8-10-1897  G.A.Bartlett,M.G.
Ridley,S.L.21 to Judia McIntire 18             2-23-1902  J.B.Elmore,J.P.
Rideout,Herman L.33 to Lillian Levenson 24     4-26-1904  C.L.Hoffman,M.G.
Right,Alfred to Polly Stewart                  5-21-1836  Ulrich Keener,Clk
Right,Benjamin to Mary Ann Moore               6-30-1860  R.C.Slagle,Reg.
Riley,Peter to Eliza Riley            Col.     -----1852  J.Reid,J.P.
Rinehart,A.M.to Elizabeth Duvall               5-25-1870  J.K.Bryson,Reg.
Rinehart,J.M.22 to I.A.Lakey 23                12-18-1881 G.W.Dean,J.P.
Rinehart,Leonard 26 to Mary E.Bell Owenby 22 12-19-1909-H.J.Hughes,M.G.
Ritchie,John 23 to Roxie Cochram 16   Col.  1- 4-1891  J.C.Hemphill,M.G.
```

Ritchie,J.T.27 to Ethel P.Penland 17	1-18-1899	T.F.Glenn,M.G.
Roads,John to Jane Roads	9- 8-1855	John Hall,Clk.
Roane,William H.to Mary F.Munday	2-19-1850	T.P.Siler,D.Clk.
Roan, John to Mary Slagle	1-20-1855	A.P.Munday.
Roane,Robert D.to Sarah E.Howard	3- 3-1858	R.C.Slagle,Reg.
Roan,J.M.to Nancy Watson	11-8-1865	John A.Green.
Roane,J.T.23 to Sarah Nichols 21	12-23-1883	M.P.Long,M.G.
Roane,Robert J.24 to Mary L.Siler 19	10-1-1884	Geo.D.French,M.G.
Roane,Charles T.34 to Mary B.Rogers 19	12-20-1893	C.D.Smith,M.G.
Roane,Frank 19 to Mamie Carpenter 16	12-31-1906	W.P.Allison,J.P.
Roane,William H.41 to Minnie A.Liner 23	1-26-1910	J.R.Pendergras,MG
Roane,Thomas E.38 to Julia E.McDowell 42	6-28-1910	Wm.P.Chedister,MG
Roane,Zeb 23 to Ivalee Waldroop 17	3-16-1913	C.S.Slagle,J.P.
Roane,Frank 28 to Allie Carpenter 20	2-26-1916	Retd.not executed
Roberts,Eli to Mary Eller	4-23-1843	J.K.Gray,Clk.
Roberts,Montraville to Jeanettie Mason	10-4-1850	Jacob Mason,M.G.
Robertson,Henry G.29 to Laura Bryson 27	4- 2-1903	Edwin L.Bain,M.G.
Robertson,Geo.28 to Elsie Woods 21 He from Brevard,N.C.	8- 3-1926	J.R.Pendergras,MG
Robison,William F.to Sarah E.Murrow	5-14-1848	D.N.Lowery.
Robison,W.A.21 to Mary E.Hawkins 21	2-24-1917	J.R.Pendergras,MG
Robinson,James to Patsy Scoggin	10-13-1840	John Hall,Clk.
Robinson,Lifurs to Mary Williams	8-20-1857	T.W.Owen,J.P.
Robinson,J.S.to A.S.Siler	10-12-1864	R.C.Slagle,Reg.
Robinson,William C.to Nancy Parker (widow)	1-10-1872	William Sloan,Reg
Robinson,Jess S.44 to Ittie Norton 30	2-15-1888	C.D.Smith,M.G.
Robinson,J.W.19 to R.E.Hasket 21	8-16-1900	J.A.Young,J.P.
Robinson,Mack 43 to Carolyn Bradley 42	12-21-1938	Lester L.Arnold.
Robbins,Jesse 19 to Louisa Griggs 19	2-13-1873	J.H.Addington,J.P
Robbins,Jasper 31 to Martha Howard 25	8- 3-1884	M.Ghormley,M.G.
Robins,H.Pinkney 22 to Sarah Joines 37	2-21-1889	S.A.Dickson.
Robins,Nathaniel 21 to Minnie A.Holden 17	4-27-1902	W.C.Mason,M.G.
Robins,George 21 to Synda Holden 35	10-16-1902	L.J.Mashburn,M.G.
Robins,George 42 to Lona Finney 18	1-21-1921	J.R.Morrison,J.P.
Rochester,Willie 25 to Jennieva Campbell 21	/6-12-1892	Summer Clark,J.P.
Rochester,Deweay 20 to Minnie Henry 20	11-28-1919	J.R.Pendergras,MG
Rodgers,John to Juliet McCasky	3- 2-1830	John Hall,C.C.C.
Rodgers,Clark to Margaret L.Reid	2-10-1855	G.W.Rogers.
Rodgers,C.L.28 to Florence Welch 18	8- 9-1906	W.T.R.Ley,M.G.
Rogle,John to Mary Ann Delozier	4-29-1866	R.C.Slagle,C.C.C.
Rogers,Newton to Carolina Lamer	2-19-1830	W.B.Hyatt,D.Clk.
Rogers,Hugh to Ruth C.Ammons	11-20-1844	J.K.Gray,Clk.
Rogers,William R.to Elizabeth Holland	7-17-1850	J.K.Gray,Clk.
Rogers,Robert to Caroline Holland	7-15-1854	John Hall,Clk.
Rogers,Jasper to Elizabeth Ford	3-10-1858	R.C.Slagle,Clk.
Rogers,Newton to Edy Holland	6-15-1858	R.C.Slagle,Clk.
Rogers,Jerry S.to Mary Millsaps	12-13-1861	R.C.Slagle,C.C.C.

Rogers,Newton to Margaret Keener	7-12-1866	R.C.Slagle,C.C.C.
Rogers,John H.to Sarah R.Deal	10-4-1866	R.C.Slagle,C.C.C.
Rogers,David 17 to Charity M.Franks 20	9-29-1872	J.D.Vinson,M.G.
Rogers,David J.23 to Mary A.Mincey 23	11-21-1872	J.S.Woodard,M.G.
Rogers,C.Melvin 23 to Letty C.Mashburn 17 He from Haywood,Co.N.C.	1- 9-1873	A.L.Wild,J.P.
Rogers,John N.26 to Mary E.Wright 23	12-13-1874	James D.Vinson,MG
Rogers,Sambo 27 to Mariah Rogers 18 Col.	12-24-1874	D.W.Wells,M.G.
Rogers,H.M.21 to Mary A.Mincey 19	9-27-1877	Hosea Moses,J.P.
Rogers,John Tyler 20 to Elizabeth Peek 20	11-15-1877	Hosea Moses,J.P.
Rogers,William M.23 to Cynthia A.Wright 19	9-21-1879	D.L.Miller,M.G.
Rogers,Geo.B.30 to S.J.Dalrymple 21 He from Cherokee,N.C.	2-26-1882	J.A.Deal,M.G.
Rogers,T.N.21 to Mary Batey 19	9- 9-1883	M.I.Skinner,J.P.
Rogers,Sam Lyle 30 to Mamie W.Addington 24	12-31-1889	W.R.Barnett,M.G.
Rogers,Wm.Masison 39 to Samantha R.Justice 17/4	-23-1891-	W.J.Grist,J.P.
Rogers,James 19 to Lou Gregory 19	11-17-1892	J.M.Keener,M.G.
Rogers,George 21 to Josephine Barnes 19	2- 5-1893	J.M.Keener,M.G.
Rogers,C.M.19 to Louisa Hall 18	10-19-1898	W.A.Peek,J.P.
Rogers,John W.29 to Rutha Conley 19	4-10-1906	J.E.Cabe,J.P.
Rogers,Robert 22 to Roxie Guffie 18	11-13-1898	Geo.Carpenter,J.P
Rogers,John T.20 to Delila B.Mathis 18	1-18-1900	G.W.Stiwinter,J.P
Rogers,James M.26 to M.S.Peek 24	1- 3-1901	G.W.Stiwinter,J.P
Rogers,William 18 to Orie E.Conley 16	2- 1-1903	L.J.Mashburn,M.G.
Rogers,John H.20 to Emma Justice 21	4- 5-1903	J.G.Bates,J.P.
Rogers,Thomas 30 to Marinda McCall 19	1-24-1904	J.H.Fulton,J.P.
Rogers,James R.24 to Ellen Houston 22	9-15-1904	J.L.Kinsland,M.G.
Rogers,William T.32 to Mattie Myers 18	3-18-1906	W.R.Bulgin,J.P.
Rogers,Benjamin 29 to Callie Tilson 23	9-12-1909	A.G.Wood,J.P.
Rogers,Charles 24 to Viola Barnes 21	5- 7-1911	Z.J.Peek,J.P.
Rogers,Wiley A.39 to Marie Renner 22	5-24-1911	M.H.Tuttle,M.G.
Rogers,Charley 20 to Clara Vanhook 18	12-11-1912	J.L.Teague,M.G.
Rogers,Neely 21 to Cora Woods 19	8- 1-1914	A.B.Miller,J.P.
Rogers,John 23 to Minnie Leopard 24	8-21-1914	J.M.Keener,M.G.
Rogers,Mack 29 to Nettie Buckner 25	10-14-1914	J.R.Pendergras,MG
Rogers,J.H.32 to Addie Miller 20	5- 9-1915	J.Z.Carver,J.P.
Rogers,H.W.38 to Zella McClure 32	12-2-1917	W.C.Ledbetter,J.P
Rogers,William H.25 to Elsie Miller 18	3-25-1922	L.J.Young,M.G.
Rogers,David 48 to Cora Bishop 35	5- 7-1933	S.J.Murray,J.P.
Rogers,John E.33 to Helen Stiles 23	5- 5-1935	E.R.Eller,M.G.
Rogers,Jamie 21 to Sarah M.Keener 19	10-21-1924	J.W.Batey,M.G.
Rogers,Wiley T.31 to Edna K.Vines 27 He from Wilmington,??.	8-25-1935	C.C.Herbert,M.G.
Rogers,Verlin 23 to Lucy Fisher 21 Both from Waynesville,N.C.	4- 2-1937	C.A.Setser,J.P.
Rogers,Kermit 27 to Ruby Ammons 21	2-19-1938	Ennis Tilson,J.P.
Rogers,Arthur L.30 to Bonnie B.Palmer 25 She from Cashiers,N.C.	3-12-1938	Geo.A.Cloer,M.G.

Roland,John to Mary A.Younce	10-30-1848	S.M.Dowell.
Roland,Calvin to Margaret Pace	3-22-1869	R.C.Slagle,Reg.
Roland,Jacob to Catherine Younce	3-28-1872	Jesse Stepp,J.P.
Roland,Columbus 16 to Mary E.Lunsford 18	10-28-1877	Z.Barnes,J.P.
Roland,Jesse 25 to Mary:A.Younce 21	2-27-1881	J.S.Woodard,M.G.
Roland,James D.21 to Martha Younce 21	10-5-1884	Z.Barnes,J.P.
Roland,J.Henry 21 to Isabel Evans 23	2- 9-1889	Z.Barnes,J.P.
Roland,Hugh E.27 to Nebraska Fouts 28	8-15-1889	Original not found
Roland,Wm.R.24 to Teresa A.Fouts 19	1-23-1890	Jno.P.Campbell,JP
Roland,Royal 25 to Texie Welch 18	9- 1-1917	J.L.Fouts,J.P.
Roland,H.P.24 to Nannie Parrish 22	11-1-1919	J.L.Fouts,J.P.
Roland,Arnold 28 to Myrtle Kimsey 23	4-10-1920	J.L.Fouts,J.P.
Rollins,Joe 22 to Jane Mason 17	2- 2-1899	W.C.Mason,M.G.
Roper,J.N.F.to Margaret Davis	3-27-1847	James Shepherd.
Roper,James to Lucinda Panther	8-19-1850	W.H.Roane,J.P.
Roper,Samuel to Martha Wilson	6-19-1853	Joe Simonds,M.G.
Roper,William to Eliza Tallent	7-20-1855	Robert Hall.
Roper,Daniel to Susan C.Fouts	2-16-1858	R.C.Slagle,Clk.
Roper,Levi to Nancy Clampet	1-16-1860	R.C.Slagle,Clk.
Roper,Samuel to Name not given	6-30-1860	R.C.Slagle,Clk.
Roper,Samuel to Malinda Tallent	1-30-1861	R.C.Slagle,Clk.
Roper,Joshua to Eliza Jones	10-12-1861	R.C.Slagle,Clk.
Roper,J.W. to Sarah E.Sheets	6-25-1865	R.C.Slagle,Clk.
Roper,D.T. to S.E.Nelson	8- 5-1870	J.K.Bryson,Reg.
Roper,Joshua to Esther A.Welch	4-14-1871	Joseph Morgan,J.P
Roper,Bary 21 to Josie Drake 19	8- 9-1879	P.C.Wild,J.P.
Roper,James 77 to Vicy Dowell 48	8-29-1879	P.C.Wild,J.P.
Roper,James E.24 to Anna Owens 17	9-21-1879	M.P.Swain,M.G.
Roper,Sidney 20 to Amanda Burnett 17	12-29-1881	Joseph Morgan,J.P
Roper,M. 22 to Martha A.Cansler 19	10-4-1883	R.A.Owens,M.G.
Roper,Samuel L.23 to Ellen J.Raby 18	10-27-1886	P.C.Wilds,J.P.
Roper,Charles R.21 to Delia C.Rowland 18	10-23-1887	A.B.Thomas,M.G.
Roper,Levi 52 to Mrs.Mary Conner 52	8-29-1889	J.A.Morrison,J.P.
Roper,Jesse M.21 to Dora Owenby 23	4- 5-1891	F.M.Morgan,M.G.
Roper,Levi 51 to Fannie Downs 44	12-27-1887	C.S.Ray,J.P.
Roper,Rufus H.27 to Jenny Downs 23	9- 6-1891	A.A.Justice,M.G.
Roper,Benjamin W.22 to Mary L.Wood 20	9-23-1891	J.Reid,J.P.
Roper,James A.21 to Alice M.Consler 18	12-00-1891?	J.E.Morgan,M.G.
Roper,Berry 34 to Mrs.Iler Huff 22	9- 8-1893	M.Ghormley,M.G.
Roper,Leverett S.26 to Eleanor H.Deal 20	12-12-1894	Fred W.Wey,M.G.
Roper,Alonzo 23 to Mary Swafford 18	7-11-1897	C.S.Ray,J.P.
Roper,John C.22 to Sarah McGaha 26	12-26-1897	M.L.Rickman,J.P.
Roper,Robert 22 to Annie Barnard 20	2-28-1899	J.P.Campbell,J.P.
Roper,W.H.19 to Beula Waters 18	10-6-1901	Mark Deweese,J.P.
Roper,Clingman C.23 to Carey Cochran 20	12-17-1902	Mark Deweese,J.P.
Roper,C.C.36 to Clara Ghormley 27	12-26-1904	A.H.Gregory,J.P.
Roper,Harlie 24 to Florence Fouts 23	5- 2-1905	J.L.Younce,M.G.

```
Roper,Robert S.17 to J.Elizabeth Rowland 19/10-2-1906    H.P.Ray,J.P.
Roper,James 50 to Martha Swafford 24        9-13-1908   M.F.Morgan,M.G.
Roper,Lawrence 19 to Carrie Tallent 20      9-29-1908   H.P.Ray,J.P.
Roper,Edd 21 to Fannie Pendergrass 20       4-24-1909   D.A.Younce,M.G.
Roper,M.E.47 to Mrs.Ellen Owenby 40         12-10-1909  W.E.Welch,J.P.
Roper,Charles Cling.31 to Sallie Owenby 34  8-31-1910   S.J.May,J.P.
Roper,Raleigh J.22 to Catherine Dills 19    6-25-1911   J.H.Grant,M.G.
Roper,Harley 22 to Bertha Garner 19         9-21-1912   G.M.Bulgin,J.P.
Roper,Arthur 22 to Emma Denny 21            7-12-1913   D.A.Younce,M.G.
Roper,Earnest 22 to Zada Wilks 19           8-10-1913   W.E.Welch,J.P.
Roper,E.E.21 to Ella Hughes 18              3- 8-1914   J.A.Morrison,J.P.
Roper,John 41 to Hyacinth Ray 26            7- 3-1916   T.J.Vinson,M.G.
Roper,V.E.21 to Arlesa Roper 18             10-1-1916   J.H.Grant,M.G.
Roper,Alonzo J.28 to Maude Owenby 22        10-15-1916  J.R.Pendergras,MG
Roper,Harvey 22 to Anna Drake 18            12-24-1916  E.G.Ledford,M.G.
Roper,Will 26 to Estella Denny 22           5-14-1918   Frank T.Gettis,JP
Roper,W.T.42 to Rebecca Houston 30          11-14-1918  J.A.Brendle,M.G.
Roper,Floyd 24 to Daisy Hughes 22           12-29-1919  J.L.Bryson,J.P.
Roper,C.C.44 to Clemmie Rowland 29          3-31-1924   Geo.Carpenter,J.P
Roper,Roby C.21 to Lola L.Bryant 18         5-17-1929   Geo.Carpenter,J.P
Roper,Franc S.24 to Grace Wood 18           7- 8-1933   Geo.Carpenter,J.P
Roper,Gordon 37 to Alfreda Simonds 16       4-17-1937   Lester Arnold,J.P
Rose,Samuel to Mary Wiley                   4-16-1838   Jona.Phillips,J.P
Rose,John to Rebecca Hensley                4-25-1836   Pierson Cooper,JP
Rose,Gideon to Francis Downs                1- 6-1840   Alfred Hall.
Rose,Joseph to Eliza Sawyers                9-14-1852   J.K.Gray,D.Clk.
Ross,W.A. to Alice Balanger                 2-16-1919   W.T.Potts,M.G.
Rouse,David 59 to Cora A.Williamson 43      1-25-1927   Geo.Carpenter,J.P
Ross,Lawson A.29 to Ruth Slagle 28          7-20-1940   Ivon L.Roberts,MG
   He from Hendersonville,N.C.
Roseberry,James D.22 to Raethel V.Olvey 21  7- 6-1925   Geo.Carpenter,J.P
   Both from Atlanta,Ga.
Rousseau,Wm.A.43 to Timoxena Crawford 25    8- 5-1934   Chesley Herbert.
   He from N.Wilkesboro,N.C.
Rouse,David 59 to Cora A.Williams 43        1-25-1927   Geo.Carpenter,J.P
Rowan,William to Catherine Brown            9-15-1845   W.P.Powell.
Rowe,John W.21 to Eddie Anderson 19         4- 2-1926   J.J.Mann,J.P.
   He from Asheville,N.C.
Rowland,William to Jane Fouts               9-21-1836   James Fouts,J.P.
Rowland,Andrew to Mary Morgan               9-11-1839   John Hall,Clk.
Rowland,Eli to Ann Morrison                 12-13-1843  John Hall,Clk.
Rowland,Wesley to Nancy Barnes              10-16-1850  Allen Adams,M.G.
Rowland,William L.to Mary Jane Trammel      12-8-1866   R.C.Slagle,C.C.C.
Rowland,Alexander 18 to Mary Johnston 19    7-24-1873   Jesse Stepp,J.P.
Rowland,Luther 23 to Catherine Garrison 18  8-22-1897   T.H.Wood,J.P.
Rowland,Harley 23 to Nora Margan 20         10-10-1903  W.A.Solesbee,M.G.
Rowland,J.B.25 to Minnie Ghormley 23        3- 6-1904   A.H.Gregory,J.P.
Rowland,W.G.24 to Maggie L.Hall 20          6-18-1910   Joseph L.Fouts,JP
```

Rowland,Harvey 21 to Nomie Teague 17	12-1-1910 J.R.Dalton,J.P.
Rowland,Berry M.27 to Alice Haney 20	6-26-1912 D.F.Howard,J.P.
Rowland,Laurence 24 to Oliatta Barnard 20	6-16-1918 A.S.Solesbee,M.G.
Rowland,Dwight 24 to Myrtle Smith 20	12-27-1920 J.R.Pendergras,MG
Rowland,Arnold to Alma Maynor She from Bridgeport,Ala.	7- 5-1942 Ray Craw,J.P.
Rucker,Oscar L.38 to Mary C.Mashburn 27	5- 5-1909 W.L.Bradley,M.G.
Rucker,Ralph 19 to Helen Catherine Holt 17	9- 9-1933 Chas.R.McCarty,MG
Runnion,N.W.to Matilda Mayfield	4-25-1853 J.F.Slagle.
Rush,George N. to Elizabeth Thomas	12-25-1854 William Allen.
Rush,N.J.27 to Laura Ledford 24	2- 5-1885 C.D.Smith,M.G.
Rush,Geo.Miller 21 to Beunia Angel 19	7-24-1895 Original not found
Rush,Geo.M.22 to Beunia Angel 20	1-10-1897 G.R.HcPherson,J.P
Rush,Geo.N.24 to Verna Penland 19	3-17-1912 T.J.Vinson,M.G.
Rush,John 26 to Lillie Corbin 20	12-31-1916 A.W.Jacobs,M.G.
Russell,Nathan N.to Chairty Jennings	9-23-1834 John Tatham,Clk.
Russell,A.J. to Roda Redmond	4-16-1836 John Tatham,Clk.
Russell,D.H. to Jane Huggins	5-29-1844 J.K.Gray,D.Clk.
Russell,A.P. to L.E.Hayes	11-7-1846 J.K.Gray,D.Clk.
Russell,John to Leaunah Vanhook	8-31-1852 T.P.Siler,D.Clk.
Russell,D.H. to Melissa Constant	11-23-1858 R.C.Slagle,D.Clk.
Russell,David M. to Statira Dowdle	1-25-1866 R.C.Slagle,C.C.C.
Russell,J.D. to Elizabeth A.Arnold	4- 4-1867 Joshua Ammons,M.G
Russell,John M. to Delphia Young	11-28-1868 E.W.Moore,M.G.
Russell,W.T.26 to Kansas Mashburn 23	11-2-1882 A.S.Bryson,J.P.
Russell,Reubin 24 to Catherine Holland 19	4-11-1883 M.Hollen,J.P.
Russell,Phillip A.23 to Emeline Raby 18	2- 4-1886 J.M.Keener,M.G.
Russell,William C.20 to Clara J.Wright 19	7-28-1886 Original not found
Russell,George H.36 to Anna L.Angel 19	11-3-1886 E.A.Sample,M.G.
Russell,John C.31 to Julia H.Penland 31	1- 8-1890 J.M.Keener,M.G.
Russell,George W.19 to Sarah C.Houston 18	6- 8-1890 J.M.Keener,M.G.
Russell,Wm.Charles 27 to Esther M.Cabe 25	5-31-1894 Samuel Holland,JP
Russell,Charlie 34 to Josephine Ammons 26	1-17-1901 J.M.Keener,M.G.
Russell,James 18 to Roxie Keener 18	4-18-1902 J.M.Keener,M.G.
Russell,Hayman 23 to Rhoda McCall 15	3-12-1911 J.M.Keener,M.G.
Russell,Leon T.32 to Mrs.Mattie B.Bell 37	4- 1-1914 J.A.Morrison,J.P.
Russell,W.H.26 to Cora Early 19	10-26-1915 J.R.Pendergras,MG
Russell,J.B.34 to Effie Jenkins 19	7- 3-1918 Geo·Howard,J.P.
Russell,Harrison 29 to Roxie Conley 28	12-26-1935 J.F.Burrell,M.G.
Sanders,John to Tilletha Stuman	4- 5-1836 Ulrich Keener,Clk
Sanders,Curtis to Margaret Hughes	8-29-1837 J.K.Gray,Clk.
Sanders,John to Mary Parker	12-5-1839 John Hall,Clk.
Sanders,Pendleton to Caroline Rogers	8-24-1846 Hiram K.Sisk.
Sanders,Wilborne to Rebecca Brendle	10-1-1849 T.P.Siler,D.Clk.
Sanders,Miles to Frances Vaun	10-10-1857 John Elmore,J.P.
Sanders,James M. to Mary A.Jones	1-20-1859 H.K.Kimsey,J.P.
Sanders,James H. to Ann L.Thomas	11-4-1863 R.C.Slagle,C.C.C.

Sanders,T.H. to Sarah Ann Oliver	2-23-1864	R.C.Slagle,Reg.
Sanders,Thomas to Mira Reid	8-28-1864	R.C.Slagle,Reg.
Sanders,T.S. to Mary Thompson	3- 9-1867	R.C.Slagle,Reg.
Sanders,John A.T.to Mary A.Lowery	3-14-1871	D.C.Harden,J.P.
Sanders,Henry to Elizabeth Curtis	11-22-1871	William Sloan,Reg
Sanders,Benjamin 23 to Martha A.Lamb 20	3-29-1873	A.L.Wild,J.P.
Sanders,Julius 33 to Lou V.Horn 23	12-2-1880	W.C.Corden,M.G.
Sanders,James E.21 to Mary M.Gibbs 19	9-18-1884	E.H.Bogle,M.G.
Sanders,A.R.24 to Lenora Nichols 16	10-2-1884	John Ammons,J.P.
Sanders,B.S.24 to M.E.Dryman 18	5- 3-1885	L.Howard,J.P.
Sanders,H.H.29 to Anna Brendle 20	9-17-1886	J.B.Elmore,J.P.
Sanders,David 29 to Sarah T.Gibbs 26	12-22-1886	M.J.Mashburn,J.P.
Sanders,Nick 39 to Rachel Beck 36 Col.	1- 1889	James Bristol,M.G
Sanders,Benjamin 27 to Hattie Oliver 20	9- 7-1890	W.C.Kimzey,J.P.
Sanders,George 21 to Lucinda Southards 18	1- 7-1894	J.T.Wade,M.G.
Sanders,J.W.23 to R.Ann Scott 19	4-15-1894	J.B.Elmore,J.P.
Sanders,George H.22 to Mary E.Coward 19	12-10-1894	J.R.Pendergras,MG
Sanders,Edward D.24 to Allie Hedden 16	8-30-1895	J.A.Brendle,M.G.
Sanders,Thomas H.22 to Ada Henson 19	9-20-1896	J.M.Farmer,J.P.
Sanders,William T.25 to Sallie Mashburn 35	2-13-1898	T.W.Angel,J.P.
Sanders,John W.32 to Lela E.Allison 25	9- 7-1898	J.T.Wade,M.G.
Sanders,M.C. 19 to Ella Jones 18	1-22-1899	W.A.Norton,J.P.
Sanders,M.A.21 to M.A.Bingham 21	4-13-1899	Robert Stamey,J.P
Sanders,Thos.H.25 to Martha Bingham 24	8-11-1899	C.W.Dowdle,J.P.
Sanders,Arthur 19 to Sallie Beeco 24	10-1-1899	C.W.Dowdle,J.P.
Sanders,Curtis 23 to Lishie Potts 26	11-17-1900	J.B.Elmore,J.P.
Sanders,T.W.21 to Ida Scott 21	10-29-1901	J.B.Elmore,J.P.
Sanders,Charles T.22 to Eula Hodgin 19	8- 9-1904	Robert Stamey,J.P
Sanders,Harley 30 to Mrs.Pauline Stamey 26	12-7-1904	Robert Stamey,J.P
Sanders,Harley M.21 to Effie T.Houston 24	9-14-1905	T.Baxter White,JP
Sanders,Thomas H.33 to Elizabeth Wadkins 30/	8-26-1906	Robert Stamey,J.P
Sanders,John 26 to Tina Anderson 17	9- 4-1906	W.P.Allison,J.P.
Sanders,C.Norman 22 to Tishia Myers 20	9-15-1907	C.L.Rickman,J.P.
Sanders,Charlie 33 to Mamie Dowdle 29	11-10-1909	W.I.Hughes,M.G.
Sanders,Zeb V.35 to Susie Bell Angel 24	12-12-1909	J.R.Pendergras,MG
Sanders,Mitchie 20 to Rosa Brendle 19	6-12-1910	Geo.Carpenter,J.P
Sanders,Fred 25 to Leona Stamey 16	9-24-1911	J.T.Watts,J.P.
Sanders,Oscar 25 to Lexie Beck 18	12-6-1911	Robert Stamey,J.P
Sanders,Robert 21 to Cora Kinsland 19	9- 9-1912	R.P.McCracken,M.G
Sanders,Uless 18 to Mrs.Nannie Maney 19	5-25-1913	C.S.Battles,J.P.
Sanders,Walter 23 to Fannie Burnett 20	7-20-1913	Geo.Carpenter,J.P
Sanders,J.B.21 to Etta Tippett 18	2-18-1914	Geo.Carpenter,J.P
Sanders,Newell 24 to Viola Addington 23 Col.	4-18-1917	J.H.Crosbey,M.G.
Sanders,Claud 21 to Leona Tippett 18	5- 5-1917	J.M.Raby,J.P.
Sanders,Raymond 22 to Maud Gregory 19	9- 8-1917	W.T.Potts,M.G.
Sanders,S.D.19 to Callie Sanders 21	7- 4-1918	J.R.Pendergras,MG
Sanders,F.H.20 to Iris Tallent 20	1-18-1919	J.R.Pendergras,MG

Sanders,Carver 24 to Oberia Downs 20	2- 5-1920	J.A.Bryson,M.G.
Sanders,Spurgeon 23 to Mary Moses 18	2- 8-1920	J.M.Keener,M.G.
Sanders,Raleigh 21 to Clarcy Moses 16	2-15-1921	J.M.Keener,M.G.
Sanders,T.C.27 to Maggie Snyder 29	2- 3-1923	Geo.Carpenter,J.P
Sanders,Sam 20 to Bertha Smith 17	5-16-1925	J.R.Pendergras,MG
Sanders,Jess 18 to Ollie M.Hastings 16	5-16-1926	Fred M.Kimsey,J.P
Sanders,Lawrence R.21 to Mary Dalrymple 21	7- 4-1935	Geo.Carpenter,J.P
Sands,Will 21 to Emily Briggs 18	4-21-1901	W.H.Morrison,J.P.
Saunders,Alfred to Harriet M.Hurst	8-21-1858	I.N.Keener,J.P.
Saunders,Patrick to Eda A.Ammons	10-6-1858	I.N.Keener,J.P.
Saunders,Noah to Susanah Waldroop	11-1-1861	W.C.Kimsey,J.P.
Saunders,H.L. to Sephrona Patton	1-25-1862	R.C.Slagle,C.C.C.
Saunders,J.B. to R.S.Russell	10-7-1865	R.C.Slagle,C.C.C.
Saunders,Harmon to Salina E.Bennett	8-17-1865	E.M.Moore,M.G.
Saunders,Nathan to Sarah McDonnell Col.	5-15-1870	H.H.Elmore,J.P.
Saunders,Cato to Eva Mitchell	2-14-1872	T.F.Glenn,M.G.
Saunders,W.C.22 to Mary A.Penland 18	1-26-1881	E.L.Long,J.P.
Saunders,Napeolean 23 to Josie Love 26	9-27-1888	W.J.Jenkins,J.P.
Saunders,J.C.21 to Flora Cabe 21	12-27-1888	John Reid,J.P.
Saunders,Alfred R.29 to Mary A.Merritt 24	9-22-1889	J.B.Elmore,J.P.
Saunders,James T.21 to Laura C.Mashburn 16	11-14-1889	J.B.Elmore,J.P.
Saunders,John A.T.53 to Margaret Haynes 31	11-14-1890	I.D.Wright,M.G.
Saunders,Matt 30 to Sallie Hughes 20	9-25-1891	J.B.Elmore,J.P.
Saunders,Cowan A.25 to Rodie E.Sanders 22	9-27-1891	W.J.Jenkins,J.P.
Saunders,H.S.50 to Reba E.McCracken 28	3-27-1929	H.C.Freeman,M.G.
Saxe,Geo.Henry 44 to Mary Eva Wright 33	6- 9-1908	A.S.Lawrence,M.G.
Savage,Frank 20 to Bessie Evans 17	9-14-1908	J.R.Pendergras,MG
Salmon,Charles D.19 to Delcenia I.Wright 17/ He from Piedmont,Ala.	12-5-1939	C.F.Rogers,M.G.
Sawyers,Alexander R.to Temperance Berry	3- 7-1836	Ulrich Keener,Clk
Sawyers,Sewallen to Eliza Chambers	12-28-1846	A.B.Welch.
Sawyers,J.L. to Louisa Welch	7- 2-1855	A.B.Welch.
Sawyers,John to Nancy Davis	7- 8-1866	R.C.Slagle,Clk.
Sawyers,James L.to Roxana P.Ashe	5- 7-1871	N.W.Vaughn,M.G.
Sawyer,Samuel B.46 to Della Cloer 18	11-8-1888	P.R.Rickman,M.G.
Sawyer,Andrew 37 to Ethel Hodgin 19	11-14-1920	G.M.Johnson,J.P.
Scales,Young 50 to Mrs.Julia Arnold 36	11-7-1888	J.M.Keener,J.P.
Schulhofer,Arthur 23 to Winnie B.Price 19 Both from Waynesville,N.C.	8-14-1927	A.P.Ratledge,M.G.
Scott,James to Letty J.Hamilton	5-12-1860	R.C.Slagle,Reg.
Scott,Robert L.22 to Jane Reid 21	2-24-1889	J.B.Elmore,J.P.
Scott,B.Hubert 23 to Addie Brendle 18	10-5-1905	C.L.Rickman,J.P.
Scott,Thomas J.,Jr.21 to Dean Matlock 15	10-7-1906	C.L.Rickman,J.P.
Scott,T.J.,Jr.32 to Nannie Brendle 19	7- 3-1917	J.B.Henry,J.P.
Scott,Claud 21 to Ruth Downs 21	7- 8-1917	A.W.Jacobs,M.G.
Scott, W.J.25 to Mattie Rickman 25	5-18-1919	R.P.McCracken,M.G
Scott,G.D.22 to Minnie Cabe 22	10-26-1919	A.W.Jacobs,M.G.
Scott,Ralph 28 to Alice Franks 22	7- 1-1934	Tom Carter,M.G.

```
Scott,Wiley B.24 to Louise Shuler 19          8-17-1935   Geo.Carpenter,J.P
Scroggs,Alfred to Leana Justus                4-10-1837   U.Keener.
Scroggs,John E.M. to Cornelia R.Wyant         2-23-1871   L.F.Glenn,M.G.
Scroggs,Alfred P.21 to Martha E.Carpenter 19/9-5-1872     W.T.Anderson,J.P.
Scroggs,William A.28 to Mary J.Green 23       3-14-1875   M.L.Kelly,J.P.
Scroggs,S.P.21 to Emma Hogsed 20              8- 5-1875   M.P.Long,M.G.
Scroggs,Wm.J.21 to Emma F.Carpenter 19        12-17-1893  G.P.Mann,J.P.
Scroggs,G.W.18 to India Carpenter 15          2-17-1897   J.D.Vinson,M.G.
Scroggs,C.A.32 to Ellen Mize 18               10-16-1902  L.H.Garland,J.P.
Scroggs,W.P.23 to Artie C.Grant 17            10-28-1902  J.L.Bryson,J.P.
Scroggs,J.Henry 19 to I.L.Miller 27           12-24-1903  D.L.Miller,M.G.
Scroggs,J.E.57 to Ivalee Mason 23             3-30-1913   Robert Stamey,J.P
Scroggs,Charles 21 to Geneva Hall 19    Col. 12-27-1914   A.B.Morrow,M.G.
Scroggs,Fleet H.23 to Margaret B.Smith 22     8-26-1926   B.C.Reavis,M.G.
Scruggs,Robert 21 to Elizabeth Vanhook 18 Col.12-27-1877-E.H.Franks,J.P.
Scruggs,William 22 to G.A.Penland 20    Col. 3-16-1880   E.T.Long,J.P.
Scruggs,William 27 to Angeline Penland 24 Col.9-6-1882   Jno.McDowell,M.G.
Scruggs,Walton 28 to Rachel McDonnell 22 Col.9-22-1892   J.M.Roane,J.P.
Scruggs,Robert 24 to Addie Bristol 24   Col. 3- 8-1894   J.Williams,M.G.
Scruggs,Charles,46 to Lassie Angel 22   Col. 1-27-1909   J.W.Elliott,M.G.
Scruggs,Dock 22 to Hallie Ritchie 15    Col. 12-16-1910  J.R.Pendergras,MG
Scruggs,Elbert 28 to Rosa Ledford 30    Col. 7- 4-1920   E.J.McKay,M.G.
Scruggs,Charles W.41 to Lula England 39 Col.3-24-1935    J.S.Thomas,M.G.
Seagle,S.A.25 to J.H.Saunders 20              8- 2-1885  L.Howard,J.P.
Seagle,Will 22 to Minnie Bradley 20           12-6-1908  J.C.Shope,J.P.
Seagle,Bascomb 23 to Ida Carpenter 19         5- 3-1914  C.S.Battles,J.P.
Sealey,G.Mitchell 52 to Minnie M.Shepherd 49/8-13-1941 J.L.Stokes,M.G.
  Both from Canton,N.C.
Seay,John A.21 to Lealer Wilbanks 18          4-18-1886  M.B.Setser,J.P.
Seay,G.W.37 to Lillie Dalrymple 32            4-27-1902  J.R.Pendergras,MG
Seay,J.W.21 to M.E.Thomas 22                  8- 4-1906  W.A.Norton,J.P.
Seay,James H.22 to Etta Raby 21               7- 6-1913  Geo.Carpenter,J.P
Seay,C.D.23 to Mell Hodgins 18                12-24-1915 G.A.Cloer,J.P.
Seay,Arvey 22 to Mary Williams 17             11-18-1917 J.M.Raby,J.P.
Sellers,George C.to Caroline Angel            12-24-1849 F.C.Siler,J.P.
Sellers,L.R. to E.S.Kelly                     1-29-1852  T.P.Siler,D.Clk.
Sellers,George to Nancy T.Bradley             2-15-1855  L.F.Siler.
Sellers,Reagan 22 to Hester A.Rogers 16       9-19-1873  Jacob Hood,M.G.
Sellers,Filmore 20 to May Guy 20        Col. 2-24-1876   Jno.McDowell,M.G.
Sellers,C.L.24 to D.M.Ledford 23              12-18-1879 C.D.Smith,M.G.
Sellers,George C. to Matilda Dowdle           1- 5-1881  G.A.Ogelsby,M.G.
Sellers,Zeb V.30 to S.Elizabeth McDowell 18/2-27-1890    W.G.Mallonee,M.G.
Sellers,Philmore 42 to Addie Love 25    Col. 12-3-1897   Jno.H.Fulton,J.P.
Sellers,W.H.27 to Sallie Stalcup 25           2-23-1898  J.A.Deal,M.G.
Sellers,J.G.29 to Fannie B.Byrd 21            5-12-1901  J.B.Elmore,J.P.
Sellers,J.C.20 to Millie Sanders 14     Col. 8-11-1904   James Bristol,M.G
Sellers,Wiley 21 to Dollie Buchanan 20        1-28-1915  J.M.Bennett,M.G.
```

```
Sellers,S.O.31 to Gladys M.Waldroop 16        11-21-1922  J.L.Teague,M.G.
Setser,John to Ann Clark                       5- 3-1839  G.M.Daniel.
Setser,Emanuel to Judith L.Redmond            11-4-1839  John Hall,Clerk
Setser,John to Bethany Holland                 7-30-1846  J.K.Gray,Clk.
Setser,J.W. to Martha Reid                    12-23-1849  J.K.Gray,Clk.
Setser,M.B. to S.J.McDowell                    1-14-1858  R.C.Slagle,Reg.
Setser,W.A.24 to C.E.Cloer 25                  1- 4-1885  James A.Bell,J.P.
Setser,C.Augustus 26 to Callie A.Johnson 21/3-24-1889  W.C.Kimzey,J.P.
Setser,Christopher 30 to Adelia Dalrymple 22/1-29-1893 Jas.C.Weaver,J.P.
Setser,L.Franklin 24 to Anna Guffee 20        12-26-1895  R.B.Shelton,M.G.
Setser,W.L.24 to Pearl Gibson 22               4-10-1910  C.W.Slagle,J.P.
Setser,J.E.34 to Buna Donaldson 18             1-22-1911  Robert Stamey,J.P.
Setser,C.A.53 to Norah Seay 36                 2- 5-1916  J.R.Pendergras,MG
Setser,J.F.27 to Harriet Slagle 21             8- 3-1918  R.H.Dougherty,M.G
Setser,Bryan 25 to Stella Justice 18          12-10-1921  J.R.Pendergras,MG
Setser,L.F.52 to Nannie Crawford 35           11-24-1923  V.B.Harrison,M.G.
Setser,J.Gilmer 26 to Nina Ray 23              9-28-1925  R.A.Truitt,M.G.
Sequine,William to Jane Thomason               1-30-1855  T.P.Siler,D.Clk.
Shady,William 23 to Georgia A.Siler 19 Col.  11-10-1885  B.G.Wild,M.G.
Shaw,Thomas J.27 to Laura D.Hall 20            4-20-1890  A.A.Justice,M.G.
Sheffield,Jessy to Elizabeth Shepherd          1-25-1870  J.K.Bryson,Reg.
Sheffield,William 23 to Buena V.E.Jenkins 16/3-29-1896 M.L.Rickman,J.P.
Sheffield,Wm.T.21 to Mayme V.Bryson 21        12-26-1918  W.W.Marr,M.G.
Shelley,J.H.29 to Kathleen Gribble 22          8-27-1917  J.Q.Wallace,M.G.
Shelton,J.M.to Mary W.Brinkley                 6-20-1865  R.C.Slagle,D.Clk.
Shelton,Robert 23 to Martha Wood 25            3-26-1899  G.W.Stiwinter,J.P
Shepherd,Joel D.to Mariah ------               8- 1-1836  Burton H.Dickey.
Shepherd,Thomas to Mary Ann Sutton             3-20-1838  Anderson Sutton.
Shepherd,Thomas J.to Polly T.Duvall           12-20-1843  J.K.Gray,Cl.
Shepherd,Calvin to Sarah Bryson                1-12-1847  J.K.Gray,Clk.
Shepherd,James to Nancy Shepherd              12-20-1848  J.K.Gray,Clk.
Shepherd,Calvin to Pheraby Ammons              8- 9-1849  T.P.Siler,D.Clk.
Shepherd,John to Mary A.Stuman                 4-17-1852  J.F.Slagle,J.P.
Shepherd,Jos.J. to Charlotte Brendle           1-20-1856  John Hall,Clk.
Shepherd,William to Mary A.Cochram             4- 6-1859  R.C.Slagle,D.Clk.
Shepherd,T.P.to C.A.Welch                     12-31-1865  James Bryson,J.P.
Shepherd,H.C.to Caroline Sanders               1-26-1866  R.C.Slagle,C.C.C.
Shepherd,Elias to Martha Queen                 7-31-1867  R.C.Slagle,Reg.
Shepherd,Leander to Harriet West       Col.    8-13-1966  J.M.Rickman,J.P.
Shepherd,Joe to Jane Poindexter        Col.   11-9-1867  R.C.Slagle,C.C.C.
Shepherd,Thomas J.to Mary J.Raby              10-27-1868  R.C.Slagle,R.D.M.
Shepherd,Joshua to Mary Paine                  7- 9-1870  J.K.Bryson,Reg.
Shepherd,John G. to Louisa A.Dalton            5-21-1871  P.R.Rickman,M.G.
Shepherd,Joseph 26 to Margaret Conley 18 Col.5-11-1873  A.L.Wild,J.P.
Shepherd,William 27 to Elizabeth Watson 21     5-27-1873  Samuel Gipson,M.G
Shepherd,J.J.21 to Winnie C.Franks 17         10-23-1873  P.R.Rickman,M.G.
Shepherd,Dave L.24 to Rebecca M.Bradley 21     3-26-1874  P.Howard,J.P.
```

```
Shepherd,Rufus 19 to Emma West 18        Col.   2- 9-1876  D.W.Wells,M.G.
Shepherd,T.C.23 to S.L.Beasley 19                8-10-1876  Thos.Mashburn,J.P
Shepherd,Jess R.18 to Eliza Siler 22             1-12-1877  E.H.Franks,J.P.
Shepherd,Jason 37 to Liddy West 31               8-19-1877  P.P.McLean,M.G.
Shepherd,Joseph 23 to Margaret A.McGaha 18      12-19-1878 John S.Gibson,J.P
Shepherd,Samuel 19 to Jane Shepherd 18 Col.  2-27-1879  John S.Gibson,J.P
Shepherd,Jas.T.19 to Nancy L.Sanders 18          8-22-1880  M.J.Mashburn,J.P.
Shepherd,J.R.28 to M.E.Jacobs 22                 9-29-1880  J.S.Gibson,J.P.
Shepherd,Rufus 22 to Ola Vanhook 18     Col.   12-12-1880 P.P.McLean,M.G.
Shepherd,H.C.38 to Rhoda Sanders 30              9-17-1882  John S.Gibson,J.P
Shepherd,James 20 to Lou Gibson 19      Col.   12-7-1882  J.E.Kilgore,M.G.
Shepherd,T.B.21 to Rebecca A.Bradley 18          11-1-1885  John S.Gibson,J.P
Shepherd,Zachariah 56 to Rachel West 45 Col.5- 2-1886  Jno.S.Gibson,J.P.
Shepherd,Thos.B.20 to Maggie Shepherd 24 Col.7-20-1886 Jno.S.Gibson,J.P.
Shepherd,John 33 to Temperance Benfield 29  9-23-1886  John Ammons,J.P.
Shepherd,Lucius 30 to Laura Mallonee 19 Col.12-22-1887 S.A.Gibson,M.G.
Shepherd,Geo.W.21 to Rebecca Hurst 22            2-26-1889  B.Elmore,J.P.
Shepherd,Leander 67 to Charity Henry 66 Col.10-28-1889 B.M.Gudger,M.G.
Shepherd,James 26 to Margaret J.Hurst 21         1-25-1891  P.R.Rickman,M.G.
Shepherd,Joshua 40 to Rosa Lee Payne 21          8-31-1891  W.J.Jenkins,J.P.
Shepherd,James 19 to Carolina Bronson 30 Col.10-10-1891 A.B.Morrow,M.G.
Shepherd,William E.25 to Harriet R.Raby 23       9-27-1894  W.R.Rickman,M.G.
Shepherd,Clingman 21 to Hattie Jenkins 19       12-31-1894 Jno.B.Carden,J.P.
Shepherd,John H.17 to Eva I.Mason 18            12-31-1894 Jno.B.Carden,J.P.
Shepherd,Burton 51 to Fannie Mallonee 18 Col.8-17-1896 J.R.Pendergras,MG
Shepherd,Sherman 20 to Octa C.Cabe 19           10-1-1896  J.B.Elmore,J.P.
Shepherd,H.B.36 to N.J.Leatherman 24             8-30-1897  P.R.Rickman,M.G.
Shepherd,Tam 19 to Mary Patterson 19            12-20-1898 P.R.Rickman,M.G.
Shepherd,Jas.L.23 to Nancy Beasley 18            1- 8-1903  Jno.Shepherd,J.P.
Shepherd,Lee 20 to Carrie Love 20        Col.  5-12-1904  J.T.Kenedy,M.G.
Shepherd,George 22 to Mell Jones 19              7-14-1907  John C.Hurst,J.P.
Shepherd,Jess 25 to Martha Shuler 22             5- 4-1909  Geo.Carpenter,J.P
Shepherd,Jesse C.27 to Charlotte M.Barker 18/2-22-1911 J.A.Lakey,J.P.
Shepherd,V.M.22 to Maud Hurst 17                 4-23-1911  J.W.Rickman,J.P.
Shepherd,Harley 29 to Arie Parrish 22   Col.  1-16-1913  S.B.Logan,M.G.
Shepherd,Richard 23 to Olie Mason 16             7-13-1913  M.L.Bradley,M.G.
Shepherd,Samuel H.24 to Flora Potts 24           8- 6-1914  T.J.Vinson,M.G.
Shepherd,James M.27 to Lillie Rhinehart 20      10-4-1914  J.A.Lakey,J.P.
Shepherd,C.G.37 to Cora Evans 22                12-5-1915  T.J.Vinson,M.G.
Shepherd,Greeley 23 to Lela Evans 17             5- 7-1916  J.L.Bryson,J.P.
Shepherd,J.F.22 to Nina Angel 18                 6-22-1916  J.L.Bryson,J.P.
Shepherd,Luther 21 to Birdie Guy 22             10-22-1916 J.A.Lakey,J.P.
Shepherd,Geo.W.73 to Jula A.Heacock 18           1-15-1917  W.T.Thompson,M.G.
Shepherd,Dock 31 to Dora Brendle 22              5-28-1917  E.O.Rickman,J.P.
Shepherd,William 21 to Icey Thomas 22   Col.  6- 4-1918  Geo.Carpenter,J.P
Shepherd,S.G.19 to Mary Allen 19                 5-24-1921  J.L.Bryson,J.P.
Shepherd,W.L.28 to Hattie Rhinehart 30           9- 7-1921  Geo.Carpenter,J.P
```

```
Shepherd,Luther 30 to Ethel Shepherd 25        12-6-1922   Geo.Carpenter,J.P
Shepherd,Weaver 27 to Mattie L.Curry 29 Col.9- 4-1924   E.S.Wikle,M.G.
Shepherd,George W.57 to Martha B.Boyd 39       11-24-1925 Geo.Carpenter,J.P
Shepherd,Charlie 36 to Elsie Jenkins 20        4-20-1929  Geo.Carpenter,J.P
Shepherd,Perry 22 to Lola Messer 18            7- 2-1934  Geo.Carpenter,J.P
Shepherd,Clyde 44 to Mrs.Daisy Buchanan 29     4- 9-1936  Geo.Carpenter,J.P
Shepherd,Sam 42 to Mrs.Zona Neal 34            7-20-1936  Geo.Carpenter,J.P
Sherrill,Ute to Elizabeth Thompson             7- 8-1831  Wm.McConnell.
Sherrill,Jessey to Margaret Queen              10-26-1833 James Tatham,Clk.
Sherrill,Asaph to Catherine Sherrill           9-30-1841  J.B.Hyde,
Sherrill,S.P. to M.D.A.Thomas                  10-12-1849 M.R.Slagle.
Sherrill,Jack 26 to Lalla Addington 15         12-24-1899  E.A.Sample,M.G.
Sherrill,Jack W.,Jr.24 to Mary L.Porter 21     2-14-1930  Robert F.Mock,M.G
Shearer,Allen to Eleonar DeHart                6-14-1833  J.W.Shearer.
Sheets,David to Mary Forester                  2-11-1854  L.F.Siler,J.P.
Shelley,J.O.32 to Minnie L.Hyat 19             11-6-1883  R.A.Owen,M.G.
Sharpe,Ruby W.48 to Sarah Gates 32             7-11-1930  Geo.Carpenter,J.P
  Both from Robinsville,N.C.
Shidell,George W.21 to Laura Calloway 20        9- 3-1899  D.R.Sellers,J.P.
Shitle,Geo.W.45 to Minnie F.Trentham 28        12-12-1921Original not found
Shirley,Carlton B.26 to Elizabeth Campbell 21/6-10-1914 W.E.Williamson.
Shields,A.J.to Name not given                  10-15-1836 John Tatham,Clk.
Shields,A.J.to Kiziah Sanders                  10-21-1865 R.C.Slagle,Reg.
Shields,J.M.to Lou Lunsford                    2- 2-1866  R.C.Slagle,C.C.C.
Shields,Asheville to Margaret Caler            9-11-1866  R.C.Slagle,C.C.C.
Shields,William W.30 to Elizabeth Mallonee 20/9-19-1873---------
Shields,Charles 19 to Susana Howard 18         12- 8-1888 M.Ghormley,M.G.
Shields,Robert W.22 to M.Etta Wilson 18        5- 7-1891  F.M.Morgan,M.G.
Shields,Marcus R.19 to Ruemma Rowland 18       4-29-1894  S.J.May,J.P.
Shields,Thomas C.20 to Cansadia Phillips 18/7- 4-1897  A.N.Wood,J.P.
Shields,Marcus R.24 to Maggie Trantham 19      5-11-1899  E.N.Dalrymple,J.P
Shields,Robt.V.21 to Mollie Lee 21             1-14-1902  John E.Norton,M.G
Shields,Mark 26 to Addie Wilds 29              2-23-1902  Mark Deweese,J.P.
Shields,William 26 to Kittie Shepherd 16       3-31-1907  J.R.Pendergras,MG
Shields,Mark 33 to Zonie Douthit 22            1-17-1909  J.L.Kinsland,M.G.
Shields,James 27 to Manda Cochran 20           5-18-1913  J.H.Grant,M.G.
Shields,C.R.21 to Elsie Duvall 24              4- 8-1915  C.R.Cabe,J.P.
Shields,James H.21 to Lucy Cole  18            7- 3-1933  J.R.Pendergras,MG
Shockley,Frank E. 20 to Ethel V.Pierson 16     3-23-1927  J.W.Baty,M.G.
  He from Walhalla,S.C.
Shook,Robert M.22 to Bell Stanfield 18         1- 9-1890  J.M.Keener,M.G.
Shook,Alexander E.23 to Jennie Stanfield 19/12-25-1894 D.L.Miller,M.G.
Shook,W.M.24 to Nellie Bryson 22               7-31-1898  G.A.Bartlett,M.G.
Shook,Alfred 21 to Bessie Gregory 19           5- 5-1912  T.J.Vinson,M.G.
Shook,L.L.20 to Ollie Mincy 18                 8- 8-1915  J.P.Moore,J.P.
Shook,Ezra 21 to Laverne Bolick 18             10-10-1933 W.G.Wood,J.P.
Shope,John to Lourena Allen                    5-27-1844  James M.Grant.
```

Shope,John B.to Emeline Deweese	8-26-1849	J.K.Gray,Clk.
Shope,Jacob to Elizabeth A.Shuler	3- 8-1852	T.P.Siler,D.Clk.
Shoap,Philip to Rachel R.McGaha	1- 1-1857	G.W.Moore.
Shope,John 50 to Martha M.Norton 37	4- 5-1874	J.H.Addington,J.P
Shope,G.L. 23 to M.L.Norton 21	4-26-1883	L.Howard,J.P.
Shope,J.C.33 to J.Mary Sellers 30	4-17-1884	S.H.Harrington,MG
Shope,Zeb V.21 to A.M.Blaine 20	1-18-1899	M.A.West,M.G.
Shope,A.M.55 to Myra Harrison 32	2-12-1902	T.N.Ford,M.G.
Shope,W.R.26 to Ellen Corn 21	3-22-1903	J.C.Shope,J.P.
Shope,E.V.25 to Lizzie Ledford 20	12-20-1903	J.C.Postell,M.G.
Shope,S.L. 21 to Vassie Ledford 19	8-31-1904	J.C.Shope,J.P.
Shope,John M.28 to Martha Ledford 24	9-29-1907	J.C.Shope,J.P.
Shope,Alex 21 to Julia Mashburn 20	2- 3-1911	Jas.L.Higdon,J.P.
Shope,Fred 30 to Maud Conley 19	3- 7-1915	W.A.Norton,J.P.
Shope,F.H.29 to Kate I.Angel 27	1- 6-1916	D.S.Richardson,MG
Shope,William 21 to Leona Bates 22	3- 7-1918	W.H.Carpenter,J.P
Shope,Bill 24 to Myrtle Chastain 19	12-24-1935	J.M.Cabe,J.P.
Shope,Woodrow 21 to Iona Waldroop 18	8-12-1936	C.S.Slagle,J.P.
Shuford,Guss 33 to Iris Downs 27	8-28-1930	J.R.Pendergras,MG
Shuler,David to Demira Berry	4-11-1840	John Hall,Clk.
Shuler,Price to Elizabeth L.Battles	12-1-1842	J.K.Gray,Clk.
Shuler,Edmonson to Margaret Newton	2-18-1843	J.K.Gray,Clk.
Shuler,John F.to Sophrona Shope	8- 2-1845	J.K.Gray,Clk.
Shuler,William G.to Elizabeth Jane Lawless	8-21-1847	J.K.Gray,Clk.
Shuler,H.P. to Narcissy Newton	2- 3-1852	T.P.Siler,D.Clk.
Shuler,E.L. to Harriet B.Battles	3- 2-1871	F.Glenn,M.G.
Shuler,J.Robert 25 to Hester Raby 20	11-4-1894	P.R.Rickman,M.G.
Shuler,John 21 to Ellen Brendle 21	6-30-1898	E.D.Franks,J.P.
Shuler,John M.25 to Julia Bradley 19	11-22-1899	W.L.Bradley,M.G.
Shuler,A.B.22 to Inda Adams 18	12-25-1901	J.B.Elmore,J.P.
Shuler,Jesse 21 to Addie Guffee 21	5-21-1905	W.A.Fisher,J.P.
Shuler,Pink 21 to Pink Fox 19	1-11-1906	S.J.Ammons,J.P.
Shuler,Sam 21 to Nannie Guffee 19	3- 3-1906	W.A.Fisher,J.P.
Shuler,J.L.64 to Jennie A.Tally 40	1- 2-1908	C.L.Rickman,J.P.
Shuler,John W.31 to Cansie Brendle 31	10-10-1909	J.R.Pendergras,MG
Shuler,Z.A.32 to Lizzie Wilson 20	1-25-1913	M.P.Alexander,M.G
Shuler,Harley 39 to Nora L.Matcalf 30 Both from Canton,N.C.	9-30-1938	Geo.Carpenter,J.P
Shuler,Glenn 30 to Ruth Morgan 31	6-21-1942	W.T.Medlin,M.G.
Siler,Julius T. to Mary J.Coleman	8-22-1844	J.K.Gray,Clk.
Siler,T.P. to Caroline E.Trotter	9-14-1848	D.N.Lowery.
Siler,L.F. to Mary Trotter	11-9-1853	John Hall,Clk.
Siler,Will to Lou Herren	Col. 9- 4-1867	R.C.Slagle,Reg.
Siler,Alfred B.to Amanda Jane Penland	Col. 9-21-1871	William Sloan,M.G
Siler,Lee 30 to Sarah Patton 22	Col. 3-21-1875	C.D.Smith,M.G.
Siler,Charles L.27 to E.E.Siler 18	Col. 12-24-1877	Thos.Warren,M.G.
Siler,Alfred 60 to Eva Sanders 32	Col. 8- 1-1880	C.D.Smith,M.G.

Siler,Jesse R.20 to Myra J.Bell 16	11-9-1880	C.Campbell,M.G.
Siler,A.T.22 to Fannie Conley 19	12-9-1880	I.D.Wright,M.G.
Siler,T.P.51 to Jane Reeves 28	12-24-1880	F.Poindexter,J.P.
Siler,J.G.22 to Ella F.Rankin 26	12-19-1883	E.H.Bogle,M.G.
Siler,Emilis 30 to Martha Carter 20 Col.	4-26-1888	M.J.Mashburn,J.P.
Siler,Frank 23 to M.Elizabeth Crawford 22	10-10-1888	W.R.Barnett,M.G.
Siler,A.L.31 to Laura C.Slagle 30	6-16-1897	D.F.Carver,M.G.
Siler,Theodore 39 to Eunice Cunningham 30	12-19-1936	J.A.Flanagan,M.G.
Sigman,Logan 26 to Margt Wikle 22	11-14-1878	John S.Gibson,J.P
Simons,Thomas to Rachel Anderson	8-22-1859	E.Allen,J.P.
Simonds,Stuart to May P.Clore	5-25-1850	J.K.Gray,Clk.
Simpkins,Eldred C.38 to N.C.Bryson 25	4-23-1891	J.R.Pendergras,MG
Simpson,Wm.Dean 21 to Lena Amelia Myers 19	9- 5-1920	J.R.Pendergras,MG
Singleton,Thos.V.30 to Montana Allen 27	1- 7-1899	T.E.Weaver,M.G.
Sitton,Floyd J.26 to Anne Lowery 28	12-14-1902	F.M.Morgan,M.G.
Sisk,R.D.22 to Emma Guy 18	9- 5-1898	J.R.Pendergras,MG
Slagle,R.C. to E.B.Hoggins	2-10-1842	J.K.Gray,Clk.
Slagle,A.H. to Hariett Siler	8-28-1845	J.K.Gray,Clk.
Slagle,Elim to Amanda R.Crawford	7-31-1849	T.P.Siler,D.Clk.
Slagle,S.A. to M.E.Crawford	3- 5-1859	R.C.Slagle,Reg.
Slagle,James S.to Mary P.Moore	10-17-1867	R.C.Slagle,C.C.C.
Slagle,J.Henry 28 to Maggie Gillespie 21	1-25-1888	J.H.Weaver,M.G.
Slagle,J.M.26 to Callie Justice 20	8-22-1888	J.S.Woodard,M.G.
Slagle,Alfred M.22 to Mary J.Anderson 25	10---1896	Jos.Morgan,J.P.
Slagle,Thos.M.45 to Laura A.Siler 34	12-28-1899	J.A.Deal,M.G.
Slagle,C.S.25 to Louise Arthur 27	10-7-1914	J.L.Teague M.G.
Slagle,Hal E.24 to Annie Lee Waldroop 22	6-24-1924	J.Q.Wallace,M.G.
Slagle,Jess W.36 to Mattie Marchman 30	6- 5-1925	A.J.Smith,M.G.
Sloan,Wm.Jr. to H.L.Siler	12-23-1856	L.F.Siler,J.P.
Sloan,Jesse S.24 to Emma R.McDowell 23	3-29-1882	M.R.Kirkpatrick.
Sloan,Wm.Neville 24 to Beulah Bidwell 21	9- 2-1913	M.H.Tuttle,M.G.
Sluder,John 33 to Lizzie Shepherd 18	1-25-1900	M.L.Rickman,J.P.
Sluder,William Jr.23 to Bonnie G.Grant 18	8-25-1936	Geo.Carpenter,J.P
He from Chatanooga,Tn.... She from Waynesville,N.C.		
Smith,Larkin to Louisa Long	3-21-1831	Anderson Vandyke.
Smith,George R.to Julyann Sellers	12-14-1837	J.K.Gray,Clk.
Smith,Merrit to Polly Sanders	8-18-1842	J.K.Gray,Clk.
Smith,Wm.C. to Nancy Reid	12-28-1854	John Hall,Clk.
Smith,J.A. to Susan Cline	7-27-1865	J.A.Green.
Smith,William W.22 to Parthena A.Hedden 20	2-23-1873	S.W.Hill,J.P.
Smith,James L.22 to Fanney Pendergrass 22	10-21-1875	Alber Siler,J.P.
Smith,William T.20 to Julia A.Taylor 22	10-31-1875	Z.Barnes,J.P.
He from Buncombe,Co.N.C.... She from Nantahala,N.C.		
Smith,B.F.22 to M.M.Dills 17	6- 1-1882	J.A.Deal,M.G.
Smith,Charles C.33 to Roxa L.Addington 31	3-10-1886	J.H.Weaver,M.G.
Smith,J.J.33 to Mary A.Chapin 31	5- 5-1886	Original not found
Smith,Samuel 22 to Emma E.Huscusson 17	5-24-1888	I.D.Wright,M.G.

```
Smith,Joseph L.25 to Sarah A.Wood 18          10-12-1890 A.A.Justice,M.G.
Smith,James B.34 to Rose A.Clark 32           1-11-1892 Original not found
Smith,Wm.Elijah 20 to Alice I.Southards 18    3- 6-1892  Jno.S.Smiley,M.G.
Smith,John A.28 to Nancy E.Allen 30           9-25-1892  J.J.McConnell,J.P
Smith,Milas K.46 to Telitha Holbrooks 19      5-24-1894  S.J.May,J.P.
Smith,J.E.26 to Ada F.Freeman 20              11-10-1895 Joseph Morgan,J.P
Smith,James B.38 to Lelia Carpenter 19        6- 3-1896  B.W.Wells,J.P.
Smith,Ancil 27 to Polly Love 21               2- 8-1899  W.A.Setser,J.P.
Smythe(Smith) Ed 23 to Rosa Byrd 19           9-28-1901  W.H.Morrison,J.P.
Smith,Frank T.44 to Virginia Crawford 30      12-31-1902 Frank Siler,M.G.
Smith,D.E.21 to Lena Cadon 19                 1-10-1904  Blurred
Smith,Carr 43 to Mrs.Nancy E.Smith 50         3-26-1905  Blurred
Smith,Laurence N.19 to Sallie N.Williamson 18/4-30-1905 Blurred
Smith,James M.25 to Sallie Jones 20           11-19-1905 S.J.May,J.P.
Smith,Virgil 22 to Carrie I.Freeman 19        1- 7-1906  W.J.Morgan,J.P.
Smith,Worth 26 to Maude Kimsey 21             9-25-1906  J.C.Shope,J.P.
Smith,Thos.J.28 to Eva Cadon 25               1- 1-1907  J.D.Vinson,J.P.
Smith,John F.21 to Allie Lewis 21             12-14-1911 T.B.Enloe,J.P.
Smith,Robert 20 to Fannie Sanders 18          1-28-1912  Geo.Carpenter,J.P
Smith,John C.25 to Leuna E.Justice 26         6-15-1913  A.W.Donaldson,J.P
Smith,Gordon 23 to Sue Crawford 21            12-13-1913 R.P.McCracken,M.G
Smith,Grady 21 to Flora Garland 18            7-11-1915  G.H.Cloer,M.G.
Smith,Pierson 20 to Eulah McGaha 18           1- 7-1917  D.C.McCoy,M.G.
Smith,L.J.33 to Gertrude R.West 18            6  3-1917  F.O.Dryman,M.G.
Smith,Vester 32 to Jennie Bryant 19           8-25-1918  W.W.Marr,M.G.
Smith,L.Crawford 19 to Sada Downs 18          9-15-1918  A.S.Solesbee,M.G.
  He from Servilla,Tenn.
Smith,H.A.36 to Celia Eda McKinney 33         4-25-1920  J.C.Umberger,M.G.
Smith,R.N.25 to Ellen Higdon 19               5- 6-1920  J.C.Owen,M.G.
Smith,E.D.25 to Myrtle Roper 19               11-28-1920 A.S.Solesbee,M.G.
Smith,James S.36 to Josephine Carson 18       3- 2-1923  J.R.Pendergras,MG
Smith,Earl 22 to Rovena Fouts 22              3- 3-1923  Geo.Carpenter,J.P
Smith,Jos.L.56 to Mrs.M.Angel Foweler 38      4- 4-1923  A.J.Smith,M.G.
Smith,Sanford 26 to Pearl Kinsland 20         9- 5-1926  D.C.McCoy,M.G.
Smith,James E.27 to Lillie A.DeHart 18        6- 6-1927  J.R.Pendergras,MG
Smith,Bruce 25 to Jane Neal 22                12-21-1927 J.M.Raby,J.P.
  Both from Nantahala,N.C.
Smith,A.J.32 to Maud Shields 20               10-29-1928 A.S.Solesbee,M.G.
Smith,Don 25 to Ruth Cabe 22                  4-28-1934  B.W.Lefler,M.G.
Smith,Jewel 30 to Gertrude Hall 27            5- 4-1936  J.F.Burrell,M.G.
Smith,Walton R.25 to Annie D.Leatherman 19    7- 3-1936  R.F.Mayberry,M.G.
Smith,Wiley G.29 to Mrs.Nettie Hensley 29     10-2-1937  C.A.Setser,J.P.
Smith,Cecil A.24 to Frances J.Jones 21        11-9-1937  W.B.Underwood,M.G
  He from Tampa,Fla.... She from Cedar Mt.,N.C.
Smith,William S.,Jr.22 to Georgeana Tessier 22/12-25-1937-J.E.Abernethey
  He from Newton,N.C.
Smith,Hoke 18 to Katharine P.Conley 17        4-28-1938  Geo.Carpenter,J.P
  He from Orlando, Fla.
```

Smart,David 38 to M.G.Stiles 40	11-24-1898	G.A.Bartlett,M.G
Smart,Robert L.23 to Floy Owen 21	11-22-1908	J.R.Pendergrás,M(
Smart,Wilson 32 to Bertha Cunningham 30	7- 2-1927	T.S.Roten,M.G.
Snyder,Odell 21 to Cora Phillips 22	11-21-1909	J.R.Pendergras,M(
Snider,Rufus 23 to Birdie Cabe 22	2- 8-1915	J.M.Bennett,M.G.
Snyder,W.H.25 to Nannie Mae Corbin 21	11-7-1917	W.W.Marr,M.G.
Snyder,John L.27 to Evelyn Buchanan 24	3-10-1918	J.M.Raby,J.P.
Snyder,Newell 28 to Martha Randall 23	7- 7-1936	Miles J.Snyder,M(
Solesbee,A. to Louisa D.Davis	10-29-1859	J.H.McLoud.
Solesbee,Asbury to Mary Davis	10-27-1871	William Sloan,Reg
Solesbee,M.L.23 to Jane Abernathy 23	1- 4-1885	W.C.Kimzey,J.P.
Solesby,Martin 29 to Lina Dills 21	2-23-1891	M.Ghormley,M.G.
Solesbee,Charles 24 to Cornelia Yonce 15	8- 6-1893	Z.Barnes,J.P.
Solesbee,A.S.25 to Bell Kilpatrick 19	12-18-1901	T.S.Denton,M.G.
Solesbee,W.S.35 to Addie Gregory 33	2-16-1902	M.Ghormley,M.G.
Solesbee,Pink 30 to Nona Alliaon 18	1-10-1907	J.F.Tippett,M.G.
Solesbee,J.P.27 to Artie Crawford 20	2-13-1907	D.A.Yonce,M.G.
Solesbee,Pat 35 to Nannie Rowland 33	4-14-1915	J.S.Yonce,M.G.
Solesbee,German 22 to Ninah V.Ramsey 15	5-14-1916	J.M.Bennett,M.G.
Solesbee,Claud 24 to Inez Owenby 19	10-4-1933	Geo.Steppe,J.P.
Solesbee,Dock 27 to Annie Guffee 22	10-14-1933	Lester Williams,J
Solesbee,Sherden 26 to Kate Roland 21 He from Nantahala,N.C.	2- 5-1935	R.M.Lambert,J.P.
Solesbee,Ralph 21 to Ruth Younce 18	3-12-1938	Geo.W.Steppe,J.P.
Solesby,Dallas 26 to Frances Rowland 18	2-18-1839	Philip H.Passmore
Sorrels,Ebenezer to Elizabeth Weeks	12-12-1849	J.K.Gray,Clk.
Sorrels,Lewis to Elizabeth Miller	7- 6-1865	R.C.Slagle,Reg.
Sorrells,Robert V.to Lou Bentley	1-21-1872	T.F.Glenn,M.G.
Sorrels,Robt.H.24 to Mollie Mashburn 17	9-27-1898	John C.Russell,JF
Sorrels,Lewis 52 to Martha J.Jones 50	11-20-1898	J.B.Elmore,J.P.
Sorrels,J.M.22 to Anna Franks 23	12-22-1901	J.D.Sitton,M.G.
Sorrels,Lester 21 to Annie Guffee 16	12-24-1920	J.R.Pendergras,MG
Sorrels,Pete 23 to Mary Williams 18	10-18-1934	A.L.Dills,J.P.
Sorrels,James C.42 to Nannie Potts 32	4-26-1935	B.W.Lefler,M.G.
Southards,Geo.W.to Sarah A.Mason	8-18-1862	R.C.Slagle,C.C.C.
Southards,William to Lucinda F.Brinkly	6-14-1871	William Sloan,Reg
Southards,Julius H.28 to Ann Vaughn 30	1-22-1885	J.D.Vinson,M.G.
Southards,Thomas 21 to Annie Battles 16	2-23-1896	Thos.M.Slagle,J.P
Southards,John Jr.23 to Mary J.Gibson 17	10-25-1897	Isaac T.Peek.M.G.
Southards,Henry 21 to Florence Battles 18	2-13-1898	H.H.Dills,J.P.
Southards,Charley 20 to Minnie Gibson 18	9-23-1900	J.P.Miller,M.G.
Southards,John 21 to Carrie Battles 18	2-17-1901	W.P.Allison,J.P.
Southards,G.W.75 to Mary Elizabeth Davis 47/3-21-1906		W.P.Allison,J.P.
Southards,Robert 19 to Hattie Carpenter 17	12-3-1906	W.P.Allison,J.P.
Southards,Chas.A.25 to Florence Sprinkles 18/2-12-1908		W.P.Allison,J.P.
Southards,Lester 20 to Martha Carpenter 16	1- 6-1918	G.W.Moffitt,J.P.
Southards,B.L.26 to Delphia Miller 18	3- 6-1921	J.M.Keener,M.G.

Southards,C.H.24 to Janie Barnes 18   8-16-1923   I.N.McCoy,J.P.
Southards,Albert 28 to Delcie I.Henry 28   12-30-1925 J.W.Baty,M.G.
Southards,John 23 to Callie Margan 22   1-25-1930   W.C.Mason,M.G.
Southards,James D.18 to Alice Ledbetter 18 8-22-1936   Sam J.Murray,J.P.
Southards,Lawrence 20 to Lena Hunnicutt 19 6- 4-1938   L.L.Arnold,J.P.
  Both from Mountain City,Ga.
Southerland,Ilet B.23 to Mary L.Slagle 23   10-15-1938 S.R.Crockett,M.G.
  He from Winston Salem,N.C.
Speed,R.D.23 to Fannie Wall 19   8-15-1895   L.H.Garland,J.P.
Speed,Lafayett 25 to Helen Beal 20   7- 9-1911   P.C.Calloway,J.P.
Speed,T.S.25 to Florence Crane 22   7-27-1919   Jesse Balew,J.P.
Speed,Doyle 24 to Bonnie Houston 20   10-25-1925 W.T.Potts,M.G.
Speights,Robert C.25 to Jessie E.DeLozier 18/1-22-1927 Geo.Carpenter,J.P
  He from Lumberton,N.C.
Spicer,Thomas to Margaret J.Jenkins   11-18-1864 R.C.Slagle,Reg.
Sprayberry,James C.35 to Emma M.Alsabrook 29/9-3-1938   J.E.Abernethy,M.G
  He from La Grange,Ga.... She from Carrollton,Ga.
Spriggs,Elmer T.45 to Grace Givens 28   6-13-1938   L.L.Arnold,J.P.
  He from Cincinnati,Ohio.
Sprinkle,M.L.22 to Maggie Carpenter 21   2-15-1884   W.L.Kimsey,J.P.
Sprinkles,John 21 to Mary Williamson 19   5-26-1889   J.O.Shelley,M.G.
Sprinkles,Leander D.22 to Mary T.Curtis 19 1- 7-1906   J.C.Shope,J.P.
Sprinkles,Daniel 20 to Flora Welch 19   9- 5-1909   Jos.L.Fouts,J.P.
Sprinkles,John H.38 to Mrs.Tina Southards 22/12-1-1910 J.T.Watts,J.P.
Sprinkles,Alex 19 to Laura Roper 19   3-26-1913   J.R.Pendergras,MG
Sprinkles,Geo.B.19 to Pearl Hodgins 18   7- 4-1915   Robert Stamey,J.P
Sprinkles,G.W.24 to Mattie Henderson 23   3-19-1916   D.S.Richardson,MG
Stalcup,William to Linney Sanders   3-29-1843   J.K.Gray,Clk.
Stalcup,Peter S.to Margaret Simons   5-15-1843   J.K.Gray,Clk.
Stalcup,Jason to Amy Mingus   11-3-1843   Wm.Stalcup.
Stalcup,Peter S. to Ruth Simons   1- 2-1847   J.K.Gray,Clk.
Stalcup,Coleman H.17 to Doxie N.Franks 16 6-21-1885   John Ammons,J.P.
Stalcup,Geo.T.21 to Jessie Wallace 21   1-10-1911   Wm.P.Chedester,MG
Stamey,W.C.18 to N.A.Moffitt 20   1-29-1885   W.C.Kimsey,J.P.
Stamey,Robert 19 to Rosetta A.Saunders 20 8- 3-1887   Wm.C.Kimsey,J.P.
  He from Habersham Co.Ga.
Stamey,Charles W.19 to Addie Fulcher 21   10-3-1889   J.M.Hilliard,M.G.
Stamey,John H.21 to Anna P.Byrd 17   1- 27-1895 G.R.McPherson,J.P
Stamey,J.G.38 to Margaret E.Shepherd 28   3- 6-1900   W.L.Bradley,M.G.
Stamey,Thomas 19 to Mary Mann 17   3-18-1900   W.L.Bradley,M.G.
Stamey,G.C.19 to Carrie Burton 18   1-31-1911   D.A.Brinkley,M.G.
Stamey,J.W.26 to Cordelia Thomas 20   10-2-1912   Robert Stamey,J.P
Stamey,C.C.20 to Lillie Brooks 18   12-15-1920 Retd.not executed
Stamey,Ernest 22 to Mrs.Allie Bates 26   5- 1-1920   J.L.Kinsland,M.G.
Stanfield,Commodore 19 to Roxana Gregory 20/8-12-1888   J.M.Keener,J.P.
Stanfield,Charles 24 to Laura Holland 25   5- 8-1897   J.M.Keener,M.G.
Stanfield,J.L.30 to F.J.Setser 23   12-29-1900 J.H.Moore,M.G.
Stanfield,W.H.28 to Conie B.Stanfield 20   10-30-1901 J.H.Moore,M.G.
Stanfield,Elias A.27 to Fannie H.McKinney 21/12-17-1901-John H.Moore,M.G.

```
Stanfield,Samuel W.22 to Lillie Rogers 18      12-24-1903 G.W.Stiwinter,M.G
Stanfield, Mack B.27 to Lula Corbin 19          6-28-1906 Retd.not executed
Stanfield,Geo.W.33 to Ittie G.McKinney 24       6- 5-1907 D.L.Miller,M.G.
Stanfield,M.B.29 to Mary Hallick 22            12-22-1907 Z.J.Peek,J.P.
Stanfield,L.S.28 to Nellie Blanche Setser 18/8-19-1914 J.L.Teague,M.G.
Stanfield,B.C.22 to Hattie Guffey 18            5-17-1919 Noah L.Jolly,J.P.
Stanford,Bedford 25 to Lonie Eliza.Cloer 17/11-16-1908 J.W.Ammons,J.P.
Starnes, John to Elizabeth Cochran              8-10-1832 N.W.Dobson.
Starrite,Mosey to Palsey Pace                   4-13-1833 John Hall,Clk.
Steele,H.L.44 to Camilla Tucker 33              1-19-1939 Ivan L.Roberts,MG
   He from Covington,Va.... She from Penick,W.Va.
Stephens,Dan S.25 to Elizabeth C.Barnes 18     1-12-1873 Jesse Stepp,J.P.
   He from Union Co.,Ga.
Stephens,Joseph M.23 to Alvira Wood 28         12-24-1905 D.F.Howard,M.G.
Stepenson,Wm.H. to Margaret Higdon              8-11-1860 T.P.Siler,D.Clk.
Stephenson,Marion 21 to Julia Holbrooks 20     4- 2-1911 J.L.Younce,M.G.
Stepp,George W.24 to Ella Wood 19               7-23-1896 J.T.Platt,M.G.
Steward,John to May Moss                        6-14-1831 John Hall,Clk.
Steward,Manley to Rhoda A.Thomas       Col.    4-29-1876 R.C.Slagle,Clk.
Stewart,R.D.27 to Sarah A.Guy 19       Col.    2-16-1882 F.Poindexter,J.P.
Steward,Logan 21 to Lucy Moore 19      Col.    11-9-1884 John D.Howard,J.P
Stewart,Rufus 32 to Lavada Henry 27            12-14-1893 J.M.Keener,M.G.
Stewart,Henry,Jr. 36to Lula McLoud 19          7- 1-1894 John Elmore,J.P.
Stewart,J.R.26 to Mattie Vanhook 20            2-18-1894 J.Williams,M.G.
Stewart,Joseph A.22 to Carrie McDonnell 18 Col.6-6-1896-J.A.Caliver,M.G.
Stewart,Henry,Sr.70 to Cassie McLoud 20        10-7-1902 J.R.Pendergras,MG
Stewart,Alvin C.37 to Kansas Berry 32          1-15-1905 J.W.Ammons,J.P.
Stewart,William 27 to Charlotte Jones 21 Col.6-7-1906 C.L.Stewart,M.G.
Stewart,Wm.G.31 to Minnie Addington 28         11-28-1908 R.E.Atkinson,M.G.
Stewart,W.W.32 to Ethel Houston 22             11-25-1923 A.B.Potts,J.P.
Stewart,Harley 25 to Pearl Moore 19            12-9-1924 Geo.Carpenter,J.P
Stewart,Charles 24 to Bess Norton 25           6- 8-1936 J.B.Tabor,M.G.
Stikeleather,Thomas H.22 to Ruth Moffitt 19/6-17-1934 E.F.Eller,M.G.
   He from Charlotte,N.C.
Stone,M.H.30 to Mrs.Estell Hooper 25           11-7-1924 W.M.Smith,M.G.
Stonecipher,Edward 18 to Mary Ramsey 22 Col.10-23-1873 D.W.Wells,M.G.
Strickling,Wm.26 to Mattie Carpenter 18 Col.10-10-1913 J.R.Pendergras,MG
Strutton,Charles 24 to S.L.Gribble 20          2- 1-1882 C.D.Smith,M.G.
Stillwell,Tilman to Susannah Carter            4-13-1832 William Ellis.
Stillwell,Ward to Susan Rowland                8-18-1866 R.C.Slagle,C.C.C.
Stillwell,James M.to Mary Poindexter           1- 2-1867 R.C.Slagle,Clk.
Stillwell,Zell 27 to Viola Drake 22            7- 5-19.. D.F.Howard,M.G.
Stiles,Lababen to Mary McConnell               11-26-1835 John Tatham,Clk.
Styles,John to Rebecca Ashe                     3-17-1836 James Cabe,
Stiles,Benjamine to Mary Hofman                 5- 4-1839 John Hall,Clk.
Stiles,C.M.to Teletha C.Conley                  4-14-1841 H.G.Woodfin,D.Clk
Stiles,B.H. to Susan Wallace                    4-20-1841 H.G.Woodfin,D.Clk
Stiles,David to Avaline Justice                 5-15-1856 J.L.Robinson.
```

Styles,Benjamin to Winnie Medlin	5-20-1860	R.C.Slagle,Clk.
Stiles,A.J. to M.M.Justice	8-31-1865	R.C.Slagle,Clk.
Stiles,John M.to Dicy M.Fulcher	1-11-1867	R.C.Slagle,Clk.
Stiles,William to Harriett McConnell	10-4-1869	R.C.Slagle,Clk.
Stiles,H.P. to Mary Ballew	2-29-1872	W.T.Ammons,J.P.
Stiles,A.W.19 to Nancy A.Cabe 21	10-24-1872	W.T.Anderson,J.P.
Stiles,A.W.30 to Nancy A.Patterson 23	1-18-1883	S.H.Harrington,MG
Stiles,Judson D.23 to E.A.Bates 16	9-25-1884	L.H.Howard,J.P.
Stiles,Robert Lee 21 to Elizabeth V.Burnett 24	10-1-1890-	A.A.Justice,M.G
Stiles,George T.33 to Bessie R.Sellers 24	3- 1-1891	S.H.Harrington,MG
Stiles,R.N.25 to Laura Beasley 21	11-12-1893	W.G.Mallonee,M.G.
Stiles,Cebarn M.23 to Emma Winstead 18	3-14-1895	G.R.McPhearson,JP
Stiles,J.H.28 to Leah Mathews 26	2- 1-1903	W.L.Higdon,J.P.
Stiles,Charley 25 to Elsie Watkins 24	12-28-1904	John H.Moore,M.G.
Stiles,E.A.26 to Nora Stiles 21	1-12-1916	J.M.Bennett,M.G.
Stiles,T.W.21 to Dell Rogers 18	1-12-1916	J.M.Bennett,M.G.
Stiles,Oliver 24 to Bettie Clark 22	10-24-1916	J.H.Gregory,J.P.
Stiles,N.H.23 to Betty Saunders 32	8-27-1927	J.R.Pendergras,MG
Stiles,R.N.60 to Cora L.Hoglen 44	8-10-1929	J.R.Pendergras,MG
Stiwinter,Jas.C.to Margaret E.Stewart	1-17-1867	I.N.Keener,J.P.
Stiwinter,George 70 to Juda Watson 40	8-23-1877	J.M.Keener,J.P.
Stiwinter,G.W.16 to M.J.Watson 16	10-13-1878	Jno.Marshall,M.G.
Stiwinter,John G.26 to Lettie M.Houston 19	11-9-1897	J.M.Keener,M.G.
Stiwinter,J.M.22 to Irphy E.Buchanan 16	12-15-1898	G.W.Stiwinter,J.P
Stiwinter,John T.26 to Texa McClure 28	8-22-1906	J.M.Keener,M.G.
Stiwinter,Frank 23 to Minnie Clark 18	11-10-1910	J.W.Ammons,J.P.
Stiwinter,Charley 26 to Lena Hedden 18	8-10-1911	Z.P.Peek,J.P.
Stiwinter,John 46 to Jennie Jenkins 42	9-12-1926	J.M.Keener,M.G.
Stiwinter,Roy 20 to Bessie Coggins 18	3-12-1934	V.C.Ramey,M.G.
Strain,Mariet to Elizabeth Bryson	2-10-1830	W.B.Hyatt.
Strain,J.L. to Mary Young	8- 9-1864	J.R.Ammons,M.G.
Strain,T.M. 23 to M.Etta Stanfield 18	8-16-1888	J.M.Keener,J.P.
Street,Peter 31 to Ida McGaha 22	12-2-1894	W.J.Jenkins,J.P.
Stockton,James to Martha Griggs	8-22-1866	R.C.Slagle,C.C.C.
Stockton,Robert to Lidey Ledford	2----1869	J.P.McConnell,J.P
Stockton,Alfred to Nancy C.Bates	11-19-1871	L.Howard,J.P.
Stockton,David M.22 to Martha Ledford 20	1-29-1873	J.H.Addington,J.P
Stockton,Alex 22 to Adelia Ferguson 20	5-24-1877	J.H.Addington,J.P
Stockton,A.B.29 to Cornelia E.McConnell 20	1-18-1883	J.H.Addington,J.P
Stockton,Henry W.22 to Mary A.Bell 20	9-15-1889	C.L.Ledford,M.G.
Stockton,Samuel R.20 to Rosa Hasting 20	11-17-1895	J.A.Brendle,M.G.
Stockton,James A.22 to Rebecca Bates 22	12-22-1895	Joseph Morgan,J.P
Stockton,D.C.21 to Nomer Ledford 19	8-20-1898	Robert Stamey,J.P
Stockton,Jess 22 to Lula Stockton 21	12-16-1900	Robert Stamey,J.P
Stockton,Jno.T.21 to Minnie McClure 23	3-19-1903	Robert Stamey,J.P
Stockton,S.V.20 to Mary Ledford 19	4- 9-1903	Robert Stamey,J.P
Stockton,Charles 24 to Maggie McClure 19	7-21-1907	Original not found

```
Stockton,Norman 20 to Ellen McClure 18          10-13-1908 Robert Stamey,J.P
Stockton,Charlie 26 to Hattie McClure 15        2-13-1910 Robert Stamey,J.P
Stockton,Grady 21 to Irene Shope 20             1- 6-1918 Robert Stamey,J.P
Stockton,C.B. 18 to Cora Wood 18                4-13-1918 O.C.Corbin,J.P.
Stockton,Daniel 22 to Lillie J.Parker 17        3-21-1921 G.W.Moffitt,J.P.
Stockton,D.C.43 to Hermie Liner 42              4-23-1924 J.J.Mann,J.P.
Stockton,Wade 20 to Edna Hall 23                4-24-1935 A.S.Solesbee,M.G.
Stuman,Marvel H.to Mary Clark                   6- 8-1847 W.B.Morgan,M.G.
Stewman,Henry to Nancy Sorrels                  1-16-1854 Joshua Ammons,M.G
Stewman,James to Cordelia Banks                 3-23-1858 John Elmore,J.P.
Stewman,M.H. to Rhoda Hughes                    9-14-1858 R.C.Slagle,Reg.
Stewman,Elijah C.21 to Lydia Blain 16           9-15-1872 W.H.Higdon,J.P.
Stewman,Charles A.20 to Ellen Crisp 20          8-18-1889 John B.Gray,J.P.
Stuman,Jess 18 to Betty A.Moore 17              1-29-1894 J.C.Russell,J.P.
Stewman,James 22 to Laura Crisp 18              12-24-1895 Jno.C.Russell,J.P
Stewman,John 45 to Nannie Dalton 40             2- 5-1902 P.R.Rickman,M.G.
Stewman,Luther 27 to Catherine Walker 18        9-25-1937 Fred Bryson,J.P.
Sullivan,J.Patrick 27 to Alice M.Linder 23      10-13-1928 E.R.Mason,M.G.
   Both from Anderson,S.C.
Sullins,A.E.30 to H.A.Stringer 35               10-5-1879 P.C.Wild,J.P.
Surrett,Thomas 29 to Annie Norton 29            12-20-1911 A.P.Foster,M.G.
Summer,Otto F.31 to Edwina M.Dalrymple 27       7- 7-1935 E.R.Eller,M.G.
Summer,Zeb V.37 to Annie Ashe 33                8-15-1912 G.M.Bulgin,J.P.
Sutton,Anderson to Mary Willson                 12-22-1834 John Tatham,Clk.
Sutton,Russell to Rachel M.Turner               11-19-1837 Joel Simons.
Sutton,Joseph to Lowenda Parton                 10-2-1846 J.K.Gray,Clk.
Sutton,James to Nancy Guilliams                 2-10-1847 J.K.Gray,Clk.
Sutton,William 22 to Nancy Garrison 24          12-6-1880 E.H.Franks,J.P.
Sutton,W.M.21 to Ollie Jones 18                 7-22-1916 Geo.Carpenter,JP
Sutton,Clement 36 to Laura Lyle 27              2-16-1924 W.M.Smith,M.G.
Sutton,Charles C.28 to Hazel V.Penland 22       9- 2-1933 G.N.Dulin,M.G.
Swafford,James 18 to Ella Crawford 18           12-3-1900 Jacob Yonce,M.G.
Swafford,W.M.21 to Nannie Crawford 20           8-28-1901 Mark Deweese,J.P.
Swafford,Perry 22 to Pearl Welch 24             12-24-1915 J.L.Fouts,J.P.
Swafford,Paul 24 to Elizabeth Poindexter 19/4- 8-1934 G.A.Cloer,M.G.
Swafford,Troy 23 to Lottie Roper 18             3- 6-1937 L.A.Jolley,M.G.
Swain,Louis H.27 to Virginia Sloan 28           6-15-1933 L.B.Hayes,M.G.
   He from Durham,N.C.
Swaney,John 36 to Laura Gibbs 23                11-5-1880 J.S.Woodard,M.G.
Swanger,A.P.21 to Cordelia Cope 17              11-17-1890 A.B.Dalton,J.P.
Swan,Robert W.25 to Victoria Queen 15           4- 4-1895 M.Ghormley,M.G.
Swanson,Walter 27 to Annie Waldroop 35          6-25-1933 Will Smith,Ord.
Sweatman,Lyman 22 to Roxie Nichols 22           4- 5-1914 C.A.Battles,J.P.
Sweatman,Joseph 23 to Issidona Dills 19         12-1-1889 W.C.Kimsey,J.P.
Sweatman,Samuel 26 to Louisa C.Jacobs 25        9-11-1895 J.T.Wade,M.G.
Sweatman,David 23 to Josie Johnson 21           10-29-1899 W.A.Setser,J.P.
Swanson,Ray M.38 to Thelma J.Welch 24           5- 3-1941 C.F.Rogers,M.G.
   He from Hayesville,N.C.
```

Sylvia,Squire to Margaret Thomas	3-24-1838	John Hall,Clk.
Sypher,Edward E.51 to Ada L.Stiles 26	2- 2-1932	O.P.Ader,M.G.
Taber,James S.to Lydia DeHart	11-4-1844	J.K.Gray,D.Clk.
Tabor,John C. to Sarah A.Elders	12-22-1846	J.K.Gray,D.Clk.
Tabor,Nathan E.to Martha Davis	2-24-1871	Wm.Sloan,Reg.
Tate,W.M.48 to Mrs.Rosa Byrd Smythe 37	6- 1-1921	J.F.Browning,J.P.
Talbott,Richard S.22 to Ethel C.Nelson 18	12-25-1918	D.A.Younce,M.G.
Tallent,Ephraim to Sarah Roper	12-28-1852	Noah Houston,J.P.
Tallent,Joshua 17 to Louisa J.Clampet 18	7-11-1872	Joseph Morgan,J.P
Tallent,Amos to Jane Gaither	8- 3-1871	William Sloan,Reg
Tallent,J.Logan to Amanda Jacobs	12-4-1871	Thos.Mashburn,J.P
Tallent,Daniel 19 to C.M.Roper 19	7-30-1878	C.Campbell,M.G.
Tallent,Emanuel 21 to Harriett Jacobs 20	10-4-1878	B.G.Wild,M.G.
Tallent,Ephriam 22 to Nancy Roper 25	11-1-1878	B.G.Wild,M.G.
Tallent,R.W.23 to Annie Reaves 19	12-27-1882	B.G.Wild,M.G.
Tallent,M.H.36 to Martha Jacobs 23	6-23-1883	R.H.Cunningham,JP
Tallent,R.W.25 ,to Jennie E.Wilds 32	2- 7-1884	E.H.Bogle,M.G.
Tallent,Eli 57 to Hariett Love 44	11-6-1884	R.H.Cunningham,MG
Tallent,James M.23 to Maggie Wilds 18	11-9-1884	J.S.Woodard,M.G.
Tallent,Charlie 23 to Amanda Reeves 24	11-5-1885	B.G.Wild,M.G.
Tallent,John W. 22 to Martha J.Key 16	1- 1-1888	John P.Campbell.
Tallent,Aaron 24 to Rebecca Willis 23	11-30-1890	J.P.Campbell,J.P.
Tallent,A.Pat 34 to Nancy C.Raby 31	3- 1-1891	J.A.Morrison,J.P.
Tallent,Ervin M.34 to Emma Deweese 27	3-11-1892	Canaro S.Ray,J.P.
Tallent,DeWitt 16 to Lavadia Ledford 16	2-18-1894	J.P.Campbell,J.P.
Tallent,Ephram 62 to Rebecca Hall 43	9- 5-1896	C.S.Ray,J.P.
Tallent,C.Charlie 22 to Jennie Sanders 21	1-12-1896	C.S.Ray,J.P.
Tallent,Elbert 20 to Addie Roper 23	10-21-1897	C.S.Ray,J.P.
Tallent,Ephriam 43 to Mary Long 37	8-28-1898	J.P.Campbell,J.P.
Tallent,Jesse 20 to Fanny Campbell 20	9-10-1899	T.E.Weaver,M.G.
Tallent,Jule 21 to Cora Scroggs 19	3- 3-1901	W.E.Sanders,J.P.
Tallent,G.H.28 to Ida Roper 19	1-14-1903	Mark Deweese,J.P.
Tallent,Noah 23 to Ilar Hall 17	2-12-1905	W.L.Bradley,M.G.
Tallent,Canaroh 21 to Martha Cabe 21	4-21-1907	W.J.Morgan,J.P.
Tallent,A.L. 22 to Nettie Reese· 21	11-8-1908	T.Baxter White,JP
Tallent,E.E. 33 to Ola Potts 37	12-24-1909	W.L.Bradley,M.G.
Tallent,Thomas 23 to Bertha Teems 20	11-14-1909	J.R.Pendergras,MG
Tallent,Aaron 24 to Florence Reeves 19	9-14-1910	Joseph L.Fouts,JP
Tallent,Henry 17 to Maude Patterson 17	10-12-1910	T.J.Vinson,M.G.
Tallent,Grady 19 to Lydia Young 18	5-19-1912	Robert Stamey,J.P
Tallent,Harve 22 to Callie Gregory 18	6- 8-1913	Robert Stamey,J.P
Tallent,Lee 20 to Roxie Welch 20	4-19-1914	Jas.L.Bryson,J.P.
Tallent,Frank 25 to Ollie Tippett 20	3-13-1915	J.R.Pendergras,MG
Tallent,John 24 to Lona Margan 20	8-22-1915	Z.Baird,J.P.
Tallent,Bill 23 to Carrie Taylor 28	4-20-1918	Geo.Carpenter,J.P.
Tallent,Edd 35 to Tallie Roper 18	3-23-1919	L.P.Roper,J.P.
Tallent,H.P.24 to Lexie Hall 18	9-14-1919	J.L.Fouts,J.P.

Tallent,Chas.59 to Pauline Willis 42	12-11-1920	J.L.Fouts,J.P.
Tallent,M.H.65 to Mrs.Sallie Gibson 42	7-16-1921	Geo.Carpenter,J.
Tallent,Norman E.24 to Laura Stewman 22	8- 5-1923	Noah Jollay,J.P.
Tallent,Lloyd 21 to Lillie M.Angel 20	12-25-1926	G.A.Cloer,M.G.
Tallent,Thomas J.28 to May Dillingham 27	1-21-1928	Geo.Carpenter,J.
Tallent,Fred to Lona Huggins	5-13-1933	Will Smith,Ord.
Talley,John to Maryan Picklesimer	10-13-1859	R.C.Slagle,Clk.
Talley,Irvin to Catherine Picklesimer	10-29-1865	Jno.Watkins,J.P.
Talley,William R.21 to Mary M.Wilson 20	9-11-1887	T.J.Vinson,M.G.
Talley,William 21 to Timmie Justice 19	10-20-1894	T.J.Vinson,M.G.
Talley,Evan 32 to Delia Picklesimer 25	1-12-1902	Milford Russell,
Talley,Jack 20 to Anna A.McCall 22	3-25-1902	T.Baxter White,J
Talley,William 32 to Dollie McGaha 32	8-16-1905	C.L.Rickman,J.P.
Talley,Henry 31 to Lillie Picklesimer 30	12-8-1907	I.H.Crunkleton,J
Talley,James 23 to Cora Beal 18	2-23-1913	R.H.Munger,J.P.
Talley,Lester 21 to Amanda Miller 19	7-18-1915	P.C.Calloway,J.P
Talley,Len 22 to Charlotte Keener 18	7-27-1917	P.C.Calloway,J.P
Talley,T.J.19 to Mattie A.Henry 20	4- 3-1924	W.T.Potts,M.G.
Talley,Ebbie 21 to Hattie Wilson 16	7-23-1924	J.W.Baty,M.G.
Talley,William D.27 to Dovie Henry 17	5-23-1926	W.T.Potts,M.G.
Talley,Leonard 22 to Emelyn Passmore 18	7-13-1936	Geo.Carpenter,J.
Talley,Arthur M.28 to Estella Chastain 19	9-26-1936	Geo.Carpenter,J.
Tatham,James W.to Martha Norton	1-11-1845	----- Tatham.
Tatham,John T.26 to Sally Hedden 18	2-12-1893	A.W.Davis,M.G.
Taylor,Garrett to Lettuce Whitaker	7-13-1838	D.Weeks.
Taylor,Andrew K.to Mary Ashe	4-29-1846	J.K.Gray.
Taylor,Buchannon 21 to Adeline Stepp 22	1-28-1877	Z.Barnes,J.P.
Taylor,Adam 22 to Savannah Sprinkles 20	10-20-1878	C.D.Smith,M.G.
Taylor,George 22 to Georgia Burch 18	2- 6-1881	E.B.Padgett,J.P.
Taylor,Jesse Z.27 to Laura J.Berry 24	11-8-1883	John Ammons,J.P.
Taylor,Carson 22 to Carrie Jones 17	12-29-1897	P.R.Rickman,M.G.
Taylor,A.J.25 to Callie Nations 18	7-25-1898	G.A.Bartlet,M.G.
Taylor,Memory 21 to Emma Stephens 18	9-16-1898	D.F.Howard,M.G.
Taylor,James B.24 to Telitha M.E.Smith 19	8-15-1899	J.A.Brauner,M.G.
Taylor,M.L.21 to Flora May 18	3-13-1902	Original not foun
Taylor,Arthur M.37 to Ella M.Smith 35	6-24-1903	J.A.Deal,M.G.
Taylor,William H.30 to Sallie Hopkins 20	9-20-1903	D.F.Howard,M.G.
Taylor,Henry Logan 23 to Polly Ann Adams 18/	2- 7-1909	Jas.M.Corbin,J.P
Taylor,James 22 to Nola Shields 21	8-28-1911	Retd.not execute
Taylor,C.A.26 to Lyda Haskett 21	1-12-1916	R.P.McCracken,M.
Taylor,Vetron 19 to Martha Brooks 18	11-28-1918	J.R.Pendergras,M
Taylor,Z.W. to Helen Crisp	4-29-1933	Will Smith,Ord.
Taylor,Walter 31 to Nancy Justice 25	2- 9-1934	F.E.Gabrels,Ord.
Taylor,Raymond J.,Jr.35 to Olive Wright 39 Both from Nantahala,N.C.	8-20-1936	Geo.Carpenter,J.
Taylor,George 22 to Exie Owenby 18	8-22-1936	Geo.W.Stepp,J.P.
Taylor,Arden G.21 to Eva Green 18	3-21-1937	N.E.Holden,M.G.

Taylor,Bob 19 to Ethel Dills 18	7-26-1938	L.L.Arnold,J.P.
Teague,Mag. to Mrs.Elviry Ledford	11-7-1835	John Tatham,Clk.
Teague,Isaac to Mira Ledford	2-10-1846	J.K.Gray,D.Clk.
Teague,John M.to Milly Ann Brown	8-26-1858	R.C.Slagle,C.C.C.
Teague,Madison to Rebecca Clampitt	6-23-1869	R.C.Slagle,D.Reg.
Teague,John L.24 to Bonnetta Taylor 24	8- 6-1874	Mark May,M.G.
Teague,A.M.40 to Carolin Hall 23	11-19-1876	Joseph Morgan,J.P
Teague,M.C.17 to Margaret Cheeks 17	1-29-1880	John D.Howard,J.P
Teague,Rufus 21 to Nevada Duncan --	9-25-1881	S.W.Hill,J.P.
Teague,Marion 22 to Nancy Webb 28	1-22-1882	S.W.Hill,J.P.
Teague,Rufus M.20 to Ollie Holland 24	10-18-1891	J.M.Keener,M.G.
Teague,Nathen R.23 to Nebraska Younce 18	8-11-1895	J.S.Woodard,M.G.
Teague,Mack 22 to Nettie McCall 45	1- 1-1899	A.G.Wood,J.P.
Teague,J.L.22 to P.A.Evans 19	11-2-1900	M.Ghormley,M.G.
Teague,John 21 to Daisy Ward 18	9- 3-1903	J.R.Pendergras,MG
Teague,G.W.26 to Mrs.Mary J.Southards 26	12-2-1904	Retd.not executed
Teague,George 25 to Emma Campbell 18	1-31-1905	W.A.Solesbee,J.P.
Teague,James A.52 to Margaret McCall 18	3-24-1907	E.P.Picklesimer.
Teague,S.P.32 to Syndia Arnold 21	6-10-1908	W.H.Guffey,M.G.
Teague,J.G.35 to Ester Billingsby 20	4-19-1916	Geo.Carpenter,J.P
Teague,Charles 25 to Clyda Ammons 19	7- 3-1922	J.R.Pendergras,MG
Teague,James N.25 to Gay Bennett 22	5- 6-1931	J.L.Teague,M.G.
Teague,Woodrow 22 to Ruth Berry 18	9-22-1934	J.L.Teague,M.G.
Teafletter,Wm.K. to Mary C.Burch	4- 7-1866	R.C.Slagle,C.C.C.
Teem,John A.26 to Lydia J.Keener 29	1-13-1889	Hosea Moses,J.P.
Teem,John A.34 to Hannah Worley 23	10-24-1897	T.R.Arnold,J.P.
Teems,William 20 to Lula Crisp 21	10-20-1910	J.L.Kinsland,M.G.
Teems,James 21 to Roxie Crisp 20	4-20-1913	T.J.Vinson,M.G.
Teems,J.H.39 to Bell Henry 21	3-29-1917	T.J.Vinson,M.G.
Teems,Gaither 24 to Flemon Lawson 23	1-23-1932	A.S.Solesbee,M.G.
Teems,Hermon W.19 to Alma L.Moses 16	1-29-1936	William Henry,J.P
Terhune,John 67 to Ellie Stanfield 26	1- 1-1906	L.P.Bogle,M.G'.
Tessier,Francis M.24 to Reby Sloan 24	12-26-1912	M.H.Tuttle,M.G.
Tetherow,Wesley 24 to L.A.Gregory 23	12-9-1897	M.Ghormley,M.G.
Thomas,Elisha to Mary Stiwinter	4-23-1832	John Hall,Clk.
Thomas,Elijah to Sally N.Lee	8-19-1834	John Tatham,Clk.
Thomas,Joseph to Elizabeth Brown	1-25-1838	W.B.Morgan,J.P.
Thomas,James to Cyntha Kerby	3-25-1839	John Hall,Clk.
Thomas,Elisha to Polly Lee	8-23-1839	S.M.Dowdle,J.P.
Thomas,Charley to Eliza A.Smith	2-24-1845	J.K.Gray,D.Clk.
Thomas,Wm.G.to E.J.Baker	8-16-1865	R.C.Slagle,Reg.
Thomas,Dock to Sarah E.Thomas	12-19-1869	E.T.Long,J.P.
Thomas,Jim to Sarah Penland	9-16-1861	William Sloan,Reg
Thomas,C.W.23 to R.A.Long,23	5- 9-1877	M.L.Kelly,J.P.
Thomas,J.W.35 to Sarah Thomas 24	12-21-1877	E.T.Long,J.P.
Thomas,Wm.N.O.19 to Flora E.Barker 22	8-26-1878	E.T.Long,J.P.
Thomas,W.G.38 to Laura E.Watts 24	10-24-1878	E.T.Long,J.P.

```
Thomas,William 26 to Mary Saunders 18          5-14-1887   R.S.Sanders,M.G.
Thomas,George N.38 to Julia McPhearson 37       12-1-1891   Robt.E.Lentz,M.G.
Thomas,Marcus P.22 to Laura A.Bingham 16        8-14-1894   J.H.Gillespie,M.G
Thomas,Samuel 24 to Liddie Kell 23              7-24-1902   D.P.Cabe,J.P.
Thomas,W.Henry 38 to Rado Patton 22    Col.     7-30-1905   Chas.Stewart,M.G.
Thomas,Eugene 23 to Ola Stewart 23     Col.     2- 3-1907   J.T.Kennedy,M.G.
Thomas,Benjamin 23 to Dona Thomas 18            2-17-1908   J.C.Shope,J.P.
Thomas,Joseph 25 to Mary Justice 19             3-10-1910   C.R.Cabe,J.P.
Thomas,Jno.L.26 to Kittie Hoglen 24             3-21-1911   Wm.P.Chedester,MG
Thomas,Marion 23 to Leona McClure 15            9-27-1911   Robert Stamey,J.P
Thomas,Loyd 22 to Addie Bronson 23     Col.     4- 1-1914   A.B.Morrow,M.G.
Thomas,Newman 22 to Iris Hodgin 18              6-13-1920   G.W.Moffitt,J.P.
Thomas,Lester 25 to Lelia Burston 16   Col.     9-16-1926   E.S.Wylie,M.G.
Thomas,Harry 24 to Della Byrd 23                9-23-1928   Geo.Carpenter,J.P
   Both from Bryson City,N.C.
Thomas,H.N.20 to Fanny Bradley 21               9- 1-1912   C.R.Cabe,J.P.
Thompson,Jas.A.to Nancy A.Battles               12-25-1847  J.K.Gray,D.Clk.
Thompson,Wm.A.to M.E.McCoy                      7-25-1859   R.C.Slagle,C.C.C.
Thompson,B.Y.to Mary Brendle                    2- 8-1860   R.C.Slagle,Clk.
Thompson,William to Mira Panther                9-11-1865   R.C.Slagle,Clk.
Thompson,William 23 to Sallie C.Angel 25        1- 4-1896   J.B.Elmore,J.P.
Thompson,Beauregard 35 to Florence Rice 23      11-28-1897  J.T.Wade,M.G.
Thompson,Sylvester 19 to Mary Long 19 Col.      7- 6-1899   J.M.Bristol,M.G.
Thompson,Wilford 23 to Alice Estes 17           1-25-1912   J.L.Kinsland,M.G.
Thompson,J.E.30 to Susie May 17                 3-20-1918   J.A.Braun,M.G.
Thompson,M.G.27 to Ethel Johnson 26             12-24-1918  J.R.Pendergras,MG
Thompson,Henry P.P.52 to Mrs.Helen L.Cleveland 32/12-29-1919=Jas.C.Mell.
Thompson,Theodore 35 to Maude Younce 21         8-31-1922   D.F.Howard,M.G.
Thompson,Lon C.26 to Grace Hooper 19            12-7-1924   J.M.Raby,J.P.
   She from Clayton,Ga.
Thompson,J.W.68 to Ada Mason 49                 3-16-1929   Geo.Carpenter,J.P
   He from Bryson City,N.C.
Thompson,Carl 24 to Anne Cagle 21               1- 2-1931   J.R.Pendergras,MG
   He from Clyde,N.C.... She from Sylva,N.C.
Thompson,Sylvester 54 to Kandas Bryson 55       2-18-1934   E.S.Wylie,M.G.
   She from Dillsboro,N.C.
Thomason,James  to Susanah Truitt               12-7-1832   John Hall,Clk.
Thomason,Levi to Sarah J.Davis                  10-15-1859  R.C.Slagle,Reg.
Thomason,Jacob L. to Nancy C.Davis              9-18-1870   William Sloan,Reg
Thomason,Claude L.50 to Nannie B.McConnell 43/12-25-1935-J.L.Teague,M.G.
Tippett,J.P.to Mary McGaha                      1-16-1858   R.C.Slagle,Reg.
Tippett,James F.to Hannah M.Raby                2- 6-1869   Meritt Rickman,MG
Tippett,H. to Louise Elmore                     3-19-1870   J.K.Bryson,Reg.
Tippett,Wm.Alfred 25 to Mrs.Lavada Reid 23      11-3-1895   John Elmore,J.P.
Tippett,A.L.28 to Mrs.Martha Jacobs 28          1- 1-1899   J.L.Franks,J.P.
Tippett,W.D.30 to Sarah L.Lowe 28               4-30-1876   P.R.McLean,M.G.
Tippett,Thomas C.22 to Brunetta Abernethey 22/2-4-1883  M.J.Mashburn,J.P.
Tippett,James F.22 to Martha L.Williams 23  9-29-1886  John Ammons,J.P.
```

```
Tippett,William 25 to Hattie Baldwin 21      1- 4-1903  Mark Deweese,J.P.
Tippett,J.A.21 to Mary Rhinehart 21          1- 2-1910  J.A.Lakey,J.P.
Tippett,Sam 24 to Belle Holland 19           3-20-1915  N.J.Jollay,J.P.
Tippett,W.C.23 to Mae Boyd 18                2-11-1917  J.L.Bryson,J.P.
Tippett,Walter 36 to Rosa B.Wilson 19        1-12-1922  J.R.Morrison,J.P.
Tippett,Buel 29 to Jennie Welch 19           12-24-1927 J.R.Pendergras,MG
Tippett,Walter 34 to Dessie West 21          6-18-1928  J.M.Raby,J.P.
Tippett,Claude R.21 to Haden Buchanan 18     12-17-1933 Lee Mason,J.P.
Tipton,Quincy A.,Jr.27 to Carrie Corpening 25/9-26-1889 W.H.Leith,M.G.
Tipton,William K.H.26 to Mary L.Siler 27     4- 2-1878  D.Atkins,M.G.
Tipton,W.W.21 to Mary Arrowood 18            11-18-1882 B.G.Wild,M.G.
Tieftyler,Chas.L.22 to Mary G.Smith 17       11-27-1891 John B.Gray,J.P.
Tilley,Lewis H.to Hannah Ford                3-25-1847  J.K.Gray,D.Clk.
Tilley,Benjamin to Cynthia Presley           2-20-1849  Thad.P.Siler,D.C.
Tilley,John W.to Louisa Johnson              3-14-1871  J.S.Woodard,M.G.
Tilley,C.S.27 to Carrie Roper 17             10-18-1914 T.F.Deitz.
Tilson,Abraham to Mary A.Franks              5- 1-1867  R.C.Slagle,Clk.
Tilson,John H.19 to Nancy C.Hurst 18         1-10-1875  E.H.Franks,J.P.
Tilson,J.C. 20 to L.H.Rogers 18              9-16-1880  D.L.Miller,M.G.
Tilson,J.Henry 19 to Zelphie Southards 21    10-17-1888 J.M.Keener,M.G.
Tilson,George W.21 to Sharlet Barnes 17      1- 5-1901  G.W.Matney,M.G.
Tilson,John T.22 to Violet Shook 22          9- 4-1904  I.T.Peek,M.G.
Tilson,Jacob F.24 to Laura Wood 18           11-22-1908 Z.P.Peek,J.P.
Tilson,D.Burt 20 to Jane Rogers 20           1- 2-1910  T.J.Vinson,M.G.
Tilson,James 40 to Betty Jane Woods 16       9- 2-1915  J.R.Pendergras,MG
Tilson,R.L.19 to Bessie Sutton 17            12-20-1919 Geo.Carpenter,J.P
Tilson,Lennie 24 to Bertha Rogers 23         12-2-1931  W.C.Wood,J.P.
Tilson,Glen A.20 to Pauline Houston 18       5-12-1935  W.P.Miller,J.P.
Tetherow,Alfred to Elizabeth Stillwell       2-29-1862  R.C.Slagle,Clk.
Totherow,John to Minerva Simons              7-30-1859  T.P.Siler,D.Clk.
Tetherow,Silas to M.V.Bird                   10-12-1865 H.H.Ray,J.P.
Totherow,Joshua to Martha Culbertson         5- 6-1870  J.K.Bryson,Reg.
Totherow,James J. to Sarah Roper             8-11-1870  James K.Bryson,Re
Totherow,William to Roxia Kilby              11-2-1871  William Sloan,Reg
Totherow,W.A.18 to Texie Gregory 19          8-28-1897  M.Ghormley,M.G.
Totherow,Alfred 19 to Mercilla Stephens 18   12-24-1902 D.F.Howard,M.G.
Totherow,Thomas 21 to Lassie Howard 21       1-19-1906  D.F.Howard,M.G.
Toomer,John V.29 to Annie Goodloe Deal 22    9-12-1910  J.A.Deal,M.G.
Townsend,J.C.22 to Laura L.Jacobs 19         7-30-1885 Original not found
Trammel,T.R. to Rebecca Pruett               2- 7-1845  J.K.Gray,D.Clk.
Trammel,I.V. to Mary Ann Morgan              11-1-1860  R.C.Slagle,Reg.
Trammel,William A.to Emaline Ray             4-19-1864  R.C.Slagle,Reg.
Trammell,Thomas 21 to Rebecca Calor 25       11-7-1875  J.M.Forrester,J.P
Travis,Theadore 24 to Alma A.Klein 19        7-31-1911  Wm.P.Chedester,MG
Traylor,Alex 52 to Hulda Sellers 34          5- 5-1897  R.B.Shelton,M.G.
Trentham,B.22 to Ida Raby 20                 1-22-1882  G.W.Dean,J.P.
Trotter,Alex 24 to Elizabeth Siler 24  Col. 11-18-1882 B.G.Wild,M.G.
```

```
Trotter,Irvin 21 to Texas Vanhook 17   Col.    4- 1-1894  James Bristol,M.G
Truitt,John W.to Frankey M.McGaha              11-19-1853 John Hall,C.C.C.
Truitt,John to Margaret Davis                  8-31-1866  R.C.Slagle,C.C.C.
Truitt,Siler M. to Dorotha I.Kilby             4- 3-1869  J.K.Bryson,Reg.
Truitt,Joshua H. to Martha A.McClure           11-20-1869 J.K.Bryson,Reg.
Truitt,M.S.22 to Georgia A.Dills 20            7- 6-1884  John S.Gibson,M.G
  He from Swain Co.,N.C.
Truitt,M.M.23 to Mrs.Ada Smith 25              8-31-1902  W.A.Solesbee,J.P.
Truitt,C.T.50 to Nannie B.Elmore 40            1- 1-1924  J.M.Woodard,M.G.
Turk,Clovis 32 to Clarica Eubanks 24           7-24-1935  J.A.Flanagan,M.G.
  He from Commerce,Ga..... She from Sales City,Ga.
Turner,John to Mary Queen                      11-8-1834  Joel Simons,J.P.
Turner,James to Sarah Brooks                   9-25-1847  Isam Franks,J.P.
Turner,R.M.G.35 to Mary G.Garland 21           7-28-1897  J.R.Pendergras,MG
Turner,Walter 38 to Lula Calloway 21           6- 5-1912  W.T.Thompson,M.G.
Turner,Walter 35 to Carrie Calloway            2- 1-1915  J.T.Houston,J.P.
Turner,John R.23 to Janett Dills 20            2-26-1938  L.L.Arnold,J.P.
  Both from Asheville,N.C.
Tyinger,Carl to Margaret H.Cunningham          7-30-1933  Will Smith,Ord.
Tyler,John T.22 to Lucinda J.Teems 22          10-2-1896  John B.Gray,J.P.
Tyler,Robert 20 to Minnie Key 19               3-28-1901  P.H.Justice,J.P.
Tyler,Jess 19 to Lizzie Crisp 18               12-25-1916 J.A.Brindle,M.G.
Ulanowsky,Paul 32 to Lucy Strom Trosdale 23 8- 3-1941  Geo.F.Taylor,M.G.
  He from New York,N.Y.... She from Savannah,Ga.
Uncel,George C.to Jane Seequire                9-14-1865  R.C.Slagle,Reg.
Underhill,John M.38 to Jura Palmer 31          7-15-1934  A.S.Solesbee,M.G.
  Both from Arden,N.C.
Underwood,William to Sarah M.Mathis            11-23-1852 Aaron Mathis,Wit.
Underwood,William J.to Manerva Lewis           11-12-1844 J.K.Gray,D.Clk.
Underwood,Lee 28 to Emmer Jennings 33 Col.     1-21-1924  L.Baird,J.P.
Underwood,William P.21 to Mary C.Pannell 16 8-19-1888  J.M.Keener,J.P.
Upton,Joseph  to Jane West                     2-19-1847  J.K.Gray,D.Clk.
Upton,John L.to Elizabeth Pilkerton            1-12-1848  J.K.Gray,D.Clk.
Upton,Andrew to Sarah J.Passmore               9-14-1869  R.C.Slagle,C.C.C.
Upton,Rufus 22 to Addie Shepherd 22    Col.    11-24-1887 W.J.Jenkins,J.P.
Upton,R.J. 50 to Lavada Mingus 50      Col.    5-16-1917  Edward Johnson,MG
Vance,Charlie 21 to Addie Smith 19             1- 7-1904  S.J.Ammons,J.P.
Valentine,Samuel 69 to Margaret Robins 21      12-23-1907 J.R.Pendergras,MG
Vandergriff,B.B.23 to Maggie Garrison 22       1- 5-1897  F.M.Morgan,M.G.
Vanhook,Mitchel to Ella Fulcher                10-27-1851 J.K.Gray,D.Clk.
Vanhook,A.C. to S.C.Russell                    9- 4-1856  J.G.Crawford.
Vanhook,A.M. to Melvina Horne                  1- 5-1860  R.C.Slagle,Reg.
Vanhook,Basil to Milly Carpenter       Col.    9- 9-1869  L.F.Siler,M.G.
Vanhook,John R.to Mary McClure                 12-28-1870 William Sloan,Reg
Vanhook,B.V. 55 to Lou Rogers 30       Col.    10-14-1880 E.H.Franks,J.P.
Vanhook,John 21 Elizabeth Cockram 23  Col.     8-11-1883  Jona.Phillips,J.P
Vanhook,Charles B.35 to Flora M.Patton 34      12-14-1892 W.G.Mallonee,M.G.
Vanhook,Henry 20 to Mollie Sanders 26          10-29-1893 J.J.McConnell,J.P
Vanhook,Edgar 29 to Lizzie Garland 23          12- 1-1897 R.B.Shelton,M.G.
```

```
Vanhook,Cary 38 to Mattie Higdon 25          2-28-1900  W.R.Rickman,M.G.
Vanhook,R.A.29 to Annie Bryson 24            11-5-1902  J.C.Postell,M.G.
Vanhook,Samuel 23 to Ida Stamey 18           12-23-1908 A.M.Ledford,M.G.
Vanhook,James 34 to Mrs.Naomi Dowdle 28      3-25-1914  J.L.Teague,M.G.
Vanhook,Charles Bun 25 to Addie Angel 24     4- 9-1914  W.G.Warren,M.G.
Vanhook,L.N.20 to Annie Justice 20           3- 7-1915  C.W.Ramey,J.P.
Vanhook,H.R.46 to Callie Jones 50            7-30-1919  Robert Stamey,J.P
Vanhook,Roy B.22 to Viola Justice 21         9-28-1919  M.L.Angel,J.P.
Vanhook,S.F.37 to Mrs.Effie Ramey 31         3- 8-1923  J.R.Pendergras,MG
Vanhook,Dee 24 to Lucille Blaine 18          8- 5-1933  A.A.Angel,M.G.
Vaughn,Archibald to Eller Kerby              2-23-1830  John D.Carne.
Vaughn,Mont to Ruth Mallonee                 12-24-1861 Henry Raby.
Vaughn,Lacy 55 to Margaret Roper (widow)40   1- 9-1873  Thos.Mashburn,J.P
Vaughn,Josiah 27 to May Houston 27           11-21-1873 J.D.Vinson,M.G.
Vaughn,A.A.,Rev.36 to Minnie Holden 21 Col.  4-10-1901  Original not found
Vaughn,H.W.38 to Lou Mass 39                 10-3-1915  W.G.Wood,J.P.
Vinson,B.L.18 to L.L.Green 16                10-28-1877 J.W.Wilson,J.P.
Vinson,Thomas J.22 to Mary C.Teague 21       3-14-1878  J.W.Wilson,J.P.
Vinson,J.J.30 to Harriet Hicks 23            12-26-1882 L.Howard,J.P.
Vinson,John R.18 to L.J.Vaughn 18            6-22-1884  D.L.Miller,M.G.
Vinson,George H.21 to Addie T.Miller 20      6-12-1888  Retd.not executed
Vinson,George H.21 to Laura J.McCall 15      11-14-1888 T.J.Vinson,J.P.
Vinson,Charles C.17 to Huldah R.Burrell 16   7-29-1894  T.J.Vinson,J.P.
Vinson,James D.35 to Mary E.Burrell 18       3-20-1898  T.J.Vinson,J.P.
Vinson,David 19 to Marinda Cabe 19           11-18-1900 A.W.Young,M.G.
Vinson,J.I.20 to Callie Peek 22              3-16-1902  J.D.Vinson,M.G.
Vinson,J.T.21 to L.B.Justice 22              2-22-1905  T.J.Vinson,M.G.
Vinson,T.Columbus 22 to Delia Scroggs 22     1-28-1906  J.D.Vinson,M.G.
Vinson,Spurgeon 22 to Sibbie Bryson 18       3-20-1910  D.L.Miller,M.G.
Vinson,Ben 24 to May Corbin 28               11-7-1912  R.P.McCracken,M.G
Vinson,John Baxter 21 to May Belle Conley 19/10-31-1913-H.O.Miller,M.G.
Waddell,James D.29 to Anna Wykle 15    Col.  9-14-1893  J.F.Houston,M.G.
Waldroop,William to Elizabeth McGaha         8-23-1835  John Tatham,Clk.
Waldroop,James to Nancy Rice                 1-15-1839  J.K.Gray,Clk.
Waldroop,Jacob to Mary Nichols               11-7-1846  J.K.Gray,Clk.
Waldroop,David to Hester A.Nichols           1-17-1852  T.P.Siler,D.Clk.
Waldroop,Joab M.to Polina H.Moffatt          12-10-1858 R.C.Slagle,Clk.
Waldroop,F.L. to Caroline Henry              9- 1-1862  R.C.Slagle,C.C.C.
Waldroop,Ambrose to Nancy West               9- 4-1864  J.R.Long,M.G.
Waldroop,Adolphus to Mary Southards          3-11-1866  W.H.Higdon,J.P.
Waldroop,Rickman to Rebecca B.Mason          11-4-1869  R.C.Slagle,Reg.
Waldroop,Alexander 17 to Roxanna Cline 20    9-22-1872  Thos.Mashburn,J.P
Waldroop,J.A.24 to Mary Truitt 27            2-19-1880  John D.Howard,J.P
Waldroop,A. 32 to Arty Lindsay 20            12-9-1880  M.J.Mashburn,J.P.
Waldroop,J.A.21 to M.L.C.Potts 19            9-22-1881  I.D.Wright,M.G.
Waldroop,T.S.30 to N.J.Allman 21             1- 5-1882  W.C.Carden,M.G.
Waldroop,L.C.30 to Mary E.Leach 21           11-24-1887 E.A.Sample,M.G.
```

```
Waldroop,Benjamin 23 to Annie O.Gribble 18      9-25-1889   I.D.Wright,M.G.
Waldroop,Gilbert 19 to Lilly Stogden 18         11-1-1889   Retd.not execute
Waldroop,Josiah A.32 to Sarah C.Potts 25        11-12-1890  C.D.Smith,M.G.
Waldroop,Gilbert 22 to Mrs.Della Frady 22       3-27-1894   J.B.Elmore,J.P.
Waldroop,Jesse 23 to Dora Dowell 23             6-21-1896   Joseph Morgan,J.
Waldroop,William H.46 to Mary Lyle 26           12-16-1896  D.F.Carver,M.G.
Waldroop,J.S.69 to Margaret Allman 35           2-13-1898   J.R.Pendergras,M
Waldroop,L.D.20 to Hattie Morrison 16           4-16-1898   J.A.Deal,M.G.
Waldroop,D.P.21 to M.L.Blain 21                 11-1-1899   E.B.Angel,J.P.
Waldroop,Lucious 22 to Mary Hicks 19            1-14-1900   D.F.Howard,M.G.
Waldroop,Henry E.25 to Pallie Gibson 21         6-18-1911   F.N.Johnson,J.P.
Waldroop,W.H.41 to Leola L.Stanfield 21         2-28-1912   J.L.Teague,M.G.
Waldroop,Arthur M.31 to Goldie Kiser 21         8-21-1912   G.M.Bulgin,J.P.
Waldroop,W.H.,Jr.26 to Florence McConnell 22/9- 4-1912 G.M.Bulgin,J.P.
Waldroop,Burnell 25 to Kate Wallace 22          1- 1-1914   Z.Baird,J.P.
Waldroop,R.P.23 to Hellen Henderson 22          3-28-1915   J.L.Teague,M.G.
Waldroop,J.S.23 to Bertha Nicholson 19          9- 5-1915   C.S.Slagle,J.P.
Waldroop,Grady 20 to Nannie Battles 17          8-25-1915   Dan Sweatman,J.P.
Waldroop,F.W.22 to Cordelia Reece 21            12-22-1915  R.H.Daugherty,M.C
Waldroop,Burt 24 to Retta Green 19              1- 2-1916   W.H.Roane,J.P.
Waldroop,B.G.25 to Laura Green 19               12-24-1916  W.H.Roane,J.P.
Waldroop,L.C.20 to Hattie Belle Kimsey 17       6-10-1918   John H.Crosby,M.C
Waldroop,J.S.20 Elizabeth Mashburn 22           12- 1-1918  W.H.Roane,J.P.
Waldroop,W.R.26 to Jennie L.Setser 24           1-29-1919   J.E.Womack,M.G.
Waldroop,Frank 21 to Ollie M.Dowell 28          6- 2-1923   J.K.Justice,M.G.
Waldroop,Charles A.27 to Kate Setser 24         10-1-1923   A.J.Smith,M.G.
Waldroop,Harley 19 to Lillie Anderson 17        11-1-1923   D.C.McCoy,M.G.
Waldroop,Harold 21 to Laura Jones 21            12-13-1924  E.J.Pipes,M.G.
Waldroop,W.J.25 to Elizabeth Anderson 21        6-15-1929   Robert F.Mock,M.G
Waldroop,Gilmer G.20 to Agnes B.Wallace 20      4-27-1937   E.J.Pipes,M.G.
Walker,Robert 20 to Mary Gray 17      Col.      3-10-1891   A.N.Norris,M.G.
Walker,W.T.57 to Janie McEachine 53             10-18-1922  J.Q.Wallace,M.G.
Wall,S.M. to Elander DeHart                     12-9-1865   Dallis DeHart,Wit
Wall,J.D.22 to Arie Donaldson 18                2-12-1905   S.S.Long,J.P.
Wall,John O.33 to Margaret Coyad ?              10-19-1940  Ivon L.Roberts,M.
Wallace,Jesse K.24 to Lou McDowell 25           4-18-1888   W.R.Barnett,M.G.
Wallace,Geo.O.22 to Lou Stallcup 18             1-10-1889   J.A.Deal,M.G.
Wallace,John 22 to Arizona Moffitt 22           6- 8-1918   J.R.Pendergras,MG
Wallace,Ernest 20 to Beatrice Green 19          9- 1-1918   J.R.Pendergras,MG
Wallace,Chas.Edwin 25 to Susan McClure 27       11-24-1938  J.A.Flanagan,M.G.
Waller,Fred C.35 to Nellie Munger 19            5-19-1934   Floyd Dendy,M.G.
Waller,Floyd 40 to Kitty Roberts 27             4-30-1938   L.L.Arnold,J.P.
Ward,G.C.44 to Mrs.Odelia Jones 36              6-26-1928   Geo.Carpenter,J.P.
  Both from Bryson City,N.C.
Warren,William 20 to Matilda Price 19           3-23-1881   Hosea Moses,J.P.
Warren,William P.41 to Mrs.L.Wittenberg 33      8-25-1919   J.G.Lawson,M.G.
Warren,H.H.18 to Zelpha C.Solesbee 19           11-25-1927  Geo.Carpenter,J.P.
  Both from Asheville,N.C.
```

Name	Date	Official
Wathen,Charles A.32 to Blanche Moore 25 He from Grayson,Ky.	7-29-1928	J.L.Teague,M.G.
Watkins,P.H.P. to Rebecah Phillips	3- 3-1835	John Tatham,Clk.
Watkins,J.J. to C.R.Dills	10-22-1860	R.C.Slagle,Reg.
Watkins,James M.to Jane B.Anderson	12-24-1867	E.W.Moore,M.G.
Watkins,William H.25 to M.J.Coggins 26	6-15-1876	P.P.McLean,M.G.
Watkins,P.T.25 to Sarah A.Burnett 19	3-21-1878	P.P.McLean,M.G.
Watkins,H.L.25 to N.A.Burnett 21	11-24-1881	C.Campbell,M.G.
Watkins,Evans 20 to Henretta Guy 21	9- 1-1882	S.W.Hill,J.P.
Watkins,John L.19 to Christy E.Green 16	2-17-1889	L.H.Garland,J.P.
Watkins,James B.20 to Mary E.Stancil 16	4-30-1889	John B.Gray,J.P.
Watkins,L.T.30 to A.Joanna Thomas 21	1- 6-1895	J.R.Pendergras,MG
Watkins,C.L.35 to Maranda Watkins 23	4- 9-1899	G.W.Stiwinter,J.P
Watkins,Silas 24 to Ollie Thomas 18	9-12-1907	J.R.Pendergras,MG
Watkins,R.W.28 to Emma Holland 18	2-16-1908	T.J.Vinson,M.G.
Watkins,Arthur 23 to Laura Garland 24	4-11-1909	T.J.Vinson,M.G.
Watkins,J.J.72 to Mary Curtis 65	6-23-1909	A.W.Jacobs,M.G.
Watkins,Elbert 22. to Lucy Briggs 20	12- 5-1909	J.A.Lakey,J.P.
Watkins,Frank 25 to Cora Howard 25	12-22-1910	J.T.Taylor,M.G.
Watkins,J.B.43 to Lula Neely 22	9-11-1913	W.T.Potts,M.G.
Watkins,W.L.24 to Myrtle Foster 15	2-22-1914	A.P.Foster,M.G.
Watkins,General 25 to Laura Dills 16	6- 7-1918	Noah L.Jollay,J.P.
Watson,James to Jane Moore	8-12-1834	John Tatham,Clk.
Watson,William to Lucinda McDowell	2-18-1836	Henry Johnson.
Watson,John H.to Lucinda Moss	10-22-1839	John Hall,Clk.
Watson,Eli G. to Sarah A.Henderson	10-14-1845	J.K.Gray,Clk.
Watson,Eli G. to Judah Sanders	9-13-1852	L.C.Hooper.
Watson,J.S. to Neomy L.Hyatt	8-29-1867	R.C.Slagle,Reg.
Watson,Henry W. to Isabella Vanhook	11-21-1869	M.Rickman,M.G.
Watson,James F.32 to Sallie L.Allen 22	6-21-1893	J.R.Pendergras,MG
Watson,E.B.27 to Ader Shepherd 20	10-9-1915	P.R.Rickman,M.G.
Watters,Samuel to Nelley Fouts	8-19-1834	John Tatham,Clk.
Waters,Michael J. to Rebecca Fouts	3-20-1838	John Hall,Clk.
Waters,John S. to Louisa Rowland	2-22-1872	Jesse Stepp,J.P.
Waters,J.J. 27 to M.J.Fouts 24	2-14-1878	Z.Barnes,J.P.
Waters,James I.23 to Mary A.Lewis 26	7-27-1884	David Prewit.
Waters,C.E. 30 to Lallie V.Garrison 22	1-22-1899	W.J.Evans,M.G.
Waters,Sam.J. 21 to Emma Cope 18	3-16-1907	D.A.Yonce,M.G.
Waters,Arthur 21 to Minnie Cowart 21	1- 7-1917	W.H.Carpenter,J.P
Waters,James 55 to Mrs.Dora Raby 45	8-17-1919	L.P.Roper,J.P.
Waters,Dewey 22 to Ethel Douthit 22	12-25-1929	Geo.Carpenter,J.P
Waters,Lawton 24 to Helen Owenby 20	11-3-1935	D.F.Howard,M.G.
Waters,Dwight 23 to Dorothy Yonce 18	12-4-1936	T.D.Denney,M.G.
Watts,Wallace to Elenor Moffett	9-25-1850	F.W.Bird.
Watts,D.M. to Ann Moffitt	9-12-1859	N.W.Yant.
Watts,William G. to Elizabeth Dills	1-20-1863	R.C.Slagle,Reg.
Watts,J.P.25 to Hester A.Waldroop 30	12-15-1874	Albert Siler,J.P

Watts,William W.46 to Adaline Carpenter 37	1-10-1878	W.H.Roane,J.P.
Watts,James T.20 to Mary E.Hodgins 16	2-28-1884	W.C.Kimsey,J.P.
Watts,A.B.18 to M.I.Stamey 15	1-29-1985	W.C.Kimsey,J.P.
Watts,F.W.23 to Dicey A.Carpenter 19	8-12-1886	L.H.Garland,J.P.
Watts,Adolphus B.38 to R.C.Jones 23	1- 5-1905	W.P.Allison,J.P.
Watts,Jake 27 to Allie Ledford 23	12-8-1912	A.M.Ledford,M.G.
Watts,J.B.27 to Emmer Parker 22	5- 2-1915	J.B.Stalcup,M.G.
Watts,William 34 to Josia Evitt 17	2-15-1917	P.C.Calloway,J.P.
Watts,Kyle 19 to Carmie Wilson 22	1-17-1933	Geo.Carpenter,J.P
Weatherman,Newton 18 to Louisa Lunsford 20	12-29-1878	Z.Barnes,J.P.
Weaver,William R. to Jane Waters	6-23-1852	M.S.Coggins.
Weaver,T.J. to Hester H.Trotter	5-16-1854	John Hall,Clk.
Weaver,James T.to Hester A.Trotter	5-10-1859	John Hall,Clk.
Weaver,John S. to Mary S.McDowell	1-20-1868	R.C.Slagle,C.C.C.
Weaver,James C.26 to Maggie Wells 19	11-2-1881	J.W.Robinson,M.G.
Weaver,C.P. 36 to Emma A.Jacobs 26 He from Buncombe Co.,N.C.	4- 2-1885	R.A.Owen,M.G.
Weaver,J.Marvin 25 to Minnie Gray 25	10-7-1903	A.W.Jacobs,M.G.
Webb,L.C. to Rhoda M.Ashe	10-16-1851	Thos.Mashburn,J.P.
Webb,James to Nancy Blackburn	12-16-1865	R.C.Slagle,Clk.
Webb,George 20 to J.Teague 15	6-24-1879	Henry Stewart,J.P.
Webb,Joseph 23 to Lou A.Sweatman 21	3-23-1882	S.W.Hill,J.P.
Webb,Hugh 21 to Caroline Cantler 15	8-13-1886	Original not found
Webb,Andrew 21 to Louisa Webb 21	10-31-1888	M.I.Skinner,J.P.
Webb,Wm.Jr.21 to Nancy L.McCall 16	1-19-1896	H.Stewart,J.P.
Webb,John 27 to N.A.Johnson 25	8-13-1898	T.N.Ford,M.G.
Webb,James 21 to Jane Loudermilk 16	3- 7-1900	J.A.Young,J.P.
Webb,Joseph 23 to Ella Webb 19	12-24-1905	I.Crunkleton,J.P.
Webb,Andrew 21 to Bashie McCall 18	4- 8-1906	H.Stewart,Jr.J.P.
Webb,George 31 to Lou Hicks 21	11-5-1908	I.H.Crunkleton,JP
Webb,James 29 to Arie Addington 23 Col.	6-26-1909	J.W.Elliott,M.G.
Webb,Harrison 22 to Fannie Russell 20	7-21-1911	J.M.Keener,J.P.
Webb,William 21 to Polly Watkins 17	3- 3-1912	E.P.Brown,J.P.
Webb,Tom 21 to Bertha Watkins 16	10-27-1912	I.T.Peek,M.G.
Webb,Joseph 29 to Gertrude Vinson 18	3-23-1913	P.C.Calloway,J.P.
Webb,Robert 27 to Edie McCall 18	6-18-1913	P.C.Calloway,J.P.
Webb,George 18 to Elsie Webb 18	8-31-1915	J.T.Houston,J.P.
Webb,John 45 to Altha Chapman 21	3- 3-1918	P.C.Calloway,J.P.
Webb,Ben,Jr.20 to Essie McCall 19	8-29-1919	Jesse Ballew,J.P.
Webb,McKinley 22 to Nettie M.Keener 15	6-20-1920	Retd.not executed
Webb,Joseph,Jr.21 to Minnie Webb 16	6- 9-1921	McKinley Webb,J.P.
Webber,Charles 37 to Mrs.Tinnie Bateman 33	3- 6-1913	D.A.Yonce,M.G.
Webster,James to Drusy Fox	3-31-1831	John Hall,Clk.
Welch,John to Mary Ann Jarrett	3-18-1832	Wm.McConnell.
Welch,Thomas to Sally Brown	3-21-1833	W.H.Thomas.
Welch,Jacob D.to Elizabeth Colvard	10-12-1833	John Tatham,Clk.
Welch,Thomas J.to Esther Tabor	3-26-1834	Alfred Truit.

Welch,Russell to Fanny Morgan	10-17-1835	John Tatham,Clk.
Welch,A.B.to Sarah Sawyers	1-18-1847	J.K.Gray,Clk.
Welch,Wilburn to Parrilla Shepherd	10-23-1847	William Drinnon.
Welch,Joseph,Jr. to Nancy Sawer	8-28-1859	A.B.Welch.
Welch,N.T. to D.A.Lakey	9-24-1861	R.C.Slagle,Clk.
Welch,E.M. to Caroline Panther	12-20-1865	W.H.Roane.
Welch,W.A. to Mira C.Ingram	8- 5-1870	R.C.Slagle,D.Reg.
Welch,John M. to Margaret M.Battle	10-23-1870	T.P.Sawyers,M.G.
Welch,Manson E.to Amanda J.Wilson	4-16-1871	P.C.Wild,J.P.
Welch,J.L. 21 to Amanda Dean 19	12-11-1878	P.P.McLean,M.G.
Welch,A.B. 17 to M.E.Justice 19 He from Swain Co.,N.C.	7-25-1880	J.S.Woodard,M.G.
Welch,F.C.20 to Lucy Dowell 17	9- 9-1880	J.S.Woodard,M.G.
Welch,John T.21 to Jane Arrowood 20	12-25-1881	J.D.Vinson,M.G.
Welch,J.C.19 to Lizzie Chastine 19	12-31-1882	John G.Gipson,J.P
Welch,J.L.27 to Sallie Canler 16	6- 9-1886	D.A.Yonce,J.P.
Welch,J.D.19 to Lucindy Deweese 18	1-25-1888	P.C.Wild,J.P.
Welch,Albert L.21 to Rebecca Shelton 20	1-23-1889	P.C.Wild,J.P.
Welch,Joseph W.19 to Alvie R.Queen 18	9- 8-1889	W.J.Jenkins,J.P.
Welch,Wm.Henry 19 to Luthenie Jones 19	4-21-1892	J.A.Morrison,J.P.
Welch,William 21 to Margaret Grant 21	3-23-1898	M.L.Rickman,J.P.
Welch,Andrew 22 to Bell Bradley 19	7-15-1900	J.B.Elmore,J.P.
Welch,W.E.27 to Alice Kimsey 16	4-27-1902	J.E.Norton,M.G.
Welch,A.J.20 to Lula Holbrooks 18	5-15-1902	J.R.Pendergras,MG
Welch,Dock 24 to Cordie Houston 20	12-31-1905	Jos.L.Fouts,J.P.
Welch,Lon 42 to Hester Raby 32	12-1-1907	W.J.Morgan,J.P.
Welch,Charles 21 to Pearl Baldwin 18	2-23-1908	Jos.L.Fouts,J.P.
Welch,Floyd 22 to Annie Ray 21	7- 3-1912	J.L.Yonce,M.G.
Welch,Austin 21 to Pearl Morgan 22	6-29-1913	J.A.Morrison,J.P.
Welch,Ell 26 to Lucilla Barnard 20	11-8-1914	J.L.Yonce,M.G.
Welch,Oscar 26 to Lillie Daves 20	11-12-1916	A.S.Solesbee,M.G.
Welch,Ed 27 to Myrtle Brendle 21	11- 8-1918	J.L.Fouts,J.P.
Welch,Robert 30 to Etta Buchanan 19	2-17-1923	J.L.Fouts,J.P.
Welch,Ralph W.21 to Ethel J.Teague 18	12-29-1926	J.R.Pendergras,MG
Welch,W.Furman 22 to Ethel A.Roper 18	8-13-1927	J.R.Pendergras,MG
Welch,Wade 21 to Eula Moore 21 She from Rabun Gap,Ga.	4-13-1929	J.R.Pendergras,MG
Wells,W.F. to M.J.Robinson	5-11-1857	J.L.Robinson.
Wells,Major 21 to Margaret Angel --- Col.	11-24-1880	E.H.Franks,J.P.
Wells,Shade 28 to Lola Bryson 20 Col.	6-22-1908	A.B.Padgett,M.G.
Wells,Carl B.46 to Margaret Fox 29	12-8-1938	J.I.Vinson,M.G.
West,Daniel to Malinda Shepherd	9-26-1833	John Hall,Clk.
West,Thomas to Mary Guire	1-14-1835	Wm.Guyer.
West,John to Elizabeth Gross	12-3-1838	George Parson.
West,Isaac to May Smith	-- --1843	J.K.Gray,Clk.
West,Leonard to Manervia Wood	5-15-1846	J.K.Gray,Clk.
West,Thomas to Mila Hicks	12-31-1846	Leonard Jones.
West,E.H.to Dorchester Medlock	5-30-1857	John Hall,Clk.

West,Isaac to Martha Henry	2-25-1858	T.P.Siler,
West,William to Matilda Mitchell	2-20-1861	T.P.Siler.
West,J.W.24 to K.M.Burnett 18	8-16-1877	P.P.McLean,M.G.
West,J.C.23 to Ada Sellers 20	3- 7-1878	P.P.McLean,M.G.
West,Jess L.22 to Pallie Parrish 19	7-16-1885	P.P.McLean,M.G.
West,Wm.J.25 to Lula E.Amburn 19	1- 3-1889	W.J.Jenkins,J.P.
West,Leon H.22 to Callie Brown 16	2-13-1889	W.J.Jenkins,J.P.
West,James F.G.20 to Iowa Welch 18	7- 3-1892	W.J.Jenkins,J.P.
West,Wm.Posey 48 to Sarah E.Cloer 36	12-6-1894	M.B.Setser,J.P.
West,J.F.24 to Minnie Poindexter 20	11-17-1901	M.L.Kelly,J.P.
West,E.L.24 to Mattie Rhinehart 19	12-25-1907	W.L.Bradley,M.G.
West,Leon 39 to Zadia Willis 26	5-22-1908	H.J.Hogue,M.G.
West,Ben S.25 to Viola Edwards 21	4-23-1910	W.L.Bradley,M.G.
West,A.J.24 to Olive Womack 19	11-20-1910	J.R.Pendergras,MG
West,H.P.20 to Dorothy Stalcup 19	10-12-1917	Geo.Carpenter,J.P
West,Frad 26 to Daisy Mingus 21 Col.	1- 3-1918	Edward J.McKay,MG
West,C.N.27 to Minnie Hyatt 19	7- 7-1918	J.C.Umberger,M.G.
West,J.C.64 to Ella Pickens 27	9- 8-1919	J.L.Bryson,J.P.
West,William E.19 to Mae Crisp 19	9-17-1921	J.R.Pendergras,MG
West,W.H.35 to Dessie Pickens 17	4- 9-1924	Geo.Carpenter,J.P
West,Henry D.53 to Elinor C.Cleavland 42	10-27-1935	J.E.Brown,M.G.
West,Adam 27 to Mrs.Daisy West 37 Col.	2- 3-1938	E.J.McKay,M.G.
West,Ben C.21 to Martha B.Duvall 19	7- 4-1938	W.G.Barker,J.P.
West,Ralph R.28 to Ruth Lenore Byrd 32 He from Bryson City,N.C.	12-20-1941	D.C.McCoy,M.G.
Whitaker,William to Jane Erwin	3-14-1831	John Hall,Clk.
Whitaker,Mac R.26 to Rannie G.Turner 24 He from Nantahala,N.C.... She from Covington,Ga.	10-4-1936	W.F.Beadle,M.G.
White,David to Elizabeth Deweese	10-30-1863	R.C.Slagle,Reg.
White,G.P.22 to Roseta Howard 20	1- 18-1885	L.H.Garland,J.P.
White,Ned 22 to Amanda J.Miller 20	12-4-1887	J.M.Keener,J.P.
White,Verlin 18 to Minnie Burgin 14	7-29-1906	D.F.Howard,M.G.
White,Charles R.30 to Ivalee Wilson 24	7- 4-1914	M.J.Mashburn,J.P.
Whitehead,Troy 25 to Edna Chambers 22 Both from Atlanta,Ga.	7-18-1927	J.R.Pendergras,MG
Whitehead,James N.32 to Nellie Nelson 24 He from Deleware City(No state given)	7- 2-1936	W.M.Burns,M.G.
Whiteside,William T.to M.A.Crisp	2-27-1860	R.C.Slagle,Reg.
Whitworth,Allen H.22 to Louise A.N.Watkins He from Seneca,S.C.	22/11-27-1938-	J.O.Nix,M.G.
Whitmire,Daniel to Nancy Zachary	3-17-1838	J.K.Gray,Clk.
Whitmire,Henry to Malinda Zachary	10-4-1842	Lon Zachary.
Whitmire,Bob 36 to Lillie McDonald 18 Col.	9-30-1895	Geo.T.Bryson,J.P.
Whitmire,Jacob B.24 to Martha J.Garland 16	2- 9-1896	J.M.Carpenter,J.P
Whitmire,R.B.39 to Anna Stewart 21 Col.	12-24-1897	W.C.Walton,M.G.
Whitner,John T.35 to Betty Guy 14	9-22-1889	M.I.Skinner,J.P.
Whittington,Edward L.23 to Hettie Raby 16	8-25-1926	E.J.Pipes,M.G.
Wigington,James 21 to Minnie Picklesimer 17/	12-14-1902	D.L.Miller,M.G.
Wiggins,Jason to Elizabeth Kirkland	8- 6-1840	John Hall,Clk.

Wiggins,Ellis 21 to Molly Green 18	11-19-1924	J.R.Pendergras,MG
Wiggins,John to Meriah Whitesidee	12-30-1867	J.S.Gibson,J.P.
Wiggins,Anderson C.43 to Josephine Owen 32	8-31-1887	J.H.Queen,M.G.
Wiggins,J.T.19 to Laura Kimsey 25	6-23-1901	Jas.N.McConnell,JP
Wike,Mathew to Jane Moss	9- 7-1834	Jesse R.Nowlen.
Wike,John to Margaret Monteath	12-25-1843	J.K.Gray,Clk.
Wike,John 22 to Hestle Rogers 18 Both from Whitter,N.C.	7- 6-1938	L.L.Arnold,J.P.
Wikel,William to Delila Mathis	1- 1-1835	----------
Wikle,Thomas to Jane Breedlove	5-10-1863	William Ammond,MG
Wikle,George 30 to Edy Carpenter 23 Col.	10-25-1874	D.W.Wells,M.G.
Wikle,John B.20 to Polly A.Beasley 17	1-23-1877	Thos.Mashburn,J.P.
Wikle,J.W.23 to Mary Walker 24 Col.	3-21-1897	E.B.Angel,J.P.
Wikle,N.C.23 to Jennie Jones 19	9-23-1897	F.M.Morgan,M.G.
Wikle,John R.25 to Bettie Jones 16	7-21-1898	F.M.Morgan,M.G.
Wikle,Samuel N.53 to Lucy J.Beasley 28	4- 5-1899	J.B.Cardon,J.P.
Wikle,W.H.26 to Sarah Beasley 18	4- 5-1902	Jno.E.Rickman,J.P
Wikle,William J.23 to Pearl Patton 18	9-27-1903	J.S.Woodard,M.G.
Wikle,Henry 27 to Lula Brooks 22 Col.	2- 6-1908	Chas.S.Stewart,MG
Wikle,Clifton T.26 to Ella Morgan 20	7- 6-1925	A.J.Smith,M.G.
Wilds,Barnett G.to Mary A.Bird	4-19-1849	M.B.Slagle.
Wilds,Alexander to Ceily Bird	3- 3-1855	A.Gregory,J.P.
Wilds,P.C. to Elizabeth Franks	2-25-1865	McLoud.
Wilds,J.M.to Rebecca Bryson	12- 6-1866	R.C.Slagle,C.C.C.
Wilds,L.F.20 to Fannie Jacobs 21	12-29-1880	W.C.Carden,M.G.
Wilds,J.Everett 18 to Laura Dean 19	2-12-1891	B.W.Justice,J.P.
Wilds,J.Henry 21 to Ellen Dean 22	3-10-1896	Jos.Morgan,J.P.
Wilds,S.B.21 to Omah Baldwin 18	3- 9-1902	Joseph L.Fouts,JP
Wilds,T.Lee 23 to Annie Gribble 20	1-15-1907	L.P.Bogle,M.G.
Wilds,Judson 20 to Delia Ray 16	5- 9-1907	Jacob Yonce,M.G.
Wilhide,R.William 27 to Francis Nolen 21 He from Andrews,N.C.	6-14-1931	J.C.Umberger,M.G.
Wilhide,C.G.23 to Elda Rowland 18	5- 4-1919	D.A.Yonce,M.G.
Wilhide,F.S.25 to Maude Rowland 20	5- 4-1919	D.A.Yonce,M.G.
Wilkins,John to Elizabeth Early	2- 8-1833	Jno.Dillingham.
Wilkeson,Isaac to Martha McDaniel	11-19-1838	J.K.Gray,Clk.
Wilks,James 19 to Malinda Reeves 17	3-28-1882	B.G.Wild,M.G.
Wilks,John E.25 to Jennie Deweese 18	2- 3-1898	Joe J.Edes,M.G.
Wilks,W.C.30 to Anna Campbell 26	5-18-1902	Joseph Fouts,J.P.
Wilks,Mack M.26 to Laura E.Willis 17	2-19-1907	Joseph Fouts,J.P.
Wilks,H.G.24 to Annie Bryant 16	12-22-1918	L.P.Roper,J.P.
Wilks,Lyman 22 to Sallie DeHart 18	6- 9-1921	J.J.Mann,J.P.
Williams,Benjamin K.to Nancy Gribble	1-22-1838	Gilbert Falls.
Williams,William to Elizabeth Lyra	10-4-1838	J.K.Gray,Clk.
Williams,Burdit E.to Mary Moore	1- 2-1844	Wibbis Guy.
Williams,J.E. to Eliza Ford	10-15-1844	N.H.Palmer.
Williams,J.K. to Mary Franks	2- 8-1860	R.C.Slagle,Reg.
Williams,Lewis D.to Martha Odum	8-18-1863	T.P.Siler,D.Clk.

```
Williams,V.A. to Mary Loudermilk             2- 4-1870  J.K.Bryson,Reg.
Williams,John A.27 to Martha S.Keener 19     12-13-1874 J.S.Woodard,M.G.
Williams,J.M.20 to Carrie A.Ridley 18        12-22-1878 W.W.Henry,J.P.
Williams,Jackson 25 to Loucinda Peek 17      5-20-1880  Hosea Moses,J.P.
Williams,P.B.24 to Mary L.Rogers 18          2-24-1881  Hosea Moses,J.P.
Williams,Thos.C.26 to Sarah C.Loudermilk 20/1- 1-1882  Hosea Moses,J.P.
Williams,Robert V.28 to Mary Barnard 21      12-14-1882 B.G.Wild,M.G.
Williams,James 34 to Hattie Stalcup 27       12-10-1895 J.T.Wade,M.G.
Williams,Frank 26 to Jane Angel 21           11-23-1898 John A.Deal,M.G.
Williams,John 33 to Margaret Ammons 28       5-17-1899  A.H.Sims,M.G.
Williams,John M.18 to Octa Browning 21       4- 4-1901  J.W.Ammons,J.P.
Williams,R.B.31 to Ruthie V.Young 19         8- 5-1902  J.W.Ammons,J.P.
Williams,John B.18 to Emma Williams 18       3-20-1904  W.H.Hasket,J.P.
Williams,Logan 23 to Fannie Young 24         12-24-1904 Retd.not executed
Williams,Joseph N.30 to Lillie Clark 21      2- 3-1906  J.M.Keener,M.G.
Williams,L.A.30 to Fannie Young 26           5- 3-1907  J.R.Pendergras,MG
Williams,Charlie 28 to Parlie McCoy 35       10-29-1908 C.L.Rickman,J.P.
Williams,L.M.27 to Mattie Holland 28         9-30-1909  J.M.Keener,M.G.
Williams,Eugene 38 to Daisy Love 18    Col. 1-14-1917  E.J.McKay,M.G.
Williams,Robert L.46 to Canvis Sorrels 35    4-22-1917  J.M.Corbin,J.P.
Williams,L.M.36 to Stella Wood 20            1- 1-1918  N.L.Jollay,J.P.
Williams,Charles A.26 to Edna H.Liner 18     4- 6-1928  A.S.Solesby,M.G.
Williams,Larrie R.18 to Mary Martin 17       6- 6-1933  J.R.Pendergras,MG
Williams,Wint 22 to Jennie Martin 17         9-24-1933  Geo.Carpenter,J.P
Williams,Victor L.38 to Mae Childs 36        7- 4-1938  L.L.Arnold,J.P.
   He from Locust Grove,Ga.... She from Jenkenburg,Ga.
Williams,Lester 20 to Jennie Nichols 19      12-8-1912  F.N.Johnston,J.P.
Williamson,Leander to Sarah Carpenter        7-20-1841  J.Robinson.
Williamson,Charles W.to Mary E.Bates         12-13-1871 J.H.Addington,J.P
Williamson,Benj.W.22 to Rhoda C.Strutton 19/12-26-1878 Albert Siler,J.P.
Williamson,David N.24 to Amanda E.Thomas 18/4-16-1888 S.A.Dickson,J.P.
Williamson,C.E.22 to Hattie L.Love 21        2-19-1902  W.A.Setser,J.P.
Williamson,F.B.25 to Mrs.R.A.Carpenter 21    12-3-1902  Robert Stamey,J.P.
Williamson,B.W.51 to Jennie Cloer 42         1-11-1903  J.W.Greenwood,J.P
Williamson,Jessie C.22 to Ethel C.Seay 18    4-11-1906  J.W.Greenwood,J.P
Williamson,Robert 23 to Mrs.Mattie Huscusson 25/8-7-1909-F.N.Johnson,J.P
Williamson,Geo.W.21 to Mamie Anderson 17     9-13-1914  C.S.Slagle,J.P.
Williamson,L.N.30 to Ester Cloer 21          12-22-1915 Robert Stamey,J.P
Williamson,John 27 to Almer Huscusson 16     10-10-1917 J.R.Pendergras,MG
Williamson,W.W.25 to Mattie Dills 17         6-27-1920  G.M.Johnson,J.P.
Williamson,James A.21 to Annie E.Blaine 21   8-31-1923  C.S.Slagle,J.P.
Williamson,Omer 22 to Irene Dyer 15          1-22-1925  J.R.Pendergras,MG
Williamson,Elmer 21 to Margie Bowers 19      2-26-1939  Robert Stamey,J.P
Willis,William E.,Jr.27 to Sarah E.Dowdle 23/6-18-1938 J.E.Abernathy,M.G
Willis,Robert to J.C.Carson                  9-27-1860  R.C.Slagle,Reg.
Willis,R.A. to Cathrene Fouts                11-24-1865 R.C.Slagle,Clk.
Willis,Jasper 22 to Mary A.Tallent 20        8-13-1873  C.Campbell,M.G.
```

```
Willis,Montavale A.19 to Margaret E.Reeves 20/10-11-1874-Thos.Mashburn,P
Willis,Charles W.18 to Rachel Wilkes 24      3- 2-1893  R.K.Wallace,J.P.
Willis,J.M.24 to Polina Hicks 23             6- 7-1903  W.A.Solesbee,J.P.
Willis,Geo.W.29 to Laura Tallent 20          6- 7-1903  Joseph L.Fouts,JP
Willis,Smith 65 to Lou Phillips 52           10-18-1903 D.F.Howard,M.G.
Willis,W.W.38 to Minnie Frady 33             1-11-1914  W.E.Welch,J.P.
Willis,Drue 25 to Annie Rowland 18           12-17-1914 J.R.Pendergras,MG
Willis,W.L.19 to Irene Tallent 15            3- 4-1917  J.L.Fouts,J.P.
Willis,F.H.25 to Cannie Morgan 25            10-7-1917  J.L.Fouts,J.P.
Willis,D.S.28 to Lelia Esther Gray 26        9- 4-1919  A.W.Jacobs,M.G.
Willis,Charles H.21 to Mary E.Poindexter 20/2-19-1939  R.L.Poindexter,MG
Willson,Alex to Sarah Harper                 1-24-1835  John Tatham,Clk.
Wilson,Barnett to Elizabeth McDanniels       4- 6-1835  John Tatham,Clk.
Willson,John to Elizabeth Anderson           12-8-1838  Wm.Anderson.
Willson,Thompson to Mary Hooper              3-23-1840  John Hall,Clk.
Wilson,Alfred to Rebecca Shook               3-20-1844  J.K.Gray,Clk.
Wilson,Jackson L.to Josbels Lee              2- 3-1849  W.H.Roane,J.P.
Wilson,Harvey to Martha Ammons               3-20-1849  J.K.Gray,Clk.
Wilson,Manson to Zilpha B.Cockram            1-16-1850  T.P.Siler,D.Clk.
Wilson,Edward to Carolin Deweese             8-12-1850  J.K.Gray,Clk.
Wilson,Elijah to Mary Hawkins                5- 2-1856  John Hall,Clk.
Wilson,Wm.to Margaret Mashburn               10-3-1857  R.C.Slagle,C.C.C.
Wilson,Jeptha to Cyntha J.Mason              11-12-1857 T.P.Siler,D.Clk.
Wilson,William D.to Susa Hughes              8- 7-1858  R.C.Slagle,Clk.
Wilson,Thomas to Hetty Deweese               11-20-1858 T.P.Siler,D.Clk.
Wilson,William to Mary Pilkinton             11-10-1860 T.P.Siler,D.Clk.
Wilson,William to Sarah Mason                12- 7-1860 R.C.Slagle,Reg.
Wilson,A.M. to Elizabeth Brown               3-28-1861  W.Picklesimer,J.P
Wilson,J.W.to M.C.Brown                      1-21-1864  W.Picklesimer,J.P
Wilson,J.W. to M.C.Brown                     11-21-1864 No other record.
Wilson,Edward to Pally A.Dempsey             6- 7-1869  Merit Rickman,M.G
Wilson,Henry S.to Elizabeth A.Mason          10-25-1869 J.K.Bryson,Reg.
Wilson,Richard L.23 to Eliza M.Pace 16       10-16-1872 J.M.Forrister,J.P
Wilson,Thomas 20 to Judy Ann Ammons 22       4-13-1874  P.R.Rickman,M.G.
Wilson,Alfred H.34 to Harriet L.Bryson 22    12-31-1874 J.W.Bowman,M.G.
Wilson,James M.21 to Manda Buckner 18        9-21-1875  Thos.Mashburn,J.P
Wilson,T.B.20 to L.E.Painter 23              7- 6-1879  P.R.Rickman,M.G.
Wilson,T.J.23 to May Adams 18                9-22-1880  E.H.Franks,J.P.
Wilson,Anthony 20 to Sarah E.Gregory 18      1-19-1881  Hosea Moses,J.P.
Wilson,J.B.27 to M.E.Roper 16                12-7-1882  M.J.Mashburn,J.P.
Wilson,Marcus 21 to Pally Lunsford 18        12-30-1883 Z.Barnes,J.P.
Wilson,John W.20 to Elen Bryson 16           10-30-1888 J.W.Wilson,J.P.
Wilson,George W.18 to Emily Passmore 18       3-26-1889  W.C.Mason,M.G.
Wilson,James 35 to Sarah Jane Mason 18        9- 5-1889  J.M.Mashburn,J.P.
Wilson,John 20 to Anna E.Gibson 15           6-25-1891  John B.Gray,J.P.
Wilson,Silas C.21 to Mary M.McMahan 17       1-17-1892  W.C.Mason,M.G.
Wilson,Christopher C.22 to Annie H.Owenby 19/1-23-1892 S.J.May,J.P.
```

Wilson,James 58 to Vira Trotter 36 Col.	3- 7-1892	W.I.Kennedy,M.G.
Wilson,Henry M.C.G 22 to Emily Martin 15	1-29-1893	W.C.Mason,M.G.
Wilson,John E.20 to Martha A.Passmore 16	4- 9-1893	W.C.Mason,M.G.
Wilson,John 23 to Harriet R.Jones 28	5-18-1894	N.J.Rush,J.P.
Wilson,Coleman 21 to Pinkie Caler 21	1-30-1896	J.R.Pendergras,MG
Wilson,John 21 to Amanda Morgan 18	12-14-1899	S.J.May,J.P.
Wilson,J.P.18 to Celia Pittman 18	3-11-1900	J.B.Justice,J.P.
Wilson,C.G. 43 to Vinnie L.Higdon 22	11-20-1902	J.W.Briggs,M.G.
Wilson,T.G.27 to Lallie Ivester 22	1-15-1903	F.M.Morgan,M.G.
Wilson,J.H.26 to Lissie Haney 19	3-12-1904	D.F.Howard,M.G.
Wilson,Richard B.21 to L.B.Carver 21	6- 5-1904	G.P.White,J.P.
Wilson,Andrew 41 to Effie Carpenter 26	12-9-1908	S.S.Long,J.P.
Wilson,T.C.28 to Lena Cantrell 22	2-19-1911	W.I.Hughes,M.G.
Wilson,Bart 27 to Lelay Mize 22	2-15-1912	H.O.Miller,M.G.
Wilson,Mack 22 to Lover Chasteaine 16	11-24-1912	R.H.Munger,J.P.
Wilson,Asbury 22 to Janie Gibson 22	1-15-1913	Geo.Carpenter,J.P
Wilson,Barnet 23 to Mebb Hicks 23	9-14-1913	W.T.Potts,M.G.
Wilson,H.A.62 to Mrs.Mattie Campbell 60	3- 5-1914	Frank T.Gettis,JP
Wilson,G.W.46 to Lizzie Morgan 28	9- 5-1916	W.C.Mason,J.P.
Wilson,Charles 21 to Maggie Higdon 14	12-3-1916	L.J.Young,M.G.
Wilson,B.E.44 to Myra Brendle 30	12-27-1916	F.O.Dryman,M.G.
Wilson,H.A.67 to Addie Forrester 50	7- 6-1918	J.W.Duvall,J.P.
Wilson,George 24 to Lula Henry 24	4-25-1920	W.T.Potts,M.G.
Wilson,Charlie 22 to Viola Sawyer 21	8- 7-1922	D.F.Howard,M.G.
Wilson,Henry 36 to Amanda Sanders 21 Both from Nantahala,N.C.	1-23-1934	P.H.Passmore,M.G.
Wilson,John E.61 to Bertie Conley 50 He from Nantahala,N.C.	4- 2-1934	Geo.Carpenter,J.P
Winfrey,Isaac McLean 24 to Cora Neal 18	12-23-1906	D.F.Howard,M.G.
Winfrey,Rand 23 to Hester Rowland 19	2-18-1912	A.S.Solesbee,M.G.
Winstead,James T.to Margaret Jacobs	2- 5-1862	R.C.Slagle,C.C.C.
Winstead,John to Elizabeth Tallent	2-20-1865	R.C.Slagle,C.C.C.
Winstead,Thaddius P.21 to Eugenia E.Fulcher	26/5-18-1886-	J.M.Carpenter,JP
Winstead,Henry A.20 to Mary E.Lee 18	1-27-1889	W.C.Kimzey,J.P.
Winstead,J.L.24 to M.E.Jones 19	4- 3-1897	J.M.Farmer,J.P.
Winstead,W.M.19 to Mary J.Patton 18	12-31-1899	C.W.Dowdle,J.P.
Winstead,Eugene 21 to Florence Key 19	11-28-1909	W.H.Roane,J.P.
Winstead,Thad 45 to Lue Dills 21	7-23-1911	Robert Stamey,J.P
Winstead,W.M.37 to Mary Young 23	4- 7-1918	W.C.Ledbetter,J.P
Winters,Z.D. to Rozena Rogers	10-29-1859	R.C.Slagle,Reg.
Wishon,Isam S.21 to Callie I.Baldwin 18	1-15-1888	M.J.Evans,J.P.
Wishon,S.G.21 to Mollie May 21	8- 9-1891	W.C.Mason,M.G.
Wishon,James 25 to Martha A.Campbell 28	11-14-1897	F.M.Morgan,M.G.
Wishon,Grover 19 to Lillian Morgan 18	7- 6-1913	D.A.Yonce,M.G.
Wishon,Gala 28 to Maud Wikle 24	9-10-1933	T.D.Denney,M.G.
Wishon,Verles 21 to Beulah Owenby 19	2-27-1936	Geo.Carpenter,J.P
Withers,Jonathan to Margaret Patterson	7-16-1836	John Tatham,Clk.
Witherow,J.J.to Sarah Ashe	10-1-1842	J.K.Gray,Clk.

Womack,Robert I.19 to Kate Hedden 18	12-22-1889	M.J.Skinner,J.P.
Womack,Anderson D.21 to Mollie J.Keener 19	12-27-1892	J.M.Keener,M.G.
Womack,Sile 27 to Ella Hughes 19	10-27-1901	M.L.Kelley,J.P.
Womack,R.T.21 to Nannie Johnson 21	3-26-1915	J.R.Pendergras,MG
Womack,J.O.33 to Sarah McIntyre 23	4-15-1917	J.B.Henry,M.G.
Womack,William G.21 to Ola B.Sprinkles 20	2-17-1918	W.W.Marr,M.G.
Wood,William to Elizabeth Arwood	9-18-1843	J.K.Gray,Clk.
Wood,Erwin to Elizabeth Jennings	7-15-1852	I.N.Keener.
Wood,John to Nancy Battle	11-3-1859	E.Collins,J.P.
Woods,R.A.to Francis Drake	9-12-1860	R.C.Slagle,
Wood,T.N. to Sarah Husten	1-16-1861	R.C.Slagle,Clk.
Wood,A.G.19 to V.E.Holland 18	10-4-1877	J.M.Keener,J.P.
Wood,Henry T.21 to Sarah M.Dockery 16	10-3-1886	Z.Barnes,J.P.
Wood,Thomas 26 to Viney Shook 17	11-20-1886	J.M.Keener,J.P.
Wood,John T.23 to Sophronia C.Keener 16	9-15-1887	M.B.Dockery,J.P.
Wood,S.M. 21 to Naomi T.Allison 16	11-27-1888	J.E.Morgan,M.G.
Wood,Osburn 22 to Dicie J.Holland 19	12-28-1889	J.M.Keener,M.G.
Wood,James E.33 to Arie McConnell 28	11-23-1890	J.M.Keener,M.G.
Wood,James T.23 to Mary J.Houston 23	5- 7-1891	Not given on orig
Wood,Newton A.24 to Jane Brown 15	12-22-1892	J.M.Keener,M.G.
Wood,Thomas N.22 to Nancy E.Neal 18	1-10-1895	M.Ghormley,M.G.
Wood,Andrew J.20 to Sarah L.McDowell 16	1-19-1896	Thos.M.Slagle,J.P
Woods,G.W.45 to Margaret A.Woods 32	2- 9-1897	J.M.Keener,J.P.
Wood,Charles 19 to Rosa Grant 17	7-31-1898	H.H.Dills,J.P.
Woods,Jabe 22 to Louise Houston 20	9- 3-1903	T.J.Vinson,M.G.
Wood,C.E.28 to Ella M.Lord 17	9- 2-1906	S.J.May,J.P.
Wood,A.G.46 to Lizie Rogers 17	12-1-1907	G.W.Stiwinter,J.P
Wood,Loyed 18 to Elma Dills 17	10-24-1911	T.J.Vinson,M.G.
Woods,Leanord 19 to Ada Barnes 18	7-14-1912	Z.I.Peek,J.P.
Wood,Jess 36 to Alice Franks 20	12-21-1913	A.B.Miller,M.G.
Woods,Arthur 21 to Georgie Hughes 18	4- 5-1914	J.A.Brawner,M.G.
Wood,Fred 21 to Manilla Crisp 18	4-17-1919	J.M.Keener,M.G.
Woods,R.A.20 to Bertha Griffin 18	1-30-1920	Geo.Carpenter,J.P
Wood,Alfred W.32 to Mary Moore 20 He from Sylva,N.C.	7- 3-1925	Geo.Carpenter,J.P
Wood,Fred B.30 to Sarah Adams 31 Both from Gainesville,Ga.	8- 5-1934	Chas.McCarthy,M.G
Wood,Obey 29 to Myrtle Crisp 23 He from Whittier,N.C.... She from Bryson City,N.C.	2-12-1937	Geo.Carpenter,J.P
Wood,Erastus 21 to Estell Morgan 18	7-16-1938	Geo.Carpenter,J.P
Woodall,C.A.60 to Dolery Talley 43	8- 4-1914	Z.Baird,J.P.
Woodall,James A.24 to Gracie C.Woodall 17	1- 9-1921	J.M.Keener,M.G.
Woodard,Samuel F. to Martha C.Franks	9-17-1868	R.C.Slagle,Reg.
Woodard,J.C. 23 to S.E.Lakey 21	3- 5-1876	Thos.Mashburn,J.P
Woodard,James R.23 to Nora Morgan 16	9- 3-1900	J.B.Justice,J.P.
Woodard,J.C.64 to Louis A.Blanton 28	1-30-1917	W.L.Bradley,M.G.
Woodard,L.D.26 to Ella Fair Calloway 15	6- 9-1921	S.H.Hillard,M.G.
Woodard,Caleb 20 to Vinnie Rogers 19	4- 7-1924	Z.Baird,J.P.

Woodard,Wm.A.37 to Bertha L.Hyatt 22	1-27-1927	J.M.Raby,J.P.
Woodard,Wm.R.23 to Nina M.Brooks 19	6- 6-1938	Lester Arnold,J.P
Woodberry,Urban 31 to Addie A.Roper 28	10-25-1905	S.J.May,J.P.
Woodfin,Samuel to Rebecca Beck	6-23-1831	N.B.Hyatt,Clk.
Woodring,Absolon to Polly Hooper	7-15-1847	J.K.Gray,Clk.
Woodward,William to Stacy Sanders	3-20-1842	Wm.Williams.
Woodward,John S.to M.M.Bailey	2- 5-1861	L.F.Siler,J.P.
Woodward,William B.25 to Jennie Bradley 16	11-1-1903	John Burnett,J.P.
Woodward,J.T.66 to Mrs.Mattie Jones 40	3-18-1905	James M.Corbin,JP
Woody,C.B.23 to R.R.Duvall 21	11-10-1879	Joseph Morgan,J.P
Woody,Thos.N.24 to Lizzie Lunsford 17	10-12-1897	T.H.Wood,J.P.
Woody,Henry 19 to Sarah Lunsford 16	11-18-1900	E.M.Evans,J.P.
Woody,Norman 26 to Daisey Solesbee 18	11-26-1916	Frank T.Gettis,JP
Woody,G.C.32 to Allie Yonce 20	3- 4-1918	J.L.Yonce,M.G.
Wooten,John E.20 to Laura A.Cabe 22	9-11-1890	J.B.Elmore,J.P.
Wooten,A.W.20 to Cora Mashburn 22	1- 8-1899	T.R.Arnold,J.P.
Wooten,Frank 23 to Dora Bell Angel 26	8- 6-1912	J.R.Pendergras,MG
Wooten,Charlie 19 to Ruth Brown 18	9-21-1827?	J.H.Strickland,MG
Worley,Jessie L.19 to Fannie Stewman 16	9-30-1897	W.A.Peek,J.P.
Worley,Jess 46 to Mabell Womack 32	6-13-1926	J.W.Baty,M.G.
Wright,Alford to Polly Stewart	5-21-1836	Ulrich Keener,Clk
Wright,James to Ninna Norton	3-12-1845	J.K.Gray,Clk.
Wright,Robert H.to Ruth E.Peake	2-17-1851	T.C.Siler,D.Clk.
Wright,Benjamin to Mary Ann Moore	6-30-1860	R.C.Slagle,Reg.
Wright,Richard to Mariah Stillwell	11-27-1870	A.A.Justice,M.G.
Wright,Aaron A.25 to Dulcina Waters 17	12-17-1876	Mark May,M.G.
Wright,Marion 32 to Julia Bryson 22	2-17-1881	C.B.Fugate,M.G.
Wright,Elford S.18 to Theodocia Ledford 18	8-14-1885	John Reid,J.P.
Wright,Barak 40 to Maggie Phillips 34	1-18-1888	J.H.Weaver,M.G.
Wright,John M.20 to Sarah L.Bryson 26	1- 9-1891	T.J.Vinson,J.P.
Wright,Wm.M.36 to Caroline C.Conley 47	9-18-1891	Retd.not executed
Wright,C.N.30 to M.L.Edwards 27	10-28-1903	J.T.Wade,M.G.
Wright,E.E.26 to Carrie M.Jarrett 19	1- 1-1906	F.L.Townsend,M.G.
Wright,Charles N.38 to Hellen P.Cabe 18	12-7-1910	T.J.Vinson,M.G.
Wright,Frank 30 to Annie S.Reece 23	10-29-1913	M.H.Tuttle,M.G.
Wright,J.C.62 to Pearl Leach 40	8-12-1915	R.H.Daugherty,M.G
Wright,Richard 30 to Maggie Jones 18	10-12-1916	W.T.Truitt,M.G.
Wright,Aus.30 to Myrtle Rowland 20	5-15-1918	D.A.Yonce,M.G.
Wyant,J.T. to R.A.Plemmons	3-17-1865	R.C.Slagle,Reg.
Wykle,Jacob R.20 to Della Slagle 18	4-30-1921	J.R.Pendergras,MG
Wykle,Wymer 23 to Irene Chavers 18 Col.	6- 2-1923	E.S.Wyly,M.G.
Yonce,Leonard to Lucy Buckner	2-11-1843	J.K.Gray,Clk.
Yonce,David to Susannah Fouts	4- 1-1846	James Fouts.
Yonce,William to Sarah Barnes	12-10-1849	T.P.Siler,D.Clk.
Yonce,Elihu 22 to Catherine Lambart 19	1-16-1873	Jesse Stepp,J.P.
Yonce,D.A.22 to A.A.Daves 16	12-2-1877	Thos.Mashburn,J.P
Younce,C.A.22 to Susie Bateman 22	1- 2-1883	Mark May,M.G.

Younce,John R.21 to Mary A.Sullens 16	2-16-1886	A.A.Justice,M.G.
Yonce,A.J.22 to Sallie Evans 19	3-17-1887	M.Ghormley,M.G.
Yonce,Robert M.34 to Alice Solesbee 17	12-12-1890	S.J.May,J.P.
Younce,Jacob M.22 to Lillie Downs 17	12-22-1891	J.T.Berry,J.P.
Younce,Joseph T.22 to Albie Hall 23	12-7-1895	Original not found
Yonce,Marcus E.25 to Amanda Cansler 25	12-3-1896	W.M.Downs,J.P.
Yonce,George 21 to Lillie Cope 19	7-11-1903	A.H.Gregory,J.P.
Yonce,Charlie 21 to Gorda Roper 22	4- 8-1906	W.L.Bradley,M.G.
Yonce,George H.24 to Callie Solesbee 24	1- 9-1908	F.M.Morgan,M.G.
Yonce,R.D.21 to Alice Duvall 22	9- 1-1918	J.A.Brendle,M.G.
Yonce,Osborne 27 to Ida S.Willis 19	6- 2-1923	Z.Baird,J.P.
Younce,Granville 20 to Laura Duvall 22	2- 1-1926	J.R.Pendergras,MG
Younce,Arthur 35 to Eula Chastain 21	8- 8-1928	Geo.Carpenter,J.P
Younce,Gay 19 to Elda Roper 18	3-10-1935	Geo.W.Stepp,J.P.
Younce,Dennis D.27 to Ella Henry 22	2-13-1936	David F.Howard,MG
York,John to Alice Curtis	2- 8-1830	W.B.Hyatt.
York,Clarke to Eliza Poindexter Col.	10-3-1866	R.C.Slagle,C.C.C.
York,Charles 27 to Fannie I.Bates 25	1-16-1936	Geo.Carpenter,J.P
Young,John to Elizabeth Phillips	11-6-1833	John Tatham,Clk.
Young,Joseph to Mary Angel	3-18-1852	J.Ammons,M.G.
Young,Wm.G.to Ruth E.Moore	12-21-1859	R.C.Slagle,Reg.
Young,Joseph to Delpha Stanfield	3-30-1861	L.F.Siler.
Young,Lewis G.23 to Catherine F.Gray 22	2-25-1872	Jacob Hood,M.G.
Young,Pinkney R.30 to Sarah L.Arnold 25 He from Buncombe Co.N.C.	11-4-1873	M.Rickman,M.G.
Young,J.A.19 to R.A.Keener,17	1- 1-1880	Hosea Moses,J.P.
Young,John 30 to Rebecca Hurst 17	4- 9-1883	John Elmore,J.P.
Young,John W.24 to Margaret A.Young 16	2-17-1888	Hosea Moses,J.P.
Young,Leander J.26 to Florida B.Parker 18	12-12-1890	S.J.May,J.P.
Young,Jacob I.26 to S.V.Dills 17	12-23-1891	P.C.Wild,J.P.
Young,Samuel P.24 to Vivian A.Dills 19	8-16-1894	J.W.Parker,J.P.
Young,William 35 to M.J.Dowell 21	1- 9-1898	T.W.Angel,J.P.
Young,James G.30 to Hattie Shuler 19	8-13-1899	A.H.Sims,M.G.
Young,James L.22 to Sallie M.Long 19	2-18-1903	E.A.Sample,M.G.
Young,Alex 35 to Callie Price 17	8-23-1905	J.W.Ammons,J.P.
Young,J.W.28 to Maggie Liner 25	10-31-1906	R.M.Taylor,M.G.
Young,W.H.28 to Nancy Williams 35	4-22-1917	J.M.Corbin,J.P.
Young,Lee 28 to Minnie Winstead 27	2-25-1919	Virgil Ramey,M.G.
Young,W.T.21 to Pink Downs 22	4-29-1919	Geo.Carpenter,J.P
Young,Donald 24 to Nell Cunningham 20	12-12-1929	J.A.Flanagan,M.G.
Young,John H.25 to Barbara L.Eskrigge 26 Both from New Orleans,La.	9-·5-1930	A.S.Thomas,M.G.
Young,Leslie J.25 to Ruby H.Henry 19	8- 1-1933	William Henry,J.P
Young,John W.38 to Martha Gregory 26	4-30-1889	J.W.Parker,J.P.
Youngblood,George to Sarah Green	10-18-1836	Jas.Robinson.
Youngblood,Ransom D.to Rachel Jones	8-31-1840	John Hall,Clk.
Youngblood,James T.to Rachail Youngblood	5-18-1847	J.K.Gray,Clk.

```
Zachary,Alexander to Isabella Wilson        6-21-1834   Alex Wilson.
Zachery,A.W. to E.A.Bryson                  12-8-1861   R.C.Slagle,Reg.
Zachary,Hal 26 to Eleanor Va. Miller 25     9- 5-1913   J.R.Pendergras,JP
Zachary,Lyman 20 to Dora Chastain 21        4-29-1917   P.C.Calloway,J.P.
Zachary,E.H.32 to Nora Moss 18              7- 3-1920   D.M.Rogers,J.P.
Zachary,C.Ross 24 to Katherine Siler 23     5-15-1933   J.A.Flanagan,M.G.
Zoellner,Carl 30 to Nellie Reece Cabe 24    10-12-1920  James C.Mell,J.P.
Zoellner,Adolph 30 to Willia May Hall 20    4-27-1927   E.J.Pipes,M.G.
```

ANGEL, Cont'd.
   Sallie C. 136; Samuel
   5; Sarah 43; Sarah E.
   24; Squire 5; Stephen
   4; Susie Bell 119; T.A.
   4; Terrill 5; Thomas W.
   5; Thos. 5; T.M. 77;
   T.W. 119,151; T.W., Jr.
   5; Virginia 49; Walter
   M. 5; W.F. 5; William
   4(2); W.L. 5; Wm. 9,106;
   W.M. 75,101,110
ANSLY, James 5; Jane 5;
   Logan 5
ARNOLD, Annie 32; Elizabeth
   A. 118; Frank 5; Fred
   M. 5; Ishmal 5; James
   5; J.J. 29,76; J.M. 45;
   J.N. 19,53,61,106,112;
   John 5(3); Mrs. Julia
   120; Lester 59,74,83,95,
   97,117,150; Lester L.
   10,24,29,30,33,36,55,58,
   88,114; L.L. 129,135,138,
   140,145,146; Lucinda C.
   35; Nancy 16; Niza 106;
   Oscar 5; Sarah L. 151;
   Syndia 135; T.R. 3,10,
   40,50,59,75,78,84,135,
   150; William 5
ARROWOOD, Boyd 5; David 5;
   Humphrey P. 5; James 5;
   Jane 143; Mary 137
ARTHUR, James S. 5; Louise
   126; T.S. 5;
ARVEY, Belle 104; Eva 19;
   J.H. 5; Julia 102; Lola
   19; Mahota 36; Otto 5;
   W.C. 6
ARWOOD, Elizabeth 149
ASHE, Amos 6(2); Annie 132;
   B.M. 6; Charley 6; Cora
   76; D.H. 6; Elcana 6;
   Ella 24; Felix 6; Hilda
   62; Ida 78; I.J. 6;
   Jesse A. 6; Lon W. 6;
   Mahala 71; Mary 134;
   Mary Bell 92; Mary Belle
   84; M.E. 5; Minnie 16;
   Minnie G. 11; Mira 11;
   Opal 35; Rebecca 130;
   Rhoda M. 142; Robert T.
   6; Roxana P. 120; Ruby
   15; Sallie 46; Sarah
   148; Sarah J. 12; T.B.
   6
ATHINS, D. 64
ATKINS, D. 137; Daniel 22
ATKINSON, Jep. 6; R.E. 5,
   130; Robt. E. 49
ATTER, Elizabeth Ann 98
AUSBURN, Adeline 26
AUTLEY, Maude 42
AXLEY, Felix 70
AYERS, Crawford 6; Lee 6

BABCOCK, Clara 104
BAILEY, Dewey 6; Emily 34;
   Goldman 6; Haseltine 42;
   H.F. 6; H. Grady 6; J.K.
   6; J.T. 6; J.W. 6;
   Laura 85; Lola 101,108;
   Martha A. 6; M.M. 150;
   Sarah R. 28; Wade 6
BAIN, Edwin L. 57,114;
   Elizabeth 70
BAINES, W.S. 6
BAIRD, Adolphus E. 6;
   Aileen 32; Eva E. 33;
   Hannah R. 22; Laura Kate
   106; Z. 13,26,73,92,133,

BAIRD, Z., Cont'd.
   138,140,149,151; Zebulon
   6
BAKER, David 6; E.J. 135;
   John B. 6; Mary 6; Robert
   6
BALANGER, Alice 117
BALDWIN, Adelia 40; Alex-
   ander 6; Bass 6; Bessie
   69; Callie I. 148;
   Daisy 42; Elizabeth 3;
   Harley 6; Hattie 137;
   Hetta 72; James 6; John
   6; Joseph 6; Kittie 72;
   Lee 6; Lillie 62; Lyle
   6; Margaret V. 78; Maud
   8; Omah 145; Pearl 143;
   Sarah F. 46; W.E. 7;
   William 6
BALEW, Elizabeth 50; Jesse
   129
BALL, George C. 7
BALLARD, Marshall, Jr. 7;
   W.S. 20,29,36,88
BALLEW, Archileus 7; Bessie
   87; Bud 7; Carl W. 7;
   Charley 7; David 7(2);
   Elizabeth 49; Flora 15;
   Jesse 66,142; Jesse J.
   7; Jessie 29; L.B. 66;
   L.J. 7; Mary 131; Mary
   J. 15; Sarah M. 23; S.C.
   7; William 7
BALOO, Elizabeth 64
BALTON, Alonzo D. 7
BANKS, Cordelia 132; J.M.
   7
BARCLAY, Richard S. 7
BARKER, Alfred 6; Charlotte
   M. 123; Mrs. Eliza 26;
   Flora E. 135; Henry 6;
   Henry S. 6; Hessie 83;
   Jason 6; J.C. 6; Warren
   6; W.G. 22,26,35,59,144
BARNARD, Annie 116; Bell
   46; H. Lackstone 7; Ida
   L. 66; J.E. 7; Jean 89;
   J. Lee 7; Launa 107;
   Lucilla 143; Mary 146;
   Mary E. 40; Maud 15;
   Oliatta 118; William D.
   7; W.M. 7
BARNES, A.B. 49; Ada 149;
   Almina 59; Andrew J. 7;
   Anna 82; C.H. 7; Elihu
   7; Elizabeth 76; Eliza-
   beth C. 130; Floyd F. 7;
   Harvey 7; James M. 7;
   Janie 129; Jas. A. 7;
   Jas. M. 28,52; J.M. 7;
   Jno. T. 63; John 7;
   John H. 7; John T. 7;
   Joseph 7; Josephine 115;
   J.T. 6,35; L.J. 76; Man-
   son 7; Mary J. 79;
   Mary R. 90; Milton 7;
   M.L. 51; Nancy 82,117;
   Nancy A. 1; Nancy B. 47;
   Robert 7; Sarah 46,56,
   150; Sharlet 137; Thomas
   7; Viola 115; William L.
   7; Z. 7,8,18,21,25,28,
   38,41,44,49,51,53,54,57,
   71,75,76,77,79,80,82,83,
   86,98,101,103,110,111,
   116,126,128,134,141,142,
   147,149; Zebada 7
BARNETT, Cynthia 90; Hubert
   7; Joseph L. 7; W.B.
   82; W.R. 12,97,107,115,
   126,140
BARR, Augustus C. 7

BARRETT, George W. 7; John
   7; Thomas 7 .
BARRIER, Claudie 90
BARRINGTON, J.C. 7
BARTLETT, G.A. 5,10,22,35,
   47,49,60,66,69,75,104,
   113,124,128,134
BASCOM, Henry M. 7
   Louise R. 7
BATEMAN, Alex 8; Archibald
   8; Arch 7; Ben 8;
   Celia 34; Charles 8; Chas.
   L. 8; Mrs. Docia 111;
   Effie 6; George 8; Howard
   8; Jacob 8; John 8; J.W.
   8; Lassie 111; Leander
   8; Martha 23,108; Maud
   40; Oma 63; Rube 8; Ruben
   P. 8; Sallie 30; Susan
   110; Susie 150; Thomas D.
   8; Mrs. Tinnie 142
BATES, Mrs. Ada E. 19; Alice
   L. 23; Mrs. Allie 129;
   E.A. 131; Fannie I. 151;
   Flora 4; h.A. 8; Hannibal
   8; Harley A. 8; Henry C.
   8; H.H. 8; Ida L. 4; Jas.
   A. 8; J.G. 8,15,101,115;
   J.R. 8; Leona 125; Louiza
   26; Mary E. 146; Nancy
   C. 131; Napolean S. 8;
   Rebecca 131; Robert H.
   8; Robert W. 8; Robt. H.
   8; S.J. 13; S.M. 8; Viana
   57; W.B. 8; W.H. 22,82;
   William J. 8(2)
BATEY, J.W. 115; Mary 115;
   Sylvester C. 8
BATHUCK, Helen A. 65
BATTLE, Eliza 3(2); Mar-
   garet M. 143; Mary Jane
   11; Nancy 149
BATTLES, Annas 96; Annie
   128; Asoph 8; B.F. 8;
   C.A. 4,132; Carrie 128;
   C.S. 7,119,121; C.
   Swain 8; Cynthia A. 49;
   Ed 8; Elizabeth L. 125;
   Florence 128; G.W. 8;
   Harriet B. 125; James m.
   8; John W. 8(2); Mary 58;
   M.T. 8; Nancy A. 136;
   Nannie 140; Sarah 96;
   Susan C. 39; Willilam 8
BATY, Augustus 8; Henry 8;
   John S. 8; John W. 8;
   J.W. 8,14,32,48,124,129,
   134,150; L.A. 72; Mally
   32; Mary A. 32; Rachel
   27
BAXTER, Andrew 9; A. Owen
   9; Mary 71
BEACH, C.W. 9
BEADLE, W.F. 81,144
BEAL, Cora 134; Helen 129;
   James 9; James H. 9;
   Robert 9
BEAM, Jess R. 9 Mary 44
BEARDEN, W.W. 9
BEASLEY, Annie S. 49; Bell
   68; Dart 45; Geo. W. 9;
   Hattie 53; Jeremiah 9;
   Laura 131; Letty C. 84;
   Lucinda 110; Lucy J. 145;
   Mary 83; Mattie 47;
   Nancy 67,84,123; Nina M.
   56; Polly A. 145; Reubin
   9; R. Van 9; Sarah 79,
   145; S.J. 9; S.L. 123;
   William 9
BEATY, John E. 9
BEAVER, George 9; Gordon 9
   Perry 9

BECK, Mrs. Addie 38;
Clemie 103; Elva 108;
James 9; John 9(2);
J.H. 9; Lawrence 9;
Lexie 119; Loucinda 80,
102; Louisa 102; Lucinda
18; Rachel 119; Rebecca
150; Samuel 9; W.M. 9
BEDINGER, R.D. 22
BEECO, Bettex 9; C.C. 9;
Sallie 119
BEEDLE, W.T. 25
BEERDINE, George 9
BELK, Charles R., Jr. 9;
Hiawatha 9; Nancy 91,103;
Zelphan 86
BELL, Ada 8; A.W. 112; B.
50; Bertha 24; B.M. 49;
Charles W. 9; E.B. 15,
25; Fannie M. 6; James
A. 122; James W. 9; J.
K. 61; Joseph R. 9; Mar-
garet A. 103; Mary A.
131; Mary E. 17; Mrs.
Mattie B. 118; Myra J.
126; Nannie L. 40;
Pauline 107; Sam H. 9;
Sarah A. 88; Sarah B. 77
BELLE, Floy 73
BENA, L.M. 36
BENFIELD, A.A. 9; E.R. 88;
J.G. 16,24; J.L. 9;
John 9; Joseph 9; L.L.
4,22; Mary I. 43;
Nancy 22; Riffie 87;
Susan E. 43; Susan
Malinda 84; Temperance
123
BENNETT, Gay 134; J.G. 9;
J.M. 61,87,88,121,128,
131; Joseph L. 9; Louisa
38; Loyed 9; M.S. 9;
Salina E. 120
BENTLEY, Cynthia 83; Lou
128; Mary M. 26; M.R. 10
BERRONG, Gladis A. 54
BERRY, Alexander J. 10;
Alma 36; Catherine 2;
Demira 125; Fred 10;
Harriett M. 62; Jack 10;
John 9; John T. 28,65;
J.P. 10; J.R. 10; J.T.
19,34,50,91,151; Kansas
130; Laura J. 134; Mrs.
Lillie E. 102; Logan 10;
Logan A. 10; Lydia C. 36;
Margaret 62; Martha 5;
Mary Ann 88; Maude E.
62; Ruth 60,135; Tem-
perance 120; W.A. 10;
William H. 9;
BERTLETT, G.A. 10
BESHEARS, James 10; R.G.
10
BETTS, Jep. L. 10
BIDWELL, Beulah 126; Frank
E. 10
BILLINGSLEY, James 10
BILLINGSLY, Ester 135
BINGHAM, Bart. L. 10; Bill
10; Callie 70; Charles
10; Cicero L. 10; C.L.
10; Cordie 78; C. Oscar
10; Emma 27; Geo. N. 10;
Geo. N. Jr. 10; G.N. 10;
G.W. 10; J.F. 10; J.N.
10; John R. 10; J. Rick-
man 10; Laura A. 136;
Lawrence 10; Lena 72;
Lillie 44; Lyda 103;
M.A. 119; Maggie 73;
Martha 119; Mersella 99;

BINGHAM, Cont'd.
Monroe 10(2); Ola 11;
Raleigh 10; R.H. 10;
R.L. 10; Rufus 10; S.E.
10; Thomas 10; Thos. A.
10; W.A. 10; William A.
10; William L. 10; W.M.
10
BINKLEY, Bertha 67
BIRCHFIELD, David 10;
George 10; Seth 10
BIRD, Ada 76; Allie 58;
Benjamin 11; Benjamin A.
11; Bonner 10; Ceily
145; Clark 11; Clearcy
L. 109; C.T. 11; Eliza-
beth 40; Ella 22; Ellen
88; Felix W. 11; Flor-
ence 50; F.W. 141; Geo.
E. 11; Jennie 48; Jno.
C. 11; Johnathan 11;
John 11; John W. 11;
Joshua C. 11; J.S. 11;
J.W. 76; Laura K. 22;
Leona 63; Louella 18;
Louisa 19; Martha J.
63; Mary A. 145; Mary
E. 22,63; M.V. 137;
Nancy 24; R.M. 41;
Robert 11; Urena C. 22;
William L. 11; W.L. 36
BISHOP, Andrew 11; Cora
115; Eva 76; Jake 11;
Tisha 47
BLACK, LaDelle 92; Robert
11
BLACKBURN, E.A. 11; J.C.
11; J.P. 11; Levi A.
11; Louisa 88; Mary 39;
Mary A. 58; Millie 46;
Nancy 142; O.C. 11;
Polly 53
BLACKWELL, David 11; Frank
11; Margaret 109
BLAIN, Arthur 11; B.F. 11;
Damaris 72; Edwin L.
32; Elizabeth 43; James
11; John 11; Lawrence
11; Louella 17; Lydia
132; M.L. 140
BLAINE, A.M. 125; Annie E.
146; Belle 80; Bertha
88; Bessie 93; Blanche
C. 88; Callie 78; Caro-
line 29; Charles L. 11;
Charles T. 11; D.W. 11;
Ella 10; Florence 5;
Florence A. 78; Frankie
10; Jessie L. 4; J.W.
11; Lucille 139; Lula
10; Margaret J. 3; Maud
67 May Hattie 53; Paul
11; Phillip 11; Ruby 21;
Sallie B. 25; S.J. 7;
T.J. 11; William 11;
Wilson N. 11
BLAKELY, Mae 69
BLALOCK, Lester 11
BLANKENSHIP, Forest 11;
Helen K. 58
BLANTON, Louis A. 149
BLECKLEY, Charles 11;
Lela 82; Thomas 11
BLEUFORT, W.M. 11
BLOXHAM, Frank 49,69,80
BLUXHAM, Frank 110
BLY, Georgia 79; Nannie 53;
Mrs. Octie 58; Q.L. 11;
Robert 11; Rosa 83
BOGAL, L.P. 67,97; E.H.
14,50,56,58,83,92,119,
126,133; L.P. 2,21,31,
43,97,99,135,145

BOLICK, Carl 12; Eliza 17;
Gabriel 11; J.A. 12;
J.C. 12; Jno. 12; John
D. 12; Laverne 124; Lela
66; May P. 42; Perry 12;
Polly S. 30; Sidney R.
12
BOLINGER, William 12
BOLTON, Claude 12
BOMAN, J.W. 1
BONA, M.S. 79
BOND, J.A. 100
BOONE, L.A. 12,27,72
BORING, James 12
BOSTON, Eugene 12; Green
12; Henrietta 104; Jesse
12; Lee 12; Mack 12;
Martha 19; William 12
BOULTON, Spencer 12
BOWERS, Charles D. 12;
Charlie 12; Mrs. Ivey
S. 74; Margie 146; Rob-
ert 12
BOWMAN, Geo. S. 12; James
12; Jane 59; J.E. 12;
Jno. W. 4,82; John 12;
J.W. 16,20,40,61,62,147;
Nancy E. 72; Sudie 26
BOYD, Carolina 109; George
Thos. 12; H.T. 12; J.A.
12; James I. 12; Julius
12; Mae 137; Margaret
34; Martha B. 124; Mary
A. 79; Nancy E. 97; Sarah
M. 102; Sudie E. 89;
Thomas W. 12; W.H. 12
BOYNTON, Chas. L. 12
BRABSON, A.C. 12; Blanche
18; John M. 12
BRACKER, Abadiah 12
BRADBURN, Addie 105
BRADFORD, George W. 12
BRADLEY, Ada 29; Alexander
13; Andrew B. 13; Angie
38; A.S. 48; Avery 13;
Bell 143; Bethel 10;
Callie 105; Callie E.
24; Carolyn 114; C.E.
82; Charles T. 13; C.N.
13; Elizabeth 12; Ella
90; Ely Morris 12; E.R.
13; Everett 13; Fanny
136; Frad 13; George 12;
G.R. 13; Hattie 95; H.C.
45; H.E. 99; Henry J. 12;
Hillard 13; I.E. 13;
Ivy 2; J.A. 13; James
12; Jennie 150; J.H.
12,40; John H. 13,18,94;
John P. 13; Joseph N. 12;
Judd 13; Julia 20,125;
L.A. 99; Laura 26; Leila
13; Leobelle 51; Levada
Bell 79; L.M. 12; Lois
113; Lucy J. 56; Mack
13; Maggie 13; Maria 36;
Marthey 86; Martin 13;
Mary 19; Mary C. 99;
Mary M. 20; Maude 108;
Minnie 121; Minnie Bell
100; M.J. 91; M.L. 48,
123; M.M. 41; Nancy T.
121; N.C. 13; Nolita 26;
Palina 50; Pearl 56;
Pleasant 86; Polly 92;
Pleasant 86; Polly 92;
Ray 13; Rebecca A. 123;
Rebecca M. 122; Riley B.
13; Rosetta G. 99; Samuel
P. 13; Sarah R. 23; S.J.
13; S.P. 12; W.A. 34;
W.L. 3,5,13,19,20,21,22.

BRADLEY, W.L., Cont'd.
26,28,33,36,42-44,56,
57,59,67,68,76,80,81,83,
96,101,109,110,113,114,
118,125,129,133,144,149,
151: W.W. 13
BRADSHAW, Horace F. 13;
James 13; John 13(2);
Mirandaa R. 65; Robert
13
BRAGG, Jane 25
BRASELTON, J.B. 13
BRAUN, J.A. 136
BRAUNER, J.A. 134
BRAWLEY, Jane 97
BRAWNER, J.A. 12,50,149
BRAZEAL, Isabella 67
BREEDLOVE, B.W. 13; Elbert
13; Harley 13; Jane 145;
Jessie 13; John 13; J.
Patton 13; Mary 109;
R.E. 13; Robert 13; T.E.
13; Wiley 13
BRENDLE, Addie 120; Alex
J.H. 14; Alfred M. 13;
Anna 119; Bertha 14;
Bessie 9; Cansie 125;
Carrie 84; Charlotte 122;
C.J. 14; David W. 14;
D.F. 14; Dora 123;
Edmund H. 14; Effie 21;
Ellen 125; Eva 85; F.M.
14; George 14; Gertrude
78; Harman D. 14; Henry
13; H.L. 12; H.T. 14;
J.A. 8,19,22,23,29,47,
94,117,119,131,151; Jas.
H. 5; J.D. 13; Joe 14;
John 13,14; John A. 14;
John D. 14; John T. 14;
Joseph 13(2) Judian 69;
Jule R. 14; L.G. 14;
Mary 34,100,136; Mathew
M. 14; Minnie 26; M.T.
14; Myra 148; Myrtle 143;
Nannie 120; Novia 42;
Parcie 97; R.D. 14;
Rebecca 118; Rebecca J.
43; Rosa 14,119; Ruth
101; Sarah 111; William
14; William T. 14; W.T.
14(3)
BRIDGERS, Rupert C. 14
BRIGGS, Emily 120; John W.
71; J.W. 5,14,75,89,148;
Lucy 141; Mary M. 76;
Wm. Robert 14
BRIGHT, T. 101
BRINDLE, Harriett 47; J.L.
56; L. Hasseltine 59;
Sarah 62
BRINKLEY, D.A. 129; Mary
W. 122
BRINKLY, Lucinda F. 128
BRISTOL, Addie 121; James/
Jas. 9,15,25,26,76,81,
89,90,104,119,121,138;
James M. 14; Jas. M. 71;
Jim 29; J.M. 2,14,56,71,
81,96,104,136
BRITON, Lorata 109
BRITTON, Lawson 14; Thomas
U. 14
BROCK, Hazel E. 69; Sarah
78
BROCKER, Abadiah 16
BRONSON, Addie 136; Albert
14; Carolina 123; Frank
14; Nan 11; Octa 11
BROOKS, Abigail 37; Bonnie
68; Candler 14; C.T.
14; Eddie 14; Elvira 17;

BROOKS, Cont'd.
James 14; John T. 14;
Jonathan R. 14; Lillie
129; Lula 145; Lydia 90;
Maggie 98; Margaret 102;
Martha 134; Martha L. 4;
Mary 98; Nina M. 150;
Paralee 17; Robert 14;
Robert C. 14; Robert P.
14; Roy 14; Sarah 138
BROOKSHIRE, Lucinda 50
BROOM, Bernice 15; Hobert
14
BROWN, Alfred 15; Annis O.
24; Aron W. 15; Bedford
15; Benj. B. 15; Bryant
15; Caleb A. 15; Callie
93,144; Carrie 58;
Catherine 117; C.D. 72;
C. Earnestine 74; Charles
15; Clarence S. 15;
Cling 15; Cornelius 15;
David 15; David A. 15;
David Carroll 16; D.F.
15; Dora 15,101; Edgar
15; Edith L. 91; Edward
15; E.H. 15; Elizabeth
110,135,147; E.P. 7,45,
64,103,106,142; F.E. 15;
Frank H. 15; G.E. 15;
George T. 15; George W.
15; G.W. 15; Harry 15;
James 14; James H. 14;
James M. 15; Jane 1,149;
J.E. 144; J.M. 15; John
15; J.W. 15,24; Lassie
54; Lee, Jr. 15; Lillie
10; Mary E. 69; Mary S.
S. 99; M.C. 147(2); Mil-
ly Ann 135; Mollie 66;
Nancy 12; Nannie 76;
Otto 15; Polly 45; R.A.
14; Ransom U. 15; Rebecca
72; Robert 15; Robert
S. 15; Romelus 75; Ruth
150; Sally 142; T.E. 15;
Thomas 15; T.W. 85; T.
Wiley 15; William 15(4);
William J. 15; William S.
15; W.S. 15
BROWNELL, Abram 13
BROWNING, Charlie 16;
George 16; Humphery 16;
J.F. 26,133; Mary I. 85;
Newton 16; Octa 146;
V.A. 16; William 16
BROWNSON, Lula 59
BRUCE, Chiman C. 16
BRYANT, Annie 145; Grady
16; Henry 16(2); Horace
16; Ida 52; Jennie 127;
J.H. 16; Lola L. 117;
Marion 16; Mark 16;
O'Dell 5; Sarah T. 57;
Virginia 108; Walter 16;
Willie 16
BRYSON, Abraham 16; Ada 25;
Miss Addie 71; A.F. 16,
17; Albert S. 16; Alice
M. 113; A.M. 16; Andrew
16; Anna 84; Annie 139;
A.S. 12,118; Bert. 17;
Bulon 17; C.A. 17; Carr
17; Charles B. 17; Chas.
S. 17; Coedelia 14;
Columbus 16; Dee 17;
Della V. 32; D.H. 17;
Dove 75; D.V. 17; E.A.
152; Edward 17; Edward
B. 17; Elbert 17; Elen
147; Elizabeth 88,97,
131; Elizabeth J. 60(2);

BRYSON, Cont'd.
Fannie 87; Felix 17;
Florence 84; Frank 17(2);
Fred 132; Genevive 110;
Geo. 81,87; Geo. E. 17;
George 28,45,106; George
T. 17,43,85,108,144; G.L.
C. 17; Harriet L. 147;
Hattie 42; Hugh B. 16;
Ida 89; Inez 113; Ivy 61;
J.A. 17,95,120; James
16,91,95,122; James H.
16; James K./Jas. K./J.K.
3,4,5,7,8,11,14,16,20,21,
27,28,35,37,39-41,44,51,
54,62,71,77,81,83,88,92,
95,97,109,112,113,116,122,
136,137,138,146,147; James
L. 16,47; James M. 16;
Jas. L. 13; J. Fred 101;
J.h. 8,29; J.L. 2,6,14,
21,35,51,68,70,76,82,83,
85,86,87,89,109-113,117,
121,123,137,144; J.M. 8,
91; Joe 17; Johnathan M.
4; John 16,17; John N. 16;
John T. 16; Joseph 16;
Joseph A. 92; J.P. 17,55;
Julia 150; Kandas 136;
Laura 81,114; Lefayett
16; L. Lee 17; Leona C.
107; Lola 143; Maggie 67;
Margaret 36; Margaret J.
107; Margaret M. 90;
Marion 17; Martha 88,110;
Mary E. 101; Mary Jane 7;
Mayme V. 122; Meekie 47;
Mildred 76; Monroe 17;
Myrtle 62; Nancy 97; Nar-
cissa 4; N.C. 126; Nellie
124; Pearl V. 109; Polly
Ann 29; Rachel 88; Ray 17;
R.E. 41,102; Rebecca 2,
145; Robert L. 17; Robert
T. 17; Roy 17(2); Ruby 6;
Sam, Jr. 17; Samuel 16
(2); Samuel N. 16; Sarah
63,122; Sarah L. 150;
Selma 17; Sibbie 139;
Simeon D. 17; T.C. 16;
Theodore 17; T.M. 17;
T.N. 17; Uel G. 16;
Virgie D. 110; Virgil 16;
W.H. 17; William 16(2);
William M. 17; Zeb 17
BUCHANAN, Bell 55; Ben E.
18; B.M. 18; Callie 59;
Charles S. 17; Cincinnati
68; C.l. 53; C.S. 6,22,
47,83; Mrs. Daisy 124;
Dan 18; Darcus 38; Dewey
18; Dollie 121; D.W. 17;
Elias 18; Ellener 31;
Ellis 18; Etta 143;
Evelyn 128; E.W. 18;
George 18; Haden 137;
Irphy E. 131; Jack 18;
James 17(2),18; James A.
18; James L. 18; James M.
18; Jane 91; Jincy 62;
J.L. 18,62; Jno. 17;
John A. 17; Joseph 17,
109; J.S. 51; J.T. 90;
J.W. 18; L.D. 17; Lillie
55; Lydia 69; Mae 77;
Martha 3,15,34,84; Mary
71; M.R. 18(2); Oscar 18;
Pearl 22; R.J. 18; Sally
3; Sarah 3,36; Susan 96;
Verlin 18; William H.
17; W.J. 18; W.L. 86
BUCKHANAN, Margaret J. 36;
Sarah 54

BUCKNER, Albin 18; Dock H.
18; Elijah 18; Louisa
56; Lucy 150; Manda 147;
M.L. 40; Nettie 115;
Sarah A. 35; S.E. 41;
Shadrick 18; William 18
BUIRL, N.L. 55
BUIST, Martha Perry 98
BULGIN, Geo. M. 18; G.M.
22,78,101,117,132,140;
G.W. 100; John 18; Law-
rence B. 18; Margaret
97; Mary E. 57; William
G. 18; W.L. 89; W.R. 5,
6,17,50,65,89,115
BULLOCK, Eugene C. 18;
Willie Mae 54
BUMGARNER, Geo. E. 18;
George 18; J.N. 18
BURCH, Barnett 18; Dyer 18;
Georgia 134; James A.
18; J.P. 18; Lee 18;
Louisa 65; Mary C. 135;
M.C. 18; Mildred 97;
M.L. 18; Nancy R. 86;
Robert H. 18
BURELL, J.F. 83
BURGESS, Adalaide 52; Austa
87; Billie 19; Charles
19; Frank 19; Grady 106;
Jennie 108; John 19;
Julia 27; Julius 18,19;
Lucinda 56; Samuel 18;
Sarah J. 72; Thomas 17,
18
BURGIN, Minnie 144; Otis
O. 19
BURLESON, Bell 6; S.L. 19
BURNES, Nancy C. 64
BURNETT, Alice I. 27;
Amanda 116; Callie 6;
Dewey 19; E.J.A. 19;
Elizabeth V. 131; Ellen
64; E.V. 19; Fannie 119;
Francis 19; Frank 19;
Fred 19; Geo. W. 19;
Henry 19(2); Henry C.
19; James 19; James W.
19; Jane 109; J.D. 19;
J.E. 19; John 19,150;
K.M. 144; M.A. 2; Mar-
garet A. 12; Mary C.
72; Mary M. 24; M.S.
19(2); N.A. 141; Pallie
Rachel M. 12; Sarah 90;
Sarah A. 141; Vernel 19
BURNS, W.F. 19; W.M. 112,
144
BURRELL, Adeline 19; B. 19;
Bettie 31; Clark Lewis
19; Eula G. 21; Huldah
R. 139; J.C. 38; J.F.
42,118,127; J.G. 19;
Lee 19; Mae B. 1; Mary
E. 139; Nora 46; Olive
31; Phebe 64; Roxana
104; Veo 21; W.L. 19
BURRES, Ethel 112
BURRESS, Dorothy Evelyn 59
BURRIS, Fernando 19
BURSTON, Agnes E. 27;
Fletcher 19; James 19;
Jerry M. 19; J.W. 9;
Lelia 136; Roxie 19;
Viola 27
BURT, Edward 19
BURTON, Carrie 129; Joe M.
19; Maybelle 78; Sudie
56; S.V. 19; Virgil 19
BUTLER, Celia 42; Elizabeth
31; Lidia 9; Mary A.
81(2); Minday 28;

BUTLER, Cont'd.
Virginia 31; W.O. 19
BYERS, Mrs. Clearinda 39
BYRD, Alice 96; Anna P.
129; Austin 19; B.A.
19; Beatrice 86; Belle
41; Beulah 37; Bula 13;
D.C. 19,20; Della 136;
Don W. 20; Dona 23;
Dora 13; Fannie B. 121;
Florence 36; Lillie
13; Perl 110; Prissilla
97; Rosa 127; Ruth
Lenore 144; Tinnie 63

CABBLE, Margaret 31
CABE, Abbie B. 29; Adaline
Addie 27; Albie 18;
Alex 21; Alma S. 65;
Amanda 23,103; Annie 21;
A.P. 21; Arie 21; Bessie
53,96; Beulah 24; Beu-
lah M. 106; Birdie 128;
Blanch A. 49; Bula 39;
Burgess 21; Cary 21;
Catherine 6; Chalmers
21; Charlie C. 20; Chas.
Chas. A. 20; Chas. S.
21; Cornelia 71; C.R.
9,15,18,21,22,24,32,
38,39,45,49,65,73,79,
82,94,100,102,106,111,
124,136; C.W. 21; David
Dicy 71; D.L. 20; D.P.
20,41,50,99,112,136;
E.C. 20; Edna 36; Elbert
N. 21; Elizabeth 13,
67,84; Ella 93; Elsie
78; Esther M. 118;
Ettie 73; Fannie 64;
Flora 120; Frank 21;
Frank L. 21; Fred D. 21;
George 20; George L.
21; George W. 20; Grady
Mae 3; Hannah 6; Harley
M. 21; Harley W. 21;
Harriet 73; Harvy G.
20; Hattie Lee 33;
Hellen P. 150; Henry
G. 21; Herschel 21;
H.G. 20; Hillard 21;
Honor 105; H.P. 20;
Ida Mae 69; Isabel 53;
Ivale 21; James 20,130;
James L. 20; James M.
20; J.E. 15,20,21,23,
29,64,75,93,94,96,115;
Jennie 80; J.H. 21;
J.H., Jr. 20; J.M. 20
92),125; Jno. L.D. 20;
John 20; John L. 20;
John V. 20; J.T. 21;
Laura 150; L.E. 20;
Leander 20(2); Lenzie 21;
Lindin 21; Lora L. 108;
Loranzo D. 20; Lorenzo
F. 20; L.R. 21; Lucenda
37; Lucius 20; Lula 99;
Mabel 108; Maggie 112;
Marinda 139; Martha 133;
Martha O. 20; Mary A.
99; Mary E. 55; Mell 20;
M.F. 39; Mrs. Millie 60;
Minnie 120; M.J. 41;
Nancy 112; Nancy A. 131;
Nellie Reece 152; Nola
62; Octa C. 123; Paschal
21; P.F. 21; Rachel A.
100; Rebecca L.D. 92;
R.L. 55; Robert 20,21;

CABE, Cont'd.
Robt. Lee 20; Ruth 127;
S.A. 48; Sallie 27; Sam-
uel 20; Samuel A. 20;
Sarah 17,60; Sarah C.
65; Sarah E. 20; Sarah T.
71; Sary S. 39; S.R. 20
(2); Stephen L. 21; Thomas
20; Thomas B. 20; Thomas
L. 21; Thomas R. 21; Tina
97; T.M. 20; Toledo 73;
W.H. 21; William 20;
William A. 20; William T.
20; William W. 20; W.R.
20; Z. 20; Zacheriah 20;
Z.P. 20
CABLE, G.W. 21
CADEN, Ethel 15; Eva 127;
Lena 127
CAGLE, Anne 136; Arthur C.
21; Ida 39; Lura 32
CAILOR, H. 33; Lettie A.
87
CALDWELL, M.C. 21; Paul 21
CALER, Kansie 16; Lillie L.
32; Margaret 124; Pinkie
148; Rutha A. 89; Texas
V. 110; Texie 6
CALHOUN, Mrs. Lillie 2; W.J.
21
CALIVER, J.A. 130
CALLAHAN, Emma 21
CALLET, H.H. 21
CALLOWAY, A.J. 22(2); A.J.,
Jr. 22; Annie M. 45; Car-
rie 138; C.L., Jr. 22;
Ella Fair 149; Esther 108;
E.T. 22; Frank 22(2);
Green 22; Harley 22; Hunt-
er 22; James 22; James J.
22; J.E. 22; Jennie 22;
J.P. 22; Laura 124; L.C.
22; Lillie 88; Lula 138;
Margaret 95; Martha N.
74; Mattie 66; M.V. 74;
Nancy 97; P.C. 17,22,51,
60,64,70,93,99,104,105,
106,108,112,129,134,142,
152; Prince 22; Rhema 101;
Robert A. 22; Sam D. 22;
Sam L. 22; Thomas 22;
William 22
CALLYER, Albert 21
CALOR, G.A. 22; Rebecca 137
CALOWAY, Albert 22; Eliza-
beth 42; Mennie J. 44
CAMPBELL, Anna 145; C. 2,28,
40,50,110,126,133,141,146;
Charles C. 22; Charles L.
22; C.M. 40,108; Edwin 22;
E.K. 22; Elizabeth 124;
Ellen 98; Emma 135; Fannie
133; G. Glen 22; Jennieva
114; Jno. P. 69,85,116;
John P. 22,133; Joseph S.
22; J.P. 7,14,22,37,50,
66,82,107,109,110,116,133
J.W. 22; Leslie 22; Lonie
22; Lula 20; Maggie 2;
Martha A. 148; Mrs. Mat-
tie 148; Nellie 80; Noraa
20; P.J. 110; Richard
22; Robert 22; Sallie 40;
Sarah 33; Thos. E. 22;
Walter 22
CANADA, Florence 100
CANLER, Sallie 143
CANNON, E.D. 22
CANSLER, Amanda 33,151;
Belle 82; Clarinda 91;
E.L. 33; John 22; Kattie
86; Martha 33; Martha A.

CANSLER, Martha A. Cont'd.
116; Mary 82; M.V. 82;
phillip 22; R.L. 22;
Sarah 22; W.B. 22(2)
CANTEY, O.L. 22
CANTLER, Caroline 142
CANTREL, John 22
CANTRELL, Eliza J. 105;
Lena 148; Vina 11
CAPPS, George 22; Z.G. 22
CARDEN, Floyd 23; James
T. 23; J.B. 23,43; Jno.
B. 123; Mary T. 82; W.C.
47,52,83,94,107,139,145
CARDIN, Wm. B. 23
CARDON, Elsie 68; J.B. 25,
34,77,145
CAREL, Rachel 72
CARGLE, John 23
CARMAN, D.H. 2
CARMICHAEL, Alice 5
CARNAM, D.H. 10
CARNE, John D. 103,107,139
CARNES, John W. 94
CARPENTER, Adaline 142;
A.J. 12; A.L. 23; Allie
114; Alma 66; Anna 61;
Arthur 24; Arthur L. 24;
Avaline 73; Balavan 23;
Barbary M. 102; Benjamin
B. 23; Bertha 49; B.H.
23; Caroline 80; Charlie
23,24; Damascus 23;
David 23; David H. 23
(2); David N. 23,24;
Dicey A. 142; D.R. 23;
Drew 24; Edna 59;
Edward E. 23; Edy 94,145;
Effie 148; E.J. 24;
Eleanore 32; Ella 61;
E.M. 23; Emma 4; Emma F.
121; Essie 77; Etta 25;
Etter 12; F.J. 24; Fred
23; G.B. 23; Geo. 1,4-6,
9-12,14-19,21,22,24,26-
31,33-37,40,42-44,48,51-
58,63,64,66-75,78,79,81,
85-93,95,97,98,100-103,
105,106,108,110-113,115,
117,119-121,123-127,129,
130,132-137,140,142,144,
146,148,149,151; Geo. B.
23; Geo. R. 23; George
23; Harley 23; Hattie
128; Henretta 29; Henry
23(2); Henry W. 23;
Humphrey P. 23; Ida 121;
India 121; Jackson 23;
Jackson T. 23; James 23;
James M. 23; Jane 73;
J.E. 23(2); J.M. 6,8,20,
23,26,63,78,92,94,112,
144,148; John 24; John W.
23; J.T. 24; Judson 23;
Julia E. 112; Lelia 127;
Letty 77; Maggie 129;
Mamie 114; Margaret H.
112; Martha 97,128;
Martha A. 77; Martha E.
121; Mary 49,99; Mary
J. 99; Mary M. 95; Mary
R. 41; M.A.T. 112; Matil-
da 11,26; Mattie 130;
May 71; M.E. 37; Milly
138; Nannie 82; Nannie
C. 43; Oscar S. 24; Paul
B. 24; Mrs. R.A. 146;
Raleigh 24; R.L. 24;
Robert L. 23; Rosa 75;
Rosetta J. 80; Sanford
23,24; Sarah 87,146;
Sarah A. 54; S.F. 12;

CARPENTER, Cont'd.
T.A. 23; Thomas 24; U.N.
23; Walter B. 24; W.D.
23; W.F. 23; W.H. 23,43,
78,125,141; W.I. 23;
William 23,24; W.J. 23;
W.T. 24; W. Vance 23
CARR, L.E. 82
CARRELL, Polly 1; Thomas
24
CARRINGER, Amanda B. 33
CARRINGTON, Alfred 24
CARROL, Absolom 24; Eliza-
beth 104; Miles 24;
Samuel 72
CARROLL, Absolom 24; Daniel
24; Margarette 65
CARSON, A.M. 24; Elizabeth
32; Jesse 24; J.C. 146;
John H. 24; Josephine
127; Martha 2; Mary 2,
89; Matilda 73; Rhoda R.
3; Richard D. 24; Susan
R. 67
CARTER, Arthur 24; Blanche
111; Bunnie 111; C.
Alberta 113; Cicero 24;
Dan 24; Elizabeth 53;
Emma L. 42; James 24;
James W. 24; Lela 17;
Martha 126; Mary 81;
M.I. 53; Roxie 19;
Susannah 130; Susey 9;
T. 26; Thomas 24;
Thomas Wm. 24; Tom 120;
Wm. Edward 24
CARVER, D.F. 2,29,61,72,
126,140; Frona 16; G.C.
24; Henry 24; J.J. 85;
J.Z. 24,93,104,115; L.B.
148; Nettie 73; Oscar 24;
Wayne 24; W.H. 24;
William R. 24
CASE, Sally 46
CASTLE, Sallie 24
CATHEY, Jane 106; Thomas
24,41
CAUTION, James 25
CAVINESS, C.H. 9,14,17
CAYLOR, Alfred 21; A.W. 21;
Elizabeth 83; Jeptha 21;
Martha L. 113; Polly L.
70; Thomas I. 21; Thomas
J. 21; Vance W. 21; W.W.
21
CERBY, Alis 103
CHAMBERS, Catherine A. 50;
Edna 144; Eliza 120;
Isaac E. 25(2); J.E. 106;
John W. 25; Lotty 22;
Moses E. 25; Phillip 25;
R.E. 61; S.R. 25; Thomas
R. 25; Thos. B. 25
CHAPIN, Mary A. 126
CHAPMAN, Altha 142; Jay F.
25
CHASTAIN, Aylor 25; C.A. 25;
D.E. 25; Dora 152; E.D.
25; Elizabeth 14; Estella
134; Eula 151; Isobeler
H. 92; James 25; Jesse
10; John D. 25; J.W. 25;
Lillie Bell 22; M.L. 25;
Myrtle 125; Thomas 25;
Zeke 25
CHASTEAINE, Lover 148
CHASTEEN, M.M. 13; Sarah
I. 15
CHASTINE, Lizzie 143
CHAVERS, Irene 150; Laura
46
CHAVIS, Arthur 25; Bob 25;

CHAVIS, Cont'd.
Charley 25; Jeff 25;
Jim 25; Lonner 99;
Thomas 25
CHEDESTER, Wm. P. 114
CHEEKS, Dora 76; Margaret
135
CHILDERS, Adna 14; Allen 25;
Annie 31; Burr A. 25;
Callie 90; Connie 43;
Edna 81; Ella 2; Herman
Lee 25; Humphrey 25(2);
Josaphine 26; Marion
25; Mary A. 23; Reuben 25;
Sarah 14; Sligah 25;
Thos. C. 25; Wm. R. 25
CHILDS, Mae 146
CHOTE, Tredele D. 25
CHRISTY, Thos. H. 25
CLAMPET, Louisa J. 133;
Mary 100; Nancy 116;
Revena 30
CLAMPETT, Ceily 69; George
25; H.T. 37; James C.
25; John 25; N.G. 25;
Rufus 25
CLAMPITT, Gertrude R. 78;
Rebecca 135
CLANTON, Alfred B. 25; Eliza
69; Emma 89; Fannie 59;
Pearl 25
CLAPP, C.G. 25
CLARK, Ann 122; Bettie 131;
Clyde 26; Edna 63; Ervin
26; Grace 73; Hiram 26;
James 26; James A. 26;
James P. 26; Jessie 103;
Jim 26; J. Logan 26;
Joanna 17; John 26; John
D. 26; Joseph 26; Laura
B. 23; Lena 56; Lillie
146; Lydia J. 18; Mar-
garet 18; Mary 70,96(2),
132; Minnie 131; Myrtle
51; Nancy C. 3; Oscar
26; Robin 26; Rose A.
127; Sarah 80; Sarah I.
40; S.J. 83; Summer 114;
T.A. 26; Ted 26; Thomas
26; W.F. 26; Woodrow 26
CLAYTON, Hattie 101; Robert
110; Robt. 51; S.M. 26
CLEAVELAND, Elinor C. 144
CLEMENT, A.B. 26; Belle 98
CLEMONS, jane 56
CLEVELAND, Evelyn E. 66;
Mrs. Helen L. 136; James
F. 26; J.D. 26; Mabel
E. 59; Martha Louisa 103;
Reppard 26; William 26
CLINE, Absolem 26; Elizabeth
69; Jane 14; Jesse 26;
John 26(3); Mae Bell 25;
Micahel 26; Roxanna 139;
Susan 126
CLOE, Mae 66
CLOER, A.J. 26; A. Jehu 26;
Andrew 27; Ava 8; C.E.
122; Charity 26; Della
120; D.W. 26; Ed. 27;
Ester 146; G.A. 13,17,
34,41,51,65,99,105,109,
111,121,132,134; Geo.
66,73; Geo. A. 115;
George 26; G.H. 127;
Grace E. 4; Hassie 38;
Hattie 15; Jacob M. 26;
James N. 26; J.C. 27;
Jennie 146; J.N. 26;
John 26; John F. 26;
Joshua 26; Lonie Eliza.
130; Lou 5; Maggie 53;

CLOER, Cont'd.
Mary 95; M.R. 25; N.J.
26; N.P. 26; P.E. 53;
Sarah 47,67; Sarah E.
144; Thad 27; Vianna 46;
William M. 26; William
R. 26; W.M. 26; W.R.
26(2)
CLORE, G.A. 4; May P. 126
CLOUSOE, M.C. 27(2); Parker
27; Timmie 36
CLURE, Elizabeth 8; Louiza
R. 1; Margaret 51
COATES, I.W. 27
COBB, Jessie M. 57; R.J.
27
COCERN, Nancy 10
COCHRAM, Amanda 48; Mary A.
122; Roxie 113; Sarah 37;
Valintia 50
COCHRAN, Aaron 27; A.J. 27;
Araṛat 27; Blenders 27;
Carey 116; Docia 41;
Dora 79; Elizabeth 130;
E.T. 27; Fred 42; Gladys
86; Hattie 25; James 27;
Jennie 15; Jerry F. 27;
J.H. 79; J.L. 27; J.M.
27; John 27; John A. 27;
Lola 86; Manda 124;
Margaret 22; Mary 86,105;
McKinley 27; Moses 27
(2); Nola 101; Pearl 25;
R.E. 27; Sallie 49; Sarah
96; Mrs. Sarah 74; Ted
27; Thelma 101; Thomas
27; Vera 101; Wash. 27
92); William 27; Wm. H.
27; W.R. 27
COCKERHAM, Aaron 27; Agnes
12,16; A.N. 27; David
27; Geo. W. 27; John 27;
J.W. 27; Madison 27;
Mira 27
COCKERHAM, Elizabeth 138;
L.R. 33; Zilpha B. 147
CODE, Baylus 58
CODY, Bell 42; Lethe 53;
Myra J. 36; Priscilla 3
COFEE, Jessie 27; John 27;
Manerva 27
COGILL, J.B. 27
COGBURN, R.L. 60
COGGINS, Bessie 131; Eldon
M. 27; Gertie 10; Lou A.
62; Lucy 27; Mary L. 113;
Mattie 68; M.J. 141;
M.S. 142; Ritter 3; Sam
E. 27; Western 27
COKER, Newton 27; W.B. 27
COLE, Garland 28; James L.
27; John 28; Laura 8;
Lucy 124; William 28(2)
COLEMAN, Benj. F. 28; E.C.
48; James 28; J.D. 28;
Jesse 28; Joseph C. 28;
Mark 8; Mary J. 125;
Nancy 75; Roxie 76;
Sarah L. 7; Simond 28
COLLATT, J.P. 28
COLLETT, Amanda 2; James 28
COLLIER, Arthur 28; C.L.
28; Henry L. 28; H.H.
28; John 28; Oscar 28;
Sallie 4; William A. 28;
William, Jr. 28; Zannie
53
COLLINS, Adolphas 28;
Andrew 28; Andrew T. 28;
B.E. 28(2); Bertha 28;
Carole 9; Charley 28;
Cora 12; E. 40,46,70,89,

COLLINS, E. Cont'd.
90,149; E.C. 28,92; Eli
82; Ellen 21; Ester B.
60; Eva 33; Flora 75;
George B. 28; George R.
28(2); Hugh E. 28; Jacob
28; Jacob A. 28; James
28; J.B. 28(3); John 28;
J.R. 28; Lucy 113; Martha
20; Martha S. 90; Mary
107; Michael W. 28; Minor
W. 28; Nancy 76; Rebia
2; Thos. A. 28; W. 28;
William 28; W.L. 28;
W.Z. 28
COLLYER, Sarah S. 77
COLMAN, Wesley 28
COLVARD, Elizabeth 142;
James 29; Mary 106
COMAME, D.H. 24
COMPTON, T.B. 29
CONLEY, Albert 29; Ann 61;
Bell 89; Belle 73; Ber-
tie 148; Burgess G. 29;
Caroline C. 150; Charles
E. 29; Clara 6; C.P. 29;
Cynthea 30; Eddy B. 29;
Edwin B. 29; Eliza 94;
Ellen V. 31; Emily 1;
Fannie 126; F.C. 29;
G.C. 29; George 29(3);
Gordie 29; Grace 74;
Hallie E. 31; Hattie 78,
81; Ingram 29; Isaac 29;
James L. 29; James M. 29;
James P. 29; Jane 21;
J.D. 29; Jess 29; Jessie
29,91; J.M. 18,73,112;
Jos. 37; Joseph A. 29;
J.W. 29; Karr 29;
Katharine P. 127; Kittie
47; Lee 29; Lester 29;
Letty 71; Louise 22;
Maggie 57; Mamie 24;
Margaret 122; Margaret M.
112; Mary C. 69; Mary E.
39; Mary V. 70; Maud 73,
125; May Belle 139; Nancy
105; Nancy E. 73; Nannie
100; N.C. 29; Nora 18;
Orie E. 115; Paradie
73; Robert Lee 29; Roxie
118; Rutha 115; Mrs.
Sallie 107; Sallie L. 79;
S.C. 29(2),66,112; S.E.
105; Sidney W. 29; Sophia
81; Teletha C. 130; W.E.
29; W. Henry 29; William
A. 29(2); Willie 23;
W.L. 29
CONNARD, Margaret 85
CONNATA, Louise H. 45
CONNELLY, C.M. 11; Jason
29; Mary E. 16; V.A. 1;
William 29
CONNELY, Jno. 41
CONNER, Edward A. 29; John
H. 29; Laura 7; Mrs.
Mary 116; W.A. 29; W.E.
102; W.H. 91; William
102; William H. 29
CONSEEN, Buck 29
CONSLER, Alice M. 116
CONSTANCE, John J. 29
CONSTANT, Melissa 118
COOK, Barnard R. 30; B.R.
81; Everett 30; H.B. 72;
H.M. 30; J.A. 30; John
29,30(2); Lon 30; S.C.
75
COOKSTON, S.M. 30
COOPER, A.F. 30; Cornelus

COOPER, Cornelus, Cont'd.
30; Jno. R. 30; J.W. 30;
Pierson 117; Risdon 34;
William C. 30
COPE, Andrew 30; Bertha 31;
Cordelia 132; Elbert C.
30; Elza 30; Emma 90,141;
Grady 30; James 30; Jane
57; Lillie 151; Margie
37; Sarah 105; Tiney 8;
Tomie 30; Will 30;
William 30
CORBETT, Edna 74
CORBIN, Annie 109; Arizona
87; Chas. Dewey 30; Eliz-
abeth 64; Emma 32; Eva
43; Georgia 62; H.D. 30;
H.L. 30; Ida 89; Ida Bell
43; Inda 110; James L.
30; James M./Jas. M.
1,3,46,58,64,134,150;
Jane M. 83; J.J. 30;
J.L. 9,38,66; J. Landon
30; J.M. 30(2), 47,146,
151; Jno. L./John L. 31,
44,45,50,59,71,88,95;
Lillie 118; Lula 62,130;
Mary 43; Mary C. 46;
May 139; M.P. 30; Nannie
Mae 128; N.J. 30; O.C.
47,64,66,93,108,132;
Pinckney 30; Sarah A.
75; S.C. 28; William 30
CORDEN, W.C. 29,81,119
CORN, Adam 46; Clyde H. 30;
Elizabeth 14; Ellen 125;
John 46; John D. 31;
L.A. 30; Rebeckah 46;
Samuel 30
CORNELIUS, Sandy 30; S.B.
55
CORNETT, Samuel 30
CORNISH, Noah 30
CORPENING, A.L. 30; Bessie
11,79; Carrie 137; Carrie
T. 25; Flora 99; J.T. 30;
Maude 73; Roscoe 30;
Will 30
COWAN, D.h. 2,15,34,82;
E.O. 56 Martha 35
COWARD, Arie 50; Carrie 5;
Claud 31; J. Shaw 31;
Mary E. 119; Nathan 30;
W.H. 31
COWART, Bertha 40; H. 99;
Minnie 141; Sarah J. 62
COWEN, Berdit 31; William
31
COWIN, Martha 17
COX, Lou 55; O.C. 31
COYAD, Margaret 140
COZAD, Henry O. 31; Mildred
15
CRAIG, B.W. 13; James 31;
Margaret 13
CRAIGE, Mary A. 27
CRAIN, Genelia 29; Ida 103
CRAINE, Pearl 22; Silla 8
CRANE, Ed. 31; Florence
129; Frank J. 31; Jane
99(2); W.A. 31
CRANSON, L.E. 98
CRAVER, W. Sandford 31
CRAW, Ray 118
CRAWFORD, Addie 84; Amanda
R. 126; Annie M. 62;
Artie 128; Cecil M. 31;
C.W. 31; E.G. 31; Ella
132; Ellen L. 52; Elmer
Wilson 31; Emerson G. 31;
Enos 31; Eugene E. 31;
George 31(2); Gilmer L. 31

CRAWFORD, Cont'd.
Harlie 31; James 31(2);
Jas. G. 31; J.G. 46,94,
107,138; J.L. 31; John
L. 31; Lee 31; L.F. 31;
Maggie 104; Martha 2;
Mattie E. 105; M.E. 126;
M. Elizabeth 126; Nannie
122,132; R.L. 31; Robt.
M. 31; Sallie Bell 62;
Sarah 94; S.N. 31; Sue
127; Timoxena 117; Vir-
ginia 127; Willie 31;
Wm. M. 31; W.R. 31
CRENSHAW, Leroy F. 31
CRISP. Amanda 16; A.P. 31;
C.E. 32; Charley 31;
Cora 96; Ed 32; Ellen
132; Ethel 89; George
31,32; G.F. 32; Helen
134; H. Grady 32; Hiram
31; H.M. 32; Iva 32(2);
Jennie 64; Joab 32;
Joel 31; John 31; J.R.
32; Julia 5; Laura 132;
Lon 32; Lula 135; M.A.
144; Madison 31; Mae
144; Mae B. 39; Manilla
Margaret 68; Mary 5;
Mary C. 64; Millard 32;
Miller 32; Molly B. 62;
M. Pinkney 32; Myrtle
149; Rachel 94; Ralph
32; Roxie 135; Simpson
131; W.T. 31
CRISPE, Merrill 31
CROCKETT, Nancy J. 93; S.R.
35,53,93,110,129
CROOK, Robt. L. 32
CROSBEY, J.H. 119
CROSBY, J.H. 58; John H.
140
CROSS, Annie 34; Elenda
61; Elijah 32; Frank
32; Jas. A. 32; J.H. 32;
Lydia 106; Mary 49;
Nancy Ann 76; Nora 3;
W.F. 32
CROWELL, George H. 32
CRUMMER, Harry J. 32
CRUNKLETON, Elizabeth 88;
Eva 8; I. 142; I.H. 134,
142; James L. 32; John
32; Melvina 74; Seth H.
32; Thos. 32; Zonie 45
CRUSE, Edward 32; Nettie
68
CRUZE, C.E. 32; L.D. 32
CULBERTSON, Martha 13,137;
Wm. 32
CUNNINGHAM, Aaron 33(2);
A.E. 33; Alice M. 111;
Altha 100; A.P. 33;
Arintha 48; Bertha 128;
Bess Irene 98; C. Ann
71; Carl P. 33; Catheryn
51; C.B. 33; Charles C.
33; C.M., Jr. 33(2);
Dewit C. 33; Dora 49;
Enoch 33; Eunice 126;
F.M. 107; Frank C. 33;
George 33; Gertrude 104;
Grady 33; Havel 33;
Howard M. 33; Jas. 33;
Jas. M. 33; J.E. 33;
Jean 33; John 33; John
B. 33; John L. 33; Julia
5; Lucinda 107; Margar-
et 107; Margaret H. 138;
Mary 69; Mary B. 62;
M.V. 28; Nell 151;
Neuton L. 33; Paul B.

CUNNINGHAM, Paul B. Cont'd.
33; Rachel 69; Reta 45;
R.H. 27,33,133; Robert
33; Robt. R. 33; Roy F.
33; Rufus 33; Sallie E.
89; Sam 33; Sarah 2;
S.C. 77; Thadius 33;
Tim 43; T.M. 33; W.A.
33; Wade 33; William 33
(2); W.R. 33
CURRIER, Marietta 10
CURRY, Mattie L. 124
CURTIS, A.J. 99; Alice 151;
Anna 65; Annie Lee 100;
Arennida 32; Asbury 32;
Charlie 32; David 32;
Edward 33; Elizabeth 46,
119; Emily 51; Emma 2;
Florence M. 57; Frank 33;
Gaston 33; G.W. 33; H.
Terrell 32; John 32;
John H. 32; Jonathan B.
32; Julius H. 32; Lelah
38; Lizzie 76; Lula 96;
Martha 23; Mary 141;
Mary T. 129; M.H. 32;
Nancy 42; Nina 33; Ora
112; R.B. 32; W.F. 32;
W.L. 32
CURTISS, Matilda 53
CYPHER, Sallie 87

DAILEY, M.H. 80
DAILY, Rhobia 98
DALRYMPLE, Adelia 122;
Allie 32; Edwina M. 132;
E.J. 67; E., Jr. 33;
Ellen 79; E.N. 6,16,45,
52,68,124; Geo. H. 34;
H.E. 51; Helen 52; Hester
E. 9; James 34; John C.
33; Julia A. 85; Kermit
33; Lillie 121; Lou 57;
Maggie J. 70; Malinda
38; Margie 8; Mary 120;
Mrs. Mary B. 85; Phebe
A. 57; Pinkie 57; Samuel
E. 34; S.J. 115; Sophrany
79; Thos. J. 34(2); T.J.
33; T.W. 33; Wm. N. 34
DALTON, A.B. 2,9,18,90,109,
132; Alfred 34; Angeline
67; B.C. 34; Beuna 69;
Carl 34; C.T. 34; C.W.
34(2); Edd 34; Ellen 80;
E.V. 101; Fred 34; Geo.
B. 34; George 34; James
34; Jane 12; J.B. 118;
J.C. 34; J.H. 43; J.
Lane 34; John H. 34,69;
John M. 34; Josephine
75; J.R. 34; Louisa A.
122; Manuel B. 34; Mary
A. 67; Nannie 132; N.E.
101; Nena 85; Nina 63;
Robt L. 34; T.E. 34;
Vallie 102; W.H. 34
DANIEL, G.M. 122
DANIELS, Chas. C. 34; James
34
DARNELL, Barbara 22
DAUGHERTY, John William
107; R.H. 140,1150
DAVES, A.A. 150; Alfred
34; Althia 35; Bell 49;
Bessie 49; C.C. 34; Early
34; Frank 34; George M.
34; G.M. 34; Hester 11;
James M. 34; Jane 40;
J.H. 34; J.M. 34; Jos-
eph 34; Kate 85; Kope 34;

DAVES, Cont'd.
Lillie 143; Maggie 75;
Mandy 27; Marcus 34; Mary
J. 100; Mollie 75; Rebe-
cca 21; Robert 34; Wm. 34
DAVIDSON, Lee 34
DAVIS, Addie 112; Alf. W.
35; Alice 38,112; Alta
42; Altha 41; Annie 54;
A.W. 2,108,134; Bessie
6,7; B.H. 1; Billie 35;
Charles H. 35; Cora 2;
D.A. 35; David 34; D.L.
35; Ephriam 35; F.C. 7;
Flonnie B. 4; F.P. 35;
Furman 35; George 35;
G.W. 35; Harriet J. 49;
Hattie 72; Henry 35;
Iowa 18; Isaac H. 35;
James L. 35; Jason 35;
Jim 35; John 35(2),47;
John B. 35; J.R. 35,108;
Kope 35; Lasaphine 8;
Laura C. 40; L.G. 35;
Lillie 41; Lois M. ?;
Louisa D. 128; Margaret
116,138; Margaret C. 67;
Martha 133; Mary 66,128;
Mary Elizabeth 128;
Mathew 35; Minnie 5;
Nancy 120; N. Don 35;
Nellie M. 59; Otis 35;
Peter 35.90; R. Franklin
35; Robert N. 35; Robt.
L. 35; Ross 35; Sandy 35;
Sarah 35,80; Thomas 34,
35; T.J. 35; T.W.P. 35;
Virgil 35; Willis H. 35;
W.M. 35
DAWKINS, Willie P. 35
DAWSON, T.J. 13
DAY, Marion 49; Mildred E.
69
DEADWYLER, J.C. 35
DEAL, Annie Goodloe 137;
Chas. 36; Eleanor H. 116;
Elizabeth P. 2; Eliza-
beth W. 71; Hattie 58;
J.A. 4,5,14,33,49,150,56,
62,71,74,87,103,104,115,
121,126,134,137,140;
James 35,36; John A. 146;
Mamie 57; Margaret A.
113; Martha 48; Martha
Jane 16; Mary Ethelwyn
71; Mattie 29; M.C. 36;
Octa 53; Ruth 77; Sarah
R. 115; T.N. 35; William
35; W.P. 36
DEAN, Alexander B. 36;
Amanda 143; Beulah 90;
Doris 17; Ellen 145;
Emily 90; Emma 7,19; Eula
24; Mrs. F.I. 105;
Furman B. 36; G.B. 36;
Geo. B. 36; George W. 36;
G.W. 11,19,40,41,44,73,
97,113,137; H.D. 36,56,
57,76,89,90; Henderson D.
36; Herman 36; Jane 11;
Jane A. 97; Jennie 95;
J.H. 36; John H. 36;
Kansas 95; Laura 145;
L.E. 91; Mary C. 107;
Mary E. 34; Myrtle M. 67;
N.C. 11; Ralston 36;
Silas J. 36; Sydney 36;
Vernon 62; Vinnie M.M.
83; Walter 36; William L.
36; Wm. B. 96
DEANNON, Nicy 91
DEATON, Jamima 95

DEAVER, William 35
DE HART, A.J. 36; Allen 36;
A.M. 36; Bryan 36;
Catherine 89; Dallas 36;
Dallis 140; D.M. 36;
Earl 36; Earnie 36;
Elander 140; Eleonar 124;
Emma 95; Esther 19; Geo.
R. 36; J.A.B. 36; Jacob
R. 36; James 36; James R.
36; Jas. W. 36; J.H. 36;
John 36; John P. 36;
John T. 36; J.P. 36; J.
Robert 36; Lillie A. 127;
L.M. 4; Lois 109; Lydia
133; Malinda 48; Martin
71,76; Mary A. 13; Mary
J. 35; Matilda 19; Min-
nie 102; Pauline 30;
Sallie 145; Sarah 13;
Sarah L. 8; T.S. 19,21,
102; William 13; Wint 36;
W.J. 36; W.R. 30; Zoah
44
DEITZ, Lorenzo 37; Nathaniel
36; Richmond 37; T.F.
137; Toban F. 36
DELOZIER/DE LOZIER, Edward
37; Elizabeth S. 29;
Jessie E. 129; J.R. 37;
Mary Ann 114; R.L. 13
DELRYMPLE, E.N. 39
DEMOSEY, Margaret 71
DEMPSEY, James 37; Pally
A. 147
DENDY, Carrie 98; Floyd 140;
Floyd E. 37
DENNEY, T.D. 141,148
DENNY, Edward 37; Emma 117;
Estella 117; T.D. 34,52,
57,86,90,101,109; T.S.
11; Will 37
DENTON, Isaac 37; T.S. 128
DERREBERRY, Cross 37
DEUVAL, B.L. 13
DEWEESE, Alie 21; Burdell
21; Carolin 147; E.A.
69,84; Elizabeth 144;
Elvie 39; Emeline 125;
Emma 133; Eunice 110;
Floyd 37; Garrett 37;
C.W. 37; Harriett 27;
Hetty 147; Jane 1; Jane
H. 41; Jennie 145; Jesse
37(2); John 37(2); John
A. 37; Joseph 37; Julean
37; L. Ann 110; Lou 22;
Louisa 35; Lucindy 143;
Mae 13; Malcomb 37;
Mark 27,37,73,78,116,124,
132,133,137; Martha 69;
Mary 51; Nettie 44; Polly
35; Rebecca 90; Theodore
37; William H. 37; Wm.
8,32,45,47,72,85,86; Wm.
D. 37; Wm. W. 37
DEWEY, Isaac 37
DEWZE, Martha J. 107
DICKERSON, Icie Ethel 74;
Mart 37; M. Carolin 99
DICKESON, M.E. 13
DICKEY, B.K. 52; Burton H.
122; Harley 37; James 37;
Jane 10; Jas. 37; S.A.
99,114,146
DIETZ, Bertha 45; Lula 54
DILL, Catherine 98
DILLARD, Arthur 37; Charlie
37; Florence 36; George
W. 37; Inez 88; Jno. M.
37; Ora 13

DILLINGHAM, Jno. 145; May
134; Tallahasee 33
DILLS, Addie 64,78; A.J.
38(2); A.L. 30,39,128;
Alice 112; Allen 38;
Allie 111; A.N. 10; Anna
47; Archie 38; Asa M.
38; Bartlett 37; Bertha
78; Berry 38; Beulah 99;
Callie 98; Carrie 75;
Catherine 117; Charlie
38; Chas. L. 38; Chas.
P. 38; Cora 68,98; C.R.
141; David B. 38; Delia
40; E.B. 38; Elizabeth
31,141; Elizabeth C. 81;
Ella 37; Elma 149; Emma
65; Erwin 37; Eta 103;
Ethel 135; Fannie 47;
Fanny 10,85; Flora 26;
Floy 111; Fred 39; Geo.
L. 38(2); George 38;
Georgia A. 138; Gladys
43,101; G.P. 38; Grady
L. 39; Hallie 4; Harley
38,39; Harlie 38; Henry
37; Henry G. 38; Henry
H. 37; Henry N. 38;
Hettie 64; Hez 38; H.H.
10,37,47,65,102,104,128,
149; Homer 38; H.T. 38;
Ida 32; Iowa A. 9;
Issidona 132; James A.
38(2); Janett 138; Jasper
N. 45; J.C. 38; Jeremiah
37; J.H. 3892); J.L. 38;
J.M. 38; John 37,39;
John, Jr. 37; John S.
37; J.R. 37; Judson 38;
Laura 141; L.E. 105;
Lester 39; Levi 37,38;
Lina 128; Lom 38; Lonnie
39; Lonnie E. 39; Lue
148; Mandy J. 84; Marga-
ret 18,38; Mary 36,76;
Mrs. Mary 60; Mary C. 54;
Matason 38; Mattie 146;
M.E. 39; Melie 91; Minnie
59; Mira 31; M.M. 126;
M.S. 38,78,91; Myra L.
41; Nancy 105; Nancy C.
81,108; Nannie 104; Net-
tie 64; Oscar 38; Parilee
4; Pearl 60; Phillips
37; Polly 53; Richard
38; Rosetta 96; Ruby 101;
Rufus V. 38; Samuel M.
38; S.E. 38; S.V. 151;
Thomas 38; Thomas S. 38;
Thos. S. 38; Vivian A.
151; W.A. 38; Wesley 38;
William 37; W.M. 38,39;
W. Sherman 38; W.T. 38;
W. Zeb 38
DITMORE, Dave 39
DIXSON, J.S. 37
DIXON, S.A. 6,13,23,89,93
DOBSON, B.W. 39; Catherine
55; Joseph W. 39; L.W.
39; Mac 39; Mary 1; M.E.
A. 4; N.W. 130; O.L. 39;
W.B. 39; W.W. 39
DOCKERY, Mamie 7; Martha J.
101; Mary J. 49; M.B. 5,
32,66,108,149; Sarah M.
149
DOCKNEY, M.B. 38
DODSON, Wm. 39
DONALDSON, A.B. 23,26; Aline
88; Annice 105; Arie 140;
A.W. 18,24,39,127; Buna
122; C.A. 39; Carie 72;

DONALDSON, Cont'd.
Carl 39; Clint 39; Elba
V. 39; Ella M. 30; Flor-
ence 112; Geo. 39; Harvey
39; Henry P. 39; H.P.
39; Ivey 39; J.B. 39;
J.C. 39; Joseph F. 39;
Lassie 55; M.N. 39;
Oscar 39; R.N. 39; W.J.
39; Wm. 39; Wm. C. 39;
Wymer 39
DONILSON, Elna 106
DONNALDSON, Rosanna L. 63
Sarah 58
DOOLEY, Summer 39
DOTSON, Bessie B. 9; Edd
39; Ella 111; Henry 39
DOUGHERTY/DAUGHERTY, R.H.
22,29,30,63,66,73,81,84,
89,107,108,111,122
DOUTHIT, A.I. 39; Alfred 39;
C.H. 39; Cleo 30; Ethel
141; Etta 32; Zonie 124
DOWDLE, Benjamin F. 40;
Bertha 100; Bulah 111;
Chas. W. 40; C.W. 11,15,
21,34,40,48,55,57,65,72,
119,148; E. 16,17,39,68;
E.A. 40; Elizabeth 65;
E.P. 40; F.A. 39; Felix
39; Felix A. 40; Geo. C.
40; George 40; J.E. 40;
J. Harve 40; J.M. 40;
Julia 15; J.W. 40; Lee
40; L.M. 92; Mamie 119;
Marcus L. 40; Mary Ann
67; Mary E. 20,58; Mat-
ilda 121; Matilda A. 55;
Mollie M. 39; Nany 94;
Mrs. Naomi 139; Peail
67; Robert T. 40; Ruby
10; Sallie 95; Sarah A.
20; Sarah E. 146; S.L.
75; S.M. 54,135; Statira
118; Susan A. 39; Thad
O. 40; Thomas 40; Thos.
C. 40; Tilman 40; Varina
98; Zoah 80
DOWELL, Dora 140; James 40;
Josie 35; Lucy 143; M.
88; Martin 40; M.J. 151;
Ollie M. 140; Richard M.
40; S.M. 98,116; Vicy
116; Wm. C. 40; W.R. 40
DOWNES, L.M. 68
DOWNES/DOWNS, W.M. 85,102,
109,151
DOWNS, Alexander 40(2);
Amanda 28; Blanche 21;
Callie 102; Catherine
47; Charles 40; Elizabeth
83; Ezekiel 40; Fannie
116; Francis 117; Ira
40; Iris 125; Jane 36,
60; Jenny 116; Lillie
151; Lilly 14; Lizzie G.
105; Lucy 105; M.C. 40;
N.B.L. 40; Oberia 120;
Pink 151; Robert 40;
Rosie 46; Ruth 120; Sada
127; Sammie 40; Sarah 2;
Thos. A. 40; Wilford 40;
William 40(2); Wm. 40;
W.W. 40; Z.A. 40; Zach-
ariah 40
DRAKE, Alice 63; Anna 117;
Arthur A. 40; Carl 40;
Ellen J. 38; Francis 149;
Joanna 33; John 40; Josie
116; L.D. 40; Nola 40;
Norman 41; Pauley 40;

DRAKE, Cont'd.
  Rebecca S. 110; Viola
  130; W.T. 40
DRENIN, Thomas 41
DRENNING, Ervin 41; Hensly
  41
DRENNON, Amanda 40
DRENON, Angalin 37; Wm. 41
DRINNON, B. 56; Mary 84;
  William 143; Wm. 41
DRINON, D.E. 41
DRYMAN, Arie 20; Cansada A.
  80; Charles 41; Cora A.
  38; Dorcas A. 80; Earl
  41; E.J. 80; Estell 39;
  F.O. 41,127,148; George
  N. 41; Harriett A. 66;
  Ida 74; Isabelle 29;
  James A. 41; J.B. 41;
  John 41; Leila 51;
  Louiza Jane 80; Marinda
  A. 13; M.E. 119; Ray 41
  92); Roy 41,82; Trixie
  40; V.M. 41; William 41;
  William J. 41; W.J. 41;
  W.M. 41; Wm. P. 41
DUCKWORTH, Robert 41
DULIN, G.N. 132; J.N. 106
DUNCAN, Daniel 41; Elisha
  41; Murray A. 41; Nevada
  135; Wm. M. 41; Yoncey 76
DUNN, Allen 41; Jno. A./
  John A. 25,31
DU PREE, R.B. 32
DURHAM, Bessie S. 31
DUVALL, Alice 151; Annie 72;
  Bascom 41; Bertha 42;
  B.L. 41(2); Caroline 82;
  C.J.A. 73; Claude 42;
  Cleaburn A. 41; Earnest
  41; Edward B. 41; Eliza
  19; Elizabeth 113; Elsie
  124; Ida 107; James A. 41;
  J.B. 41; J.M. 42(2); John
  41; Joseph K. 41; Joshua
  41; J.R. 41; J.W. 3,57,
  89,98,101,148; Laura 151;
  Lee 42; Lewis 41; Martha
  86; Martha B. 144; Moses
  41; Nina 71; Polly T. 122;
  R.M. 33; Robert R. 41;
  R.R. 150; Steve 42; S.W.
  41; W.H. 42; William 41;
  William L. 41
DYER, Irene 146

EARLS, Sarah J. 50
EARLY, Cora 118; Elizabeth
  145; John 42(2); William
  M. 42
EASTON, Irvin L. 42
EDES, Joe J. 145
EDMONSON, Mary 83
EDMUNDSON, Robert 42; W. 42
EDWARD, J.J. 35,108
EDWARDS, A.C. 42; A.J. 42;
  Andrew E. 42; Carrie 37;
  Elizabeth 111; F. Darrell
  42; George 42; Grover D.
  42; Irene M. 112; James
  G. 42; James M. 42; John
  R. 42; John W. 7,8; J.R.
  42,61; J.W. 42; Lem 42;
  Loyd 42; Mack D. 42;
  Mimie Z. 42; M.L. 150;
  Paralee 41; Phillip 42;
  Ralph 42; Viola 144; W.I.
  42; Wilbur J. 42; W.M.
  42; W. Robert 42; W.W.
  42

ELDERS, Ada 3; A.M. 26;
  Bob 42; C.L. 42; Eliza
  36; Rachael 9; R.L. 42;
  Sarah A. 133; Teletha 59;
  Thurman 42
ELIAS, Isabell 72; K. 42;
  Thomas J. 42
ELLARD, Lamar M. 42
ELLENBURG, Luther 42
ELLENBY, John C. 42
ELLER, E.R. 15,24,75,100,
  111,115,130,132; Eugene
  R. 75; J.A. 42; Martin
  42; Mary 114
ELLIOTT, Charley 43; Chas.
  W. 43; Elva 32; Eugene
  A. 42; Geo. W. 42,43;
  Henry 43; Hester 40;
  James 43(2); Jesse 43;
  Joseph 43; J.W. 121,142;
  Lillia A. 94; Lillian
  60; Mary 10; Nannie E.
  104; Oscar 43; Perceval
  43; Robt. 43; Robt. J.
  43; Roxanna 87,88; W.A.
  43; Walter 43; Walter D.
  43; William 43
ELLIS, William 130
ELLISON, Lonie Belle 67
ELMORE, B. 123; Berdie 113;
  Bertha 23; Cora Lee 101;
  Dollie 108; Fannie 36;
  H.H. 16,47,75,81,94,120;
  Hugh H. 43; James M. 43;
  J.B. 1,6,22,26,28,38,43,
  46,47,55,60,64,68,75,85,
  86,90,112,113,119,120;
  121,123,125,128,136,140,
  143,150; J.B., Jr. 43;
  Jemima E. 18; J.H. 94;
  John 3,10,14,20,28,33,
  35,43,47,52,59,66,70,76,
  80,87,88,93,95,101,113,
  118,130,132,136,151;
  John C. 43; Louise 136;
  M.A. 79; Martha 36,64;
  Martha M. 6; Nancy C. 86;
  Nannie B. 138; Omar 43;
  William 43
EMERSON, Henery 12
EMORY, Bessie 4; Furman 43;
  James 43; James P. 43;
  John 43(2); Robert 43
ENGLAND, Adalin 5; Clifton
  43; Gus 43; H.P. 43;
  John P. 43; Lavada 87;
  Lon 43; Lula 121
ENGLISH, Augustus 43
ENLOE, A. Slice 88; G.O.
  43; James T. 43; J.T. 43;
  L.H. 10,43; Mary L. 10;
  Sarah Ann 49; T.B. 38,
  43,75,92,127; W.A. 43;
  William W. 43
ENSLEY, Rebecca 67
ERVIN, Clifton 81,92; G.C.
  31; G. Cliff. 104
ERWIN, Ira 31,32,63,69,89;
  Jane 144; Mercer 43
ESKRIGGE, Barbara L. 151
ESSANSA, Mrs. Josie 20
ESTES, Alice 136; Alonzo
  44; Asbury 43; Callie 26;
  C.L. 43; D.E. 43; G.
  Willy 44; Harriett 13;
  James D. 44; Jess L. 44;
  Mamie 42; Mary M. 53;
  William A. 43; Zelmer 64
ESTIS, Mennie 53
ESTRIDGE, Jesse E. 44;
  William 44
EUBANKS, Clarica 138

EVANS, Abratham L. 44;
  Albert 44(2); Andrew J.
  44; Bessie 120; Carl 44;
  Celia E. 8; Charles 44;
  Claud 44; Clıne 44; Cora
  123; E.M. 109,150; E.N.
  16,44,79,101; Erastus N.
  44; Isabel 116; J.A. 44;
  Jackson 44; Jesse 44;
  J.M. 44; John 44; J.S.
  44; Lasca 66; Lela 123;
  Leona 17; Lexie 49;
  Lillie 2; Martha 26;
  Mary 73; Mary L. 92;
  Maude 68; M.J. 148; Nicy
  28; Norman H. 44; P.A.
  135; Pearl 30; Reuben P.
  44; Sallie 151; Shirdan
  44; Susan C. 7; Thomas
  44; William J. 44; W.J.
  8,27,28,82,85,110,141;
  W.R. 44
EVETT, Eliza H. 111
EVIT, Lucinda P. 70
EVITT, Columbus 44; D.M. 44;
  Dock 44; Jackson C. 44;
  James 44; J.C. 44; Josia
  142; Lethie Ann 97;
  Martha 22
EXRINE, John M. 44

FAGG, T.H. 44
FAIR, James A. 44; Pearl 27;
  Pinkney 44
FALLS, Gilbert 145
FARLEY, William 44
FARM, L.A. 24
FARMER, Blanche 104; Caro-
  lyn 73; E.H. 44; George
  44; Hettie 31; J.C. 4;
  J.F. 44; J.M. 19,44,119,
  148; John 44; Lexie 78
FARRISS, C.F. 28
FEEZELL, Asbury 45
FERGUSON, Adelia 131;
  Beulah M. 12; Charles
  45; E.G. 45; John C. 45;
  Lewis 44; Mary 2; R. 45
FESSENDER, Prier D. 45
FIELD, J.E. 45
FINCHER, S. 5
FINE, Peter L. 45
FINNEY, A.D. 45; Lona 114
FISH, A.C. 45; Bessie 108;
  Charlie 45; Dorothy 48
FISHER, Anna V. 28; Clara
  Mae 35; Ella B. 64; Lucy
  115; Sue 104; W.A. 125
FLANAGAN, J.A. 12,15,17,18,
  19,26,29,30,31,33,35,41,
  44,51,53,54,62,66,75,79;
  86,99,112,126; 138,140,
  151,152; J.L. 45
FLANNAGAN, J.A. 42
FLEMING, J.G. 77; J.H. 63
FLOOD, James 45
FLOWERS, A.R. 45; Cordelia
  85; Jessie 45; Lydia 45;
  Patty 45; William P. 45
FLOYD, T.J. 30
FLYNT, John W. 45
FOGARITE, Jas. E. 7
FOGARTIE, Jas. E. 63
FOISTER, Jonathan 45
FORD, Eliza 145; Elizabeth
  114; Hannah 137; Horatio
  45; Jackson 45; James 45;
  John B. 45; Jonathan 45
  (2); Landon C. 45; Mary
  A. 14; Mary Ann 30; Nan-
  nie 56; Thos. 45;

FORD, Cont'd.
T.n. 7,15,43,45,49,51,55,
94,125,142
FORE, Horrace 45; Joseph U.
45; Morris 45; Thomas 45
FORESTER, Andrew J. 45;
Carolina 84; Jack 65;
J.m. 49,51,57,58,82,98,
100; John A. 45; J.P. 45;
Martha A. 93; Mary 124;
M.C. 45; Rosetta 93;
Sarah 11
FORGARTIE, J.E. 7,113
FORISTER, Sarah 51
FORRESTER, Addie 148;
Beulah 30; Caroline 16;
Caroline E. 80; Clingman
45; D.C. 45; Eli 45;
Elizabeth 77; Harriette
L. 45; H.S. 45; James 45;
James M. 45; J.M. 28,38,
45,84,88,137; Loucinda
47; Martha 68; M.M. 45;
Wm. A. 45; Wm. C. 45
FORRIESTER, Elizabeth 86
FORRISTER, J.M. 147
FORTENBERRY, James H. 46
FORTINS, William 46
FOSS, Mary D. 112
FOSTER, A.B. 46; Adam 46;
A.P. 37,65,88,99,132,141;
Frances 93; F.S. 45;
Margaret R. 37; Mary 56;
Myrtle 141; Ray 45
FOUSE, Earnest 46
FOUST, Pauline M. 92
FOUTS, Addie 28; Adie 110;
A.E. 46; Bertha 100;
Blanche 30; Brag 46;
Cathrene 146; C.H. 46;
Cleo 8; C.R. 110; D.C.
46; Emma 22; Florence
116; Green T. 46; Jacob
46; James 117,150; James
L. 111; Jas. E. 46; Jas.
L. 40; Jane 117; J.H. 46;
J.L. 8,16,44,57,63,67,69,
70,73,91,102,110,116,132,
134,143,147; John 46;
Joseph 145; Joseph L. 13,
17,22,25,28,36,40,41,42,
46,63,73,74,86,109,117,
133,145,147; Josephine
110; Jos. L. 31,56,59,95,
111,113,129,143; Lalie M.
95; Leah 46; Lucy 102;
Margaret 104; Mary 69;
M.J. 141; Nebraska 116;
Nelley 141; Noah 46;
Rebecca 141; Rovena 127;
Sicero 46; Susan C. 116;
Susannah 150; Tall 46;
Teresa A. 116; Toliver
46(2); William 46;
William P. 46; W.T. 46(2)
FOWLER, Mrs. M. Angel 127
FOWLER, E.W. 46(2); J.M. 80
Leina 109
FOX, Drusy 142; Elisha 46
(2); George 46; G.n. 46;
Hattie 34; Henry 46;
James 46; James W. 46;
J.W. 46; Lola 1; Luther
46; Lydia 1; Margaret
143; Margie 64; Mattie
91; Nana 74; Peggie 54;
Pink 125; Robert 46;
Robert L. 46; Thos. L.
46(2); Wm. R. 46; Zollie
46
FRADA, Charity 59

FRADY, A.J. 46; Alvire 1;
Annis 47; B.F. 47; Cole-
man 47; Coleman M. 47;
Mrs. Della 140; Edmond
46; Erwin 46; G.J. 47;
G.L. 47; G.W. 46,47(2);
J.A. 47; Jackson 47;
Kelse 47 Levi 46; Mar-
garet 28; May 66; Minnie
147; Rebecca 92; Rhoda J.
47; R. Jane 104; Samantha
A. 77; Solomon 46; Thomas
47; William 46; Wm. A.
47; W.S. 47
FRANCIS, J.m. 47
FRANKLIN, Catherine 75;
John 47; Joseph 47; L.A.
72; W.F. 47
FRANKS, Alice 120,149;
Anna 128; Anner 5; Annie
92; Belle 66; Charity M.
115; David 47; D.M. 18;
Doxie N. 129; E.D. 47,99,
125; E.H. 1,4,5,12,20,22,
28,37,39,42,47,71,76,88,
90,103,106,108,121,123,
132,137,138,143,147;
Elizabeth 145; Elmira 60
Ethel 60; Mrs. Eva 80;
Everett D. 47; G.F. 47;
Harrison 47; Henry 47,103;
Isam 47,138; J.A. 47;
Jake 47; James D. 47;
J.D. 9; Jessie 33; J.I.
47(2); J.L. 136; John 47;
John A. 47; John H. 47;
John R. 47(3); John T.
47; Josiah 47; J.T. 47;
Martha C. 149; Mary 145;
Mary A. 137; Mattie 62;
Minnie A. 49; M.J. 47;
Modena 30; Nancy A. 11;
Nancy C. 47; Pheriba O.
9; Sarah A. 28(2); S.C.
47; S.h. 47,103; Tillman
48; Virginia 27; William
47(2); William F. 47;
Winnie C. 122; Wm. J. 47;
W.R. 47
FRANZINE, C.J. 48
FRAZIER, Ellen 4; Marie 103;
Mary A. 37; Milton 48;
Norah H. 21; Van 48
FREEMAN, Ada F. 127; Allen
48; Carrie I. 127; Glen
48; Hasteline 61; H.C.
15,33,58,60,66,120; John
48(2); John L. 48; Lee
48; Lee 48; Martha A. 49;
Minnie 75; Robert H. 48;
Samuel 48(2); Sarah 13;
Thos. M. 48; T.W. 48
FREEZELL, Asbury 48
FRETWELL, H.B. 48; Jeff 48;
Maggie 15
FRENCH, Geo. 63; Geo. D. 30,
31,40,66,114
FRIZEL, John A. 48
FRIZELLE, Jane 47
FRIZLE, Margaret C. 46
FRIZZLE, Mack 48; Malinda 6
FROST, C.L. 48; Mrs. Meta N.
56; S.O. 63
FRY, Joseph 42
FUGATE, C.B. 97,150; Chas.
B. 18
FULBRIGHT, John 48; Johnie
F. 48; Robt. L. 48
FULCHER, Addie 129; A.E.
10; Amanda 20; Dicy M.
131; Eddie 48; Elenor 20;
Ella 138; Ethel 33;

FULCHER, Cont'd.
Eugenia E. 148; Fanny
79; J.A. 48; James B. 48;
J.B. 48; J.C. 48; Lanna
79; Mamie 15; Matilda
20; Nannie 63; Naomi 40;
Wm. 48
FULLER, J.B. 48; John 48;
Lucy 15; Mary 6; M.C. 44;
Sam 48(2); Sela H.L. 71
FULTON, J.H. 15,16,22,54,
59,74,115; Jno. H. 121;
John H. 5,48,50,84; Mack
48; Margarite 60; Mary
M. 105; Nancy M. 66
FURR, Susa 37; W.E. 48

GABBY, Daniel, Jr. 48
GABRELS, F.E. 134
GAITHER, Jane 133
GALBRATH, James M. 48
GALION, Mary L. 13
GALLIAN, James 48
GALLOWAY, Alonzo 48; P.C. 8
GAREY, Edward M. 48
GARLAND, Ada 23; Adda E. 78;
Andy 49; Barnet 49; Chas.
L. 49; David L. 49; Doc
49; Elizabeth 68; Flora
15,127; Geo. M. 49; Geo.
W. 49; G.L. 49; H.L. 49;
H.P. 49; Humphry 48;
H.W. 49; Jane 99; J.m.
49; John 48; Julia 32;
Laura 141; Lee 49; L.H.
11,15,25,39,43,49,53,58,
65,80,87,96,102,104,105,
111,121,129,141,142,144;
Lizzie 138; L.M. 101;
Lulah 94; Mae 41; Maggie
8; Margaret L. 57; Martha
44; Martha J. 144; Mary
E. 55; Mary G. 138; M.C.
55; Mrs. Minnie A. 108;
Noah L. 49; R.J. 49;
Robert L. 49; Sallie 77;
William 99; William M.
48; William P. 48
GARNER, A. Jackson 49;
Augusta 106; Bertha 117;
Dora Lee 24; James Grady
49; Lois V. 29
GARRET, Elizabeth 12
GARRETT, Andrew 49; James
F. 49; Jane 68; Julius
49; L.N. 62; Mary C. 40;
S.G. 16; Walter V. 49;
William R. 49
GARRIS, Arnold 49
GARRISON, Alice S. 44;
Caleb 49; Catherine 117;
Elvira E. 21; Henry I.
64; Hurshel 49; Ida 61;
John 49; Lallie V. 141;
Lela 54; Maggie 138;
M.J. 65; Nancy 132; O.L.
49; R.B. 49; R.P. 8,69;
R.Q. 28; Samuel 49
GASH, Alla 49; Mary A. 100
GASTON, Bertha W. 108;
Elizabeth L. 32; Mary 32;
Parley C. 49
GATE, Sarah 124; Virginia
L. 7
GATHER, Jacob 49
GAY, J.E. 61,67; Margaret
H. 61
GAZIWAY, John 49
GELISPIE, Mary S. 58
GENNETT, N.W. 49
GENTRY, A.E. 49; Emmer 49

GEORGE, Louisa 12
GETTIS, Frank T. 6,31,49,
  58,62,117,148,150; F.T.
  49,86
GHORMLEY, Alma 13; Clara
  116; Mrs. Lula D. 106
GHORMLEY/GHOMLEY, M. 1,2,
  13,16,21,25,44,50,57,
  61,65,72,76,81,83,89,
  90,96,105,109,114,116,
  124,128,132,135,137,149,
  151; M.D. 49(2); Minnie
  117; W.D. 49
GHRMLEY, Emma 11
GIBBS, A.C. 112; Andrew 49;
  Bryan 49; Charles W. 49;
  C. Virginia 14; J.A. 3;
  Jane G. 97; John N. 49;
  John W. 49; Laura 132;
  Mary M. 119; Orrie G.
  14; Ruth 97; Sarah T.
  119; Sophria 35; Susanah
  8; William 49
GIBBY, Bryant 50; Elisha
  50; James C. 50; J.S.
  50; Logan C. 50; Mar-
  garet 7,77; Mary 82;
  William 50
GIBSON, Alexander 50; Anna
  E. 147; Asbury 50; Ben-
  jamin 50,51; Birdell 57;
  Caroline 56; Carrie 89;
  Dora E. 21; D. Walter
  50; Elias P. 50; Elijah
  50; Ellen 72; Ellis 51;
  Emeline 50; Emily A. 34;
  E.T. 50; Florence 12;
  Frank W. 51; Georgia A.
  56; G.H. 50; Harrison
  50; Hiram 50; H.L. 50;
  H.M. 50; Hugh 50; Ira
  D. 51; Isaac 50; Jake
  50; Janie 148; Jas. G.
  50; Jason 50; Jaunita
  57; Jay C. 50; J.C. 50;
  John 50,95; Jno. S./John
  S. 13,19,50,62,63,69,
  79,84,85,101,102,109,
  113,123,126,138; John L.
  50; John P. 50(2); John
  T. 86; Joseph 50(2);
  Joseph R. 51; J.S. 2,50,
  85,109,123,145; J. Thomas
  51; Leander 50(2); Lillie
  6,25; Lona 73; Lou 123;
  Luther 51; Maggie 85;
  Mammie B. 112; Margaret
  37; Margaret A. 24;
  Mary J. 128; Mattie 22;
  Minnie 73, 128; Mrs.
  Minnie 51; N.A. 23; Neil
  51; newton G. 50; N.F.
  51; Nobia 92(2); Nola
  36; Pallie 140; Pearl
  63,122; Rhody 50; Robt.
  J. 50; Roda 55; Rosetta
  22; Roy C. 51; Ruby Lee
  13; Mrs. Sallie 134;
  Sam 9,50; Sandy A. 50;
  S.A. 123; Samuel 67,98;
  S.B. 50; S.W. 50; Thomas
  E. 50; Vina 77; W.A. 50;
  Walter 50; Weaver 51;
  W. Henry 50; Willie 51
GILBERT, Margaret S. 57
GILLESPIE, Abrigail 31;
  Cecilla 86; Henry 51;
  J.H. 136; J.M. 32; Lola
  78; L.T. 51; Maggie 126;
  Marion 51; Nancy 41;
  Nellie 49; Nina 76;
  Nora L. 53; Obra 34;

GILLESPIE, Cont'd.
  Sarah A. 41; W. Frank
  17,51
GILLIAM, Daniel 51
GILLILAND, Robert E. 51
GIPSEN, Eliza A. 36
GIPSON, Catherine E. 50;
  Elizabeth J. 51; James
  50; Joe Dendy 50; John
  G. 143; Joseph 50; Josie
  4; Mary 38; Mary L. 60;
  P.A. 50; Sallie 55;
  Samuel 122
GIVENS, Grace 129
GLASE, Nancy 47
GLAZE, G.M. 51
GLEEN, T.F. 58
GLENN, F. 125; L.F. 24,121;
  T.E. 2; T.F. 15,20,55;
  114,120,128
GLIDEWELL, Callie 43; C.M.
  23; Sarah R. 20
GLIDWELL, Ada 61; Ida 49;
  J.H. 51; T.A. 51
GLIMPES, Leonard 51
GLYMPS, Mary C. 40
GODFRED, Frank 76
GODWIN, E.M. 51; Sidney 51
GOODE, Elizabeth 85
GOODSON, Joseph 51
GORMLEY, M. 38
GOSS, Louie J. 51
GOTTWALS, John Z. 51
GRAHAM, Althea Z. 112; James
  H. 51; Swan 51
GRAHL, Harriet E. 77;
  William M. 51
GRANT, A.B. 51; Alice 26;
  Arthur 52; Artie C. 121;
  A. Sherman 52; Balm 52;
  Bonnie G. 126; Chas. T.
  52; D.A. 52; Daphine 27;
  Eliza Ann 67; Elizabeth
  52; Eliza F. 61; Ellen
  100; Faney W. 52; Frank
  Fred 52; G.C. 51; G.W.
  52; Henry 51; James 51;
  James M. 52,124; James
  S. 52; Jessie 51; J.H.
  6,27,30,32,48,52,84,98,
  101,117,124; J. Henry
  52; J.J. 52; John 51,52;
  John P. 51; John S. 52;
  Joseph 51; Joseph A. 51;
  J.R. 51; J.W. 52; Lelia
  103; Louisa 22; Manda 37;
  Margaret 143; Margaret E.
  23; Mart 52; Martha M.
  100; Mary 23; Maude 52;
  M.E. 52; Minnie 21; Nany
  35; Noel 52; Olsen A. 52;
  Rachel 13; Rachel A. 52;
  R.E. 38; Richard 52;
  Rosa 149; Sarah 76; Tho-
  mas 52; V.D. 52; V.M. 52;
  W.C. 52; Wilkey 51; Wil-
  key N. 52; William 52;
  William C. 51; William
  H. 51; William M. 51;
  W.M. 51
GRASTY, M.C. 52; Shirley 9;
  Taylor 52
GRAY, Addie A. 55; Annie I.
  32; Carolin 1; Catherine
  F. 151; Clifford 53;
  Dallas 52; Elmira 8;
  Emma D. 113; Enos 52;
  E.T. 39; Ethel 93; Eula-
  la 94; Fannie 24,52;
  George W. 52; H.E. 81;
  Henretta 33; H.R. 52;
  Isaac 52; James 54;

GRAY, Cont'd.
  James G. 52; James K. 52;
  Javan J. 52; J.B. 70,97;
  J.E. 53,67,104; J.J. 107;
  J.K. 1-4,6-16,18-21,24-27,
  29-31,33-37,39-41,43,45-
  51,53-56,58,59,61,73-71,
  73-77,80-86,88,90-99,102-
  194,196,111,112,114,117,
  118,122,125,126,128,129,
  132-139,143,145,147-149,
  151; Jno. P. 52; Joe 52;
  Jno. B./John B. 9,32,46,
  56,66,70,72,77,88,101,
  103,132,137,138,141,147;
  John J. 52; Joseph Burk
  53; J.S. 53,57; Julia
  Ann 94; Lelia Esther 147;
  Louisa 28; Lucy Sue 31;
  Margie A. 35; Martha A.
  80; Mary 140; Mary A. 45,
  50; Mary C. 3; Mary Lou
  68; Minnie 142; M. Louisa
  69; Matilda 41; Myrtle
  E. 45; Sarah E. 8; Sue
  36; Thomas R. 52; Thos.
  R. 52; W.H. 52; William
  52(2); William H. 52;
  Zettee 68
GREEN, A. Judson 53; Arthur
  L. 53; Beatrice 140;
  Cecil S. 53; Chris. C.
  53; Christy E. 141; C.M.
  E. 53; E.H. 53; Eliza V.
  36; Elmer D. 53; Eva
  134; Flora 68; Hillard
  53; Homer C. 53; J.A.
  53,126; J.H. 102; John
  A. 41,53,99,114; John S.
  44; Joseph 53; Jourdan
  53; Laura 140; L.F. 97;
  Lizzie 47; L.L. 139;
  Luther 53; Maggie 76;
  Margaret 64; Martha S.
  25; Mary J. 121; Mary M.
  71; Maud 11; Minerva 17;
  Molly 145; Pleasant 53;
  R.C. 5393); Retta 140;
  Robert 53; Sarah 151;
  Silas 53; Silas J. 53;
  Philip L. 95; T.F. 48;
  Thad. M. 53; William 53;
  W.T. 53; W. Thomas 53
GREENWOOD, Ada 92; Clarence
  G. 53; Betty 4; F.M. 53;
  G.H. 53; Ice 58; Isabell
  79; Jas. W. 53; John D.W.
  53; Josa 28; J.W. 38,146;
  Lethea 59; Madison 53;
  Maggie B. 24; Maria 88;
  Mary M. 68; Thomas 53(2);
  W.H.A. 53; William 53;
  William H. 53
GREGGS, William 54
GREGORY, A. 145; Addie 128;
  Adolphus 54; A.H. 49,54,
  65,76,103,116,117,151;
  Alice L. 46; Andrew 53;
  Archabald 53; Asbury 54;
  Bell 38; Bessie 124;
  B.H. 54; Birdie 33; Calli
  133; Charley 54; Charley
  M. 54; Chas. M. 54; Dicy
  R. 66; Dora 12; E. Caro-
  line 66; Geo. L. 54;
  George 54; George W. 54;
  Henry 53; J.A. 54; J.C.
  54; J.H. 5492; 57,131;
  J.M. 54; John 54(3);
  John C. 53; Joseph W. 54;
  J.W. 11,44,103; L.A. 135;
  Laura 108; Laura C. 3;

GREGORY, Cont'd.
Lou 115; Lucy 97; Lydia
41; Maden 54; Maggie 17;
Martha 68,151; Mary 56;
Mary Bell 95; Mary C.
68; Mary J. 67,91; Maud
119; Minnie 18; Nerva
10; R.A. 54; Roxana 129;
Sallie 18,72; Sallie E.
68; Sarah 64; Sarah E.
147; Susan 50; Texie 137;
W. Alex 54; William 54
(2); William R. 54; Wil-
lie 1; W.J. 54; Wm. T.
54
GREY, Coradine 60
GRIBBLE, Addie 55; Annie
145; Annie O. 140; James
L. 54; Jno. J. 54; John
54(2); J. Wilburn 54;
Kathleen 122; Lucius M.
54; Margaret 26; Margaret
J. 97; Mary C. 110; Nancy
145; Rachel E. 4; Robert
W. 54; S.L. 130; Ted 54;
Thomas 54; Virginia 28;
William A. 54(2); William
M. 54
GRIFFIN, Alfred 54; Bertha
149; J.H. 54; Lawrence
54; Lawson 54; Patsy 89
GRIGGE, Leaner 104
GRIGGS, Altha 10; E.L. 55;
Ella 78; James 104; J.M.
24,55,88,104; Loas 70;
Louisa 114; Martha 131;
R.A. 55; W.L. 26,63,78,
105,108; Woody 54; W.T.
40
GRILLIANY, Mary A. 53
GRINGSTAFF, C.S. 55
GRISHAM, A.F. 55; Daisy 111;
Jule 55
GRIST, A.J. 55; Meril 61;
Viola 21; William J. 55;
Willie 111; W.J. 22,29,
105,115
GROSS, Elizabeth 143; George
W. 55
GROVES, William 55
GUDGER, Benjamin M. 55;
Bishop 55; B.M. 123;
Eva 65; Hattie 14;
William 55
GUESS, James C. 55
GUEST, Charlie 55; Geo. A.
55; George 55; Ida 106;
James 55; Mary D. 75;
R. Holland 55
GUFFEE, A.A. 94; Addie 125;
Anna 122; Annie 128(2);
Ben 55; Bessie 103; Dav-
id 55(2); E.N. 55(2);
Fannie B. 39; Hattie 43;
Henry 55(2); James 55;
Jennie 5; Jesse R. 55;
J.L. 55(2); John H. 55;
Joseph E. 55; Lassie 83;
Mrs. Lassie 99; Lizzie
5,52; L.J. 78; Martha M.
72; Mary 49,65; Nancy 82;
Nannie 125; Samuel 55;
Susie 45; Thomas 55;
William 55; William C. 55
GUFFEY, Callie 8; Ellen 20;
Emma 38; Flora 29;Hattie
130; Henry L. 55; Martha
77; Mary E. 20; O.B. 55;
Pearl 36; Rachel 83;
Rolen S. 55; Sarah M. 40;
W.H. 16,135

GUFFIE, Mrs. Lassie 45;
Roxie 115
CUILLIAMS, Nancy 132
GUILLIAMS, William B. 55
GUINN, Ben 55; Hiley 55;
James W. 55; Jerry 55
GUIRE, Mary 143
GULLETH, Guy A. 51
GUNTER, T.B. 55
GUY, Albert 56(2); Beecher
Betty 144; Birdie 123;
Clark 56; Daniel 56;
D.N. 56; Ed 56; Elizabeth
A. 50; Ella 104; Emma
126; Furman 56; George
56(2); Henretta 141;
Henry 56; Ida 78; James
56; Johnston 56; Joseph
56; Josephine 50; Joshua
R. 56; Margaret A. 96;
Martha Ann 56; Mary E.
29; May 121; Minnie 41;
Nannie 10; R.E. 8; Reb-
ecca 56; Sallie 79;
Sarah A. 130; Timox 26;
William 56(2); William
P. 56; Willie 79; W.W.
56
GUYE, Irene 26
GUYER, Catherine 40; David
56; Elizabeth 18; G.H.
56; James 56; Luthenia
42; Margaret 88; Phillip
56; Sarah 42; Wm. 143
GUYNN, Bertha 30

HACKET, Nancy 110
HADGCOCK, Martha 92
HAGG, T.E. 43
HALDERMAN, Dan 56
HALL, A. 41; Albey 56;
Albie 151; Aleck 56;
Alford 2; Alfred 56,117;
A.M. 56; A.W. 57; Callie
Carolin 135; Cary McD.
56; Clingman 56; D.A. 56;
David L. 56; David R. 56;
Delphia 27; Dewitt C. 56;
Edna 132; Elbert 56;
Eliza J. 94; Elna 13;
Fannie Bell 95; F.H. 57;
Furman 57; Geneva 121;
Gertrude 127; H.A. 56;
Hattie 22,29,78; Helen
75; Ida 6; Ilar 133;
James 57; James A. 56;
Jamison 56; Jane 61,75;
John 1,2,4-9,12-20,22-
24;26-33,35,36,39,40,43,
44-53,56-58,61,64,65,69,
71,73,76,77,79,81-83,87,
89,90,92,94,97,99,100,
102,104-107,110,112,114,
117,118,122,125,126,130,
133,135,138,141,142,143,
144,147,151; John M. 57;
John W. 56(2); Lassie
105; Laura 102; Laura D.
122; Lena 56; Lester 57;
Lexie 133; Ligah 57;
Louisa 115; Lucinda 41;
Maggie 19; Maggie L. 117;
Mary A. 17,74; May 95;
M.M. 5692); Nannie C. 97;
Oliver V. 57; Rebecca
20,133; R.H. 56; Robert
116; Robert S. 56; R.
Sam 57; Rufus 57; Rufus
H. 56; Sarah 27; Tudor N.
57; Tudor T. 56; Will 57;
Willia May 152; Wm. G. 57

HALLECK, Joseph 57
HALLICK, Mary 130
HALLOWAY, Champ 57
HAMBY, John C. 57
HAMILTON, F.A. 57; Gilbert
A. 57; Letty J. 120;
Robert 57
HAMPTON, B.F. 57; E.R. 57;
John 57; Mary F. 47; Mary
J. 21; Ollie 44; Robert
57; Thomas G. 57
HAMRICK, W.C. 36
HANCOCK, Ethie 66
HANEY, Alice 118; Ambrose
57; Annie 25; Charles 57;
Charley W. 57; D.C. 16;
Ellen 44; Frank 57; I.B.
57; J.H. 57; J.M. 57;
J.N. 57; John 57; Laura
25; Lissie 148; Mark 57;
Mathew 57(2); Paralee 58;
Riley 57; Sarah 16; W.C.
57
HANNER, James 57
HANRICK, W.C. 37,81,86
HANSON, Eli 61
HARBISON, Thomas C. 57; Thos
G. 57
HARDEN, D.C. 88,119
HARDIE, William E. 57
HARDIN, J.C. 45
HARDMAN, John B. 57
HARKINS, Jeefia 57
HARNESS, Richard 58
HARPER, Mary 89; Ollie 81;
Sarah 147; W.B. 58;
William B. 58
HARRELL, Clifford 58
HARRINGTON, S.F. 43; S.H.
16,18,23,29,47,58,60,57,
75,103,105,107,109,125,
131
HARRIS, Bessie 60; Charley
58; Delia 27; E.J. 17;
Hettie 42; Jas. G. 58;
John H. 58; Lydia 29;
Will 58
HARRISON, Allie 101; Benja-
min 58; Bettie 69; Earl
M. 58; E.L. 58; Hattie
110; Horace 58; Jeramiah
58; J.M. 58; John O. 58;
Mary 9; Myra 125; Ryle 5
Sallie 29; V.B. 61,94,11
HARSHAW, Ann E. 45; Cale 55
Jesse 58
HARTNESS, Hiram 102
HARWOOD, Patton 58
HASCUSSON, Malinda 38
HASKET, Andrew C. 58; Cathe
rine 22; D.A. 18; J.C. 5
John T. 58; Levi 58;
Nancy 1; R.E. 114; W.H.
18,30,41,146
HASKETT, Lizzie 104; Lorena
103; Lyda 134; Margaret
46; Mary E. 47; Otelia
62; Parker 58; Sarah Ann
16
HASTIN, Franklin 58
HASTING, Albert 58; Eliza-
beth 91; F. Columbus 58;
Ida 85; Jason A. 58; Jo
58; Leona 36; Rosa 133;
Wimer 58
HASTINGS, Fanny 105; H.A.
96; Ollie M. 120; Rosa
HAUSER, Love H. 58; Therma
58
HAUSIER, Luther 58
HAWKES, B.H. 58

HOLBROOKS, Cont'd.
A.H. 63; Ann 66; Bettie
A. 38; Ezra 63; Fannie
113; F.h. 63; Henry 63;
Ira L. 63; James H. 63;
Jerry M. 63; John, Jr.
63; Jonah 63; J.R. 63;
J.S. 63; Julia 130; Lark-
in S. 63; Laura 40; Luc-
ella 68; Lula 143;
Martha 91; Mary A. 105;
Mary C. 88; Moses 63;
Octie 8; R.C. 71; Teli-
tha 127; Vinnie Alice 35;
William 63(2); W.M. 63;
Wm. F. 63; Wm. T. 63;
W.P. 63
HOLCOMB, Caleb 109; Mary
109
HOLDEN, Alice 98; Alma 84;
Arthur H. 64; Coburn 64;
Cora 84; H.F. 64; Isaac
T. 64; J.R. 64; Lindia
85; Madison J. 63; Maggie
67; Minnie 139; Minnie A.
114; M.J. 64; N.E. 57,73,
134; Pallie 85; Robt. H.
63; Synda 114; Ticia 96;
Wm. F. 64
HOLEBROOKS, R.V. 74
HOLLAND, Allafair 95; Anth-
ony 64(2); Belle 137;
Benjamin 64(2); Bertha
90; Bertie 39; Bessie
107; Bethany 122; Bright
64; Caroline 114; Cath-
erine 118; Cecil 64;
Charlotte 105; Cora 84;
Coralee M. 38; Cordelia
19; David G. 64; Dicie
J. 149; Drucilla 95;
Edy 114; Elizabeth 114;
Emma 141; Frank 64;
Frank W. 44; Girlie 64;
Hallie 95; Harlie 64;
Heerble 9; Ivalee 17;
James 64(2); James H.
64; J.M. 64; John 64;
Laura 34,129; Lee H. 64;
L.L. 64; Lora C. 31;
Maggie 53; Marvin 64;
Mary J. 42; Mattie 10,
146; M. Troy 64; Nora 91;
Ollie 135; Perry 64;
Radford 6492); R.L. 64
(2); Rosetta 91; Sallie
54; Samuel 100,118;
Sarah Ann 75; Sarah E.
38; Soloman 64; Sophronia
38; Tillman 64; T. Luther
64; Vallie 54; V.E. 149;
William J. 64; W.M. 64
(2); W.S. 64
HOLLEN, M. 118; Martha 74
HOLLOWAY, J.G.W. 111
HOLT, Andrew 64; Bonnie 82;
Elizabeth 63; George 64;
Helen Catherine 118;
John M. 64; Martha 98;
Marvin 64; Ruth 9; Thelma
35
HONEYCUTT, Margarie 31
HOOD, Americas 95; Iseral P.
64; Jacob 121,151; James
N. 64; William 64
HOOPER, Andrew 65; B.H. 65;
Edward 65; Eloise 75;
Mrs. Estell 130; F.A.
12; Grace 136; James M.
65; Joseph 65; L.C. 65,
141; Martha 104; M.M.
65; Polly 150; Rebecca

HOOPER, Rebecca, Cont'd.
76; Sallie 89; Thos. J.
65; Wm. 65
HOPE, Radford 65
HOPKINS, Carry 63; Dora
52; Ellis 65,66; F. Ray
66; James 65; John 65;
Louisa 102; Mary S. 80;
Nancy 12; Raleigh 66;
Sallie 134; Sam L. 65;
Samuel T. 65; S.O. 65;
William 65; William E.
65; W.R. 65
HOPPAR, Allie 59
HOPPER, Andrew 66; Geo. 66;
Jasper 66; Joseph 66;
Mary 13; Rachel 20;
William 66
HORN, Alfred W. 66; Edward
F. 66; Leonard 66; Lou
V. 119; Mary E. 70;
Wm. 66
HORNE, Melvina 138
HORSLEY, James W. 66
HORTEN, Molly 3
HORTON, David 66
HOUK, G.L. 66
HOUSTON, Alexander 66;
Allie Fair 26; Amanda
54; Ann 104; Bella 73;
Bertha 32; Beulah Z. 60;
Bonnie 129; Calvin 66;
Calvin C. 66; Charlie
I. 66; Chas. P. 66;
Cordie 143; Cuba 67;
Don 66; Effie T. 119;
E.G. 66; Ellen 115;
Emily 38; Emulus G. 66;
Ethel 130; Eula 60;
Eva 81; Fannie 45; Floyd
66(2); Geo. I. 66;
George W. 66; G.S. 66;
Grady 66; Hulda J. 64;
Isaac 66; Jane 72; J.F.
139; J.T. 138,142; J.
Thomas 66; J.W. 66;
Lavada 46; Lelia E. 60;
Lettie M. 131; Louise
149; Lydia 95; Mary J.
149; Mattie 95; May 139;
Mel 66; Monroe 66; Noah
133; Parthena 102; Paul-
ine 137; Pearl 74;
Rebecca 117; R. Hensley
66; Richard H. 66;
Robert H. 66; Rosa 40;
Rosetta E. 44; Ruth 109;
Sarah 15; Sarah C. 118;
Susie 22; W.A. 66
HOVIS, G.A. 60
HOWARD, Addie F. 29; Alex
65; Alexander 65; Arie
Ella 96; Carl 65; Cora
141; David F. 16,28,58,
151; D.F. 16,18,19,20,
21,28,49,54,57,58,62,
63,65,66,67,68,79,81,
90,96,98,101,105,111,
118,130,136,137,140,141,
144,147,148; Elizabeth
13; Geo. 118; Geo. E.
65; George 65; Georgia
S. 49; Hattie 100; Hester
R. 101; John 24,45,80,
94; John D. 7,72,130,
135,139; L. 13,21,23,
39,57,65,78,80,99,101,
119,125,131,139; Lafay-
ette 65; Larence 65;
Lassie 137; Levada R.
58; L.H. 131; Martha
114; Martha A. 82;

HOWARD, Cont'd.
Marvin 65; Mary 61;
Mary J. 13; May 98; M.C.
21; Mercilla 93; M.M.
37; Nancy M. 99; Nichol-
as F. 65; Noah I. 65;
P. 20,29,65,122; Pearl
79; Robert 65; Robert L.
65; Rosetta 144; Rosetta
S. 99; Sam 99; Samuel 20,
30,65; Sarah E. 114;
Susana 124; Virgil 65;
William 65; Wm. A. 65;
W. Sylvanus 65; W.W. 65,
106
HOWE, R.S. 17
HOWELL, A.R. 65; Denver 65;
D.V. 45; E.W. 54; Harry
65; Henry 65; John 65;
John D. 64; Luke 65;
Mattie 73; R.S. 86;
Thelma 59
HOWIE, Robt. 40
HUBBARD, Jenny 9; J.G. 66;
Lewis McBride 66
HUCKABY, John 66
HUDSON, Arthur S. 66; Maud
100; Mike 66; Vera 60
HUDSPETH, Leonard R. 66
HUFF, Mrs. Iler 116
HUGGINS, Betty 34; Cather-
ine S. 55; Desda 25;
D.F. 80; E.A. 67; Mrs.
Elizabeth 72; F.L. 95;
Georgia E. 83; Hattie
70; Hattie P. 57; James
67; Jane 40,118; J.L.
100; John 67; John H. 67;
J.W. 67; Lona 134;
Margaret 70; Mary M. 40;
Robert 107; Sarah L. 87;
Sophia 55; W.A. 67
HUGHES, Andrew H. 67; Bell
25; B.M. 67; Daisy 117;
Ed. 67; Ed. T. 67; Ella
117,149; Frank 67; G.D.
67; George 67; Georgie
149; Gilbert 67; Heab
67; H.J. 113; H.L. Grady
67; Jackson 67; James W.
67; Jane 84; J.B. 67;
John E. 67; Laura 95;
Mack 67; Margaret 4,118;
Margie 40; Mary 8; Mary
E. 63; Pansy 19; Ralph
67; Rhoda 132; Robert
67; Sallie 120; Susa 147
Walter M. 67; W.I. 22,
39,40,67,80,100,101,105,
107,119,148; William P.
67; W.V. 67
HUGHSTON, Elizabeth 87;
John W. 66,67
HUMPHREY, Chas. G. 67;
George 67; Glenn 67;
J.H. 67; John D. 67;
Maggie 97
HUMPHREYS, Allie 6; Wil-
liam 67
HUNEYCUTT, Josiah 67;
Leonard 64
HUNNICUTT, Dorthy 14; Lena
129; May 31
HUNT, J.B. 67; T.R. 67
HUNTER, Jason H. 67;
Lavina 5; Mitchel 67;
Nicholas A. 67; Pheoba
47
HURST, Albert T. 68; Arden
110; B.J. 67; B. Judson
68; Belle 50; Carie A.
52; Caroline 24; Chas.

HURST, Chas. T. Cont'd.
68; Edith 106; Elizabeth
29; Emlis 68; Fannie 45;
Geo. B. 68; Geo. Bascomb
68; G.J. 68; G.N. 67;
Harriet M. 120; Hattie
53; Horace C. 68; Horace
J. 68; Iona 36; Ivlee
34; James 3 67; J.D. 68;
Jesse C. 68; J.M. 68;
John A. 67; John C. 52,
68,77,85,103,108,123;
Judith A. 69; Louisa 34;
Lucinda M. 43; Madison
67; Margaret J. 123;
Maud 123; Myrtle 107;
Nancy C. 137; Nancy E.
79; Nora 86; Rebecca 123,
151; R.M. 1; Sarah C.
108; Valzora 77; William
67; William T. 67
HUSCUSSON, Almer 146; Della
53; Emma E. 126; Mrs.
Mattie 146
HUSSCUSSON, B.H. 68; Harley
68; John 68; Wm. Taylor
68
HUSKEY, Cecil G. 68
HUSTEN, Sarah 149
HUSTON, Elbert I. 68; Hens-
ley 68; James C. 68;
James R. 68
HUTSON, J.H. 68; Thos. 68
HYAT, Minnie L. 124
HYATT, Ann Eliza 74; Bertha
L. 150; Clare Faye 110;
Early M. 68(2); Edgar
68; Eva Mae 35; Filetes
68; John 68; Mary 9;
Mary A. 88; Minnie 144;
N.B. 24,150; Neomy L.
141; Robert B. 68; Seth
H. 4; S.H. 12,68; Shad-
rick 68; Telecha 81;
W.B. 6,12,16,80,81,108,
114,131,151
HYDE, Catharine 26; David
68; Elizabeth 26,56;
Jane C. 56; J.B. 124;
H.H. 65; John B. 68;
Nancy T. 102; Perley 68;
Rachel 15,69; William 68
HYLTON, N.J. 68

ICENHOWER, Berdie 63; J.C.
68; Loyd 68; Mamie 109
INGRAM, Anne E. 58; John 9,
68(2); Mary 16; Mary A.
24,78; Mira C. 143;
Nancy 109; Octie 109;
Vina 66
INMAN, Bessie 47; L.L. 68
IRISH, Eleanor 83
IVAN, John 68
IVESTER, Julius P. 68;
Lallie 148; Sidney J. 68

JACKSON, Andrew 69; Eliza
48; G.H. 27,56; James S.
69; Nancy 80; Oscar H.
69
JACOBS, Amanda 133; A.T.
69; A.W. 2,11,32,40,41,
47,68,69,74,95,108,110,
111,113,118,120,141,142,
147; Bettie 101; Bird 69;
B.P. 69(4); Callie N. 92;
Cary 22; Chas. E. 69;
Chas. T. 69; Cora 50;
C.S. 69; David 69; David

JACOBS, David A. Cont'd.
A. 69; Edith 33(2); Elen
33; Eliza 28; Elizabeth
22; Emma 33; Emma A. 142;
Fannie 145; Florence 84;
Frank 69; Geo. A. 97;
G.L. 69; Harriett 133;
Hattie 6; Jas. P. 69;
J. Logan 69; John 69;
John M. 69; J.T. 69;
Laura L. 137; Louisa C.
132; Lucinda 3; Margaret
107,148; Martha 133; Mrs.
Martha 136; Mary 56;
Maud E. 73; M.E. 123;
Minnie 33,80; Mittie 46;
Nannie B. 81,92; Ollie
2; Rhoda 70; R.P. 69;
Sol 69; Solomon 69(2);
W.B. 69; William A. 69
JACOBSON, W.D. 63
JAMES, Andrew J. 69; Anna
89; Benjamin 69; Charles
69; Dank 69; John 69;
Lawton F. 69; Samuel 69
JAMERSON, T.P. 94
JAMES, Earnest 89; M.H. 54
JAMESON, T.P. 69
JAMISON, Carl 69; Essie
109; Grover 69
JARRETT, A.A. 92; Carrie M.
150; Daniel 69; D.H. 14;
H.I. 109; John 69; Mary
Ann 142; Robt. F. 69
JARROTT, Devereaux 69
JAYNES, Zelma 65
JEMKINS, Dora B. 43
JENKINS, Amanda J. 103;
Buena V.E. 122; Burdelle
111; Butler 70; Charley
70; Effie 118; Elsie 124;
F.M. 70; George 70; J.
Allen 70; Hattie 123;
Jennie 131; John 70(3);
Jonas 69; Lawson 70;
Lillian M. 68; Margaret
J. 129; Mary 50,65,68;
Melvill 70; Peter 69;
Silas 70; S.W. 70; Thomas
69,70; W.A. 12; W.B. 70;
W.J. 2,7,14,34,37,75,79,
82,85,86,87,90,95,102,
120,123,131,138,143,144;
Wm. J. 70; W.R. 2; Zelma
88
JENNINGS, Allie 89; Burdell
105; Charity 118; Charles
C. 70; Dolly 50; E.C.
70; Elizabeth 149; Elmer
70; Emmer 138; James 70;
James J. 70; Jessie 39;
J.J. 70(2); John 70(2);
Martha 35; Mary 74;
Sarah 47; V.V. 70; W.I.
60; W.T. 3,60,74,79,102
JENNINS, James 70
JENTRY, John 70; Nancy 92;
Polly 70
JEROME, C.P. 70; Robert L.
70
JOHNS, Martha 109
JOHNSON, Alfred A. 70;
Birdie L. 68; Callie A.
122; Claude 71; Clyde
71; Edward 138; E.L. 70;
Ellen D. 9; Elmer 70;
Ethel 136; F.N. 28,30,
72,100,140; Geo. M. 70;
G. Frank 71; G.M. 4,39,
120,146; Henry 141;
Homer D. 70,71; Jackson
113; Jacob L. 70; James

JOHNSON, James C., Cont'd.
C. 71; James·Riley 70;
John 70(3); Josie 132;
Julia 1; Lealer 12; L.H.
70; Lillie 87; L.J. 71;
Louisa 137; Lowellen 78;
Luther 70; Lydia M. 4;
Mira 6; N.A. 142; Nannie
149; P.N. 70; Ruby 74;
S.M. 71; T.B. 70,111;
Thomas H. 70; W.I. 70;
Willard 71; William 70;
Wm. S. 70;
JOHNSTON, Allen 71; Amanda
A. 87; Benjamin 71; Chas.
D. 71; Elizabeth 79;
F.N. 39,79,112,146; G.M.
30,99; Grover 71; Harvey
71; H.C.C. 71; Henry H.
71; Jackson 71; James H.
71; James L. 71; Jane 23;
John L. 71; Lynn 66;
Mandy 83; Margaret 68;
Martha 18; Mary 2,117;
M.M. 18; Reid 71(2);
Roe 71; Silva A. 27;
Thos. J. 71; Thos., Jr.
71
JOLLAY, Beulah C. 102;
Emma 99; John G. 71;
Lyman 71; N.J. 137; Noah
134,97; N.L. 93,96,146;
Noah L. 106,141; Rebecca
77
JOLLEY, L.A. 132; N.L. 64
JOLLY, Marshall A. 71; N.L.
34,89; Noah 71; Noah L.
61,130
JOINES, Sarah 114
JONES, Addie 19; A. Jackson
72; Alfred L. 72; Arie
89; Artelia 20; Arthur
73; B.C. 73; Benjamine
72; Bettie 145; B.H. 92;
Callie 23,62,139; Carrie
134; C.D. 78; Charley
72; Charley N. 72; Char-
lotte 130; Chas. A. 72;
Cora 16; Cora A. 78;
Dolly 14; E.J. 71; Elcie
101; Elias 71; Eliza 55,
116; Elizabeth 8,93;
Ella 119; Elsie 1; Ema-
line 91,97; Emily 77;
Emma 54,111; Fannie J.
74; Fenton 72; Frances
J. 127; Francis 106;
Frank H. 73; G.A. 72;
Geo. A. 72; Geo. L. 73;
George 73; George A. 72;
George L. 73; Gilmer A.
73; G.L. 14,45; H. 71;
Hannah 109; Harriet R.
148; Harriett C. 55;
H.C. 71; Henderson 71;
Henrietta A. 99; Henry
R. 73; Hester 62; H.F.
72; Ida 85; James 72,73;
James A. 72; James S.
72; Jane 86; Jennie 101,
145; Jim 73; J.M. 71;
Joe 72; Joe Brown 72;
John F. 72; John G. 71;
John S. 71; John W. 72
(2); Joseph D. 71,72;
Joshua 71; Kate 87; L.A.
73; Larkin 72; Laura 140;
L.C. 73; L.E. 72;
Leanard 71; Leonard 143;
Lewis 72; Lillie B. 51;
Lucy 33; Lusinda 48;
Luthenie 143; Maggie 150;

JONES, Cont'd.
Mamie 50,98; Marcus 72;
Margaret 50,63; Margar-
et J. 75; Maria 108;
Martha Ann 99; Martha
J. 128; Martin F. 72;
Mary 25,71; Mary A. 118;
Mary B. 38; Mary E. 28,
90; Mrs. Mattie 150;
M.C. 64; M.E. 148; Mell
123; M.W. 72; Myrtle
33; Nancy 82; Nancy C.
80; Nichols W. 72; Nora
L. 92; Mrs. Odelia 140;
O. Howard 73; Olivia 16;
Ollie 132; Oscar 72;
Rachel 151; R.C. 142;
Richard 71; Riley 72;
Robert 72; Rufus 71;
Sallie 127; Samuel 72,
103; Sarah 13,99; S.J.
72; Stephen 71; Stephen
D. 71; Susan V. 94;
Thelma 42; Thomas 72(2);
Thomas C. 72; Thos. S.
72; T.J. 71; Vincen 73;
Virgil L. 72; W.A. 72;
W.H. 72; William 71,72,
(2); William R. 72;
Wilson Taylor 71;
Winnie 37; W.L. 72; W.M.
72; Wm. L. 72; Zeb 72,73
JORDAN, F.M. 26
JUSTICE, A.A. 7,19,36,40,
41,43,52,67,73,75,82,83,
110,116,122,127,131,150,
151; Addie 60; A.E. 15;
A.J. 3; Alex 73; Allen
73; A.M. 73(2); Andrew
73; Andrew J. 73; Ann
53; Anna M. 91; Annie
112,139; Avaline 130;
Badger 73; B.W. 145;
Callie 126; Charlotte
76; Clara 71; Elizabeth
7; Ella 21; Emma 115;
Emory 73; Harriett 64;
Helen 3; Henry N. 73;
Henry P. 73; Hesper 32;
Horace 73; Isaac 72,100;
James 73; Jane 11; J.B.
41,83,86,90,110,148,149;
J.D. 73; J.K. 140; J.M.
73; John B. 73; John W.
73; Julia 43; J.W. 73;
L.B. 139; Lelia C. 49;
Lester 73; Leuna E. 127;
Lillie 47; Manson L. 73;
Mary 7,29,112(2),136;
Mary A. 29; Mary J. 47;
Mattie E. 49; M.E. 143;
Minnie 41; M.M. 131;
Nancy 50,134; Nannie 20;
P.H. 4,13,19,20,75,85,
96,138; Rufus 73; Sadie
29; Samantha R. 115;
Samuel 64; Sarah E. 22,
80; Sharlotte 18; S.P.C.
73(2); Stella 122; T.B.
73; T.C. 73; Timmie 134;
Trixie 110; Viola 139;
Wm. A. 73; W.V. 73
JUSTIS, Amos A. 73
JUSTUS, Leana 121; Martha
A. 21

KANNEDY, Jas. T. 1
KEE, T.A. 74
KEENER, Alex 74; Alex I.
74; Amanda J. 58; Annie
59; Annie Mae 100;

KEENER, Cont'd.
Ben I. 74; Brownlow 74;
Charlie 74; Charlotte
134; C.M. 88; Effie 112;
Elizabeth 57; Eliza J.
104; Ella 72,105; E.N.
74; Ernestine 4,24; Fan-
nie 91; F.B. 18; Frances
93; Geo. 74; Henry 74;
Hiram A. 74; I.N. 12,38,
44,46,50,54,60,62,64,67,
87,93,120,131,149; Isaac
74(2); Isaac N. 74; J.
70; James C. 74; James
M. 74; J.M. 1,3,7,12,17,
18,19,26,27,32,38,42,44,
45,56,48,54,59,62,64,66,
67,68,70,71,72,74,84,87,
89,91,92,93,95,98,101,
102,104,105,108,111,115,
118,120,124,128,129,130,
131,135,137,138,142,144,
146,149; J.N. 46; Jno.
S. 74; J.U. 74; J.W. 17,
64; Lydia 19,95; Lydia
J. 135; Margaret 115;
Margaret G. 66; Martha
S. 146; Mary 3; Mary M.
74; May Bell 106; Mollie
J. 149; Nellie O. 22;
Nettie M. 142; Nettie
M. 142; Nettie M.B. 25;
R.A. 74,151; Randolph
74; Rosa 61; Roxie 118;
Sarah A. 32; Sarah M.
115; Sophronia C. 149;
T.M. 74(2),87,111; T.
Maud 1; Truman 74; U. 15,
20,31,34,63,74,77,93,97,
100,103,121; U1. 63;
Ulrech 74; Ulrich 92,95,
113,118,120,150; W.A.
74,84,105; W.C. 74;
William P. 74; William
W. 74; Wm. A. 74
KEENON, Robert T. 74
KEEVER, W.C. 74
KELL, Ida 23; James F. 74;
J.R. 74; Leonard 74;
Liddie 136; Mathew 74;
M.L. 74
KEELEY, Marcus L. 74; M.L.
20,23,24,48,55,149
KELLY, Adeline 1; E.S. 121;
Jane 34; Mary R. 2; M.L.
15,61,72,80,85,94,96,99,
100,101,121,135,144;
Octa 53; Sarah 1
KELPIN, Sara 31
KELSEY, Laura O. 7; S.T.,
Jr. 74
KEMP, Homer Robert, Jr. 74
KENEDY, Jas. T. 14; J.T.
48,50,123
KENNEDY, J.T. 44,64,89,136;
Virginia 91; W.I. 148
KERBY, A.F. 74; Alvey F.
74; Cynthia 135; Eller
139; Emily 50; May 9;
Nancie 56; Precilla 16;
Susan 56; Wm. R. 74;
W.W. 74
KESTERSON, J.W. 43
KEY, Florence 148; Francis
55; Frank 75; James 75;
James A. 75; James Henry
75; Jas. Albert 75; John
75(2); John F. 75; Laura
52; Martha J. 133; Min-
nie 138; Samuel 75; T.L.
75; William 75
KILBY, Dorotha I. 138;
Roxia 137

KILGORE, J.E. 29,50,71,87,
108,123
KILLIAN, Carrie L. 58; Flora
L. 80; Miles 95; Mirian
26; W.B. 75
KILLPATRICK, Taxas 7
KILPATRICK, A.A. 75; Addie
49; Annie 56; Athen 5;
B.E. 75; Bell 128; Elisha
A. 75; Elizabeth 89;
Elizabeth A. 70; Felix
109; Florence 84; Hulda
88; J. 34; J. Morgan 75;
Julia 34; Lydia 89; Mary
84; M.E. 65; Sallie 98;
W. Francis 75
KIMSEY, Alice 143; Charles
O. 75; David 75; Effie
46; Elisha L. 75; Fred
M. 120; Harold D. 75;
Hattie Belle 140; H.K.
52,118; Ida 87; Laura
145; Marshall P. 75;
Maude 127; Myrtle 116;
Thos. J. 75; T.J. 50;
W.C. 10,26,32,44,68,94,
96,103,120,129,142;
William B. 75; W.L. 129;
Wm. C. 26,129
KIMZEY, A.E. 20; Amanda 33;
Charles R. 75; Lizzie
39; W.C. 63,75,87,88,100,
119,122,128,148; Wm. C.
63
KIMZY, W.C. 23,38,44
KIMZEY, Wm. 38; Wm. C. 9
KING, Allen L. 75; C.T. 68'
Eula Lee 74; Jackson 75;
J.W. 75; Mahalie 16;
Martin 75; Peter 75;
S.W. 33; T.C. 2,11,14,
15,46,60;62,77,105; W.H.
75(2)
KINGREE, Nancy J. 34
KINNEBREW, Edwin R. 75;
Mildred A. 93; Nannie
Mae 30
KINSLAND, A.G. 75; Carrie
60; Charley 75; Cora 119;
E.C. 75; Ella 47; Fannie
55; Ida 43; Inda 106;
Jane 95; J.L. 21,24,27,
32,33,34,37,38,39,42,43,
47,68,75,78,94,102,103,
115,124,129,135,136;
John 75(2); John L. 75;
Martha 55; M.G. 75; Paul
75; Pearl 127; Roy 75;
Sophronia 47; Tiny 6
KIRBY, Jess B. 74; Mary 50
KIRKLAN, Mary M. 85
KIRKLAND, Elizabeth 68,107,
144; James 76; Pat 76;
Rachel 9; Rody 26
KIRKLEY, Ethel Howell 66
KIRKPATRICK, M.R. 12,126
KIRLPATRIC, M.R. 97
KISER, Goldie 140; J.B. 76;
T.W. 76; Vastie 79
KITCHENS, Jason 76
KLEIN, Alma A. 137
KNIGHT, Dora 106; James 76;
J.H. 76; Mary 23; Narvel
76; R.A. 3; Sallie27
KNOX, Cornelius 76
KROM, Stanford 76

LACKEY, Lloyd 76; Frances
C. 67; W.A. 76
LADD, Ed. L. 76
LADFORD, Angie 32; Martha 4

LOUDERMILK, Cont'd.
Mary 16,146; Sarah C.
146; S.L. 3,89; William
80; W.W. 80
LOVE, Addie 121; Andrew 80,
81; Andrew B. 81; And-
rew J. 81; Annie W. 77;
Ben 81; Berryman 81;
Burton 81; Carrie 123;
Charley S. 81; Daisy 146;
Dillard 67; D. Wimer 81;
Effa 108; Eliza 46; Ella
Mae 43; Essie 43; Eva 1;
Francis 56(2); Gertrude
97; Geter 81; Grace 111;
Graham 81; G. Washington
81; Hariett 133; Harry
81; Hattie L. 146;
Henrietta 79; Ida 112;
Isam 81; James 81; James
M. 81; James T. 81;
Jesse 81; J. Frank 81;
John A. 81; John C. 81;
John E. 81; Josie 120;
J.W. 81; Lennie 5;
Lexie 101; M.A. 5,30,43,
47,54,60,75,88,100,104;
Martha 27,37; Martha C.
108; Mary 48,88,91; Mary
A. 83; Mary Will 106;
Maud 29; M. Dillard 81;
Nancy 81; Nicodemiss 81;
Ola 68; Otto A. 81;
Polly 127; Rebecca M. 55;
Samuel P. 81; Susan M.
52; Theodor T. 81;
Thomas G. 81; Vick 19;
W.F. 19,37; William L.
81
LOVELL, Lucea 57
LOVINGOOD, Harmon 81; Lena
M. 58
LOW, Betsy Ann 51; D.H. 81;
Emma J. 47; Jesse 81(2);
Jess N. 81; J.N. 81;
John L. 81; Mary L. 51;
Nathen 81; W.F. 81
LOWDERMILK, G.W. 80;
Joseph I. 80
LOWE, Adam 81; Ed 81;
Elizabeth 32; Hattie 40;
James N. 81; Lillie 98;
Polly Ann 109; Sarah L.
136
LOWERY,Anne 126; Charles A.
81; Cora 98; D.N. 114,
125; Elizabeth 61; Jane
105; J.B. 81; Margaret
55; Mary A. 119; May
105; Olivia 71; R.R. 81;
T.A. 81
LOWMAN, Carl M. 82
LOWRY, Martha 55
LOYD, Frank 100; John 82
LUNCEFORD, Elizabeth 37
LUNSFORD, Annie 98; D.M.
81; Doshia 57; John 81;
John W. 81; Lizzie 150;
Lou 124; Louisa 142;
Mary A. 79; Mary E. 116;
Maud 150; May 7; Micayah
81; Michael 81; M.M. 81;
Nora 54; Pally 147;
Sarah 150; Sophronia 28;
Texie 16; Thomas 81;
Thos. 81,82; William 81;
William R. 81; Willie
81; W.R. 70
LUTHER, Kittie 86; Kittie
E. 86; Lilly May 23;
Mattie 111

LYLE, Daniel 81; J.M. 81;
John 81; Laura 132;
Leona L. 16; Lilly E. 72;
Mary 140
LYRA, Elizabeth 145
MC AFEE, A. McDuffie 82,92;
Fannie 92
MC CALEY, Raymond D. 92
MC CALL, Andy 93; Anna A.
134; Augustus 81; Bashie
142; Cassie 17; Charlotte
B. 39; Clara 70; D.A. 53,
92; Dorothy 21; Dovie 41;
Edie 142; Elmire 7; E.S.
93; Essie 142; Eveline
60; George W. 92; Harley
M. 93; Harry E. 93; Hulda
A. 46; Ida E. 60; J.A.
92; James A. 92; Jane
106; Jasper 93; John 92,
93; Julius 93; Julius W.
92; Latha 70; Laura J.
139; Lucy 60; Luther 93
92); Margaret 64,135;
Margaret D. 14; Marinda
115; Mary A. 66; May 53;
Minnie L. 21,33; Nancy
L. 142; Nettie 135;
Rebecca 91; Rhoda 118;

Rosa 73; Rufus 92; S.C.
92; S.J. 92; Temperence
O. 94; Thomas C. 93;
Thomas J. 92; Thomas R.
92; T.T. 92; Tyra 93;
Urella 85; Vest 93;
William M. 92; Wm. R. 45
MC CALLISTER, Charley 93
MC CARTHY, Chas. 149
MC CARTY, Chas. R. 42,57,
88,93,118; C.R. 32; S.L.
57,113
MC CASKY, Juliet 114
MC CINNIS, Jamima 101
MC CLAIN, Minnie 30
MC CLASKY, Elizabeth 69
MC CLOUD, J.H. 11
MC CLURE, Ada 48; A.L. 93;
Andrew 93; Ann 75; Bertha
E. 35; Bynam M. 92; Cal-
lie 65; Carey 93; Chas.
H. 93; E.H. 93; Elizabeth
L. 41; Ellen 132; Ervin
93; Estell 20; Fannie
108; Flora 63; George
69,93; Hattie 132; James
93; Jasper 93; J.E. 93;
Jessey 93; John 93(2);
John T. 93; Jos. 53;
Julia M. 82; Lamb 93;
Laura 15,40; Lee 93;
Leona 136; L.J. 93;
Maggie 131; Martha A.
8,138; Mary 55,138; Mary
A. 104; Masrus L. 93;
Millie 74; Minnie 131;
Nancy C. 20; Norman 93;
Oscar 93; Otto 93;
Parker 93; Reubin 93;
Rosa A. 45; Rosie 92;
Sofiah 52; Susan 140;
Texa 131; W.D. 93;
Willard 93; William 93;
W.M. 93(2); Wm. H. 93;
Zeb 93; Zella 115
MC COMBS, J. Thomas 94;
Mary 9; William 94(2);
W.M. 94
MC CONLEY, Martha 16
MC CONNELL, Albert N. 94;
Arie 149; Arizona 40;
Arthur 95; Benjamin T. 94;

MC CONNELL, Cont'd.
Bessie R. 70; C.A. 94;
C.B. 94; Chas. W. 94;
Cora H. 94; Cornelia E.
131; D.A. 94; David 94;
Dewey 94; E.C. 94;
Edward 94; Elisha W. 94;
Eloise 76; E.M. 94;
Florence 140; George, Jr.
95; George R. 94; G.R.
94(2); Harley M. 94;
Harriett 131; Harve 94;
Ida 44,93; Irene 45;
James M. 94; Jane 48;
Jas. 80; Jas. N. 10,39,
68,94,145; J.C. 94(2);
J.J. 3,9,13,20,23,38,93,
94,127,138; J.M. 94(2);
Jno. C. 94; John A. 94;
John C. 94(2); John D.
94(2); John P. 94; J.P.
81,87,131; Judson 94;
Launa 98; Lillie 5; Lona
45; Loran 94; Mamie 41;
Martha 20; Mary 19,52,
130; Mary A. 93; Mary
S. 101; Maye 70; Nancy
42; Nellie 94; Orah 52;
Patience 23; Rachel 39,
41; Robert 94; Samuel
H. 94; Sarah 23; Sarah
E. 106; W.A. 94; W.D.
94; Wiley B. 94; William
94(2); W.M. 55,94; Wm.
26,45,124,142; Wm. A.
94; W.R. 94
MC CORD, H.I. 95; Winifred
H. 32
MC COY, Bessie 64(2); Beu-
lah 64; Brunettie 93;
Callie 36; Candis 36;
Carl 95; Caroline 97;
Catherine M. 21; C.E.
95; D.A. 95; Daniel 95;
David 95; David M. 95;
D.C. 3,4,13,16,28,36,42,
51,53,76,81,83,85,91,97,
104,108,127,140,144; D.
Commodore 95; Dearl 95;
D.W. 95; Edgar 95; Emma
25,66,80; Ethel 13; Eva
earl 108; Evie 47; E.W.
95; H.L. 95; H.P.P. 95;
Hugh H. 95; I.N. 129;
Isaac 95; James 95; James
C. 95; J.D. 12,105; J.J.
4,25,90,102; John W.
95(2); Josie 56; J. Welch
95; Mrs. Lala M. 22;
Lettie 38; Lou 37; Louisa
C. 40; Lula 66; Lydia 66;
Margaret 56; Martin 95;
Mary 93; Mary C. 32;
M.E. 136; Mell 95; Milton
16,95; Minnie 21; Mont-
gomery 95; Parlie 146;
Paul 95; Pauline 11;
Pearlie F. 110; Pearl R.
113; S.E. 95; S.J.W. 75;
Theo. 13; Theodore 2;
T.L. 64; Tolitha 87;
Ulucus 95; Verlin 95;
William 95; Wilson 95;
Wm. N. 95; Wm. S. 95
MC CRACKEN, C.T. 95; D. 74;
David 112; Ella 27; Ezra
11; J.M.L. 95; Leota 66;
Reba E. 120; Reva 43;
R.P. 17,48,49,51,60,76,
78,89,108,119,120,127,
134,139; R.T. 95; W.R.95

MC CULLUM, Phil 93; Ruth M. 55
MC CURRY, Martha 56,58
MC DADE, R.E. 95
MC DANIEL, Andrew 95; James 95; Martha 145; Mary 94; T.H. 95
MC DANNIELS, Elizabeth 147
MC DONALD, Adam 95; Jennie 59; Joe 96; John 34,95; Josephine V. 45; Lillie 144; Martha 37; Mary J. 82; Richard 96; Texie 111
MC DONNALL, Elizabeth 65
MC DONNEL, Georgia L. 18; Samuel 96
MC DONNELL, Abner 96; Allean 50; Ben 95; Carrie 130; Ella 81; H.A. 55; Harriett 88; Hassie 25; L. Anna 103; Lassie 89; Laura 55; Lena A. 105; Lester 96; Lillie A. 88; Lou 68,88; Lula 6; Maggie N. 44; Margaret 96; Martha 66; Rachel 121; R.D. 96; Samuel 96; Sarah 120; Thomas 95; Thomas H. 96; Wilburn 96; Wm. T. 96
MC DOWELL, Ab. D. 96; A.D. 96; Addie 104; A.L. 96; Altha 99; Anna 99; Arie A. 89; Charley 96; Elizabeth A. 39; Elizabeth C. 93; Emma 62; Emma R. 126; Francis 44; Georgea A. 30; H.h. 96; Indiana 20; James F. 96; James H. 96; Jane 89; Jas. E. 96; Jas. M. 96; J.E. 96; Jno./John 4,8,11,23,39,58,86,96, 97,105,121; John L. 96; Joseph 96; Julia E. 114; Lassie 65; Lou 140; Lucinda 141; Maggie 94; Maria Ann 93; Mary 12; Mary P. 3; Mary S. 142; Millard 96; S. 83; Sarah 13; Sarah L. 149; S. Elizabeth 121; Silas 44, 49; Siler 11; S.J. 122; T.D. 8; Texas 25; T.L. 55; T.M. 96; W.F. 96
MC DOWLE, Sarah 71
MC EACHINE, Janie 140
MC FALL, Edward 96
MC FALLS, Dochia 39; Tisha 91
MC FARLAND, Sarah 98
MC GAHA, Adlee 48; Alfred 96; Artie 34; Boyd 97; Charles 96; Charley 96; Dollie 134; Elizabeth 139; Eulah 127; Frankey M. 138; Fred 97; George 96; Harriett L. 52; Harvey 97; Ida 131; James T. 96; Jane A. 83; John 96; Joseph 97; J.R. 96; Jud 97; Lilly 52; Mrs. Maggie 109; Margaret A. 123; Mary 28,37,136; Mary Bell 102; Mira M. 98; P.K. 96; Rachel R. 125; R.M. 96(2); Samuel 96(2); Sarah 107,116; Velma 29; William A. 96(2); William C. 96; Wm. T. 96; W.T. 96

MC GAHAY, Alfred 96
MC GAHEY, James 96
MC GATHEY, Elizabeth 26
MC GAUGHTY, James 97
MC GEE, Allie 58; Charles 97; E.S. 97; Georgina 24; G.W. 97; James 1,15; James W. 97; Jas. 54; John 97; M.A. 88; Margaret 88; Mary 71
MC GILL, M.W. 97
MC GINNIS, Mary 6
MC GUFFEY, Alexander 97
MC GUIRE, Fred 97; J.M. 9; Louise 109; Margaret 30; Mildred 18; Thomas J. 97; Virginia A. 18; William B. 97; Wm. B. 97
MC GUYER, Joseph 97
MC HAFFEY, D.F. 97
MC HAN, Burchet 97; Ellis 97; James H. 97; Noah 97; Sarah 19; William A. 97; W.J. 97
MC HARD, Nancy 33
MC HARGEN, W.P. 97
MC INTIRE, Judia 113
MC INTYRE, J.S. 97; Oma 11; Sarah 149;
MC KAY, Edward J. 144; E.J. 26,36,59,73,78,79,83, 121,144,146; E. Jno. 1; E. Johnson 21,27; Johnson 74
MC KEE, Eli 97; W.F. 97,102; William 16,97; William F. 51
MC KELWAY, A.J. 81
MC KIMSEY, William W. 97
MC KINNEY, Caroline 20
MC KINNEY, Carrie Edna 104; Celia Eda 127; C.J. 23; Eula Bell 108; Fannie H. 129; Helen Lee 26; Ittie G. 130; James 81; Jennie 1; J.P. 97; J.S. 50; Mack H. 97; N.H. 97; R.S. 45; Ruth E. 99; Sarah H. 86; Thomasm G. 97; Zeb. V. 97
MC KINNISH, Lillie 35
MC KINZEY, Airy 54; William 97
MC LANE, Daniel S. 97
MC LAUGHLIN, John G. 97
MC LEAN, A.L. 97; Bertha 35; Melvin 97; Pinkney P. 97; P.P. 28,34,51,84, 89,96,102,107,123,141, 143,144; P.R. 136; Zena 17
MC LEON, P.P. 70
MC LEOW, P.P. 101
MC LOUD, Cassie 130; E. 97; James H. 97; J.C. 76; Jesse M. 98; J.H. 19,27, 37,95,128; Lula 130; Mason 97; Roxana J. 94; Tilman W. 98; T.W. 98; William M. 98
MC MAHAN, Albert 98; Amanda 52; Anner 82; Clara 64; Curtis 98; Delphia 85; Fred 98; J.C. 98; J.L. 98; John 98(2); Lucius 98; Mary M. 147; Robert 98; Ruth 22
MC MAN, Leander 98
MC MULLEN, Jason 98
MC NAB, William H. 98
MC NABB, Lloyd T. 98
MC PHEARSON, G.R. 9,31,43,

MC PHEARSON, G.R., Cont'd. 61,131; Julia 136; Ollie 40
MC PHERSON, Daisy L. 22; Eugene R. 98; Geo. R. 63,70; G.R. 7,15,19,33, 52,58,59,75,78,86,93, 94,98,99,112,118,129; John E. 98; Lila 6; Mary L. 1; Robert B. 98; Robert H. 98

MACK, Horace 82; Robert 48
MADCAP, Anna 56
MADEN, G.A. 112; G.H. 61
MAGAHA, Elizabeth 55; Margaret B. 83
MAHAFFEY, D.F. 82
MAIDEN, Geo. A. 1,65
MAJOR, Chas. S. 82
MALLONEE, Abraham 82; Charles R. 82; Comodore B. 82; D. 98; E. Harley 82; Elbert S. 82; Elizabeth 124; Fannie 16,56,123; Jack 82; Jackson 82; John 82(2); Laura 123; Mary 95; Nannie 50; Ruth 139; Sarah 33; W.G. 5,29,46,49,50,65, 67,75,82,88,101,104,121, 131,138
MALONEE, Adam 82; Conie 87
MANEY, Mack 82; Mrs. Nannie 119
MANLEY, Ben 82; John 82(2); Mrs. Nancy 92
MANN, Annie L. 29; Effie 98; Elizabeth 42; G.P. 23,24, 80,82,121; H.C. 82; James L. 21,82; J.C. 82; J.H. 82; J.J. 10,39,40,59, 117,132,145; L.M. 23; Mary 129; Mary A. 20; M.E. 89; Rachele 86; Sarah 39; S.E. 94; W.H. 20,82
MANNING, Eugenia E. 2
MANSFIELD, Thos. W. 45
MANTOOTH, John 82
MARCHMAN, Mattie 126
MARCUSS, Ruphus 82
MARETT, Stella G. 19
MARGAN, Callie 129; Lona 133; Nora 117
MARR, Benj. F. 82; Cordelia 85; Dicy 57; Joseph 82; Lambert 83; Lemuel 82; Martha 28; Minnie 22; Thomas 82; William 83; W.W. 10,12,15,31,36,63, 68,83,102,122,127,128, 149
MARROW, A.B. 95; Elizabeth A. 45
MARSHALL, George D. 83; Jno. 131
MARTIN, Alice 65,66,100; Annie 93; Ben C. 83; B.F. 83; Blanche 34; Catherine 106; Charley R. 83; Dan 83(2); Delia 22; Ellis James 83; Emily 148; Eva 89; Harley 83; Henry 83; H.Z. 83; Jane 4; Jefferson 83; Jennie 146; J.F. 83; John 83(2); John J. 83; John M. 83; Joseph 83; Josephine 14; Julia 101; Lillie 30,67; Lillie C.

MARTIN, Lillie C. Cont'd.
81; L.J. 101; Mary 146;
Mary L. 72; Milley 7;
Nancy M. 51; Nathaniel
83; Richmond 83; Riley
83; Sarah 74; Tiny A. 52;
T.J. 61; T.P. 83; Walker
83; W.D. 83
MASHBURN, A.J. 84; Alfred
83; Allen 84; Amos 84;
Ann 64; Bertha E. 1;
Burt 84; Clara V. 51;
C.M.S. 66; Cora 150;
David 83; Drury W. 83;
D.W. 83; Eddie 84;
Elbert 84; Elizabeth 140;
Ella 11; Emma 33; Evy 48;
Fanny B. 5; F.E. 84;
George 84; George W. 84;
Gertrude 101; Gilbert
83,84; Harley 84;
Harriett 69; Hattie 72;
H.L. 83; H. Leander 83;
Ida 3; Isaac 84; James
M. 83; Jane E. J.D. 84;
Jesse 83; J.F. 11,28,92;
J. Harvey 83; J.H., Jr.
84; J.M. 147; Jno. F./
John F. 56,71; John R.
84; Julia 127; Kansas
118; Larce 84; Laura 10;
Laura C. 120; Letty C.
115; L.H. 84; L.I. 38,
47,52,64,71,81,98; L.J.
32,38,114,115; Louis 83;
Louiza 70; L.S. 83; Lu-
cinda 88; Manson 83;
Margaret 147; Mary C.
118; Mathew A. 83; M.C.
34; M.E. 84; Menervia
83; Mira 25; Mira M. 26;
M.J. 14,16,19,22,23,28,
34,47,52,56,57,59,67,68,
69,71,72,75,81,83,84,87,
90,92,101,102,107,108,
110,112,119,123,126,136,
139,144,147; Mollie 128;
Myra 70; Nellie 111;
Nora 39; Odas 84; Rebe-
cca 96; Rosie 38; R.R.
84; Sallie 119; Sarah
43; S.J. 85; T.A. 84;
Thomas 84(2); Thomas/
Thos. 2,28,33,52,61,67,
69,72,79,84,92,96,97,107,
123,133,139,142,145,147,
149,150; Tina 92; T.W.
83(2); W.C. 84; W.G. 84;
William P. 83(2); W.J.
14; W.W. 84
MASON, Ada 136; A.M. 84;
Amanda 136; Andrew A. 85;
Arie 63; Arthur 85;
Azalee 103; Buel 85;
Bulah 44; Charlie 85;
Cordelia 102; Cynthia J.
147; Cynthia 81; Dan
85(2); Edward 85; E.J.
49; Elizabeth 28,45,81;
Elizabeth A. 147; Ella
7; Ella M. 21; Emeline
19; E.R. 132; Eva T. 123;
Felix 85; Gilbert P. 84;
Harley 85; Henry 85;
Isaac 84; Isabella 43;
Ivalee 121; J.A. 84;
Jacob 84(2),114; Jacob
M. 84; James 84; James
H. 84; Jane 116; Jean-
ettie 114; Jesse J. 85;
J.N. 85(2); John 84,85,
(2),John T. 84; Joseph

MASON, Joseph B., Cont'd.
B. 84; Julia 63; Kanzada
38; Laura 6; Lee 106,137;
Lillie 45,70,85; Lorina
23; Louisa J. 67; Lydia
O. 58; Malinda E. 105;
Marion 85; Marion W. 85;
Martha 36,45; Martha J.
72; Martin 85; Mary 52,
81,83; Mary L. 98; M.C.
83; Melvina 84; Nancy
77; Nancy J. 98; Nevada
4; Nobia 1; Olie 123;
Olive 73; Oscar 85;
Peter 84(2); R.A. 85;
Rachel 64; Ralph 85;
Rebecca B. 139; Rosa B.
86; Rosey 38; Ruby 18,
75; Samantha 84; Sarah
38,147; Sarah A. 128;
Sarah C. 45; Sarah Jane
147; Sheridan 85; Sissie
113; Theadocia 88; Thomas
85; Thos. C. 84; Wavery
85; W.C. 29,38,39,42,45,
52,57,63,64,68,75,82,84,
85,90,98,100,103,105,114,
116,129,147,148; William
C. 84 William, Jr. 84;
William M. 84; W.R. 85;
Zettie 90
MASS, Lou 139
MATCALF, Nora L. 125
MATENY, G.W. 57
MATHASON, Jno. A. 49
MATHESON, A.I. 90; D.M. 10,
61,78; D.W. 60; E.P. 85;
Wm. F. 85
MATHEW, Callie 27
MATHEWS, David 85; Elizabeth
T. 54; James 85; John 85;
Leah 131
MATHIS, Aaron 138; Andy
85; Christine 85; Corde-
lia 91; Delila 145;
Delila B. 115; Exie 14;
Grover 85; G.W. 85;
Henry C. 85; James 85;
Jane 16; J.D. 85; Kansas
113; Levi 85; Nancy 46;
Sarah M. 138; Tom 85;
W.M. 85; Wm. W. 85
MATLOCK, Andrew 85; Cora
B. 108; Dean 120; D.P.
109; E.B. 107; Jennie
70; J.H. 85; John B. 85;
Martha 19; Nannie 17;
Rebecca T. 16; Thomas
85(2); Vinnie 97; G.W.
7,14,51,59,60,82,95,98,
106,113,137
MATTHEWS, Charlotte 62
MATTOX, A.M. 92
MAULDIN, H.L. 86
MAUNEY, Selene 91
MAY, Anna 12; Emma 36; Etta
72; Flora 134; Florie
81; James B. 86; John
86; Lou Rany Bell 72;
Lucindy C. 100; Marcus
M. 86; Mark 7,8,18,33,
34,38,41,45,46,86,98,103,
135,150; Martha 7;
Martha R. 100; Mary 49;
M.J. 86; Mollie 148;
Ollie 76; Palmer 86;
Ruth 100; Sam 86; S.J.
21,25,27,30,38,41,44,
46,48,52,67,72,85,86,
97,105,108,117,124,127,
147,148,149,150,151;
Susie 136; Tim A. 86;

MAY, Cont'd.
W.B. 86; William O. 86
MAYBERRY, R.E. 107; R.F.
14,45,113,127
MAYFIELD, Jane 50; Matilda
118; Moris 69; Moses W.
86; Nancy 51
MAYNOR, Alma 118
MAYSON, Isaac 84; Mary 6
MEADOWS, Crude 86; Daniel
86; Della 19; Emlius 86;
Fannie 57; Lucy J. 73;
Margaret 91; Seth 86;
Willis 86
MEDFORD, A.T. 58,79; C.H.
86; Elmer 86; James B.
86; Ruth 35
MEDLIN, Franklin 86; William
86; Winnie 131; W.T. 125
MEDLOCK, Dochester 143
MEEKINS, J.B. 43
MELL, James C. 42,60,93,152;
Jas. C. 136; J.C. 6
MERONEY, W.R. 86
MERRITT, Mary A. 120; Mel-
vill 86; M.J. 101; S.E.
55; William 86
MESSER, Charles 86; Cora
78; Granvill 86; Henry
86; Jason 86; John L.
86(2); Lola 124; Mary 32;
Thadus 86; W.J. 86; W.T.
86
MIDDLETON, Elizabeth 34
MILES, John A., Jr. 86
MILLER, Aaron B. 87; Aaron
H. 87; A.B. 66,115,149;
Ada 4; Addie 112,115;
Addit T. 139; Amanda 134;
Amanda J. 144; Archie 87;
A.W. 18; Bynum 87; Charles
87; Clare 74; David 87;
David F. 87; David L.
104; Delphia 128; D.I.
87; D.L. 1,8,9,17,25,34,
47,56,60,87,90,93,95,
101,104,112,115,121,124,
130,137,139,144; D.L.,
Jr. 87; Docia 27; Edgar
87(2); Eleanor Va. 152;
Eliza 60; Elizabeth 74,
128; Ella M. 68; Elsie
115; Evit 87; Geo. B.
87; Geo. L. 87; Hattie
25; Henry 86(2), 87;
H.O. 9,12,17,19,41,74,
87,101,139,148; Ida 97;
I.L. 121; Isabell 83;
Jeremiah 87(2); J.I. 87,
95; Joel B. 87; John 87;
John A. 87; John K. 86;
Joseph I. 87; J.P. 128;
Lemuel 87; L.M. 66,67;
Lula D. 95; Margaret L.
36; Martha I. 13; Mary
M. 66; Noah 86; Ollyan
79; Pearl 74; Rachel 21;
Sarah 112; W.E. 87; W.P.
137
MILLS, James 86
MILLSAP, John T. 87
MILLSAPS, Logan 87; Lucin-
day 45; Mary 114
MINCEY, James A. 87; J.H.
27,101; Mary A. 11592);
Minnie 10
MINCY, Charles G. 87; C.M.
27; Darkey J. 89; David
M. 87; Henry R. 87; J.H.
34; Lester L. 87; Lizzie
E.C. 14; M.A. 54; Ollie
124; O.V. 87

MINGUS, Amy 129; Bert 87;
Daisy 144; Ed 87; Frank
87(2); Lavada 138; Shan-
non 87
MINTERS, William M. 87
MISNER, Anora 48
MITCHELL, Eva 120; E.W., Jr.
87; George 87; J.W. 87;
Matilda 144
MIZE, Ellen 121; Lelay 148;
Mary 94; Nancy C. 80;
Nancy J. 7; Nathan 87;
Ray 87
MIZNER, Mrs. Nina Porter 49
MOCK, Cora Lee 25; Lila T.
91; Robert 35; Robert F.
Robt. F. 5,21,25,71,92,
104,106,111,124,140;
Will 87
MODDER, C.W. 17
MOFFAT, Margaret 111
MOFFATE, L.K. 88
MOFFATT, A.A. 18; Polina
H. 139; William S. 87,
88
MOFFETT, Elenor 141;
Howard R. 88
MOFFIT, J.W. 58
MOFFITT, Ann 141; Arizona
140; B.M. 88; Carolina
94; Charles 88; Dillard
88; Earnest 88; Elizabeth
94; Etta May 94; Geo.
Lester 88; Geo. W. 11,87;
G.W. 24,88,94,128,132,
136; Ida 78,79; John
87; John M. 88; Josiah
87; Julia A. 63; Laurence
88; Lester 88; L.K. 88;
Lonie 79; N.A. 129; O.
C. 88; Ruth 130
MONGER, R.H. 82
MONROE, Washington 88
MONTEATH, Margaret 145;
Nancy 48
MONTEITH, D.W. 88; J.C. 88;
W.O. 88
MONTGOMERY, Bulah 94; Oscar
88
MOODY, C.T. 88; Francis C.
62; William H. 88
MOONEY, Lucius P. 88
MOORE, Ada 96; A.J. 88;
Albie 81; Alex 89; A.M.
11; Amilea J. 100;
Andrew 89; Andrew J., Jr.
89; Anna Jean 19; Arie
19; Artie E. 21; A.T.
88; Betty A. 132; Blanche
141; Burt 89; B.W. 88;
Carl 89; Carrie 17,53;
Cathrine 60; C.E. 89;
C.G. 89; Charles M. 89;
Charley 89(2); C.J. 107;
Clifford 89; Cora 94;
Cyntha 16; David D. 89;
Elizabeth 64,86; Ellen
40; Elsie 97; E.M. 120;
Emma 52; E.S. 107; Ethel
44; Eula 143; E.W. 2,94,
118,141; Fannie 14; Mrs.
Ferry 57; Fred S. 89;
Geo. W. 89; Grace E. 71;
G.W. 94,125; G.W.J. 88;
G.W.Q. 26; Hallie 30;
Hariet 83; Harvey 89;
H.M.J. 71; Howard A. 89;
H.W. 88; Isaac 88; James
A. 89; James C. 89; Jane
61,62,103,141; Jane M.
11; J.B. 89; J.D. 88;
J.E. 72; Jesse S. 36;

MOORE, Cont'd
J.H. 17,20,28,40,46,58,
81,89,99,129; J.L., Jr.
88; J. Marion 89; Joab
89; John 88(2); John H.
2,15,33,40,52,63,65,104,
129;131; John J. 88;
John J., Jr. 89; John P.
88; John W. 88; Josiah
88; J.P. 1,3,18,27,36,42,
46,58,60,62,84,87,91,103,
108,124; J.S. 88; J.W.
89; Kate A. 112; Larken
A. 89; Laura 56; Lavina
28; Lidia 54; Lillie F.
107; Lucinda Jane 92;
Lucy 130; Lydia 75; M.A.
60; Maggie 97; Margaret
26; Margaret A. 49;
Margaret E. 6; Margaret
R. 21; Marharett H. 15;
Marion 88; Martha 68,72;
Martin 88; Mary 145,149;
Mary A. 9; Mary Ann 113,
150; Mary E. 110; Mary
P. 126; May 87; M.J. 58;
Nancy C. 83; Nannie A.
82; Parker 88; Patt 88;
Parchina 105; Pearl 130;
R.S. 40; Rufus Alex 89;
Ruth E. 151; Salina 111;
Sallie 30; Sarah 1,16,
33; Sary A. 63; Selah 13;
Simon 89(2); S.W. 89;
Temperance 64; T.H. 88;
T.L. 88,89; U. Emerson
89; Virginia R. 18; Visa
102; Wendell Wm. 89;
William 88(3),89(2);
William J. 89; W.L. 89;
W.M. 88; W.T. 89
MOOSE, Joe 91; Mary I. 83
MORELAND, John 91
MORGAN, A. 66; A.C. 90;
Alf 90; Alice 36; Alley
83; Amanda 148; Arthur
90(2); Arthur M. 90; A.
Rufus 100; Barthew 89;
Bertha 71; B.L. 89; C.A.
90; Cannie 147; Cara 72;
Charley 90; E.A. 67;
E.J. 90; Ella 145; Est-
elle 149; Ethel 86,98;
Eula E. 103; Fanny 143;
F.D. 90; F.M. 4,6,9,12,
13,21,36,37,40,49,52,53,
62,63,67,72,74,76,83,85,
86,89,90,95,100,103,108,
112,116,124,126,138,145,
148,151; Frank W. 90;
G.A. 90; George 90(2);
Harriet H. 105; Horace
J. 90; Irena A. 13; Iris
18; James 89; James J.
90; James L. 90; James
R. 90; James W. 90; Jane
43,92; Jason 90; J.B.
90; J.E. 17,44,47,63,75,
105,116,149; Jeff 90;
Jennie 41; Jerusha 27;
Jesse 90; J.h. 49,83;
John H. 90; Jonathan M.
90; Jos./Joseph 5,30,38,
40,41,48,52,56,63,73,77,
90,91,102,116,126,127,
31,133,135,140,145,150;
Joseph W. 90; J.W., Jr.
90; Laura C. 110; Laurine
106; Leeman 90; Lillian
148; Lillie 41,75; Lizzie
148; Louisa 110; Lucy 47;
Margaret 85; Margaret E.

MORGAN, Margaret E., Cont'd
48; Martha A. 9; Martin
Van 90; Mary 117; Mary
Ann 137; Matilda 80; M.F.
117; M.J. 48,102; M.P.
89; Nora 149; Pearl 143;
R. 67; Rachel 83; R.C.
90; Robert 89; Ruth 125;
Sallie 38; Sallie E. 89;
Sarah 103; Texie 41,63;
T.M. 22; W.B. 132,135;
Willard 90; William 89,
90; William B. 89; William
C. 90; William R. 90;
W.J. 9,13,19,90,96,127,
133,143; Wm. 109; W.R.
90; Zeb 90
MORRIS, Ben 90; Dovie 96;
John M. 90
MORRISON, A.J. 63; Alfred 90
Alice 25; Amanda 107;
Ann 117; Arie 28; E. Etta
35; Elizabeth 51; F.D.
91; Harley R. 91; Hattie
140; J.A. 17,24,27,40,51,
56,95,96,109,116,117,118,
133,143; J.A.J. 52; James
90(2); James A. 91; James
M. 91; Jas. A. 16; Javan
90; j. Don 91; Jennie 96;
J.H. 5,11; John 90,91;
Jos. 25; Joseph 90,91;
J.R. 98,109,114,137; Juan
91; L.J. 12; Lucy 11,56,
69; Margaret 96,113; Mary
6,16; Mary A. 11; Mary
S. 16; Minnie 56; Sarah
E. 41; Susie S. 107; W.H.
11,43,76,91,120,127;
William 90(2),91; W.S. 91
MORROW, A.B. 11,19,25,37,57,
58,65,121,123,136; E.G.
91; Isabel 53; James 91;
James H. 91; Jane 86;
Jim 91; John P. 91; Judeth
Ann 67; Mary 91; Nancy 48;
Patterson 91; Sarah A.
75; Susannah 42; William
91
MORTON, Georgia Lee 110
MOSELEY, Sarah 105
MOSES, A.B. 91(2); Alma L.
135; Anson B. 91; Arthur
91; Athen 91; Byard 91;
Caroline 60; Clarcy 120;
Clarence 91; Cynthia 93;
David J. 91; Eva M. 21;
Fay 84; Helen A. 51; Hosa
16,18,27,47,54,58,72,74,
75,91,96,108,112,115,135,
140,146,147,151; Ida 2;
L.A. 102; M.A. 102;
Martha 47; Mary 120;
Minnie 91; O.E. 62,87;
Oleney 91; Oliney 91;
Oliver H. 91; P.N. 60,91;
R.C. 91; Sarah J. 1; Thur-
man 91; W.H. 91; William
A. 91; Zachary 91
MOSS, Alma 12; Callie V. 9;
Charles 91; Elizabeth 15;
Frank 91; Fred J. 92;
Henry 91; Howell 91; Jane
104,145; John 91; Lucinda
141; Malinda 15; Margar-
et 59; May 130; Milton 92;
Nora 152; Olive 111; Tho-
mas 91; T.M. 91; William
91(2); W.W. 60,72
MOSTELLER, Arthur 60,62,105;
Jesse 92

MOULDEN, F.P. 88,96; T.P. 29
MOZELEY, James 92; Thomas 92; W.E. 92
MOZELY, Edith 46
MOZINSKY, Rose 70
MOZLEY, W.E. 49
MULL, Benjamin 92; Johnston 92; William E. 92
MULLINS, Asa 92
MULLIN, Sarah 100
MULLINS, Sarah E. 80
MUNDAY, A.P. 92,114; Boice 92; Ella C. 1; Mary F. 114; T.S. 92
MUNGER, Fred W. 92; James S. 92; Marion 48; Nellie 140; R.H. 9,15,61,87,92, 97,134,148
MURPHY, F.C. 92
MURRAY, Mrs. Amey 113; Elizabeth 62; Frank I. 92(2); James W. 92; Jas. M. 109; John W. 92; Joseph 92; Linsey 107; Sam 95; Sam. J. 1,4,7, 30,45,66,73,84,89,103, 129; S.J. 17,76,92,115
MURROW, Anderson 92; Sarah E. 114
MYERS, Anna V. 86; Bertha 52; D.A. 92; E. 92; Ellie 29; George B. 92; Jacob T. 92; James E. 92; John C. 92; Lena Amelia 126; L.P. 92; Lucy 42; Mary N. 56; Mattie 115; Maude 22; Minnie 47; Nannie 69; Nannie M. 36; Nina 5; Pinkney P. 92; Tishia 119

NAGG, T.E. 107
NALL, A.R. 98
NATIONS, Callie 134; Flora 28; Samuel A. 98
NEAGLE, Alice 81
NEAL, Annie 65; Artie 82; Bellzora 65; Cora 148; Flora 54; Geo. W. 98; Homer 98; James 98; James A. 98; Jane 127; John H. 98; John W. 98; Lucy 105; Nancy E. 149; R. 48; Samuel 98; Sarah 54; Thomas 98; W.D. 98; Mrs. Zona 124
NEEL, Andrew J. 98; Sarah S. 36
NEELY, Alice 92; Effie 67; G.Y. 98; Harry 98; H.B. 98; Lula 141; Margaret 99; Mollie 5; Stinson 98
NEIL, Jane 101
NEILL, Jonathan 17
NELSON, Ethel C. 133; Hughey 98; Lillie 103; Nellie 144; S.E. 116; W.L. 98
NEVELS, Mattie 4
NEW, Albert 110
NEWELL, I.C. 98
NEWMAN, John 98; Willie M. 12
NEWSON, Emmett E. 98
NEWTON, D.C. 70,109; John 98; Margaret 125; Narcissy 125; Solomon 50
NICHELSON, Mary G. 7
NICHLES, May 70
NICHOLDS, Nancy S. 83

NICHOLS, Beulah 79; Catherine 100; Charles D. 99; D.I. 99; Elenor 4; Elizabeth 58; Floyd 99; George L. 99; G.R. 99; Henrietta 37; Hester A. 139; H.M. 100; James 98; Jennie 146; J.F. 99; John H. 99; J.T. 99; Lenora 119; L.O. 11; Margaret 13; Margaret A. 100; Martha R. 38; Mary 23,90,139; M. Dore 112; Minnie 102; Robert L. 99(2); Rosetta 78; Roxie 132; Sarah 4,114; W.R. 99
NICHOLSON, Bertha 140; Hattie 46
NICKLES, Amy 77; Daniel 99; Jane 68; P.B. 99; Susannah 99; Wesly M. 99; William 99
NICKS, Oscar 99
NIGHT, May E. 46
NIX, J.O. 60,69,71,98,144; Mary 70; Pearl 29
NOLEN, Allie O. 58; F.H. 99; Francis 145; Horace T. 99; H.W. 99; Ruth 19
NORMAN, John 99
NORRIS, A.N. 140; E. 90; Ephram 77; H.H. 99; I.C.J. 99; Ida 111; Isaac 99; J.R. 99; J.W. 99; Lafayett 99; Laura 87; L.D. 99; L.S. 99; Mary A. 39; Mary J. 113; Minnie 21; N.C. 99; Ora 61; Ornessie 61; R.H. 80; Texie A. 53
NORTON, Ada 24; Albert 99; Alice 24; Amanda 96; Annie 132; Bell 20; Bess 130; Burrus 99; C.A. 99; Calib 99; Charley 99; Cora 96; Cordelia 65(2); Earnest B. 100; Ed. L. 100; Effie 113; E.J. 93; Elias 106; Elizabeth 71; F. 99; Fannie 45; Flora 30; Frank H. 100; Fred 100; Hattie S. 15; Homer 100; Ida 24; Ittie 114; James 99; J.E. 143; Jennie 23; John E. 124; J.P. 99, 100; L.A. 65; Laura 38, 73; Lena 30; Leonard 99 (2); Lillian 30; Lula 13,59; M.A. 93; Mann 100; Martha 51,134; Martha M. 125; Mary 78; May 18; Meta 48; M.L. 125; Nathan 9992; Ninna 150; Olive G. 35; P. Lafayett 99; Rebecca 106; Robert L. 99; Sarah 23; T.N. 99; Virgil Z. 99; W.A. 13,23,24,29,32,33, 46,61,65,74,78,80,112, 119,121,125; William 99; William P. 99; Zeb L. 100
NOULAND, Sarah 45
NOWLAND, James H. 100
NOWLEN, Jesse R. 145
NUNN, E. Getty 105; James G. 100; W.L. 100

OBE, Callie 1
OBEY, Elizabeth 89
O'DELL, Ed 100
ODUM, I.A. 33; Martha 145
OFFICER, Marsh 100
OGDEN, Jonathan 100
OGELSBY, G.A. 37
OGLESBY, G.A. 1,69,96,121
OLDHAM, John 100
OLDRIDGE, J.E. 100
OLIVER, Allie Z. 78; Ann 77; Burt 100; Florence C. 5; Fred S. 100; Geo. W. 100; Hattie 119; Henry Ellis 100; Hugh 100; James M. 100; J.C. 100; Jesse 100; Joseph 100; Martha 44; Mary 30,77; Mary A. 72; Milus N. 100; M.J. 28; N.C. 100; Ollie 98; Sarah Ann 119; Thomas W. 100; T.V. 73; William P. 100; Zack 100
OLVEY, Raethel V. 117
OOCUMMA, Anna 29
ORMOND, Alfred N. 100
ORR, Fifill 100; James R. 100
OSBORN, Ezekiel 100; John G. 100
OVERCASH, Hayes E. 100
OVERSTREET, William C. 100
OWEN, Bessie 96; Emma L. 50; Floy 128; Hariett 97; Henry M. 101; J.C. 28, 127; John A. 101; Josephine 145; Julia H. 89; M.A. 80; Mary A. 87; R.A. 12,30,43,80,94,98,106, 111,124,142; T.W. 26,46, 114
OWENBEE, Martha M. 103
OWENBEY, Tally 52
OWENBY, Addie 39,101; Agrie 101; Alex 100; Alfred F. 100; Annie H. 147; Beuford 101; Beulah 148; Carolina 52; David 101; Dora 116; Dora E. 101; Eckel 101; Edgar R. 101; Eleanor M. 103; Elizabeth 8; Mrs. Ellen 117; Ellender 103; Elmer 101; Elmyra L. 74; Exie 134; Gladys 101; Hassie 39; Helen 141; Inez 128; John E. 100; J.R. 101; Leander 100; Lester 101; Lillie 85; Lillie T. 90; Lornzo 100; Lorenzo 100; Mary B. Bell 113; Maude 117; O.A. 37; Pauline 73; R.L. 100; Roxie 103; Roy 101; Sallie 117; Samuel 100; Thomas 100; T.M. 101; T.V. 108; Vixie 41; Voyd 101
OWENS, Anna 116; Bruenettie 93; Evan 101; Jesse C. 101; Jesse G. 101; John W. 101; Lela 93; R.A. 40, 116; Sarah 100; Thomas W. 101; William J. 101; William S. 101; Zena 93
OWENBY, Mary 73

PACE, C.A. 101; Eliza M. 147; Margaret 116; Palsey 130
PADGET/PADGETT, E.B. 40,61, 65,72,75,76,134

PADGETT, A.B. 52,143;
Elijah B. 101; J.F. 110
PAINE, Dink 101; Mary 122
PAINTER, Ada 65; Annie 75;
Cordelia E. 36; Eastman
101; James C. 101; John
101(2); J.P. 67; Kansas
75; Latishu 84; L.E.
147; Mrs. Minnie 34;
Myrtle 14; Polly 61;
Robert 101; Sarah 109;
S.G. 101; William L. 101
PALMER, Amy E. 99; Bonnie
B. 115; Carrie E. 92;
Francis 108; Frank 101;
Jake F. 101; James A.
101; J.F. 101(2); Joe
101; Jura 138; Mattie
69; Minnie 87; N.H. 4,
15,98,145; T. Jane 103;
W.T. 101
PANLAND, A.E. 4; Kate 104
PANNEL, Amanda 43
PANNELL, A.E. 101; Arthur
101; Elias 101; Glady
Lorine 75; Harrison 102;
Hattie 98; James 101;
Mary 44; Mary C. 138;
William 101; W.T. 101;
W.T. 101
PANTER, John 102; S.C. 102
PANTHER, Aurzema 102;
Caroline 143; Jacob 102;
Lousea 50; Lucinda 116;
Mira 136; Robert E. 102
PARDON, Pascal L. 102
PARHAM, Gladys 15
PARIS, Jackson 102
PARKER, Alexander L. 102;
Alice 58; Booth 102;
C.A. 11; C.L. 102; C.W.
102; D.B. 102; Dock 102;
Elvira 14; Emmer 142;
Florida B. 151; Franklin
102; Homer 102; Isabel 3;
Jacob W. 60; Jacob Wm.
102; John 102(2); Julia
A. 84; J.W. 1,3,6,14,27,
41,54,58,59,60,65,70,87,
103,151; Kansada 101;
Ledger 102; Lillie J.
132; Mabel 107; Mary
18,118; Mary E. 54; Mary
M. 3; Nancy 114; Nettie
63; Queen Vashti 108;
Samuel 102(2); Temple
85; William 102; William
M. 102; Wilma 102; W.M.
102
PARKS, Cyntha L. 61;
Jefferson 102
PARRISH, Aletha A. 36;
Alice M. 75; Arie 123;
Avaline 24; Carl 102;
Carrie A. 82; Della 86;
E.H. 102; E.W. 102;
Francis 51; Fred 102;
G.B. 13; Geneva 7;
George 102; Geo. W. 102;
Green 102; G.W. 41,102;
H. 40; Hallie B. 41;
Henry 102; Inez 66;
James A. 102; James R.
102; John 102; J.R. 102;
Julia E. 22; J.W. 102;
Lelah 76; Lorenda 36;
Louisa 29; Major 102;
Mamie 36; Martha 58;
Nancy 110; Nannie 116;
Nathaniel H. 102; N.H.
102; Pallie 144; R.P.
102; Susy A. 82; Tema-

PARRISH, Temasure, Cont'd.
sure 95; William M. 102
PARSON, George 143; Ione
53; James 35
PARTER, Otelia 26
PARTON, G.W. 103(2); James
103; Lowenda 132;
Marion F. 103
PASE, Lelah Ann 90
PASSMORE, Alice E. 76;
Catherine 28; C.P. 103;
Dave 103; David 103;
Elisha 52,103; Emeline
76; Emelyn 134; Emily
147; Fred 103; Harden
103; Homer 103; Hugh D.
103; James L. 103; John
103; J.T. 103; Leona 75;
Lillie 92; Lou 83; Mar
tha A. 148; Maud 39;
M.E. 50; Meranda 100;
Modene 45; Nancy 107;
Nancy M. 74; N.H. 103
(2); P.H. 52,62,73,86,
90,103,148; Phil./Phillip
37,101; Philip H. 128;
Ray 103; Robert 103;
Roxie 27; Sarah J. 138;
S.H. 103; S.T. 103;
Thomas J. 103; Thos. M.
103; Travis L. 103; Troy
C. 103; W.C. 103; William
F. 103; Wm. C. 103; Wm.
Thomas 103
PATE, Monroe 103
PATRICK, Jessie C., Jr. 103
PATTERSON, Bertha L. 62;
Flomire M. 111; Hawlass
103; J.C. 103; J.D.A.
103; John 103(2); John
A. 103; John H. 103;
Lora 112; Margaret 148;
Mary 123; Maude 133;
M.C. 104; Nancy A. 131;
Polk 104; Sam 103; Sarah
5; W.E. 103; William
104; W.S. 103
PATTON, Alfred S. 104; A.P.
105; Arthur 104; Bartlett
104; Belle 10; Caroline
96; C.B. 104; Cornelia
97; Dicy C. 63; Dulcena
15; Elizabeth R. 29;
Ellen 102; Ervin 104(2);
Flora M. 138; George B.
104; George R. 104; Hanna
88; Hattie 78; Ida 40;
John 10492); John B. 104;
J.T. 81; J. Thad 10492);
L.A. 104; Margaret A. 91;
Mary 18,38; Mary Ann 4,
81; Mary J. 148; Matilda
96; Nancy A. 37; Nina
E.P. 79; N.M. 14; Pearl
145; R. 104; Rado 136;
Robert A. 104; Sallie
52; Sarah 125; Sephrona
120; T.W. 104; William
104(2); William J. 104;
William, Jr. 104; W.
Ramsey 104
PAUL, Guy 104; Hiram 104;
Hiram T. 104; M. Francis
59
PAYNE, Caledonia 26; Clay
104; Cley 104; Dora 109;
Oma M. 43; Rachel 37;
Rosa Lee 123; Samuel 104;
Sarah A. 104
PEACOCK, Sophie E. 33
PEAK, Ruth 92
PEAKE, Ruth E. 150

PEARCE, Ed. 104
PEARSON, Jefferson 104;
Lillian S. 98; Moses 104;
W.D. 104
PEBELEY, J.A. 104
PEEK, Callie 139; Carl 105;
C.T. 45; Delena 32; D.L.
104; Elizabeth 77,115
Eliza J. 60; Flora 12;
Frank 59,66,105; G.R.
105; Harriet 6; Henry
104; I.H. 104; Isaac 104;
Isaac T. 104,128; I.T.
17,20,27,50,64,74,87,92,
112,137,142; James 105,
108; James M. 104; Jane
16; Jas. M., Jr. 104;
J.K. 104; John M. 105;
Josephine 104; J.T. 22,
38; Juda 38,95; Jula 95;
Latha 91; Laura A. 56;
Loucinda 146; L.V. 50;
M.A. 72; Manerva 35,91;
Margaret A. 104; Martha
A. 17; Martin J. 105;
Mary 87,95; Milley 59;
Millie 44; M.S. 115;
Parazadie 87; Paul 105;
Rutha 38; Sophronia 59;
Susan C. 87; Thedocia 87;
Truman 105; U.A. 54;
Vina 108; W.A. 11,18,105,
115,150; William C. 104;
William P. 105; Wm. M.
104; Z.I. 149; Z.J. 51,
91,104,115,130; Z.P. 7,
54,131,137
PEELER, J.A. 15
PELL, Hampton A. 105
PENDERGRAS/PENDERGRASS, J.R.
1,2,4-11,13-15,17,19,21-
27,30-37,39-51,53-56,
60-62,65-104,106-119,
120-126,128-138,140,141,
143-152
PENDERGRASS, Agness 90;
Alex. 105; Annar 6; Ber-
nice 95; Bonnie 57; C.L.
105; Dollie 44,71; Eliza-
beth 54; Eliza G. 3;
Fanney 126; Fannie 117;
Florence 103; Floyd 105;
Fred C. 105; George 105;
Hariett R. 3; Henry M.
105; Humphery 105; Jacob
D. 105; Jane 38,58; J.D.
105; Jesse 105; Jesse
R. 105; John 10592);
John S. 105; Julia 90;
Leona 105; L.T. 3;
Margaret 38; Margaret R.
81; Martha 6; Matilda 24;
Miles 105(2); Minnie 85;
M.M. 82; Mollie 52;
Polly 77; Susan 82; Troy
105; Wiley 105; William
105
PENLAND, Addie 46; A.H. 92;
Amanda Jane 125; Angeline
121; Bertie 21; Bida 19;
Bland 21; Carrie 19;
Chamberlain 105; Chas. M.
82; David W. 105; Eddy
C. 105; Elbie 104; Eliza-
beth 20; Ellen 101; Emma
I. 20; Enoch 105; Ethel
P. 114; Fred 106; G.A.
121; Geo. N. 105; Ham
105; Hazel V. 132; Hellen
R. 111; Henry A. 105;
Homer 105; Homer R. 105;
H.P. 105; Ida M. 94;

SMITH, Cont'd.
Bertha 120; B.F. 126;
Bruce 127; Carr 127;
C.C. 83; C.D. 1,2,5,10,
24,29,35,39,41,45,49,54,
58,68,75,77,79,88,89,94,
96,97,98,104,105,106,
110,111,114,118,121,125,
130,134,140; Cecil A.
127; Charles C. 126;
D.E. 127; Don 127; Dora
P. 35; Earl 127; Ed
(Smythe) 127; E.D. 127;
Eliza A. 135; Ella M.
134; Ellen 85; Emily V.
52; Emma D. 6; Esther
90; Fannie 92; Frank A.
24; Frank T. 127; George
R. 126; Gordon 127; Grady
127; H.A. 127; Hoke 127;
Ila 6; J.A. 126; James
B. 127(2); James E. 127;
James L. 126; James M.
127; James S. 127; James
T. 88; J.C. 62; J.E. 127;
Jennie 39,57; Jewel 127;
J.J. 126; John A. 127;
John C. 127; John F. 127;
Joseph L. 127; Jos. L.
127; Lane 97; Larkin 126;
Laura 98; Laurence N.
127; Lavada 86; L. Craw-
ford 127; Lillian 110;
Lillie 110; L.J. 127;
Mae 26; Margaret B. 121;
Martha 30,85; Martha A.
79; Mary 92,96; Mary G.
137; May 143; M.C. 57;
Merrit 126; Milas K. 127;
M. Rebecca 58; Myrtle
118; Mrs. Nancy E. 127;
Nettie 83; Norah 109;
Paul 68; Pierson 127;
R.N. 127; Robert 127;
Robt. 50; R.P. 32; Sam-
uel 80,126; Sanford 127;
Sarah 40,51; Sarah C.
81; S.C. 38; S.D. 21;
Stella 22,110; Telitha
M.E. 134; Thos. J. 127;
Vester 127; Virgil 127;
Walton R. 127; Wiley
127; Will 9,14,17,21,25,
33,39,44,62,74,132,134,
138; William S., Jr. 127;
William T. 126; William
W. 126; Wm. 132; Wm. C.
126; Wm. Elijah 127;
W.M. 15,42,73,107,130;
Worth 127
SMYTHE, Mrs. Rosa Byrd 133
SNIDER, Rufus 128
SNYDER, John L. 128; Jose-
phine 25; Maggie 120;
Mary E. 31; Mattie 69;
Miles J. 128; Newell
128; Odell 128; Pauline
81; W.H. 128
SOLESBEE, A. 128; Alice 151;
A.S. 7,27,30,34,37,39,
48,49,51,54,57,64,82,91,
105,107,110,118,127,128,
132,135,138,143,148;
Asbury 128; Callie 151;
Charles 128; Claud 128;
Daisey 150; Dock 128;
Elsie 37; Florence 76;
German 128; J.P. 128;
Loula 49; M.L. 128; Pat
128; Pink 128; Rachel
37; Ralph 128; Sherden
128; Tallie 42; W.A. 8,

SOLESBEE, W.A., Cont'd.
11,30,34,37,54,67,71,72,
111,117,135,138,147;
W.H. 6; W.L. 8; W.S. 128;
Zelpha C. 140
SOLESBY, A.S. 16,44,146;
Dallas 128; Martin 128
SOMEX, Palina 26
SORRELLS, Mattie 65; Robert
V. 128
SORRELS, Addie 50; Belle 5;
Callie 54; Canvis 146;
Ebenezer 128; Elizabeth
26; Emma 47; Hattie 50;
James C. 128; J.M. 128;
Laura 55; Lester 128;
Lewis 128(2); Mary J.
113; Minnie 95; Nancy
132; Pete 128; Robt. H.
128; Sallie 50
SORRELLS, Lester 40
SOUTHARD, Margaret 60
SOUTHARDS, Albert 129;
Alice I. 127; Ann 91;
B.L. 128; C.H. 129;
Charley 128; Chas. A. 128;
Dovie 66; Eliza 101;
Emma C. 24; Eva A. 99;
Geo. W. 128; G.W. 128;
Henry 128; James D. 129;
John 128,129; John, Jr.
128; Julius H. 128; L.A.
47; Lawrence 129; Lester
128; Lillie 24; Lucinda
119; Martha L. 60; Mary
8,139; Mrs. Mary 2 135;
Nancy 87; Robert 128;
Thomas 128; Mrs. Tina
129; William 128; Zelphie
137
SOUTHERLAND, Ilet B. 129
SPARROW, Geo. A. 94
SPEARS, John 41
SPEED, Doyle 129; Jenely
22; Lafayett 129; Lena
6; R.D. 129; T.S. 129
SPEIGHTS, Robert C. 129
SPICER, Thomas 129
SPIVY, Narcissis 82
SPRAYBERRY, James C. 129
SPRIGGS, Elmer T. 129
SPRINKLE, M.L. 129
SPRINKLES, Alex 129;
Daniel 129; Florence 128;
Geo. B. 129; G.W. 129;
John 129; John H. 129;
Leander D. 129; Ola B.
149; Savannah 134
STALCUP, Alma E. 73; Amanda
27; Coleman H. 129;
Dorothy 144; Geo. T. 129;
Harvy 70; Hattie 146;
Jason 100,129; Maggie
33; Maggie A. 38; Peter
S. 129(2); Sallie 121;
William 129; Wm. 129
STALKUP, Margaret 69
STALLCUP/STALCUP, J.B. 1,
62,62,77,111,142; Lou
140; Rufus 100
STAMEY, Bessie 57; C.C.
129; Charles W. 129;
C.L. 31; Delia 72;
Ernest 129; G.C. 129;
Ida 139; Ivey 30; J.G.
129; John H. 129; J.W.
129; Leona 119; M.I.
142; Mrs. Pauline 119;
Robert/Robt. 5,8,9,10,
12,25,27,28,31,36,38,39,
44,47,48,52,58,59,61,
63,78,85,88,93,94,106,

STAMEY, Robert, Cont'd.
119,121,122,129,131,132,
133,136,139,146,148;
Sarah B. 94; Sarah M.
72; Thomas 129; W.C. 129
STANCIL, Mary E. 141
STANFIELD, B.C. 130; Bell
124; Charles 129;
Commodore 129; Conie B.
129; Delpha 151; Dollie
E. 43; Elias A. 129;
Ellie 135; Fannie 54;
Geo. W. 130; Jennie 124;
J.L. 129; Leola L. 140;
Lillie 74; L.S. 130;
Lula 78; Mack B. 130;
M.B. 130; M. Etta 131;
M.G. 96; Minnie 34;
Samuel W. 130; W.H. 129
STANFORD, Bedford 130
STANLEY, Helen 45
STARBUCK, N.h. 26,29; V.H.
32,80
STARNES, J.F. 17,21,70;
John 130
STARRITE, Mosey 130
STEED, G.A. 109; Geo. C.
1,58,86,102; Geo. M.
58
STEEL, Sarah H. 14
STEELE, H.L. 130
STENSON, James 79
STEPENSON, Wm. H. 130
STEPHENS, Basha A. 75; Dan
S. 130; Emma 134; Eva
45; Joseph M. 130;
Mercilla 137; Virginia 41
STEPHENSON, A.E. 57; Marion
130
STEPP, Adeline 134; Alcy
A. 83; Bessie 67; Elmira
101; Geo. 71,101; Geo.
W. 5,7,37,52,67,85,101,
134,1519also STEPPE);
George W. 130; Ivy 111;
Jesse 76,77,116,117,130,
141,150; Ollie 62
STEPPE, Geo. 128; Geo. W.
128
STEVENS, Sallie 5
STEWARD, Addie 44; John 130;
Logan 130; Manley 130
STEWART, Alvin C. 130; Anna
144; Callie 42; Charles
130; Chas. 30,136; Chas.
L. 6,52,66,88,111; Chas.
S. 145; C.L. 17,25,26,
46,53,58,59,83,94,96,
99,130; Ella 78; Elsie
30; Emely Jane 24; Geor-
gia 95; H. 38,142; Harley
130; Henry 44,64,66,72,
93,142; Henry, Jr. 22,
70,85,130; Henry, Sr.
130; H., Jr. 32,142;
Ida 59; Joseph A. 130;
J.R. 130; Margaret E.
131; Mary Samantha 89;
Mildred 60; M.J.L. 96;
Ola 136; Polly 113,150;
R.D. 130; Rufus 130;
Saphrona A. 31; Sarah S.
89; Stacy P. 108; William
130; Wm. G. 130; W.W. 13
STEWMAN, Addie 74(2); Carri
60; Charles A. 132;
E.C. 18,34,109; Elijah
C. 132; Fannie 150;
Henry 132; James 132(2);
John 132; Laura 134;
Luther 132; Mary J. 1;
M.H. 132; N.M. 42;
Rebecca 62

WADKINS, Cont'd.
Ethel 102; Jane 23
WAGG, T.E. 70,99
WAIN, M.P. 50
WALDROOP, A. 139; Adolphus
139; Alexander 139;
Ambrose 139; Angeline 56;
Annie 132; Annie Lee 126;
Arthur M. 140; Artie 63;
Benjamin 140; Betty 103;
B.G. 140; Birdell 111;
Burnell 140; Burt 140;
Charles A. 140; David
139; D.P. 140; D.T. 101;
Emeline 71; F.L. 139;
Florence 50; Frank 140;
F.W. 140; Gilbert 140
(2); Gilmer G. 140;
Gladys M. 122; Grady 140;
Harley 140; Harold 140;
Henry E. 140; Hester A.
141; Iona 125; Ivalee
114; J.A. 139(2); Jacob
48,139; James 139; Jennie
79; Jesse 140; Joab M.
139; Josiah A. 140; J.S.
140(3); L.C. 139,140;
L.D. 140; Leona 89;
Lucious 140; Margie 111;
Mary 112; Nancy A. 75;
Nellie 113; Oma 104;
Rickman 139; R.P. 140;
Sarah Ann 2; Sarah C. 84;
Susanah 120; T.S. 139;
W.H. 140; W.H., Jr. 140;
William 139; William H.
140; W.J. 140; W.R. 140
WALKER, Catherine 132;
Janny 27; Mrs. Leona 73;
Louise 30; Mary 145;
Robert 140; W.T. 140
WALL, Alice 5; Fannie 129;
J.D. 140; John O. 140;
S.M. 140
WALLACE, Agnes B. 140;
Chas. Edwin 140; Ernest
140; Eunice S. 29; F.W.
11,81; Geo. O. 140; Jesse
K. 140; Jessie 129;
John 140; J.Q. 5,6,10,
15,18,31,35,46,53,57,58,
59,69,73,97,100,109,110,
122,126,140; Kate 140;
Mrs. Louisa J. 89; R.K.
147; Ruth 53; Susan 130
WALLER, Floyd 140; Fred C.
140
WALLIS, Maria 103
WALTEN, C.W. 50
WALTON, C.W. 89,92; W.C.
144
WARD, Daisy 135; G.C. 140;
R.E. 65,89; Robert E. 53,
69,100
WARDLOW, H.G. 98
WARE, Joseph T. 7
WARLICK, M.C. 103
WARREN, H.H. 140; Thos. 23,
31,125; W.G. 7,16,22,34,
94,101,139; William 140;
William P. 140; W.J. 93
WASHINGTON, G.W. 67
WATERS, Arthur 141; Beula
116; Catherine 62; C.E.
141; Dewey 141; D.P. 70;
Dulcina 150; Dwight 141;
Florence 34; James 141;
James I. 141; Jane 142;
J.J. 141; John S. 141;
Lawton 141; Lillie 85;
Malia 8; Martha 62;
Michael J. 141; Rebecca
44; Sam. J. 141; S.H.

WATERS, S.H., Cont'd.
79; Susie 111
WATHEN, Charles A. 141
WATKINS, Annie 108; Arie F.
77; Arthur 141; Bertha
142; Beulah 17; Carrie
64; C.L. 141; Elbert 141;
Elizabeth 106; Ellen 80;
Elsie 131; Evans 141;
Fanny 76; Frank 141;
General 141; H.L. 141;
James B. 141; James M.
141; J.B. 141; J.J. 141
(2); Jno. 134; John L.
141; Julia Ann N. 87;
Lela E. 97; Louise A.N.
144; L.T. 141; Lucenda
70; Maranda 141; Margaret
87; M. Jenney 91; Nancy
R. 111; Pallie L. 111;
P.H.P. 141; Polly 142;
P.T. 141; Ruth A. 53;
R.W. 141; Silas 141;
William H. 141; W.L. 141
WATSON, Callie Mae 100;
E.B. 141; Eli G. 141(2);
Elizabeth 122; Henry W.
141; Ibby 48; James 141;
James F. 141; Jane 28;
John H. 141; J.R. 79;
J.S. 141; Juda 131; M.J.
131; Nancy 114; Sarah
65; William 141
WATTERS, L.J. 90; Metilda
92; Samuel 141
WATTS, A.B. 142; Adaline
85; Adolphus B. 142;
Annie M. 59; Blanche 65,
94; D.M. 141; Effie 15;
Elza 11; Flora Ann 78;
F.W. 142; Hester A. 103;
Jake 142; James T. 142;
J.B. 142; J.P. 141; J.T
4,10,23,24,39,47,78,82,
86,88,111,119,129; Juliet
M. 93; Kyle 142; Laura
E. 135; Lou Ellen 80;
Martha Ellon 111; May
102; Nellie May 78;
Viola 8; Wallace 141;
William 142; William G.
141; William W. 142
WEATHERMAN, Newton 142
WEAVER, Chas. C. 59; C.P.
142; James C. 15,142;
James T. 142; Jas. C. 24,
51,56,109,111,122; J.C.
4,104; J.H. 48,106,126,
150; J. Marvin 142;
John S. 142; T.E. 6,126,
133; T.J. 142; William
R. 142
WEBB, Andrew 142(2); Mrs.
Arie 31; Ben, Jr. 142;
Betsey 70; Bettie 60;
Candes 109; Creasy 70;
Dora T.J. 60; Elizabeth
92; Ella 142; Elsie 142;
George 142(2); Harrison
142; Hugh 142; Ivey 70;
James 142(3); Jane 31;
Jennie 70; John 142(2);
Joseph 142(3); Joseph,
Jr. 142; L.C. 142; Louisa
142; McKinley 60,142(2);
Mindy 93; Minnie 142;
Myra 37; Nancy 135;
Rebecca 85; Robert 142;
Ruth 1; Sarah 70; Teli-
tha 38; Telitha Jane 85;
Tom 142; William 142;
Wm., Jr. 142

WEBBER, Charles 142
WEBSTER, James 142
WEEKS, D. 45,107,134;
Elizabeth 128; Winny 81
WELCH, A.B. 31,50,68,93,120,
143; Ada B. 110; A.J.
143; A.L. 39; Albert L.
143; Andrew 143; Angeline
28; Austin 143; Bertha
113; Bulah 42; C.A. 122;
Carey 96; C.C. 35,95;
Charles 143; Dock 143;
Ed 143; Elizabeth 82;
Ell 143; E.M. 143; Eme-
line 1; Emily A. 95; Emma
100; Esther A. 116; Ethel
67; F.C. 143; Flora 129;
Florence 104,114; Floyd
143; Ida 67; Iowa 144;
Jacob D. 142; J.C. 143;
J.D. 143; Jennie 137;
J.L. 143(2); John 142;
John M. 143; John T.
143; Jonah 82; Joseph
25,31; Joseph, Jr. 143;
Joseph W. 143; Lizzie
J. 56; Lon 143; Louisa
120; Maggie 72; Manson
E. 143; Maron 41; Martha
98; Mary E. 100; M.C.
86; M.E. 47; Myrtle 13;
Nora M. 113; N.T. 143;
Oscar 143; Pearl 132;
Pearlie M. 89; Ralph W.
143; Robert 143; Roxie
133; Russell 143; Ruth
95; Texie 116; Thelma
J. 132; Thomas 142;
Thomas J. 142; Thos. 103;
W.A. 143; Wade 143; W.E.
16,66,111,112,117,143,
147; W. Furman 143;
Wilburn 143; William 143;
Wm. Henry 143
WELDES, J.M. 37
WELLS, A.W. 95; B.W. 1,57,
60,127; Carl B. 143; D.W.
25,27,35,59,81,82,88,95,
115,123,130,145; Maggie
142; Major 143; O.W. 64;
Shade 143; W.F. 143
WEST, Adam 144; Ader 76;
A.J. 144; Alvira J. 85;
Amanda 102; Arie 91;
Ben C. 144; Ben S. 41,
144; Berdie 55; Callie
82; C.N. 144; Mrs. Daisy
144; Daniel 143; Dessie
137; E.H. 143; E.L. 144;
Elizabeth 85,95; Emma
123; Emma V. 97; Frad 144;
Gertrude R. 127; Grady
92; Hariet L. 55; Harriett
G. 96; Harriet 122;
Henry D. 144; H.P. 144;
Ida Roxana 25; Isaac
143,144; James F.G. 144;
Jane 81,138; J.C. 144(2);
Jess L. 144; J.F. 144;
John 143; J.W. 144; Leon
144; Leonard 143; Leon
H. 144; Liddy 123; Mae
67,111; M.A. 10,15,32,
72,99,125; Mamie E. 30;
Margaret 82; Mary 29,49;
Mary E. 96; Melinda 11;
Molly J. 62; Myrtle 36;
Nancy 139; Nannie 16;
Nannie May 74; Nora 17;
Phoeba 61; R.A. 110;
Rachel 123; Ralph R. 144;
Sarah 49; Susan 109;

WOLF, Margaret Ann 44
WOMACK, Anderson D. 149;
Annie 4; Fannie K. 100;
Hulda 65; J.E. 24,33,44,
73,79,140; J.O. 149;
Lillie 113; Mabell 150;
Nellie M. 83; O. 111;
Olive 144; Robert I. 149;
R.T. 149; Sile 149;
William G. 149
WOOD, A.G. 12,74,88,115,
135,149(2); Alfred W.
149; Alice 91; Alvira 130;
A.N. 124; Andrew J. 149;
Carrie 62; C.E. 149;
Charles 149; Cora 132;
Dovie 18; Ella 130;
Erastus 149; Erwin 149;
Etta 7; Fred 149; Fred B.
149; Grace 117; Hattie
46; Hattie M. 58; Henry
T. 149; Iowa T. 75;
James E. 149; James T.
149; Jess 149; John 149;
John T. 149; Julia 54;
Laura 137; Laura A. 39,
64; Loyed 149; Manervia
143; Martha 122; Mary L.
116; Nellie 59; Newton
A. 149; Obey 149; Ollie
61; Osburn 149; Rouie
59; Roxie 93; Sarah A.
12,127; S.M. 149; Stella
146; Thomas 149; Thomas
N. 149; T.H. 117,150;
T.N. 149; W.C. 137; W.G.
7,12,70,91,105,124,139;
William 149
WOODALL, Arzela 32; C.A.
149; Gracie C. 149; James
A. 149; May 7; Sallie A.
7
WOODARD, Caleb 149; Eva 87;
J. 28; James R. 149; J.C.
149(2); J.D. 95; J.M. 62,
104,138; J.S. 1,2,3,8,12,
13,14,27,30,36,46,47,52,
58,62,72,73,88,97,110,
112,113,115,116,126,132,
133,135,137,143,145,146;
J.T. 23; L.D. 149; Lena
88; Nancy 6; Samuel F.
149; Wm. A. 150; Wm. R.
150
WOODBERRY, Urban 150
WOODFIN, H.G. 5,7,13,16,17,
23,28,35,37,43,46,51,55,
56,61,63,68,69,70,75,83,
98,103,106,108,109,110,
130; Samuel 150; W.G. 46
WOODRING, Absolon 150; Sarah
65,66
WOODS, Arthur 149; Betty
Jane 137; Clara 32; Cora
115; Elsie 114; Emalin
98; G.W. 149; Jabe 149;
Jane 12; Leanord 149;
Leroy 53; Lillie 45;
Lillie D. 65; Margaret
A. 149; Martha 7; Mary
98; R.A. 149(2); W.G. 56;
Zettie 32
WOODWARD, I.S. 16; John S.
150; J.S. 12,59; J.T. 150;
William 150; William B.
150
WOODY, A.B. 73; C.B. 150;
G.C. 150; Henry 150;
Norman 150; Thos. N. 150
WOOLUM, Dee 51
WOOSLEY, J.E. 14,22,99,113
WOOTEN, A.W. 150; Charlie

WOOTEN, Cont'd.
Frank 150; Hattie 43;
John E. 150; Nancy A.
60; Velma 44
WORLEY, Hannah 135; Jess
150; Jessie L. 150;
Malinda 9
WRIGHT, Aaron A. 150;
Alford 150; Amelia 17;
Aus. 150; Barak 150;
Benjamin 150; Mrs. Carrie
M. 28; Charles N. 150;
Clara J. 118; Clarissa
104; C.N. 150; Cynthia
A. 115; Delcenia I. 120;
E.E. 150; Elford S. 150;
Elie I. 49; Frank 150;
I.D. 49,55,77,78,80,86,
91,102,120,126,139,140;
James 150; Jane 104;
J.C. 150; J.D. 26,39,52;
John M. 150; Laura 77;
Marion 60,150; Mary E.
106,115; Mary Eva 120;
Nancy 29; Olive 134;
Rebecca 82; Richard 150
(2); Robert H. 150; Wm.
M. 150
WYANT, Cornelia 121; Harriet
94; J.T. 150; Mary J. 8
WYATT, Sarah A. 29
WYKLE, Anna 139; Bulah 88;
C.A. 1; Jacob R. 150;
Vergie 58; Wymer 150
WYLEY, Thomas 79
WYLIE, E.S. 136
WYLY, E.S. 59,77,87,150

YANT, N.W. 141
YARBOROUGH, J.P. 68,72
YODEN, S.B. 33
YONCE, Adaline 34; A.J. 151;
Allie 150; Belle 31;
Charlie 151; Cornelia
128; D.A. 30,42,44,62,
67,85,90,100,101,103,
105,111,128,141,142,143,
145,148,150; David 150;
Dora 8; Dorothy 141;
E.C. 61; Effie 101;
Elihu 150; George 151;
George H. 151; G.W. 79;
Jacob 47,54,132,145;
Jacob L. 46; J.L. 31,
42,43,107,111,143,150;
J.S. 128; Leonard 150;
Maggie 42; Malinda 9;
Marcus E. 151; Minnie
71,111; Osborne 151;
Palace 103; R.D. 151;
Robert M. 151; Rose 44;
Sarah 46; William 150
YORK, Charles 151; Clarke
151; John 151; Viola 57
YOUNCE, Arthur 151; Birdie
62; C.A. 150; Catherine
116; D.A. 6,8,34,117,133;
Dennis D. 151; Docie 8;
Elizabeth 53; Gay 151;
Gordia 20; Granville 151;
Jacob 107; Jacob M. 151;
J.L. 7,13,22,28,41,98,
116,130; John R. 151;
Joseph T. 151; Martha 116;
Mary A. 116(2); Maude 136;
Nebraska 135; Ruth 128;
Sallie B. 82
YOUNG, Adelia 112; Alex 151;
A.W. 17,23,41,73,139;
Clarissa 109; Dallas 33;
Delphia 118; Donald 151;

Ella A.,
(2); Frona 41; I.E. 49;
J.A. 17,39,102,114,142,
151; Jacob I. 151; James
G. 151; James L. 151;
Jane 54; John 151(2);
John H. 151; John W.
151(2); Joseph 151(2);
J.W. 151; Leander J. 151;
Lee 151; Leslie J. 151;
Lewis G. 151; L.J. 54,
60,83,84,89,104,108,115,
148; Lula 15; Lydea 91;
Lydia 133; Margaret 16;
Margaret A. 151; Mary
35,131,148; Mary E. 74;
Minnie 29; Nancy 98;
Nancy V. 88; Nina 97;
Omah 108; Pinkney R. 151;
P.R. 29,52; Ruthie V.
146; Samuel P. 151; Sarah
60; S. Clementine 80;
Selma 71; Tabitha 45;
Tolietha 48; W.H. 151;
William 151; Wm. G. 151;
W.T. 151
YOUNGBLOOD, George 151;
James T. 151; Rachail 151;
Ransom D. 151

ZACHARY, Agness 62; Alexander
152; Mrs. Alice 99; C.
Ross 152; E.H. 152; Eliz-
abeth 2; Ethel 94; Flor-
ence Lena 97; Hal 152;
Helen G. 108; Lon 144;
Lyman 152; Malinda 144;
Nancy 144; Ruth 107;
Susan 99; Virginia 33
ZACHERY, A.W. 152
ZOELINER, Louise 27
ZOELLNER, Adolph 152; Carl
152; Margaret 58

END

www.ingramcontent.com/pod-product-compliance
Lightning Source LLC
Chambersburg PA
CBHW021906020426
42334CB00013B/506